New Technologies and Renaissance Studies IV

NEW TECHNOLOGIES IN MEDIEVAL AND RENAISSANCE STUDIES 12

SERIES EDITOR Raymond G. Siemens

New Technologies and Renaissance Studies IV: The Changing Shape of Digital Early Modern Studies

Edited by
Randa El Khatib and Caroline Winter

Iter Press
NEW YORK | TORONTO
2025

Printed in the United States of America

978-1-64959-119-7 (paper)
978-1-64959-120-3 (pdf)
978-1-64959-121-0 (epub)

Library of Congress Cataloging-in-Publication Data

Names: El Khatib, Randa, editor. | Winter, Caroline, editor.

Title: New technologies and Renaissance studies IV : the changing shape of digital early modern studies / edited by Randa El Khatib and Caroline Winter.

Other titles: Changing shape of digital early modern studies

Description: New York : Iter Press, 2025 | Series: New technologies in medieval and Renaissance studies ; 12 | "Contributions to this volume build on presentations at the NTRS-DH@RSA (2020) event or for the New Technologies and Renaissance Studies panels of the 2020 RSA Annual Meeting."--CIP galley. | Includes bibliographical references. | Summary: "Contributors to this volume engage with digital scholarship in several ways: by creating digital projects, often in multidisciplinary, collaborative environments; by applying digital methodologies and tools to explore research questions; and by speculating about the potential directions that digital scholarship can take to tackle existing research areas that could benefit from new perspectives. Together, the chapters demonstrate how various digital approaches--from network analysis to web mapping, VR and AR technologies, digital editions, databases, and archives--are all contributing in creative and effective ways to expand our knowledge of the past, to help ask and answer questions at a scale that was unimaginable before the digital turn, and to reshape early modern studies in the twenty-first century"-- Provided by publisher.

Identifiers: LCCN 2024002709 (print) | LCCN 2024002710 (ebook) | ISBN 9781649591197 (paper) | ISBN 9781649591203 (pdf) | ISBN 9781649591210 (epub)

Subjects: LCSH: Renaissance--Study and teaching (Higher)--Congresses. | Archival materials--Digitization--Congresses. | Manuscripts, Renaissance--Data processing--Congresses. | Digital humanities--Congresses. | Electronic publications--Congresses. | Educational technology--Congresses. | BISAC: LITERARY CRITICISM / General | COMPUTERS / Design, Graphics & Media / General | LCGFT: Conference papers and proceedings. https://id.loc.gov/authorities/genreForms/gf2014026068

Classification: LCC CB361 .N494 2025 (print) | LCC CB361 (ebook) | DDC 940.2/10711--dc23/eng/20240513

LC record available at https://lccn.loc.gov/2024002709

LC ebook record available at https://lccn.loc.gov/2024002710

Cover Illustration

Shuper, Alex. "An Aerial View of a Blue Lake Surrounded by Mountains." Digital image. Unsplash. Web. 26 June 2024 <https://unsplash.com/photos/an-aerial-view-of-a-blue-lake-surrounded-by-mountains-SF95uM_t_Jk>.

Cover Design

Maureen Morin, Library Communications, University of Toronto Libraries.

Contents

Introduction: The Changing Shape of Digital Early Modern Studies

Randa El Khatib
University of Toronto Scarborough

Caroline Winter
University of Victoria

Amid a broader cultural turn toward digital modes of knowledge production, the humanities have seen a marked expansion of digital and open-access practices. Although the degree and extent of change in the way we work and live since early 2020 has been unprecedented,[1] the field of early modern studies continues to change too, partly in response to new technologies that alter not only how we go about research, writing, and teaching but also how we approach our objects of study and the very kinds of questions we are able to ask. Sitting at the intersection of the two fields, this volume engages with this notion of change in early modern studies and digital humanities. In what follows, we offer a brief snapshot of current discourses in digital humanities from which we can extrapolate the state of digital early modern studies research.

Many in the digital humanities (DH) community have pointed out that although the community itself may be open and inclusive, the notion of DH as a "big tent," a metaphor that gained currency over a decade ago as the theme of the Alliance of Digital Humanities Organizations (ADHO) conference DH2011 (ADHO n.d.),[2] tends to elide the institutional and structural factors that keep the entrance of the tent shut to many people (Bailey et al. 2016; Booth and Posner 2020; Svensson 2012; Terras 2011). Instead, reflections on the state of the field are increasingly calling for a digital humanities that is critical and transformative. These calls build upon movements such as #transformDH, which has interrogated, for example, the erasure of people of color from early modern and Renaissance paintings (Lothian and Phillips

[1] Contributions to this volume build on presentations at the NTRS-DH@RSA (2020) event or for the New Technologies and Renaissance Studies panels of the 2020 RSA Annual Meeting.

[2] The metaphor of the "big tent" is drawn from nineteenth-century religious gatherings and invites associations with circus tents. In the context of DH, it was intended to emphasize the openness and inclusiveness of the field, including its methodological diversity (Booth and Posner 2020; Terras 2011).

ISBN 978-1-64959-119-7 (paper) ISBN 978-1-64959-120-3 (pdf) ISBN 978-1-64959-121-0 (epub)
New Technologies in Medieval and Renaissance Studies 12 (2025) 1–14

2013; #transformDH 2014), and Global Outlook::Digital Humanities (globaloutlookdh.org), a special interest group of the ADHO that recognizes and promotes the global nature of digital humanities (Risam 2016). Additionally, these calls have inspired the formation of initiatives and collaborations that are informed by critical digital humanities values and methodologies, such as the Critical Digital Humanities Initiative (dhn.utoronto.ca) at the University of Toronto, which emphasizes anti-racist, queer, feminist, non-binary, and decolonial research that addresses questions of social justice and power.

In their introduction to *Debates in the Digital Humanities 2016*, Lauren Klein and Matthew Gold (2016, ix) proclaim that "digital humanities, as a field, has arrived." In the introduction to the 2019 volume in that same series, they consider how the field has matured, arguing that not only has its expansion into other fields continued, but that critical attention has now turned toward the field itself (Gold and Klein 2019). Christie Carson and Peter Kirwan (2014a, 1) introduce their volume on digital Shakespeare, for instance, by drawing on this idea of critical digital humanities to "assert the mutual importance of the 'digital' as a context that influences the study of Shakespeare and, conversely, the importance of Shakespeare as a case study to understand the developing nature of the digital world." Critical attention is also increasingly being paid to the very structures in which digital humanities is embedded.

Klein and Gold (2016, x) note that, although the big tent idea has been interrogated and challenged since 2011, no other model has yet emerged to replace it. They propose a conception of digital humanities as an "expanded field," drawing on the art historian Rosalind Krauss's notion of the expanded field of postmodern sculpture—a field whose defining structures are not binary but relational,[3] "constructed by the relationships among key concepts, rather than by a single umbrella term." Unlike the metaphor of the big tent, which evokes a structure into which the field must fit (no matter how flexible or how big) with a point of entry that necessitates a binary view of "who's in and who's out," understanding DH as an expanded field means imagining its structure as emergent, something created from within the field itself: not the

[3] Krauss (1979, 36–37) situates sculpture alongside landscape and architecture, arguing that, by the 1960s, sculpture had become "a kind of ontological absence"—something that was "not-landscape" and "not-architecture." Using a conceptual model called a Klein set or Piaget group that expands a conceptual framework or field defined by binary relationships (landscape/architecture) into quaternary ones (landscape/not-landscape; architecture/not-architecture), she theorizes the field of sculpture as part of this "logically expanded" conceptual field at the intersection of not-landscape and not-architecture.

neat, contained circle of a pie chart but the messy, amorphous shape of the network graph. Klein and Gold (2016) argue that the notion of the expanded field is a particularly useful way of understanding the history and current definition of digital humanities as its theories, methods, and practices expand into individual fields. Élika Ortega (2019, 179) builds on the idea of the expanded field of digital humanities by noting that, as the field diversifies and expands in scope, an equally important consideration is the "explosion" of work practiced in DH communities around the world. Similar to Svensson's (2012) conception of digital humanities as a meeting place or trading zone, Ortega (2019, 180–81) argues for understanding the field as comprising a heterogeneous assemblage of praxes, intersecting at "zones of contact" to form "ecology of knowledges" that are inherently and consciously social. In the introduction to their edited volume about digital humanities infrastructures, Anne McGrail, Angel David Nieves, and Siobhan Senier (2021, ix) also emphasize the intersectionality and relationality of the digital humanities, a "contact zone" where technology, humanistic inquiry, and institutional structures and cultures "collide."

Like Svensson and Klein and Gold, William Thomas views the next phase of digital humanities as being defined by its relationship with the humanities disciplines. Thomas (2016, 527) notes that whereas the first phase of digital humanities involved "reassembling the human record in digital form," the second phase will be more concerned with critical and hermeneutic interventions, "creating discipline-based interpretive scholarship in digital form." Similarly, Gold and Klein (2019) argue that as the idea of the expanded field has solidified, digital humanities has been reaching into other disciplines to the extent that we now find digital humanities articles in disciplinary journals (such as *PMLA*); at the same time, the internal contours of the field have been deepening and its niches becoming more defined. Because DH is now being taken up in the disciplines—as it has been in early modern studies for some time—the question is no longer how to define the field (a top-down approach) but rather how the field is constituted and shaped by the disciplines (a bottom-up approach).

By nature heterogeneous, interdisciplinary, and linguistically diverse, early modern studies offers strong examples—some of which are published here—of how digital tools and methodologies are applied in innovative ways that, in turn, help to shape the field itself. Today, digital early modern studies has reached the point where "computational methods, information technologies, and digital resources have become parts of our regular academic toolbox" (Jenstad, Kaethler, and Roberts-Smith 2018a, 2), to which the RSA's long and growing list of digital resources for research and teaching in a wide variety of early modern subfields can attest (RSA n.d.). However, according to Matthew Steggle (2008, 83), there is no scholarly consensus about the origin of the digital revolution in early modern studies: some trace the origins to long-standing projects such as Early English Books Online (EEBO), whereas others trace it to the publication of digital editions such as the e-text of *Paradise Lost*, or even more informally to the use of email by early modernists. This dispersed history points to a branch of scholarship that began, and in many ways continues to develop, through largely siloed projects that are brought together under the umbrella of a scholarly volume such as this one, through digital humanities panels at disciplinary conferences such as the RSA or the Sixteenth Century Society and Conference, or through large organizations or early modern centers connected to universities or libraries that have dedicated intellectual and physical spaces for digital scholarship.

The expanded field of digital humanities in early modern studies also often occurs in subdisciplinary clusters, many of which have a long history, such as lost play studies (Steggle 2015); paleography (Magni 2020); theater history (Bloom 2020); and Milton studies (Cunningham and Quamen 2021). Another is Shakespeare studies (Bell and Borsuk 2020; Carson and Kirwan 2014b; Estill 2019; Jenstad, Kaethler, and Roberts-Smith 2018b; Valls-Russell 2016), to which John Misak and Kevin LaGrandeur's chapter in this volume contributes. To the subfield of digital early modern women studies (Baranda 2018; Guénette 2019), this volume adds chapters by Catherine Medici, Gerit Quealy, and Elena Brizio and Luis Meneses. To book history (Greteman 2021), this volume contributes chapters by Giuditta Cirnigliaro and Crystal Hall. In addition to adopting digital approaches in existing early modern subfields, this volume also engages with research subfields that are by nature digital and were only later brought into early modern studies, such as game studies seen in the chapter by John Misak and Kevin LaGrandeur, virtual reality in the chapter by Thomas Herron, and social network analysis in the chapters by Catherine Medici, Crystal Hall, and Jessica Marie Otis.

Traditional forms of scholarly publications such as the aforementioned recent volumes and special issues only offer a partial view of the actual work taking place in the expanded field of digital early modern studies. Arguably, the bulk of research in the field is in the form of digital projects published in a wide variety of mixed-media digital formats, ranging from websites to digital editions, archives, databases, virtual and augmented reality, other software applications, and beyond. In addition to online searches and curated lists, such as the RSA list of digital resources, scholarly venues such as *Early Modern*

Digital Review (*EMDR*)—a journal aimed at reviewing digital projects that study the early modern world—point to this rich production of knowledge through special issues that draw together digital projects under a disciplinary, thematic, or methodological umbrella. For instance, *EMDR* recently published a special issue by Pedro Germano Leal and Mara R. Wade (2022) on "Digital Emblematica," which is the first issue in the field that reviews 10 major digital scholarly resources that study digital emblematica; another issue by Darren Freebury-Jones (2021) on "Computational Approaches to Examining Early Modern Texts" looks at 13 digital resources that offer new possibilities for research using computational methodologies; Randa El Khatib's (2021) special issue on "Spatial Humanities" showcases 10 spatial projects that expand our knowledge of the early modern period and global cartographic advancements through web mapping technologies; and Bi-qi Beatrice Lei's (2021) special issue, "Digital Representations of Contemporary Shakespeare Performances," traces global digital adaptations of Shakespeare on the stage since the onset of COVID-19. While the authors in this volume present complete arguments and insights into their fields of study, most chapters engage with digital resources and methodologies that extend beyond the context of this work; require collaboration, skill, and labor to be built and maintained; and are valuable contributions to knowledge in and of themselves.

This volume comes several years after the *Early Modern Studies after the Digital Turn* volume in this series edited by Laura Estill, Diane Jackacki, and Michael Ullyot. The work in that volume "orient[ed] us toward the extensible future of early modern scholarship after the digital turn" (2016, 7). Now, we ask, "Where has the digital turn taken early modern studies?" This question is explored in this volume, which adopts a threefold goal: to demonstrate how digital methods are brought to bear on early modern research questions; to demonstrate how digital mixed-media approaches are being used to reconstruct our knowledge of the past in a wide variety of early modern subfields; and to lay the foundation for the future innovations and discoveries that will continue to reshape early modern digital humanities.

The chapters in this volume have been clustered according to shared methodologies, but, as noted both above and in the brief summaries that follow, they resist easy categorization, displaying sets of intersecting methods, topics, and disciplinary foci in addition to those by which they are clustered: networks, digital editions, maps, databases and archives, as well as virtual and augmented reality (VR and AR). In addition to numerous forms of history, including the history of science, women's history, and art history, the volume is also shaped by intersecting areas of study including environmental studies, archeology, linguistics, musicology and sound studies, literary studies, and scholarly communication, with many chapters engaging multidisciplinary research.

Emerging from these intersecting fields, topics, and methodologies, these "zones of contact" (Ortega 2019) offer a rich variety of themes and ideas. Many of the chapters describe how digital technologies enable us to see our objects of study in new ways and to understand the past differently. Some discuss how digital technologies enable us to draw on those objects to create reconstructions of the past, whether through maps, data, or virtual simulations. Several engage in a critical examination of digital tools, methods, and infrastructure, as well as the relationship between humanistic studies and the digital. Running through the essays is the idea that digital technologies enable various forms of multiplicity: multilingualism, multimedia, multidimensional representation, and an openness to a multiplicity of voices and perspectives. Evoking the conceptual, ideological, and technological model of digital humanities that Alan Liu (2003, 135) describes as a "diversity stack," this openness to and embracing of multiplicity seems to enable greater diversity and inclusivity in early modern studies as it shapes and is reshaped by the digital. We see an opportunity for future digital early modern studies to extend this linguistic and methodological multiplicity geographically as well, continuing Rila Mukherjee's (2021) interrogation of the "global early modern."

Finally, the essays in this collection discuss applications the contributors envision for their research, which include the preservation and archiving of the cultural record, the development of tools and methods that can be taken up and built upon by other researchers, and the pedagogical applications of digital tools, methods, and projects. Several chapters discuss how digital tools and technologies enable us to engage with the past in order to better understand the challenges we face today, highlighting the continued importance and relevance of the humanities and social sciences. Gold and Klein (2019, xiii) write that the "principal task" of digital humanities "may no longer be to define or defend digital humanities to skeptical outsiders, but instead to translate the subtleties of our research to others within the expanded field—a project that can help DH matter beyond itself." Most of the digital projects described in this volume are open and public facing, and several chapters—including those by Sarah Banschbach Valles and Sarah J. Sprouse; Steven Bednarski et al.; Herron; and Misak and LaGrandeur—explicitly address the ways in which digital scholarship facilitates a kind of early modern scholarship that engages with our own historical moment.

All of the chapters in the first cluster apply network analysis methodologies to offer insights into early modern political and scholarly communities, as well as the social networks of current practitioners in disciplines that study the historical period. Catherine Medici's chapter, "Visualizing the Sidney Network: Using Network Analysis to Understand Women's Place," applies network analysis to track and visualize the correspondence of 657 letters sent to and from the Sidney family in order to uncover the central role that women played in social and political networks, as well as to identify and restore the role of individual players within these networks. Crystal Hall's chapter, "Print Networks of Early Modern Astronomy in Galileo's Library," also employs network analysis, tracing the information found on the title pages of 152 books in Galileo's library that together represent "microhistories" of early modern print networks in Italy, while also contextualizing the environment in which Galileo's own works were printed and distributed. Jessica Marie Otis looks at contemporary social networks in "The Republic of Tweets," which focuses on the semi-formal communication of scholars in annual digital, early modern, and disciplinary conferences on the social media platform X, formerly known as Twitter, to trace the evolving scholarly discourses and intersectionalities within and across traditional disciplinary boundaries over time.

The chapters in the second cluster, focused on digital scholarly editions, demonstrate how such editions draw upon the editorial traditions of the past and push them forward. In "Opening Up the Scriptorium: The Theory and Ethics of Transcription Methods from the Handwritten Page to the Web Page," Sarah Banschbach Valles and Sarah J. Sprouse trace similarities between digital scholarly edition production and medieval scribal practices in order to work toward a positive definition of what a digital scholarly edition is and what it could be. They argue that digital scholarly editing practices—including crowdsourced transcription—are founded upon the social and collaborative scribal practices of the scriptorium through which early modern codices were produced and understood. Like Banschbach Valles and Sprouse, Nadia Cannata in "New Solutions for Old Problems: Digital Publication, the Linguistic Study of Medieval Vernacular Texts, and the EDV Project" argues that the digital medium makes possible forms of scholarly editing and research that could not be achieved through print. She discusses the Epigraphic Database of Inscriptions in Italian Vernaculars (EDV) project, which comprises a corpus of medieval Italian vernacular inscriptions and a comprehensive archive of edited and encoded texts that pave the way for new discoveries in historical sociolinguistics and the new discipline of vernacular epigraphy. In "Moving Images and Text on Leonardo's Codices: The

Evolution of Drawing a Digital Edition," Giuditta Cirnigliaro introduces the LiLeo Beta: Word-and-Image Leonardo Digital Edition project. Combining traditional artistic tools with digital archival practices, LiLeo examines how the drawings in Leonardo's codices interact with the textual and other elements on the page, and in doing so presents a new reading of the role of the drawings in Leonardo's scientific studies. Whether layering numerous versions of a single text, bringing together a heterogeneous corpus of texts into a digital archive, or facilitating the study of texts and images taken together, these chapters demonstrate the affordance of digital tools to bring together, edit, and interpret multiplicities of texts.

The next cluster of chapters focuses on digital mapping—in particular, how web mapping technologies are currently being employed to reconstruct early modern historical moments. Francesca Bortoletti, Giuseppe Gerbino, Beatrice Gobbo, and Tommaso Elli's chapter, "FRIDA: A Multilevel Digital Atlas for the Ephemeral Renaissance, La Serenissima Venice, 1450–1550," addresses the complexities of reconstructing early modern festival events, such as political performances and religious ceremonies that engulfed entire cities, when the visual and textual records resulting from such events are today often fragmented across different historical archives. Bortoletti et al. walk readers through a mixed-media project that helps overcome the fragmentation of records, allows the reconstruction of early modern festivals while preserving their ephemerality, and supports dynamic forms of engagement with said materials. In "'Dear Galileo': Letters as Data on Astronomy," Caterina Agostini traces 370 of Galileo Galilei's correspondents on astronomical topics, using locational information and web mapping technologies to trace the extent of Galileo's influence within Italy and around the world. The project also tracks the free circulation of ideas and competing astronomical theories before Galileo's 1633 Inquisition trial and the subsequent stifling of scientific freedom after the Catholic Church's 1633 Copernican ban. Gerit Quealy's "Penelope Rich: Mapping the Mobility of a Sixteenth-Century Aristocratic Woman" examines the travel patterns of Penelope Rich, one of the most influential and well-traveled women in early modern England. By tracing Rich's travels, the project also sheds light on the mobility of upper-class women in sixteenth-century England and the circumstances that authorized them to travel—a practice that was otherwise reserved for men. While the chapters in this cluster use varying web mapping approaches, they all demonstrate how organizing research around locational anchors can be a useful method in shedding light on early modern historical events, in this case reconstructing the complexities of festivals, tracing the circulation of scientific knowledge, and uncovering social attitudes about female mobility.

While all of the essays in this volume concern data, the chapters in the next cluster engage particularly with the affordances of databases and the roles of data in digital early modern studies. In "GEA: Invisible Sienese Women Made Visible," Elena Brizio and Luis Meneses describe how the relational database at the core of the GEA project makes possible a new view of the role of women in Siena between the 1450s and the 1570s. They explain how the database enables the bringing together of pieces of data from across a variety of archival sources and how the GEA project's methods and tools might benefit other DH researchers. In "Beyond a Digital Catalog: Rethinking Musical and Cartographic Sources through Digital Humanities," Angela Fiore and Sara Belotti describe how they have drawn upon digital collections of musical and cartographic resources as well as geographic information systems (GIS) for the Este Soundscape project, an online reconstruction of the historical soundscape of Modena in the seventeenth century, in order to enable a new understanding of Modena's changing culture. In "Interacting with Big Historical Data of the Dutch Golden Age: Golden Agents and Virtual Interiors," Charles van den Heuvel presents a critical examination of the digital infrastructures that enable historical research using big data. Through a study of two projects that employ big data, databases, and linked data, van den Heuvel addresses concerns about the roles of programmers and humanists in DH projects, and the value that can be realized by large investments in digital infrastructures. Through their discussions of the uses and affordances of data, these chapters emphasize that putting data in conversation—whether in relational databases, digital collections, or linked data—makes possible new insights into the early modern past.

The final cluster of chapters in this volume discusses the reconstruction of the early modern past through the technology of VR and AR. In "Northeye (Re)Constructed: Augmented Reality of an Abandoned Medieval Village," Steven Bednarski, T. C. Nicholas Graham, Robin Harrap, Zack MacDonald, and Andrew Moore discuss the development of *Virtual Northeye*, a game that draws together archival and archeological evidence, artistic evidence, and geospatial evidence with AR and 3D computer graphics to enable students to experience a simulation of a medieval village. Focusing on the game's pedagogical applications, Bednarski et al. show how the game uses augmented reality to create immersive experiences to help students better understand the connection between environmental change and human settlement, and to draw connections between past and present challenges. Like Bednarski et al., Thomas Herron discusses pedagogical applications, critically examining how the experience of reading within a virtual space can be optimized with VR. In "The Place of Reading in VR: Pedagogy, Spenser's Kilcolman

Castle, and *Amoretti* 65," Herron presents three ways of reading Spenser's *Amoretti* 65 in a 3D simulation of Kilcolman Castle, arguing that the experience of reading in virtual spaces can offer insights into the texts and into VR technology itself. Gamified pedagogy is also at the forefront of "Designing an Educational Video Game for Shakespeare's *Hamlet*," in which John Misak and Kevin LaGrandeur discuss a game they co-developed titled *Perchance*. According to the authors, a gamified version of *Hamlet* engages students and enables them to work through the density of Shakespeare's literature. The authors also explore how gaming can be employed to improve student experience and increase engagement in order to reach the learning goals embedded into the game. In the final chapter of the volume, "Does the *kunstkammer* Need a Digital Future?," Andrea M. Gáldy argues for a new approach to study the *kunstkammer*—a type of display room that also figured as an early form of museum—through digital reconstructions. Recreating the *kunstkammer* in virtual reality would allow scholars to replicate decorative elements as closely as possible without needing to loan and invest in the exhibition elements, while also foregoing considerations of space, accessibility, and safety—considerations that have become especially relevant with the pivot toward working in virtual environments and which will no doubt continue to inform early modern digital humanities in the future.

Contributors to this volume engage with digital scholarship in several ways: by creating digital projects, often in multidisciplinary, collaborative environments; by applying existing digital methodologies and tools to explore research questions; and by speculating about the potential directions that digital scholarship can take to tackle existing research areas that could benefit from new perspectives. Together, the chapters demonstrate how various digital approaches—from network analysis to web mapping, VR and AR technologies, digital editions, databases, and archives—are all contributing in creative and effective ways to expand our knowledge of the past, to help ask and answer questions at a scale that was unimaginable before the digital turn, and to reshape early modern studies in the twenty-first century. Figures and videos mentioned in this volume can also be found on the volume's companion website.[4]

[4] See https://iterpress.org/books/supplementary-materials/nt12/.

WORKS CITED

Alliance of Digital Humanities Organizations (ADHO). n.d. "General CFP." DH2011. Accessed 7 July 2023. dh2011.stanford.edu/?page_id=97.

Bailey, Moya, Anne Cong-Huyen, Alexis Lothian, and Amanda Phillips. 2016. "Reflections on a Movement: #transformDH, Growing Up." In *Debates in the Digital Humanities 2016*, edited by Matthew K. Gold and Lauren F. Klein, 71–80. Minneapolis: University of Minnesota Press. doi.org/10.5749/j.ctt1cn6thb.11.

Baranda, Nieves. 2018. "Studying Early Modern Women Writers: The Digital Humanities Turn." *Early Modern Women* 13 (1): 163–71. doi.org/10.1353/emw.2018.0059.

Bell, Henry, and Amy Borsuk. 2020. "Teaching Shakespeare: Digital Processes." *Research in Drama Education* 25 (1): 1–7. doi.org/10.1080/13569783.2019.1704241.

Bloom, Gina. 2020. "Theater History in 3D: The Digital Early Modern in the Age of the Interface." *English Literary Renaissance* 50 (1): 8–16. doi.org/10.1086/706213.

Booth, Alison, and Miriam Posner. 2020. "Introduction—The Materials at Hand." *PMLA* 135 (1): 9–22. doi.org/10.1632/pmla.2020.135.1.9.

Carson, Christie, and Peter Kirwan. 2014a. "Shakespeare and the Digital World: Introduction." In *Shakespeare and the Digital World: Redefining Scholarship and Practice*, edited by Christie Carson and Peter Kirwan, 1–7. Cambridge: Cambridge University Press. doi.org/10.1017/CBO9781107587526.001.

———. 2014b. *Shakespeare and the Digital World: Redefining Scholarship and Practice*. Cambridge: Cambridge University Press. doi.org/10.1017/CBO9781107587526.

Cunningham, Richard, and Harvey Quamen, eds. 2021. "Digital Approaches to John Milton." Special issue, *Renaissance and Reformation / Renaissance et Réforme* 44 (3). doi.org/10.33137/rr.v44i3.37988.

El Khatib, Randa, ed. 2021. "Spatial Humanities." Special issue, *Early Modern Digital Review* 4 (3). doi.org/10.33137/rr.v44i3.37994.

Estill, Laura, ed. 2019. “Digital Shakespeare Texts.” Special issue, *Early Modern Digital Review* 2 (3). doi.org/10.7202/1066363ar.

Estill, Laura, Diane Jackacki, and Michael Ullyot, eds. 2016. *Early Modern Digital Studies after the Digital Turn*. Tempe: Arizona Center for Medieval and Renaissance Studies.

Freebury-Jones, Darren, ed. 2021. “Computational Approaches to Examining Early Modern Texts.” Special issue, *Early Modern Digital Review* 4 (4). doi.org/10.33137/rr.v44i4.38645.

Gold, Matthew K., and Lauren F. Klein. 2019. “Introduction: A DH That Matters.” In *Debates in the Digital Humanities 2019*, edited by Matthew K. Gold and Lauren F. Klein, ix–xiv. Minneapolis: University of Minnesota Press. doi.org/10.5749/j.ctvg251hk.3.

Greteman, Blaine. 2021. *Networking Print in Shakespeare’s England: Influence, Agency, and Revolutionary Change*. Stanford, CA: Stanford University Press. doi.org/10.1515/9781503627994.

Guénette, Marie-France, ed. 2019. “Women’s Authorial Agency and Print Culture.” Special issue, *Early Modern Digital Review* 2 (4). doi.org/10.7202/1068579ar.

Jenstad, Janelle, Mark Kaethler, and Jennifer Roberts-Smith. 2018a. “Introduction.” In *Shakespeare’s Language in Digital Media: Old Words, New Tools*, edited by Janelle Jenstad, Mark Kaethler, and Jennifer Roberts-Smith, 1–8. Abington: Routledge. doi.org/10.4324/9781315608747.

———, eds. 2018b. *Shakespeare’s Language in Digital Media: Old Words, New Tools*. Abingdon: Routledge. doi.org/10.4324/9781315608747.

Klein, Lauren F., and Matthew K. Gold. 2016. “Digital Humanities: The Expanded Field.” In *Debates in the Digital Humanities 2016*, edited by Matthew K. Gold and Lauren F. Klein, ix–xv. Minneapolis: University of Minnesota Press. doi.org/10.5749/j.ctt1cn6thb.3.

Krauss, Rosalind. 1979. “Sculpture in the Expanded Field.” *October* 8 (Spring): 30–44. doi.org/10.2307/778224.

Leal, Pedro Germano, and Mara R. Wade, eds. 2022. “Digital Emblematica.” Special Issue, *Early Modern Digital Review* 5 (2). doi.org/10.33137/rr.v45i3.40432.

Lei, Bi-qi Beatrice, ed. 2021. "Digital Representations of Contemporary Shakespeare Performances." Special issue, *Early Modern Digital Review* 4 (2). doi.org/10.33137/rr.v44i2.37527.

Liu, Alan. 2020. "Toward a Diversity Stack: Digital Humanities and Diversity as Technical Problem." *PMLA* 135 (1): 130–51. doi.org/10.1632/pmla.2020.135.1.130.

Lothian, Alexis, and Amanda Phillips. 2013. "Can Digital Humanities Mean Transformative Critique?" *E-Media Studies* 3 (1). doi.org/10.1349/PS1.1938-6060.A.425.

Magni, Isabella, ed. 2020. "Digital Paleography." Special issue, *Early Modern Digital Review* 3 (2). doi.org/10.33137/rr.v43i2.34800.

McGrail, Anne, Angel David Nieves, and Siobhan Senier. 2021. "Introduction." In *People, Practice, Power: Digital Humanities outside the Center*, edited by Anne McGrail, Angel David Nieves, and Siobhan Senier, vii–xxi. Minneapolis: University of Minnesota Press.

Mukherjee, Rila. 2021. "The Global Early Modern." *Journal of Early Modern History* 25 (6): 534–46. doi.org/10.1163/15700658-bja10044.

Ortega, Élika. 2019. "*Zonas de Contacto*: A Digital Humanities Ecology of Knowledges." In *Debates in the Digital Humanities 2019*, edited by Matthew K. Gold and Lauren F. Klein, 179–87. Minneapolis: University of Minnesota Press. doi.org/10.5749/j.ctvg251hk.18.

Renaissance Society of America (RSA). n.d. "RSA Digital Resources: About." Humanities Commons. Accessed 7 July 2023. rsadigitalresources.hcommons.org.

Risam, Roopika. 2016. "Navigating the Global Digital Humanities: Insights from Black Feminism." In *Debates in the Digital Humanities 2016*, edited by Matthew K Gold and Lauren F. Klein, 359–67. Minneapolis: University of Minnesota Press. doi.org/10.5749/j.ctt1cn6thb.32.

Steggle, Matthew. 2008. "'Knowledge will be multiplied': Digital Literary Studies and Early Modern Literature." In *A Companion to Digital Literary Studies*, edited by Ray Siemens and Susan Schreibman, 82–105. Oxford: Blackwell. doi.org/10.1002/9781405177504.ch4.

———. 2015. *Digital Humanities and the Lost Drama of Early Modern England: Ten Case Studies*. Burlington, VT: Ashgate. doi.org/10.4324/9781315577180.

Svensson, Patrik. 2012. "Beyond the Big Tent." In *Debates in the Digital Humanities*, edited by Matthew K. Gold, 36–72. Minneapolis: University of Minnesota Press. dhdebates.gc.cuny.edu/debates/text/22.

Terras, Melissa. 2011. "Peering Inside the Big Tent: Digital Humanities and the Crisis of Inclusion." *Melissa Terras' Blog*, 26 July 2011. melissaterras.blogspot.com/2011/07/peering-inside-big-tent-digital.html.

Thomas, William G., III. 2016. "The Promise of the Digital Humanities and the Contested Nature of Digital Scholarship." In *A New Companion to Digital Humanities*, edited by Susan Schreibman, Ray Siemens, and John Unsworth, 524–37. West Sussex, UK: John Wiley & Sons. doi.org/10.1002/9781118680605.ch36.

#transformDH. 2014. "Peter Lely, Portrait of Elizabeth Murray." Reblogged from thesoftghetto. Tumblr, 4 March 2014. transformdh.tumblr.com/post/78545012051/thesoftghetto-medievalpoc-heartsalchemy.

Valls-Russell, Janice. 2016. "Digital Shakespeare: An Expanding Universe in Search of Itself." *Cahiers Élisabéthains* 91 (1): 82–87. doi.org/10.1177/0184767816663126.

Chapter 1: Visualizing the Sidney Network: Using Network Analysis to Understand Women's Place

Catherine Medici
University of Nebraska

Network analysis provides an exciting opportunity to better understand early modern women's social, political, and professional networks. Network analysis can make visible that which we have not previously been able to see because it can reveal the agency of lesser-known actors. This method can highlight women's agency and, in some cases, recover women's roles within early modern networks that had been lost or obscured because of archival and historical practices that dismissed or ignored women outside the home. It can also provide new or additional information about the centrality of some members over others and the roles of less visible members, including women, in already recognized networks.

Visualizing the Sidney Network uses network analysis and visualization on a printed collection of 657 letters written to and from members of the Sidney family, who were prominent in England's politics and literature in the sixteenth and seventeenth centuries, to highlight the role of women in the family political network. Tracking correspondence and social connections as well as information exchanged within the letters from Elizabeth I's reign, it locates the place of women within an important early modern political and familial network. While still in development, Visualizing the Sidney Network is already recovering the place of women within an early modern political network. To understand the significance of these early findings, it is important to understand the scope and parameters of the project as well as the basics of network analysis. I will begin with a discussion of the project's data source, move on to an explanation of network analysis and its use in early modern studies, explain my process, and then conclude with the findings of the project so far, which, using network measures, show the significance of women to the network as well as point to future research directions.

Visualizing the Sidney Network

My project, Visualizing the Sidney Network, locates the place of women within an important early modern political and familial network. The project

ISBN 978-1-64959-119-7 (paper) ISBN 978-1-64959-120-3 (pdf) ISBN 978-1-64959-121-0 (epub)
New Technologies in Medieval and Renaissance Studies 12 (2025) 15–34

is an outgrowth of my research into the women of the Dudley-Sidney family as political actors that largely focuses on these women's roles within early modern familial and political networks and finds that the women played important roles as connectors or brokers within patronage, information, and religious networks. Because of the prominence of the Sidney family, it will be a resource for scholars in history, literature, and early modern and British studies.

The Sidney family was influential in politics and literature in Tudor and Stuart England. Henry Sidney's political service to Queen Elizabeth, his son Philip's renown as a poet and his tragic early death, and subsequent generations following within this tradition of government service and literary production have made the family well-known within the study of Tudor and Stuart England. At one time during Elizabeth's reign, between their own properties and the lands they managed through government offices, the Sidney family controlled one-quarter of all English land (Brennan 2006, 39). This immense amount of control gave the family incredible political importance. However, it was not just the male members of the family who created this political and literary legacy: Sidney women were central to this work. While this has been acknowledged with respect to the family's literary legacy, women's roles in politics have been overlooked.

Because of the important role of the Sidney family, its political and literary networks have been studied in more traditional ways. Scholarship on the political network has largely examined the central male members of the network: the Dudley brothers Ambrose and Robert, Mary's husband Henry Sidney, and Katherine's husband Henry Hastings (Adams 2002; Cross 1967; Brennan 2006). However, the women of the family were central participants too. The Sidney women's roles in the family literary network are better studied and acknowledged (Crawford 2014; Hannay 1990, 2010; Kinnamon and Brennan 2003), but these studies often leave out the place of women in political networks and the depth of the political aspects of their involvement in literary networks. When it comes to studying the literature and politics of Philip Sidney or Robert Sidney, it is widely understood that the Sidney's familial and political networks were intertwined, but these networks were also interwoven among male and female family members.

The Letters

The source material for this project is 657 Sidney family letters collected, edited, and published by Arthur Collins in 1746 as *Letters and Memorials of State: In the Reigns of Queen Mary, Queen Elizabeth, King James, King Charles the First,*

Part of the Reign of King Charles the Second, and Oliver's Usurpation, a two-volume work. Collins utilized records from the Sidney family seat at Penshurst in Kent as well as the Office of Papers and Records for Business of State ("Office of State Papers"). The records range from the time of Sir Henry Sidney's lord deputyship in Ireland in 1567, through his son Robert Sidney's various terms of government service, to Robert's son Algernon in the 1660s. Transcriptions of letters comprise the bulk of the two volumes of *Letters and Memorials* and also account for the value of Collins's work alongside biographies and occasionally other documents from the lives of the Sidneys. Although manuscript letters from the family exist in public and family archives in the UK, for the purpose of this project, Visualizing the Sidney Network only considers the letters printed in *Letters and Memorials*, which acts as a closed dataset.

In the extensive full title, Collins acknowledged some of the beneficial aspects of his work. He stated that the letters share information on various negotiations with foreign powers, "intrigues of the several courts of Queen Elizabeth, King James, and King Charles the First," as well as "some remarkable transactions, both at home and abroad, during those times, not hitherto known" (Collins 1746, title page). Henry Sidney's letters, especially those from his time serving as lord deputy of Ireland, comprise the majority of the first volume of *Letters and Memorials*, but both volumes also contain many letters written between Robert Sidney and his secretary, Rowland Whyte, while Robert was serving on diplomatic missions throughout Europe, particularly in the Netherlands. These letters shed light on the "news and intrigues of court" and on English foreign policy during the end of the reign of Elizabeth I and the early reign of James I (Collins 1746, 1:[6]). The letters of the first two generations of the men of the Sidney family thus make up the great majority of the content of *Letters and Memorials*. The continued role of subsequent generations of Sidney men in the courts and governments of James I and Charles I, during the Civil War and the Interregnum, and then again in the reign of Charles II provide more accounts of significant state actions and diplomatic affairs as well as the workings of the court.

The letters included in the book were selected from the Sidney family collections and the early version of the Office of State Papers based on their "political" relevance in the eighteenth century. As such, very few letters by women that are part of the Sidney family archives held in Kent are included in the collection, as their content was likely deemed "domestic" by compliers. James Daybell (2016, 213–15, 217) notes the motivations for archival practices that largely excluded women's letters, including that institutional recordkeeping and familial recordkeeping centered on estate records. He additionally notes that there seems to have been an archival practice to separate women's letters as unrelated to those of public interest. Familial correspondence might have also been kept and recorded as a family history or monument. In the case of the Sidney letters, this can certainly be seen in *Letters and Memorials*, which opens with biographical notes on the family. These notes, however, further suggest the exclusion of women's letters, as they overlook and exclude female family members. Finally, the later construction and organization of archives overlooked women's records (Daybell 2016, 236). A survey of journal articles available on JSTOR shows that *Letters and Memorials* is a frequently cited source for both historians and literary scholars. The letters in *Letters and Memorials* are a common source for the history of the court and its workings. *Letters and Memorials* proves a valuable primary source for Elizabethan and Stuart history, as it has since its publication in the eighteenth century.

Initially this project will use the letters from the reign of Elizabeth since they comprise the bulk of the collection and allow for analysis of change over time. This includes 657 letters beginning in 1565 on 380 folio pages in volume 1 and 270 folio pages in volume 2. As noted above, the majority of the letters are from Sir Henry Sidney or his son, Sir Robert Sidney.

Why Network Analysis?

Since the late 1980s, women's kinship and social networks have received attention in scholarship on women's families, communities, and alliances. Examinations of aristocratic women's political, familial, and patronage networks by critics such as Barbara Harris (2002) and Sharon Kettering (1989) were some of the earliest. Among others, James Daybell (2006, 2016) has produced extensive scholarship on early modern English women's political and epistolary networks (see also Daybell and Gordon 2016). In addition, women's literary communities, networks, or circles have been central to understanding early modern women. The works of Margaret Hannay (1990) and Mary Ellen Lamb (1990) on the Sidney Circle, and the more recent scholarship of Julie Crawford (2014) on the same, participate in network studies, as does Micheline White's (2011) collection on English women's literary circles. Digital network analysis compliments and adds to this area of inquiry about early modern women.

Network analysis uses techniques that incorporate large amounts of data to present a more complete view of a network as a whole than can be found through other methods. This method uses data about individuals or objects and their relationships to provide information about the way a network functioned. It can also provide new or additional information about the centrality of some members over others and the roles of less visible members, including women, in already recognized networks.

This study of networks is based on the understanding of the laws of networks developed from studies in sociology, math, and physics, which found that many kinds of real-world networks follow an underlying order (Barabási 2002). Network analysis was first developed in the social sciences and began to be used in the humanities in the 1980s in the work of Bruno Latour and John Law in the history of science field. Latour and Law developed actor network theory, which proposed a relational understanding of networks of humans and things. This understating of networks emphasizes the importance of adding context and description to explain the web of relations that create a network (Latour 2007; Law 2009). Network analysis has only recently been applied to early modern studies.

In the 1990s, historians gradually began to use network analysis: one of the earliest instances for the early modern era was John Padgett and Christopher Ansell's (1993) examination of the Medici family to understand its political power; they found that women in the family connected the network through marriage, which was the unique factor that granted the family sustained and exceptional political influence. Focused on recreating the early modern social network as a whole, the Six Degrees of Francis Bacon project (sixdegreesoffrancisbacon.com) uses the *Oxford Dictionary of National Biography* as its dataset (Warren et al. 2016). In similar fashion, the Mapping the Republic of Letters project (republicofletters.stanford.edu) uses a series of network analysis case studies to understand the realities, extent, and evolution of the social, physical, and correspondence networks of the Republic of Letters of the Enlightenment. Ruth and Sebastian Ahnert's (2014) work on the letters of Protestant Marian martyrs is among the most significant projects in terms of its use of network analysis to study early modern women, while Michael Morrissey's (2015) study of a French-Indian community in colonial Mississippi has examined the value of social network analysis for social history, finding that women were among the most central and highly connected in the network. The Reception and Circulation of Early Modern Women's Writing project (recirc.universityofgalway.ie), led by Marie-Louise Coolahan, uses network analysis to understand the place of women and their writings in the broader context of early modern writing. Like the RECIRC project, Intertextual Networks by the Women Writers Project (wwp.northeastern.edu/

intertextual-networks) encompasses a number of projects for which scholars are utilizing network analysis to explore early modern women's writing. Ruth and Sebastian Ahnert, together with Kim Albrecht, also created Tudor Networks (tudornetworks.net), which examines the correspondence network represented in the State Papers during the reigns of the Tudors. They have not only discovered broad patterns of communication but are also able to predict people involved in conspiracies and illicit intelligence (Ahnert and Ahnert 2019, 28).

Visualizing the Sidney Network is part of a larger group of early modern network analysis projects that focus on or incorporate gender into their inquiries. This includes Evan Bourke's (2017) work on the women of the Hartlib Circle as well as the RECIRC and Women's Writers projects. Ruth and Sebastian Ahnert's work on the letters of Protestant Marian martyrs influentially used network analysis to highlight the role of women and encourages others to do the same. Large scale projects such as Six Degrees of Francis Bacon and Mapping the Republic of Letters have also addressed issues of gender in their respective networks.[1]

Network analysis uses algorithms to understand the structure of a network. Algorithms highlight figures who were important hubs or connectors in networks. These and other centrality measures can be used to assess women's importance in the networks and the strength of their ties and their roles in the infrastructure of the networks. Network analysis thus offers the ability to highlight women's agency and lost or obscured places within early modern networks.

Networks were a central aspect of early modern politics, especially in regard to patronage, diplomacy, and information sharing, so getting a better idea of the social and political network of the Sidney family will provide useful information about early modern English politics. Using network analysis visualization provides the opportunity to better understand the network that has been the focus of many scholars. Network analysis of an archive of letters, as represented by Collins's collection of the Sidney letters, creates a view of the family's community, albeit one centering on Henry and Robert Sidney.

The work of Ruth and Sebastian Ahnert has been particularly informative about the possibilities provided by network analysis on a collection of letters.

[1] For a more complete and detailed discussion of early modern network analysis projects focused on women or gender, see Medici 2018.

They analyzed 289 letters written by or to Protestants in England during the reign on Mary I to find the social organization of the Protestant community. In addition to the roles of well-known Protestant leaders, Ahnert and Ahnert (2015, 3) show that there was an infrastructure of financial sustainers, copyists, scribes, and carriers who all enabled imprisoned Protestants' letters and writings to reach those in England and in Europe. Their work on the letters of Protestant martyrs points to the centrality of women in the network and their importance to the network's infrastructure, highlighting the strength of their role sustaining the network. This work on the letters of the martyrs is a critical resource for its explanation of network analysis using correspondence. Additionally, Ahnert and Ahnert's (2014, 2015) use of information about individuals discussed within the letters and not just the senders and recipients demonstrates how, with more detailed information, network analysis can reveal the women of the network, who are often obscured because women's letters were kept and archived at a much lower rate than men's. They argue that letters are a "textual witness to social relations and structures," and that network analysis can help uncover the structures, noting the additional benefits of applying network analysis techniques because of their potential to provide additional information about the centrality of members and the roles of less visible members (Ahnert and Ahnert 2015, 2). Importantly, they speak specifically to how network analysis can show women's participation and central place in these networks that have been overlooked.

Before Visualizing the Sidney Network project began, I ran a test analysis and visualization using a randomly selected letter from which I manually extracted individuals and their relationships. In the visualization, a number of women appear as important connectors within the network. This suggests that the project's scope has the potential to show the role of a large variety of women in one of the most significant political networks of Elizabethan England. Additionally, within the visualization it is apparent that women and men are interacting within the same network. Women's and men's networks are often treated separately, but in the case of this letter and the Sidney network as a whole, the relationships and involvement of both genders within networks is significant and presents an important view of the social and political function of the early modern period. The outcome of the test visualization supported two major hypotheses about the Sidney network—(1) that men and women share connections, and (2) that women play a key role within the network—and encouraged further work.

How Network Analysis Works

Networks are created out of *nodes* and *edges* (Fig. 1). *Nodes* are entities or units of information, such as people, locations, or objects. In this project, nodes are people mentioned in the letters. *Edges* are the links or connections between those items. In the case of the Sidney network, edges are the relationships between two people in the network. Network analysis uses statistical analysis and algorithms to provide information about the nodes and edges in the network. These are the most basic aspects of a network, and by adding information to these nodes and edges, networks can become more complex and convey additional information. Edges can be weighted, which shows the different strengths of connection between nodes, which adds complexity to a network as a whole. For example, individuals who are connected many times, like Robert Sidney and his secretary Rowland Whyte, have a heavily weighted connection. Connections can also be directed or not. Directed networks assume that connections occur in a certain way, while undirected networks assume connections are reciprocal or go in both directions. This is, for example, the difference between caring about who wrote a letter and who received it versus being concerned with any connection existing between the two. Additionally, nodes can be categorized, creating a bipartite network where edges go between different kinds of nodes, such as between people and books or objects. These attributes are meaningful for how network measures, which provide information about each node, are calculated.

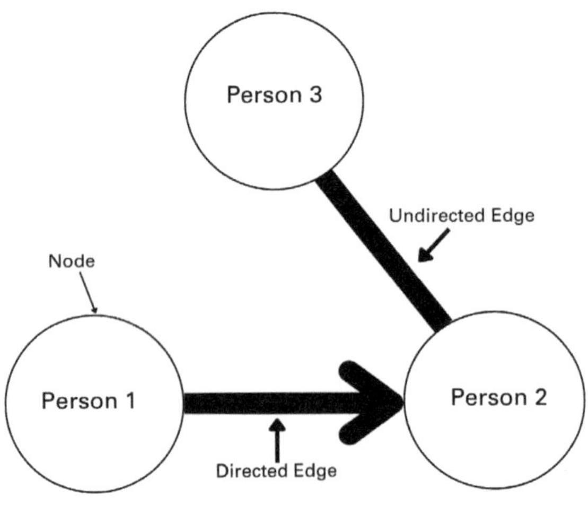

Figure 1. Node and edge diagram.

Network analysis uses algorithms to compute various statistics about the nodes and edges in the network. *Degree* measures the number of connections a node has. Many networks, including the Sidney network, are made of many small degree nodes with a few high degree nodes. High degree nodes act as hubs within the network because they are connected to the most people. In many cases, these connections are expected and might be attributed to the context of the data. In the case of the Sidney letters, we expect a Sidney family member or two to be the highest degree nodes because their letters form the center of the collection. A *shortest path calculation* measures how closely connected every node is in the network. The diameter of the network is the measure of the longest shortest path. The measure of *betweenness* is how many shortest paths pass through a node. A node with high betweenness is important in the network because of the connections it facilitates within the network and its ability to act as a bridge connecting disparate parts of the network. Measuring betweenness highlights nodes of structural importance because they create a path between different parts of the network, which may have been invisible without analysis. These bridges within the network are essential but not necessarily prominent in other methods of analysis. Weak ties or bridges in networks allow for the diffusion of information and the overall strength of the network (Granovetter 1973, 1366, 1368). Significantly for the study of early modern women, this understanding of networks expresses the importance of seemingly marginal actors within a network. In the case of the Sidney network, Katherine Hastings has a high level of betweenness that has not formally been known. *Eigenvector centrality* measures a node's importance based on the importance of its neighbors, essentially a measure of the quality of a node's friends or connections. Hubs often have a high eigenvector measure, but nodes with few connections to other important nodes can also have a high eigenvector score and importance to the network. Nodes that have high eigenvector scores but low betweenness indicate the strength of the network because power is dispersed through the network. Lady Essex—that is, Frances Devereux (nee Walsingham)—holds this role in these years of the Sidney network. Women also frequently show high eigenvector scores because of their relationships to important figures within the network, making them important to the strength of the network (Bourke 2017, 8, 10).

Some of these items become apparent when a network is visualized. For example, a hub in a network is obvious because it has more edges connected to it, and a bridge is a node that creates a link between two parts of a network. If these nodes are removed from the network, it greatly affects the network's integrity and survival; without them, the network collapses or shrinks.

However, measures like eigenvector are not immediately apparent. Network measures reveal the figures who were most important to the network and provide a new kind of evidence for understanding the agency and importance of early modern women in their networks.

Network analysis presents especially interesting possibilities for studying early modern women. Using the theory of triadic closure to predict relationships within a network may address one of the key issues in researching early modern women: the missing sources. Triadic closure is the understanding that if one node is strongly connected to two other nodes, then there must be a connection between the two other nodes as well. In a correspondence network, triadic closure can suggest what the network might look like if we had the letters from other individuals—such as replies to letters or letters that were not saved—and pushes us to examine the possible existence of letters between seemingly unconnected individuals. For example, within the Sidney family network, Henry Sidney has strong correspondence connections with his wife, Mary Dudley Sidney, and William Cecil, leader of the privy council and both a friend and superior to Henry. So, even though Mary's letters were not saved and archived in the same way because her letters were not seen as politically significant by later generations, we may still infer a connection between Mary and Cecil. In fact, letters from Henry Sidney to William Cecil that are part of the Irish State Papers include commendations from Mary Sidney to Cecil (Sidney 1566).

Network analysis can also identify groups within a network using modularity, which finds nodes that are highly connected within the larger network. In the Sidney network, three main letter writers—Henry Sidney, Robert Sidney, and Rowland Whyte—are each at the center of a modularity group; there are also smaller groups centered on Queen Elizabeth and Turlough O'Neill, an Irish lord and clan leader (Fig. 2). We expect the network to have groups centered around the first three men based on the conditions of the collection. The queen is also rather unsurprising because we would expect her to be at the center of a political network. More unexpected, however, is O'Neill, whose modularity suggests his influence over Irish politics.

As with all historical work, it must be acknowledged that our sources are not complete, and thus historical network analysis presents one image of the past rather than an authoritative, objective truth. As Kate Davison (2019, 480) notes, network analysis of the past must be used critically and as a starting point to understanding and further investigation. By highlighting certain individuals, network analysis also points out gaps in research. Figures that have surprising network measures or whose network measures indicate a previously unknown importance in the network may warrant further investigation. Thus, network analysis acts as a type of finding aid to guide scholars to overlooked but significant early modern women, or to confirm suspicions and inferences about their significance.

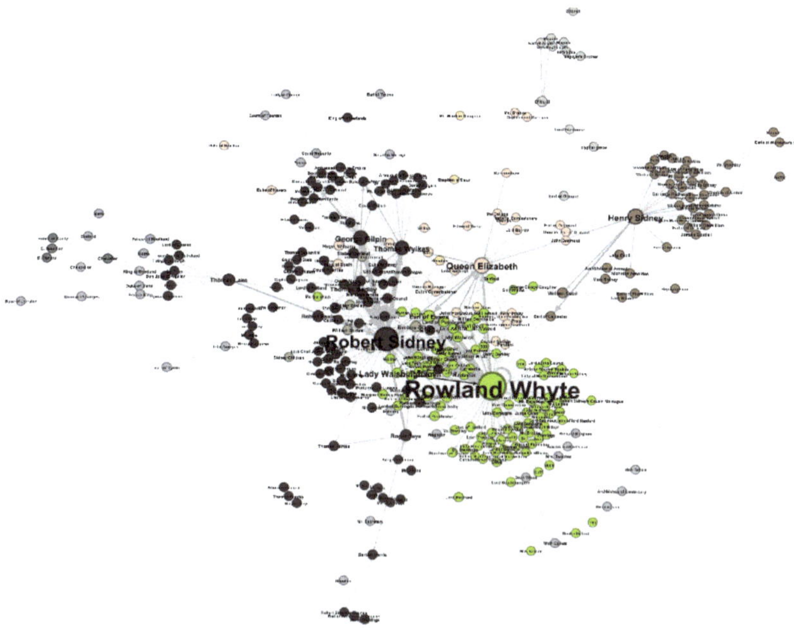

Figure 2. The Sidney network colored by modularity. The colors/shades represent the five distinct groups within the network centered on Robert Sidney, Rowland Whyte, Henry Sidney, Queen Elizabeth, and Turlough O'Neill.

The Process

To create the network, I hand curate the metadata from the letters. Using a digital copy of Collins's *Letters and Memorials*, I read over each letter and manually enter every relationship into a datasheet, recording the type of relationship, gender of both individuals, date, and location, if possible. The categories for connections are based on Ahnert and Ahnert's study of the letters of Protestant martyrs, with a few changes. Connections are categorized into social and letter links including connections created by sending or receiving a letter, acting as a messenger, or meeting in person. There are also commendation links, which are created when a compliment is paid or greetings are passed on from sender to recipient or other party; implied links, which are when a compliment or greeting is passed from recipient to sender or other party; and requested links, which are requests to make a connection with a sender or recipient. Finally, a news link indicates that someone passes along news or information generally, and a reported link indicates when this information is passed directly to a sender or recipient. These connections create directed edges between the nodes of individuals within the network to show the flow of information and connections between individuals.

While manually entering letters into a datasheet is time consuming, technology does not yet exist that can read the letters and extract the social connections, which are what I am most interested in. Existing technology can extract the named individuals or the correspondents but cannot identify and categorize the other social links in the letters. With machine reading, we would know who sent and received letters and largely who was mentioned within them, but we would be unable to distinguish between someone who was a direct contact and gossip about the king of Spain. Just about 9 percent of the links in the sample data years (see below) are letter links, and these are the only links current text analysis or text mining tools are able to extract from the source text.

In addition to being able to extract social links, manual curation has a few other benefits including that it makes the data "cleaner" from the start. "Cleaning" is the process of correcting spellings as well as disambiguating individuals or sometimes putting them back together: recognizing, for example, that at certain points the lord secretary is Francis Walsingham, and the "Earl of Essex" is the same as "Lord Essex." Common problems with early modern documents are that one person may be referred to in multiple ways by name, aristocratic title, and/or office; the fact that titles, offices, and office holders change; and the frequency of variant spellings. However, Rowland Whyte's use of a unique alphanumeric coding system for some individuals within some letters is a more unique cleaning issue. I fix some of these issues immediately while entering data, assisted by my familiarity with the letters and the Sidneys; others are addressed in a later cleaning process with the aid of reference works on the Sidneys and the *Oxford Dictionary of National Biography*. Moving forward, the open data of individuals in early modern England from the Six Degrees of Francis Bacon project will also be used. Another benefit of hand curating the data is that I get to read all the letters and have found trends and information I otherwise would not have, such as Robert Sidney and Rowland Whyte's discussion of the marriage prospects of young courtiers that rivals those between characters in a Jane Austen novel, or seeing the extent of information about women in Ireland with information about the elopement of a Irish clan leader and the daughter of an English official (see Medici 2020).

The years 1565/66, 1590, and 1595 are the three complete years I have worked through this process so far. I then enter the data in the Gephi network analysis program, which creates visualizations of the data but also, often more importantly, runs network analytics to produce network measures. I chose to use Gephi because of the analytics and network measures and visualizations it provides, and because I have received training on the program. In the visualization (Fig. 3) it is easy to see the types of connections and the gender breakdown of the network because I color coded each relationship type as well as colored male nodes gray and female nodes orange. There are currently no non-binary or people with unknown gender in the dataset, but they would be represented as yellow nodes.

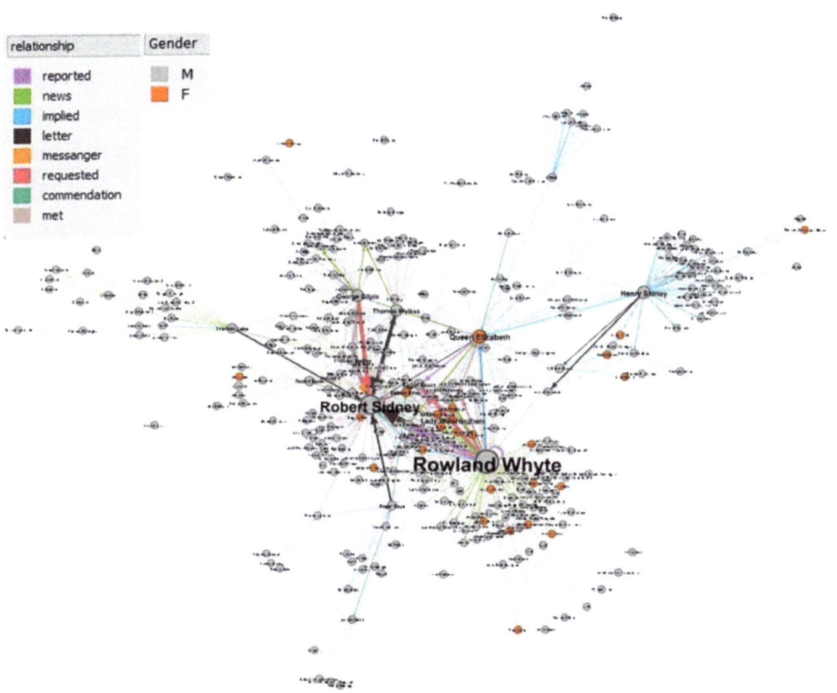

Figure 3. The Sidney network from 1565/1566, 1590, and 1595 visualized using Gephi. Edges are colored according to connection type, and nodes are colored by gender (men are gray, women are orange).

Findings

In addition to being fun to look at, the visualizations can help guide further research questions. Because I have colored men gray and women orange, I can see on closer examination that there is a cluster of women between Robert Sidney and his secretary Rowland Whyte, as well as between Whyte and the queen (Fig. 4). That suggests further investigation should be done on those women and the letters in which they appear, which we can now identify and find because of the data curation. This is especially true when thinking of the eigenvector centrality measure, as these women are connected to three of the most important individuals in the network and may have high betweenness rankings if they connect individuals to these network hubs. As it turns out, the women served as information sources for Whyte, who passed along the information to Robert Sidney in the Netherlands. For example, Katherine Hastings provided information to Whyte about the queen's intentions regarding Robert's requested leave from his position as governor in the Netherlands (Whyte 1746, 354), and Lady Warwick acted as a strong connector in the network and created requested links between Whyte/Robert Sidney and Queen Elizabeth, the Lord Admiral Charles Howard, and Robert Cecil. Lady Warwick's place at court as one of the gentlewomen of the queen's privy chamber and one of the queen's close confidants helped her make these connections.

Other findings from these sample years suggest the significant role of women within the Sidney network. As we would expect based on whose letters were collected and why they were chosen, the highest degree nodes are Robert Sidney, Rowland Whyte, Queen Elizabeth, and Henry Sidney, but within the top 25 members of the network for their number of connections are Barbara Sidney, Lady Warwick, Lady Essex, and Katherine Hastings. When considering weighted degree or multiple connections to the same person, the women's places in the network rise to within the top 15 members of the network. Others in the top 25 highest degree nodes of the network suggest the power and influence that make up the center of the Sidney network, including the Lord Treasurer, the Earl of Essex, the queen's favorite, and the Secretaries of State and leaders of the privy council William and Robert Cecil. The high degree rankings of the four women show how well connected they were within the network, making them central figures within it, while the other high degree nodes suggest that this located them in a place of political significance. Robert Sidney, Rowland Whyte, and Queen Elizabeth are the top for both betweenness and eigenvector centrality rankings, but among other notables for betweenness, including both William and Robert Cecil and the

Earl of Essex, is Katherine Hastings. Katherine's high betweenness shows the large number of connections she facilitates within the network. In terms of hubs, Lady Warwick ranks just above Queen Elizabeth as the sixth largest hub in the network, suggesting her important role as a connector. Lady Essex and Katherine Hastings are also in the top 10 for eigenvector centrality because of the importance of their connections to the network overall. Lady Warwick has a high eigenvector score but a low betweenness score, indicating the strength of the network and that she plays an important infrastructural role. While women account for only 8 percent (28 of 344) of the individuals in the network, these network measures suggest that women included in the network were significant for its function. From their network measures it is apparent that these women held important roles within the network and were significant factors in the network's infrastructure.

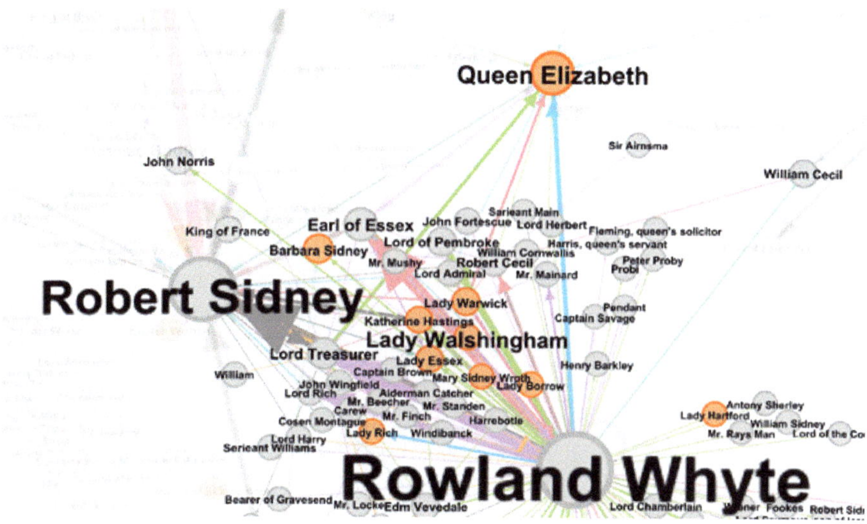

Figure 4. A group of ladies—Barbra Sidney, Katherine Hastings, Lady Warwick, Lady Walsingham, Lady Essex, Mary Sidney Wroth, and Lady Borrow—are between Robert Sidney, Rowland Whyte, and Queen Elizabeth.

In addition to their network measures that suggest their central place within the network, these women have something else in common. Barbara Sidney was Robert Sidney's wife (Gray 2004). Lady Warwick was Ann Russell Dudley, the wife of Ambrose Dudley, sister-in-law to Henry Sidney, and aunt to Robert Sidney (Adams 2004). Katherine Hastings, Countess of Huntingdon, was sister of Mary Sidney, Henry Sidney's wife and Robert's mother; she was also at one time the guardian of Robert, and the two had a close relationship (Cross 2004). Lady Essex was Frances Walsingham, who had a complex kin relationship to the Sidneys. Her first husband was Philip Sidney, son of Henry and bother of Robert, and her second husband, the Earl of Essex Robert Devereux, was a ward of Katherine Hastings and also step-son to Robert Dudley, a brother-in-law and uncle to the Sidneys (Tsakiropoulou 2019). The women in positions of importance in the network, holding infrastructural roles that help the network function, were also all part of the extended Sidney family network. But as the network measures make clear, they were also part of the Sidney political network as recorded in political letters. While there are other women in the network, in the years of this study they do not rank highly in network measures, suggesting they did not have key roles in the network. These network measures are a significant indication that more work should be done on the roles of women in the Sidney political network. For example, Katherine Hastings has been either overlooked or dismissed as peripheral to the network, but network measures indicate that she was in fact central to the network in terms of the number and importance of the connections she had and facilitated.

Some other trends have become apparent through the data. Visualizations of the sample years 1565/66, 1590, and 1595 show higher betweenness and eigenvector scores for women in the later years of Elizabeth's reign than in the first decade, suggesting that their place within the network and the politics of Elizabethan England shifted. Moving forward, it will be interesting to trace the changes that occur over time in the network and its measures through Elizabeth's reign and investigate the causes, including if they are a feature of the Sidney network or represent a broader shift in Elizabethan politics. Importantly, while the letters within Collins's collection are almost entirely to and from men, within them women and men share and ask for information about and make social connections with both genders. The social connections show a more complex picture of the network. As hypothesized, tracing both social and letter connections shows that women and men function within the same network, and tracing the social connections brings out the women within the network. While we cannot make up for archival practices and the historical loss of women's letters, this more in-depth method of tracing a social network through letters helps to reconstruct the mixed-gender networks that early modern people functioned within.

In addition to individuals, geographical issues are apparent when looking at the network. The wives of Irish lords or clan leaders appear frequently in the letters of Henry Sidney during his time as lord deputy of Ireland, and they make the English very anxious. Keeping an eye on the locations where women appear will also be important moving forward. Eventually this may point to areas where women are more likely to be active within the political network and perhaps within politics more broadly. Like the significance of the network itself, these trends can only be explained if one moves from the distant reading of larger patterns to a close reading of specific connections and relationships.

Conclusions

Network analysis creates algorithmic network measures that can highlight and bring to prominence women who held important structural roles or were central within networks, many of whom other methods of network study have overlooked or obscured. Using the methods of network analysis, Visualizing the Sidney Network recreates the Sidney family political network from a collection of political letters and finds just this. Hand-curated data of three sample years has already suggested the significant place of women in the network through both network measures and visualization and subsequent investigation. Additionally, it is clear this is a mixed-gender network with men and women sharing connections. Ultimately, the goal of Visualizing the Sidney Network is to provide support for a new understanding of early modern politics that recognizes women's influence and place within networks of power by explaining the roles that women had in the Sidney network, who these women were who held important roles, and how this changed throughout Elizabeth's reign.

The planned end point of the project includes an interactive network visualization and access to the dataset. I would like the project to be useful as a dataset of connections within the Sidney network for scholars studying their connections, as well as a source of information about the letters such that the data can be used to understand the family's movements and temporality using the location and date information in the data. For scholars more broadly interested in Elizabethan England or early modern women, I plan to make the data and visualizations searchable by individual, location, and date so that other people of interest can be located and analyzed. I foresee this being especially useful for the women in the network. I hope that the project will provide detailed information about the Sidney network for Sidney scholars as well as further our understanding of the impact of analyzing and visualizing gender within early modern networks.

WORKS CITED

Adams, Simon. 2002. *Leicester and the Court: Essays on Elizabethan Politics.* Manchester: Manchester University Press.

———. 2004. "Dudley [*née* Russell], Anne, Countess of Warwick (1548/9–1604), Courtier." In *Oxford Dictionary of National Biography*. Oxford: Oxford University Press. doi.org/10.1093/ref:odnb/69744.

Ahnert, Ruth, and Sebastian E. Ahnert. 2014. "A Community Under Attack: Protestant Letter Networks in the Reign of Mary I." *Leonardo* 47, no. 3 (June): 275. doi.org/10.1162/LEON_a_00778.

———. 2015. "Protestant Letter Networks in the Reign of Mary I: A Quantitative Approach." *English Literary History* 82, no. 1 (Spring): 1–33. doi.org/10.1353/elh.2015.0000.

———. 2019. "Metadata, Surveillance and the Tudor State." *History Workshop Journal* 87 (Spring): 27–51. doi.org/10.1093/hwj/dby033.

Barabási, Albert-László. 2002. *Linked: The New Science of Networks*. Cambridge, MA: Perseus.

Bourke, Evan. 2017. "Female Involvement, Membership, and Centrality: A Social Network Analysis of the Hartlib Circle." *Literature Compass* 14, no. 4 (April): 1–17. doi.org/10.1111/lic3.12388.

Brennan, Michael. 2006. *The Sidneys of Penshurst and the Monarchy, 1500–1700.* Burlington, VT: Ashgate. doi.org/10.4324/9781315237060.

Collins, Arthur. 1746. *Letters and Memorials of State: In the Reigns of Queen Mary, Queen Elizabeth, King James, King Charles the First, Part of the Reign of King Charles the Second, and Oliver's Usurpation.* 2 vols. London: T. Osborne.

Crawford, Julie. 2014. *Mediatrix: Women, Politics, and Literary Production in Early Modern England*. Oxford: Oxford University Press.

Cross, Claire. 1967. *The Puritan Earl: The Life of Henry Hastings, Third Earl of Huntingdon, 1536–1595*. London: St. Martin's Press.

———. 2004. "Hastings [*née* Dudley], Katherine, Countess of Huntingdon (c. 1538–1620), Noblewoman." In *Oxford Dictionary of National Biography*. Oxford: Oxford University Press. doi.org/10.1093/ref:odnb/69739.

Davison, Kate. 2019. "Early Modern Social Networks: Antecedents, Opportunities, and Challenges." *The American Historical Review* 124, no. 2 (April): 456–82. doi.org/10.1093/ahr/rhz253.

Daybell, James. 2006. *Women Letter-Writers in Tudor England.* Oxford: Oxford University Press. doi.org/10.1093/acprof:oso/9780199259915.001.0001.

———. 2016. "Gendered Archival Practices and the Future Lives of Letters." In *Cultures of Correspondence in Early Modern Britain*, edited by James Daybell and Andrew Gordon, 210–36. Philadelphia: University of Pennsylvania Press. doi.org/10.9783/9780812292930-012.

Daybell, James, and Andrew Gordon, eds. 2016. *Women and Epistolary Agency in Early Modern Culture, 1450–1690.* New York: Routledge. doi.org/10.4324/9781315546919.

Granovetter, Mark S. 1973. "The Strength of Weak Ties." *American Journal of Sociology* 78, no. 6 (May): 1360–80. doi.org/10.1086/225469.

Gray, Madeleine. 2004. "Sidney [*née* Gamage], Barbara, Countess of Leicester (c. 1559–1621), Noblewoman." In *Oxford Dictionary of National Biography.* Oxford: Oxford University Press. doi.org/10.1093/ref:odnb/67993.

Hannay, Margaret P. 1990. *Philip's Phoenix: Mary Sidney, Countess of Pembroke.* Oxford: Oxford University Press.

———. 2010. *Mary Sidney, Lady Wroth.* Burlington, VT: Ashgate. doi.org/10.4324/9781315594095.

Harris, Barbara. 2002. *English Aristocratic Women, 1450–1550: Marriage and Family, Property and Careers.* New York: Oxford University Press.

Kettering, Sharon. 1989. "The Patronage Power of Early Modern French Noblewomen." *The Historical Journal* 32, no. 4 (December): 817–41. doi.org/10.1017/S0018246X00015727.

Kinnamon Noel, and Michael Brennan. 2003. *The Sidney Chronology, 1554–1654.* New York: Palgrave Macmillan.

Lamb, Mary Ellen. 1990. *Gender and Authorship in the Sidney Circle.* Madison: University of Wisconsin Press.

Latour, Bruno. 2007. *Reassembling the Social: An Introduction to Actor-Network-Theory.* Oxford: Oxford University Press.

Law, John. 2009. "Actor Network Theory and Material Semiotics." In *The New Blackwell Companion to Social Theory*, edited by Bryan S. Turner, 141–58. New York: Wiley-Blackwell. doi.org/10.1002/9781444304992.ch7.

Medici, Catherine. 2018. "Using Network Analysis to Understand Early Modern Women." *Early Modern Women* 13, no. 1 (Fall): 153–63. doi.org/10.1353/emw.2018.0058.

———. 2020. "Becoming a Scot and Cross-Cultural Marriages in *Outlander* and the Early Modern British Isles." *Nursing Clio* (blog). 5 March 2020. nursingclio.org/2020/03/05/becoming-a-scot-and-cross-cultural-marriages-in-outlander-and-the-early-modern-british-isles.

Morrissey, Robert Michael. 2015. "Archive of Connection: 'Whole Network' Analysis and Social History." *Historical Methods* 48 (3): 67–79. doi.org/10.1080/01615440.2014.962208.

Padgett, John F., and Christopher K. Ansell. 1993. "Robust Action and the Rise of the Medici, 1400–1434." *The American Journal of Sociology* 98, no. 6 (May): 1259–1319. doi.org/10.1086/230190.

Sidney, Henry. 1566. "Lord Deputy Sidney to Sir William Cecil." The National Archives of the UK. SP 63/17 f.37.

Tsakiropoulou, Ioanna. 2019. "Devereux, Frances [*née* Walsingham; *Other Married Names* Sidney and Burke], countess of Essex and of Clanricarde (c. 1568–1632), Noblewoman." In *Oxford Dictionary of National Biography*. Oxford: Oxford University Press. doi.org/10.1093/odnb/9780198614128.013.112779.

Warren, Christopher, Daniel Shore, Jessica Otis, Lawrence Wang, Mike Finegold, and Cosma Shalizi. 2016. "Six Degrees of Francis Bacon: A Statistical Method for Reconstructing Large Historical Social Networks." *Digital Humanities Quarterly* 10 (3). doi.org/10.17613/M6B020.

White, Micheline, ed. 2011. *English Women, Religion, and Textual Production, 1500–1625*. Burlington, VT: Ashgate. doi.org/10.4324/9781315579818.

Whyte, Rowland. 1746. "Rowland Whyte to Robert Sidney, 8 October 1595." In *Letters and Memorials of State*, edited by Arthur Collins, 354. Vol. 1. London: T. Osborne.

Chapter 2: Print Networks of Early Modern Astronomy in Galileo's Library

Crystal Hall
Bowdoin College

In August 1640, Galileo Galilei (1564–1642) found himself once again responding to a problem that had dogged him nearly his entire writing career: disassociating himself from something he had not written. This time, instead of recovering phrasing and intentions that had been garbled by an opponent, possibly intentionally, he was correcting the memory of a well-regarded colleague, Fortunio Liceti (1577–1657). By then Liceti was a philosophy professor at the University of Bologna, but he had known Galileo since they overlapped as faculty members at the University of Padua in 1609. Extant correspondence between the two philosophers documents a respectful, although not entirely philosophically aligned, intellectual friendship, and Galileo owned more works by Liceti than by any other author. Liceti's printed texts are ambitiously and meticulously annotated and glossed with sources and attributions, either by Liceti or his publishers. Yet, he had made a mistake in a letter that he sent to Galileo about the nature of light. In his response, Galileo praises Liceti's critical style, but he is compelled to address the misidentification: "I am surprised that you attribute to me something indicated by [Giulio Cesare] Lagalla, that I thought light to be a material and corporeal thing, while you yourself read that the same author says that I was always unable to penetrate its nature."[1] Lagalla (1576–1624) was a Neapolitan, a Jesuit working primarily in Rome, committed to most, but not all, Aristotelian precepts (similarly to Liceti), and a frequent correspondent of Galileo. How could Liceti have confused Lagalla for Galileo? Even without quantitative analysis of Latin works by the two authors, it is evident that style does not link the two.

[1] The Italian letter reads: "mi sono maravigliato che ella per cosa accennata dal filosofo Lagalla mi atrribuisca che io habbia tenuto il lume essere cosa materiale e corporea, mentre che ella medesima legge nell'istesso autore che io mi era sempre tenuto tanto inhabile a poter penetrare che sia il lume" (Galilei 1890–1900, 18:223). All translations are my own unless otherwise indicated. Liceti (1642, 167) includes part of Galileo's reply.

ISBN 978-1-64959-119-7 (paper) ISBN 978-1-64959-120-3 (pdf) ISBN 978-1-64959-121-0 (epub)
New Technologies in Medieval and Renaissance Studies 12 (2025) 35–60

Theme is similarly unlikely, since Galileo did not publish treatises on light or speculate about its nature in print.

The answer to Liceti's confusion lies in the early work of a large, collaborative project in development: Galileo's Library (research.bowdoin.edu/galileos-library). As developer of this project, my goal has been to document, digitize, and curate the books in Galileo's personal library (Hall 2015). Because a clean, full text is unavailable for this complete set of books, a preliminary phase of curation has focused on the data presented on the books' title pages.[2] While the data currently exist as a spreadsheet, continued work aspires to the usability of an interface similar to the Early Modern Dramatic Paratexts project at the Folger Shakespeare Library (paratexts.folger.edu). Literary theorist Gerard Genette (1997) has called aspects of the book, such as the title page paratext, the "threshold" for entering or crossing into a book; that is, all of the materials, experiences, and words that we encounter before we start to read the content of a book.[3] The paratext, like other material traces of an early modern book, tells an important story about the history of the challenges that an author faced once the manuscript was complete: financing the labor and supplies for printing, acquiring available legal protection in the form of copyright for reprinting and sales, securing permissions from imperial or papal censors, getting distribution through publishers and booksellers, crafting advertisement through at least the title page, and establishing associations with prestigious individuals to increase the apparent authority and value of the work (Maclean 2009, 132–33; Smith 2011). Treating the title page as a micronetwork of individuals and the sites of their labor opens the possibility to connect one volume to others at scale without full text. The title pages can thus document the network of labor, associations, and gatekeeping surrounding late Renaissance information, which offers the missing interpretative layer that conflates the works of Galileo and Lagalla.

This study is based on the people, institutions, and places named on the title pages of 152 books in Galileo's library, described in more detail in the

---

[2] This method, for now, overlooks the possibility that different names might appear on the title page and in the colophon of a book. Given the scarcity of documentation about non-bound print materials in Galileo's collection, the corpus knowingly omits, for the time being, an investigation of ephemeral prints such as brochures, flysheets, handbills, pamphlets, and other newly minted print genres from this period (see Dackerman 2011; Walsby 2013, 11–14).

[3] Helen Smith and Louise Wilson (2011) offer an overview of this theory in the Renaissance context as well as a significant bibliography.

next sections. This paratext contains the bibliographic information (the metadata) that helps us locate each volume in a modern physical or digital repository, but it can also create a navigational tool for the collection as a whole.[4] When seen together, the nodes on title pages represent networks of authors, printers, patrons, editors, commentators, and printing centers (including pseudonyms, false imprint locations, and other deliberately misleading metadata).[5] In the case of the books authored or owned by Galileo, the category of patron carries added interpretative weight. Mario Biagioli (1994) has done revealing work to establish an understanding of the courtly practices in Italy, the social network that prominently underlies the production of printed materials in Galileo's collection. Yet, patrons were only one piece of the puzzle. Isabelle Pantin (1999) has highlighted how printers and print formats shaped the potential reception of Copernican ideas outside of Italy, and how the paratextual materials were essential attributes of making public the relationships between authoritative arbiters of knowledge and the content of a volume. Pantin highlights Galileo's early missteps in this regard, which created challenges for publishing his final work, *Two New Sciences*, outside of Italy in 1638. Building on this work, Renée Raphael (2012) has documented the network of printers, publishers, and even stationers who worked as intermediaries and collaborators in the efforts to put that work into print. Yet, each of these material layers can only offer a glimpse of the broader system of promoting and disseminating new and controversial information.

Examining the layers together from a perspective of digital network analysis both reinforces the conclusions drawn by microhistories of early modern print in Italy and reveals new paths for exploration. Historians of science often speak figuratively of networks of knowledge and production in relation to printed books; the Galileo's Library project is an opportunity to represent printed volumes as such.[6] The title page documents this network of exchange, and this chapter builds upon that concept to convert title page

[4] This study resists adding ontologies to the data but is complementary to the surveys by Inga Söderlund (2010) and Nick Kanas (2011).

[5] Yves Gingras (2010) has conducted a similar study using names mentioned in letters. Stefano Gulizia (2016) has explored the ways in which print and instrument-making cross diverse networks of audiences.

[6] Matteo Valleriani (2017) and his team (Kräutli and Valleriani 2018) have done something similar, but with a focus on just one title that saw multiple reprints, Johannes de Sacrobosco's *Sphere*. Valleriani's work represents a possible next step for database development for titles in Galileo's library for which we do not have specific bibliographic details.

information into network data in order to better understand the contexts in which Galileo's works were composed and interpreted. There is also a prevailing narrative that printers of what historians have labeled "key texts" in the history of science are responsible for ushering in the revolutionary shifts in epistemology and philosophy that preceded the Enlightenment. But even the partial network offered by information on the title pages reveals how the local stories at smaller presses are sites of exchange across genres, forms, and collaborators in late Renaissance cultural expression.

We will see that this paratextual space shaped Liceti's recollection and confusion of Galileo and Lagalla. When contextualized in the network of print production of texts that used terms associated with astronomy on their title pages, not only can Liceti's slip be forgiven, but we can evaluate whether or not this paratext contributed to other framings and (mis)identifications of Galileo's work. We can ask where each book connects with works on astronomy and, eventually, with works on other subjects in the library. We can see what or who is not present. We can see the margins more clearly and start asking questions about their relationship with the center. This method also allows us to put Latin and Italian works into conversation with one another at scale in ways that text analysis does not easily permit. In so doing, the corpus of these printed volumes in Galileo's library pushes against methodologies of digital humanities, history, and literary analysis that rely on post hoc categories of genre, distinctions of form, and separation of labor. The title page offers traces of how those boundaries blurred or disappeared altogether, leaving something more heterogeneous than just relationships of correspondence or financial transactions. The resulting network of people, places, and institutions that share a title page is an abstraction of the geopolitical, practical, and conceptual environments in which Galileo operated. While this network has navigational capacity, pointing us toward interesting questions, its descriptive power is limited, since it immediately and always points to other possible networks.[7] For instance, Paula Findlen (2019a) has documented the role of Jesuit authors in Europe as brokers of knowledge arriving from and being sent to Jesuit missionaries in India, China, and Japan. Only part of their work is seen through this examination of title pages. Even with these limitations, the network represented essentially by proper nouns on title pages that use astronomical terms in Galileo's library expands the contexts in which to interpret historical and literary expressions of the period.

[7] For an overview of the multiple network layers in this context, see Findlen 2019b.

A Micronetwork of Contexts

The people, places, and institutions appearing on the title page of Galileo's *Sidereus nuncius*, or *Starry Messenger*, published in Venice in early 1610, provide a clear example of nodes in a network of ideas, agents, and sites of activity in early modern discourse in print and help to answer the question of Liceti's confusion. The *Starry Messenger* presents Galileo's observations of heavenly bodies with his modified telescope and offers an example of how this contextual network is structured. In addition to observing what he correctly interpreted as mountains and craters on the moon's surface, Galileo also documented his observation of four previously unseen stars that he determined to be orbiting Jupiter. The imperfect lunar surface and the appearance of apparent stars orbiting something other than earth undermined Aristotelian and Ptolemaic conceptions of the structure of the cosmos and lent controversial weight to the Copernican hypothesis of heliocentrism. The novelty of applying a military device to the study of celestial phenomena, combined with the technical skill involved in improving a device brought to the Veneto by a Dutch traveler, made the rush to the press more intense because of the value, both economic and social, that it carried for Galileo's career.

The *Starry Messenger* underscores the importance of choices made at every level for selecting and expressing each detail that readers would have encountered on the title page (Fig. 1).[8] The title page, translated by Stillman Drake, reads as follows:

> The *Starry Messenger* revealing great, unusual, and remarkable spectacles, opening these to the consideration of every man, and especially of philosophers and astronomers; As observed by Galileo Galilei Gentleman of Florence Professor of Mathematics in the University of Padua, With the aid of a spyglass lately invented by him, In the surface of the Moon, in innumerable Fixed Stars, in Nebulae, and above all in Four Planets swiftly revolving around Jupiter at differing distances and periods, and known to no one before the Author recently perceived them and decided that they should be named The Medicean Stars. (Galilei 1957, 23)

Galileo initially proposed calling the satellites "Cosmici" (cosmics) or the "Medicea Sydera" (Medicean stars) as a way to honor Grand Duke of Tuscany Cosimo II de' Medici in a bid for, or in recognition of, late-breaking patronage (Biagioli 2006). In addition, by applying Biagioli's (1994) work on Galileo's

[8] For a parallel study on a book in Galileo's collection, see Gattei 2015.

efforts to establish himself as a courtier, we notice the relative sizes of the data of value: "patritio florentino" (gentleman of Florence) and "perspicilli," the Latin term for the telescope, and the much larger advertisement of the "Medicea Siderea," the Medicean stars.

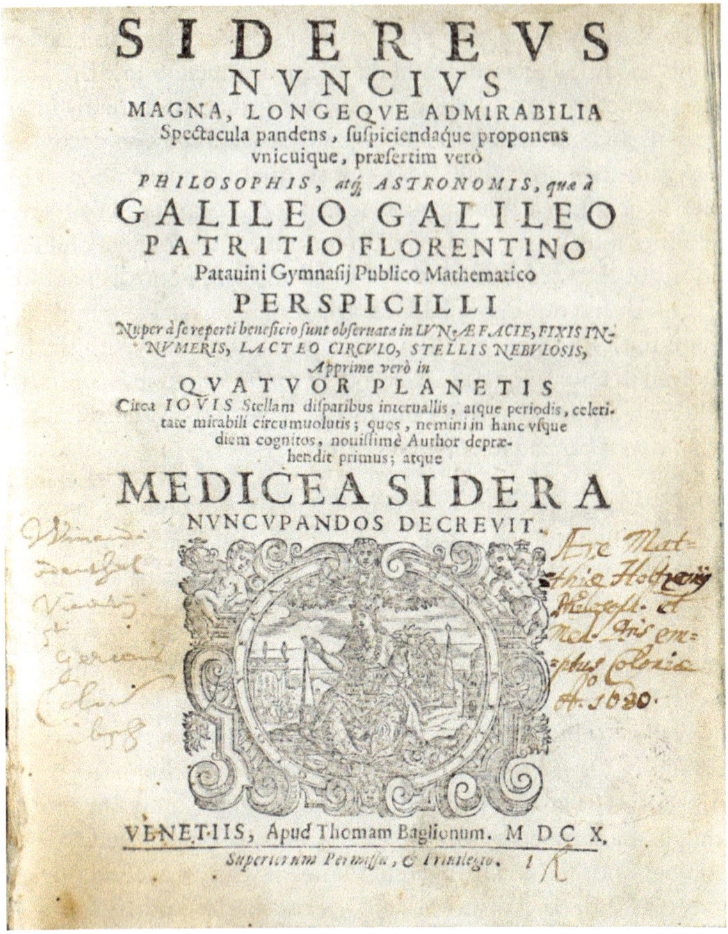

SIDEREVS
NVNCIVS
MAGNA, LONGEQVE ADMIRABILIA
Spectacula pandens, suſpiciendaque proponens
vnicuique, præſertim verò
PHILOSOPHIS, atq; *ASTRONOMIS*, quæ à
GALILEO GALILEO
PATRITIO FLORENTINO
Patauini Gymnaſij Publico Mathematico
PERSPICILLI
Nuper à ſe reperti beneficio ſunt obſeruata in LVNÆ FACIE, FIXIS INNVMERIS, LACTEO CIRCVLO, STELLIS NEBVLOSIS,
Apprime verò in
QVATVOR PLANETIS
Circa IOVIS Stellam diſparibus interuallis, atque periodis, celeritate mirabili circumuolutis; quos, nemini in hanc vſque diem cognitos, nouiſſimè Author deprehendit primus; atque
MEDICEA SIDERA
NVNCVPANDOS DECREVIT.

VENETIIS, Apud Thomam Baglionum. M D C X.
Superiorum Permiſſu, & Priuilegio.

Figure 1. Title page of the first edition of Galileo's *Sidereus nuncius* (1610), known in English as the *Starry Messenger*. Image credit: *Sidereus nuncius magna, longeque admirabilia spectacula pandens* [. . .] *Galileo Galileo* [. . .]: *nuper a se reperti beneficio sunt observata in lunae facie, fixis innumeris, lacteo circulo, stellis nebulosis, apprime vero in quatuor planetis circa* [. . .]. Venetiis: Thomam Baglionum, 1610. ETH-Bibliothek Zürich, Rar 4342: 1, doi.org/10.3931/e-rara-695/Public Domain Mark.

Directing our gaze to the bottom of the page we see the printer's mark and the final nodes for this book's micronetwork. Nick Wilding's (2014) painstaking research on the material history of the first printing of the *Starry Messenger* has not only prevented a recent multi-million-dollar auction of a forgery of the work but has also shown that Tomaso Baglioni's name on the title page was "legally irregular" (95). By tracing the heritage of books printed by Baglioni along with printers' marks and woodcuts, Wilding has convincingly shown that Galileo deliberately chose a press, printer, and publisher for the *Starry Messenger* who could insert his work into a particular network of rebellious Venetian intellectuals. The printer and bookseller Roberto Meietti was known for selling banned books (which provoked his excommunication in 1606). With Baglioni's help, he had established an extensive network in Germany and Austria for procuring and transporting these and other less scandalous volumes. As a result, his bookstore was an intellectual hub in Venice. In 1607, Baglioni printed Galileo's defense of his intellectual property regarding his manual for using a geometric compass, which had been plagiarized by local Baldassare Capra. Wilding (2014, 105) suggests that Galileo and Giovanni Francesco Sagredo likely purchased many of their pre-1602 books printed beyond the Alps from Meietti's store. Their work was often as controversial in its support of heretical ideas as it was licentious in its distribution of erotica. Wilding's work was laborious because he needed to reconstruct shared groups of printers' blocks from printed evidence that had been dispersed across Italian libraries over the course of four centuries. Frequent Venetian book buyers would have likely already been aware of the visual and verbal cues hidden in the book's metadata.

Liceti's confusion of Lagalla for Galileo adds evidence to this conjecture about the recognition of the cultural values associated with these markers. Baglioni also published Lagalla's *De phoenominis in orbe lunae* (On the phenomena of the lunar orb) and *De luce et lumine* (On light and illumination) as two books in one volume in 1612 (Fig. 2). The work represents the Neapolitan physician's response to the *Starry Messenger* and to experiments with the telescope and the luminescent "Bologna stone" in Rome in April 1611. Lagalla's association with the heretical press is surprising, even though Candida Carella (2016) and Alberto Martinez (2018) have shown his engagement with Giordano Bruno's theories in the work. Lagalla was born in the southern province of Salerno, near Naples, he was a professor of Aristotelian philosophy at the Collegio Romano and La Sapienza and published all of his several other works in Rome, and he was physician to Cardinal Pietro Aldobrandino (Gallo 1986, 1987). The founder of the Accademia dei Lincei, Federico Cesi, had considered inviting Lagalla to join because of the potential symbolic victory that Lagalla's presumed

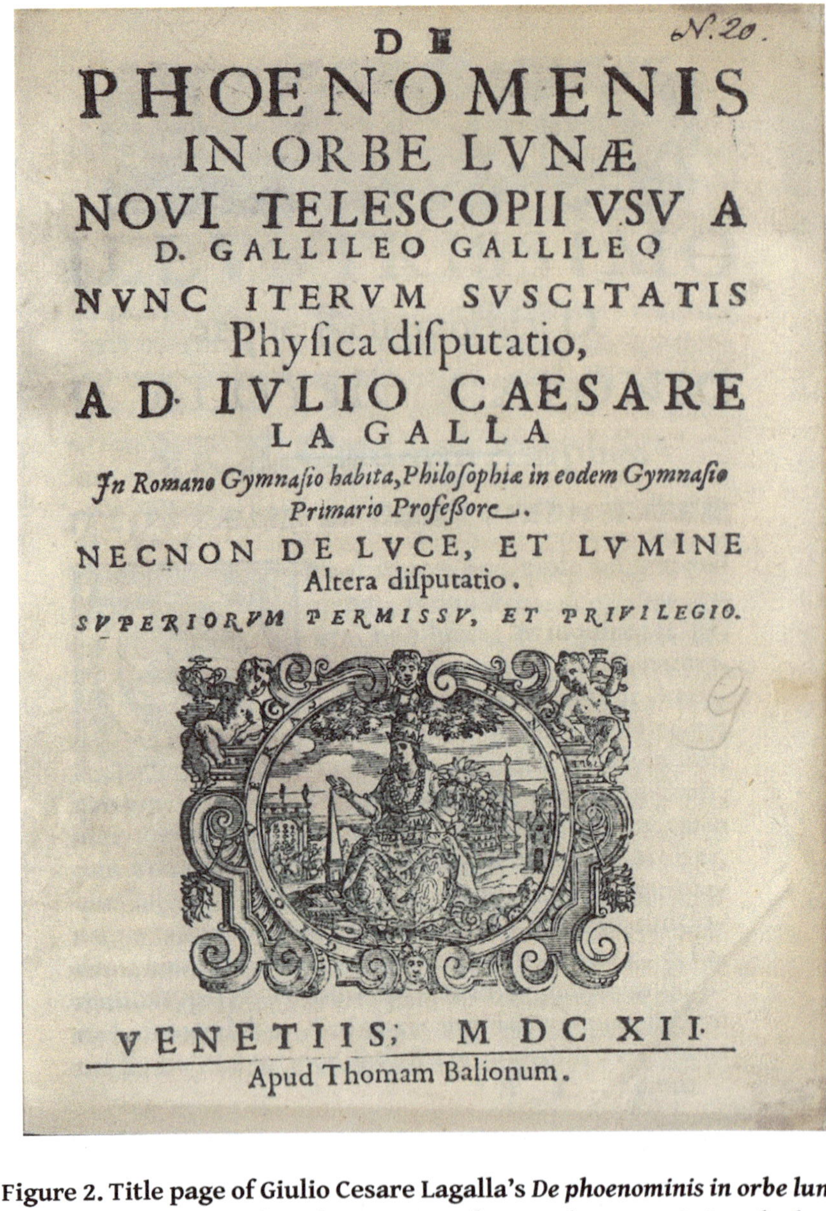

DE
PHOENOMENIS
IN ORBE LVNÆ
NOVI TELESCOPII VSV A
D. GALLILEO GALLILEO
NVNC ITERVM SVSCITATIS
Phyſica diſputatio,
A D. IVLIO CAESARE
LA GALLA
In Romano Gymnaſio habita, Philoſophiæ in eodem Gymnaſio Primario Profeßore.
NECNON DE LVCE, ET LVMINE
Altera diſputatio.
SVPERIORVM PERMISSV, ET PRIVILEGIO.

VENETIIS, M DC XII.
Apud Thomam Balionum.

Figure 2. Title page of Giulio Cesare Lagalla's *De phoenominis in orbe lunae* and *De luce et lumine* (1612). Image credit: *De phoenomenis in orbe lunae novi telescopii usu a* [. . .] *Gallileo Gallileo nunc iterum suscitatis physica disputatio: necnon De luce et lumine.* Venetiis: Thomam Balionum, 1612. ETH-Bibliothek Zürich, Rar 2076, doi.org/10.3931/e-rara-14760/Public Domain Mark.

anti-Aristotelianism would represent for the new natural philosophy academy (Caredda 2008, 121–31).[9] Ultimately, Lagalla's text was not as pro-Galilean as Cesi had hoped, and he laments in a letter to Galileo in September 1611 that he had not been able to see a copy prior to publication because Lagalla "was having it sent to be printed outside [of Rome]."[10] Cesi's expression suggests that the Lincei were cut out of the publishing conversation. Lagalla's connection to Baglioni in Venice must have taken considerable effort on behalf of his social network, since the Jesuits had been expelled from the region in 1606.[11] The choice of printer places much emphasis on the value of that association for the dispute and Lagalla's desires to leave Rome. The result also clarifies why Liceti had interchanged the two treatises: material and topical similarities along with the connotations of the press that produced them.

Modern scholarship has listed Baglioni as the printer of Lagalla's two-book volume without other remarks. Seeing him in this Galilean network brings to light the potential value placed on his press that has not survived in correspondence or other documentation. While this connection is easily established without a network representation or analysis, adding this layer of context allows us to probe the extent to which these connotations scale or can be found at other presses. The people, places, and institutions represented on the two title pages can serve as nodes (or points) with their connections represented by edges (or lines) in an example of how the overall network is constructed (Fig. 3).

When we see the Baglioni micronetwork in the context of the overall collection of books with astronomy terms on their title pages (to be described in more detail in the next section), our local knowledge of Baglioni then prompts questions about the other connections to his press in Galileo's library (Fig. 4). These volumes are by authors—Cesare Cremonini and Marc Antonio de Dominis[12]—known for what the Catholic Church would deem their heretical,

---

[9] Lagalla's earliest biographer, his student Leone Allacci (1586–1669), rushes quickly past his early philosophical works, choosing to focus predominantly on Lagalla's later treatises on the soul (Allacci 1644, 9–10).

[10] "mandava a farlo stampar fuori" (Galilei 1890–1900, 11:210).

[11] It is possible Emilio Sarli and Vincenzo Maria Pinto (2015) touch upon the details of what follows, but their volume has proven impossible to access in the US, complicated by COVID-19 personnel restrictions.

[12] Galileo's successor for the chair of mathematics at the University of Padua also published two geometrical works with Baglioni's network, but there is no evidence that Galileo owned these.

anti-clerical positions, and, in that sense, they align well with the overall themes of anti-Jesuit literature and mild erotica that Meietti's press issued. In addition to his 1613 treatise on the motions of the heavens, which Galileo owned, Cremonini had published other work with the team at the press. Galileo also owned Marco Antonio de Dominis's 1611 treatise *De radiis visus et lucis in vitris* (On the sight of rays and light in glass), which analyzed rainbows and provided a mathematical description of Galileo's telescope. De Dominis is most frequently remembered for his anti-clerical stance, which resulted in his posthumous execution as a heretic in 1624, having died a natural death before the sentence could be carried out on the verdict (De Mas 1983). Seeing Baglioni's local case in an even larger context can help us to ascertain the extent to which books with astronomical terms were distributed across such microsituations or otherwise clustered around only a few specialist presses.

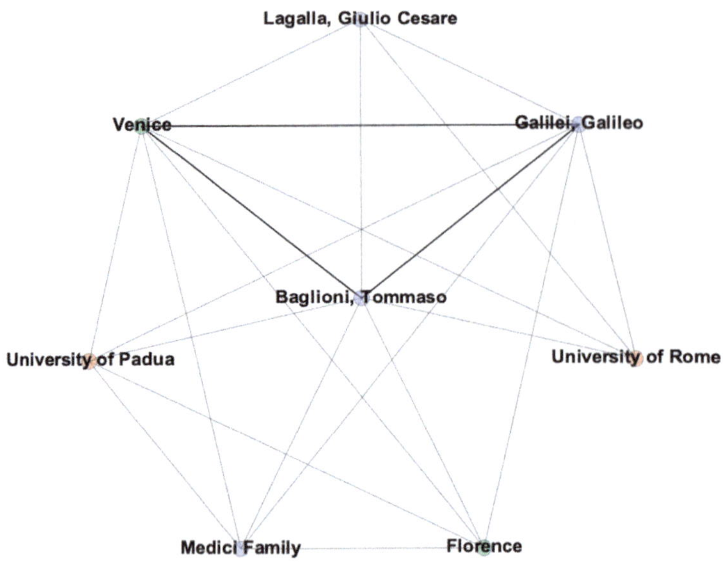

Figure 3. Gephi network representation of the title pages of Galileo's *Starry Messenger* and Lagalla's *De phoenominis in orbe lunae*, which highlights interpersonal and geographic relationships facilitated by Baglioni's press (center) and less connected sites of direct exchange (i.e., the universities). Nodes in the color image are categorized by person (purple), place (green), or institution (orange). Edges between nodes indicate that they are mentioned together on a title page; thickness of the line is relative to the number of times the nodes are mentioned

together. Node and label size are uniform. The Fruchterman-Reingold layout algorithm has been used for legibility. Image credit: Crystal Hall.

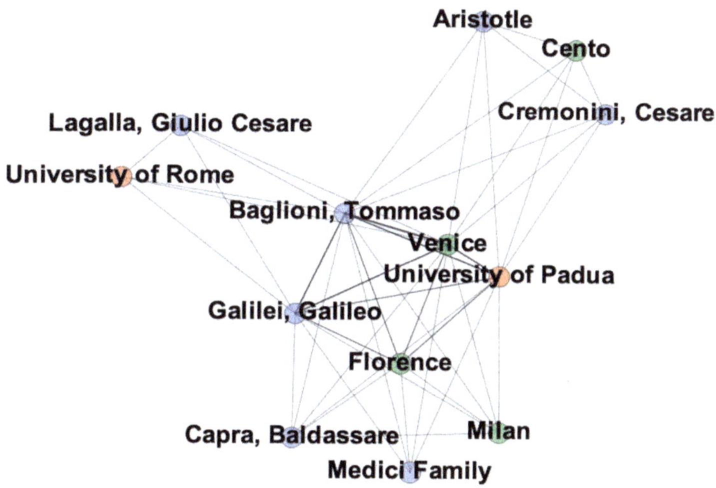

Figure 4. Partial view of a Gephi network of title pages of the 152 books of astronomy in Galileo's library, highlighting connections to the press of Tommaso Baglioni and representing the geographic differentiation of intellectuals alongside connective capacity of the printer Baglioni. Nodes in the color image are categorized by person (purple), place (green), or institution (orange). Edges between nodes indicate that they are mentioned together on a title page; thickness of the line is relative to the number of times the nodes are mentioned together. Node and label size are uniform. A Force Atlas layout algorithm was used to visualize interconnected subgroups. Image credit: Crystal Hall.

The Network at Scale

Scaling up immediately raises a number of questions related to the books, converting them to data interpretable by network analysis software, and other decisions about bringing together this information: What counts as a book? What counts as astronomy? And what cannot be counted? In the spirit of Julia Damerow and Dirk Wintergrün (2019), it feels necessary to document what data has or has not been used to create this preliminary navigational tool for the network. Until now, I have used laborious phrasing to describe my corpus, taking care not to talk about "books on astronomy." For inclusion in my subset of volumes from Galileo's library, the title page of a work had to include at least one variant of several keywords or phrases related to astronomy in Galileo's lifetime (with an * to indicate truncation for wildcard searching): *astro**, Brah*, *cael*/coel**, *ciel*/celest**, *comet**, Copernic*, *cosmo**, *ephemerid**, *perspecillio*, *pianet** (or names of the five classical planets), *sider**, *sole*, *sphaer**, *stell**, *system* mund*/mond**, *telescopio*, *terr* moviment**, *univers**, *zodiac**. Given that most of the data about Galileo's library was preserved in basic inventories, this subset does not include banned titles, manuscript notes about books, or books that might have been bound with other books, a common practice in the period. Moreover, the keyword search approach distinguishes self-declared volumes on astronomy from the more complex body of classical and medieval texts that was adopted by practitioners of natural philosophy as witnesses to and authorities on astronomical events. These include, in Galileo's library, Cicero's *De natura deorum* (On the nature of the gods), Ovid's *Metamorphoses*, Plato's *Timaeus*, and Virgil's *Georgics*. Galileo also owned Giovanni Pico della Mirandola's commentary on Genesis, but paratextual information does not advertise a cosmographical framing of his glosses.

This analysis privileges the ways in which books were trying to advertise themselves to potential readers through the visual and lexical cues on their title pages. That means that works are included such as Rafaelle Gualterotti's *L'universo, ovvero il Polemidoro* (The universe, or Polemidoro), the heroic poem first published in 1600 that Gualterotti hoped to revise decades later once he had learned of Galileo's findings. Yet, we will not see Antonio Rocco's *Esercitationi filosofiche* (Philosophical exercises) of 1633, a direct response to Galileo's *Dialogo sopra i due massimi sistemi del mondo* (Dialogue concerning the two chief world systems) that provoked intensive commentary by Galileo, likely in preparation for a rebuttal in print that was never produced. Also omitted are a handful of works on astronomy known to be in Galileo's library, but for which detailed information is sparse: tables of predictions of celestial motion, foundational sixteenth-century works on cosmography, and three works by Ptolemy. Overall, the astronomy books are the best documented in terms of bibliographic information, yet these gaps invite a next phase of research to understand why these volumes in particular escaped detailed records in the archive.

I pause here to acknowledge what cannot be visualized or has been left out of the subset because of the consequences it holds for what the graph can ultimately reveal. Using the keyword searches in a small ($n = 461$) dataset with which I have been working for over a decade brings to light the benefits and challenges of developing a method for exploring subsets of larger collections. My specialist knowledge allows me to quickly identify non-astronomical uses of a term on a title page and to recognize the absence of books that would have been consulted for content related to cosmography. Rather than take the book at its literal word, I could rely on later, modern bibliographic additions of subject headings or editorial tags to create a filter, but that would answer a different research question. I am interested in how material aspects of books signaled possible participation in a broad conversation, not in how later readers have inserted them into those discussions. So, in spite of the margin of error for false inclusion or omission, I retained the resulting 152 books, which, overall, are texts written for the purpose of measuring, charting, predicting, or explaining the location or movement of planets and stars.

By comparison, on the advent of the comet of 1577 alone, 111 separate items were written and circulated, prompting scholar C. Doris Hellman (1934, 41), the compiler of the bibliography of these tracts and treatises, to write, "I should not be at all surprised to learn of another 20 of which I am at present ignorant." Hellman identified materials as diverse as those in this subset from Galileo's collection: prayers, observations, logical works, theological treatises, predictions, and calculations. They were printed across Europe in Latin, English, Flemish, French, German, and Italian. The subset from Galileo's library is less linguistically diverse: 110 are in Latin, 42 in Italian.

Galileo's corpus represents 94 authors, 25 of whom account for over half (83) of the titles, but it is not an exhaustive representation of works on astronomy printed in Europe in this period. The German astronomer and natural philosopher Johannes Kepler (1570–1631), a prolific author unto himself, wrote the most titles in this subset of Galileo's collection: nine. Galileo himself wrote eight titles that meet our criteria. The remaining 23 authors who have more than one title in this dataset are a who's who of European astronomy in the late Renaissance: foundational thinkers such as Ptolemy, Regiomontanus, Copernicus, and Brahe; a catalog of Galileo's opponents; and a select group of his Italian supporters.[13]

The books represent 160 years of print history centered on the period from 1575 to 1625.[14] They neatly encapsulate the three generations of scientific writing that Miriam Chrisman (1982) has outlined: editions and translations of early work (1500–20), new material alongside a reassessment of the old (1527–43), and publications by academics (post-1570). The volumes stretch

---

[13] The individuals, institutions, and locations represent 22 modern nations.

[14] The median birth date for individuals (when available) is 1573; the median death date is 1624. My thanks to Camila Argueta Angulo (Bowdoin College Class of 2022) for assistance cleaning this data.

from two incunables from 1492 to one volume only known to have been printed in 1653, over a decade after Galileo's death. Books that extend past Galileo's lifetime speak to the organic nature of the library, which includes rare volumes that circulated for generations prior to arriving in his collection as well as books that authors, friends, or family members sent to later generations in the Galilei family to add to its representative capacity. The 1653 volume turns out to be an actual "false positive" for astronomy, since "Mercury" is in the title but is really an allusion to the genre of contemporary history chronicles.

The few other false positives are also opportunities to investigate surprise. Among the spurious inclusions in this subset are a volume printed at a press that operated at "insegna alla Stella" (the sign of the star), Eutoch's geometric treatise on spheres, the 1589 *Tesoro celeste* (The celestial treasure) on indulgences, and five books from the Cecconcelli press dedicated to the Medicean stars, only one of which mentions an astronomy keyword in the title. The so-called Medicean stars were the satellites that Galileo had discovered orbiting around Jupiter during his first period of observation with the telescope in late 1609 and early 1610, as reported in the *Starry Messenger*. The imprint invites us to look further at the network represented by Cecconcelli's press and its authors (Fig. 5).

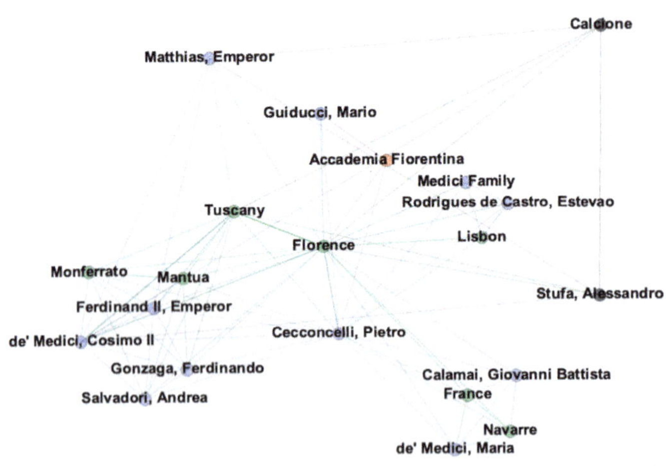

Figure 5. Partial view of a Gephi network of title pages of the 152 books of astronomy in Galileo's library, highlighting connections to the press of Pietro Cecconcelli and representing the geographic differentiation of intellectuals and patrons and the role of Cecconcelli's press at the

center. Nodes in the color image are categorized by person (purple), place (green), or institution (orange). Edges between nodes indicate that they are mentioned together on a title page; thickness of the line is relative to the number of times the nodes are mentioned together. Node and label size are uniform. A Force Atlas layout algorithm was used to emphasize interconnected subgroups. Image credit: Crystal Hall.

The findings here add four titles and other examples of printer's devices to Oddone Longo's (2004) presentation of Cecconcelli, who printed for Galileo's patrons, the Grand Dukes of Tuscany Cosimo II and Ferdinando II de' Medici, in the period from 1619 to 1633 using variations of a dedication to the Medicean stars on several of the title pages of works from his press.[15] Most scholarly attention for the press has been given to the *Discorso delle Comete* (Discourse on comets; 1619) written by Galileo's disciple, Mario Guiducci, with significant intervention from Galileo. The printer's device on the title page explicitly links Cecconcelli to the Galilean project and the Medici family for readers aware of the discovery of the "stars" orbiting Jupiter (Fig. 6).

Figure 6. Printer's device on the title page of Mario Guiducci's *Discorso delle Comete* (1619) showing a diagram of four stars in orbit around a

[15] Future work will need to determine the relationship between Cecconcelli and the printing partners Amador Massi and Lorenzo Landi, who used at least one of the blocks in a later work also owned by Galileo, Margherita Costa's *Flora feconda* (1640).

larger central star, presumably Jupiter, framed by the six Medici *palle* (balls). Image credit: *Discorso delle Comete di Mario Guiducci fatto da lui nell' Accademia Fiorentina nel suo Medesimo Consolato.* In *Firenze: Nella Stamperia di Pietro Cecconcelli* [. . .], 1619. ETH-Bibliothek Zürich, RAR 1950, doi.org/10.3931/e-rara-417/Public Domain Mark.

Cecconcelli does not make these visual connections to Galilean cosmography on every title page of books that he prints, but he does highlight their connection to the broader intellectual network in other ways.[16] Aside from Guiducci's *Discorso*, the other four texts are unlikely members of the astronomy subset: Alessandro Stufa's *Esequie* (Funeral rites; 1619) for Emperor Matthias of Austria celebrated by the Grand Duke; Andrea Salvadori's *Il Medoro* (1623); Giorgio Calamai's *Il Parto della Vergine, Poema eroico* (The virgin birth, heroic poem; 1623), and Portuguese Estevao Rodrigues de Castro's ethical treatise for students, *Philomelia* (1628).[17] The association with Cecconcelli's press invites an investigation beyond the title. First, Stufa's description of the funeral held in Florence for Matthias, an otherwise lugubrious text published during the first year of Cecconcelli's operation, includes a metaphorical use of a popular debate topic for Galileo: sunspots (see Stufa 1619, 6). Next, Salvadori's 1623 libretto about the protagonist of an episode in Ludovico Ariosto's epic poem *Orlando furioso* (Orlando enraged; 1532) superficially seems of interest to Galileo simply due to its status as fan fiction drawing on his favorite literary work. Yet, the ornamentation at the opening of act 2 of *Il Medoro* holds another key (see Fig. 7). Salvadori had earlier written a *canzonetta* in praise of the Medicean stars, which Galileo had corrected, and the ornamental block visually instantiates those ties.

Figure 7. Ornamentation at the head of folio 13r in Salvadori's *Il Medoro* (1623) showing a variation of Cecconcelli's printer's device. Image credit: Thomas Fisher Rare Book Library, University of Toronto.

[16] For a similar analysis in the British print context, see Silva 2020.

[17] Galileo owned at least one more title published by Cecconcelli: Alessandro Adimari's *La Polinnia* (1628), a collection of sonnets that, upon close reading, does not seem to contain overt references to astronomy or Galileo.

The same block appears in Calamai's (1623, fol. 2r) poem and Castro's (1628, fol. 2v) treatise. In the case of Calamai, this suggests further depth to a relatively undocumented relationship between this poet and Galileo. Another layer of the paratext adds more context for these associations. Calamai's poem includes prefatory poetry by Salvadori and diverse members of the Florentine literary world and Galileo's extended circle: Carlo Bocchineri (future father-in-law to Galileo's son), Lodovico delle Colombe (Galileo's frequent opponent), Giovanni Battista Doni (correspondent), Rafaele Gualterotti (one of the earliest builders of a telescope in Florence), Filippo Salviati (future namesake of Galileo's fictional interlocutor in his later dialogues), and Giovanni Battista Strozzi (correspondent). Calamai's otherwise non-astronomical text is still a declaration of the inroads of Galilean cosmography in Florentine culture and also the reciprocal framing that these poets, librettists, and court figures offered to his new discoveries. Similarly, Castro's text places him in the Galilean circle a few years before the Portuguese doctor's conflicts with Liceti erupted and before the extant letters that he exchanged with Galileo.[18] In short, these "false positives" were anything but. Pending available, reliable, full-text resources, the network offered a way to bring to light documents that have been overlooked for their importance in advancing the agenda of the new science based on Galileo's discoveries.

Connecting Micronetworks

As a concept map, the overall network belies the framing principle of Galileo's collection of works in this subset. Galileo is the most connected person in this paratextual network despite not being the most prolific author. His prominence is due to the fact that he is mentioned 13 times on the title pages of authors' works (Fig. 8).

Galileo is as prominent as the publishing centers of Florence and Venice, and the layout helps to outline the opposition between Venetian and Paduan institutions against those in Rome, while Florentine concerns are connected more frequently to people and places north of the Alps. Seeing the full network puts our opening problem of Liceti's confusion into context. Who published a theory of light with anti-Aristotelian underpinnings at the heretical press in Venice? Yes, Lagalla did, but Galileo was the most obvious choice given his connections in the print network. The network helps us to see the intensity of the struggle to articulate and maintain an authorial voice in such a system. We have the context for understanding Galileo's surprise

---

[18] On Liceti and Castro, see Boffitto 1941.

and exhaustion at once again having to redraw intellectual boundaries that he thought had been established by his texts.

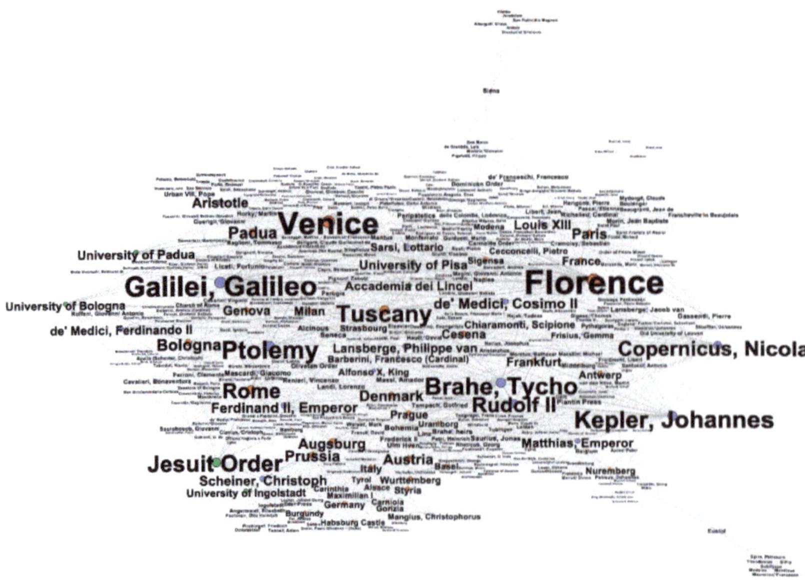

Figure 8. Gephi network of title pages of the 152 books of astronomy in Galileo's library (a searchable, interactive version is available at bowdoin.edu/~chall/AstroNtwk/index.html). Node color is uniform. Edges between nodes indicate that they are mentioned together on a title page; thickness of the line is relative to the number of times the nodes are mentioned together. Node and label size indicates degree (number of connections). A Force Atlas layout algorithm was used to emphasize interconnected subgroups with Label Adjust for clarity. Image credit: Crystal Hall.

Galileo's subset of this network is striking in its comprehensiveness as a synecdoche for his biography as well as in the breadth of the intellectual and print territory his work encompassed. This portion of the overall graph helps to orient us within the expansive network of making, distributing, and then buying these books within which Galileo operated (Fig. 9). Given Galileo's work and living patterns, Florence and Venice are two of the most connected hubs in the library.[19] Not only does it reflect the institutions where Galileo

[19] The network currently does not distinguish between sites of printing and use of a city as a descriptor (e.g., a press in Florence and an author who is identified as Florentine).

and his opponents, as well as his and their patrons, worked, but it also reveals the breadth of the European intellectual and print market for astronomy into which he made inroads during his lifetime: Augsburg, Frankfurt, Paris, Prague, and Strasbourg (where three translations of his work were printed).

Figure 9. Subgraph of the Gephi network of title pages of the 152 books of astronomy in Galileo's library, highlighting connections to Galileo. While Italian sites are prominent, multiple European cities are at the periphery alongside contemporary Austro-German natural philosophers. Of the 2,386 edges in the full graph, Galileo's texts account for 175 (7.3 percent). Node color is uniform. Edges between nodes indicate that they are mentioned together on a title page; thickness of the line is relative to the number of times the nodes are mentioned together. Node label size indicates degree (number of connections). A Force Atlas layout algorithm was used to emphasize interconnected subgroups with Label Adjust for legibility. Image credit: Crystal Hall.

Of the 77 nodes connected to Galileo, 19 are printers, 9 of whom worked outside of Italy, signaling the intense national and European contexts of the debates in which he was involved. This is a fraction of the 123 printers and publishers identified on the title pages of the 152 volumes in this subset, indicating a broad distribution of the conversation across presses. In terms of European context, Andrew Pettegree's (2010, 274) comprehensive study has suggested that the material demands of printing scientific works limited production to high-end top producers who already controlled much of book culture in the period. Pettegree focuses on Basel and Nuremberg, part of the heart of printing centers in Central Europe. While Nuremberg does play a role in this astronomy network, it is not central. Rather, it may point to another press like Baglioni's, or to a printing center more generally, which held interest for Galileo's detractor Simon Mayr. The sixteenth-century Nuremberg printer Johannes Petreus—a specialist in alchemical, mathematical, and Lutheran texts—is exemplary of the threat posed by certain publishers from over the Alps (*oltrealpe*) (Maclean 2009, 138). Alternatively, one of the most prominent printers in Galileo's collection of books on astronomy is Gottfried Tampach, who operated in Frankfurt. Tampach produced Tycho Brahe's work (likely at the insistence of Johannes Kepler), several of Kepler's works that Galileo did not own, and the treatises of Tommaso Campanella, including his 1622 defense of Galileo.

To a certain extent, we might be able to see Pettegree's observation about powerful printers by contextualizing the astronomy subset against the rest of Galileo's library. As leading printers in Italy at the time, the Florentine offices of the Giunti brothers appear in many of the books in Galileo's library (17 works), but only four of the works of astronomy or mathematics that he owned. Through 1570, the Giunti printed very few works related to astronomy and mathematics. They printed a portable ottavo of Ptolemy in 1525, Ignazio Danti's work on constructing an astrolabe in 1569, and two editions of an arithmetic text in Italian (Pettas 2012). Similar observations prevail about Giacomo Mascardi, whose Roman press produced 14 books in Galileo's collection, only three of which are in this subset on astronomy; Amador Massi and Landi, popular in the collection overall (10 titles) account for just one astronomy volume. This invites a consideration of the ways in which publishing centers may have been points of resistance or bottlenecks to engaging debates in print. The print networks in Galileo's library suggest that smaller, regionally connected (and currently understudied) presses like Baglioni's and Cecconcelli's bore a significant amount of the material and labor costs necessary to broaden access to a proliferation of ideas about astronomy. The gatekeepers for facilitating or debilitating an idea's ability to gain traction, or at least find space in the debate, are more diffuse and perhaps less specialized than research on the most prolific presses suggests.

The cross section we see here suggests a predominantly Italian conversation, not a European one, and one that involves many smaller presses like Baglioni's and Cecconcelli's. Established European intellectual centers and Roman institutions populate this graph, but they are flanked by the dynamism of the interconnectedness of presses within Italy as represented by this collection of books. Marginal and mainstream ideas about astronomy and cosmography are being exchanged locally and rapidly. Still, many of these theories only gain traction and become a dominant force in another language and culture entirely with the work of Isaac Newton. Is this jumbled space of debate a proving ground or a quagmire?

Other than those in Venice, the Italian printers that produced the debates that gave rise to Galileo's articulation of the new natural philosophy are typically not considered major centers in early modern Europe. For instance, an intriguing "satellite" in this network is an anonymous Jesuit treatise on the comets of 1618, the *Assemblea celeste* (Celestial assembly; 1619), which stages a letter to the so-called Spassionato (the Impartial), an "Academico Italico" from an "Academico Danico" nicknamed the Riposato (the Undisturbed). Attributed to Giovanni Rho, the letter's tone and its support for Tycho Brahe provoked Galileo and his student Guiducci (from the Cecconcelli case study) to prepare a witty response that was never published (Besomi and Camerota 2000). This is the only book related to astronomy printed in Milan in Galileo's library. The printer, Marco Tullio Paganello, printed at least one other treatise related to these comets, Pietro Maria Castiglione's *Discorso sopra l'apparsa cometa nel mese di novembre, del anno 1618* (Discourse on the comet that appeared in the month of November in the year 1618). Castiglione identifies himself as part of the Accademia della Morte (Academy of Death), with the nickname "il Vegliante Ardito" (the Bold Vigil Holder). Castiglione's other works are medical treatises, emphasizing kidney function. The one extant copy of Castiglione's *Discorso* (held by the University of Pavia) is bound with the *Assemblea celeste*. Milan was often the site for printing anti-Venetian treatises and pamphlets during the Interdict years early in the century; it was also the native city of one of Galileo's earliest opponents, the plagiarist of the geometric compass manual, Baldassare Capra. Regionalism may have played a part in the production of and desire to respond to the *Assemblea celeste*. These repeating patterns in the network provoke questions about what the other print spaces for debate may have been for other topics and other countries.

Connecting to Other Networks

This paratextual network allows us a glimpse of the heterogeneous layers of interpretation surrounding Galileo during his lifetime. Liceti's confusion about Galileo was facilitated by Baglioni's identity as a printer. Cecconcelli's press was signaling the breadth of integration of Galilean natural philosophy in Florentine and Medici culture. The location of printers in this network becomes a way to enter an interpretive conversation with a local framing, particularly in light of the relatively minimal role of the most notable presses in participating in the debates that honed and otherwise shaped late Renaissance theories of cosmography.

This network graph of paratextual information is an invitation, not a declaration. For instance, we might let network metrics prompt us to evaluate why the use of variants of "Jesuit Order" is more interconnected with Austrian locations than Italian, and specifically Roman, ones. By adding more nuance to the category of places, we could study the export of ideas from the place of origin of an author to the location of the press where a work was printed. Integration with semantic network analysis similar to that of Pereira et al. (2011) could reveal other layers of associations between individuals, locations, and concepts. Another step would be to highlight patrons in the way that printers have been presented here, since without the patronage of princes and dukes, the costs of printing these texts often fell on the shoulders of the authors themselves, with the added constraints of presses that were responding to market tendencies. As digital editions of early modern Italian and Neo-Latin texts become more readily available, we could expand this paratextual network to include dedicatees, authors of prefatory works, censors and inquisitors, marginal glosses, and internal citations. As historians of science Deryc Painter, Bryan Daniels, and Jürgen Jost (2019, 541) highlight in their analysis of citations, once there are more networks for comparison, we can better understand formal properties that they may share and systemic relations across different domains. By returning to local microhistories of print that are similar across dimensions of the network, we can recreate organically the overall macro patterns that lend themselves to interpretation and evaluation. In the case of Galileo, such networked interpretations were pivotal to the fortunes of his ideas and his person.

WORKS CITED

Allacci, Leone. 1644. *Iulii Cesaris Lagallae philosophi romani vita, a Leone Allatio conscripta*. Paris: Johann Bessin.

Besomi, Ottavio, and Michele Camerota. 2000. *Galileo e il Parnaso tychonico: Un capitolo inedito del dibattito sulle comete tra finzione letteraria a trattazione scientifica*. Florence: Olschki.

Biagioli, Mario. 1994. *Galileo, Courtier: The Practice of Science in the Culture of Absolutism*. Chicago: University of Chicago Press.

———. 2006. *Galileo's Instruments of Credit: Telescopes, Images, Secrecy*. Chicago: University of Chicago Press.

Boffitto, Giuseppe. 1941. "Battaglie di marche tipografiche di Stefano della Bella e l'ultima memoria scientifica dettata da Galileo Galilei." *La Bibliofilia* 43 (7/9): 145–56. jstor.org/stable/26210249.

Calamai, Giorgio. 1623. *Il Parto della Vergine, Poema eroico*. Florence: Cecconcelli.

Caredda, Barbara. 2008. *Aspetti e momenti del dibattito astronomico nella prima Accademia dei Lincei (1603–1616): Tesi di Dottorato in Storia, Filosofia e Didattica delle scienze*. Cagliari: Università di Cagliari.

Carella, Candida. 2016. "All'ombra del rogo: Riferimenti bruniani nella Roma degli inizi del Seicento." In *Altro Seicento: Arte a Roma tra eterodossia, libertinismo e scienza: Atti del convegno di studi, Accademia di belle arti di Roma 14–15 maggio 2015*, edited by Dalma Frascarelli, 55–70. Rome: L'Erma di Bretschneider.

Castro, Estevao Rodrigues de. 1628. *Philomelia*. Florence: Cecconcelli.

Chrisman, Miriam Usher. 1982. *Lay Culture, Learned Culture: Books and Social Change in Strasbourg, 1480–1599*. New Haven, CT: Yale University Press. doi.org/10.2307/j.ctt211qxqq.

Costa, Margherita. 1640. *La Flora Feconda, poema*. Florence: Massi and Landi.

Dackerman, Susan, ed. 2011. *Prints and the Pursuit of Knowledge in Early Modern Europe*. New Haven, CT: Yale University Press. doi.org/10.37862/aaeportal.00097.

Damerow, Julia, and Dirk Wintergrün. 2019. "The Hitchhiker's Guide to Data in the History of Science." *Isis* 110, no. 3 (September): 513–21. doi.org/10.1086/705497.

De Mas, Enrico. 1983. "Il *De Radiis visus et lucis* un trattato scientifico pubblicato a Venezia dalla stesso editore del *Sidereus Nuncius*." In *Novità celesti e crisi del sapere: Atti del Convegno internazionale di Studi galileiani*, edited by Paolo Galluzzi, 159–66. Florence: Istituto e Museo di Storia della Scienza.

Findlen, Paula. 2019a. "How Information Travels: Jesuit Networks, Scientific Knowledge, and the Early Modern Republic of Letters, 1540–1640." In *Empires of Knowledge: Scientific Networks in the Early*

Modern World, edited by Paula Findlen, 57–105. London: Routledge. doi.org/10.4324/9780429461842.

———. 2019b. "Introduction—Early Modern Scientific Networks: Knowledge and Community in a Globalized World, 1500–1800." In *Empires of Knowledge: Scientific Networks in the Early Modern World*, edited by Paula Findlen, 1–22. London: Routledge. doi.org/10.4324/9780429461842.

Galilei, Galileo. 1890–1909. *Le opere di Galileo Galilei: Edizione nazionale sotto gli auspicii di sua maesta il re d'Italia*. Edited by Antonio Favaro and Isidoro del Lungo. 20 vols. Florence: Barbéra.

———. 1957. *Discoveries and Opinions of Galileo*. Edited and translated by Stillman Drake. New York: Anchor Books.

Gallo, Italo. 1986. "Filosofia e scienza agli albori del Seicento: Giulio Cesare Lagalla tra Aristotile e Galileo." *Rassegna storica salernitana* 3 (2): 55–75.

———. 1987. "Il filosofo padulese Giulio Cesare Lagalla tra Aristotile e Galileo." *Studi umanistici piceni* 7:111–25.

Gattei, Stefano. 2015. "The Phoenix and the Architect: The Frontispiece of Kepler's *Tabulae Rudolphinae*." In *Scienze e rappresentazioni: Saggi in onore di Pierre Souffrin*, edited by Pierre Caye, Romano Nanni, and Piere Daniele Napolitani, 469–94. Florence: Biblioteca Leonardiana.

Genette, Gerard. 1997. *Paratexts: Thresholds of Interpretation*. Translated by Jane E. Lewin. Cambridge: Cambridge University Press. doi.org/10.1017/CBO9780511549373.

Gingras, Yves. 2010. "Mapping the Structure of the Intellectual Field Using Citation and Co-Citation Analysis of Correspondence." *History of European Ideas* 36 (3): 330–39. doi.org/10.1016/j.histeuroideas.2010.04.002.

Gulizia, Stefano. 2016. "Printing and Instrument Making in the Early Modern Atlantic, 1520–1600: The Origin and Reception of Pedro de Medina's Navigational Manual." *Nuncius* 31:129–62.

Hall, Crystal. 2015. "Galileo's Library Reconsidered." *Galilaeana* 12:25–78.

Hellman, C. Doris. 1934. "Bibliography of Tracts and Treatises of the Comet of 1577." *Isis* 22, no. 1 (December): 41–68. doi.org/10.1086/346871.

Kanas, Nick. 2011. "Celestial Maps and Frontispieces in the Time of Mercator." In *A World of Innovation: Cartography in the Time of Gerhard Mercator*, edited by Gerhard Holzer, Valerie Newby, Petra Svatek, and Georg Zotti, 215–31. Newcastle upon Tyne: Cambridge Scholars Publishing.

Kräutli, Florian, and Matteo Valleriani. 2018. "CorpusTracer: A CIDOC Database for Tracing Knowledge Networks." *Digital Scholarship in the Humanities* 33, no. 2 (June): 336–46. doi.org/10.1093/llc/fqx047.

Liceti, Fortunio. 1642. *De lunae subobscura luce*. Udine: Schiratti.

Longo, Oddone. 2004. "Un'impresa galileiana: L'emblema della Stamperia alle stelle medicee." In *Scritti su Galileo e il suo tempo*, edited by Oddone Longo, 67–81. Padua: Esedra.

Maclean, Ian. 2009. *Learning and the Market Place: Essays in the History of the Book*. Leiden: Brill. doi.org/10.1163/ej.9789004175501.i-460.

Martinez, Alberto. 2018. *Burned Alive: Giordano Bruno, Galileo and the Inquisition*. London: Reaktion Books.

Painter, Deryc T., Bryan C. Daniels, and Jürgen Jost. 2019. "Network Analysis for the Digital Humanities: Principles, Problems, Extensions." *Isis* 110, no. 3 (September): 538–54. doi.org/10.1086/705532.

Pantin, Isabelle. 1999. "New Aspects of Old Prejudices: Aspects of the Reception of Copernicanism in a Divided Europe." *Studies in History and Philosophy of Science* 30, no. 2 (June): 237–62. doi.org/10.1016/S0039-3681(98)00049-1.

Pereira, H. B. B., I. S. Fadigas, V. Sennaa, and M. A. Moreta. 2011. "Semantic Networks Based on Titles of Scientific Papers." *Physica A* 390, no. 6 (March): 1192–97. doi.org/10.1016/j.physa.2010.12.001.

Pettas, William A. 2012. *The Giunti of Florence: A Renaissance Printing and Publishing Family*. New Castle, DE: Oak Knoll Press.

Pettegree, Andrew. 2010. *The Book in the Renaissance*. New Haven, CT: Yale University Press. doi.org/10.12987/9780300168358.

Raphael, Renée J. 2012. "Printing Galileo's *Discorsi*: A Collaborative Affair." *Annals of Science* 69 (4): 483–513. 10.1080/00033790.2011.644192.

Salvadori, Andrea. 1623. *Il Medoro*. Florence: Cecconcelli.

Sarli, Emilio, and Vincenzo Maria Pinto. 2015. *Giulio Cesare Lagalla: Un aristotelico che dialogava con Galilei*. Battipaglia: Laveglia & Carlone.

Silva, Andie. 2020. *The Brand of Print: Marketing Paratexts in the Early English Book Trade*. Leiden: Brill. doi.org/10.1163/9789004410244.

Smith, Helen. 2011. "'Imprinted by Simeon such a signe': Reading Early Modern Imprints." In *Renaissance Paratexts*, edited by Helen Smith and Louise Wilson, 17–33. Cambridge: Cambridge University Press. doi.org/10.1017/CBO9780511842429.002.

Smith, Helen, and Louise Wilson, eds. 2011. *Renaissance Paratexts*. Cambridge: Cambridge University Press. doi.org/10.1017/CBO9780511842429.

Söderlund, Inga Elmqvist. 2010. *Taking Possession of Astronomy: Frontispieces and Illustrated Title Pages in 17th-Century Books on Astronomy*. Stockholm: The Center for History of Science.

Stufa, Alessandro. 1619. *Esequie della Maestà Cesarea dell'Imperador Mattia celebrate dal Serenissimo Cosimo Secondo Gran Duca di Toscana*. Florence: Cecconcelli.

Valleriani, Matteo. 2017. "The Tracts on the *Sphere*: Knowledge Restructured Over a Network." In *The Structures of Practical Knowledge*, edited by Matteo Valleriani, 421–73. Berlin: Springer. doi.org/10.1007/978-3-319-45671-3_16.

Walsby, Malcolm. 2013. "Book Lists and Their Meaning." In *Documenting the Early Modern Book World: Inventories and Catalogues in Manuscript and Print*, edited by Malcolm Walsby and Natasha Constantinidou, 1–24. Leiden: Brill. doi.org/10.1163/9789004258907_002.

Wilding, Nick. 2014. *Galileo's Idol: Gianfrancesco Sagredo and the Politics of Knowledge*. Chicago: University of Chicago Press.

Chapter 3:
The Republic of Tweets

Jessica Marie Otis
George Mason University

Since Twitter's creation in 2006, the social media platform has become a high-profile conduit for the public dissemination of information during academic conferences.[1] Conference tweeting began as an informal back channel but has since been adopted by professional societies as a semi-formal means of communication, with the creation of society Twitter accounts, official conference hashtags, social media guidelines, Twitter prizes, and even dedicated Twitter translators.[2] In addition to becoming a robust avenue for scholarly communication, conference Twitter networks have also become recognized objects of study in their own right.[3] Studies of academic networks have often focused on formal connections, but conference Twitter networks let us examine avenues of informal scholarly communication at scale and in more-or-less real time. While some tweets simply vanish into the Internet void, others provoke lively conversation within the conference community or are retweeted to signal boost them into adjacent or similar communities. The networks formed by these tweets—a twenty-first-century "Republic of Letters" written 140 or 280 characters at a time—reveal interdisciplinary patterns of association among early modern and digital scholars within wider humanist and librarian networks. This chapter analyzes the structure of early modern, digital, and disciplinary conference Twitter networks to demonstrate how professional networking on social media enables scholars

[1] This chapter was originally written before the acquisition of Twitter, Inc. by Elon Musk and subsequent, significant changes to the platform in late 2022 and 2023.

[2] The Society for the History of Authorship, Reading and Publishing (SHARP) conference in 2017 had dedicated social media translators who live-tweeted language presentations in 12 languages (SHARP2017 2017; SHARP 2017: Technologies of the Book 2017).

[3] For examples of conference Twitter network analysis, see Gilbert and Paulin 2015; Himelboim et al. 2017; Kimmons and Veletsianos 2016; Lee et al. 2017; Quan-Haase, Martin, and McCay-Peet 2015; and Ross et al. 2011. This is a subset of a wider genre of Twitter network analyses that covers everything from politics (Del Valle and Bravo 2018) to vacation advertising (Bokunewicz and Shulman 2017).

ISBN 978-1-64959-119-7 (paper) ISBN 978-1-64959-120-3 (pdf) ISBN 978-1-64959-121-0 (epub)
New Technologies in Medieval and Renaissance Studies 12 (2025) 61–84

to form continuously evolving communities that share knowledge across traditional disciplinary boundaries.

Data Collection and Methods

This study focuses on 31 academic conferences that occurred between 2016 and 2020. The core of the dataset is formed by the 2016–19 Renaissance Society of America (RSA) conferences, both because of the conference's active Twitter contingent and because the RSA is my primary early modern professional affiliation. The 2019 conferences of the Sixteenth Century Society and Conference (SCSC) and the Shakespeare Association of America (SAA) were also included to increase the breadth of early modern scholars covered by the network. In order to study the role of explicitly digital scholars in conference network formation, the dataset also includes the international digital humanities (DH) conference, hosted by the Alliance of Digital Humanities Organizations (ADHO), from 2017 to 2019; the Digital Library Federation (DLF) conferences from 2016 to 2019; and the Association for Computers and the Humanities (ACH) and Current Research in Digital History (CRDH) conferences in 2019. To study communication patterns within the broadly recognized disciplines of history, library and information science, and literary studies, the dataset further includes the 2017–20 midwinter conferences of the American Historical Association (AHA), the American Library Association (ALA), and the Modern Language Association (MLA). Finally, the 2016–19 conferences of the Society for the History of Authorship, Reading and Publishing (SHARP)[4] were included in the dataset in order to compare the communication patterns of early modern scholars and digital humanists with those of another interdiscipline, specifically book historians.

The data for this analysis was collected by iteratively searching Twitter for publicly available tweets that included specific conference hashtags, using Martin Hawksey's Twitter Archiving Google Sheet (TAGS) and imposing temporal limits of seven days before and after the official conference dates.[5] This excludes public tweets that might have been related to the conference but which did not include the conference hashtag, including subtweeting, parts of Twitter conversations that began using the hashtag but dropped it as they evolved, and threaded tweets that included the hashtag in the first

[4] SHARP maintains a public archive of its 2011–18 conference tweets at sharpweb.org/main/conferences.

[5] Twitter limits free access to historical tweets, as selling access is part of its core business model. Hawksey's TAGS is an easy and free "set and forget" method for collecting Twitter data over time. For more on Hawskey's TAGS, see tags.hawksey.info.

tweet but failed to include it in subsequent tweets.[6] While it is possible to find public replies to tweets using the conference hashtag through Twitter's in_reply_to_status_id_str metadata field, many people who drop the hashtag do so deliberately as a way to move a conversation out of the publicly broadcast conference Twitter feed and into a more private side channel.[7] This can be considered analogous to the difference between asking a question in the official Q&A at the end of a conference session, which invites further discussion and questions from the rest of the session attendees, and asking a question in the hallway or at a reception after the session ends, which still occurs in a public space but is intended to be more limited in audience. Because the volume of data collected was so high—including tweets from or mentioning over 53,000 Twitter handles—and the network relationships created by these tweets is generally already attested to in tweets that included the conference hashtag, I have chosen to systematically exclude these tweets rather than attempt to gain explicit consent for their inclusion in the dataset.[8]

Following collection, the tweets were algorithmically deduplicated and then transformed into a network edge list.[9] Each Twitter account became a node

---

[6] I do include common "variants" of official conference hashtags; for example, #dh2017 and #dh17 refer to the same ADHO conference, DH 2017. While hashtag typos and uncommon variants have not been included, it is unlikely that they would have played a structurally significant role in the network. Furthermore, while I vigorously reported spammers to Twitter when live-tweeting some of these conferences, I made no attempt to identify and remove spammers from the dataset post-collection. In my experience, many spam tweets are images or lists of hashtags and do not include other Twitter handles, meaning they would automatically be excluded in the process of constructing the network. Colladon and Gloor (2019) have shown spammers to have minimal impact on Twitter network structures.

[7] Many people "follow" a conference by searching the hashtag and thus end up seeing tweets from people they do not follow and would not usually see. This is often done through dashboard applications like TweetDeck and Hootsuite.

[8] This approach is consistent with that of organizations that archive tweets on the conference hashtag and various conferences' social media policies that delineate how speakers and other attendees can opt out of live-tweeting. See, for example, AHA n.d.; Digital Humanities Summer Institute (DHSI) n.d.; and SHARP 2016. For more on the ethics of analyzing publicly available social media, see Jules, Summers, and Mitchell 2018.

[9] TAGS sometimes collects the same tweet twice, however it is easy to find and remove duplicate tweets by using Twitter's unique identifiers for each tweet. All code for this, and other parts of the project, can be found on GitHub at github.com/jmotis/twitter-networks.

in the network, with its Twitter handle serving as its unique identifier, and its associated edges were formed by tweets from or mentioning its Twitter handle.[10] The network edge list thus consists of pairs of Twitter handles, specifically the two nodes connected by each edge. This is a directed network; for each tweet, the Twitter handle that wrote the tweet became the source node, and edges were created from that source node to all Twitter handles mentioned in a tweet (the target nodes).[11] Repeat edges were usually summed, so each node's weighted degree gives the total number of edges originally generated to and from that node. Self-loops—edges that connect a node to itself rather than to another node—were allowed, corresponding to the case of Twitter handles that replied to their own tweets, while tweets with no target nodes in them were discarded from the network.

Additionally, individual Twitter handles were algorithmically sorted into 1 of 25 categories based on their conference tweeting patterns. First, they were assigned to an overarching group based on inferred disciplinary association as a librarian, literary scholar, or historian. Twitter handles whose weighted degree were highest in a library conference network (ALA midwinter conference or DLF Forum) were considered librarians; those whose highest weighted degree were in the MLA annual meeting network were considered literary scholars; and those whose highest weighted degree were in the AHA annual meeting network were considered historians. Each of these three overarching groups was then subdivided into 8 categories (24 categories total) according to whether or not the Twitter handle also interacted with a digital humanities conference, early modern conference, or book history conference (Fig. 1). As a shorthand, I use "non-interdisciplinary" to mean only that a Twitter handle did not interact with one of the three interdisciplinary conferences.[12] The final category was for Twitter handles whose categorization was unclear. The 25 categories ranged in size from 4 (early modern book history librarians) to 22,108 (non-interdisciplinary librarians).

---

[10] In networks where the nodes do not already have unique identifiers associated with them, scholars commonly assign numerical unique identifiers to each node instead.

[11] For comparison, Facebook forms undirected networks—to "friend" someone, they must agree to "friend" you back.

[12] I recognize that many of these nodes are likely associated with other interdisciplines besides the three studied here.

digital historian	digital librarian	digital literary scholar
early modern historian	early modern librarian	early modern literary scholar
book historian	book history librarian	book history literary scholar
digital early modern historian	digital early modern librarian	digital early modern literary scholar
digital book historian	digital book history librarian	digital book history literary scholar
early modern book historian	early modern book history librarian	early modern book history literary scholar
digital early modern book historian	digital early modern book history librarian	digital early modern book history literary scholar
non-interdisciplinary historian	non-interdisciplinary librarian	non-interdisciplinary literary scholar

Figure 1. List of 25 node categories (excluding the final "unclear" category).

While this method produces some oddities surrounding low degree nodes and organizations—for example, tweets about conference travel led to the accounts of major airlines such as Delta, Frontier, Southwest, and United being categorized as librarians—spot checking individuals' Twitter handles provided the expected results based on their known affiliations and disciplinary backgrounds. These categorizations were compared with network modularity classes—an algorithmic way to find communities within a network—using Jaccard indices—a measure of the overlap between two sets calculated by dividing the size of their intersection (nodes in both sets) by their union (nodes in either set)—to search for meaningful patterns of community formation in the conference networks.

Global Characteristics of Conference Twitter Networks

While conference Twitter networks can vary significantly due to characteristics of their sponsoring organizations, and even vary from year to year based on conference location and attendance, they share some general characteristics. Examining these characteristics enables us to both establish the normal parameters of a "typical" academic humanities conference, as well as identify potentially meaningful deviations from those norms. Consider the following subset of the 25 conference Twitter networks generated between 2016 and 2020, listed in Figure 2 below. This includes one conference hosted by the

ACH; four by the AHA; four by the ALA, with the hashtag #alamw--; three by the ADHO, with the hashtag #dh20--; four by the MLA; four by the RSA, with the hashtag #rensa--; four by SHARP; and one by the SAA, with the hashtag #shax2019.[13] They were all generally three- to four-day conferences that encouraged live-tweeting, and the networks formed by their tweets range in size from 420 nodes and 739 edges (#rensa17, the RSA conference in 2017) to 8,309 nodes and 22,681 edges (#alamw19, the ALA 2019 midwinter meeting).[14]

Several network metrics in this subset vary consistently based on the size of the conference network. The number of tweets, nodes, and edges are in almost perfect positive correlation to one another; these metrics were likely determined by the number of people tweeting at the conference, and a future conference with a similar number of tweeters would have similar metrics. The number of tweets, nodes, and edges also have very strong positive correlations to the number of connected components; in other words, the larger the conference network, the more tweeters generate subnetworks that fail to connect to tweeters participating in the main conference network. This is logical, given that people tweeting at conferences are provided the hashtag by the sponsoring organizations rather than organically discovering an ongoing conversation using that hashtag and adopting it as they join that conversation. Small subnetworks—often just of two or three nodes each—form when someone uses this organization-provided conference hashtag while tweeting to someone else, who likewise never tweets to (generates edges to) the rest of the participants in the conference network. But while the number of connected components among the conferences in this set ranges from 3 to 101, an average of 94.2 percent of the nodes (range: 85–99.5 percent) and 98.1 percent of the edges (range: 93.4–99.9 percent) are in the giant connected component for each network, meaning the vast majority of people and tweets using the conference hashtag do end up connected by the end of a conference. If they are not central to the network, they interact with someone—or interact with someone who has interacted with someone—who is.

[13] Prior to the switchover year of 2018, the SAA infamously used the hashtag #shakeass-- at its conferences. Data for #shakeass13 through #shakeass18 are available via sarahwerner.net/blog/a-compendium-of-resources.

[14] Conferences encouraged tweeting by providing free Internet access in conference spaces, establishing hashtags, and/or creating social media guidelines. Internet access, in particular, is a key prerequisite for supporting a conference Twitter network.

Hashtag	Tweets	Nodes	Edges	Components	% Nodes in Giant Component	% Edges in Giant Component	Graph Density	Avg. W. Degree	Avg. Path Length	Diameter
#ach2019	9549	1498	7766	10	98.4	99.72	0.003	9.605	3.173	7
#aha17	10837	2676	6653	68	91.14	96.78	0.001	3.497	4.352	11
#aha18	10087	2812	7362	69	91.79	97.31	0.001	3.373	4.919	13
#aha19	14424	4578	12293	56	96.29	98.73	0.001	3.526	4.389	14
#aha20	12363	3638	9941	32	96.37	98.37	0.001	4.119	3.59	10
#alamw17	28293	7851	20505	101	96.08	98.89	0	3.595	5.359	14
#alamw18	24719	8032	18184	97	96.71	98.82	0	3.027	5.314	14
#alamw19	27944	8308	22681	84	97.57	99.38	0	3.634	5.389	14
#alamw20	22293	7132	18706	91	96.57	98.88	0	3.631	5.204	13
#dh2017	16691	2681	12319	36	95.34	99.13	0.002	7.358	3.607	9
#dh2018	16249	3042	13141	27	90.83	97.76	0.001	6.869	3.398	8
#dh2019	14258	2554	11816	19	97.22	98.93	0.002	7.094	3.671	9
#mla17	19692	3440	9912	72	94.62	98.31	0.001	5.165	4.377	12
#mla18	11874	2884	7753	74	91.92	96.38	0.001	3.871	4.662	12
#mla19	11535	3588	9175	58	93.84	97.29	0.001	3.414	4.837	13
#mla20	9576	2700	7174	40	94.56	97.55	0.001	4.669	4.668	13
#rensa16	4947	619	1897	14	93.54	98	0.005	6.758	3.47	9
#rensa17	1414	420	739	23	85.48	93.37	0.004	2.357	3.408	8
#rensa18	2013	530	1204	10	94.72	98.01	0.004	3.289	4.143	10
#rensa19	3700	716	1972	12	95.81	98.58	0.004	4.116	4.181	10
#sharp16	6755	917	2791	25	88.11	96.7	0.003	6.234	3.528	7
#sharp17	8358	989	3973	33	84.93	96.12	0.004	8.832	3.209	7
#sharp18	3301	441	1743	5	97.96	99.71	0.009	7.746	2.906	5
#sharp19	5735	870	3292	3	99.54	99.94	0.004	7.395	3.131	7
#shax2019	7329	954	4008	17	94.97	99	0.004	6.604	3.539	8

Figure 2. Conference network metrics, by hashtag.

The number of tweets, nodes, and edges also have a very strong negative correlation to graph density; these conference Twitter networks are all very sparse (low-density) networks, but the larger networks are even sparser than the smaller ones. All but two of the networks have graph densities at or below 0.004, which means these networks contain at most 1 out of every 250 possible edges. SHARP 2018's density of 0.009 is an intriguing outlier for this set of networks—and likely attributable to the conference being hosted in Australia, whereas the rest of the conferences in this set took place in North America or Europe—but it is still nowhere near close to a densely connected network such as might be formed during a small workshop or class, in which most nodes would be connected to most other nodes.[15] While information can and is passed freely from one side of a conference Twitter network to the other—since an average of 19 out of 20 people participating in the network participate in a single connected component—most people directly interact with less than 1 percent of the other people tweeting on the conference hashtag. Just as a scholar might chat in the halls with 1 in 1,000 of their fellow attendees at a massive disciplinary conference, so too scholars on Twitter only interact with a tiny fraction of their fellow digital attendees.

Other characteristics of conference networks similarly correlate to the network's size, although not as closely, and seem to also be influenced by characteristics of the sponsoring organization. The network's diameter and average path length are very strongly positively correlated to the number of nodes; strongly positively correlated to the number of tweets and edges; and almost perfectly positively correlated with one another.[16] Of all the conferences, SHARP networks generally have the shortest diameter (7, except for the anomalous 2018 conference, which had a diameter of 5 and suggests that Australian conference attendees were an unusually tight-knit group compared to attendees of the North American and European conferences). The first biannual ACH conference, in 2019, had a similarly short diameter, but there are no other years with which to compare it, so it is unclear if this will be a normal feature of the ACH conference. The DH conference generally has a diameter of 8 or 9, while the smaller RSA conference ranges from 8 to 10.

---

[15] These low-density, low-isolate conference networks are thus examples of what Himelboim et al. (2017) call "community clusters."

[16] The diameter is calculated by first finding the shortest possible path (hopping from node to node by way of edges, like finding the friend or the friend of a friend who already knows and can introduce you to someone you would like to meet at a conference) between every pair of nodes in the network; the longest of these shortest possible paths is the network diameter. If the network diameter is 1, every node is already connected to every other node. If the network diameter is 2, every node is at most a "friend of a friend" to every other node. If the network diameter is 3, every node is at most a "friend of a friend of a friend" to every other node, and so on. This is the longest possible path length, but there will always be shorter path lengths (e.g., two nodes are directly connected to each other, even if two other nodes are three connections apart). The average path length is the average of all these shortest path lengths.

Among the larger conferences, the AHA conference has been the most variable, with a diameter ranging from 10 to 14, the largest being in 2019 when the AHA and MLA conferences happened concurrently, in the same city, and had a significant overlap in attendees that impacted this metric. In other words, the conjunction of the two conferences made for a less tightly knit group of attendees, as people attended sessions across their usual disciplinary boundaries, encountering new scholars and participating in conversations that normally would have happened outside their social circle. The MLA conference has had a diameter of 12 or 13 over the years, while the largest of the conferences, the ALA midwinter conference, had a consistent diameter of 14 for three years, but in 2020 had a slightly smaller diameter of 13. Thus, while larger conferences tend to create networks with longer path lengths, resulting in longer diameters and average path lengths, the conference networks generated by any specific professional society (e.g., SHARP networks, MLA networks) also seem to be relatively stable from year to year despite network size fluctuations. More tightly knit Twitter networks associated with a particular conference remain tightly knit, even as attendance rates at the conference rise and fall, while more sprawling networks do the same.

Of all the network characteristics in the above chart, average weighted degree—averaging the weighted degree of all nodes in the network—is the least correlated to network size and thus has the potential to shine light on more qualitative aspects of conference networks. Indeed, removing the large ALA midwinter conferences from the dataset leaves average weighted degree uncorrelated to network size, suggesting any apparent correlation is a product of this study's small sample size.[17] The numbers for the full dataset suggest there is a weak negative correlation to the number of tweets and edges and a moderate negative correlation to the number of nodes. Weighted degree follows a power law distribution: the vast majority of nodes have a low weighted degree, while an exponentially decreasing number have a higher weighted degree, with just a few nodes having the highest weighted degrees. It is thus plausible that larger conferences might attract larger numbers of low degree tweeters, thereby decreasing the average weighted degree. However, a closer examination of the individual conferences suggests something else is going on here. The RSA and SHARP conferences have the smallest conference networks in the set, with the RSA ranging in size from 420 to 716 nodes and

---

[17] Removing the ALA midwinter conferences from the set and recalculating leaves the average weighted degree with only a weak negative correlation to the number of nodes. The average weighted degree becomes completely uncorrelated to the number of tweets and edges, at 0.08 and 0.03, respectively, as opposed to its previous -0.25 and -0.28.

SHARP ranging in size from 441 to 989 nodes. Yet the RSA conferences range in average weighted degree from the lowest in the set—2.357 in 2017, when the network was also its smallest at 420—to the seventh highest—6.758 in 2016, when the network was only its second largest at 619 nodes. By contrast, SHARP had three of the top four highest average weighted degrees in the set—at 7.4, 7.7, and 8.8—coming in behind only the mid-sized ACH conference at 9.6. Conversely, the ALA midwinter networks, which are by far and consistently the largest networks, have average weighted degrees in the low to mid 3s, which is generally a bit higher than those of the AHA, even if they are also a bit lower than those of the MLA. The average weighted degree thus seems to be the main metric for these networks that correlates to some characteristic of the conferences *other* than size.

Closer examination shows that the top conferences, ranked by average weighted degree, are all either digital humanities conferences (ACH and DH) or SHARP conferences. Given digital humanists' strong early interest in the digital, including social media, and SHARP's similarly early adoption and support of conference tweeting through Twitter prizes, their high average weighted degrees make sense on qualitative rather than quantitative grounds.[18] Similarly, the anomalously high (for RSA) average weighted degree of RSA 2016 is likely attributable to a strong contingent of digital humanists who live-tweeted the conference that year—particularly, but not exclusively, associated with the three Folger Digital Agendas panels sponsored by the Folger Shakespeare Library—and who exponentially boosted their metrics through retweeting each other. In 2016, the top four nodes had weighted degrees of 645, 618, 578, and 439, respectively, and were significant outliers compared to the rest of the nodes in both the 2016 network as well as in subsequent years. Of these four, only one live-tweeted the conference in 2017 and had the highest weighted degree in the 2017 network at a mere 130. Not all prolific tweeters are digital humanists, but digital humanists tend to tweet more than other humanists, and thus the attendance (or absence) of more digitally inclined scholars appears to be a causal factor for increased average weighted degree.

While it is useful to think of each conference as an individual event, and to analyze each conference network independently of the other networks, it is important to remember that each discrete event is also part of a series of annual (or biannual) events. While many people only attend conferences sporadically due to conferences' shifting geographical locations and the expense

[18] SHARP began awarding its Twitter prize in 2011 (SHARP 2019).

of attendance, others attend the same conference year after year.[19] When the tweets from an annual conference series are combined into a single network, summing edges from across conferences, the number of nodes in the combined network are substantially fewer than they would have been had each node only tweeted at one conference. As seen in Figure 3, the MLA conference has the most nodes that occur in more than one annual network, with its combined network consisting of only 76.8 percent of the number of nodes it would have had if every node only interacted with one year's MLA conference. The AHA and ALA midwinter conferences have almost as many repeat nodes, followed by the RSA and DH conferences, while SHARP has the fewest repeat nodes. It is likely that the expense of international travel depressed the number of repeat nodes for the intercontinental conferences: the DH conferences were held in Canada, Mexico, and the Netherlands, while the SHARP conferences were held in France, Canada, Australia, and the US. While the RSA also has intercontinental conferences, all RSA conferences in this analysis met in North America, leading to the strong possibility that North American members of the society could afford to attend the conference in multiple years.[20]

Despite having the fewest repeat nodes, SHARP actually had the most repeat edges at 8.4 percent compared to 4.3–5.5 percent for the other conferences. Fewer people might have engaged with the SHARP Twitter networks in multiple years, but those who did were twice as likely to reinforce preexisting network ties as other conferences' tweeters. For the remainder of the conferences, however, somewhere between one-fifth and one-fourth of the nodes in the combined conference networks participated in more than one year of their respective conferences, and about 1 in 20 edges are repeat edges across conferences. While this is enough to make the average weighted degree of the combined conference networks higher than their individual conference networks for every conference except RSA (whose combined network has a lower average weighted degree than that of the anomalous RSA 2016

---

[19] Although physical attendance at a conference is not a requirement for interacting with its Twitter network, it does make such engagement more likely. While I have deliberately excluded the Twitter networks of 2020 conferences that went online during the COVID-19 pandemic from this analysis, these conferences showed a dramatic decrease in Twitter engagement. For example, despite actively working to create an engaging online conference experience and removing the financial barrier to attendance caused by international travel, the DH 2020 network contained only 796 nodes and 2,218 edges, and thus had less than one-third of the nodes in the DH 2019 network and less than one-quarter of the nodes in the DH 2018 network.

[20] The 2015 RSA conference was in Berlin, Germany, and the 2021 RSA conference was scheduled for Dublin, Ireland (RSA n.d.).

conference), it is still only a small fraction of the overall edges. The majority of nodes in the conference Twitter networks interact with only one year, and the overwhelming majority of edges are creating new connections from conference to conference. While the in-person experience of a conference can feel "cliquey," and newcomers may find it awkward or impossible to join conversations being held within established social groups, the Twitter networks continuously make space for—and multi-year participants make connections to—new participants from year to year.

Hashtag	Years	Possible Node	Possible Edges	Nodes	Edges	Percent Nodes	Percent Edges	Components	% Nodes in GCC	% Edges in GCC	Graph Density	Avg. W. Degree	Avg. Path Length	Diameter
AHA	4	13704	36249	10609	34286	77.4	94.6	118	96.27	98.97	0	4.71	3.904	10
ALAMW	4	31323	80076	24256	75887	77.4	94.8	196	97.89	99.49	0	4.478	4.748	13
DH	3	8277	37276	6672	35611	80.6	95.5	65	93.44	98.6	0.001	8.804	3.637	9
MLA	4	12612	34014	9683	32153	76.8	94.5	125	95.62	98.41	0	5.555	4.321	13
RenSA	4	2285	5812	1817	5562	79.5	95.7	35	94.55	98.42	0.002	5.428	4.41	15
SHARP	4	3217	11799	2693	10813	83.7	91.6	53	91.09	97.88	0.001	9.024	3.442	8

Figure 3. Multi-year conference network metrics. Possible nodes = the total number of nodes that could be in the combined network if no node attended more than one year. Possible edges = the total number of edges that could be in the combined network if no edges recurred in more than one year. Nodes = actual number of nodes in the combined network. Edges = actual number of edges in the combined network. Percent nodes = nodes / possible nodes. Percent edges = edges / possible edges.

Interdisciplinarity and Modularity in Disciplinary Conferences

Humanities and library conferences with an active Twitter presence not only generate networks that share a number of structural characteristics, but they also generate overlapping networks that demonstrate interdisciplinary patterns of association among tweeting scholars. Even just looking at the networks generated by the three major US disciplinary conferences that happen every January—the AHA annual meeting, the ALA midwinter meeting, and the MLA annual meeting—shows significant overlap between historians, literary scholars, and librarians. In Figure 4 below, nodes that primarily tweet at the

AHA are colored in green and mostly located in the lower right-hand corner; ALA nodes are colored in red and mostly located in the upper left-hand corner; MLA nodes are colored in blue and mostly located in bottom center. Even though the librarian subnetwork is more distinct *as* a subnetwork than the visibly overlapping historian and literary scholars subnetwork, all three share extensive network ties with one another, and there are a significant number of nodes scattered throughout each of the three subnetworks that categorically belong to a different discipline. While only 368 nodes tweeted to hashtags associated with all three disciplines—split about equally between institutions and people—an additional 3,556 nodes—most of which were people—tweeted to conferences for two of the three disciplines and together constitute 9.3 percent of the nodes in the network.

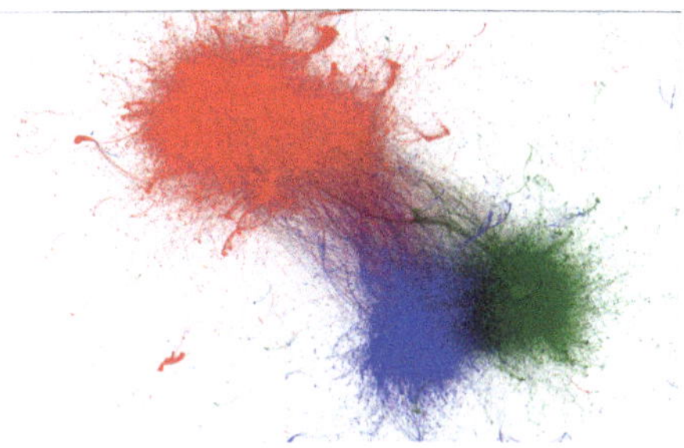

Figure 4.

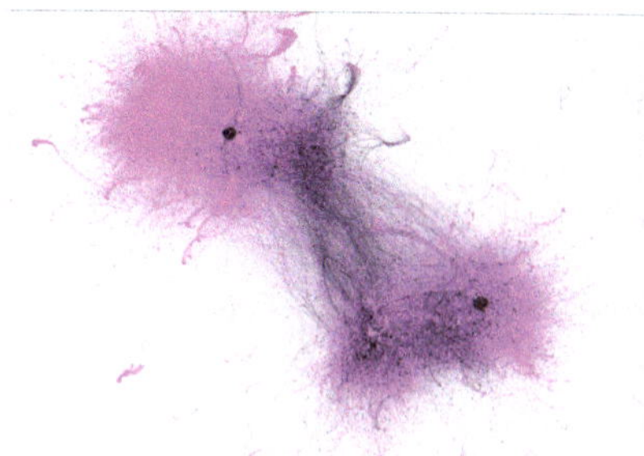

Figure 5.

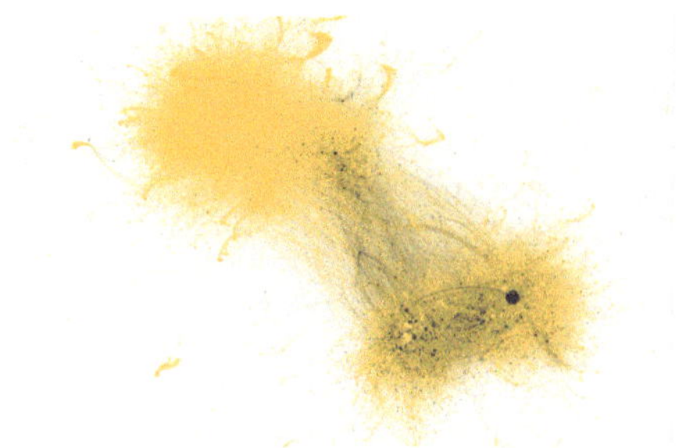

Figure 6.

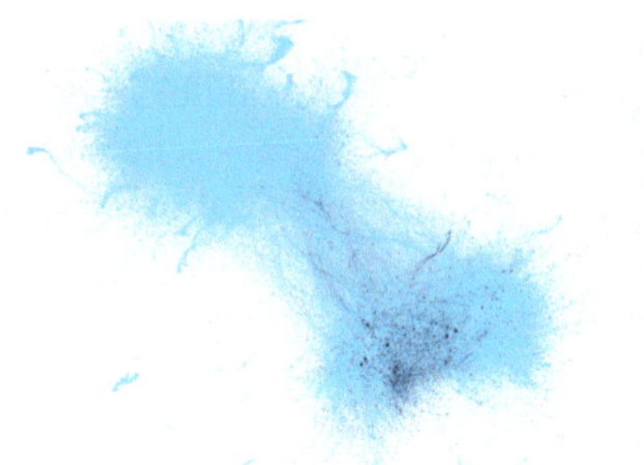

Figure 7.

Figures 4–7. The AHA-ALA-MLA network. Figure 4 shows the network colored by conference affiliation. Figures 5, 6, and 7 highlight digital scholars, book history scholars, and early modern scholars, respectively.

The other three visualizations show the same network but recolored so that the black nodes stand for digital scholars (Fig. 5), book history scholars

(Fig. 6), and early modern scholars (Fig. 7), respectively.[21] These three interdisciplines remain highly integrated with the three disciplinary subnetworks—that is, they do not form distinct subnetworks in the combined network—and they play a clear role in keeping the historians and literary scholars connected to the librarian subnetwork. Indeed, if there is any distinct subnetwork formed by these interdisciplines, it is the subnetwork of librarians who do *not* participate in them, and who cluster to the upper-left corner of all three visualizations.

This visual reading of the network can be reinforced by using Jaccard indices to compare the disciplinary categories of nodes with the network's modularity classes (see Fig. 8).[22] Of the 22,108 librarians who do not participate in the interdisciplinary conference networks, 18,019 (or 81.5 percent) of them share a single modularity class—the largest in the network—and they have the largest overlap of all categories and modularity classes in the network, with a Jaccard index of 0.796.[23] The division between digital and non-digital librarians is also particularly visible, with only 23 digital librarians sharing this modularity class. Instead, another modularity class is home to 79.6 percent of the digital librarians and also contains 16.6 percent of the non-interdisciplinary librarians, leaving a bit less than 2 percent of the non-interdisciplinary librarians to be scattered among the remaining modularity classes. Thus, while a few non-interdisciplinary librarians are embedded in social networks shared by historians and literary scholars, and a larger percentage engage with digital librarians, the vast majority of them form their own distinct subnetwork.

By contrast, the digital librarians share strong ties with numerous book history and digital literary scholars—and through them, the digital historians—which can be seen in both the visualizations and the Jaccard indices. A third modularity class contains 13.3 percent of digital librarians, and 50 percent of the book history librarians then reach across the disciplinary divide to connect them with 94 percent of the book history literary scholars, 91.2 percent of the digital literary scholars, 30 percent of the early modern literary scholars, and 22.9 percent of the non-interdisciplinary literary scholars. This class also contains a strong contingent of digital book historians (55.3 percent) and digital historians (41 percent), marking this as a diverse collection of nodes that coalesced around the intersection of the disciplines and interdisciplines.

21 These categories are not mutually exclusive. Some digital scholars are also book history scholars, some book history scholars are also early modern scholars, and so on.

22 Modularity classes were generated using Gephi's standard, built-in algorithm.

23 Jaccard indices range from 0—when two groups share no members—to 1—when two groups are identical.

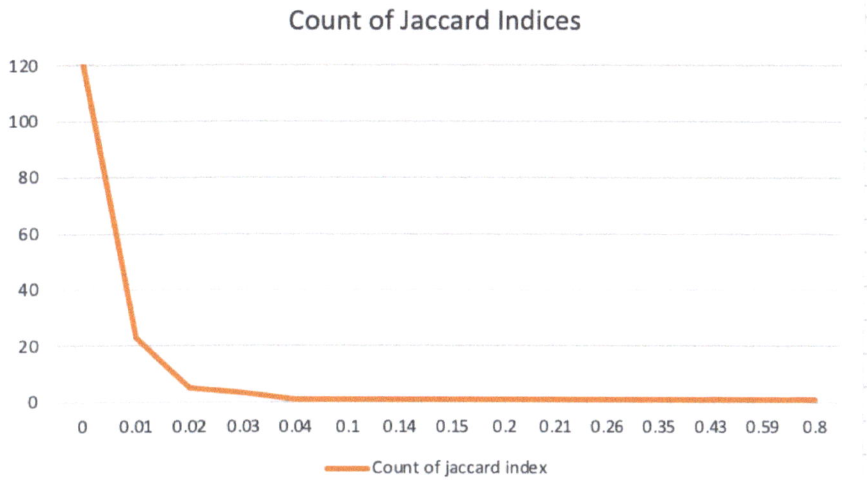

Figure 8. Size distribution of Jaccard indices.

While there are a few historians in the aforementioned modularity classes, 90 percent of the non-interdisciplinary historians and 48.2 percent of the digital historians are in a fourth modularity class, along with the plurality (43.4 percent) of the non-interdisciplinary literary scholars and various subcategorizations of historians. The overlap of this modularity class and the non-interdisciplinary historians has the second highest Jaccard index in the network, at 0.592, making this primarily, but not exclusively, a modularity class of historians. The Jaccard index of its overlap with the non-interdisciplinary literary scholars is 0.202, making them a particularly significant minority in the modularity class. This, then, is a modularity class of historians and those literary scholars interested in work at the intersection of historical and literary methods of analysis.

Of the remaining modularity classes, only one is large enough and has significant enough overlap with the disciplinary and interdisciplinary categorizations to be worth examining in detail here. This final class is primarily a class of early modernists, containing 61.7 percent of the early modern literary scholars along with another 25.1 percent of the non-interdisciplinary literary scholars (Jaccard indices 0.236 and 0.208, respectively). It also contains 31.2 percent of the early modern historians, although they are fewer in number than the literary scholars, and eight additional early modern librarians. Of all the interdisciplines, the early modernists are thus least connected to the librarian subnetwork and instead concentrated primarily—but not exclusively—in the modularity class that can be visibly seen in Figure 7 as occupying the lower right-hand corner of the literary scholar subnetwork and in the intersection of the literary scholar and historian subnetworks.

Overall, the librarians are the only one of the three main disciplines to form their own disciplinary modularity classes, with the majority of the non-interdisciplinary librarians in the upper left-hand corner of the network, and the digital librarians with a subset of the non-interdisciplinary librarians in the lower right-hand corner of the librarian subnetwork. Librarians and literary scholars—and to a lesser degree historians—interested in the digital and in book history form the basis of the connection between the librarians and the two humanities disciplines. Looking back to the digital and book history visualizations, it is clear that while there are fewer book history scholars than digital scholars, they connect along many of the same edges across the disciplines, and several key book history nodes are also digital nodes. By contrast, the early modern nodes come closest to forming a distinct subnetwork; while a few high degree nodes are visible in the same regions of the network that contain the book history and digital scholars, the plurality of early modern nodes cluster to the bottom and to the literary side of the intersection between the literary and historian disciplinary networks. Despite the prominence of some digitally inclined early modernists, in general people tweeting at early modern conferences are more closely aligned with non-digital humanists and exist firmly within the intersection of historians and literary scholars.

In-Discipline and Out-Discipline Network Ties at Interdisciplinary Conferences

While modularity classes are a useful way of analyzing how nodes create subcommunities in networks, just because a node shares a modularity class with nodes from other disciplines or other interdisciplines does not mean that node itself has edges connecting it to nodes from other disciplines or interdisciplines. In real world terms, scholars may be in communication with other scholars who cross disciplinary boundaries, and thus obtain access to information and scholarship through those boundary-crossing scholars without crossing any boundaries themselves. Similarly, just because a scholar participates in an interdisciplinary conference does not mean that the scholar crosses disciplinary boundaries to do so. An early modern literary scholar and an early modern historian may both attend the RSA conference but fail to interact with one another, as the former attends panels on Donne and Milton, while the latter attends panels on religion in Venice. Although they share an interdiscipline, they do not have to participate in it interdisciplinarily.

When colored by discipline (red = librarians; green = historians; blue = literary scholars; white = unknown), the networks formed by the digital conferences (ACH, DH, DLF) in Figure 9, the book history conference (SHARP) in Figure 10, and the early modern conferences (RSA, SCSC, SSA) in Figure 11 all appear to be highly interdisciplinary, with variously colored nodes thoroughly intermixed. While there is clear visual separation between the ACH and DH conferences (upper left) and the librarian-centric DLF conferences (lower right) in Figure 9, the librarians do not cluster into a subnetwork in the DH portion of the network, nor do the humanists cluster in the DLF portion—a pattern that remains when their annual networks are considered individually—and there is significant overlap and intermixing between the two. The book history conferences are similarly intermixed in Figure 10, while the early modern conference in Figure 11 shows only the slightest visual separation between the historian and literary scholar nodes, due to the predominance of literary scholars clustering together in the lower right-hand corner of the visualization. But despite these promising visual results, there are too many nodes and the visualizations are too cluttered to determine whether these nodes are genuinely interacting across disciplinary boundaries without turning to counting.

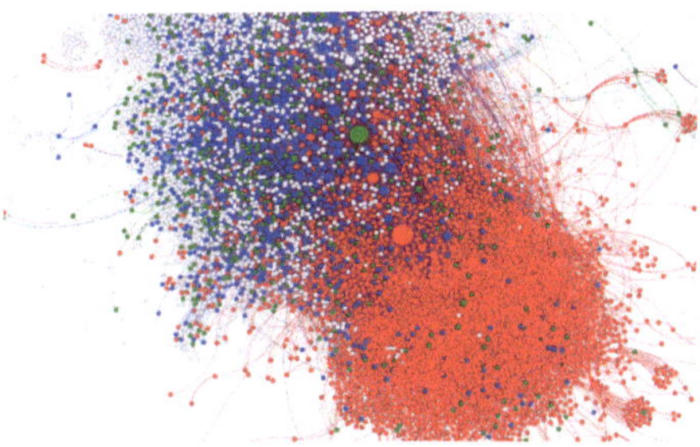

Figure 9.

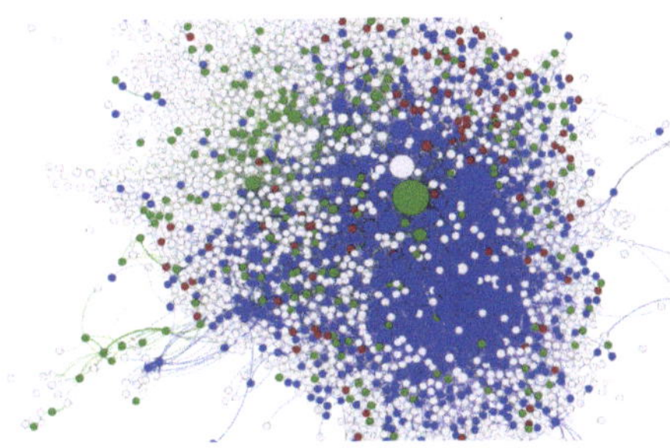

Figure 10.

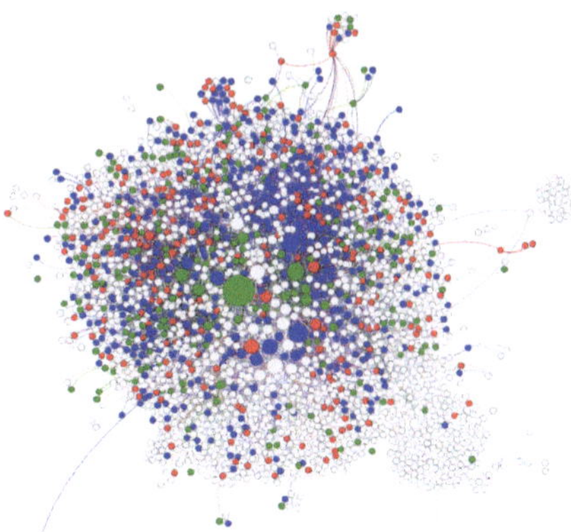

Figure 11.

Figures 9–11. Digital, book history, and early modern conference networks colored by discipline.

In Figure 12, we see a count of the edges in the network of all digital conferences, divided by whether the source and target node are classified as belonging to the same global discipline ("in-discipline" connections, as seen in the first four bars) or not ("out-discipline" connections, whose various permutations can be seen in the remaining 12 bars). For example, two literary scholars tweeting to one another create an "in-discipline" edge, while a librarian tweeting to a historian creates an "out-discipline" edge. The digital conferences include the librarian-centric DLF, accounting for the high proportion of librarians—3,688 nodes—in the network as compared to historians and literary scholars—625 and 994, respectively. The nodes categorized as unknown discipline outnumber them all, at 5,076. This is due in part to the inclusion of the international DH conference, most of whose attendees have no cause to attend the American-centric AHA, ALA, and MLA conferences. For example, the top "unknown" nodes by degree include an American librarian, the official Twitter accounts for the DH2018 and DH2019 conferences, the pan-European organization DARIAH (Digital Research Infrastructure for the Arts and Humanities), and a French classicist. While the number of in-discipline edges among the unknown nodes is striking, it unfortunately does not provide any information about disciplinarity. Their out-discipline edges privilege literary nodes and historian nodes over library nodes, a pattern also seen in the out-discipline edges of historians and literary scholars. The library nodes, by contrast, connect to literary nodes more often than could be accounted for by the nodes' percentage of the network. Literary nodes also have significantly more in-discipline edges (40 percent) than nodes from the other two disciplines, in part because they generated more edges than any other discipline. Historians and librarians, by contrast, connect slightly more with literary nodes than nodes within their own discipline, at 19 percent and 25.2 percent, respectively. Excluding uncategorized nodes, the majority of categorized edges formed interdisciplinary connections, particularly for historians and librarians. People attending these digital conferences more often communicated across disciplinary boundaries rather than within them.

The book history and early modern networks tell a similar story. The network formed by the SHARP conferences has 222 historians, 272 librarians, 445 literary scholars, and 1801 unknown nodes, with scholars from Australia, Canada, the UK, and Germany forming the top of the list of unknown nodes by degree.[24] Of the categorized connections, 17.1 percent of librarians' tweets were in-discipline, 21.4 percent of historians' tweets were in-discipline, and

---

[24] The next highest "unknown" node by degree is a playful, anonymous account, @SharpIceCream, whose geographic and disciplinary homes are a mystery.

38.2 percent of literary scholars' tweets were in-discipline. Among the early modern conferences, there are only 107 librarians, along with 245 historians, 550 literary scholars, and 1,673 unknown nodes, with top nodes including American scholars and British project-based accounts. A mere 7.6 percent of librarians' connections were in-network, in part reflecting their small percentage of tweeters. The historians' in-discipline edges were in line with the other networks, at 19.2 percent, and the literary scholars' in-discipline edges significantly increased to 61.9 percent, in line with the clustering of literary scholar nodes in the visualization. While early modern scholars remain committed to interdisciplinary communication, there is a subset of literary scholars whose communication is primarily within their own discipline.

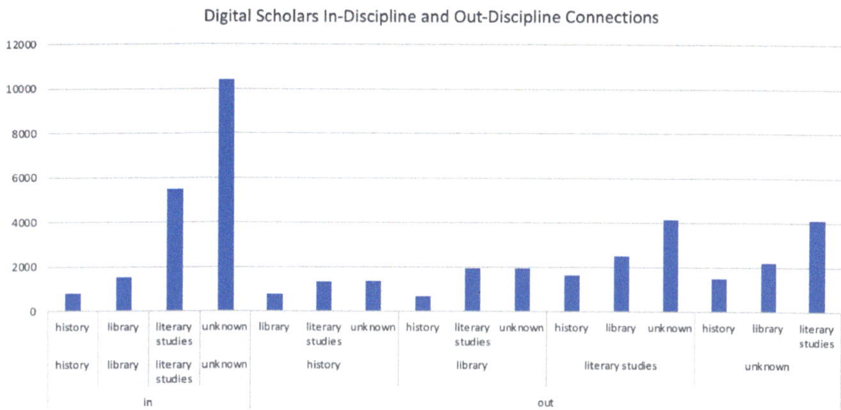

Figure 12. Digital scholars' in-discipline and out-discipline connections.

By the numbers, discipline still matters in each of the interdisciplinary conferences. While this seems particularly true for literary scholars, it is possible this is mainly an artifact of their greater numbers; to take the case of the early modern conferences, 245 historians could create a potential 60,025 in-discipline edges, while 550 literary scholars have the potential to create five times that many, or 302,500 in-discipline edges.[25] Although conference tweeters generate a significant number of disciplinarily inward-facing edges, they also generate an almost equal number of outward-facing edges.

[25] Because edges are directed, meaning Person A tweeting to Person B does not automatically create an equivalent edge of Person B tweeting to Person A, every node in a network has the potential to create an edge with every other node in the network, and the number of potential edges in a network with X nodes is $X \times (X - 1)$. Allowing self-loops increases that number to $X \times X$ or X^2.

Reincluding uncategorized edges, 47.8 percent of early modern edges, 46.8 percent of digital edges, and 58.4 percent of book history edges crossed disciplinary boundaries. Thus, scholars who tweet at the big three disciplinary conferences do not attend interdisciplinary conferences to communicate exclusively to their disciplinary cohort. Rather, they come to have a combination of disciplinary and interdisciplinary conversations with other digital, book history, or early modern scholars.

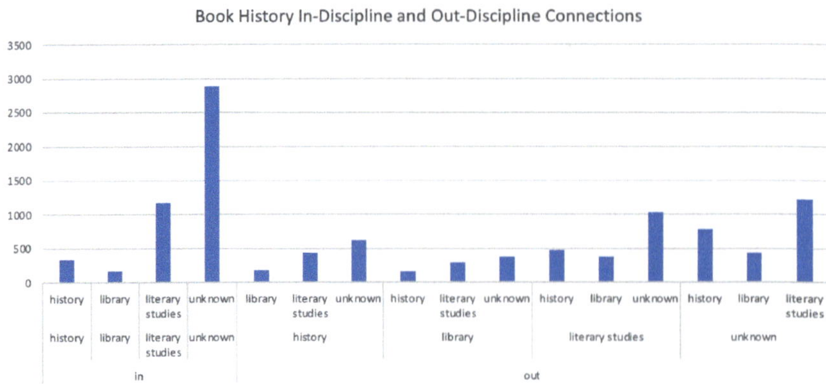

Figure 13.

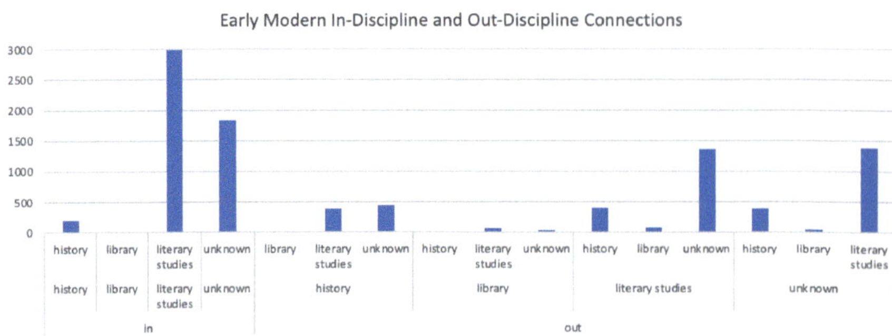

Figure 14.

Figures 13–14. Percentage of book history and early modern scholars' in-discipline and out-discipline connections.

Conferences, Social Media, and Scholarly Communication

Academic conferences create sparse social networks on Twitter, in which attendees interact with only a tiny fraction of other attendees. Nevertheless, they manage to generate a community that includes 19 out of 20 Twitter handles and 98 percent or more of their connections in a single network component. Information has the potential to travel rapidly through such a network. Like the famous six degrees of separation theory suggests, the average shortest path between any two nodes in even the largest of these Twitter networks is less than six, and in the case of the Australian SHARP 2018 conference, no two nodes in the network were separated by more than five degrees; any particular conference tweeter might not know everyone else in the network, but they know someone who knows someone who knows someone who knows someone. And while conference size impacts the structure of the network, just as it impacts the in-person conference experience, a conference's commitment to encourage tweeting can also increase the size of a network and decrease the distance of a network. But as conferences like the RSA in 2016 and 2017 demonstrate, who attends a conference matters, too. Particularly for smaller and mid-sized conferences, the presence or absence of prolific tweeters—often, but not always, digital scholars—can have an outsized impact on the network.

While conference Twitter communities have a consistent core of tweeters, with between 1 in 4 and 1 in 5 Twitter handles occurring in multiple years of a conference, they remain welcoming and open to newcomers. A mere 1 in 20 edges repeat across the years; instead, the majority of the connections are new ones formed among both established and new members of the network. The social conventions—and thus the shape—of these Twitter conversations form a sometimes stark contrast to face-to-face conversations, where eavesdropping on and attempting to join an ongoing conversation between strangers can be the height of rudeness. Instead, the public-facing nature of Twitter conversations ensures that even as old friends and colleagues reconnect over shared interests, there remains space for newcomers to enter existing conversations or start new ones.

These conversations have the potential to spill across the boundaries imposed by traditional conference attendance. While most people who interact with a Twitter conference hashtag are attending the conference, not all are, and signal-boosting a conversation onto the Internet creates the potential for those who do not attend the conference to engage with those who do. Particularly with respect to disciplinary conferences, this encourages conversations and ideas to pass across disciplinary boundaries. For the case of the AHA, ALA, and MLA, digital scholars—and, to a lesser degree (because they are fewer in number), those scholars interested in book history—connect the three disciplinary conferences. Perhaps unsurprisingly, given the history of DH and librarians' and literary scholars' great interest in book history, these ties are more numerous between librarians and literary scholars than historians. But the two humanities disciplines are also tightly connected, with early modernists forming a coherent subnetwork almost completely within the intersection of literary studies and history. And these trends continue with tweeters at interdisciplinary conferences, who create edges across disciplinary boundaries as often as within them.

Over the past decade, social media has become a vital avenue of scholarly communication at academic conferences and beyond. Academic networks still derive and gain strength from formal and face-to-face connections—co-authorship, citations, mentorship, and shared committees, institutions, and memberships—but social media provides a new avenue for generating and supporting network ties. Twitter networks cross traditional academic boundaries of discipline and class, connecting professors and librarians, students and retirees, projects and institutions, funders and independent scholars, and members of the public at large. By examining these networks, we can begin to see how twenty-first-century scholars are crossing and re-crossing disciplinary boundaries to share ideas, expand on conferences as a traditional method of scholarly communication, and transform the way they form professional, scholarly networks in a newly digital and interdisciplinary world.

WORKS CITED

American Historical Association (AHA). n.d. "Guidelines for Tweeting at the Annual Meeting." Accessed 1 September 2020. historians.org/annual-meeting/resources-and-guides/guidelines-for-tweeting-at-the-annual-meeting.

Bokunewicz, Jane F., and Jason Shulman. 2017. "Influencer Identification in Twitter Networks of Destination Marketing Organizations." *Journal of Hospitality and Tourism Technology* 8 (2): 205–19. doi.org/10.1108/JHTT-09-2016-0057.

Colladon, Andrea Fronzetti, and Peter A. Gloor. 2019. "Measuring the Impact of Spammers on E-mail and Twitter Networks." *International Journal of Information Management* 48 (October): 254–62. doi.org/10.1016/j.ijinfomgt.2018.09.009.

Del Valle, Marc Esteve, and Rosa Borge Bravo. 2018. "Echo Chambers in Parliamentary Twitter Networks: The Catalan Case." *International Journal of Communication* 12:1715–35.

Digital Humanities Summer Institute (DHSI). n.d. "Accessibility and Social Media Guidelines." Accessed 12 January 2023. dhsi.org/accessibility-social-media-guidelines.

Gilbert, Sarah, and Drew Paulin. 2015. "Tweet to Learn: Expertise and Centrality in Conference Twitter Networks." In *2015 48th Hawaii International Conference on Systems Science*, 1920–29. doi.org/10.1109/HICSS.2015.231.

Himelboim, Itai, Marc A. Smith, Lee Rainie, Ben Shneiderman, and Camila Espina. 2017. "Classifying Twitter Topic-Networks Using Social Network Analysis." *Social Media + Society* 3, no. 1 (January–March): 1–13. doi.org/10.1177/2056305117691545.

Jules, Bergis, Ed Summers, and Vernon Mitchell Jr. 2018. *Ethical Considerations for Archiving Social Media Content Generated by Contemporary Social Movements: Challenges, Opportunities, and Recommendations*. docnow.io/docs/docnow-whitepaper-2018.pdf.

Kimmons, Royce, and George Veletsianos. 2016. "Education Scholars' Evolving Uses of Twitter as a Conference Backchannel and Social Commentary Platform." *British Journal of Educational Technology* 47, no. 3 (April): 445–64. doi.org/10.1111/bjet.12428.

Lee, Mi Kyung, Ho Young Yoon, Marc Smith, Hye Jin Park, and Han Woo Park. 2017. "Mapping a Twitter Scholarly Communications Network: A Case of the Association of Internet Researchers' Conference." *Scientometrics* 112, no. 2 (August): 767–97. doi.org/10.1007/s11192-017-2413-z.

Quan-Haase, Anabel, Kim Martin, and Lori McCay-Peet. 2015. "Networks of Digital Humanities Scholars: The Informational and Social Uses and Gratifications of Twitter." *Big Data & Society* 2, no. 1 (January–June): 1–12. doi.org/10.1177/2053951715589417.

Renaissance Society of America (RSA). n.d. "Past Meetings." Accessed 1 September 2020. rsa.org/page/Pastmeetings.

Ross, Claire, Melissa Terras, Claire Warwick, and Anne Welsh. 2011. "Enabled Backchannel: Conference Twitter Use by Digital Humanists." *Journal of Documentation* 67 (2): 214–37. doi.org/10.1108/00220411111109449.

SHARP (@SHARPorg). 2019. "Since 2011, we've been awarding the annual conference Twitter prize and there have been over sixty winners." Twitter, 14 July 2019, 7:04 a.m. twitter.com/SHARPorg/status/1150360395170963458.

SHARP 2017 (@SHARP2017). 2017. "Don't forget that Social Media Translators will be tweeting in languages other than English throughout #sharp17!" Twitter, 7 June 2017, 1:55 p.m. twitter.com/SHARP2017/status/872512272043737089.

SHARP 2017: Technologies of the Book. 2017. "Social Media." web.archive.org/web/20170722065516/http://www.sharp2017.com/about/social-media.

Society for the History of Authorship, Reading and Publishing (SHARP). 2016. "SHARP Social Media Guidelines." sharpweb.org/main/social-media-guidelines.

Chapter 4: Opening Up the Scriptorium: The Theory and Ethics of Transcription Methods from the Handwritten Page to the Web Page

Sarah Banschbach Valles
Dalhousie Manuscripts Project

Sarah J. Sprouse
West Texas A&M University

In the introduction to his edition of two works by Giraldus Cambrensis,[1] the late nineteenth-century editor James F. Dimock provided a brief stemmatic history[2] of the manuscripts available for producing the edition. In those introductory notes, Dimock made a startling comment: "A large number of the manuscripts . . . are late, and some of these very worthless" (Dimock 1868, ix).[3] The context, of course, is the desire to produce an edition that most closely renders authorial intention by capturing the earliest, most complete copies of the texts. In his effort to trace authorial intention, however, Dimock comes to ignore most of the extant manuscripts. Of the 31 manuscripts containing Giraldus's works, 22 are from the fifteenth through eighteenth centuries. While authorial intention is surely best sought in those earliest manuscripts, ignoring the later manuscripts is tantamount to obscuring a significant trend in the production and circulation of the texts

[1] Giraldus Cambrensis, better known as Gerald of Wales, was a late twelfth-century Cambro-Norman writer, historian, and archdeacon. The two works referenced above are the *Itinerarium Kambriae* (Journey through Wales) and the *Descriptio Kambriae* (Description of Wales), both of which were written at the end of the twelfth century.

[2] A stemmatic history charts the relationships of known extant manuscript copies of the same text and often places them into formal variant "families." The record of such a history is usually accompanied by a visual chart or "stemma."

[3] It should be noted that despite its age, Dimock's edition is still the most current. Cambridge University Press recently commissioned a new series of Giraldus Cambrensis editions.

ISBN 978-1-64959-119-7 (paper) ISBN 978-1-64959-120-3 (pdf) ISBN 978-1-64959-121-0 (epub)
New Technologies in Medieval and Renaissance Studies 12 (2025) 85–108

Dimock edited.[4] This editing conundrum—authorial intention or a complete sociological survey and history—is one endemic to print editions. The static nature and economics of the medium usually permit approximately one edition of a text, even when there may exist hundreds of manuscript copies. Further, the stemmatic mindset that prizes the earliest copies of a text most often results in an edited text based on a group of manuscripts, and thus the product is a simulacrum that does not directly represent any one manuscript. So editorial principles and intentions can impact the generations of scholarship that rely on the edition. If an editor chooses to emphasize a set of early manuscripts or a particular author represented in one manuscript, then the resulting scholarship is likely to follow the editor's biases. Editorial principles and the medium of the edition have consequences.

Dimock's perspective is not necessarily unusual in textual editing prior to the digital era. Author-centrism is conceptually linked to a focus on canonical literature, though such emphasis has indeed shifted in the last 50 years. The desire for the "perfect" edition of an author's work is a byproduct of canonical emphasis. Authors whose oeuvre first appeared in print are somewhat less affected by intentionalist editors. For writers whose works appeared in manuscript cultures, an editing criterion that prioritizes origins ultimately relies largely on conjecture. Further, author-centrism obfuscates not just the companion works that inevitably accompany the "primary" text but also the social, cultural, and historical value of the manuscript itself. In other words, privileging the author greatly impairs the perceived value of an individual manuscript. But as digital editions have come to the fore over the last few decades, there has been a subtle yet growing shift in editorial focus. While many digital editions do concentrate on a single author's work or body of work, there seems to be a mechanism inherent to the digital realm that resists, and indeed prohibits, author-centrism at the expense of the material object. In the digital environment, the materiality of the text itself can come into focus and, in doing so, the (im)materiality of the digital can come under scrutiny as well. The digital mirrors and amplifies the physical not just in product but, even more fascinatingly, in the very *processes* of production.

---

[4] Literary scholars are well versed in the multivalent challenges associated with seeking authorial intention, however the matter is especially fraught in the case of Giraldus. These texts survive in multiple versions, each from a different decade, suggesting not just revision but a change of attitude toward the material in those texts over a long period of time. When seeking authorial intention, the question here becomes, "Which Giraldus?" The Giraldus who wrote the first versions? Or the Giraldus of later recensions?

The shift in editorial values over the last 50 years can perhaps best be seen in placing a foundational scholar of textual editing in company with a theorist of digital editing. In 1992, David Greetham forecasted the advent of digital editions:

> Such editions might properly be called *post-critical*, in that the editor does not establish a text nor does he or she simply reproduce a previously existing text. Such editions provide the raw materials (through hypertext) for a series of possible conflated editions, in a manner very different from the fixing of text usually associated with critical editions. (Greetham 1992, 357; emphasis added)

On the emerging end of the digital era, Greetham had an understandably cautious skepticism of the editorial paradigm shift that the new medium would facilitate. Conversely, in 2016 Patrick Sahle cast Greetham's idea of "post-critical" as a positive achievement of digital scholarly editing. Sahle (2016, 29) touts digital editorial theory as allowing the edition to abandon "its recognisability as an authoritative, final statement. Instead, it becomes a permanent but potentially always changing documentation of an ongoing examination and processing of the objects in question. In this way, the edition as a publication is a *process rather than a product*" (emphasis added).

The editorial transition from author-centrism to text-as-object is fraught with its own possible pitfalls, such as using the new medium as an end in itself. The "MLA Statement on the Scholarly Edition in the Digital Age" cautions that "[t]he digital is neither inherently a site of innovation nor a necessarily useful innovation in itself" (MLA Committee on Scholarly Editions 2016, 5). Or, as Dot Porter (2016) of the Schoenberg Institute of Manuscript Studies argues, "Data over interface." The interface is subject to the wear and tear of stagnation associated with the expiration of software and add-ons absent regular technical maintenance. The data, if coded well, can persist beyond the interface itself. What these caveats point to is that an editorial purpose must still exist when using the digital medium. In this way, Greetham's concern over the critical value of digital editions is mitigated because the digital editor still curates, organizes, directs, emphasizes, researches, positions, and prioritizes with the intent of transparently sharing such work as well as the data accrued in those editorial choices. Sahle (2016, 31) celebrates that "one effect of this change in methodology, [is that] the edited text is relativised and the multiple text is facilitated." Because the multiple text has multiple articulations, some of which have surely not been imagined as yet, it is difficult to properly articulate a comprehensive definition of the digital scholarly edition (DSE).

Too often with new technologies users find themselves thinking in the old medium while working in the new. Early print incunabula are but one book history example of this skeuomorphic tendency, while contemporary web page interfaces frequently mimic the codex. The present moment is still the era of invention, of discovering possibilities, of realizing poly-texts. No one DSE is like another because each one speaks to a unique object. Thus, most attempts at defining a DSE think in terms of negative space—what it is *not* rather than what it is. In this chapter, we demonstrate how the production methodology of DSEs mimics medieval scribal practices and how the DSEs themselves can exhibit the multiplicity inherent in scribal practices. We see the definition of a digital edition as one of possibilities, multiplicities, and multivalences that encompasses both the fluidity of the texts themselves as well as the continued progression of digital tools that make new ways of reading possible.[5] In other words, we see digital editing as a continuance of the ongoing, millennia-long effort of meaning-making and knowledge preservation, so we look to the practices of the past in order to think forward the ethics of digital editing, both in practice and presentation.

It is our contention that such expansive efforts afforded by the digital have a long history spanning back to the scriptoria of medieval Europe. In most cases, many participants were necessary to produce a single codex. Depending on the size and scope of a digital project, it is still true that many participants are necessary, particularly in cases where the project lacks funding or direct institutional support. We argue that modern digital editing is grounded in medieval precedents and that successful digital projects benefit particularly from forms of crowdsourcing that are similar to the many scribes involved in manuscript production. Moreover, digital workflows present possible answers to two ethical dilemmas faced by potential editors—the *ethics of presentation* and the *ethics of work*. A critical component of ethical presentation is the desire to resist "perfecting" a manuscript, instead celebrating the scribal deviations in texts rather than moderating them. This effort highlights the

[5] The MLA itself struggles to articulate one succinct definition for a DSE. They offer a set of minimum standards in lieu of one concrete definition, further emphasizing the inherent plurality and possibility of the DSE (see MLA Committee on Scholarly Editions 2016, 5–8).

potential value of representing the "sociology of the text"[6] and manuscript rather than deferring to the grand notion of an author (McKenzie 1999). The Donne Variorum project is a critical example of such efforts.[7] The Donne Variorum endeavors to represent in digital facsimile and textual edition every single manuscript and print copy of the works of John Donne, thus permitting scholars the ability to trace relationships between the poems and their social and historical contexts. The project is expansive in its study. The other concern, the ethics of work, is particularly a matter of inclusivity and transparency not only in the work product but also in the sense of providing opportunities to graduate students, early career scholars, and particularly scholars from underrepresented backgrounds. Crowdsourcing and delegation of a variety of associated tasks allows for the inclusion of many potential participants. Instead of working across the manuscript to make it fit a set of editorial standards, a digital edition has many tools available to facilitate participants' communication *with* the manuscript. The flexibility of the digital accommodates a manuscript, or series of manuscripts, with greater transparency than a print edition. The editorial principles of a digital edition can adapt as necessary to accommodate the peculiarities of a particular material object, ultimately making room for greater context and better representation of such an object.

Philosophy of Medieval Continuance

In her monograph, *Collaborative Meaning in Medieval Scribal Culture*, Elizabeth Bryan (1999, 5–6) complicates critical scholarly assumptions about "texts" rife in modern scholarly print editions of premodern works that are based largely in poststructuralist ideas about consciousness and authorship. She argues that meaning is not just made by an author or a scribe but rather in multiple and continuing processes that extend to the modern reader, editor, and translator who access the text in a variety of forms. Bryan theorizes the concept of the "continuance of a text," which she defines in this way:

> The emphasis of this particularly configured medieval scribal textual community is not only on the object of the text but on the process between text and reader, a process of collaboration among first authors, scribes, illuminators, correctors, annotators, and other

[6] D. F. McKenzie argues for interplay of the material form of the text with the text's meaning; in other words, the how, what, where, and when of a text affects its meaning.

[7] Digital Donne: The Online *Variorum* (donnevariorum.dh.tamu.edu) is the virtual branch of the ongoing *Variorum Edition of the Poetry of John Donne* published by the Indiana University Press. It is an ongoing digital project.

> readers. The continuance of such a scribal text did not mean exactly repeated "mechanical" reproduction, but instead a renegotiation among meaning and words of preceding models and current writers and readers every time a codex was reproduced. (45–46)

Traditional scholarly editing prizes the earliest, fullest version of a work as a means of approaching authorial intention; however, such practices neglect the inherent value of multiplicity contemplated in "continuance." Premodern manuscripts, both medieval and early modern, are complicated by the many hands involved in their production and meaning-making; each manuscript copy of a text is unique in ways that cannot be fully captured in a stemmatic study of relationality. Lauryn Mayer (2004, 10) describes such efforts as a "*simulacrum* in the truest sense of the word: a textual production announcing itself as a reproduction, yet with no original." In other words, the product—the printed edition—is a constructed form of the text that does not exist elsewhere. Such an edition palimpsests material realities of manuscript culture and premodern print. It is a strange continuance of the text that cannot fully realize the peculiarities of communities of early textual production.

We suggest that a continuance of not just the text but of the scribal methodologies that produced manuscripts is possible in the fluidity of digital space beyond the rigid, flat, and hierarchical print edition. Digital standards such as the Text Encoding Initiative (TEI) and the International Image Interoperability Framework (IIIF) make a fuller rendering of the individual material realities of a manuscript and its texts possible.[8] Of course, while digital tools can provide greater access to the materiality of a manuscript, they can also palimpsest important qualities such as size of the object. Matthew Evan Davis (2018, 100) noted one such anecdote in which a computational specialist working with a team to produce a "large scale, multi-person collaborative research project to digitize, transcribe, annotate, and describe medieval manuscript texts" only later encountered the physical objects after spending considerable time with their digital facsimiles and "expressed surprise that

[8] TEI is a set of guidelines for encoding texts. The standardization offered by TEI allows for the data created to be used across a wide range of digital tools as well as endless combinations of TEI-encoded texts from any source. Large pools of data can be collected and studied together. Guidelines and tools can be found at tei-c.org. IIIF offers similar standardization for coded digital images of manuscripts and books, which are anchored in Application Programming Interfaces (API). Collections can be produced of manuscript images from any and all sources in order to comparatively study multiple manuscripts at once. More info can be found at iiif.io.

they were not all the same size." Such examples point to the need to account more fully for the physical realities of manuscripts as objects. Porter of the Schoenberg Institute tackled one such problem with the VisColl project, which allows for the digital modeling of the physical collation of manuscript (Porter, Campagnolo, and Connelly 2017).[9] VisColl seeks particularly to address the digital presentation of physical objects, which often do not provide images of the binding nor a collation formula. By modeling the collation formula in XML, the project is able to shape that data into diagrams that render the size, binding, and collation of a manuscript as a material object.

Historical Interventions in Editing

A digital edition, or set of digital editions, can destabilize the monolithic value placed on the earliest, most complete manuscript. Andrew Zurcher (2017) characterizes the divide between print and digital in this way:

> Until recently, scholarship advanced by the obliviation of its ephemerised texts; until recently, new editions cut their teeth on the carcasses of their predecessors. Today, as our publishing practices have begun to shift out of paper toward electronic processes of transcription, collation, correction, composition, and dissemination, we face a future in which scholarly editions may never be superseded. (171)

Virtual space is only limited by the capacity of servers and the time and effort of the editors. If the editors of a project so choose, all the relevant manuscripts could be rendered in the same project with coded text that permits comparative study using algorithmic and analytical tools. Of course, such efforts are time-consuming, and, in a case where dozens or even hundreds of manuscripts are available, the editors could not possibly tackle the work alone. But conventions of the digital realm offer a host of other solutions including a variety of forms of crowdsourcing. The collaborative processes of digital editing can not only better account for the material realities of the manuscript as an object, but they can also more fully continue the scribal methodologies that first produced the manuscript. Methods such as crowdsourced transcription have the same effects for a digital edition that scribal production had for the manuscript itself, including faster production time

[9] Porter's collaborators on the project include Alexandra Gillespie, Alberto Campagnolo, Conal Tuohy, the University of Toronto Libraries, and the Old Books New Science Lab. The VisColl project is located at viscoll.org, and the open-access code is available on GitHub.

and inclusivity. The concept of modern methodologies replicating those of premodern scribal practices will be investigated over the course of the three case studies below. We trace such practices from the medieval scriptorium to eighteenth-century transcription practices and finally to a study of digital, crowdsourced projects. Together these case studies demonstrate a temporal continuance of both texts and the methodologies that produced them.

The Medieval Scriptorium

The medieval scriptorium largely informs the twenty-first-century practices that we argue operate as a continuance of both the texts themselves and the methodologies involved in crowdsourcing. The scriptorium took many shapes, informed by location, time period, and even monastic rule. The common thread of these various forms is that the scriptorium was where books were made in an extensive, collaborative process that included parchment-makers, rubricators, scribes, and illuminators. Most often texts were copied from exemplars, either from a monastery's own collection or borrowed from elsewhere. The scribal work was performed by teams of literate monks. Vernacular scribal practices had many of their own peculiarities that distinguish them from the Latin in greater use in cathedral and monastic settings. In brief, we will discuss Latin scribal practices in England in the century or so after the Norman Conquest, which was a period marked by increased codicological output.

The physical space of a scriptorium was not always a certain reality for every monastery. In some locations, particularly in the early Middle Ages, the "scriptorium" was more of a conceptual plan than a designated physical space (Edler 1931; Horn and Born 1986; Kwakkel 2018). In these cases, monks would often perform their work either in their individual cells or in the cloisters. Even modern scholars use the term beyond the bounds of physical space; a *scriptorium* in such parlance is most often used to describe the collective known output of a particular monastery (Stones 2014). Such use facilitates the stemmatic grouping of families of manuscripts. Whether the scriptorium was a specific location in the monastery or not, the scribal practices were similar.

Prior to the Norman Conquest, many English monastic libraries were missing key patristic texts that were widely available and in use on the Continent. William I's installation of Norman bishops and abbots fueled a campaign for greater development of the monastic libraries, including classical works as well as patristic texts (Thomson 2008, 140–41). Such development necessitated a systematized plan for copying. An especially demonstrative example of this development is the case of Bishop Osmund (1078–99) and his oversight of the scriptorium at the Old Sarum Cathedral. The chronicler William of Malmesbury remarked that "Osmund gathered gifted writers about him and personally worked side by side with his scribes, not only in the copying but also in the binding of new books" (quoted in Drueke 2001, 508). This description paints a picture of what we commonly think of as a traditional scriptorium. Osmund brought together a group of (presumably Norman) monastic scribes in order to produce an extensive collection for the Old Sarum Cathedral library, which paved the way for a new campaign of monastic learning (Drueke 2001, 506–7). Approximately 70 manuscripts survive from this scriptorium prior to the 1120s, which demonstrates a remarkably prolific period of production set in motion by Osmund (Thomson 2008, 139). Across those 70 manuscripts, 26 separate scribes have been identified, 3 of whom were also involved in the production of the Exon Domesday book (c. 1086) (Thomson 2008, 140). The manuscripts are largely inexpert in execution, described by Jeanetta Drueke (2001, 506) as "messy texts, copied hurriedly in crooked lines on rough, unevenly cut parchment."

The number and varying quality of individual hands in each manuscript gives clues to their method of practice. Scribes would work separately on the leaves of parchment, which were later collated and bound together. Osmund himself oversaw production as a supervisor; there would, of course, have been many other participants in the production, including rubricators, correctors, illuminators, annotators, and binders. Stephen G. Nichols (2008) illustrates another key role—the master scribe who would have reported directly to Osmund. The master scribe was the one

> who "designed" the manuscript—the codex—by laying out the pages or leaves, called folios. His was no easy task. In addition to deciding whether to create two columns or three of text on each page, the designer also had to determine where to place the . . . "illuminations." He had to fit each of these with their caption, and then to place the . . . "rubrics" . . . throughout the manuscript. . . . Once the page layout was planned, it was next the master scribe's job to supervise the team of scribes and artists that would actually carry out the design.

The scribes worked to the collective plan by copying a text from their exemplar, thus giving shape to the plan of the master. Of course, each scribe had their own proclivities and made their own errors, which would be inevitable when one works for hours each day carefully copying a lengthy text by hand.

These errors and little distinctions (small illustrations, the addition of comments and complaints in the margins, short lines of poetry, etc.) contribute to the uniqueness of each individual copy of a text and highlight the value in studying the whole manuscript as a material object. The collective picture is of a collaborative effort for each manuscript, which is precisely the same methodology contemplated in crowdsourcing transcriptions for a digital edition. Many hands contribute to the effort of producing a single virtual edition of a manuscript; each volunteer transcriber participates in reproducing the digital exemplar. The digital hearkens back to the medieval.

An Eighteenth-Century Encounter with *Beowulf*

By the eighteenth century, print reigned supreme. The British Museum was founded in 1753 and afterwards became a hub for scholarly study of medieval manuscripts. These early scholars laid the foundations for what would become standard print editing practices. In doing so, however, they enacted their own scribal practices that functionally became continuances of the texts in those manuscripts. Grímur Jónsson Thorkelin, an eighteenth-century Icelandic-Danish scholar tasked with unearthing historical records of the Danes, produced the first published edition of *Beowulf* (Kiernan 1986, 1–41). His efforts at finding Danish records in the libraries of the British Isles took him several years, and he combed through numerous manuscripts and rolls. Early into that work, Thorkelin discovered the *Beowulf* poem in London, British Library Cotton MS Nero A.xv. Rather than make his own transcription, Thorkelin hired a currently unknown amanuensis to make a copy, which is now known as the Thorkelin A transcript. The scribe produced a surprisingly accurate copy (Kiernan 1986, 97–151), which has been attributed to the scribe's apparent unfamiliarity with the Carolingian and Uncial scripts that dominate the manuscript. The Thorkelin A scribe carefully reproduced the exact letterforms, including a crude attempt at the Carolingian style, thus demonstrating his inexpert understanding of the material before him. He simply copied what he saw, and the accuracy of his transcript improved the further he progressed through the manuscript. Thorkelin later made his own copy, now known as the Thorkelin B transcript, which contained many more errors precisely because Thorkelin had a strong working knowledge of Old English and the Carolingian script. Thorkelin anticipated certain orthographical forms and grammatical constructions, which biased the accuracy of his transcription (Gerritsen 1999). As he prepared his edition of *Beowulf*, Thorkelin made notes and corrections on both transcriptions, though he did not ultimately collate the two.

Aside from the awareness of Thorkelin's method arising out of medieval scribal practices, there is a significant lesson to be learned from his case. The Thorkelin A amanuensis had no knowledge of *Beowulf* or Old English, nor even a familiarity with the Carolingian script in which the poem was written. That lack of additional context forced the amanuensis to pay closer attention to the exact letterforms and spelling conventions present in the manuscript before him. Conversely, prior knowledge can prejudice a scribe by leading him to assume certain phrasings or spellings from the text before him rather than closely examining the contents of the manuscript itself. Such a lesson can be brought forward to a crowdsourced or double-blind model of digital transcription when volunteers and citizen scholars are involved. If one of the volunteer scribes looks at an edition, they may miss alternate phrasing or variant spelling conventions in the manuscript (effectively "palimpsesting" the text as they get it wrong). Asking such volunteers to avoid searching for other editions of a poem can help prevent contamination of the work. Even as the text of the medieval manuscript of *Beowulf* survives, in part due to Thorkelin's transcripts, the process of its production was also carried forward through the work of both the amanuensis and Thorkelin himself. Further damage to the manuscript after Thorkelin encountered it has also necessitated scholarly collation of the Thorkelin transcripts with the primary text of *Beowulf*. So, the Thorkelin transcripts ultimately became continuances of the manuscript as well as of the scribal process that produced it.

Digital Humanities and the Crowdsourced Edition

These earlier models of transcription and production have continued resonance for textual studies in the digital age. Democratized shared labor—in the sense that it is possible for experts, novices, and everyone in between to contribute in large or small ways—is a through line in the practices of the scriptorium to the digital edition. Projects that rely on crowdsourcing explicitly engage in this kind of shared labor as a means of more speedily producing a digital edition of a text, engaging public interest and support, as well as ensuring the quality of the edition. Crowdsourcing can be defined as an "online, distributed problem-solving and production model that leverages the collective intelligence of online communities to serve specific organizational goals" (Brabham 2013, xix). Specifically, crowdsourcing asks "the public to undertake tasks that cannot be done automatically, in an environment where the tasks, goals (or both) provide inherent rewards for participation" (Ridge 2013, 437). While there are examples of pre-Internet crowdsourcing prototypes, effective crowdsourcing is best suited to an online environment. The Internet lowers barriers to information, professional knowledge, tools, and communities, while also shortening the intervals of space and time; thus, active participation is easily enabled and attained (Mika, DeVeer, and Rinaldo 2017, 61). Furthermore, for a project to be truly crowdsourced rather than just collaboratively created, there must be an interplay between the management who organizes or directs the work and the volunteer crowd who generates content (Brabham 2013, xxi). In this sense, Wikipedia is not a crowdsourced enterprise because the commons is created by the community, and the community itself is the source of checks and balances.

The top-down/bottom-up dynamic of crowdsourcing has, from the coining of the term in 2006 by Jeff Howe, led many to assume that "the crowd" is primarily composed of amateurs, whose contributions must necessarily be somewhat lacking, while the management system of a project is filled with specialists (Howe 2006). However, a review of research studies shows that the crowds are typically more than "just" a collection of amateurs. Rather, any given crowd is more often than not "a self-selecting group of experts and professionals with a keen interest in a given task," and thus, "participatory-culture arrangements like crowdsourcing call into question what defines an amateur or a professional in the first place" (Brabham 2013, 73). While "self-selecting" implies a measure of self-aware agency in determining one's level of contribution, it is worth noting that the reality is likely more pragmatic at heart, since individuals who lack the time, skills, resources, knowledge, or aptitude eventually cease participating in a project. "Crowd-sifting" may thus be a more accurately descriptive term (Ridge 2014, 4). Additional alternative labels for crowdsourcing such as "community-sourcing," "targeted crowdsourcing," and "micro-volunteering" have been variously used as a means of addressing the nuance of the identity of "the crowd." For those concerned with the value, quality, and rigor of crowdsourced humanities projects, this general data on the credentials of contributors is a soothing balm, which specifics from the Transcribe Bentham project fully support (Causer and Terras 2014). Moreover, evidence from national initiatives that promote citizen scientists (citizenscience.gov), citizen archivists (archives.gov/citizen-archivist), and (more loosely) citizen historians (archinternational.org/projects/citizen-historians) show overwhelmingly positive, high-quality results from their volunteers.

The sciences have long recognized that crowdsourcing the production of knowledge is a useful tool for advancing the field. Galleries, libraries, archives, and museums have also been using crowdsourcing techniques for many years. For textual scholarship and scholarly editions, however, especially for rare manuscripts, various protective measures, gatekeeping, and elitism have historically prevented crowdsourcing from developing as a viable avenue of knowledge creation. But in the digital age those barriers are minimized, and with greater access has come greater opportunities for public engagement with rare manuscripts. Major platforms such as Transkribus (formerly tranScriptorium, a delightfully self-aware name),[10] FromThePage,[11] the Smithsonian Transcription Center,[12] Zooniverse,[13] the Folger Shakespeare Library's Dromio,[14] and Scripto+Omeka[15] are but some samples of the technological boom of transcription software developed for crowdsourced projects.

These digital tools dovetail with medieval scriptorium practices in that they provide opportunities for both users and contributors to connect with manuscripts in a variety of ways. Print facsimiles and print editions of manuscripts can only provide so much interaction with a manuscript. In such cases, the manuscript is fully dependent on a static iteration of its contents and *mise-en-page*—an iteration filtered through an editor's hierarchy of importance coupled with the two-dimensional limitations of the print medium. Creating a print edition of a manuscript takes on the nature of a Procrustean bed; something is inevitably lost in the process. In practice, what this means is that

> while printed editions, due to economic restrictions, usually come without facsimiles as a visual counterpart to the typographic text, digital editions usually start with visual representations ... [and] while printed editions normally give exactly one version of a text, the deeply marked up textual code of the digital edition theoretically covers several views of the text and may lead to various presentations generated by specific algorithms. (Sahle 2016, 27)

Though print editions of manuscripts have and still do serve essential roles in scholarship and in the classroom, a digital edition affords more opportunities to work *with* the manuscript as a dynamic actor rather than *across* it as

---

[10] Transkribus (readcoop.eu/transkribus) offers manual transcription tools as well as AI text, image, and structure recognition.

[11] FromThePage (fromthepage.com) is a free software for transcribing documents online.

[12] The Smithsonian Transcription Center (transcription.si.edu) is a public engagement program that aims to make the Smithsonian's collections more accessible.

[13] Zooniverse (zooniverse.org) is one of the largest crowdsourcing research platforms. It has the capability to host transcription projects.

[14] Dromio (transcribe.folger.edu) is the transcription interface for Early Modern Manuscripts Online.

[15] Scripto+Omeka (omeka.org/classic/plugins/Scripto) allows for crowdsourcing transcription for Omeka content.

a solidified, authoritative object subjected to rigid rules. In this sense, a DSE of a text is a potentially more ethical approach than a print edition, for it seeks to uphold the continuance of the text in its own right rather than as an interpreted palimpsest of itself.

If the digital environment provides the opportunity for the continuance of the text, so too does it provide the context for the continuance of its production ethos. Fluidity, flexibility, and a widely dispersed process are hallmarks of crowdsourced digital editions as well as of scriptorium practices. The digital environment, in a sense, thus creates a simulacrum of medieval and early modern manuscript practices. Any digital edition or project that utilizes crowdsourced transcription of manuscript materials recreates the scriptorium milieu by means of dispersed work across a gradation of specialties and proficiencies. Even non-humanities, non-medieval/early modern projects such as Old Weather (oldweather.org), Biodiversity Heritage Library (biodiversitylibrary.org), and Trove (trove.nla.gov.au) rely on scriptorium methods in their online communities for crowdsourced transcriptions, coding, and item descriptions. Because digital editions by nature destabilize the long-standing idea of "the single omniscient editor . . . to the team of specialists with differentiated roles," every person who contributes to the edition is essential in the shaping of a "fundamentally collaborative endeavor" (Sahle 2016, 30).

While there are many crowdsourced digital projects, the *Social Edition of the Devonshire Manuscript* (en.wikibooks.org/wiki/The_Devonshire_Manuscript) shows incredible self-consciousness in utilizing the possibilities of digital technology to create a multivalent crowdsourced project. The *Social Edition* is a Wikibooks-hosted digital edition of the Devonshire Manuscript (London, British Library Add. MS 17492). This sixteenth-century verse miscellany from the court of Henry VIII is largely composed of poetry by Thomas Wyatt; however, new attention is being paid to the other poets in the manuscript not only due to greater accessibility but also due to the desire in textual scholarship to move away from stable, author-centric models of analysis and toward social, plural, multi-vocal, dynamic texts that engage literary and historical contexts (Marcus 2009, 82). The digital medium assists with this movement toward plurality or versioning of a text because there is greater flexibility in representing the text itself, as well as in representing the cultures who made the text or who made the text their own. In this instance, we see how internet-based textual scholarship and editing "[erode] the boundary between an implicit hierarchy of traditional canonical literature and other forms of cultural production" (Marcus 2009, 94) while also allowing for a reiteration of the very practices that created the miscellany in the first place.

The editors of the *Social Edition of the Devonshire Manuscript* consciously sought to enter the spirit of the collaborative production of the Devonshire Manuscript by emphasizing open access and transparency, as well as by utilizing social media and social platforms to invite the contributions of citizen scholars (Siemens et al. 2016, 138). In doing so, the *Social Edition* deliberately reconfigured scholarly contributions. The editorial group of the *Social Edition* maintained that by using social media and adopting an outward-facing, transparent modus operandi, their goal was to "change the role of the scholarly editor from the *sole authority* on the text to a *facilitator* who brings traditional and citizen scholars into collaboration through ongoing editorial conversation" (Siemens et al. 2016, 158). Theirs was a calculated move to model early modern scriptoria or coteries in order to honor and embody the shared, social activities that resulted in the creation of the Devonshire Manuscript as a text and object (Siemens et al. 2018, 193). For the *Social Edition*, the "sociology of the text" is applied in a reflexive metalevel to emulate patterns of production. Thus, it seems that the continuance of a text is intimately related to the continuance of collaborative work.

Many humanities projects skillfully use crowdsourcing to accomplish a variety of work, yet crowdsourcing is often used for a particular end: the transcription of handwritten documents. While consortiums such as READ[16] work toward developing automatic Handwritten Text Recognition (HTR) software, there is still a need for human intervention in deciphering manuscript pages. And yet, even between human transcribers, there can be error and discrepancy. Error can be minimized by having each page of a manuscript transcribed by multiple people. As seen in the Thorkelin study, ranges of scholarly experience can affect the quality of a transcription in various ways. And in the *Social Edition of the Devonshire Manuscript*, the editorial group required each page to be transcribed by two different members working independently; any discrepancies in this blind system were resolved using a collation program (Siemens and Leitch 2009, 121).

The Folger Shakespeare Library's Dromio transcription platform includes a collation tool that assists in checking work from transcribers. The Dalhousie Manuscripts Project (dalhousiemssproject.com), for example, utilizes the Dromio capabilities to review work from their variety of volunteers. While the project is freely open to any volunteers who wish to participate, the editors decided to institute a carefully moderated form of crowdsourcing

---

[16] READ (readcoop.eu) is a European Cooperative Society created to develop the Transkribus platform.

transcriptions. Since the Dalhousie project has a limited scope, the crowd-sourcing model has carefully structured controls in place to keep track of who is transcribing which page and when. Two volunteers transcribe each page in a blind system. A collation protocol is implemented at a later stage when the editors note information for the critical and textual apparatuses such as changing scribal hands, unusual orthography, text identifications, and so on. This process is augmented with a weekly email to volunteers apprising them of the progress of the project and sending new assignments. These review processes ensure not only necessary accuracy and scholarly rigor, but they also help to maintain regularity across the whole body of work. By implementing collation and review procedures, standardized methods of coding markup and diplomatic editing practices ensure consistency is maintained across each page. Marrying scholarly rigor to volunteer participation necessitates a transparent statement of editorial practices and methodologies. To that end, the Dalhousie Manuscripts Project website includes a list of volunteers, a coherent accounting of collation processes, digital tools used by volunteers, and the TEI documentation for download.

Ethical Considerations in the Digital Environment

The case studies above demonstrate a continuance of workflow processes across nearly a millennium of scribal outputs and editing. Moving scribal methodologies into the digital realm carries the possibility for democratizing the editing process while also ensuring scholarly rigor for the edition itself. Further, digital editing permits an ongoing, active engagement with the manuscript(s) as new participants enter the conversation in a variety of ways including contributing transcriptions, assisting with coding and other web-based tasks, adding to living bibliographies, and producing new scholarship based in part on studies of the edition itself. In its statement on scholarly editions, the MLA notes that

> [d]igital modalities open up important opportunities for alternative uses of scholarly editions. First, they allow the data in an edition to be used as the basis for other editions, as transcriptions that can be compared using collation tools, as a contribution to a digital repository, and as part of a text corpus that might support quite different types of analysis. Second, digital modalities make it possible to support features such as user annotation, commentary, citation, and the creation of additional layers of information. Third, digital modalities allow edition interfaces to serve as environments for manipulation and exploration of the edition's textual space,

> so that the user can occupy the role of a contingent editor. (MLA Committee on Scholarly Editions 2016, 1)

In other words, the digital environment permits a continuance of both the text and the process that produces it. Readers, editors, and transcribers can engage with the primary source in new ways afforded by an interface that permits new modes of analysis not previously possible. The adaptability of digital space echoes the medieval scribal approach to reproduction, adaptation, and translation of the materials in their exemplar. Whereas print editions make static a single critical perspective on the premodern text they edit, the digital reminds us that a text is always in process. Several applications of premodern scribal methods endemic to a digital environment are apropos in promoting the ethics of work and the ethics of presentation.

Ethics of work refers both to the ability of crowdsourcing to create an inclusive environment and to the digital environment's potential for transparency. Crowdsourcing in an online environment lowers the entry threshold to present opportunities for greater access for more people across space. Institutional gatekeeping structures are minimized on the Web, expertise is easily shared, information circulates more quickly, hierarchies are less entrenched, gendered division of labor is less likely to occur, and more voices can contribute to a conversation. This means that knowledge creation can proceed rapidly yet still retain the integrity of scholarly rigor; it also means that more people acquire the skills necessary to empower them in their own projects and intellectual life. For each of the foregoing attributes, we suggest that digital editors consider the following issues as they design their workflow operating procedures:

1. *Institutional gatekeeping.* It is possible to actively cultivate public engagement by moving beyond traditional academic circles. Public interest is vital to maintaining funding for research; sharing, showing, and inviting people into the kinds of work accomplished by academics builds rapport and appreciation for that work.[17]

[17] The emergent practice of open science provides an example of "virtual witnessing" whereby trust is generated: "The opportunities for transparency, authenticity, and timeliness of the record created by open science could both reveal the scientific process in real time and allow claims to be viewed within the context of their underlying data. Open science thus has the potential to contribute to the substantiation of the relationships that are central both to people's trust in science and to science's trust in people" (Grand et al. 2012, 681). The arts and humanities could take a cue from open science and develop their own trust-inducing strategies.

2. *Shared expertise.* Contributors across a wide range of abilities can learn from each other. By opening up the editing process, a digital project creates more opportunities for more people to share their expertise. The dynamism of a digital project adapts itself to the skill sets of interested contributors, who in turn increase the sophistication of the project.[18]

3. *Information circulation.* The more a person understands about a project, the more likely it is that they will be invested in its success. Transparency in work methodology is necessary to generate an inclusive environment where each contributor is valued for their work. Sharing details of operational policies, infrastructure, resource management, collation, vetting, quality control measures, and problems and solutions with contributors creates an atmosphere of trust that further incentivizes work on a project. Sharing information may seem an extra step for an editor to pursue, yet effective management of an inclusive environment requires transparency to promote insightful, thoughtful work.[19]

4. *Hierarchy.* A less rigid sense of command structures enabled by the digital allows for more contributions from more people. More experiences and more types of knowledge and skills can carry greater value in a less hierarchical arrangement. Women and people of color are less likely to be tied to administrative, organizationally supportive work in a democratized system (see Siemens et al. 2016). Additionally, actively cultivating visibility measures such as providing space in a digital edition for public recognition of contributors, including them in discussions of design, or even inviting them to take part in academic and/or public forums such as conferences is vital in ensuring that participants are appropriately credited for their invaluable labor.

Ethics of presentation is another dimension of digital transparency. In TEI coding, the critical apparatus and editorial notes are built into the code itself; in essence, TEI is a map of decisions, a record of scholarly methods. TEI allows for substantial insight into editorial choices, and it also allows for different

[18] Digital tools facilitate engagement across a spectrum of ability and "can support the evolution of roles, allowing members of different communities to develop a critical awareness of the process and context of research" (Grand et al. 2016, 16).

[19] For theoretical underpinnings, see Grand et al. 2016. For an example in action, see Siemens et al. 2018.

manipulations of the text via data mining. Additionally, the digital space presents the opportunity for texts to be seen as they exist. Though issues do arise when considering how to represent the scale of a physical text in the digital environment, overall the text is filtered much less by medium and editor than otherwise. The editors of a digital edition cannot alter the physical text, and they can only offer so much in terms of an interpretive framework. The text itself as a physical object remains at the center of attention. This transparency, this restrained mediation of a text, creates the possibility for new interpretations and new kinds of scholarship. We propose that digital editions, unlike their print forebears, continue to resist the urge to perfect a manuscript and instead remain focused on adequately presenting the manuscript as is, rather than seek for ways to create an ideal manuscript.

Any individual can be a participant in these processes of a digital scriptorium. All that is necessary is a computer and access to the Internet. From citizen scholars to graduate students, the possibilities of inclusion are nearly endless. Indeed, unfamiliarity with the text to be transcribed can be a boon rather than a hindrance, as seen in the case of the Thorkelin A scribe, who more accurately transcribed *Beowulf* due to his inability to predict what a poetic line *might* say or what an Old English word *should* be. With some basic guidance on the scribal hand, the uninformed citizen scholar could more accurately render the page than an expert with both the training and extensive knowledge of the author's works. In this way, the digital edition opens up new possibilities for inclusion.

Beyond accessibility to the citizen scholar and emerging scholars, the production of a digital edition also facilitates the inclusion of those scholars in positions of precarity and/or from underrepresented backgrounds. This is yet another reason why visibility measures such as public credit are necessary. The humanities fields are currently undergoing a moment of reckoning, encouraging the reexamination of inequal positions of power and the racism and bigotry that underlie hiring practices, tenure promotion, and field-specific opportunities in publishing, research, and grants (Bellamy and Mosley 2020; Laland 2020). While we would not argue that digital editing is a remedy for such massively systemic inequities, we do suggest that advocating for digital scholarly editions as a viable metric for hiring and tenure promotion carries the possibility of greater inclusion of such underrepresented voices in the field. Further, pushing the field toward wider acceptance of the fruitful possibilities of digital editing could facilitate greater representation of underrepresented authors, texts, and manuscripts. The process of digital editing, like Osmund and his team of scribes, permits active involvement of participants with a range of skills and areas of expertise that could enhance the usability of the edition and its applications. The VisColl project discussed above further emphasizes the fluidity of digital editing and the opportunities available for development of new tools to better represent a manuscript as both the site of a text and as a material object.

Conclusion

From handwritten page to web page, this chapter has suggested that there is a spirit of continuance in both the production protocols and readerly interactions with a text in manuscripts and in digital editions of those manuscripts. It has promoted the idea that carrying forward the principle of shared labor across a gamut of expertise produces an environment where the text itself remains the center of study, both as a work of literature and as a physical object. The digital era has afforded the opportunity for the material object to be reunited with its contents in meaning-making activities. Digital editions are thus an important attempt at tackling the challenge of ethically presenting a text. The editor of a digital edition is better able to present a text on its own merits and on its own terms rather than acquiescing to the economics (the politics!) of the canon, the influence of a static medium, or Urtext ideology. Questions of usage between a print edition of a manuscript and a digital edition of the same manuscript also collide in that the possibilities of interpretation are expanded when the "body and spirit" of a text are unified. More scholarship can be done by more people when there are more entrances to a text.

Editing has always been a tricky business, and digital editing has its own intrigues to overcome. Digital editing is not simply an innovation by merit of technological advancement. When the aspirations of digital editing are more expansive, they have the potential "to change literary history: to change our collective organization of the intertextual spaces of the past, and by doing so to change the kind of intertextual spaces that may be created by future readers, critics, writers. To change our reading of the past, in order to change the future of reading" (Taylor 1993, 143). The manifold possibilities envisioned in digital editing can significantly alter literary history and truly affect the multivalent intertextual spaces of textual usage by "getting out of the way" as much as possible—or rather, by not speaking over the text, not telling the text what it should be or how it should behave. A digital edition of a text better allows it to be the object that it is rather than what the canon needs it to be. Even so, "[e]diting in the early twenty-first century is full of paradoxes. The editor has a responsibility both to the politics of the dead author and the author's society, and to the politics of the contemporary audience; the editor is a parasite on the text, and also the reason for that text's continuing existence; s/he is both guardian of text and constructor of text, both guardian and maker of meaning" (Maguire 2016, 92). But in the flexible, fluid space of a digital interface the editor can better accommodate the past, present, and future readers of a text; can be less parasitical and craft a more symbiotic relationship; and can guard a text not to keep people out but to let them in to make their own meaning. While the scriptoria of the past were limited in the wider reach of the manuscripts they produced, adapting their models of production to transcription and editing in digital space permits a level of accessibility and immediacy the scribes could never have imagined. Opening up the scriptorium of the past as a model for future textual scholarship in the digital age provides not just work-flow pragmatics but also allows for a less controlling ethos of use and interpretation. The sociology of the text expands again.

WORKS CITED

Bellamy, Pearis L., and Della V. Mosley. 2020. "A Tale of Two Towers: An Open Letter and Call to Action." Academics for Black Survival and Wellness, 5 June 2020. academics4blacklives.com/call-to-action/a4bl-call-to-action/call-to-action-our-letter-to-academics.

Brabham, Daren C. 2013. *Crowdsourcing*. Cambridge, MA: MIT Press.

Bryan, Elizabeth. 1999. *Collaborative Meaning in Medieval Scribal Culture: The Otho Layamon*. Ann Arbor: University of Michigan Press. doi.org/10.3998/mpub.15209.

Causer, Tim, and Melissa Terras. 2014. "'Many Hands Make Light Work. Many Hands Together Make Merry Work': *Transcribe Bentham* and Crowdsourcing Manuscript Collections." In *Crowdsourcing Our Cultural Heritage*, edited by Mia Ridge, 57–88. Burlington, VT: Ashgate. doi.org/10.4324/9781315575162.

Davis, Matthew Evan. 2018. "Content Is Not Context: Radical Transparency and the Acknowledgement of Informational Palimpsests in Online Display." In *Meeting the Medieval in a Digital World*, edited by Matthew Evan Davis,

Tamsyn Mahoney-Steel, and Ece Turnator, 93–122. Amsterdam: Arc Humanities Press. doi.org/10.1515/9781641891936-008.

Dimock, James F. 1868. "Preface: Part I., Manuscripts." In *Giraldi Cambrensis Opera*, ix–xxxii. Vol. 6. London: J. S. Brewer.

Drueke, Jeanetta. 2001. "St. Osmund's New Legacy: The Scriptorium Informs Electronic Text." *Libraries & Culture* 36, no. 4 (Fall): 506–17. jstor.org/stable/25548952.

Edler, Florence. 1931. "The Monastic Scriptorium." *Thought: Fordham University Quarterly* 6 (2): 181–206.

Gerritsen, J. 1999. "What Use Are the Thorkelin Transcripts of *Beowulf*?" *Anglo-Saxon England* 28 (December): 23–42. doi.org/10.1017/S0263675100002246.

Grand, Ann, Richard Holliman, Trevor Collins, and Anne Adams. 2016. "'We muddle our way through': Shared and Distributed Expertise in Digital Engagement with Research." *Science Communication* 15, no. 4 (June): 1–23. doi.org/10.22323/2.15040205.

Grand, Ann, Clare Wilkinson, Karen Bultitude, and Alan F. T. Winfield. 2012. "Open Science: A New 'Trust Technology'?" *Science Communication* 34, no. 5 (October): 679–89. doi.org/10.1177/1075547012443021.

Greetham, David C. 1992. *Textual Scholarship: An Introduction*. New York: Garland Publishing. doi.org/10.4324/9780203821220.

Horn, Walter, and Ernest Born. 1986. "The Medieval Monastery as a Setting for the Production of Manuscripts." *The Journal of the Walters Art Gallery* 44:16–47. jstor.org/stable/20169021.

Howe, Jeff. 2006. "The Rise of Crowdsourcing." *Wired*, 1 June 2006. wired.com/2006/06/crowds.

Kiernan, Kevin S. 1986. *The Thorkelin Transcripts of* Beowulf. Copenhagen: Rosenkilde and Bagger.

Kwakkel, Erik. 2018. "Where Are the Scriptoria?" In *Books before Print*, 211–15. Leeds: Arc Humanities Press. doi.org/10.2307/j.ctvg251fm.38.

Laland, Kevin N. 2020. "Racism in Academia, and Why the 'Little Things' Matter." *Nature* 584 (August): 653–54. doi.org/10.1038/d41586-020-02471-6.

Maguire, Laurie E. 2016. "Feminist Editing and the Body of the Text." In *A Feminist Companion to Shakespeare*, edited by Dympna Callaghan, 77–97. Malden, MA: John Wiley & Sons. doi.org/10.1002/9781118501221.ch4.

Marcus, Leah. 2009. "Textual Scholarship." In *Women Editing/Editing Women: Early Modern Women Writers and the New Textualism*, edited by Ann Hollinshead Hurley and Chanita Goodblatt, 75–102. Newcastle upon Tyne: Cambridge Scholars Publishing.

Mayer, Lauryn S. 2004. *Worlds Made Flesh: Reading Medieval Manuscript Culture*. New York: Routledge.

McKenzie, D. F. 1999. *Bibliography and the Sociology of Texts*. New York: Cambridge University Press. doi.org/10.1017/CBO9780511483226.

Mika, Katherine, Joseph DeVeer, and Constance Rinaldo. 2017. "Crowdsourcing Natural History Archives: Tools for Extracting Transcriptions and Data." *Biodiversity Informatics* 12 (November): 58–75. doi.org/10.17161/bi.v12i0.6646.

MLA Committee on Scholarly Editions. 2016. "MLA Statement on the Scholarly Edition in the Digital Age." Modern Language Association. mla.org/content/download/52050/file/rptCSE16.pdf.

Nichols, Stephen G. 2008. "'Born Medieval': MSS. in the Digital Scriptorium." *Journal of Electronic Publishing* 11, no. 1 (Winter). doi.org/10.3998/3336451.0011.104.

Porter, Dot. 2016. "'What is an edition anyway?' My Keynote for the Digital Scholarly Editions as Interfaces Conference, University of Graz." *Dot Porter Digital* (blog), 24 September 2016. dotporterdigital.org/what-is-an-edition-anyway-my-keynote-for-the-digital-scholarly-editions-as-interfaces-conference-university-of-graz.

Porter, Dot, Alberto Campagnolo, and Erin Connelly. 2017. "VisColl: A New Collation Tool for Manuscript Studies." In *Kodikologie und Paläographie im digitalin Zeitalter 4*, edited by Hannah Busch, Franz Fischer, and Patrick Sahle, 81–102. Norderstedt: Books on Demand.

Ridge, Mia. 2013. "From Tagging to Theorizing: Deepening Engagement with Cultural Heritage through Crowdsourcing." *Curator* 56, no. 4 (October): 435–50. doi.org/10.1111/cura.12046.

———, ed. 2014. *Crowdsourcing Our Cultural Heritage*. Burlington, VT: Ashgate. doi.org/10.4324/9781315575162.

Sahle, Patrick. 2016. "What Is a Scholarly Digital Edition?" In *Digital Scholarly Editing: Theories and Practices*, edited by Matthew James Driscoll and Elena Pierazzo, 19–40. Cambridge: Open Book Publishers. doi.org/10.11647/OBP.0095.02.

Siemens, Ray, Constance Crompton, Daniel Powell, Alyssa Arbuckle, and Maggie Shirley. 2016. "Building a Social Edition of the Devonshire Manuscript." In *Digital Scholarly Editing: Theories and Practices*, edited by Matthew James Driscoll and Elena Pierazzo, 137–60. Cambridge: Open Book Publishers. doi.org/10.11647/OBP.0095.

Siemens, Ray, Constance Crompton, Daniel Powell, Alyssa Arbuckle, Maggie Shirley, and the Devonshire Manuscript Editorial Group. 2018. "Social Editing and the Devonshire Manuscript." In *A Handbook of Editing Early Modern Texts*, edited by Claire Loffman and Harriet Phillips, 193–98. New York: Routledge.

Siemens, Ray, and Caroline Leitch. 2009. "Editing the Early Modern Miscellany: Modelling and Knowledge (Re)Presentation as a Context for the Contemporary Editor." In *New Ways of Looking at Old Texts, IV: Papers of the Renaissance English Text Society, 2002–2006*, edited by Michael Denbog, 115–30. Tempe, AZ: Renaissance English Text Society.

Stones, Alison. 2014. "Scriptorium: The Term and Its History." *Perspective* 1:113–20.

Taylor, Gary. 1993. "The Renaissance and the End of Editing." In *Palimpsest: Editorial Theory in the Humanities*, edited by George Bornstein and Ralph G. Williams, 121–49. Ann Arbor: University of Michigan Press.

Thomson, Rodney M. 2008. "Monastic and Cathedral Book Production." In *The Cambridge History of the Book in Britain*, edited by Nigel Morgan and Rodney M. Thomson, 136–67. Vol. 2, *1100–1400*. New York: Cambridge University Press. doi.org/10.1017/CHOL9780521782180.011.

Zurcher, Andrew. 2017. "Parting 'with much wee know': Digital Editing and the Early Modern Text." In *A Handbook of Editing Early Modern Texts*, edited by Claire Loffman and Harriet Phillips, 171–75. New York: Routledge.

Chapter 5:
New Solutions for Old Problems: Digital Publication, the Linguistic Study of Medieval Vernacular Texts, and the EDV Project

Nadia Cannata
Sapienza Università di Roma

Introduction

I should like to briefly discuss the advantages of digital publication in relation to the linguistic study of medieval texts. The context for this is the publication of the results of a ten-year project—*EDV: Epigraphic Database of Inscriptions in Italian Vernaculars (IXth–XVth c.)*—which records all extant vernacular inscriptions produced in Italy from the middle of the ninth to the end of the fifteenth century that were displayed publicly and composed in any language other than Latin.

The database used for the storage, study, and eventual publication of the corpus, available at edv.seai.uniroma1.it, records general features (date, place of origin, location, type of object, material, language(s) used, function, and script) and the complete bibliography available to date for each inscription. Its texts are published in diplomatic transcription as well as critical edition and are marked up in EpiDoc XML for the purpose of making them available for detailed linguistic analysis. The database currently records around 570 inscriptions spread across the whole period (ninth to fifteenth century) and the whole Italian peninsula (Cacchioli, Cannata, and Tiburzi 2016; Cannata 2018a, 2018b).

The aim of the study is fundamentally threefold: (1) to preserve a record of a significant and hitherto largely unknown corpus of medieval texts of a non-literary nature; (2) to provide an archive of documentary evidence of the uses of language(s) other than Latin in public script in late medieval and early modern Italy; and (3) to devise a powerful research tool to study such languages, or linguistic varieties, which are—in their vast majority—all lacking a standard and a canon. Related to this final objective are two important research questions for which the project may be able to give some form of answer:

ISBN 978-1-64959-119-7 (paper) ISBN 978-1-64959-120-3 (pdf) ISBN 978-1-64959-121-0 (epub)
New Technologies in Medieval and Renaissance Studies 12 (2025) 109–26

1. Is there a way to help describe (even partially) the languages used in Romance Europe outside of the strict categories of "Italian," "French," and "Spanish" after the demise of "Latin"?
2. Can we develop a methodology that allows us to map the hitherto scarcely charted territory connecting written and spoken language?

It is my contention that the first two aims are best served by traditional forms of publication, in print and in book form, while the research potential unleashed by the possibility of interrogating texts marked up in XML may offer a reason for it to become an integral part of the research methods of historical sociolinguistics. In order to address the complex issues involved in studying medieval Romance languages, scholars may harness the potential of digital tools and methodologies to enable a fruitful dialogue across disciplines as well as test against each other the historical methods of historical linguistics, sociolinguistics, and paleography. Digital tools can support an innovative interaction between historical linguistics and the history of writing by allowing the cross-referencing of huge amounts of textual data, which, through their sheer volume, may give us better grounds to infer the relation between sign and sound in recording languages with a very limited written tradition.

In this chapter, I shall first discuss the context in which the study falls, the need for an interdisciplinary approach combining language studies with studies in paleography and the history of written culture, and the function of digital tools to this effect. I will then present some of the results of the EDV project.

Retracing Lost Languages

As a philologist and textual critic mostly engaged in the study of languages and literary traditions in Romance Europe (with particular reference to Italy and its vernaculars), I have often wondered through what methods—other than those that historical linguistics and Romance philologists in particular have passed down to us—we might be able to add to our knowledge of the languages actually spoken in medieval and early modern Europe given that the available documentation testifying to the linguistic culture of that time and place is constituted by written records. In any society—medieval, early modern, or contemporary—written records come to be written in the ideal space occupied by whichever languages hold the necessary prestige in a community, and therefore only a few of the many languages and language varieties available in a community achieve a written transmission (Cannata

2016). When the objects of scholarly attention are languages in current use, we have the means to retrieve the oral voices actually used in speech, and we can therefore try to account for their varieties and forms. Attempting to engage in historical sociolinguistics is much harder, however, since it is uncertain whether the languages whose use was solely, or mostly, oral and confined to everyday exchanges are somehow accounted for in writing, or if—as one would be inclined to conclude—they have mostly fallen through the net of historical memory, since they were sparsely written, or not written at all.

It is a known fact to sociolinguists that any sociolinguistic investigation depends on the ability to engage with a comprehensive dataset, and to contextualize the linguistic document under scrutiny into the wider picture of general language use or, to put it in terms I prefer, the linguistic culture into which it falls. Context in sociolinguistics—and all the more in historical sociolinguistics—is paramount (Hernández-Campoy and Conde-Silvestre 2012; Romaine 2009; Varvaro 1982). Moreover, when studying documents written in languages that were not standardized, the relationship between spelling and pronunciation is often less mediated than in learned or literary production and may therefore betray—through the occasional inadvertencies of the writers—information about the natural speech actually in use. Similarly, one might see more clearly the influence of the standard on common usage, and of the usage on the perceived standard. If we can compare the *scripta* (i.e., the written forms acquired by a language) of these writers with contemporary texts of a different nature and function—literary texts or documents of a legal nature—the complex "linguistic culture" the document belongs to will appear more clearly, making it possible to identify language uses that, because of their marginality or lack of prestige, may well have escaped our attention.

Interestingly, we lack the appropriate terms to describe the oral varieties in most frequent use in the period and places under consideration. Our description of the languages of Italy in the Middle Ages is based on categories that were not shared by the communities whose languages are the focus of our attention. "Italian" and "Latin" are terms often used by Dante—the first major European author to openly discuss language matters—to refer to the peoples of Italy, but they seem to refer to a cultural belonging rather than to specific languages (Alighieri 2011). As regards contemporary languages, he only refers to two major categories: *gramatica* (i.e., Latin) and *vulgares* (i.e., vernaculars). Not only for Dante but in all of Romance Europe, from Ireland to the shores of northern Africa, the Latin adjective *vulgaris, -e* applied to the description of any language, serving as a blanket term up until at least the thirteenth century for any modern language in use at the time that was distinct from Latin. Although the term described languages profoundly different from one another, according to medieval linguists these languages shared a fundamental sameness constituted by their common identity as "natural" languages. Latin and Greek, on the other hand, were seen as "artificial" languages devised by mankind to counteract the nefarious effect of the destruction of the Tower of Babel, which had brought about linguistic diversity (Alighieri 2011; Tavoni 1999; Tomasin 2015; Vineis and Maierù 2014). The "nations" that constituted the preferred groupings in medieval universities across the fourteenth and fifteenth centuries did not in any way coincide with the nations as we know them today, or indeed with any idea of a common birthplace as the etymology of the name would suggest (Bruni 2010, 109–12).

Such cultural history attached to the word still echoes, since in most Romance languages *vulgaire*, *volgare*, *vulgar*, or its synonymous *vernacular*, is still used in reference to mother tongues commonly spoken in medieval Europe. Moreover, the term is adopted extensively by Romance philologists faced with the conundrum of naming those Neo-Latin or Proto-Romance languages in use in the past that did not enjoy a written transmission and therefore lack a proper nomenclature—from "vulgar" Latin down to the vernaculars of Italy, France, Spain, and so on.

Even if we consider the linguistic history of Italy alone, we must register that during the fifth to fifteenth century an array of vernaculars, some varieties of which are unknown to us today, were in use (van Moos 2008). We should also bear in mind that epigraphic documentation reveals beyond a doubt that already in fifth-century Rome, Latin phonology had evolved to the point that the quantitative vowel system was no longer in place, the case system was heavily reduced (the accusative used extensively in lieu of the nominative), and verb terminations were similarly subjected to reduction and change. The possibility of observing contextually the linguistic features of a very significant number of Christian funerary inscriptions up to the fifth century allows us to conclude that although the language in use in Rome at the time could not be defined as "Latin," we would nevertheless be unable to define it as anything *but* Latin; there is no evidence that the authors of the records documenting such irreversible linguistic change and irretrievable distance of their language from Latin had any awareness that they wrote anything but it (Cannata 2014; Maiden, Smith, and Ledgeway 2013).[1] We record the birth of vernacular languages when we can document the birth of such an awareness: in Italy this happened no earlier than the ninth century.

There are therefore around five centuries of linguistic usage—from the fifth to at least the ninth—that appear unaccounted for, since we would be quite unable to answer this simple question: "What language(s) were spoken in Italy in the fifth, sixth, seventh, and eighth centuries?" We define languages in use in Italy after the ninth century by using the dominant literary vernaculars at the time—Sicilian, Tuscan, Provençal, Old French, Catalan, and so on—which does not help with the issue of how to account for languages not graced with a written tradition but nonetheless widely used by local communities (Cannata 2016; Castellani 1984, 2000; Lepschy 2015). Even when we move forward in time to consider the period between the tenth and the fifteenth centuries, we are at pains to find names for the languages recorded by epigraphy or in documents of a legal nature (which are widely understood to record "natural" everyday language more faithfully than other kinds of text) and those supposedly spoken in vernaculars other than Tuscan, Central Italian, Sicilian, and so on.

Roger Wright and Michel Banniard, among others, have argued extensively about the need to devise a new paradigm to understand language change and its periodization, and to deal with the issues that the rigid protocols of nineteenth-century philology seem to have passed onto us, in particular the very conception of a "vernacular Latin" distinct and diverse with respect to "classical Latin," which was to be regarded as the true progenitor of Romance. Such an idea, which brought the welcome acknowledgement that even in antiquity languages had different registers and varieties, has been applied in a rather mechanical fashion. The idea that there were two different Latin languages, the definition of the vernacular variety appearing at best slippery and at worst confused, has hindered our understanding of linguistic and cultural change in Neo-Latin Europe. In this context, I believe that digital interrogation of marked-up texts could contribute to our finding answers to the issues raised above.

---

[1] The full database of Christian inscriptions up to the eighth century is EDB: Epigraphic Database Bari (edb.uniba.it), which is to be found in the Electronic Archive of Greek and Latin Epigraphy (EAGLE), which collects and makes fully available the impressive documentation resulting from several long-established projects: the Epigraphische Datenbank Heidelberg (EDH), the Epigraphic Database Roma (EDR), the Hispania Epigraphica (HE), and the Epigraphic Database Falsae (EDF).

Linguistics, Paleography, and Digital Tools

These issues may seem of a "pure" philological and linguistic nature, but they can only be addressed if we look at language questions in the wider perspective of cultural history. The gap separating written records and oral culture widens significantly whenever major cultural shifts occur, as was indeed the case in the centuries spanning the end of the Roman dominion and early modern Europe; that is, between the fifth and fifteenth centuries. Latin gave way—albeit in different ways and through various dynamics across the so-called Romània—to other languages that became gradually acceptable as suitable means for written communication. Translating language into script is not a mechanical process, as every society dealt with it differently: diversifying scripts on a functional basis, using different alphabets, entrusting certain sectors of society with the task of preserving memory, and eventually electing one linguistic variety as the best suited for the task. For nearly a millennium in most of Europe this language was Latin, and as a consequence of its dominance, we know very little about the wide variety of languages spoken in the 1,000 or so years of Roman rule in Europe. In the early modern period, more languages graduated to writing, and we date their birth based on their written records. These records do not, however, document the birth of new languages (which were alive long before any of them came to be written) but rather, more crucially, the establishment of a written tradition for modern languages, a cultural milestone in any society, which always had wide-ranging consequences. Written languages acquire names and prevail on other languages that may be in use in that community, which in turn tend to recede to a somewhat subordinate position and may be forgotten. Written languages are not a reproduction of speech; they are, however, preserved for history in a form (writing) that is quintessentially different from their most common (oral) use, which remains somewhat mysteriously volatile for us.

Neo-Latin languages (i.e., all modern languages deriving from Latin), which had previously existed in a countless variety of oral usages, started to be written around the ninth century, with their literary traditions being established significantly later. Modern Europe was born multilingual. Romance languages, different as the chronology of their appearance and later developments may have been, developed a written form not earlier than the second half of the thirteenth century. Very few manuscripts bearing Romance texts (mostly Anglo-Norman) are datable before then (Careri, Ruby, and Short 2011; A. Petrucci 1988). Naturally, not all Romance languages came to be written, but when they did, they reached wider communities and were adopted for writing even when other vernaculars continued to be used orally.

Writing has had the formidable task of constituting the fundamental means for the composition, reading, transmission, and preservation of texts. All written documents are also linguistic documents, and they survive thanks to a material support. It follows that any critical approach to the study of text and language cannot ignore either textual transmission or, indeed, paleography and the study of the history of writing in its material aspects. The relationship between a history of written culture and oral and written text transmission, be it for documentary or artistic purpose, constitutes, if seen from this viewpoint, an object of study to the historical understanding of which the competence of paleographers, linguists, and scholars of literature must concur. More generally, this is an area of vital interest to all scholars whose main scientific concern is the written or spoken word (Cannata and Signorini 2014). It is my contention that it would be impossible to study and understand fully any written message if we were unable to decode not just the components that form it but the grammar of writing presiding over the way in which that language is written. The grammar of paleography, in other words, is essential to understanding the components that constitute the linguistic variety that any written document preserves and transmits.

We acknowledge the birth of new languages only when they acquire a written form. Yet to understand what actually is encoded into writing linguistics alone is insufficient. Since no European language that has a name attached to it lacks a written tradition, and since writing preserves language by fundamentally changing its nature from voice to sign, historical linguistics should consider as a direct object of study not just linguistic documents as such but also the processes through which languages have acquired a written form. This is what the EDV project does by integrating the study of historical linguistics and paleography. There appears, therefore, to be a further research question that begs to be answered: Is there a way to separate the issues of "how they spoke" from "how they wrote"?

Recently, there have been renewed discussions about the nature of language use in medieval Italy and the existence (or not) of *koinai*, or intermediate languages between local vernaculars and Latin and later local vernaculars and Tuscan (Sanga 1990). It was argued that there had been a stark reduction from around 1,000 vernaculars to just 100 in the years spanning from the tenth to the fifteenth century (Maiden and Perry 1997). The ensuing situation would point, according to some scholars, to a significant difference between the language spoken "on the street," written language, and some standardization in between at the level of the so-called *scriptae*. Others have argued for the close relationship between Italian vernaculars, especially evident in syntax, and for the existence of an *italiano tendenziale* (basic common Italian) as early as the thirteenth century (Vincent 2006). Be that as it may, the fact remains that all such discussions are inevitably based on the written sources history has preserved.

Digital publication constitutes an important innovation in the methods of textual and linguistic analysis, and for the historical interpretation of our linguistic past. This is linked both to the potential for interrogation of marked-up texts, and to the fact that important datasets, acquired independently by different teams of scholars across time and space, are significantly expanding the corpora of texts available to scholars and open to digital interrogation.[2] Once interoperability of the available datasets is made possible, we will be able to digitally interrogate an ever-growing body of linguistic data, a powerful tool for historical linguistics. A change in the means of documenting the past cannot but result in an important improvement in our abilities to interpret it. We will be able to engage in analysis and cross-referencing of textual and linguistic (sometimes even material) features of medieval Romance texts in the numerous languages in which they were composed and gauge our findings in a wider context. As more information is made available for linguistic analysis, significantly increasing the linguistic data brought to our knowledge, we will be able to bring to light and better understand linguistic cultures of the past.

New methodologies in digital philology allow us not only to revisualize medieval texts in their original contexts (putting aside the filter of centuries of cultural transmission) but also to rethink the way we interpret them. The connection between textual and material features of the handwritten manuscripts exceeds the mere reproduction of the texts. Material philology (and that of the digital code) allows us to explore relations between the texts and the written codes they adopt—in terms of syntax, morphology, phonology, graphic solutions, and spellings—which may give precious indications, once a significant amount of data is put together, of trends internal to particular *scriptae* and thus enlighten us of the linguistic features hidden behind them.

EDV: Italian Medieval Epigraphy in the Vernacular

Let us furnish a few examples. At the time of writing, EDV has published 120 inscriptions from Central and Southern Italy. Since the texts are marked up

---

[2] Some subjects, such as ancient and medieval epigraphy, can boast having most of its documentation online and marked up for interrogation. This is the result of over 30 years of fruitful collaboration across languages and civilizations in the field.

through a complex system that was developed at the start of the project, the website generates (and updates whenever a new inscription is uploaded) a complex indexing of spelling systems and linguistic features, which in turn allows us to catalog important information for the interpretation of the linguistic data gathered in the corpus.

Latin did not have palatal sounds, which developed around the fifth century if not before. As a consequence, modern Romance languages have adopted a variety of different solutions to represent them. They varied greatly in time from area to area and according to the script adopted, albeit not as haphazardly as one may think. As an example, numerous Christian inscriptions display the form COIUX for "spouse," written without an *N* or the required abbreviation for it, known as the *titulus*. Yet the numerosity of such inscriptions does not warrant the current explanation that this is simply due to the writer having forgotten to carve (or paint) the required *titulus*. The frequency with which it slipped from the chisel would encourage one to believe that the *I* may have been perceived as a possible representation of the palatal sound. Such an interpretation is further supported by the fact that in later Latin and vernacular documents the use of *I* for words for which we are quite certain of an *ɲ* pronunciation is frequent, and by the fact that in the Beneventan script (largely used in Southern Italy from the eight to at least the thirteenth century) capital *I* is used when small *i* would be expected to signal the palatal *ɲ* (Signorini 2009). Should this interpretation prove to be correct, as I believe it is, it would invite the inference that the palatal had developed much earlier than current scholarship allows, and that written culture strove to accommodate it.

Graphic solutions adopted in Christian inscriptions, studied systematically, have yielded significant information about language development in Rome in the fifth to ninth century by allowing relations that have resulted in the identification of phenomena belonging to Romance linguistic varieties at a very early stage. They were not, however, recorded in script, and therefore linguists ascribe them to the realm of late or vernacular Latin, or else Proto-Romance, not that of a modern language.

Similarly, the possibility of digitally interrogating thousands of texts would allow us to better understand the history of sound change. Through the study of the ways in which palatal and affricate consonants (/ts/ and /dz/) are represented in writing and how the *scriptae* cover the varying distance over time of sound and sign, the differing graphic solutions for /ʃ/ /ʎ/ /tʃ/ /dz/ suggest for certain areas the development of an affricate rather than the palatal. We have noticed, for example, developments of spellings specific to certain regions, which have to do with the cultural influence of Tuscan as opposed to Spanish or French. In texts originating from Southern Italy, for example, /tʃ/ is mostly represented as *ch*, while in Central Italy the grapheme *ch* usually stands for /k/. Similarly, in Southern *scriptae*, *cz* as opposed to *ç* or *z* is generally used for /ts/. The correctness of these hypotheses of pronunciation is warranted either by the frequency of use that poses no doubts as to the pronunciation of certain words, or by the presence of words in rhyme with others whose pronunciation we are certain about. These hypotheses may also be strengthened through metalinguistic remarks present in contemporary texts.

The main feature of the EDV corpus lies in its complex variety in terms of time, space, form, function, language, and scripts. The inscriptions were written in 15 different varieties of Romance vernaculars, as well as in Sardinian, Catalan, Provençal, and Old French, nearly always with more or less extended portions in Latin. Some are informal notices, others are inscriptions solemnly celebrating patronage. Many were inscribed in stone or engraved on metal, some are casually scratched on plaster. Quite a few are painted on wood or canvas—sometimes openly displayed, sometimes disguised in the picture or else discreetly placed to indicate the authorship of a painting or the biblical source of a scene. Those cut in stone were in most, if not all, cases not created by the authors of the texts they bear; others are written or scratched by whomever devised the messages they convey. In all cases they show a degree of skill in using script, ranging from the barely literate to the highly professional.

According to St. Augustine, walls can function as an open book, and throughout the Middle Ages they did, since texts and images were often used to enrich the walls of churches, private homes, public palaces, and other seats of power to divulge shared narratives regarding different aspects of the life of the community that produced them. Vernacular was used in inscriptions intended for religious establishments or for sites dedicated to pilgrimage and prayer: biblical verses engraved on archways or on doors leading into churches; inscriptions in cloisters or in porches that carried admonitions of a moral nature or rulings in matters regarding indulgencies; lives of saints; *laudae*; quotations from the Scriptures in paintings and frescoes; and so on. Progressively, biblical and liturgical sources gave way to stories or admonitions regarding civic virtues and public life. The introduction of these new themes seems to reflect a slow but unstoppable change in social life that is deeply intertwined with the birth and growth of a vernacular linguistic culture.

The approximately 570 inscriptions in Italian vernaculars produced (and preserved) in Italy spanning the ninth through fifteenth centuries that constitute our EDV database are a meaningful statistical sample for the study of common languages in medieval Italy. Inscriptions are practical texts with a known function. They are also dated or easily datable, which helps us to place them firmly in their sociocultural context. As such, we arranged our records into four different categories according to function:

1. Public inscriptions (laws, edicts, public assertions of patronage, etc.)
2. Funerary inscriptions
3. Narrative captions in paintings, artists' signatures, admonitions, and proverbs
4. Script of a more private nature (graffiti and inscriptions on objects of everyday use)

The text they carry, set against the Latin and vernacular written standards, helps in drawing a general picture of the sociolinguistics of writing in the late Middle Ages. The inscriptions date as far back as the ninth century and are written in about 20 different vernaculars, some in Greek alphabet, most in Latin script. Progressing in time into Renaissance Italy, we still find texts that could not be further from the Tuscan linguistic standard, and which contradict our commonly accepted perception that it was the main linguistic variety in Italy (Cannata, 2018a; Ciociola 1997; D'Achille 2012; L. Petrucci 2010). It is interesting to note that a similar sociolinguistic context can be observed in Medieval France and Spain.[3]

The number of inscriptions so far identified and recorded in the database widely exceeds our previous knowledge of the extent to which the language of the *illiterati* (i.e., those who did not know Latin) was used in public contexts. To this body of data we are currently adding a comprehensive catalog of graffiti. Once the comprehensive corpus is ready and available for study, we will be able to look at the historical phenomenon of public script produced in languages other than Latin in early modern Italy in its entirety.

[3] Estelle Ingrand-Varennes's "Écritures Exposées: Discours, matérialité et usages" is a research project jointly coordinated by the École des hautes études hispaniques et ibériques (EHEHI), the Grupo de Investigación Lectura, escritura, alfabetización (LEA), the Seminario Interdisciplinar de Estudios sobre Cultura Escrita (SIECE), the Centre d'Etude des Littératures et Langues Anciennes et Modernes (CELLAM), and Groupe de recherche sur culture écrite et société (GRECES).

We will then be able to produce a comprehensive and valuable inventory of "common" languages in use both in communities and privately to an extent not possible before. In this respect, the systematically collected, cataloged, and edited materials, marked up to account analytically for their material and linguistic features, constitute a component for a new discipline, vernacular epigraphy, the study of which—as is widely acknowledged for its sister discipline, classical epigraphy—will be of crucial relevance to historical studies, very broadly intended: for epigraphists, linguists (with interests in both Latin and Romance), and paleographers, of course, but also for the advancement of learning in fields of enquiry as diverse as anthropology, the history of art and architecture, and culture studies.[4]

Digital publication of EDV materials allows us to assemble online and interactive libraries of texts. The texts of the inscriptions are marked in EpiDoc, a subset of the Text Encoding Initiative's standard for the representation of texts in digital form using Extensible Markup Language (XML).[5] We use EpiDoc to enable the indexing and subsequent interrogation of phonological features, spelling vs. pronunciation, morphology, syntax, and lexicon. EDV critically edits and indexes the linguistic features of epigraphic texts written in the medieval vernaculars in use in Italy up to the fifteenth century. The standardized marking up in XML makes it possible to cross-reference this body of texts with other corpora of texts located and dated with a reasonable degree of accuracy in order to trace chains of influence between Latin and modern vernaculars, and across the vernaculars. This in turn is helping us appreciate the sociolinguistics and the sociology of writing in late medieval

---

[4] Over 50 years ago, Augusto Campana advocated for the need to establish an epigraphic discipline for early modern inscriptions. The interest in vernacular epigraphy flourished only somewhat later, even though it yielded its first results at a quicker pace. In 1995, an exhibition and conference, *Visibile parlare* (see Ciociola 1997), effectively signaled the start of a dedicated scholarly interest for this body of texts. There has also been some pioneering work done on the use of script in Renaissance art (see, for example, the periodical *Opera Nomina Historiae*, launched by the late Maria Monica Donato at the Scuola Normale in Pisa: onh.giornale.sns.it). In the past 20 years, many new projects have been undertaken, mostly as a result of interests in local history and linguistics. Particular attention has been devoted to Rome and the Lazio, to Venice and the Veneto, as well as to the earliest examples in Tuscany and elsewhere. A relatively recent volume catalogs all vernacular inscriptions produced up to the thirteenth century (L. Petrucci 2010), and other similar cataloging initiatives are also being undertaken outside of Italy (see Ingrand-Varenne 2017).

[5] More information can be found at epidoc.stoa.org/gl/latest.

and early modern Italy as well as the multilingual reality in communities in which Latin and vernaculars coexisted and nurtured each other. At the same time, relating the language of the available documents "horizontally" to each other helps us understand what language(s) or varieties were in use and why, rather than relating the language of each written document to ideal linguistic standards that had not yet been established.

Epigraphic material is commonly used as documentation for the protohistory of Romance languages. But what kind of documentation do these inscriptions actually provide? Do they testify to a lack of knowledge of Latin by Latin speakers, or to their inability to write it properly, or to the distance that separated writing from speech? And does such distance mark the development of a new language, or is it evidence of the contextual use of different linguistic varieties of Latin? Is there even a difference?[6] The truth is that we do not have the necessary categories and terminology to define such languages other than as Proto-Romance or late Latin, which is evidently nonsensical if we adopt the viewpoint of the speaker of the time and not the teleology of the historian who has already fixed a paradigm that moves from "Latin" toward "Italian" (or "French," "Spanish," etc.).

As philologists, we try to elicit from written records information regarding the making of literary languages and written textual transmission, as well as the history and making of languages, historical grammar, linguistic varieties, orality, and speech. This may represent a curious paradox: we are forced to avail ourselves of sources that cannot provide first order evidence for the information we need, and yet we carry on asking for it through them. If we did not, we would have to acknowledge the impossibility of continuing with research on linguistic cultures from the past, and we could no longer pursue the questions of language variation and change that are the foundations of all our understanding of linguistic behavior.

The long process through which Romance vernaculars became languages fit to be written alongside Latin happened in a continuum. It entailed, inevitably, a progressive search and definition (both conscious and unconscious) of new linguistic and graphic norms. The process through which such norms were established and ultimately accepted can be revealed better from the vantage point of the *Umgangssprache*, defined as the most common functional

[6] Some answers to such questions may be found in Banniard 1992, 2003; Maiden, Smith, and Ledgeway 2013; and Wright 2002, 2012. However, I believe that such issues are complex and involve a reassessment of the methodologies of historical linguistics, which I have recently attempted in Cannata 2022.

style of speech (Spitzer 1922), and provides insight into the spoken languages that the project is designed to explore and ultimately reveal.

Expected Results and Sustainability

Digital publication allows us to capitalize on the sheer wealth of data it has the potential to make available and contextually searchable for a wider community of scholars. Such data acquisition is instrumental for the development of a new theoretical framework to guide the historical interpretation of written documents from the late Middle Ages and early modern period. We have come to consider that a series of events, facts, or documents are part of a history only when such a series belongs to a recognizable context, reveals a pattern, and therefore constitutes a narration, or better, a narrative. A digital library of thousands of "substandard" texts written in the various languages in use at the time—and the marking up of their linguistic features and the graphic solutions adopted to represent them in writing—definitely helps create a new narrative. It enables a systematic and extended interrogation of texts, and their cross-referencing with "standard" texts, so as to bring to light and lift from oblivion aspects of medieval linguistic culture and reveal hitherto unknown evidence for Romance linguistics.

In the best-case scenario, databases of encoded texts might reveal new stages of linguistic change and prove an effective and sound methodology for retrieving the memory of oral languages. In any case, they furnish data to the scholarly community upon which scholars will be able to build and use the material retrieved for developing their own methods of inquiry. Issues relating to the sustainability—technical and economical—of the digital means through which such knowledge circulates are also to be taken into account; digital humanities is costly and requires a significant initial investment that must be sustained by strong institutional commitment to ensure that its benefits are carried into the future. Such investments must fulfill three concurring purposes: (1) the preservation and dissemination of the results of advanced research; (2) the edition of the texts; and (3) access to critical tools, which traditional publication cannot afford, by indexing all the linguistic and material features of the documents and providing bibliographies, localization, and vocabularies.

Although the flexibility and open-ended nature of digital projects ensures that data can be constantly updated and mistakes or inaccuracies immediately corrected, such projects have a downside in their significant costs as well as in questions about their sustainability over time.[7] The issue of the long-term preservation of the outcomes of such projects is therefore a pressing one (Cannata 2020). An integration of digital and traditional means of publication might help address such issues and allow for the wide dissemination and accuracy of data—as well as its durability over time—thus ensuring that the very significant investment of time and resources that normally go into big digital projects reap their expected rewards.

WORKS CITED

Alighieri, Dante. 2011. *De Vulgari eloquentia.* Edited by Mirko Tavoni. Milan: Mondadori.

Allegrezza, Stefano, ed. 2020. "Pegagogy, Teaching, and Research in the Age of Digital Humanities." Special issue, *Umanistica Digitale* 8 (May). umanisticadigitale.unibo.it/issue/view/863.

Banniard, Michel. 1992. *Viva voce: Communication écrite et communication orale du IVe au IXe siècle en Occident Latin.* Turnhout: Brepols.

———. 2003. "Latinophones, romanophones, germanophones: Interactions identitaires et construction langagière (VIIIe–Xe siècle)." *Médiévales* 45 (Autumn): 25–42. doi.org/10.4000/medievales.753.

Bruni, Francesco. 2010. *Italia: Vita e avventure di un'idea.* Bologna: Il Mulino.

Cacchioli, Luna, Nadia Cannata, and Alessandra Tiburzi. 2016. "EDV—Italian Medieval Epigraphy in the Vernacular (9th–15th Century): A New Database." In *Off the Beaten Track: Epigraphy at the Borders. Proceedings of VI EAGLE International Event (24–25 September 2015, Bari, Italy)*, edited by Antonio E. Felle and Anita Rocco, 91–129. Oxford: Archaeopress.

Cannata, Nadia. 2014. "Le parole sono pietre: *Lingua communis* e *lingua literata* in alcune epigrafi romane (secc. IV–VI)." *Studj Romanzi* 10:281–310.

[7] Interesting contributions across the spectrum of issues relating to digital humanities and its sustainability can be found in the recent proceedings of the 8th Annual Conference of the AIUCD (Associazione per l'Informatica Umanistica e la Cultura Digitale) that took place in Udine, Italy, in January 2019 (see Allegrezza 2020).

———. 2016. "Lontano da dove? Tradizioni culturali e coscienza linguistica in Europa." *Critica del testo* 19 (1): 63–91.

———. 2018a. "EDV—Italian Medieval Epigraphy in the Vernacular Some Editorial Problems Discussed." In *Crossing Experiences in Digital Epigraphy: From Practice to Discipline*, edited by Annamaria De Santis and Irene Rossi, 179–90. Berlin: De Gruyter. doi.org/10.1515/9783110607208-015.

———. 2018b. "Scrivere per tutti: Il volgare esposto in Italia (secc. IX–XV)." *Critica del testo* 21 (1): 43–76.

———. 2020. "Memory and Loss: Digital Tools and the Writing of History: A Few Considerations." *Digital Philology: A Journal of Medieval Cultures* 9 (1).

———. 2022. "Il corpo della lingua: Nomi, forme e limiti della rappresentazione di un'idea." *TranScript* 1, no. 2 (October): 215–58. doi.org/10.30687/TranScript/2785-5708/2022/02/001.

Cannata, Nadia, and Maddalena Signorini, eds. 2014. "Scrivere, leggere, conservare: A colloquio con Armando Petrucci." Special issue, *Studj Romanzi* 10.

Careri, Maria, Christine Ruby, and Ian Short. 2011. *Livres et écritures en français et en occitan au XIIe siècle: Catalogue illustré*. Rome: Viella.

Castellani, Arrigo. 1984. "Terminologia linguistica." *Studi linguistici italiani* 10:153–61.

———. 2000. *Grammatica storica della lingua italiana*. Florence: Sansoni.

Ciociola, Claudio, ed. 1997. *Visibile parlare: Le scritture esposte nei volgari italiani dal Medioevo al Rinascimento*. Naples: Edizioni Scientifiche Italiane.

D'Achille, Paolo. 2012. *Parole: Al muro e in scena. L'italiano esposto e rappresentato*. Florence: Franco Cesati Editore.

Hernández-Campoy, Juan M., and J. Camilo Conde-Silvestre, eds. 2012. *The Handbook of Historical Sociolinguistics*. Chichester: Wiley-Blackwell. doi.org/10.1002/9781118257227.

Ingrand-Varenne, Estelle. 2017. *Langues de bois, de pierre et de verre: Latin et français dans les inscriptions médiévales*. Paris: Classiques Garnier. doi.org/10.15122/isbn.978-2-406-07129-7.

Lepschy, Giulio C. 2015. "Ethnicity and Language in Italy." In *L'Italia allo specchio: Linguaggi e identità italiani nel mondo*, edited by Fabio Finotti and Marina Johnston, 97–112. Venice: Marsilio.

Maiden, Martin, and Mair Perry, eds. 1997. *The Dialects of Italy*. London: Routledge. doi.org/10.4324/9780203993880.

Maiden, Martin, John Charles Smith, and Adam Ledgeway, eds. 2013. *The Cambridge History of Romance Languages*. Cambridge: Cambridge University Press. doi.org/10.1017/CHO9781139019996.

Petrucci, Armando. 1988. "Storia e geografia delle culture scritte (dal secolo XI al secolo XVII)." In *Letteratura italiana: Storia e Geografia*, edited by Alberto Asor Rosa, 1193–292. Vol. 2, *L'età moderna*. Turin: Einaudi.

Petrucci, Livio. 2010. *Alle origini dell'epigrafia volgare: Iscrizioni italiane e romanze fino al 1275*. Pisa: Edizioni Plus.

Romaine, Suzanne. 2009. *Socio-Historical Linguistics: Its Status and Methodology*. Cambridge: Cambridge University Press. doi.org/10.1017/CBO9780511720130.

Sanga, Glauco, ed. 1990. *Koinè in Italia dalle origini al Cinquecento: Atti del convegno di Milano e Pavia 25–26 settembre 1987*. Bergamo: Lubrina.

Signorini, Maddalena. 2009. "Il *ritmo cassinese*: Cultura grafico-libraria e qualche proposta di correzione." In *Scrivere il volgare fra Medioevo e Rinascimento*, edited by Nadia Cannata and Maria Antonietta Grignani, 1–26. Pisa: Pacini.

Spitzer, Leo. 1922. *Italienische Umgangssprache*. Bonn: K. Schroeder.

Tavoni, Mirko. 1999. "Storia della lingua e storia della coscienza linguistica: Appunti medievali e rinascimentali." *Studi di grammatica italiana* 18:205–31.

Tomasin, Lorenzo. 2015. "Sulla percezione medievale dello spazio linguistico romanzo." *Medioevo Romanzo* 39 (2): 268–92.

van Moos, Peter, ed. 2008. *Entre Babel et Pentecôte: Difference linguistiques et communication orale avant la modernité (VIIIe–XVIe siècle)*. Berlin: LIT Verlag.

Varvaro, Alberto. 1982. "Sociolinguistica e linguistica storica." In *Actes XVI Congrés internacional de lingüística i filologia romàniques*, 191–201. Vol. 1. Palma de Mallorca: Moll.

Vincent, Nigel. 2006. "Languages in Contact in Medieval Italy." In *Rethinking Languages in Contact: The Case of Italian*, edited by Anna Laura Lepschy and Arturo Tosi, 12–24. Oxford: Legenda.

Vineis, Edoardo, and Alfonso Maierù. 2014. "Medieval Linguistics." In *History of Linguistics*, edited by Giulio C. Lepschy, 134–345. Vol. 2, *Classical and Medieval Linguistics*. London: Routledge.

Wright, Roger. 2002. *A Sociophilological Study of Late Latin*. Turnhout: Brepols.

———. 2012. "Romance Languages as a Source for Spoken Latin." In *A Companion to the Latin Language*, edited by James Clackson, 59–79. Chichester: Wiley-Blackwell. doi.org/10.1002/9781444343397.ch5.

Chapter 6: Moving Images and Text on Leonardo's Codices: The Evolution of Drawing a Digital Edition[1]

Giuditta Cirnigliaro
Roma Tre University

Leonardo da Vinci's codices are a unique resource for understanding early modern artistic culture, as they represent the biggest gathering of sheets compiled by the same hand in the Renaissance. They comprise notes and drawings of various kinds—from grocery lists and color recipes to majestic sketches for ambitious projects such as *The Last Supper* and the never completed largest equestrian statue in the world, the Sforza monument. The codices, which were mainly preserved at the Biblioteca Ambrosiana in Milan under the patronage of Cardinal Federico Borromeo, are now held at many prestigious European institutions. The Codex Arundel, which is found at the British Library, London, contains miscellaneous sheets originally scattered on Leonardo's writing desk (c. 1478–1518). The Codices Forster I, II, and III (Victoria and Albert Museum, National Library of Design, London) feature drawings and notes on hydraulic machines, stereometry, architecture, and the mechanics of weight; transcriptions; recipes; fables, facetiae and prophecies; and figurative notes on *The Last Supper* (c. 1478–1505). The Codices Madrid I and II (Biblioteca Nacional de España, Madrid) include studies of

[1] This paper evolved from a conference presentation delivered at the NTRS–DH@RSA Virtual Conference in 2020 on an ongoing project on Leonardo's manuscripts and drawings, which was launched as part of my dissertation at Rutgers University and is currently hosted by Roma Tre University. I wish to thank Randa El Khatib and Caroline Winter for organizing this virtual event as well as the contributors to the project—Professor Luca Marcozzi, project tutor; Professor Manfredi Merluzzi, director of the Roma Tre Digital Humanities Laboratory; Professor Maurizio Fiorilla, scientific coordinator of the Laboratorio informatico di Italianistica; and Dr. Marco Guarracino, technical lab coordinator—for their insights throughout the development of the project and for their technical and institutional support. A special thanks to Professor Carlo Vecce, scientific advisor at the University of Naples L'Orientale, Professor Paolo Galluzzi, former director of the Museo Galileo in Florence, Professor Andrea Bernardoni, Dr. Dinni Rolfo, and the staff of the Museo Galileo, who took the time to discuss this project in its early stages and offered helpful commentary.

ISBN 978-1-64959-119-7 (paper) ISBN 978-1-64959-120-3 (pdf) ISBN 978-1-64959-121-0 (epub)
New Technologies in Medieval and Renaissance Studies 12 (2025) 127–48

mechanics, geometry, stereometry, painting, optics, perspective, and architecture; lists of books; and notes on the war of Pisa, the change of the course of the Arno River, and the melting of the Sforza monument (c. 1493–97). The Codex Atlanticus (Biblioteca Ambrosiana, Milan) gathers various writings and drawings, which were mounted on 401 bigger support sheets by the sculptor Pompeo Leoni at the end of the sixteenth century (c. 1478–1519). The Codex Trivulzianus (Biblioteca Trivulziana, Milan) contains lexical lists, drawings and studies on architecture, proverbs, fables, and facetiae (c. 1488–90). The Codices A, B, C, D, E, F, G, H, I, K, L, M (Institut de France, Paris) include texts for *A Treatise on Painting* and for other scientific and technical books; various transcriptions; notes and drawings on military arts, geometry, physics, mechanics and the science of weight, architecture, and city planning; studies on light and shadow, natural elements and phenomena, hydraulics and hydrology, water, motion, and percussion, the flight of birds, and botany; grammar notes; a bestiary; proverbs; notes and drawings for emblems and allegories; notes of trips around Milan, Tuscany, Marche, and Romagna at the service of Cesare Borgia; and surveys of cities and fortifications (c. 1486–1515). The Codex Leicester (Collection of Bill and Melinda Gates, Seattle) features materials for a treatise on water and the science of earth (c. 1505–8). The Codex on the Flight of Birds (Biblioteca Reale, Turin) gathers studies and drawings on the flight of birds (c. 1505). Finally, a corpus of 600 documents and drawings, including the notebooks on anatomy, is preserved at the Royal Library of Windsor, Berkshire (Vecce 2017, 195–97).[2] These codices remained completely unknown to both the community of scholars and the wider public until their first publication as one of the earlier phototype editions by Charles Ravaisson-Mollien in 1881–91 (Paris: A. Quantin). Subsequently, the first anthology of Leonardo's writings was published by Jean Paul Richter in 1883 (London: Sampson Low), and the editions of the Codex Trivulzianus in 1891 (Milan: Hoepli), the Codex on the Flight of Birds in 1893 (Paris: E. Rouveyre), the Codex Atlanticus in 1894–1904 (Milan: Hoepli), the Windsor sheets in 1898–1901 (Paris: E. Rouveyre), and the Codex Leicester in 1909 (Milan: Cogliati) (Cursi 2020, 13–30, 161–79; Vecce 2017, 15–17, 2021).

Among the several publications on Leonardo, scholarly contributions are not so numerous, and they mainly focus on art and science, leaving aside the field of literature and, particularly, his fables. However, Leonardo's codices

[2] Other relevant institutions that preserve Leonardo's works and sources include the Museo Galileo and the Biblioteca Centrale in Florence, the Biblioteca Vaticana in Rome, the Bibliothèque nationale de France in Paris, the Warburg Library in London, the Bodleian Libraries in Oxford, and the Metropolitan Museum of New York.

show a lively interest in literary studies, which is mostly documented by fragmentary notes, apparently not attributable to a precise form or discipline—neither literary, philosophic, scientific, nor artistic. The most organic of Leonardo's notations are certainly those devoted to painting, which were gathered in 1651 by Raphaël du Fresne in what might be considered an actual handbook, *A Treatise on Painting*. This publication left out any other hybrid or incomplete materials that were considered less relevant or off topic, facilitating a reductive interpretation of Da Vinci's thought. Significant problems in deciphering and offering a critical interpretation of Leonardo's textual and visual notes were also due to his mirror writing, in addition to the apparent disorganization and overlay of research approaches and materials (Frosini 2020, vii–viii).

Considering the multifaceted materials contained within Leonardo's codices, one gets the sense that connections between words and pictures are accidental or deeply subconscious rather than purposeful, as a wide branch of scholarship in the field has claimed. The art historian Ernst Gombrich (1976) argued that Leonardo's sketches were just unconscious "doodles" and, accordingly, Sigmund Freud (1960) interpreted them as the expression of his interior and psychic life. From this perspective, the artist's hand had a consciousness of its own, capable of bypassing the mind. Kenneth Clark (1967, 71) spoke about Leonardo's pictures as "images his hand created when his attention was wandering" and used them as evidence of an unconscious process. Similarly, David Rosand (2002, 1–111) defined Leonardo's drawings as the "handwriting of the self" and considered the repetition of figures in the artist's manuscripts not as preparatory drawings or studies for his projects but as a restless activity (see also Barkan 2011, 2, 9–10).

Furthermore, the "mythical" use of Leonardo promoted by scholars such as Giovanni Battista Venturi (1797) and Fritjof Capra (2007) has favored the exaltation of grand artistic and scientific achievements as representative of the public face of Leonardo's production, much to the detriment of his sketches, notes, and unfinished works. In his unsurpassable book *La mente di Leonardo*, Cesare Luporini (1953) already observed how nineteenth-century revisionism of Leonardo's image as a romantic genius merged into a gradual reconsideration of the notion of Renaissance—Rinascimento Italiano, in particular—as the most innovative epoch and generator of modernity. Indeed, Leonardo dealt with most of the problems that came to define present-day culture: nature, science and scientific methods, experiment, machines, work and its impact on humanity, art as a cognitive and realistic technique, and the relationship between art and science (Frosini and Nova

2013; Luporini 1953, 4–6, 117–54). A recent initiative for the reassessment of Leonardo's image as "universal genius" was the *Leonardo 1939: La costruzione di un mito* symposium held at the Museo Nazionale della Scienza e della Tecnologia Leonardo da Vinci in Milan on 18 January 2018 in occasion of the homonymous exhibit (see Beretta, Canadelli, and Giorgione 2019).

Following Leonard Barkan's interpretation, in this chapter I assert the cultural value of Leonardo's art and artwork and argue that each element on the page in Leonardo's manuscripts should not just be celebrated for its individual artistic genius but rather needs to be appreciated and understood in relation to all the other elements on the same page. Thanks to the interaction of his sketches, notes, and unfinished works, Leonardo was able to make sense of the complexity of nature in both textual and visual terms.

> In the case of Leonardo, there is a kind of paradox: on the one hand he was a doodler; on the other hand, he was a thinker who aspired to the kind of systematic investigative processes that would eventually produce experimental science. . . . Yet what is common to all these cases is that image and text have been conceived as purposefully interrelated. Indeed, it is this double presence, however variously it emerges on the page, that nearly always signals the opposite of the doodle—that is, an attempt to make the kind of definitive statement about nature, technology, or art that requires both the mimetic or diagrammatic qualities of the picture and the discursive or descriptive qualities of the text to nail down the truth. (Barkan 2011, 12, 14)

As Robert Zwijnenberg (1999, i) observed, Leonardo's embodied practice of jotting down notes in the shape of words and images activated and secured his understanding of things: "The fragmentary and chaotic nature of the manuscripts must have had a functional value for Leonardo in giving form to and in elaborating his ideas and thought about science and art."

This chapter conceptualizes Leonardo's manuscripts as complex and multimodal texts, with the aim to uncover the intimate links between different means of early modern inquiry and presentation of knowledge. By blending a traditional object-based approach with digital technologies, I focus on Leonardo's compositional methods in his drawings and literary writings and investigate their relationship with technical-scientific studies. The comparative analysis of these materials shows that literary, figurative, and scientific components in Leonardo's manuscripts present similar structures and purposes by suggesting a common interpretation of nature. The project began with the creation of analytical drawing tables to examine recurrent patterns in Leonardo's manuscripts and sources featuring fables, emblems, and scientific diagrams. Subsequently, the analytical drawing tables were digitized as part of the Omeka[3] platform LiLeo: Leonardo Library Archive, which finally evolved into the LiLeo Beta: Word-and-Image Leonardo Digital Edition, developed in collaboration with Rutgers and Roma Tre Digital Humanities Laboratory. Drawing upon recent work on the digital archives of Leonardo's codices, this project provides original insights for early modern research on intertextual languages by making available original sources of early modern culture, and by presenting an innovative way to interrogate and interrelate them by means of traditional interdisciplinary research and innovative trends in digital humanities.

Moving Images and Text on Leonardo's Codices: Fables, Emblems, and Scientific Diagrams

The combination of literary, artistic, and scientific analysis is at the core of Leonardo's fables (Bisanti 2019; Cirnigliaro 2013, 2019b, 2023; Cirnigliaro and Vecce 2019; Marsh 2004; Vecce and Cirnigliaro 2013). The fables are a collection of fragments that are modeled on different traditions, such as the works of Aesop and Pliny the Elder, and entail various modes of interaction between words and pictures. In a few cases—such as in the fable of the spider (Codex Atlanticus, fol. 820v)—we find fables translated in the form of emblems, which are a kind of hermetic language composed of an image (*figura*) and a caption (*motto*) that concurrently suggest a hidden meaning (Arbizzoni 2007; Bolzoni and Volterrani 2008; Giovio 1555, 6; Lippincott 1990, 49–76).[4] Other times, fables feature beside images acting as clarifying illustrations, which create a sequential narrative with the scientific notations adjacent to them; exemplary, in this case, is the folio on Leonardo's fables on plants (Codex Atlanticus, fol. 207r). This sheet is organized in three columns, each containing eight interrelated elements. On the left, we see fables on plants, while the central column features corresponding illustrations showing the

[3] Omeka (omeka.org) is a free open-source web-publishing platform for sharing digital collections and creating media-rich online exhibits in library, museum, archive, and academic settings.

[4] On Leonardo's emblems and word-and-image combinations, see Bambach 2019, 1:117–26, 482–500, 3:110–23; Marinoni 1954, 1983; Residori 2019; Reti 1959, 1964; Salsi and Alberti 2019; Schirg 2015; Vecce 1993, 1995, 173–83, 2000; Versiero 2019, 96–98, 119–56.

plants' attitudes in the fables, often in contrast with natural laws. The sequence is completed, on the right, by botanical observations condemning those who aim to oppose the workings of nature, thus explaining the moral of the fable in scientific terms (Fig. 1).

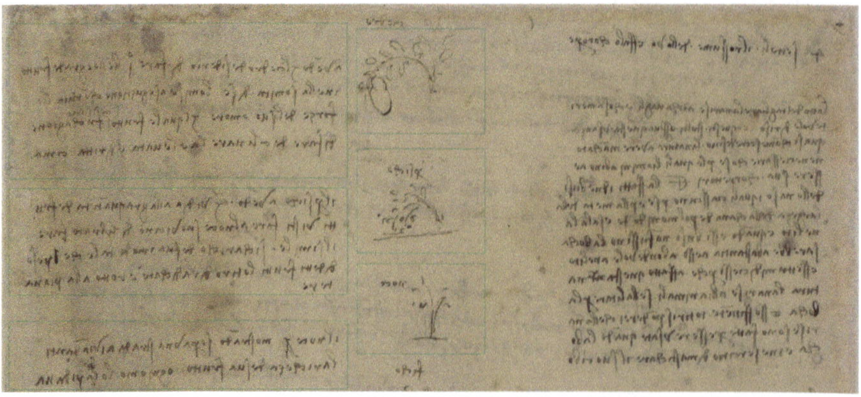

Figure 1. Leonardo da Vinci, fables of the citron, the peach, and the nut, with corresponding illustrations. Codex Atlanticus, fol. 207r. c. 1490. Biblioteca Ambrosiana, Milan.

Finally, fables can appear among scientific diagrams on similar topics, which evolve in emblematic representations found in other codices, as the fable of the lily clearly exemplifies (Manuscript H, fol. 44r). By staging a natural picture of a lily bowing down in the face of the river's current, the fable illustrates the failure of a small biological force (the lily) to oppose a greater physical power (the current). Intriguingly, the fable appears on a folio entirely dedicated to diagrams of mechanic devices called dynamometers, which reflect upon the same issue by explaining, to the contrary, how lesser forces can win over greater forces. A sheet from the Royal Collection of Windsor (RL 12,700v) completes Leonardo's process of reasoning by showing a series of emblems that re-enacts the structure of both the fable and the scientific diagrams to express in words and images the simultaneity of the causes and the effects of the depicted situation (Fig. 2).

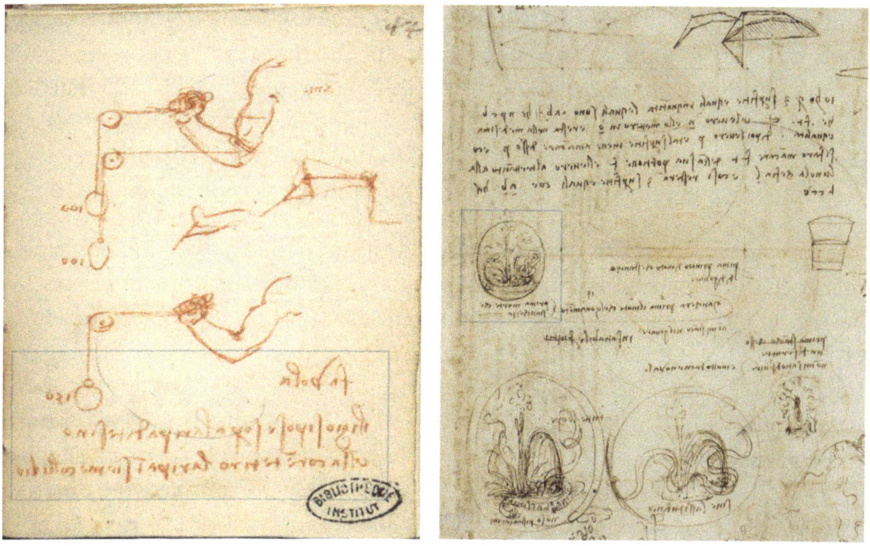

Figure 2. Left: Leonardo da Vinci, fable of the lily and dynamometers. Manuscript H, fol. 44r. 1493–94. Bibliothèque de l'Institut de France, Paris. Right: Leonardo da Vinci, emblem of the lily and diagrams and notes on geometry. RL 12,700v. 1508–10. The Royal Collection of Windsor, Berkshire.

Situated within the long-standing word-and-image debate in art history and literary studies, my work concentrates on the chaotic character of Leonardo's notes and considers both the "factual content" and the "tangible form" (Zwijnenberg 1999, 8) of his thought traced across his manuscripts. From this perspective, Leonardo's fable fragments are forms in relation with, whether the artist intended it or not, the scientific diagrams that over time layered beside them. Similarly, emblems are not only a codified genre with a clear high-culture audience, but—as Karen Pinkus argues—pictographs belonging to the repertoire of images that circulated in the early modern workshop. In particular, Pinkus problematizes interpretations of Renaissance emblems that privilege the discursive component of the emblem as the interpretive key of the visual: "A text is supposed to provide information about some painterly enigma" (Pinkus 1996, 160). Her argument does not aim to place the visual over writing in a new hierarchy but suggests instead a reconsideration of images at the center of humanism in order to understand how "in a general and a theoretical sense the explicit values and implicit ideologies of humanism are expressed in the visual" (Pinkus 1996, 173). Furthermore, she addresses the compactness of time expressed in emblems as reflecting the unity of time and drama in Aesopian fables. The essence of emblems lies in their capacity to express the simultaneity of the depicted actions—to make events simultaneous, regardless of their political destination. Leonardo's conglomerates of words and pictures that belong to different discourses are part of this tradition: text and image are in dialogue primarily because they are found on the same page and contribute to suggest a concealed meaning.

The increasing diversification and specialization in the analysis of Leonardo's manuscripts produced comprehensive catalogs and collections of essays focusing on either his scientific-technical projects (Galluzzi 1987; Nanni 2014), or his artistic (Marani 1989; Bambach 2019) and literary (Marinoni 1952; Vecce 1992) works. Between the 1940s and 1980s, excellent studies by Erwin Panofsky (1940), Ernst Gombrich (1969), and Carlo Pedretti (1973) on both the scientific and artistic aspects of Leonardo's research were published. The gradual access to his works and the opportunity to compare his creative and scientific projects signaled a fresh scholarly interest in the relationship between art, science, and technology in Leonardo's oeuvre. As a result, the last century witnessed a huge spread of major scholarly contributions on the "interdisciplinary Leonardo"—among them the works of Giovanni Gentile (1941), Cesare Luporini (1953), and Leonid Batkin (1988)—sounding the philosophical component of this interaction. Even more recently, scholars have attempted to examine Leonardo's thought by connecting his activities as scientist, engineer, inventor, and artist—I particularly refer to Martin Kemp (1981) and Claire Farago (1992).

However, wholly transdisciplinary research is still needed to initiate dialogue about this multifarious material as well as to enlighten us about Leonardo's reasoning concerning different compositional forms found in his codices. The international conference Leonardo on Nature, organized by Fabio Frosini and Alessandro Nova at the Kunsthistorisches Institut in Florenz in 2013, introduced a significant change in Da Vinci scholarship by promoting collaborative projects across disciplines with the aim of reconstructing Leonardo's philosophical thought and the sources of his creative process (Frosini and Nova 2013, 11–31). As Barthes perfectly outlines, word-and-image studies are a privileged field to conduct interdisciplinary research: "It is not the discipline which needs to be exchanged, but the objects: there is no question of 'applying' linguistics to the picture, injecting a little semiology into art history; there is a question of eliminating the distance (the censorship) institutionally separating picture and text" (quoted in Barkan 2013, iii). Thanks to digital humanities scholarship, we can now focus on the picture and text—the "form" and "content" of Leonardo's annotations—and draw connections between every element on the page of his codices to make sense of the artist's aims and combinatory devices.

Analytical Drawing and Digital Models: The LiLeo Archive

As part of my PhD project at Rutgers University, I designed a diagrammatic model that blends an object-based approach with digital humanities research to track the evolution of forms through different media and underline recurrent patterns in Leonardo's research. The material component of this work is a set of analytical drawing tables that visually and textually translate Leonardo's manuscripts. Each table shows a folio in its original size onto which I layer two combinable tracing pages. The first page contains the transcriptions of Leonardo's writings featured in the original manuscript position, readable from left to right. The second page concerns diagrammatic notes on recurrent aesthetic and scientific patterns and visual and textual connections on the space of the manuscript (Fig. 3).

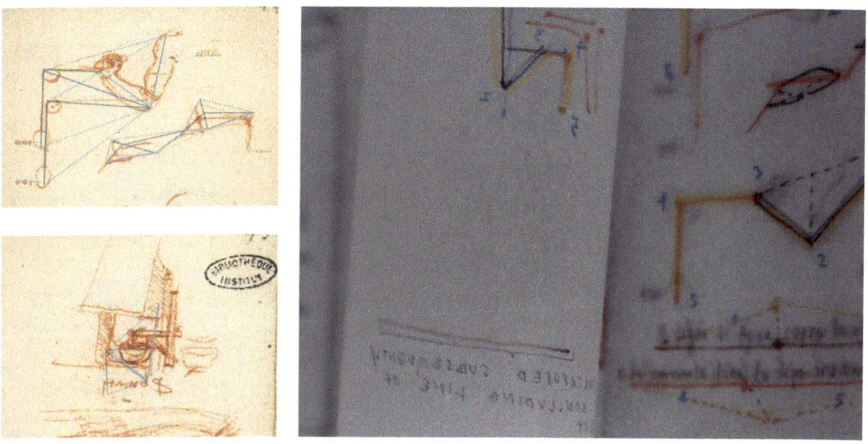

Figure 3. Leonardo da Vinci, fable of the lily and dynamometers (top left), and the water well and the laundry cauldron (bottom left). Right: analytical drawing tables with diagrammatic notes. Manuscript H, fols. 44r, 43r. 1493–94. Bibliothèque de l'Institut de France, Paris.

In compiling the tables, my methodology consisted of highlighting with the same color (e.g., yellow) a recurrent form, shape, or pattern featured in both visual and textual representations but belonging to different fields of investigation, such as scientific diagrams and notations, emblems and fables, or life drawings. Subsequently, two colors (e.g., red and blue) and letters (a and

b) were chosen to underline the binary structure of each examined form with the aim of identifying, respectively, the two forces analyzed: the protagonists of the fable and the emblem, and the causes and effects of a situation. Numbers were also used to label subsections of textual and visual forms. For instance, the fable of the lily is composed of two coordinate clauses following the cause–effect model: the lily (force a) stands before the waves of the current (force b) and is immediately overwhelmed (Manuscript H, fol. 44v). The scientific diagrams or dynamometers show a parallel conflict, that of the human arm (a) opposing the weight (b). In the pages of the manuscript that follow and precede the fable, we find related visual and textual notations, such as a sketch of the mechanical arm of the water well (force a) contrasting the weight of the laundry cauldron (force b) (Manuscript H, fol. 43r). In a similar way, the emblem of the lily re-enacts a visual depiction of the fable with a corresponding scheme, showing the flower standing upright (a) and then bowing down (b) (RL 12,700v).

Diagrammatic notations in each drawing table may vary in relation to the subjects shown on the investigated set of folios, as they are modeled on Leonardo's process of reasoning, which often develops according to no other constrains than the paper's spatial limits. In addition, Leonardo generally employs tools and creates forms that are unique to the specific problem he is trying to solve. Therefore, I decided to consider each sheet as a work that stands on its own by developing a methodology for compiling the drawing tables that could be as flexible as possible. The primary purpose of this methodology is to make explicit formal and conceptual connections among Leonardo's drawings and writings and, eventually, to create a vocabulary of recurrent textual and visual forms.

The diagrams identified by means of the analytical drawing tables were subsequently cataloged as part of the digital platform LiLeo: Leonardo Library Archive (lileo.libraries.rutgers.edu). The LiLeo Archive is composed of three basic sections. The first two sections—item and collection—serve to classify and organize the data. Items, visualized under the title of the manuscript to which they belong, are gathered into collections that are named after the physical archives where they are preserved (Fig. 4). The exhibit section is devoted to the analysis and interpretation of the data, specifically the evolution of Leonardo's fables into emblems and the development of Leonardo's sources into his textual and visual narratives (Cirnigliaro 2019a, 132–42).

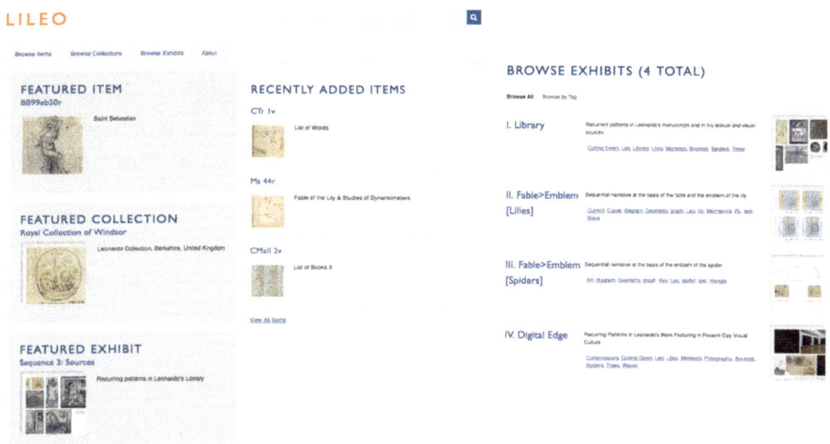

Figure 4. The LiLeo: Leonardo Library Archive home page, with the three featured sections—item, collection, and exhibit—which serve, respectively, to classify, organize, and interpret the data.

The publication of the LiLeo Archive was followed by the 2019 Garzanti edition of *Leonardo da Vinci: Favole e profezie* (fables and prophecies), which I curated with Carlo Vecce. By focusing on Leonardo's literary writings in relation to the context in which they were produced, this edition aimed to enlighten the connections between Leonardo's fables, their visual and textual sources, and related projects conducted by Leonardo and other contemporary artist-technicians.

LiLeo Beta: Word-and-Image Leonardo Digital Edition

While working on the LiLeo Archive and the Garzanti publication, it became clear that a digital edition would have been the best possible option to fully represent, track, and examine the complex interconnections between textual and visual materials in Leonardo's codices. Therefore, with the Roma Tre Digital Humanities Laboratory, I began to work on a digital edition of Leonardo's drawings and writings. As part of this project—provisionally entitled LiLeo Beta: Word-and-Image Leonardo Digital Edition—I am cataloging subjects that feature both in Leonardo's codices and in his textual and visual sources, and I am grouping them according to their typology, format, and field of investigation. Subjects are being considered both as single items and as part of the original manuscript folio, each supplied with transcriptions and English translations. My goal is to digitally enable the juxtaposition and layering of drafts belonging to similar projects in Leonardo's works and sources in order to identify aesthetic and scientific patterns in his output, uncover the origins of his interdisciplinary research, and reveal his creation of a hieroglyphic language. The final project will show digital editions of the work of Leonardo, his sources (Aesop, Pliny, etc.), and the work of his contemporaries (such as Giuliano da Sangallo and Francesco di Giorgio), which feature related visual and textual structures (Fig. 5).

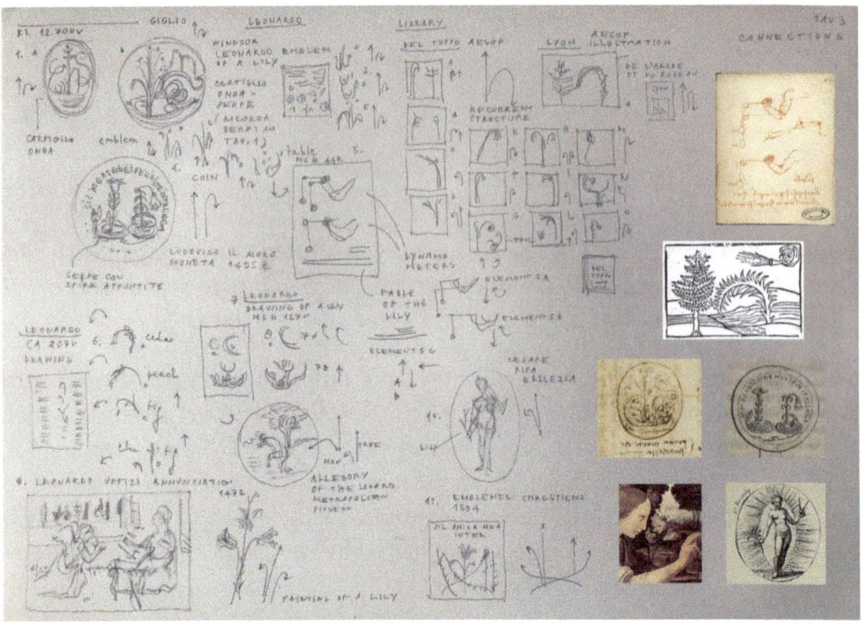

Figure 5. Table of Connections. Works by Leonardo, his sources, and contemporary cultural objects that feature related visual and textual structures on the subject of the lily.

The LiLeo Beta Digital Edition is a highly interdisciplinary project, which entails the creation of a hyper-medial critical edition developed by a team of research fellows who specialize in the textual, visual, and scientific fields of Leonardo's investigation, library science technical staff, and a research assistant with experience in digital humanities. An important early stage of the project was the discussing and testing of different digital languages and platforms in order to identify a model for our digital edition.

The Biblioteca Leonardiana and the Museo Galileo have developed exemplary work with the aim of broadening access to Leonardo's codices and contributing to academic research in this field. I particularly refer to the e-Leo Digital Archive of History of Technology and Science (leonardodigitale.com) and digital La Biblioteca di Leonardo (bibliotecadileonardo.museogalileo.it). Thanks to these initiatives, Leonardo's digital facsimiles and library sources are now freely consultable, and it is possible to identify and examine recurrent terms in his codices. However, digital projects on Leonardo have been focusing primarily on the textual component of his manuscripts, without taking into consideration the mobility and materiality of his textual and visual annotations (Vecce 2017, 2019).

The examination of the various typologies of Leonardo's textuality revealed that Text Encoding Initiative–compliant Extensible Markup Language (TEI-XML)[5] would be the best option to solve technical problems related to the representation and interpretation of textual and visual movements across codices, including writing and rewriting the same portion of text, corrections, and re-elaborations of artistic-technical ideas (Fig. 6). In addition, TEI-XML experimentation allowed us to reflect on the relationship between words and images, the connection of Leonardo's work to his sources, and indexing for the creation of a linguistic, thematic, and interpretive database (Mancinelli and Pierazzo 2020; Pierazzo 2015).

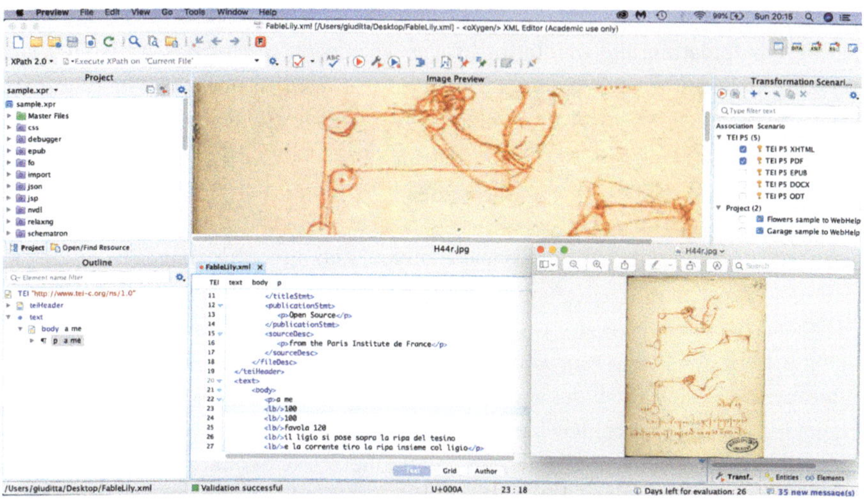

Figure 6. TEI-XML transcription of the fable of the lily.

[5] "The Text Encoding Initiative (TEI) is a consortium which collectively develops and maintains a standard for the representation of texts in digital form" (tei-c.org).

With regard to the visual component of the LiLeo Beta Digital Edition, we realized that International Image Interoperability Framework (IIIF) compliant resources and platforms, such as Omeka and Project Mirador, would allow us not only to publish digital collections and exhibits but also to juxtapose, annotate, and actively interact with both images and text on Leonardo's codices.[6] These are very intuitive platforms and tools, which guarantee the usability of our product not only by academics but also by a wider audience, such as museum users, school teachers, and students, making it interoperable with other systems. Particularly, thanks to Omeka S, we aim to integrate and connect our work with other relevant projects, such as e-Leo, and multiple online resources and collections where Leonardo's codices and sources are preserved, including the Biblioteca Ambrosiana in Milan and the Royal Collection of Windsor (see Cirnigliaro and Robson 2022).[7]

After defining the standards and naming conventions for directories and files in relation to each format of work (e.g., manuscript, incunabulum, drawing),

---

[6] IIIF (iiif.io) is a growing community of the world's leading research libraries and image repositories, which collaborate to produce an interoperable technology and community framework for image delivery. IIIF provides uniform and rich access to image-based resources hosted around the world; it also develops interfaces that support interoperability between image repositories and technologies for viewing, comparing, manipulating, and annotating images. The Omeka platform is available in two versions: Omeka Classic (see note 3 above) is for individual projects and educators, and it served as the basis for the LiLeo Archive; Omeka S (omeka.org/s), created for institutions managing a shareable resource pool across multiple sites, is being employed for the development of the LiLeo Beta Digital Edition. Project Mirador (projectmirador.org) is an open-source, web-based, multi-window image viewing platform with the ability to zoom, display, compare, and annotate images belonging to different repositories.

[7] Leonardo's manuscripts are preserved at multiple repositories, which use different standards for image reproductions and metadata and, therefore, do not easily interoperate. Online databases and platforms that inform the project on both a methodological and a practical level are the e-Leo Digital Archive of History of Technology and Science (leonardodigitale.com), La Biblioteca di Leonardo (bibliotecadileonardo.museogalileo.it), Codex Atlanticus (codex-atlanticus.it), the Warburg Institute Iconographic Database (iconographic.warburg.sas.ac.uk), BnF Gallica Digital Library (gallica.bnf.fr), Emblematica Online (emblematica.grainger.illinois.edu), Universal Short Title Catalogue (ustc.ac.uk), Incunabula Short Title Catalogue (data.cerl.org/istc), Internet Archive (archive.org), Europeana (europeana.eu), and Galassia Ariosto (galassiaariosto.sns.it).

we collected and organized the image files to be included in our digital edition. Subsequently, while developing the TEI-compliant XML text files conversion, we created derivative images containing selected texts and pictures from the original files as well as spreadsheets for tracking project metadata and for bulk upload of items to the digital database. Then, we finally began the site mock-up and demo (Fig. 7).

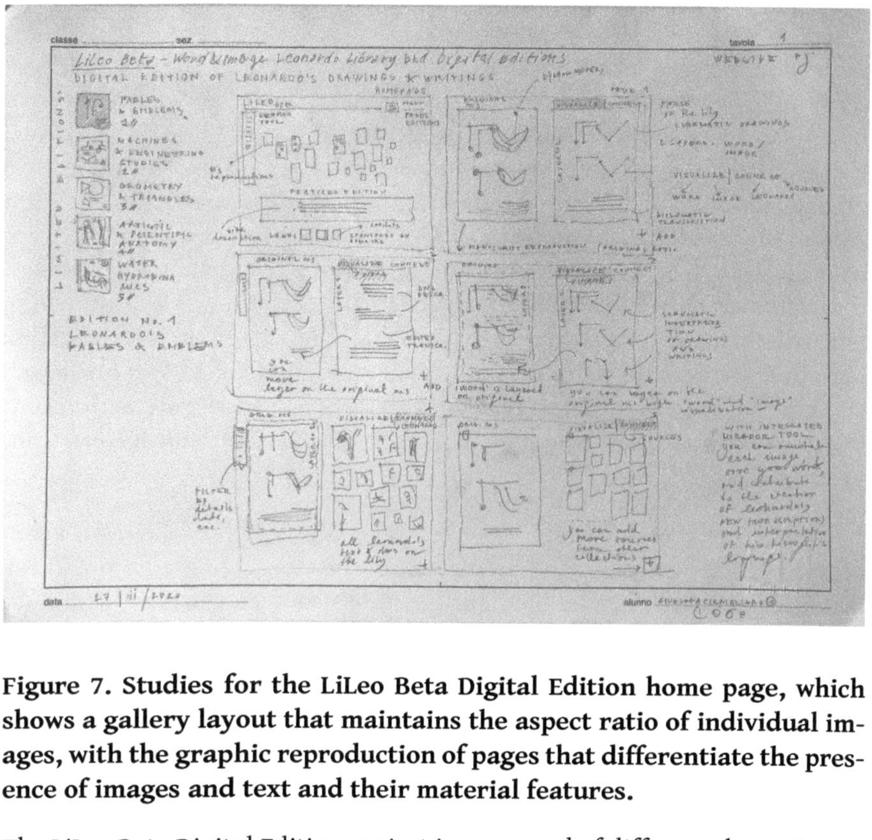

Figure 7. Studies for the LiLeo Beta Digital Edition home page, which shows a gallery layout that maintains the aspect ratio of individual images, with the graphic reproduction of pages that differentiate the presence of images and text and their material features.

The LiLeo Beta Digital Edition project is composed of different thematic sections that we intend to publish separately. We are now preparing the first publication focusing on Leonardo's fables and emblems, which will likely be followed by a thematic publication on machines and engineering studies. The home page shows a gallery layout that maintains the aspect ratio of individual images, with the graphic reproduction of pages from the featured edition on Leonardo's fables and emblems.[8]

[8] The LiLeo Beta Digital Edition home page is modeled on Marco Cursi's (2018, 238,

The graphic reproductions formally differentiate the presence of images and text and their material features—brown for ink, black for charcoal, and red for red chalk. Thanks to the banner on the left, you can browse items by specific information, such as date, title, and collection, and identify recurrent words and pictures. The top-right site menu allows you to browse different codices and editions. By moving the cursor on each image file, you can visualize the original manuscript page. Then, if you click on the image file, a new page opens, and you enter the digital edition.

Each edition page features two windows. The first window shows the manuscript folio—containing, for instance, the fable of the lily—while the second is devoted to its transcription. The transcription is composed of two layers that highlight, respectively, textual and visual portions of the file in the form of diplomatic and schematic drawing transcriptions. Thanks to the top-right menu, you can either visualize the different components of the folio or connect the folio to other items. The "Visualize>word" tool allows you to view the edited transcription of the text and the description of the drawings; "Visualize>image" allows you, instead, to view the schematic interpretation of both drawings and writings. Both the textual- and visual-window layers can be overlapped on the original manuscript page to allow simultaneous viewing of textual and visual structures with the option to multiply adjacent visualizations (Fig. 8).

With the "Connect>Leonardo" tool, you can connect the folio with Leonardo's related drawings and writings (for instance, emblems on lilies); "Connect>sources" focuses then on Leonardo's sources (such as his library books). This allows the user to link dispersed sources and reconstruct collections scattered around various institutions, including folios belonging to the same booklet or project, and items from Leonardo's library and workshop. Finally, we aim to integrate the Project Mirador tool to let users add and compare sources belonging to different collections, annotate the image files, save their work, and contribute to the implementation of Leonardo's textual and visual transcriptions. By allowing users to interact with the website materials on different levels, the project aims to bridge the gap between the results of academic research and dissemination. Furthermore, it provides a best practice standard for using technological tools to engage the larger public with products of scientific investigation, having members of the public as co-creators of knowledge (Fig. 9).

---

240) material description of Leonardo's manuscripts, and on the digital project Petrarchive (dcl.slis.indiana.edu/petrarchive).

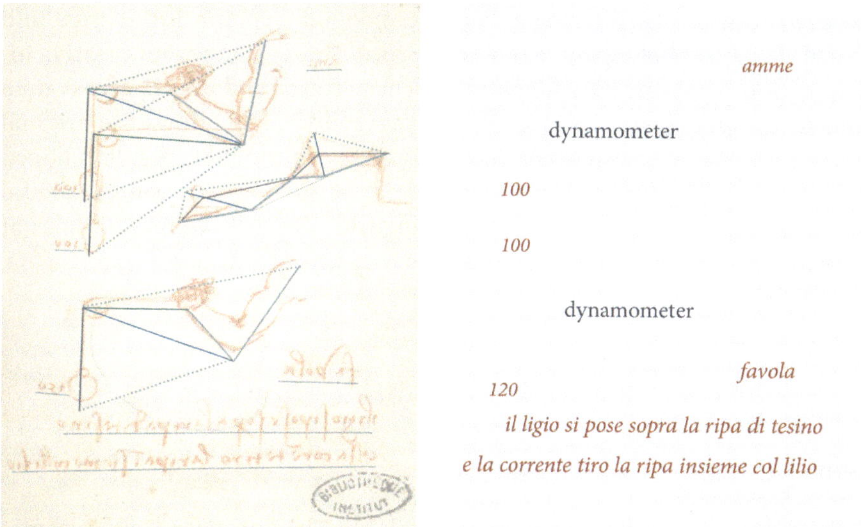

Figure 8. The LiLeo Beta Digital Edition tools for visualizing diagrams (Visualize>image tool) and transcriptions (Visualize>word tool).

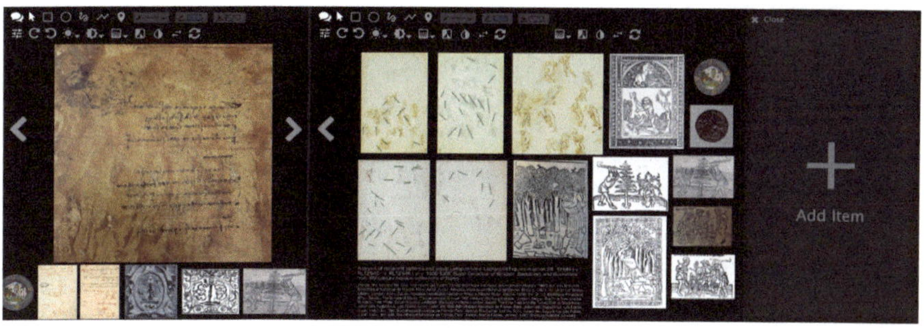

Figure 9. The LiLeo Beta Digital Edition tools for connecting Leonardo's folios with related drawings and writings (Connect>Leonardo tool) and his sources (Connect>sources tool).

To conclude, by combining new approaches in the digital humanities with traditional artistic tools, the LiLeo Beta Digital Edition expands the work of the already existing digital archives on Leonardo's codices and makes original sources of early modern culture available to a wider public. Furthermore, it provides original insights for early modern research on intertextual languages by defining their verbal, visual, and spatial relations. This project facilitates research in the fields of Leonardo studies and interdisciplinary early modern research by offering a reusable model for comparing textual and visual structures belonging to the same process of reasoning and creative investigation. The identification of recurrent patterns and motifs across time and space informs studies on early modern sources and allows the original texts under investigation to be reconnected to their archetypes. It is hoped that the final outcome will be an interoperable, durable, and scalable digital product—one that not only explores Leonardo's transdisciplinary modes of investigation but is also open to multiple uses across different forms, media, and fields of study.

WORKS CITED

Arbizzoni, Guido. 2007. "Imprese as Emblems: The European Reputation of an 'Italian' Genre." In *The Italian Emblem: A Collection of Essays*, edited by Donato Mansueto, 1–32. Glasgow: Glasgow Emblem Studies.

Bambach, Carmen. 2019. *Leonardo da Vinci Rediscovered*. 3 vols. New Haven, CT: Yale University Press.

Barkan, Leonard. 2011. *Michelangelo: A Life on Paper*. Princeton, NJ: Princeton University Press.

———. 2013. *Mute Poetry, Speaking Pictures*. Princeton, NJ: Princeton University Press. doi.org/10.1515/9781400844784.

Batkin, Leonid. 1988. *Leonardo da Vinci*. Bari: Laterza.

Beretta, Marco, Elena Canadelli, and Claudio Giorgione, eds. 2019. *Leonardo 1939: La costruzione del mito*. Milan: Editrice Bibliografica.

Bisanti, Armando. 2019. "Violenza, frustrazione, vanità: La visione pessimistica di Leonardo nel Bestiario e nelle Favole." *Rivista di Letteratura Italiana* 37 (2): 47–54.

Bolzoni, Lina, and Silvia Volterrani. 2008. *Con parola brieve e con figura: Emblemi e imprese fra antico e moderno*. Pisa: Edizioni della Normale.

Capra, Fritjof. 2007. *The Science of Leonardo: Inside the Mind of a Great Genius of the Renaissance*. New York: Doubleday.

Cirnigliaro, Giuditta. 2013. "Le Favole di Leonardo da Vinci: Struttura e temi." *Rivista di Letteratura Italiana* 31 (2): 23–43.

———. 2019a. "The Digital Reconstruction of Leonardo's Library: Revealing Formal Patterns in Early Modern Thought." *Studies in Digital Heritage* 3 (2): 128–43. doi.org/10.14434/sdh.v3i2.27719.

———. 2019b. "Gli 'Esopi' di Leonardo: L'ascia e il noce." *Rivista di Letteratura Italiana* 37 (2): 57–67.

———. 2023. *Leonardo's Fables: Sources, Iconography and Science*. Leiden: Brill. doi.org/10.1163/9789004527195.

Cirnigliaro, Giuditta, and Glen Robson. 2022. "Manuscript Linking, Comparison, and Visual Annotation with IIIF: A Case Study on Leonardo's Codices." *The Italianist* 42 (3): 1–20.

Cirnigliaro, Giuditta, and Carlo Vecce, eds. 2019. *Leonardo da Vinci: Favole e profezie: Scritti letterari*. Milan: Garzanti.

Clark, Kenneth. 1967. *Leonardo da Vinci: An Account of His Development as an Artist*. Rev. ed. Baltimore: Penguin.

Cursi, Marco. 2018. "Leonardo da Vinci: Books." In *Collecting, Organizing, and Transmitting Knowledge: Miscellanies in Late Medieval Europe*, edited by Sabrina Corbellini, Giovanna Murano, and Giacomo Signore, 233–48. Turnhout: Brepols.

———. 2020. *Lo specchio di Leonardo: Scritture e libri del genio universale*. Bologna: Il Mulino.

Farago, Claire. 1992. *Leonardo da Vinci's Paragone: A Critical Interpretation with a New Edition of the Text in the Codex Urbinas*. Leiden: Brill. doi.org/10.1163/9789004246744.

Freud, Sigmund. 1960. *Complete Psychological Works*. Vol. 6, *The Psychopathology of Everyday Life*. London: Hogarth.

Frosini, Fabio. 2020. *"Artefiziosa natura": Leonardo da Vinci dalla magia alla filosofia*. Rome: Edizioni di Storia e Letteratura.

Frosini, Fabio, and Alessandro Nova, eds. 2013. *Leonardo da Vinci on Nature: Knowledge and Representation*. Venice: Marsilio.

Galluzzi, Paolo. 1987. *Leonardo da Vinci: Engineer and Architect*. Montreal: Montreal Museum of Fine Arts.

Gentile, Giovanni. 1941. *Il pensiero di Leonardo*. Florence: Sansoni.

Giovio, Paolo. 1555. *Dialogo dell'imprese militari et amorose di Monsignor Paolo Giovio vescovo di Nucera*. Rome: Antonio Barre.

Gombrich, Ernst H. 1969. "The Form of Movement in Water and Air." In *Leonardo's Legacy: An International Symposium*, edited by Charles Donald O' Malley, 131–204. Berkeley: University of California Press.

———. 1976. "The Grotesque Heads." In *The Heritage of Apelles*, 57–75. London: Phaidon.

Kemp, Martin. 1981. *Leonardo da Vinci: The Marvellous Work of Nature and Man*. London: Dent.

Lippincott, Kristen. 1990. "The Genesis and Significance of the Fifteenth-Century Italian Impresa." In *Chivalry in the Renaissance*, edited by Sydney Anglo, 49–76. Woodbridge, UK: Boydell.

Luporini, Cesare. 1953. *La mente di Leonardo*. Florence: Sansoni.

Mancinelli, Tiziana, and Elena Pierazzo. 2020. *Che cos'è un'edizione scientifica digitale*. Rome: Carocci.

Marani, Pietro Cesare. 1989. *Leonardo: Catalogo completo dei dipinti*. Florence: Cantini.

Marinoni, Augusto, ed. 1952. *Leonardo da Vinci: Scritti letterari*. Milan: Rizzoli.

———. 1954. *I rebus di Leonardo da Vinci raccolti e interpretati, con un saggio su una virtù spirituale*. Florence: Olschki.

———. 1983. *Leonardo da Vinci: Rebus*. Milan: Silvana.

Marsh, David. 2004. *Renaissance Fables: Aesopic Prose by Leon Battista Alberti, Bartolomeo Scala, Leonardo da Vinci, Bernardino Baldi*. Tempe: Arizona Center for Medieval and Renaissance Studies.

Nanni, Romano. 2014. *Leonardo and the Artes Mechanicae*. New York: Skira.

Panofsky, Erwin. 1940. *The Codex Huygens and Leonardo da Vinci's Theory of Art*. London: Kraus.

Pedretti, Carlo. 1973. *Leonardo: A Study in Chronology and Style*. London: Thames and Hudson.

Pierazzo, Elena. 2015. *Digital Scholarly Editing: Theories, Models and Methods*. Farnham: Ashgate. doi.org/10.4324/9781315577227.

Pinkus, Karen. 1996. *Picturing Silence: Emblem, Language, Counter-Reformation Materiality*. Ann Arbor: University of Michigan Press.

Residori, Matteo. 2019. "Appunti su Leonardo 'morale': Il tema dell'ingratitudine fra parole e immagini." In *Nodi, vincoli e groppi leonardeschi*, edited by Frederique Dubard de Guillarbois and Oliver Chiquet, 108–36. Paris: Spartacus IDH.

Reti, Ladislao. 1959. "Non si volta chi a stella è fisso: Le imprese di Leonardo da Vinci." *Bibliothèque d'Humanisme et Renaissance* 21 (1): 7–48.

———. 1964. "Tal è 'l mal che non mi noce, quale il bene che non mi giova: Interpretazione dell'impresa della lampada." *Raccolta vinciana* 20: 325–30.

Rosand, David. 2002. *Drawing Acts: Studies on Graphic Expression and Representation*. Cambridge: Cambridge University Press.

Salsi, Claudio, and Alessia Alberti. 2019. *La sala delle Asse del Castello Sforzesco: Leonardo da Vinci all'ombra del Moro*. Milan: Silvana.

Schirg, Bernhard. 2015. "Decoding da Vinci's *Impresa*: Leonardo's Gift to Cardinal Ippolito d'Este and Mario Equicola's *De opportunitate* (1507)." *Journal of the Warburg and Courtauld Institutes* 78 (1): 135–55. doi.org/10.1086/JWCI26321951.

Vecce, Carlo, ed. 1992. *Leonardo da Vinci: Scritti*. Milan: Mursia.

———. 1993. "Leonardo e il gioco." In *Passare il tempo: La letteratura del gioco e dell'intrattenimento dal XII al XVI secolo. Atti del convegno di Pienza, 10–14 settembre 1991*, 280–86. Rome: Salerno.

———. 1995. "La parola e l'icona: Dai rebus di Leonardo ai 'fermagli' di Fabricio Luna." *Achademia Leonardi Vinci* 8: 173–83.

———. 2000. "Parola e immagine nei manoscritti di Leonardo da Vinci." In *Percorsi tra parole e immagini (1400–1600)*, edited by Angela Guidotti and Massimiliano Rossi, 19–35. Lucca: Maria Pacini Fazzi.

———. 2017. *La biblioteca perduta: I libri di Leonardo*. Rome: Salerno.

———. 2019. *Leonardo e i suoi libri: La biblioteca del genio universale*. Florence: Giunti.

———. 2021. *La biblioteca di Leonardo*. Florence: Giunti.

Vecce, Carlo, and Giuditta Cirnigliaro. 2013. *Leonardo: Favole e facezie. Disegni di Leonardo dal Codice Atlantico*. Novara: De Agostini.

Venturi, Giovanni Battista. 1797. *Essai sur les ouvrages physico-mathématiques de Léonard de Vinci, avec des fragmens tirés de ses manuscrits, apportés de l'Italie: Lu à la première Classe de l'Institut National des Sciences et Arts*. Paris: Duprat.

Versiero, Marco. 2019. *Leonardo in "chiaroscuro": Politica, profezia, allegoria, c. 1494–1504*. Mantua: Oligo.

Zwijnenberg, Robert. 1999. *The Writings and Drawings of Leonardo da Vinci: Order and Chaos in Early Modern Thought*. Cambridge: Cambridge University Press.

Chapter 7: FRIDA: A Multilevel Digital Atlas for the Ephemeral Renaissance, La Serenissima Venice, 1450–1550

Francesca Bortoletti
University of Parma

Giuseppe Gerbino
Columbia University

Paolo Ciuccarelli
Northeastern University
Politecnico di Milano

Beatrice Gobbo
Politecnico di Milano

Tommaso Elli
Politecnico di Milano

Digital humanities and design have recently partnered in developing robust methods and effective visual tools to make data accessible and usable to help understand the complexity of historical phenomena. But what happens when scholars want to restore the materiality of ephemeral historical practices, such as performative events, political celebrations, oral performances, and religious ceremonies, which present intangible, yet crucial, aspects of political, artistic, and social life? Organized by patrons and featuring a dynamic community of humanists, artists, and performers, these festive events embodied political and social tensions and transcultural exchanges across Europe and the Mediterranean and led to a flourishing of new forms of performing arts that became avant-garde in Renaissance culture. During these performing rituals, the whole city was transformed into a theater: the city gate became the architectural stage for triumphal entrances accompanied by solemn music; the piazza was the setting for tournaments and jousts; and the palace was the site of "private" shows, including mise-en-scènes of mythological fables, classical comedies, and new plays. The model for these festivals stems from antiquity, which humanists rediscovered through existing Greco-Roman artworks as well as through the study of classical poems, reviving them into the framework of festivals. Although the poetic, figurative, and musical materials involved were often short-lived, these multimedia events produced objects that held a collective memory of the festival. Yet, these materials are now scattered in historical archives. How can we overcome the fragmentation of the historical record? Moreover, if we consider the ephemeral nature of these events as an essential part of their materiality and value,

ISBN 978-1-64959-119-7 (paper) ISBN 978-1-64959-120-3 (pdf) ISBN 978-1-64959-121-0 (epub)
New Technologies in Medieval and Renaissance Studies 12 (2025) 149–96

how can we reconstruct these experiences and restore their cultural genesis together with their political, social, and artistic implications?

The complex and transitory nature of these events requires a new epistemological system and novel information technology tools that will allow scholars to investigate a large number of materials and a dynamic form of knowledge. This chapter presents the preliminary outcomes of a dynamic platform, Festivals in Renaissance Italy: A Digital Atlas (FRIDA), designed by an interdisciplinary team of historians of theater, music, and the arts along with information designers and specialists in digital humanities.[1] The pilot project for the Atlas is the city of Venice, which will eventually be joined by Florence, Rome, Naples, and the northern courts of Milan, Mantua, and Ferrara. By mapping festivals from 1450 to 1550 for each of these geographic areas, FRIDA allows the complexity of these political and festive events to be revived, investigated, and visualized through the integration of three levels of analysis—Event, Backstage, and Memory—and three related visual layers—*cartographic visualizations*, *social network diagrams*, and *clusters of texts and images* (Fig. 1).[2] This multilevel system of visual representations offers a method and a tool for overcoming the ephemeral nature of these ritual

---

[1] This study received support from the Gladys Krieble Delmas Foundation and the University of Minnesota's Consortium for the Study of the Premodern World–Andrew W. Mellon Foundation Award. The principal investigator (PI), Francesca Bortoletti, in collaboration with co-PIs Giuseppe Gerbino and Paolo Ciuccarelli, assembled an interdisciplinary team, bringing together the combined strength of specialists in the history of theater, literature, music, and art; librarian curators; and experts in information design and digital humanities. Together with collaborators Beatrice Gobbo and Tommaso Elli of the Density Design Research Lab (Politecnico di Milano) who produced the digital diagrams and related texts, this research team developed the design of the digital Atlas described in this chapter. The results have been previously published in an article (Bortoletti et al. 2018) and presented at panel conferences (Renaissance Society of America 2019, 2020), international symposia (Fondazione Cini), and workshops (Kessler Institute; University of Minnesota). Core elements of the Atlas were also included in an exhibit at the Bell Library of the University of Minnesota in 2018. A special thanks to Patricia F. Brown, Raimondo Guarino, Rachel McGarry, Edward Muir, Paola Ventrone, and Piermario Vescovo for their valuable feedback on this project, to David Lemke for editing and translations, and to the Italian Academy for Advanced Studies, Columbia University, which supported the beginning of this project during a residential fellowship of the PI.

[2] All figures can be found at the end of the chapter.

performances and restoring their original multimedia in a digital environment.[3] In particular, the research team is creating a front-end prototype to enable the visual exploration of all data and content by generating a series of multimedia historical stories of performing festivals that will be made freely and publicly available. This system will optimize our comparative and interdisciplinary approach, while the standard metadata will contribute to the use of the Atlas by a broader community of scholars and students as well as a general audience.

Following a brief description of the design and functionality of the Atlas, as well as of the methodology and strategies for gathering, digitizing, and populating the Atlas, this chapter will focus on Venice as a case study of this digital project and will ultimately present some of the results and preliminary considerations of our research for future development of the FRIDA Atlas.

Incipit: Design and Functionality of the Atlas

As early as 1978, André Chastel (1978, 1:417) noted that "l'orientation fructueuse donnée a l'étude de la culture de la Renaissance par la simple considération de la fête . . . mais manque de substance et d'articulations au stade où en sont maintenant les connaissances." Since then, great contributions have been made in theater and performance studies. Building on those contributions, FRIDA is designed as a "virtual laboratory" that capitalizes on vast interdisciplinary scholarship on performing rituals and festivals (Burckhardt [1860] 2002; Jacquot 1956; Warburg [1932] 2004–8; Yates 1959);[4] human-

---

[3] This platform will be hosted by the University of Parma and linked to the Italian Academy's International Observatory for Cultural Heritage at Columbia University (italianacademy.columbia.edu/content/international-observatory-cultural-heritage). A demo video demonstrating the capabilities of the Atlas can be found on the Italian Academy website, which offers an overview of the project (italianacademy.columbia.edu/content/frida).

[4] These works significantly expanded the field of sociopolitical analysis of the festival (Casini 1996; Strong 1984; Tafuri 1992; Trexler 1980) and stimulated interest in the study of symbolic forms as a constitutive part of the visual, poetic, and performative imaginary of the festival program. There is a large biography on the topic. See, in particular, Cruciani 1972, 1983; Cruciani, Falletti, and Ruffini 1994; Decroisette and Plaisance 1993; Guarino 1988; McGowan 1973; Mitchell 1979, 1986; Pieri 1983; Povoledo (1969) 1975; Ventrone 1992; L. Zorzi 1977. And more recently, Bortoletti 2008, 2012, 2020; Plaisance 2008; Ventrone 2013, 2016. See also the studies sponsored by the Society for European Festivals Research (SEFR) book series: Mulryne, Aliverti, and Testaverde 2015; Mulryne and Goldring 2002; Mulryne et al. 2004. Specifically, on the

istic studies on archives and atlases (Didi-Huberman 2004, 2010; Foucault 1982); and decades of digitization, which have made a wealth of material available online.[5] We are also indebted to a new wave of visual methods that emphasize the need for new hybrid forms of thinking and making between designers, historians, and archivists (Bach et al. 2018; Caviglia, Ciuccarelli, and Coleman 2012; Ciuccarelli and Elli 2019; Mauri and Ciuccarelli 2016).[6] In particular, if the emergence of digital resources and projects on festivals, rituals, and theater have demonstrated the value of digital humanities for the study of performing arts, the increasing development of new digital atlases has validated the effectiveness of these interactive digital platforms for the visual representations of complex phenomena.[7] The primary purpose in

---

study of memory and memorialization, see Bolzoni 1995; Carruthers 1990; Freedberg 1989; Praz 1971; Settis 1986. On musical studies of the festival, see Fenlon 2007; Gallo 1992; Gerbino 2009; Guidobaldi 1995; Lockwood 2009. Finally, the most important documentary source remains D'Ancona (1877) 1891.

[5] In particular, Aby Warburg's Atlas, *Bilderatlas Mnemosyne* (warburg.sas.ac.uk/archive/bilderatlas-mnemosyne), which defined Warburg's theories on how ideas, rituals, images, and words persist throughout history, significantly informed the conception of our digital Atlas. See also Ohrt and Heil 2020.

[6] According to Caviglia, Ciuccarelli, and Coleman (2012, 1), "Digitization, the process of encoding information in a machine-readable format, has provided new modes of accessing and working with traditional materials. Moreover, the cultural and social dimensions of software and hardware constitute new and challenging fields of study for traditional and emerging humanities disciplines." See also Berry 2012; Burdick and Willis 2011; Fuller 2008. On the question of how the design of digital tools supports humanities research, see Burdick et al. 2012; Drucker 2011. For a specific focus on history and literary studies as well as cultural heritage, see McGann and Samuels 2004; Moretti 2005; Pope 1995; Ruecker, Radzikowska, and Sinclair 2011. On design theory as an interdisciplinary and integrative discipline, see Friedman 2003.

[7] Important digital collections include the festival collections at the Warburg Institute (warburg.libguides.com/archived-collections), the Getty Institute (getty.edu/research/special_collections/highlights/festivals), and the British Library (bl.uk/treasures/festivalbooks); digital projects such as the Newberry Religious-Venice (publications.newberry.org/venice), the AHRC-funded Early Modern Soundscape (emsoundscapes.co.uk), the University of St. Andrews' Theatre in Saint-Domingue (theatreinsaintdomingue.org), and the Oxford Archive of Performances of Greek and Roman Drama (apgrd.ox.ac.uk); and specific resources focusing on Venice such as Visualizing Venice (visualizingvenice.org), EPFL/Cini Replica (actu.epfl.ch/news/replica), and Venice Time Machine (epfl.ch/research/domains/venice-time-machine). For other digital atlases, see, for example, the Density Design's Atlante Calvino

designing FRIDA is to create a digital atlas that can serve as an interactive visual environment for scientific investigation.

At the core of our digital Atlas is a relational database composed of five categories of objects:

1. *Festivals* (~90 events, including political celebrations; civic, religious, and liturgical rituals; weddings; carnivals; occasional festivals commemorating a visit by an illustrious guest; triumphal entrances; processions; funerals; jousts; banquets; dances; musical performances; and theatrical stagings of comedies, farces, and tragedies)
2. *Poems* (historical accounts; archival material; letters; literary and musical works; and plays)
3. *Artworks* (paintings; statues; tapestries; maps; coins; medals; and emblems)
4. *Actors* (patrons; artists; poets; performers; and social organizations)
5. *Places* (private/public urban spaces)[8]

These elements are integrated in a system of cross-analysis, combining spatial, relational, and temporal data. Three different levels of investigations (Event, Backstage, and Memory) with their related visual layers capture in multimedia settings the circulation of people, topics, and artifacts (Fig. 2).

The "Event" level creates *cartographic visualizations*, reconstructing itineraries of multi-day festive events against the backdrop of an abstract rendition of historical maps—Jacopo de' Barbari's *View of Venice* in our case study (Fig. 3).[9] Details from these maps are used to highlight the most important stages

---

(atlantecalvino.unige.ch) and Baldessari (baldessari.densitydesign.org/persone), and Harvard University's Digital Atlas of Roman and Medieval Civilizations (darmc.harvard.edu).

[8] Documents are scattered in historical archives, including Archivio di Stato (Venice); Biblioteca Nazionale Marciana (Venice); Biblioteca Museo Correr (Venice); Biblioteca Fondazione Cini (San Giorgio Maggiore, Venice); Doge's Palace (Venice); Galleria Palazzo Cini (Venice); Getty Museum (Los Angeles); James Ford Bell Library (University of Minnesota, Minneapolis); Library in the Scuola Grande di San Marco (Venice); Morgan Library and Museum (New York); and Gallerie dell'Accademia (Venice). FRIDA Atlas aims at both drawing together artifacts from various resources as well as making available previously undigitized materials.

[9] I would like to thank the Department of Prints and Drawings at the Minneapolis

and venues (*places*) in the itinerary of the *festa* (Fig. 4). Single visualizations give the user the option to move from a "realistic" view of the itinerary within the urban setting to a diagrammatic representation of the event (Fig. 5), which facilitates chronological and geographical comparisons. In addition, the system offers the possibility of visualizing data for multiple festivals and itineraries in a comparative perspective (Figs. 6–7). These visualizations provide detailed and multimedia representations of each event, including visual/textual/audio materials (*poems/artworks*) collected in the Atlas (Figs. 8–10). Their function is to bring to light the geography and role of specific performing practices within the larger sociopolitical context of Venice (Figs. 11–15).

The "Backstage" level uses *social network diagrams* to recreate the social/performative network of the *actors* involved in the production of these events (Uboldi et al. 2013). These dynamic network diagrams (Figs. 16–18) show how artists, humanists, performers, patrons, and social groups collaborated in the planning and execution of one or more festivals—available also in a timeline format (Fig. 19). Finally, users have access to biographies, transcriptions of documents, and related multimedia materials (Figs. 20–22). The network diagrams aim to reveal relationships between individuals, communities, spaces, themes, types of events, and webs of patronage involving aristocratic and religious-civic networks (Fig. 23).

The "Memory" level presents *clusters of texts and images* (*poems/artworks*) reflecting the classical heritage of Renaissance festivals, which allows us to examine the physical traces left by these festivities on the artistic and political life of the city. A series of hyperlinks allows users to browse the entire body of documents and explore different historical lineages of cultural heritage (Fig. 24). Our intent is to capture the ephemeral but rich world of the performing arts and encourage the study of the traces that such performances left in written/figurative sources and in the broader culture of the time. Specifically, this section will highlight the manipulation of classical heritage in relation to aristocratic prestige, political agenda, and the process of creation of new genres in the performing arts. The uniqueness of this visual model allows scholars to investigate early modern rituals as a "performing archive" for the transmission of ancient culture (Figs. 25–26).

These three levels and accompanying visual layers have been identified on the basis of the data and research questions informing FRIDA. They aid our

Institute of Art for providing a digital copy of the de' Barbari *View of Venice* included in their collection.

understanding of the principles that framed the creation and perception of these historical events as well as their impact on collective memory and on the ruling classes of Europe and the Mediterranean. In other words, the Atlas visually reconstructs festivals as a complex symbolic system of texts and images related to political, artistic, and cultural programs. The final product—"historical-analytic" and "geographical-visual" histories of Renaissance festivals—will be freely and publicly available. We are paying particular attention to the way users—researchers and students as well as a general audience—can move across different visual representations, visual diagrams, and maps. Users will actively create their own paths through the historical stories, having access to the entire body of documents and a wide-ranging dataset in a multimedia setting of texts, images, and sounds. The generous interface will also enrich interpretation by revealing relationships within the collection. Finally, the platform will utilize the principles of universal design to create a user-friendly interface.

La Serenissima Venice: Preliminary Outcomes

The Republic of Venice represents an extraordinary case study for our Atlas because of its cosmopolitan nature, diplomatic relations, and geographic position as a major crossroads between Europe, Asia, and Africa. The fifteenth- and sixteenth-century Venetian ceremonial calendar promoted an ideal of civic life and political equilibrium via multimedia spectacles, mostly described in Marino Sanudo's *Diarii*, a 58-volume manuscript[10] covering almost 40 years of Venetian history that we are investigating along with other historical accounts and the coeval poetical, aural, and visual culture.[11] While Venice has been praised for the regularity of its rituals, as Francesco Sansovino (1581, 168r) noted, "in private *feste*, altogether different things happen." There was a fervent community of artists and intellectuals who operated within the civic (public and private) context of the festival and experimented with new forms and techniques of the performing arts. This section will focus on this experimentation and present a preliminary analysis made possible by our three-level Atlas.

---

[10] The original autograph copy can be found at the Bibloteca Nazionale Marciana: Bibl. Marciana, Ital. Cl. VII, 228–86 (9215–73). Selections from Sanudo's *Diarii* have been translated into English by Linda L. Carroll (see Labalme and Sanguineti White 2008).

[11] In addition to the studies mentioned above in note 4, see Chastel 1978; Crouzet-Pavan 1992, 1999; Infelise 2016; Matino 2017; Muir 1981; Muraro 2004; Puppi 1980; Salzberg 2014; Urban 1966, 1968, 1969, 1988; Venturi (1909) 1983. See also the valuable work of Patricia Fortini Brown (1988, 1996).

Event: Festival Locations in Venice—Itineraries

Venice's natural environment features a number of locations that have served as the setting for processions, social rituals, and other celebrations of the city-state. The majestic Piazza San Marco, the Basilica, and the Piazzetta on the lagoon are the most important sites. These are the "theaters" of the public's religious and civic celebrations: locations that highlight the power of the Republic as embodied in the processional order assigned to the magistrates, the doge's delegations, and even the lay and religious guilds. Additional locations were also progressively introduced in the festival program. This variety speaks to the diverse occasions for festivities and the participation of diverse social groups (schools, confraternities, guilds, artists, etc.) that took on new political roles in these events. In turn, these groups modified the urban landscape of Venice in accordance with their representational needs. These locations include the Bacino di San Marco, the Canal Grande, and even the Due Castelli on Lido at the mouth of the Adriatic Sea, as in the case of the ceremony of the Festa della Sensa (Feast of the Ascension), one of the most important civic celebrations in Venice.

The Festa della Sensa began as a blessing of the sea, as originally mandated by Doge Orseolo (991–1009), but it was subsequently transformed into a much more complicated event that celebrated Venice's maritime power and its dominion over the sea. By the fifteenth century, this ceremony appeared to be well codified even to the eyes of contemporary foreigners: as Isabella d'Este wrote, "it seems to me that they have a mold for their ceremonies" (quoted in Luzio and Renier 1890).[12] Starting from the pages of Sanudo's *Diarii*, and from the valuable studies of Venitian ceremonies by Lina Urban (1968) and Edward Muir (1981), among others, we have reconstructed the stages of the Festa della Sensa on an abstract map of Venice, creating a preliminary visual model of the festival.

The ceremony began at the dock of the Palazzo Ducale with a solemn procession of boats, guided by the doge's ship, called the *bucintoro*, and proceeded to Sant'Elena, the Due Castelli, and the Chiesa of San Nicolò before returning to the market in Piazza San Marco where the festivities would conclude with a banquet in front of the Palazzo Ducale. While many aspects of the ceremony were repeated each year (in particular, its aquatic setting in the lagoon, the mobile scenes on the *bucintoro*, and the Marriage of the Sea ceremony), there

---

[12] See also Branca 1983; Fenlon 2007; Guarino 1995; Muir 1981; Padoan 1978; Povoledo (1969) 1975; L. Zorzi 1977.

were slight variations that resulted from historical and political events and/or intentional attempts to transgress the uniformity of the rituals. These transgressions came into conflict with the edicts of the Council of Ten, which continually appealed to the need for uniformity in rites and ceremonies (Crouzet-Pavan 1992, 538–61).[13] These variations are represented in the four itineraries of Figure 7, in which each point is a stage of the festival itinerary.

During the Festa della Sensa of 1497, for example, the doge's court, returning from the ring ritual on Lido, stopped at San Lio to witness a tournament of the Stradioti (mercenary light cavalry corps of Greek, Albanian, and Slav origin) and other feasts (Fig. 7.1). In contrast, the Sensa of 1509 was much more reserved, given that it coincided with the tragic defeat of Venice in the Battle of Agnadello. Sanudo notes that "only a few people attended the *festa de la Sensa*" because "everybody was nervous and stayed at the ducal palace for the whole day to hear news about the battle" (Sanudo, *Diarii* 8, col. 257) (Fig. 7.2). Finally, for the Sensa of 1520, Sanudo reports that the regular ceremonial stages were followed by a number of famous guests including the Marquis Federico II Gonzaga, his brother Ercole (who returned for the same occasion in 1526), Eleonora, his sister and duchess of Urbino, and her husband, Francesco Maria della Rovere, along with a group of women from Mantua (Sanudo *Diarii* 8, col. 257). During this festival, the actors of the Compagnia della Calza, called Immortali, organized more entertainments and performances throughout the city (in both public and private locations), extending the festival period to the Tuesday after Easter (Fig. 7.3).[14]

After the Mass at San Marco, "given from the grand altar," the Marquis Federico Gonzaga, alongside other members of his family, took part in "a triumphant public *festa*," organized in their honor by the Immortali who had welcomed the marquis as a member of their company. Having been granted the use of the *bucintoro*, on which they held luxurious banquets and dances, the Immortali organized two regattas (one for men and one for women), which wound their way down the Canal Grande following the path of the Festa della Sensa with the addition of jousts and *palii* with boats. These regattas were

[13] On the Festa delle Marie, see Casini 1996, 288–94 and 301.

[14] Compagnia della Calza were theatrical associations in Venice in the fifteenth and sixteenth centuries set up by groups of young noblemen who actively collaborated in the organization of public festivals, private feasts, and theatrical representations. Their name comes from the trousers they wore that make each company recognizable thanks to the Company's insignia imprinted on the trouser leg or the hood of their cloaks (Casini 1996; Guarino 1995; Venturi [1909] 1983).

repeated on several occasions during the days following the Sensa (Sanudo, *Diarii* 28, col. 529–30).

On this occasion, the Immortali organized two more feasts: one at Ca' Foscari in San Simon, and another at Ca' Corner de la Piscopia, reserved for the Compagnia members and 50 invited ladies. A *solero* (a covered stage), featuring dances and banquets, descended the Canal Grande going first "to a dinner at the Giudecca in Ca' Dandalo" and then to Piazza San Marco, where two *soleri* were built with the approval of the doge: "a big one for the ladies and gentlemen, and another for a [new] *momaria*" (Sanudo *Diarii* 28, col. 530).[15] The director was maestro Pellegrin (a teacher of dance).[16] As Sanudo noted, "the celebration shall be in Piazza San Marco at night: a *new and unusual* event" (Sanudo, *Diarii* 28, col. 532–62; emphasis added). This "new and unusual event" was the result of long negotiations between the Compagni and the Signoria. These negotiations simultaneously exceeded the restrictions of the ceremonial calendar and extended the festivities of the Immortali from aristocratic homes into the Piazza San Marco, a place that was traditionally reserved for the doge's celebrations.

The *momaria* "conquered" institutional spaces as a result of the Compagnie della Calza's political and social actions. These Venetian spectacles were eventually staged alongside triumphal entrances in honor of the doge, processions of the confraternities, and even jousts and tournaments. Historical accounts documented mise-en-scènes of the *momaria* even in the halls of the Maggior Consiglio and in the courtyard of the Palazzo Ducale. In 1487, for instance, as a part of the festivities for Alfonso d'Este, the Compagni of the Modesti staged a complex indoor *momaria* in the hall of the Consiglio with the endorsement of the state (see Biblioteca del Museo Correr, Cod. Cicogna 2977). In 1493, in honor of the visit of Beatrice d'Este and Eleonora d'Aragona, a similar show was staged at the Palazzo Ducale, adapting the mythological scene for political purposes. Using mobile scenes that resembled those used in aquatic ceremonies, the ancient story of Meleagro was introduced into the frame of the *festa*, which was represented with dances from the beginning to the end of the spectacle.[17]

---

[15] The *momaria* was a form of mythological spectacle that assumed "a hegemonic role" in Venetian ceremonies around the end of the fifteenth century (Urban 1966, 1969).

[16] The name of maestro Pellegrin appears several times in the *Dirarii*, in entries for 24 January 1513 (15, col. 511); 20 February 1528 (46, col. 611); 17 July 1530 (53, col. 355); and 20 February 1533 (57, col. 530–32). See Labalme and Sanguineti White 2008, 495.

[17] Evidence is found in Sabellico 1502, 17v–18r as well as in a letter by Beatrice d'Este

In the public and private ceremonial locations of the Serenissima, artists had a variety of figurative and thematic strategies for embedding mythological motifs in the visual/poetic program of the festival. Still in 1520, a few months before the festivities marking the Ascension, on the occasion of Carnival, the Compagnia of the Immortali sponsored a solemn spectacle at Ca' Foscari in San Simon on the Canal Grande in honor of their new member Federico Gonzaga. The Immortali proposed additional performances, dances, and banquets in different locations of the city, as we have reconstructed in a preliminary visual model based on the de' Barbari map. This cartographic representation marks a new mode of representing urban space in which each quadrant represents a stage of the festival (Fig. 4 and Video 1 on the companion website). The itinerary is also represented in a straight line, with the type of each performance marked in each stage (Fig. 5–6). This structure is oriented in such a way as to allow the construction of dynamic narrative models that combine a series of visual representations with a specific set of texts, images, and sounds from the poetic/visual/sonic program of the festival (Figs. 8–10 and Video 2).

According to Sanudo, the Carnival of 1520 began on a partially covered mobile *solero* connecting Ca' Foscari with the Chiesa di Santa Maria in Nazareth degli Scalzi through some *burchielle* (little boats). The procession then proceeded down the Canal Grande to the church of Cannaregio, where a *momaria* was staged and directed by maestro Marco Tonin.[18] The show represented mythological scenes featuring Laocoön and the story of Troy set atop mobile stages carried by six porters, who danced alongside a king, his daughter, and men dressed as peasants. The guest of honor was Francesco Sanudo (son of Angelo), who had been accepted as part of the company alongside the Marquis Gonzaga and two other Venetian nobles, Stefano Querini and Federico di Priuli. Venetians ran to view the spectacle from along the walls, from balconies, and even from the sea in small and medium-sized boats. The *momaria* then continued on water, traveling to the Chiesa del Corpus Domini in the district of Cannaregio before returning to the bridge at Ca' Foscari, where a dinner was set for 350 people and a comedy *alla villanesca* was staged in *pavano* (Paduan dialect) by Angelo Beolco (better known as Ruzante). The same day, in the court of Ca' Loredan in San Marcuola, the actors of the Compagnia della Calza of the Trionfanti performed Terence's *Adelphi*. The next day, they staged *Aulularia* (Sanudo, *Diarii* 28, col. 248, 253–56, 561).

(Molmenti 1880, 627–30) and Eleonora d'Aragona (Chiappini 1956, 84–85).

[18] A teacher of dance, whose name appears two more times in the *Diarii*: 3 July 1524 (36, col. 457–58) and 28 February 1527 (44, col. 172).

The Trojan myth was a theme with high symbolic value for the mythical origin of Venice and was used often throughout this period.[19] The Trojan cycle appears, for instance, in the admirable *momaria* staged by the Compagnia della Calza of the Eletti in the hall of the Maggior Consiglio of the Palazzo Ducale, after the usual procession on the *bucintoro*, the regattas, and the jousts, organized in honor of Anna di Foix of Candale in 1502.[20] The Trojan stories were proposed again in 1515 for the Carnival at Ca' Pesaro in San Benedetto, where "a representation of the story of Paris and those goddesses to whom he gave the apple" was staged (Sanudo, *Diarii* 19, col. 443). The spectacle was preceded by a staging of Plautus's *Miles Gloriosus* by the Immortali and included interludes performed by the *buffoni* Zuan Polo and Domenico Tajacalze as well as choreographed nymph dances.[21] The Trojan myth also appears in the *momaria* of 1524, given in the presence of the Duke of Urbino. On this occasion, the Compagnia della Calza of the *Valorosi* staged the story of the rape of Helen by Paris in an outdoor setting at the *fondamenta* of Cannaregio. Maestro Marco Tonin was the director of this *momaria*, as in the Carnival of 1520 (Sanudo, *Diarii* 36, col. 459).

By highlighting a few historical "events," we can trace the movement of the *momaria* between institutionalized centers of civil ceremonies and alternative sites of entertainment and leisure within the urban spaces of Venice. This is visible in the topographic map of de' Barbari (Fig. 11), which illustrates the indoor and outdoor locations of the *momaria* in Venice between 1450 and 1550. These locations are further tied to other representations of the "ancient fable" and the legacy of classical comedy that had been reappearing in convent schools and humanistic educational programs since the middle of the 1400s. A variety of theatrical representations also included alternative dramatic forms, like Ruzante's comedy *alla villanesca*, or new kinds of performances, like those of the *buffoni* Zuan Polo and Domenico Tajcalze, and even allegorical fables, farces, or musical performances.[22] This variety of

[19] Venetians claimed their descent from Troy. See M. Zorzi 1996, 833–34.

[20] The theatrical representation is described by the humanist patrician Angelo Gabriel. See Guarino 1995, 119–46. A list of sources related to the "entrances" of Anna di Foix can be found in Mitchell 1979, 144–45.

[21] Only a few days before, in the refectory of Santo Stefano, a "great" recitation of Plautus's *Asinaria* was staged in the vernacular by "some learned men" (Sanudo, *Diarii* 19, col. 443).

[22] See the topographic tables reconstructed in Crouzet-Pavan 1992, 1–18. Ruzante was a very popular actor and playwright; Zuan Polo (Liompardi) and Domenico Tajaclaze were two well-known actors who appear in many of the performances of this period. See Guarino 1995.

extraordinary images, words, and sounds contained the seeds of a new form of theater.

In this section, we have attempted to offer a preliminary mapping of these performing practices that reconstructs their times, locations, and models in order to untangle and visualize the multiplicitous and stratified object of the festival (Figs. 13–15). The result is a varied geographic and cultural topography—an assemblage of indoor and outdoor theatrical stages on which a variety of types of performances were held, as Sanudo, Sansovino, and other historians and humanists have described. Our Atlas attempts to reconstruct this topography by visualizing their words in a dynamic sequence of representations that will include a targeted selection of texts, images, and sounds of the poetic, visual, and sonic program of the festival in order to reconstruct a multimedia geographic and historical narrative of the festival. This reconstruction will help uncover hidden relationships between the use of public and private spaces and the forms of performances and theatrical representations that these spaces, whether occasionally or recurrently, hosted. This analysis will also demonstrate how individuals in these locations affirmed their own social position and/or political prestige by importing their own specific performative and organizational skills into the festival context.

Backstage: The Social Networks of the "Ancient Fable"

In order to study temporary creations, such as festive rituals, it is necessary to go behind the historical events so we can also investigate them as co-creative processes rather than simply products, thus reconstructing what we call the "Backstage" of festivals. As we note above, this section aims to articulate the social and performative network of the *actors* involved in the event by generating network diagrams, which explore the dynamics of interaction of the "micro-society" of the *festa*. Sansovino offers an exemplary view of the backstage of the *festa*, which we will analyze in this section alongside the two festivals of 1520 (for Carnival and Ascension Day) organized by the young members of the Immortali in honor of the Gonzagas.

In "private *feste*," as Sansovino (1581, 168r) states, there were "altogether different things." Different, that is, from the institutional rituals that recurred throughout the Republican festive calendar. These different forms of entertainment, which animated the "licentious times" of the "private *feste*" (private spaces of aristocratic entertainments) brought together writers, artists, performers, and dancers, and included—as we have seen above—indoor and outdoor stagings of myths, the revival of ancient comedies, and other "new" theatrical forms. In these spaces, Sansovino continues, "comedies had been performed for years, as the ancient poets did in the past, in order to teach the rules of civil life through the allegories of fables." However, according to the Venetian historian, in these "private *feste*," the classical model was at risk of "contamination" or "corruption" because of the inclusion of "ridiculous inventions and characters" by "performers, who knew little of the original classical matter" (Sansovino 1581, 168v). Sansovino exposes a contradiction between the theoretical framework of the humanists, their intention of reviving the classics for a pedagogical and moral function in society, and the actual performative practices taking place in private spaces.

Yet not all of these "inventors" earned Sansovino's scorn. In his introduction to Francesco de' Nobili from Lucca, better known as Cherea, Sansovino (1581, 168v) reports, for example, the appreciation that Venetian nobles (and Pope Leo X) had for this "inventor of new things in performing comedies." Cherea, a diplomat and performer, introduced in Venice a large repertoire of vernacular translations of Plautus's comedies, eclogues, and farces that he performed in the spaces of elite entertainment throughout Italy: in Rome, where he had even taken his nickname Cherea from a performance of a Plautine comedy; in Naples, at the theatrical court of the Sanseverino, where Cherea became acquainted with the poet Caracciolo; and in Ferrara, where he defined the theatrical repertoire that he eventually performed in the houses of Venetian patricians and in the convents of the Serenissima.[23] Cherea's name is mentioned in Sansovino's (1581) list along with other "nobili ingegni":

> Antonio da Molino, called Burchiella, a pleasant man, who spoke in Greek and *lingua schiavona* [Slavic] corrupted with Italian and with the most ridiculous and strange inventions and chimeras in the world; Frate Armonio of the *Ordine de' Crococchieri*, organist at San Marco; Valerio Zuccato dal Mosaico, Lodovico Dolce and other

[23] Cherea's first stay in Venice was in 1508, recorded by his request to the Senate and the Council of Ten to print his theatrical repertoire and by the comments on his performances in the peripheral private houses of the aristocracy in San Cancian in Biri and Ca' Corner. He also attempted, but failed, to perform in the Rialto market: the vibrant center of the civic and economic life of the city and of its merchant oligarchy. He returned in 1522 and proposed a comedy at the convent of the Crosechieri, including a performance by Zuan Polo and his son as interlude during a feast. Finally, he appears on the occasion of the *giovedì grasso* (fat Thursday) in 1525 (Sanudo, *Diarii*, 7, col. 701; 14, col. 325; 15, col. 531; 16, col. 548).

> artists, among all a noble performing lady, called Polinia (Polonia di Vicenza), who was the wife of the mentioned Valerio. (168v)

Burchiella, a multilingual poet and dramaturg, is recognized as the first to have "translated" the classic comedies and vernacular plays into more theatrical languages. Lodovico Dolce recalled him as a cofounder of a well-known music academy in Venice along with his friend Friar Armonio, who in turn was well-known by the humanists as the author of the comedy *Stephanium*, an original play written on the model of classical comedy and represented by his students at the Crociferi's convents.[24]

Sansovino's overview concludes by mentioning the noted mosaicist Valerio Zuccato and his future wife, the celebrated actress and comedian Polonia, as well as Lodovico Dolce "and others" (see also D'Ancona [1877] 1891, 1:403, 2:112n, 2:458; Vescovo 1996, 2016). Working with his brother Francesco in the composition of the mosaics of the Basilica di San Marco, Valerio was the son of Sebastiano, who ran one of the most influential workshops in Venice. This is also recorded by Dolce (1557, 54v–55v, quoted in Donati 2014, 34–37), who mentions a "troubled" Titian "who could not stand the dry and stentorian style of Gentile," arousing the ire of his teacher who, for his part, did not want him to "distance himself" from the traditional path.[25]

We could continue adding more and more names to this list in order to recreate a richer and even more finely articulated mosaic of the writers, poets, artists, dancers, and musicians who transformed the "ancient fables" by corrupting them and, in so doing, created a new practice of theater. Thus, in addition to the diaries and chronicles of humanist writers and noble men and women, the Atlas contains data from archival notes, edicts from the state (that these practices sought to control), and many other documents. These

[24] Burchiella is also praised for his great ability as a performer, dancer, musician, and writer who could compete both with the art of the Roman actor Roscio (Quintus Roscius Gallus) as well as that of the great poets of the fourteenth century (Guarino 1995, 111–18; Sabellico 1502, 52r, 68r–70r).

[25] Dolce's memory of Titian highlights the same experimental tension that Sansovino recognized in the "nobili ingegni" of the comedies. Perhaps he had in mind the feasts at Titian's house that the Zuccato brothers attended along with Giulio Camillo, Jacopo Sansovino (the father), Jacopo Nardi, the architect Serlio, and several noble women including Paola Sansovino, Giulia da Ponte, and her daughter-in-law, Irene da Spilinbergo (Molmenti 1880, 407). Arentino was almost certainly also part of this group, given his now well-known ties with Jacopo Sansovino and Titian.

allow us to trace the nodes and connections of the living and complex micro-society of the *festa*. We accomplish this by tracing through a schematic analysis reconstructing the social, artistic, and cultural networks that performers used in the course of their work. We then put those networks in relationship with the forms, styles, and locations featured in the new dramaturgies they proposed for the festivals.

As a result, our narrative combines a cartographic analysis of the locations of the festival-event identified in our dataset (level 1, the "Event" level) with an analysis of the relationships between the communities, spaces, and types of ceremonies that made up the festival program (level 2, the "Backstage" level). This combination shows how the relationships between social actors, locations, and events evolved within the chronological arc of the Atlas, illustrating a significant intensification of networked connections beginning in the last three decades of the fifteenth century (Fig. 23).

We have created a more detailed, although still provisional, view of these relationships beginning with the two festive events of 1520: the Carnival and the Festa della Sensa, respectively. Focusing on these two events, we have begun an initial reconstruction of this micro-society in network diagrams that connect the *actors* of 1520 with other festive events (Figs. 16–17 and Video 3).

This reconstruction is organized around a specific analytic focus, as the four images of Figure 18 show. First, we have distinguished the presence of these protagonists in this festival from those performers who also worked on other festivals, tied in this case essentially to Loredan's and Gritti's reigns as doge (Fig. 18.1). We also limited the body of festivals on the basis of the type of event, thus selecting a thematic key (i.e., the Trojan cycle) and putting the network of actors of these festivals in relation with other events that, like Carnival in 1520, used the Trojan myth as the nucleus of the mythological staging. In this way we have registered a network of actors whose presence in the "Trojan events" of 1502, 1515, 1520, and 1524 recurs in a consistent manner (Fig. 18.2), as in the focus on the Immortali, for example, whose presence is noted in four different festivals (Fig. 18.3), or on the Ruzante (Fig. 12.4).

The preliminary network of the 1520 events shows a significant degree of contamination between performers with different specialties, as Sansovino noted in the passage above. Through the progressive insertion of new data, which at the moment follows in the mode privileged by Sanudo and Sansovino, we can begin to trace a labyrinth of connections configured according to the form, metaphorical and conceptual, of the network. This produces a map of the complex circulation of cultural and human material, and of the presence of microcommunities or individuals in the political, cultural, and performative universe of Venetian festivals and elite entertainment. This section also includes information about contributors (Fig. 20), specific festival events, and short biographies, transcriptions of documents, and a selection of multimedia material (Figs. 21–22 and Video 4).

The system of analysis of the social networks of the *actors* on which we are working allows for the possibility of rendering visible nodes (or "vertices") and edges (or "arcs") of the festival, which reveal the circulation of people, knowledge, and actions that are not always visible from a broad view. These first visualizations on the social network of the festival do not represent the final result of the study and analysis of networks, but they allow us to recognize a few initial structural properties, which will be analytically developed and quantitatively implemented by creating new explorations of relations' networks. These analyses are also supported by another analytic tool and visual layer that is complementary both to the system of social networks (level 2) and the cartographic representations (level 1). This additional visual layer moves—as we shall see in the next section—on an interdisciplinary terrain and allows the reconstruction of the co-creative process of these ephemeral events, their transformative power, and their "significance" and impact (level 3, the "Memory" level).

Memory: The Forms of the "Ancient Fable"

This section introduces a visual interdisciplinary matrix that works as an "interlinked library," interconnecting the texts, sounds, and images (*poems/artworks*) that shaped these events and exploring both the durable material that they generated and their effects in the artistic and political life of Venice and collective memory.

The passage, quoted above, that Sansovino wrote at the end of the sixteenth century on Venetian ceremonies and festivals testifies to a profound contrast between the ideals of Latin and vernacular humanism and the contemporary reception and interest in antiquity, which dated back to the vernacular practices of the fourteenth century. In this tension, Sansovino places the experiments of artists, performers, and playwrights, who were attempting to renew classic theater. While they first performed in the "licentious times" of entertainment, they eventually became woven into public and institutional ceremonies, as documented by the events of 1520.

As we have seen so far, classical stories and characters appeared on the festive stage alongside the multilingual comedies of Burchiella and Ruzante, the performances of the married Zuccatos or the buffoons Tajacalze and Zuan Polo, and the stagings of Cherea and the Compagni della Calza. The result was a kind of "mythology in action." Performative practices open to contamination were staged without fear of the philological humanistic norm. This practice of recreation (in the double meaning that this term holds as both a form of entertainment and a re-envisioning of antiquity) was not only a part of theatrical experimentations within the festival program but also traceable in the visual arts, literature, and even in Venetian prints. As a result, these experimental practices led to a new level of relationship between "letter," "figure," and "form"—a level on which Ludovico Dolce (one of the "nobili ingegni" of Sansovino's list), for instance, worked with his *Trasformationi* (1553), based on the Latin texts of Ovid's *Metamorphoses*.

Therefore, to recreate an important part of the process of selection, adaptation, and dissemination of the visual and poetic imaginary of antiquity that made up the public and private festival programs—their significance, their contents, and their memory—we have to create an associative system that makes it possible to comprehend the vast and complex set of works, genres, forms, and styles that first shaped the performance during the festival and then eventually generated new art and poetry. We must do this while referring to the figurative and literary culture of the time and the contamination of ancient stories—including those of Ovid and Virgil and the comedies of Plautus and Terence—published in illustrated books in Latin and in vernacular languages (Guarino 1995, 102).

After all, Venice is the city that birthed the illustrated book, which offered a "figurative version" of antiquity. Renewed by the publication of the 1497 Giunta edition of the *Ovidio Metamorphoseos vulgare*, written in the 1370s by Giovanni dei Bonsignori, this mediated knowledge of antiquity made classic myths available and accessible to vast areas of literature, music, and the figurative and performing arts (Guthmüller 2008, 154–75). In the gap between the work of rewriting the ancient fable and the humanistic reception of the *Metamorphoses* there are established links between the oral and written tradition and the visual culture that emerge in the festival.[26]

---

[26] An important example of a new theater was the *Fabula di Orfeo* of Angelo Poliziano (Bortoletti 2012, 225–66; Carrai 1990; Ventrone 1992). Following this example, the end of the 1400s and the beginning of the 1500s featured a new series of dramatic texts, inspired by Ovid's stories, staged in Ferrara, Mantua, Milan, and finally in Venice.

There is evidence of this in the relationships we found between the spectacles included in our database and the vernacular editions published during the sixteenth century. In particular, the edition of the *Metamorphoses* written by Niccolò degli Agostini (1522) along with the work of Dolce (1553) confirmed the central role that Venice played in shaping how mythological terms were used in literature and theater (Guthmüller 2008, 189).[27] Through this analysis we have noted a connection between thematic innovations in Agostini's edition (published by Zoppino) and the themes staged during Venetian festivals.

In the introduction and conclusion, for example, Agostini retells the story of Jason and the Golden Fleece and, right at the end, introduces a personal comment. Agostini enriched the story with new details based on the model of Bonsignori and other collections of myths, specifically for the scenes of "greetings, receptions, and banquets" or themes of "love" and the "hunt" (Guthmüller 2008, 227–28). This also happened in the story of Perseus and Andromeda, in that of Meleagro, and even in the story of the Fall of Troy.

These selections are significant. These are the Ovidian stories that Venetians saw "happen" for real in the lagoon, or staged in the *campi*, in the "private" houses and palaces, or in Piazza San Marco and the Palazzo Ducale. Jason and the Golden Fleece was the theme of the *momaria* represented by the Immortali in Campo San Polo in honor of the marriage of Luca da Lezze and the daughter of Giovanni Battista Foscarini in 1507 (Sanudo, *Diarii* 6, col. 161). At the Palazzo Ducale, four triumphant carriages, each with four or five figures dancing, were used to represent "the life of Meleagro . . . from birth until death" at the conclusion of the celebrations in honor of the visit of Isabella and Beatrice d'Este in 1493 (*Lettre* by Beatrice d'Este, in Molmenti 1880, 627–30). Extremely beautiful, "with dances and mirable sounds," and praised by bystanders, the story of Andromeda and Perseus was performed in the *momaria* of the Compagni in the court of the Palazzo Ducale for the Carnival of 1527 and then staged again in the Piazza San Marco. This spectacle was directed by maestro Tonin, the same dancing teacher who staged the Trojan

---

The body of dramatic texts is made up of the *Fabula de Cefalo* by Niccolò da Correggio; the *Pasitea* of Gasparo Visconti; the *Danae* by Baldassarre Taccone; the *Noze de Psiche*; and *Cupidine* of Galetto del Carretto. See further Tissoni Benvenuti and Mussini Sacchi 1983; Vescovo 2005.

[27] The illustrated edition of Bonsignori, published by Giunta and presented in luxurious and well-decorated volumes, is imposed as the literary and figurative model in Venice during the early 1500s despite the scandal generated by the xilographies, which depicted naked female figures, as was done in antiquity.

myth in the Carnival of 1520, and then again in 1524 in the presence of the Duke of Urbino.

The thematic coincidence is even more interesting in this final case, if we note on the one hand the chronology of these theatrical events—preceding for the most part Agostini's edition by Zoppino—and on the other hand the fact that the introduction of the Trojan War represents an innovation of Agostini even in respect to the Bonsignori edition. This new theme is likely tied to the theatrical representations of the Trojan story staged on the occasion of Venetian festivals—or at least to the oral repertoire of the *cantari*, traditionally performed in *ottava rima* by *canterini* (street singers) and poets in the *campi* or at the court (see further Guthmüller 1997, 187–212; Ugolini 1933, 135). At this point, the distance from the Latin original of the mythological stories appeared to be inevitably "compromised" and "corrupted" as Sansovino, indeed, stated.[28]

We are now at the stage of proceeding to catalog literary and iconographic sources on the basis of a datasheet model that we are progressively sharpening—indexing literary and figurative subgroups, themes, motives, stories, characters, sources, styles, expressive categories, and allegories—and analyzing them in relation to the political, cultural, and artistic context of the festival. This datasheet model and relative level of analysis of the festival—the third and final level of our Atlas—will allow the user to explore the entire body of the documents through multiple points of access (Fig. 24). All the works (*poems/artworks*) are positioned according to an interactive, dynamic, and configurable matrix (like double-entry bookkeeping). This matrix has filters that can highlight particular intersections between typologies of different sources, their contents, genres, themes, and other properties tied to the events, to which more levels of interrelationships can be progressively added in order to retrace the meme of the festival (Figs. 25–26).

The analysis becomes more compelling in the case of the editions of illustrated books, or even in the book of emblems, another fundamental genre on which our Atlas is focusing (Bortoletti and Sacchi 2018). By examining textual material alongside iconography, we can verify the correspondence between word and image within the text, or between more texts, or even between texts and the visual material tied to contemporary artistic culture. Similarly, the examination of Venetian artworks (from the narrative system

[28] At least until the new versions of *Metamorfosi* were added, including that of Dolce (published by Gabriel Giolito) in the middle of the century. See further Dionisotti 1999, 140–55; Guthmüller 2008, 243–64.

of the paintings to the stories of the wedding chests to the most important commissions) takes place on a complex terrain of visual concepts, symbols, and modules common both to the universe of the arts as well as the contemporary stagings, testifying to the fecundity of a mobile culture that found its formal unity within the festival (Settis 1986).

Epilogue: Toward an Atlas of the Theatrum mundi

The encyclopedia of images, texts, people, places, and cultures that made up the festival featured the magnificence of Venice, as well as the "recreative" and experimental work of Venetian artists of the fifteenth and sixteenth centuries. These ephemeral events conceptualized and practiced a vision of a *Theatrum mundi*: an idea of the theater, which the theories and practices of the art of memory had taken on as much as a metaphor as an experience of reality. This idea is materialized—as documented in the drawing in Gradenigo's manuscript (Fig. 27)—in the spectacle of the temporal theatrical building that flutters in the waters of the lagoon from Piazza San Marco along the Canal Grande for special occasions of ceremony, performing rituals, and theatrical representations. This idea and practice carried with it a complex visual, poetic, and political program that, in selecting and reviving the inheritance of the ancient world and mythology, became in those festive events and spectacles an amphibious occasion of synthesis and refraction of a universal knowledge, putting before the eyes of the spectators—as Giulio Camillo would have said—"all the human concepts."

This Atlas is conceptualized as a flexible platform, in constant evolution, from which we will compose a series of historical-geographic stories and "dynamic perspectives" by investigating and recomposing the festival itineraries, the analyses of social networks, and a system of associations of texts and images that make up the material of the Atlas. The objective of this architecture is to make it possible to quickly access the information contained in the datasets of the festival events, allowing an efficient visual exploration of the collected contents. Following the locations, the material, and the metaphor of this *Theatrum mundi*, our FRIDA Atlas is presented as a laboratory of data, texts, images, and sounds put together to encourage an "intermedial" analysis of the ritual of the *festa*. The Atlas is not meant to be viewed as a simple repository of "things" that constantly disappear (as we understand the archive) but as an act of survival and at the same time as a tool of reappearance, in this way investigating alternative structures of memory (Fig. 26 and Video 6).

This multilevel digital Atlas will offer new methodologies and digital tools for approaching the immateriality of performing historical events—such as festivals—by investigating and visualizing their materiality as a cultural experience of bodily effects and perceptions. Materializing the materiality of festive and ritual performance within their historical, social, and political context or in relation to their social and artistic networks and their legacy, this Atlas has the potential to produce multidisciplinary reflections on artistic performances and other historical phenomena with complex performative structures in a range of times and places, and to explore their implications as both aesthetic objects and efficacious performative enactments.

Tripartite Architecture of the Atlas and Related Visual Layers

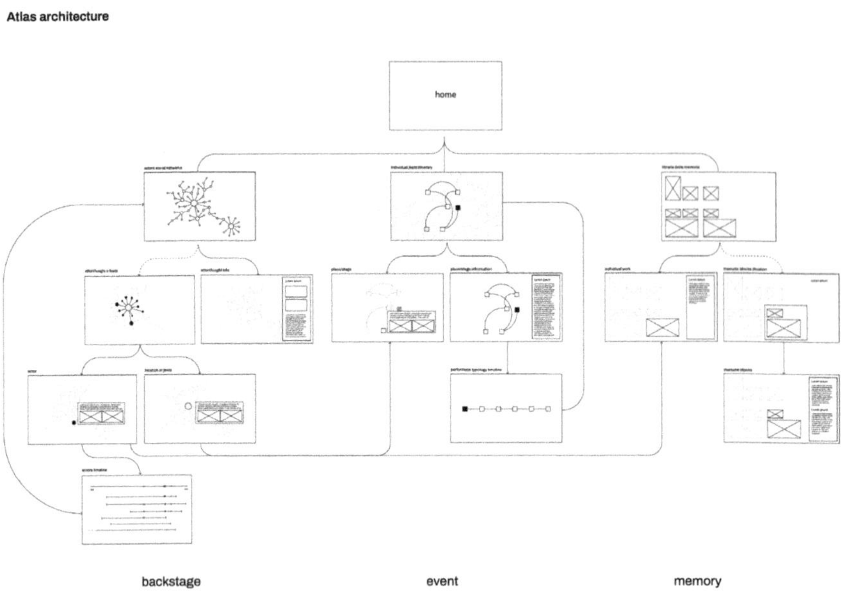

Figure 1. FRIDA is divided into three fully interactive sections: Event, Backstage, and Memory.

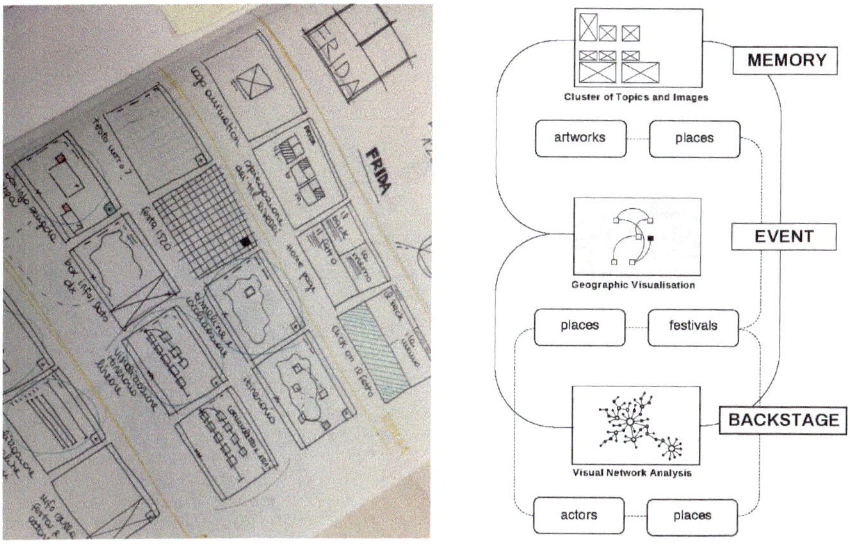

Figure 2. (1) *Cartographic visualizations* of the festivals' itineraries, recreating the multimediality of the "Event"; (2) *Social network diagrams* of social/political/performative communities, retracing the "Backstage" of the festivals; (3) *Clusters of texts and images*, restoring the "Memory" of the festive event.

THE EVENT

Cartographic Visualizations

Figure 3. We overlapped a current geographical map with the historical Jacopo de' Barbari's *View of Venice* (1500).

Animated Itineraries and Timelines

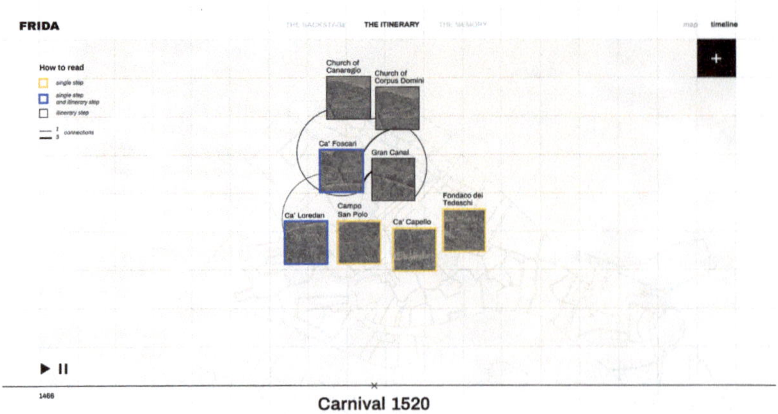

Figure 4.

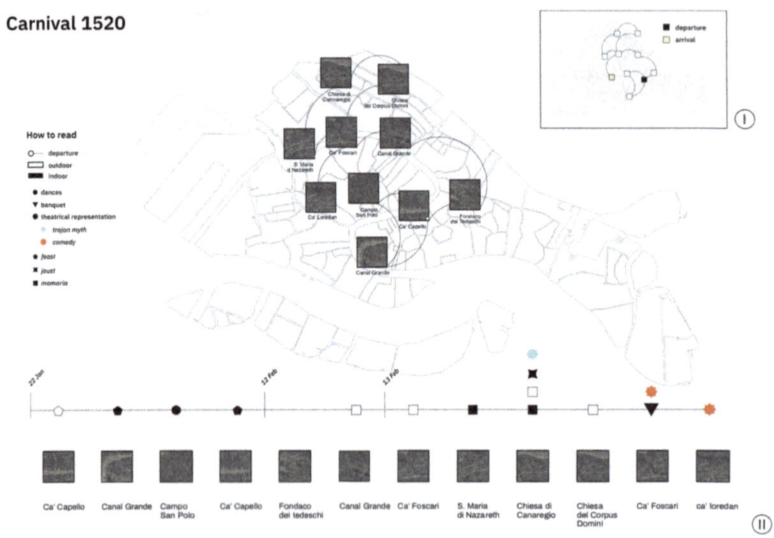

Figure 5.

Figures 4–5. An animation describes the movement of the festival participants between locations of importance, creating a virtual itinerary by using icons from de' Barbari's *View of Venice* that highlighted the most important stages and venues (Fig. 4). Users can see the chronology of a particular Event in a timeline format (Fig. 5). See also Video 1 on the companion website.

Comparing Itineraries

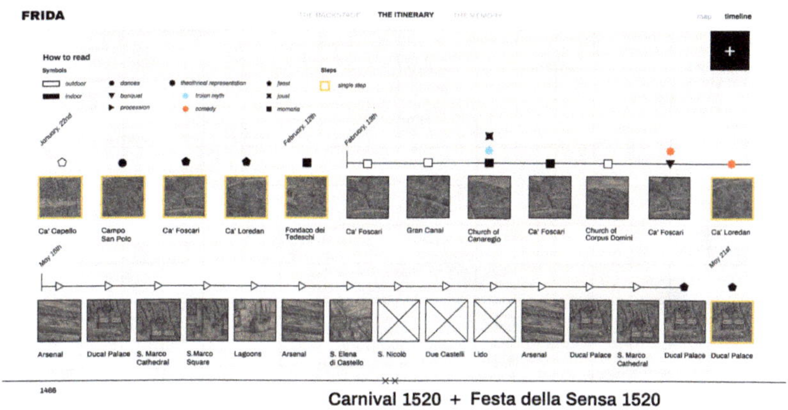

Figure 6.

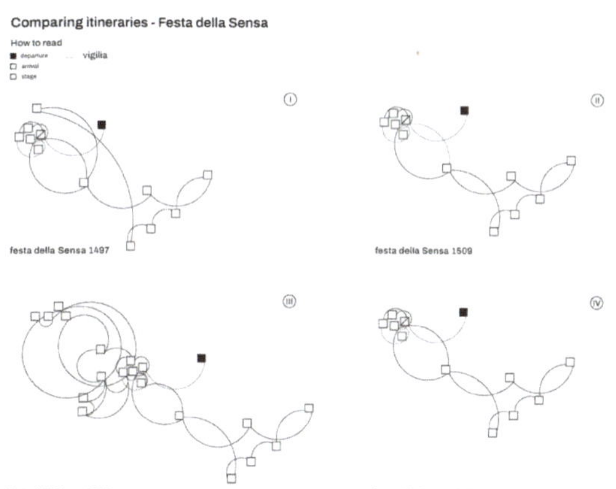

Figure 7.

Figures 6–7. The timeline format arranges the festival diagrammatically and allows for comparisons between locations, events, and itineraries of different festivals (Fig. 6). The system offers the possibility of visualizing data for multiple itineraries, which can be also visualized in the map itinerary (Fig. 7). In this case, the representation of four itineraries shows elements of variability of the canonical ritual of the Festa della Sensa, reconstructing four different temporal moments. Political facts or social strategies modified traditional itineraries and use of the urban space. See also Video 2 on the companion website.

Multimedia Stories

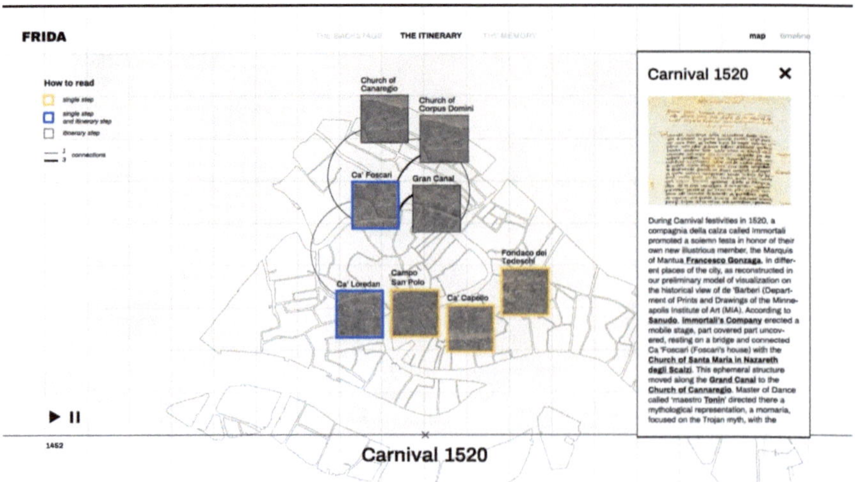

Figure 8.

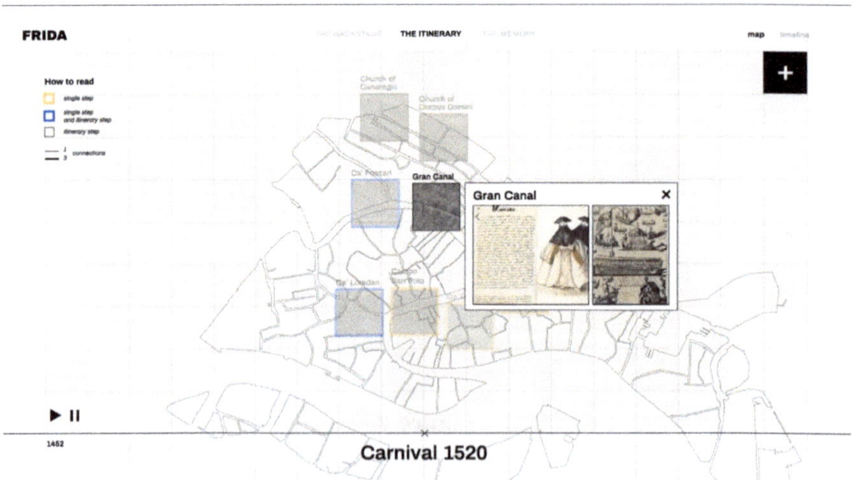

Figure 9.

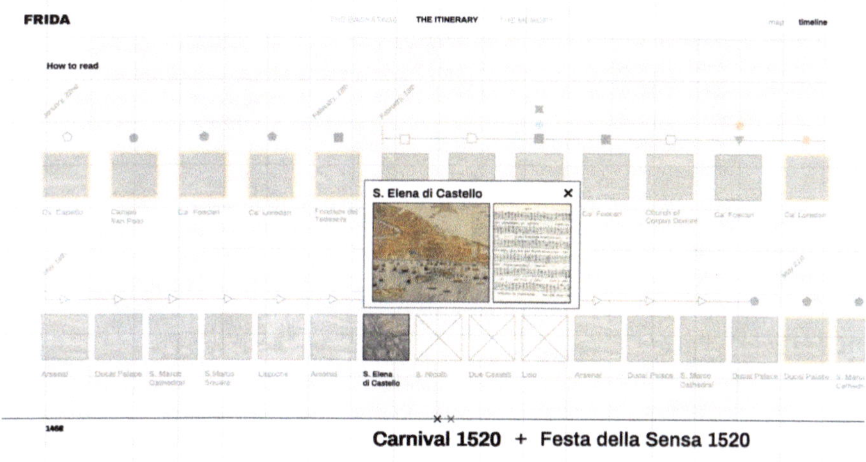

Figure 10.

Figures 8–10. Additional information including visual and textual materials that are collected in the Atlas can be easily accessed by clicking each of the de' Barbari icons (Figs. 8–10). Here is a description of Carnival 1520 from the fifteenth-century manuscript of the *Diarii* by the historien Marin Sanudo and a transcription of the document (Fig. 8). Users will be able to access other historical accounts, chronicles, letters, and literary works related to the event as well as visual material (Fig. 9), maps, and music works (Fig. 10). We are now working on the integration of music registration.

The Geography of the *festa*: Themes and Performances

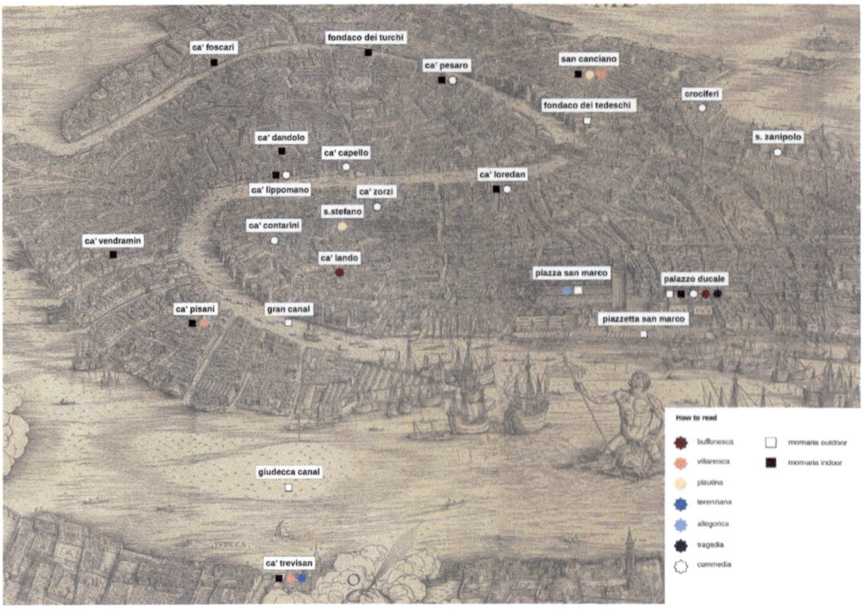

Figure 11.

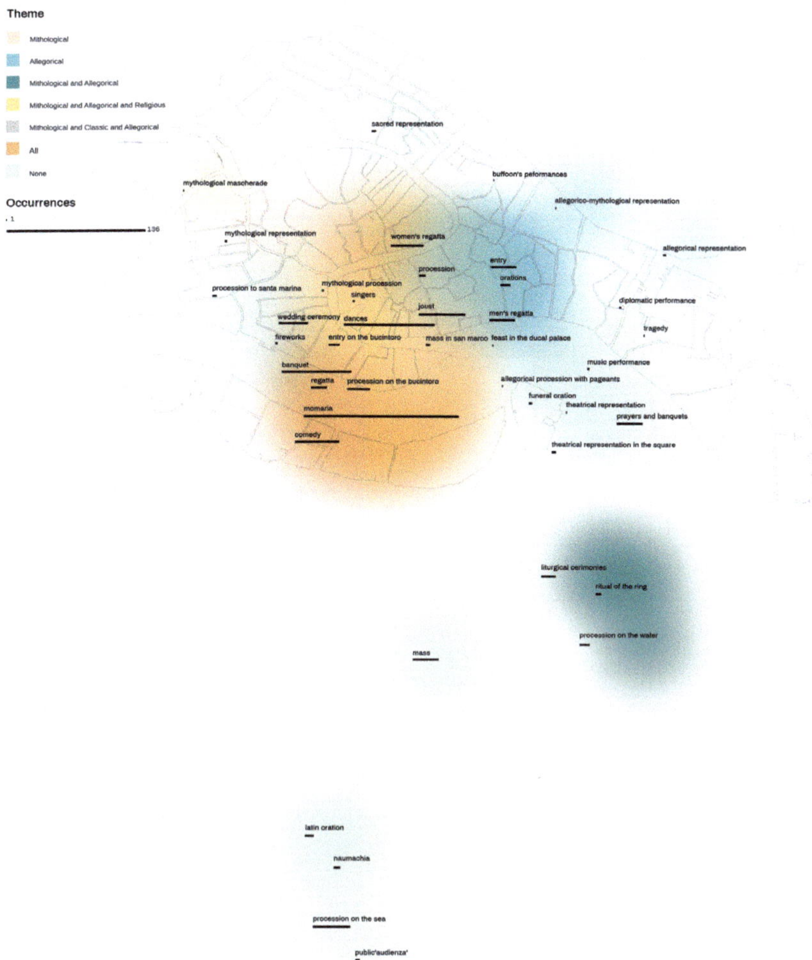
Theme
Mithological
Allegorical
Mithological and Allegorical
Mithological and Allegorical and Religious
Mithological and Classic and Allegorical
All
None
Occurrences
1
136
sacred representation
buffoon's peformances
mythological mascherade
allegorico-mythological representation
mythological representation
women's regatta
allegorical representation
entry
procession
orations
procession to santa marina
mythological procession
singers
diplomatic performance
joust
men's regatta
wedding ceremony
dances
tragedy
fireworks
entry on the bucintoro
mass in san marco
feast in the ducal palace
music performance
banquet
allegorical procession with pageants
regatta
procession on the bucintoro
funeral oration
theatrical representation
momaria
prayers and banquets
comedy
theatrical representation in the square
liturgical cerimonies
ritual of the ring
procession on the water
mass
latin oration
naumachia
procession on the sea
public'audienza'

Figure 12.

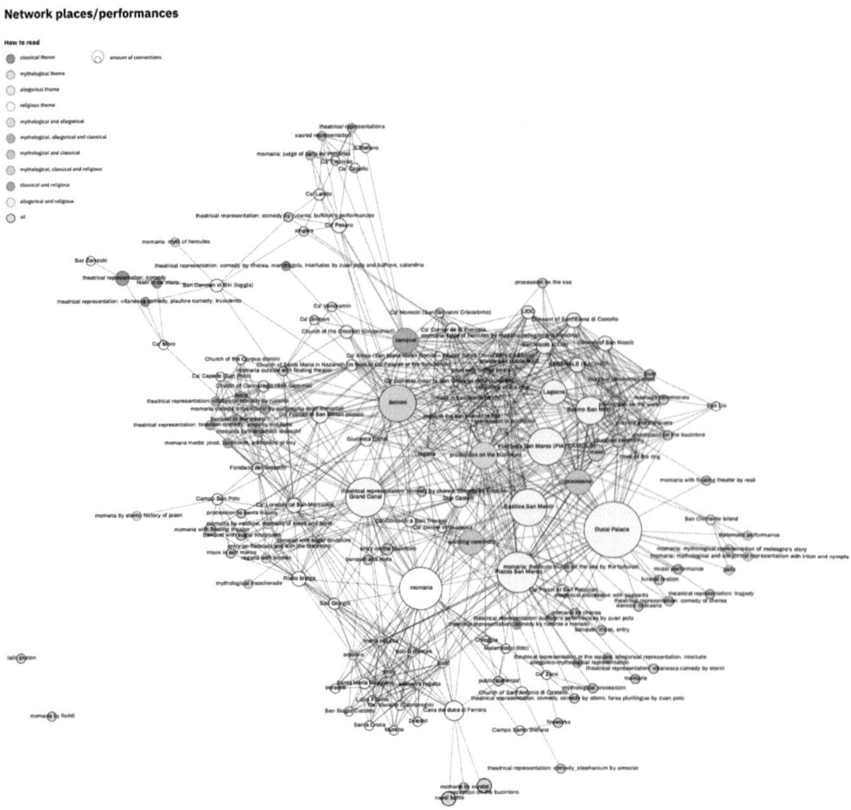
Network places/performances
How to read
Ducal Palace
Grand Canal
Basilica San Marco
momaria

Figure 13.

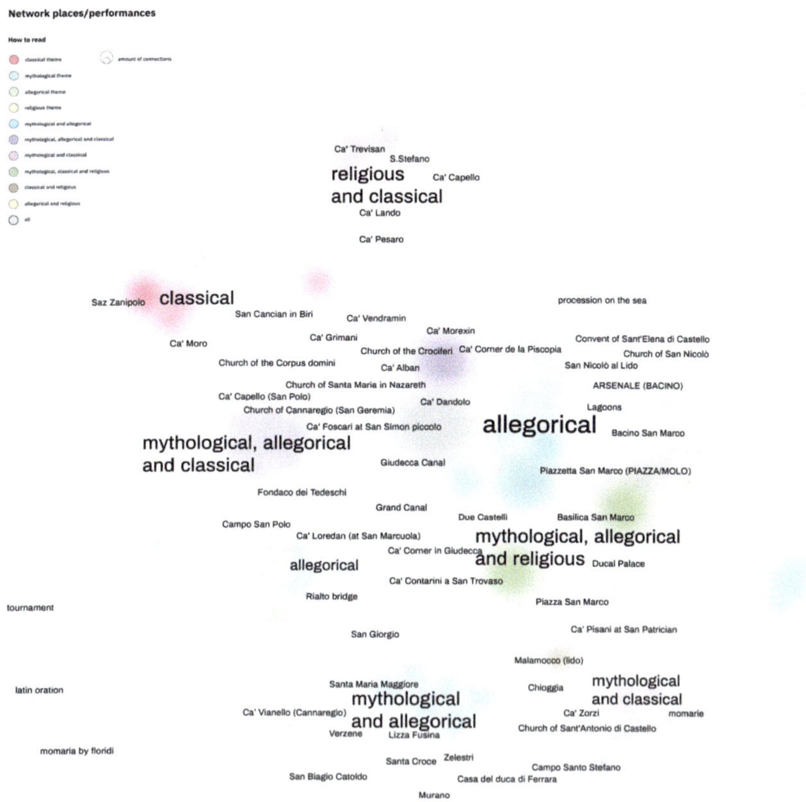
Network places/performances
How to read
classical theme
amount of connections
mythological theme
allegorical theme
religious theme
mythological and allegorical
mythological, allegorical and classical
mythological and classical
mythological, classical and religious
classical and religious
allegorical and religious
all
Ca' Trevisan
S.Stefano
religious and classical
Ca' Capello
Ca' Lando
Ca' Pesaro
Saz Zanipolo
classical
San Cancian in Biri
Ca' Vendramin
procession on the sea
Ca' Grimani
Ca' Morexin
Ca' Moro
Church of the Crociferi
Ca' Corner de la Piscopia
Convent of Sant'Elena di Castello
Church of San Nicolò
Church of the Corpus domini
Ca' Alban
San Nicolò al Lido
Church of Santa Maria in Nazareth
ARSENALE (BACINO)
Ca' Capello (San Polo)
Ca' Dandolo
Church of Cannaregio (San Geremia)
Lagoons
Ca' Foscari at San Simon piccolo
allegorical
Bacino San Marco
mythological, allegorical and classical
Giudecca Canal
Piazzetta San Marco (PIAZZA/MOLO)
Fondaco dei Tedeschi
Grand Canal
Due Castelli
Basilica San Marco
Campo San Polo
Ca' Loredan (at San Marcuola)
mythological, allegorical and religious
Ca' Corner in Giudecca
allegorical
Ducal Palace
Ca' Contarini a San Trovaso
Rialto bridge
tournament
Piazza San Marco
San Giorgio
Ca' Pisani at San Patrician
Malamocco (lido)
latin oration
Santa Maria Maggiore
Chioggia
mythological and classical
mythological and allegorical
Ca' Vianello (Cannaregio)
Ca' Zorzi
momarie
Verzene
Lizza Fusina
Church of Sant'Antonio di Castello
momaria by floridi
Santa Croce
Zelestri
Campo Santo Stefano
San Biagio Catoldo
Casa del duca di Ferrara
Murano

Figure 14.

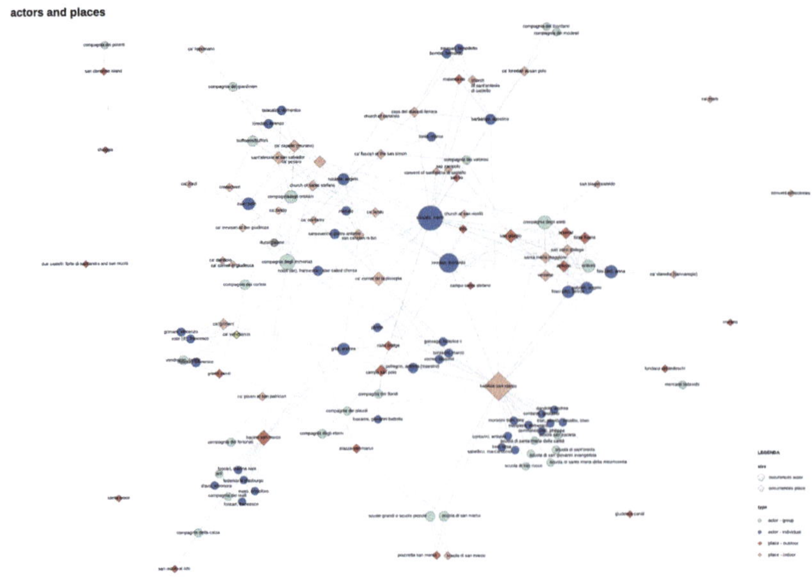

Figure 15.

Figures 11–15. A georeferenced network shows the relation between (private and public) spaces and types of ceremonies, entertainment, and performances (Figs. 11–12). The bars show the number of occurrences for each type of festive event; the themes that composed the visual, musical, and poetical program of the festive events; and the group and individuals who participated in different ways at different events (*actors*) (Figs. 13–15).

THE BACKSTAGE

Social Networks Diagrams

Actors/Festivals

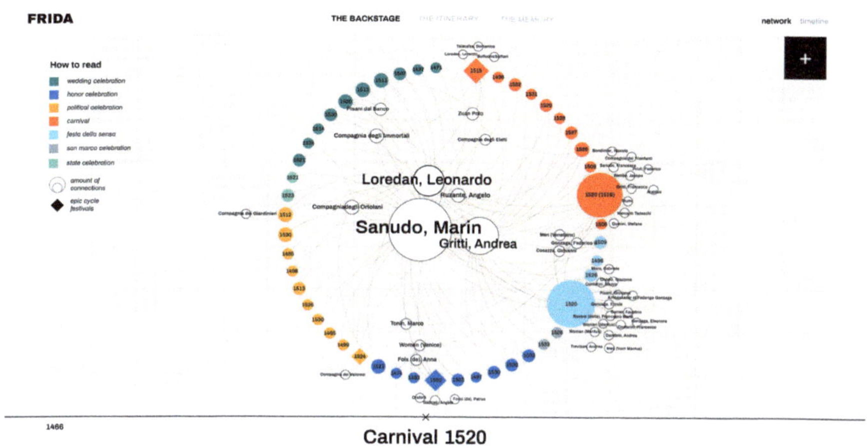

Figure 16.

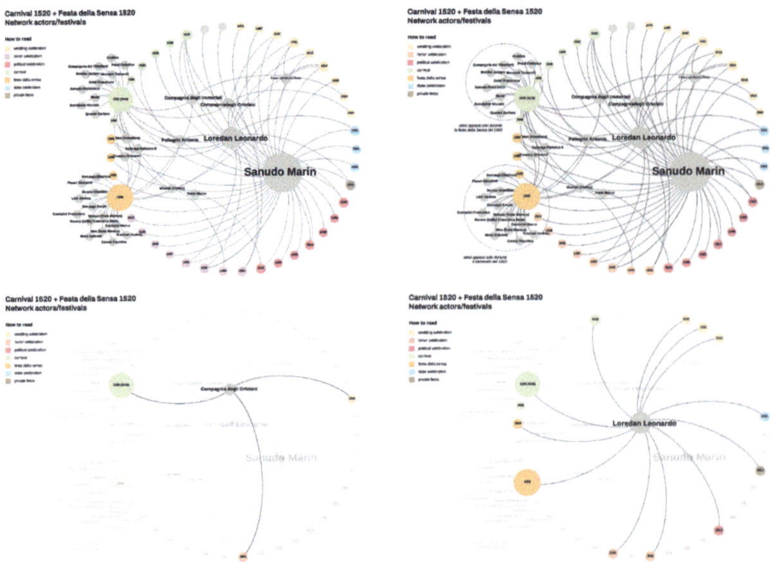

Figure 17.

Figures 16–17. An animation of network views describes a vibrant microcommunity of the *actors* (social subjects, performers, and patrons). In particular, for the Carnival and the Festa della Sensa in 1520, we compared and connected the social network of the actors active during these two events with other festive occasions, specifically over the governors of Venice, Loredan, and Gritti (Fig. 16). The user can identify a single actor and visualize his/her own activity/role in different events through a series of visual diagrams and dynamic network views, which will make visible a web of relationships and circuits of people, knowledge, and actions that are not always perceptible in an overview (Fig. 17). This investigation will reveal an increasing number of interconnections as we increase the number of festivals analyzed, and will also reveal hidden connections between individuals, communities, spaces, and types of the ceremonials that composed the festive program. See also Video 3 on the companion website.

Actors/Festivals and Themes—Focus on the Trojan Cycle

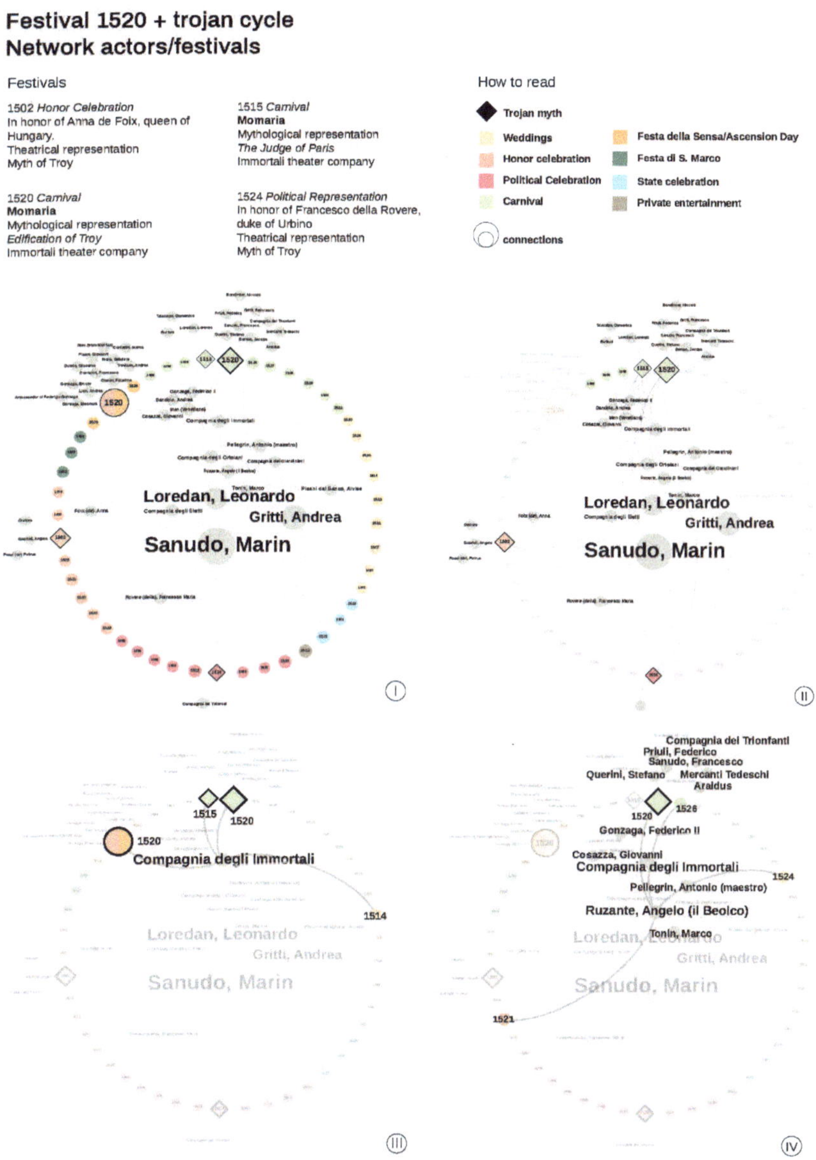

Figure 18.

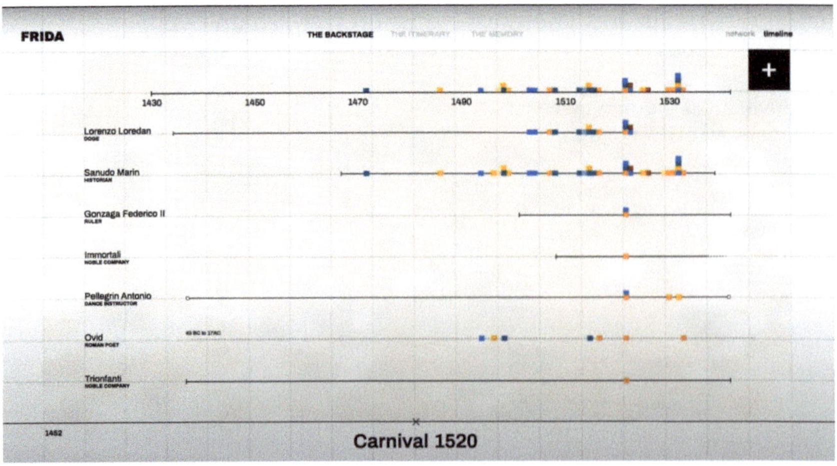

Figure 19.

Figures 18–19. The network diagrams identify the corpus of festivals based on the typology of events. In this case, the visual diagrams describe the theme of the Trojan cycle, relating the network of actors who contributed to four festivals (in 1502, 1515, 1520, and 1524) that used the Trojan myth as a dramaturgical core of the mythological staging (Fig. 18.1). It is possible to identify a single actor or group of actors and visualize their role in the selected events and investigate the connections between actors, themes, genre, and models (Fig. 18.2–4).

Multimedia Stories

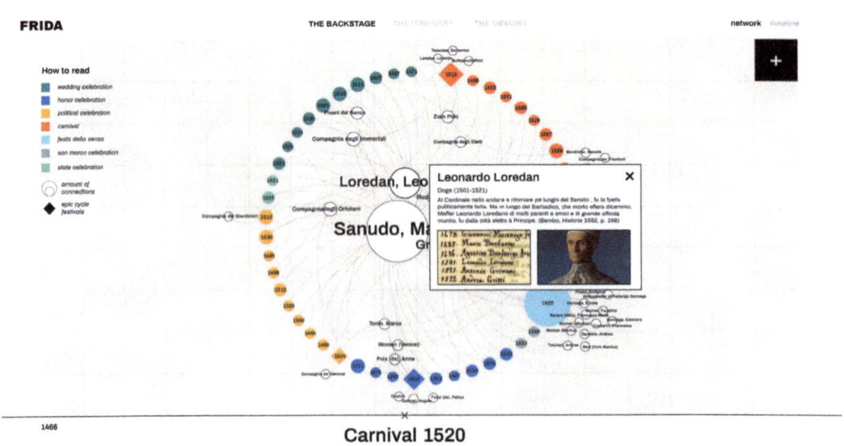

Figure 20.

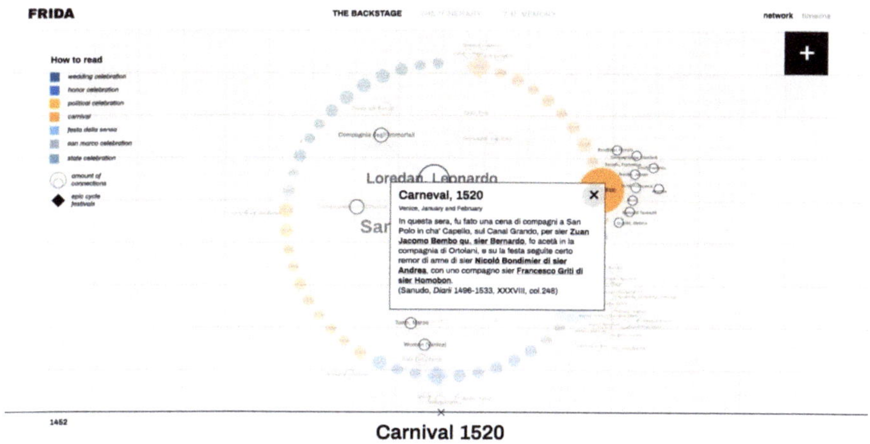

Figure 21.

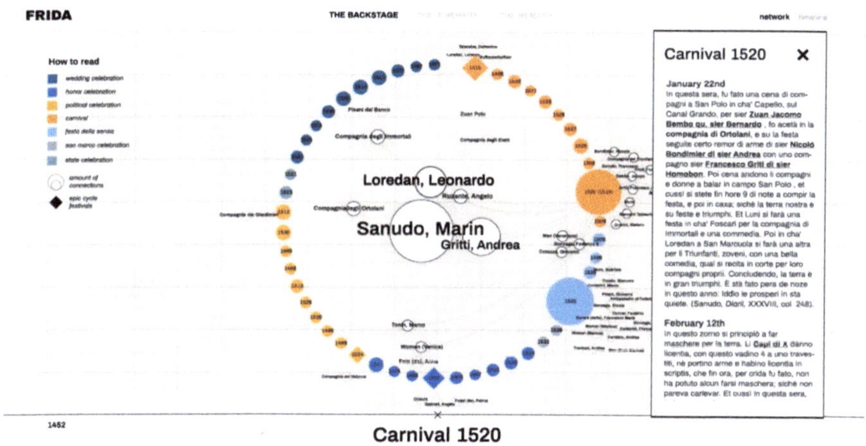

Figure 22.

Figures 20–22. Additional information about contributors (Fig. 20) and specific festival events (Figs. 21– 22) can be viewed by the user. Information includes short biographies, transcriptions of documents, and a selection of multimedia material. Information may also be viewed in a timeline format. This provides a chronological reference of both festivals and contributors. See also Video 4 on the companion site.

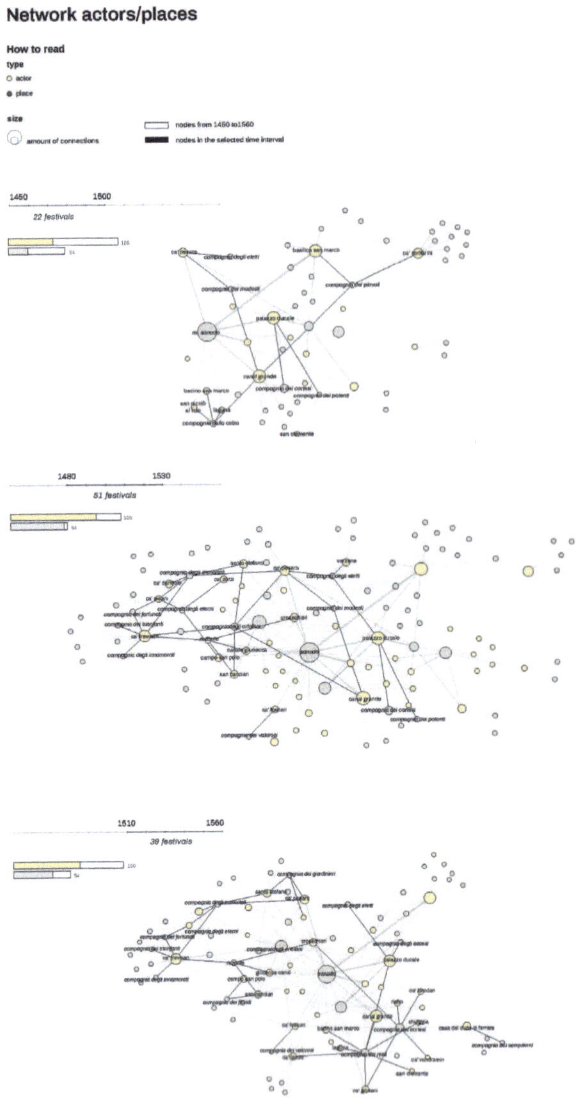

Figure 23. This visualization shows how the actor/places network has changed over time from 1450 to 1560. The visualization is composed of three views; each view focuses on a time frame of 50 years. The bar charts visualize the relation between the number of actors or places involved in the ceremonies of the selected intervals. In particular, the central time interval (1480–1530) is the most flourishing, indicating an increasing number of events and actors involved.

THE MEMORY

Cluster of Texts and Images

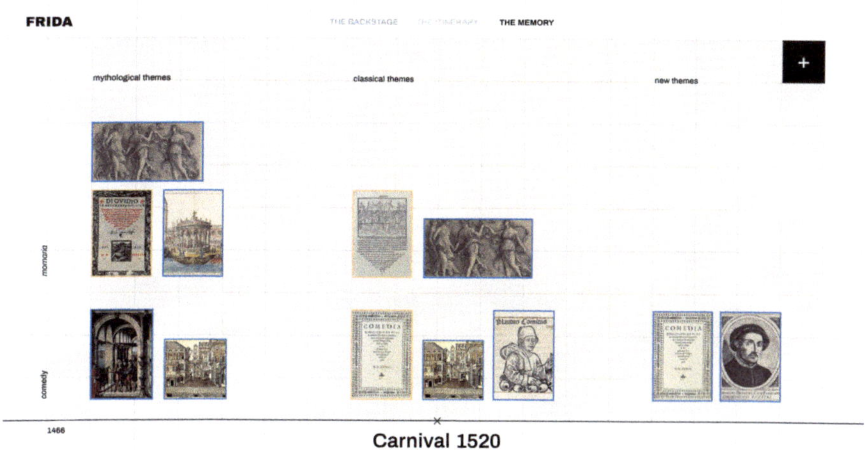

Figure 24.

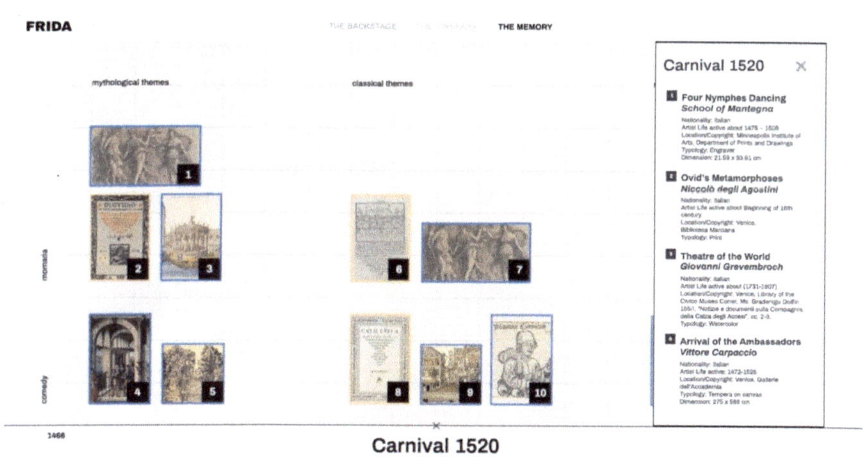

Figure 25.

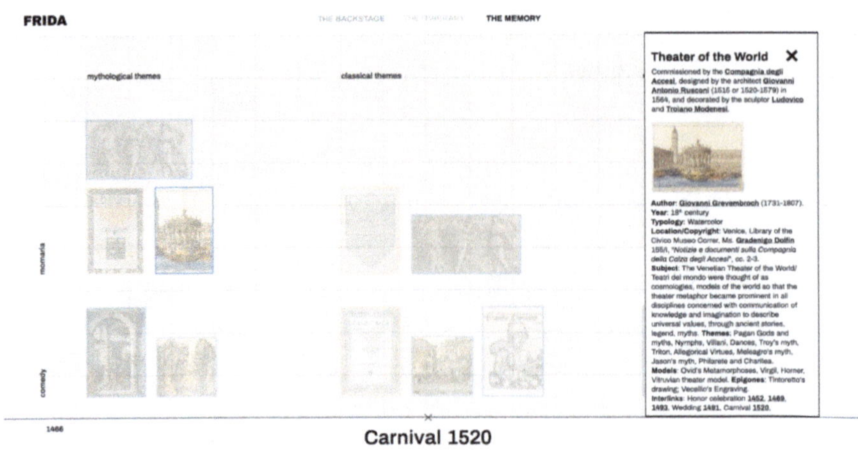

Figure 26.

Figures 24–26. A hierarchically organized thesaurus includes a series of keywords, tags, and subcategories that will compose the model of the datasheet for each artefact and a related interlinked system of visual associations (Fig. 24). Each sheet includes a detailed description of fine art (Figs. 25–26), written accounts, poetry, and music related to a specific festival. See also Videos 5 and 6 on the companion website.

Figure 27. Correr Library, Venice, Ms Gradenigo Dolfin 49, sixteenth century.

WORKS CITED

Bach, Benjamin, Mortitz Stefaner, Jeremy Boy, Steven Drucker, Lyn Bartram, Jo Wood, Paolo Ciuccarelli, Yuri Engelhardt, Ulrike Köppen, and Barbara Tversky. 2018. "Narrative Design Patterns for Data-Driven Storytelling." In *Data-Driven Storytelling*, edited by Nathalie Henry Riche, Christophe Hurter, Nicholas Diakopoulos, and Sheelagh Carpendale, 107–34. Boca Raton, FL: CRC Press. doi.org/10.1201/9781315281575.

Berry, David M., ed. 2012. *Understanding Digital Humanities*. New York: Palgrave Macmillan. doi.org/10.1057/9780230371934.

Bolzoni, Lina. 1995. *La stanza della memoria*. Turin: Einaudi.

Bortoletti, Francesca. 2008. *Egloga e spettacolo nel primo Rinascimento: Da Firenze alle corti*. Milan: Mimesis.

———. 2012. *L'attore del Parnaso*. Milan: Mimesis.

———. 2020. *I mestieri di Orfeo: Memoria, Politica e Teatro nel primo Rinascimento*. Milan: Mimesis.

Bortoletti, Francesca, Beatrice Gobbo, Tommaso Elli, Giuseppe Gerbino, and Paolo Ciuccarelli. 2018. "Venezia, la 'Festa Mobile': Per un Atlante in fieri." *La Rivista di Engramma* 160 (November): 47–88.

Bortoletti, Francesca, and Annalisa Sacchi. 2018. *La performance della memoria*. Bologna: Baskerville.

Branca, Vittore. 1983. "Momarie veneziane e 'Fabula di Orfeo.'" In *Poliziano e l'umanesimo della parola*, 55–72. Turin: Einaudi.

Brown, Patricia Fortini. 1988. *Venetian Narrative Painting in the Age of Carpaccio*. New Haven, CT: Yale University Press.

———. 1996. *Venice and Antiquity*. Cambridge: Cambridge University Press.

Burckhardt, Jacob. (1860) 2002. *The Civilization of the Renaissance in Italy*. London: Modern Library Classics.

Burdick, Anne, Johanna Drucker, Peter Lunenfeld, Todd Presner, and Jeffrey Schnapp, eds. 2012. *Digital Humanities*. Cambridge, MA: MIT Press.

Burdick, Anne, and Holly Willis. 2011. "Digital Learning, Digital Scholarship and Design Thinking." *Design Studies* 32, no. 6 (November): 546–56. doi.org/10.1016/j.destud.2011.07.005.

Carrai, Stefano. 1990. "Implicazioni cortigiane nell'Orfeo del Poliziano." *Rivista di Letteratura Italiana* 8:9–23.

Carruthers, Mary. 1990. *The Book of Memory: A Study of Memory in Medieval Culture*. Cambridge: Cambridge University Press. doi.org/10.1017/CBO9781107051126.

Casini, Matteo. 1996. *I gesti del principe: La festa politica a Firenze e Venezia in età rinascimentale*. Venice: Marsilio.

Caviglia, Giorgio, Paolo Ciuccarelli, and Nicole Coleman. 2012. "Communication Design and Digital Humanities: Visualizations and Interfaces for Humanities Research." Paper presented at the Fourth International Forum for Design as a Process, Belo Horizonte, Brazil, 19–22 September 2012.

Chastel, André. 1978. *Fables, Formes, Figures*. 2 vols. Paris: Flammarion.

Chiappini, Luciano. 1956. *Eleonora d'Aragona prima duchessa di Ferrara*. Rovigo: S.T.E.R.

Ciuccarelli, Paolo, and Tommaso Elli. 2019. "Beyond Visualization." In *Reassembling the Republic of Letters in the Digital Age: Standards, Systems, Scholarship*, edited by Howard Hotson and Thomas Wallnig, 299–314. Gottingen: Universitätsverlag Göttingen. doi.org/10.17875/gup2019-1146.

Crouzet-Pavan, Elisabeth. 1992. *"Sopra le acque salse": Espaces, pouvoirs et société à Venise à la fin du Moyen Age*. Rome: École française de Rome, Istituto storico italiano per il Medio Evo.

———. 1999. *Venise triomphante, les horizons d'un mythe*. Paris: Albin Michel.

Cruciani, Fabrizio. 1972. "Per lo studio del teatro Rinascimentale: La festa." *Biblioteca teatrale* 5:1–16.

———. 1983. *Teatro nel Rinascimento: Roma 1450–1550*. Rome: Bulzoni.

Cruciani, Fabrizio, Clelia Falletti, and Franco Ruffini. 1994. "La sperimentazione a Ferrara negli anni di Ercole I e di Ludovico Ariosto." *Teatro e storia* 16:131–217.

D'Ancona, Alessandro. (1877) 1891. *Origini del teatro italiano*. 2 vols. Turin: Loescher.

Decroisette, Françoise, and Michele Plaisance, eds. 1993. *Les fêtes urbaines en Italie à l'époque de la Renaissance: Verona, Florence, Siena, Naples*. Paris: Klincksieck, Presses de la Sorbonne nouvelle.

Didi-Huberman, Georges. 2004. "Knowledge: Movement." Foreword to *Aby Warburg and the Image in Motion*, by Philippe-Alain Michaud, 7–19. New York: MIT Press.

———. 2010. *Atlas: How to Carry the World on One's Back?* Madrid: Museo Nacional Centro de Arte Reina Sofía.

Dionisotti, Carlo. 1999. "Tradizione classica e volgarizzamenti." In *Geografia e storia della letteratura italiana*, 125–78. Turin: Einaudi.

Dolce, Lodovico. 1553. *Le Trasformationi*. Venice.

———. 1557. *Dialogo della pittura*. Venice: Gabriel Giolito de' Ferrari.

Donati, Andrea. 2014. "Sebastiano Zuccato." In *San Sebastiano: Bellezza e integrità nell'arte tra Quattrocento e Seicento*, edited by Antonio D'Amico and Vittorio Sgarbi, 34–37. Milan: Skira.

Drucker, Joanna. 2011. "Humanities Approach to Interface Theory." *Culture Machine* 12:1–20.

Fenlon, Iain. 2007. *The Ceremonial City: History, Memory and Myth in Renaissance Venice*. New Haven, CT: Yale University Press.

Freedberg, David. 1989. *The Power of Images: Studies in the History and Theory of Response*. Chicago: Chicago University Press.

Friedman, Ken. 2003. "Theory Construction in Design Research: Criteria: Approaches, and Methods." *Design Studies* 24, no. 6 (November): 507–22. doi.org/10.1016/S0142-694X(03)00039-5.

Foucault, Michel. 1982. *The Archeology of Knowledge*. New York: Pantheon.

Fuller, Matthew. 2008. *Software Studies*. Cambridge, MA: MIT Press.

Gallo, Franco Alberto. 1992. *Musica nel castello: Trovatori, libri, oratori nelle corti italiane dal XIII al XV secolo*. Bologna: Il Mulino.

Gerbino, Giuseppe. 2009. *Music and the Myth of Arcadia in Renaissance Italy*. Cambridge: Cambridge University Press.

Guarino, Raimondo, ed. 1988. *Teatro e culture della rappresentazione: Lo spettacolo in Italia nel Quattrocento*. Bologna: Il Mulino.

———. 1995. *Teatro e mutamenti: Rinascimento e spettacolo a Venezia*. Bologna: Il Mulino.

Guidobaldi, Nicoletta. 1995. *La musica di Federico: Immagini e suoni alla corte di Urbino*. Florence: Olschki.

Guthmüller, Bodo. 1997. *Mito, poesia, arte: Saggi sulla tradizione ovidiana nel Rinascimento*. Rome: Buzoni.

———. 2008. *Ovidio Metamorphoseos vulgare*. Fiesole: Cadmo.

Infelise, Mario. 2016. "Aldo Manuzio tra storia e bibliofilia." In *Aldo Manuzio: La costruzione del mito*, edited by Mario Infelise, 9–22. Venice: Marsilio.

Jacquot, Jean, ed. 1956. *Les fêtes de la Renaissance*. Paris: Centre National de la Recherche Scientifique.

Labalme, Patricia H., and Laura Sanguineti White, eds. 2008. *Venice, Cità Excelentissima: Selections from the Renaissance Diaries of Marin Sanudo*. Translated by Linda L. Carroll. Baltimore: Johns Hopkins University Press.

Lockwood, Lewis. 2009. *Music in Renaissance Ferrara 1400–1505: The Creation of a Musical Center in the Fifteenth Century*. Oxford: Oxford University Press. doi.org/10.1093/acprof:oso/9780195378276.001.0001.

Luzio, Alessandro, and Rodolfo Renier. 1890. *Delle relazioni di Isabella d'Este Gonzaga con Ludovico e Beatrice Sforza*. Milan: G. Prato.

Matino, Gabriele. 2017. "Il ciclo dell'Albergo della Scuola Grande di San Marco: Una nuova prospettiva." In *La Scuola Grande di San Marco a Venezia*, edited by Gherardo Ortalli and Salvatore Settis, 117–33. Vol. 1. Modena: Panini.

Mauri, Michele, and Paolo Ciuccarelli. 2016. "Designing Diagrams for Social Issues." In *Proceedings of DRS2016: Design + Research + Society - Future-Focused Thinking*, edited by Peter Lloyd and Erik Bohemia, 941–56. Vol. 3. Brighton: University of Brighton.

McGann, Jerome, and Lisa Samuels. 2004. "Deformance and Interpretation." In *Radiant Textuality*, 105–36. New York: Palgrave Macmillan.

McGowan, Margaret 1973. *Renaissance Triumphs and Magnificence*. London: Routledge.

Mitchell, Bonner. 1979. *Italian Civic Pageantry in the High Renaissance*. Florence: Olschki.

———. 1986. *The Majesty of the State*. Florence: Olschki.

Molmenti, Pompeo. 1880. *La storia di Venezia nella vita privata dalle origini alla caduta della repubblica*. Turin: Roux e Favale.

Moretti, Franco. 2005. *Graphs, Maps, Trees: Abstract Models for a Literary Theory*. London: Verso.

Muir, Edward. 1981. *Civic Ritual in Renaissance Venice*. Princeton, NJ: Princeton University Press.

Mulryne, James Ronald, Maria Ines Aliverti, and Anna Maria Testaverde, eds. 2015. *Ceremonial Entries in Early Modern Europe: The Iconography of Power*. London: Routledge. doi.org/10.4324/9781315571140.

Mulryne, James Ronald, and Elizabeth Goldring. 2002. *Court Festivals of the European Renaissance: Art, Politics and Performance*. London: Routledge. doi.org/10.4324/9781315259086.

Mulryne, James Ronald, Helen Watanabe-O'Kelly, Margaret Shewring, Elizabeth Goldring, and Sarah Knight, eds. 2004. *Europa Triumphans: Court and Civic Festivals in Early Modern Europe*. London: Ashgate.

Muraro, Maria Teresa. 2004. *Scena e Messinscena*. Venice. Fondazione Cini.

Ohrt, Roberto, and Axel Heil, eds. 2020. *Aby Warburg: Bilderatlas Mnemosyne—The Original*. Berlin: Hatje Cantz.

Padoan, Giorgio. 1978. *Momenti del Rinascimento veneto*. Padua: Antenore.

Pieri, Marzia. 1983. *La scena boschereccia nel Rinascimento italiano*. Padua: Liviana.

Plaisance, Michele. 2008. *Fêtes, spectacles et politique à l'époque de la Renaissance*. Manziana: Vecchiarelli.

Pope, Rob. 1995. *Textual Intervention: Critical and Creative Strategies for Literary Studies*. London: Routledge.

Povoledo, Elena. (1969) 1975. "Origini e aspetti della scenografia in Italia: Dalla fine del Quattrocento agli intermezzi fiorentini del 1589." In *Li due Orfei: Da Poliziano a Monteverdi* by Nina Pirrotta, 337–460. Turin: Einaudi.

Praz, Mario. 1971. *Mnemosine: Parallelo tra letteratura e le arti visive*. Milan: Mondadori.

Puppi, Lionello. 1980. *Architettura e utopia nella Venezia del Cinquecento*. Milan: Electa.

Ruecker, Stan, Milena Radzikowska, and Stefan Sinclair. 2011. *Visual Interface Design for Digital Cultural Heritage: A Guide to Rich-Prospect Browsing*. London: Ashgate. doi.org/10.4324/9781315547961.

Sabellico, Marco Antonio. 1502. *Opera Mar. Ant. Sabellici*. Venice: Albertinum de Lisona Vercellensem.

Salzberg, Rosa. 2014. *Ephemeral City: Cheap Print and Urban Culture in Renaissance Venice*. Manchester: Manchester University Press. doi.org/10.7228/manchester/9780719087035.001.0001.

Sansovino, Francesco. 1581. *Venetia città nobilissima et singolare* [. . .]. Venice: Jacopo Sansovino.

Sanudo, Marino. 1879–1903. *I Diarii di Marino Sanuto*. Edited by Federico Stefani, Nicolò Barozzi, Rinaldo Fulin, and Guglielmo Berchet. 58 vols. Venice: Fratelli Visentini.

Settis, Salvatore. 1986. "Continuità, distanza, conoscenza: Tre usi dell'antico." In *Memoria dell'antico nell'arte italiana*, 373–486. Vol. 3, *Dalla tradizione all'archeologia*. Turin: Einaudi.

Strong, Roy. 1984. *Art and Power: Renaissance Festival, 1450–1650*. Berkeley: University of California Press.

Tafuri, Manfredo. 1992. *Ricerca del Rinascimento: Principi, città, architetti*. Turin: Einaudi.

Tissoni Benvenuti, Antonia, and Maria Pia Mussini Sacchi, eds. 1983. *Teatro del Quattrocento: Le corti padane*. Turin: Unione Tiografico-Editrice Torinese.

Trexler, Richard C. 1980. *Public Life in Renaissance Florence*. Ithaca, NY: Cornell University Press.

Uboldi, Giorgio, Giorgio Caviglia, Nicole Coleman, Sébastien Mantegari, Glauco Heyman, and Paolo Ciuccarelli. 2013. "Knot: An Interface for the Study of Social Networks in the Humanities." *ACM* 15:1–9.

Ugolini, Francesco. 1933. *I cantari di argomento classico*. Florence: Olschki.

Urban, Lina. 1966. "Teatri e 'teatri del mondo' nella Venezia del Cinquecento." *Arte Veneta* 20:137–46.

———. 1968. "La festa della Sensa nelle arti e nell'iconografia." *Studi veneziani* 10:291–353.

———. 1969. "Apparati scenografici nelle feste veneziane cinquecentesche." *Arte Veneta* 23:145–55.

———. 1988. *Il Bucintoro. La festa e la fiera della "Sensa" dalle origini alle caduta della Repubblica*. Venice: Centro Internazionale della Grafica di Venezia.

Ventrone, Paola. 1992. *Le Temps revient—Il tempo si rinnova: Feste e spettacoli nella Firenze di Lorenzo il Magnifico*. Milan: Silvana.

———. 2013. "Simbologia e funzione delle feste identitarie in alcune città italiane fra XIII e XV secolo." *Teatro e Storia* 34:285–310.

———. 2016. *Teatro civile e sacra rappresentazione a Firenze nel Rinascimento*. Florence: Le Lettere.

Venturi, Lionello. (1909) 1983. *Le Compagnie della Calza: Sec. XV–XVI*. Venice: Filippi Editore.

Vescovo, Piermario. 1996. *Da Ruzante a Calmo: Tra "signore commedie" e "onorandissime stampe."* Padua: Antenore.

———. 2005. "Il teatro del Rinascimento: Il mito e la favola cortigiana." In *Il mito nella letteratura italiana*, edited by P. Gibellini, 535–51. Vol. 1, *Dal Medioevo al Rinascimento*. Brescia: Morcelliana.

———. 2016. "Terentius cum figuris (preliminari a una ricerca)." *Drammaturgia* 13 (3): 313–46. doi.org/10.13128/Drammaturgia-22041.

Warburg, Aby. (1932) 2004–8. *The Renewal of Pagan Antiquity*. Los Angeles: Getty Research Institute.

Yates, Francis Amelia. 1959. *The Valois Tapestries*. London: Warburg Institute.

Zorzi, Ludovico. 1977. *Il teatro e la città: Saggi sulla scena italiana*. Turin: Einaudi.

Zorzi, Marino. 1996. "Dal manoscritto al libro." In *Storia di Venezia: Dalle origini alla caduta della Serenissima*, edited by Alberto Tenenti and Ugo Tucci, 817–958. Vol. 4, *Il Rinascimento: Politica e cultura*. Rome: Istituto dell'Enciclopedia Italiana.

Chapter 8:
"Dear Galileo": Letters as Data on Astronomy

Caterina Agostini
Indiana University Bloomington

Galileo Galilei (1564–1642) wrote books wherein he described his scientific discoveries, the motions of celestial bodies, and the structure of the universe. In addition to publishing books, he exchanged numerous letters on scientific topics with scholars, scientists, and artists. Thousands of letters, to and from Galileo, have been included in volumes 10–18 of the Italian edition of Galileo's collected works, *Le opere di Galileo Galilei*, edited by Antonio Favaro (Galileo 1890–1909, hereafter *OG*) and recently digitized by Museo Galileo (bibdig.museogalileo.it/Teca/Viewer?an=328457). Though not all the correspondence is published in Favaro's edition, or even extant, the high volume of letters documented in the Italian national edition, and now available in a digital format, invites further investigation into early modern scientific writing in Italy through the medium of correspondence. Science in Italian history and public memory has come to the fore in recent years, especially with the rise of new digital projects such as Mapping the Republic of Letters (republicofletters.stanford.edu), which tracks letters by famous thinkers and scientists in Europe (see Midura 2019); in that context, Paula Findlen and Hannah Marcus examined Galileo's correspondence in relation to networks of intellectuals (republicofletters.stanford.edu/casestudies/galileo.html). My project develops thematic directions in geospatial information through a thematic layer, the topic of astronomy, and for letters addressed to one person: Galileo.[1]

When I surveyed letters sent to Galileo, I found that he received over 2,700 letters discussing astronomy from 1588 to 1642. Given this high volume of letters, epistolary communication is clearly an important means to study

[1] On the use of geospatial technologies in the humanities, Patricia Murrieta-Flores and Bruno Martins (2019, 424) have recently commented that "(a)lthough technologies such as Geographic Information Systems have been used in Humanities fields such as Archaeology for over four decades, it has been only in recent years that the development of new technologies and methods have led to the emergence of the field that is now more commonly known as the Spatial Humanities, often also referred to as GeoHumanities." See also El Khatib and Schaeben 2020.

ISBN 978-1-64959-119-7 (paper) ISBN 978-1-64959-120-3 (pdf) ISBN 978-1-64959-121-0 (epub)
New Technologies in Medieval and Renaissance Studies 12 (2025) 197–226

where Galileo's scientific ideas on astronomy circulated beyond the official publication of his books. Computational tools in geospatial digital humanities have helped me select and build a database of letters information, and this chapter will discuss letters as data in astronomy, and digital maps as the medium to integrate Galileo's correspondence within early modern scientific knowledge.[2] My digital project, "Dear Galileo": Letters as Data on Astronomy, intends to map places from which letters on astronomical topics were addressed to Galileo. This digital project maps letters sent to Galileo with the goal of understanding the impact and influence he exerted through his correspondents in Italy and in the international scene. Since I chose to build a dataset emphasizing themes and places as the key features of correspondence, representing those locations on a digital map serves as the spatial anchor to the varying locations in which Galileo's correspondents lived and traveled. There seems to be a wide geographic distribution in Italy and Europe, thus complementing historical information on the circumstances in which Galileo and his correspondents found themselves, with most mail coming from the Italian peninsula and occasional mail addressed to Galileo from Asia and Africa. Digital maps have not been used to visualize this correspondence information in such detail before. Among Galileo's correspondents, 11 were women: his daughter, Sister Maria Celeste Galilei, and other family members and friends; artists Artemisia Gentileschi and Anna Maria Vaiani; poet Margherita Sarrocchi (Ray 2016); and Caterina Riccardi Niccolini, the Florentine ambassador's wife and sister to the Roman censor. By concentrating on the places from which letters were sent, new information is added to help understand the scientist's international network, with the related geospatial information revealing how far Galileo's books and ideas circulated in both his native Tuscany and internationally in the years in which he actively worked on astronomy.

In this project, digital geographic perspectives benefit from a timespan of over 50 years, a *longue durée*, which the French Annales school argued was necessary to understand and discuss historical events (Braudel 1980, 25–33). First, I address methods and the implications of representing humanistic

[2] I presented part of the current study at the New Technologies and Renaissance Studies panel organized by ITER: Gateway to the Middle Ages and Renaissance. The panel was held online after the Renaissance Society of America conference was canceled in April 2020. For my presentation, titled "Before the Eclipse: Corresponding with Galileo Galilei on the Topic of Astronomy," I am very grateful to the Ms. Elena Petronio Scholarship, Rutgers Digital Humanities Initiative and Lab, and Rutgers University Libraries and Rutgers Rare Books and Special Collections.

data in digital formats. Then, I examine astronomical observations from Galileo's correspondence in order to discuss the role of local and international correspondents in Galileo's research and writing process in the difficult circumstances of the Inquisition trial against him and during his house arrests. Such perspectives contribute to understanding scientific debates before unanimous theories on astronomy were determined.

Visualizing Digital Data through Maps

Visualizing the places mentioned throughout a corpus has been proven as a method in the digital humanities with digital cartography. There are several digital tools for map visualizations that can benefit humanistic inquiries. A web-based tool readily available to humanists is Palladio (hdlab.stanford.edu/palladio), developed by the Humanities + Design research lab at Stanford University for scholars to investigate and visualize multidimensional data.[3] There was no available dataset for Galileo's correspondence, so I annotated the volumes in the Favaro edition of Galileo's collected works manually in order to transfer information on correspondence into digital formats. Data collection for this project involved various considerations, the result of which is my dataset structured around geographic information by correspondents, with the dates and locations for all letters and additional bibliographic information from the Favaro edition of *Le opere di Galileo Galilei*. Letters are central, textual items to study in this project, thus confirming David Wrisley's (2017, 151) views that "(a) text-centered approach to mapping means that the locatable places can be compared visually on a digital map interface as a way of performing a 'spatial reading' of those texts—alone, comparatively, or in the aggregate." To develop my project, I transcribed geographic information contained in each letter discussing astronomy in the corpus of letters written to Galileo, entering those details in a spreadsheet so as to have the information organized into a tabular form that is machine-readable.

Exploring letters as texts and data on astronomy from a geographical perspective is a valuable practice, adding to previous textual, literary, and historical interpretations by contextualizing a study of the letters themselves and the historical circumstances of their production, communication, and circulation through copies. By looking at Galileo's corpus of letters, one can find out from where correspondents wrote; their institutional affiliations; their cultural, religious, or political beliefs; their scientific education; and how far back their support of Galileo went. Additionally, it is possible to

[3] For historical gazetteers, data organization, and application in case studies, see World Historical Gazetteer (whgazetteer.org); Southall, Mostern, and Berman 2011.

notice changes in letter frequency after the 1633 Inquisition trial, which in terms of literary expression corresponds to open, as opposed to secretive, communication, thus confirming insights that Marcus and Findlen (2019) have shown through the analysis of cryptographic techniques used by Galileo and his correspondents to maintain epistolary communication. The present study examines where, when (before and after the Inquisition trial), and how often locations are mentioned in the collection of Galileo's correspondence with 370 individuals interested in scientific topics, in particular astronomy. The number of people involved in a cultural phenomenon, the connections among them, and the degrees of connection are all relevant factors to consider in collective cultural enterprises, as was the case for the French Enlightenment encyclopedia in what Melanie Conroy (2017) considered to be "knowledge networks." When Galileo wrote letters, it was from Pisa, Padua, Venice, Florence, and the nearby towns of Arcetri and Bellosguardo where he lived and worked. Furthermore, having such a set of geospatial information integrates with the knowledge we have about where Galileo published his books: Venice and its mainland university at Padua, but also Florence, Rome, and Leiden, where prestigious universities advanced scientific knowledge, thus showing epistolary communication to be more frequent within higher education areas in the European scientific community.

Visual representations of the dataset through Palladio allow one to select spatiotemporal and multivariate data through the digital map and the underlying facet, timeline, and timespan filters. At the geospatial level, visualizations of the letters' locations are circles of varying dimensions based on the number of letters sent from each location. The resulting digital map on Palladio is thus based on underlying concepts of centrality and eccentricity and shows associations and peculiarities through points on a map, in this case representing the locations of all 370 correspondents (Fig. 1).

The process behind building the dataset involves tracking the name of the locale where a letter was written (e.g., Florence, Prague) as part of the context for that letter, as well as compiling information regarding material aspects of the letter, usually found on the back of the envelope and in a letter's opening lines. By choosing to include such geographic information as textual and material evidence of correspondents' whereabouts, an implicit statement exists—no falsification occurred about the locations where letters were written, so that we assume no one writing to Galileo would have pretended to be elsewhere. For those reasons, mapping place-names supplies a view of Galileo's letters that privileges his correspondents as people who were determined to start, and maintain, a conversation with the scientist.

Figure 1. A map visualization of the locations from where people wrote to Galileo, with points proportionally sized based on the numbers of letters sent locally. Therefore, more letters sent from a location correspond to a bigger dot, for a total of 2,700 letters written by 370 correspondents discussing astronomy from 1588 to 1642; 11 of those correspondents were women. In a further development of this project, I intend to also trace distance between sender and recipient, so that letters sent locally are marked visually. Letters traveling a greater distance after the Inquisition trial and Copernican ban would have faced greater challenges, and those instances highlight the present digital project beyond mapping and network visualization goals.

When I prepared digital datasets transcribing geographic information contained in the corpus of letters written to Galileo, I entered those details into a spreadsheet so that I could have the information organized in a tabular form that is machine-readable.[4] The tabular form thus contains data structured so that the information can be converted into machine-readable formats, starting with Pelagios Recogito (recogito.pelagios.org), an exploratory tool for digital mapping and annotation that converts place-names (toponyms)

[4] Working with digital media informs and impacts the "data culture" and deriving knowledge systems, so that the control of information flows and the "differentiation" of media and ideas inform a "cultural geography" (Gitelman 2014, 9, 12, 19).

and textual descriptions of places into geographic identifiers, namely coordinates with latitude and longitude (geocoding) to research the location of each place and the corresponding latitudes and longitudes using decimal GPS coordinates. The places in the database, then, are associated with present-day locations, keeping older city names and variants. Recogito allows users to annotate texts and maps and to visualize geographic information through linked, built-in Recogito digital gazetteers, so that locations and geographic points are matched automatically and can be checked later for accuracy. What follows is a screenshot of one visualization generated from the exploration of project data on a digital map via Recogito (Fig. 2). The map displays the points to express a geographic representation for a gazetteer of early modern places accurate for Galileo's lifetime in ways that allow viewers to access the map.[5] This might help us understand the data better and reevaluate the assumption that people wrote regularly to Galileo at all times, when in fact correspondence was actually more frequent around the time of his discoveries with the telescope, shortly before and after the publication of his books, and during the Inquisition trial.

Figure 2. An exploratory map visualization of the areas from where people wrote to Galileo. Galileo lived in Pisa, Florence, the neighboring small towns of Bellosguardo and Arcetri, and Padua.

[5] See the dataset here: drive.google.com/drive/folders/1Z16_lGtTGqdbF54lUKWCY-uzE7bf1feHa?usp=sharing.

Map visualizations serve as the starting point for new considerations of how locales were distributed in the early modern period for the circulation of scientific ideas. Features of space for modern cartography cannot be fully captured and recreated on early modern maps, where naming conventions and state borders change within the historical time for this project, so I chose not to use georeferenced base maps, for which digital images have been rectified to align with GPS coordinates. As Øyvind Eide (2015) argued, geographic and textual information are not interchangeable, and though their contents refer to the same entities in the natural world, georeferencing decisions need to be thoughtful because their information modes differ. Thus, digital maps visualize geographical information on a physical map or, alternatively, on an aerial view or urban grid to complement the texts of letters sent to Galileo, not to replace the type of humanistic information found in them.

The social network of 370 correspondents in Galileo's letters on astronomy ranges from writers, artists, and scholars who participated in the editing and publishing process of Galileo's most influential books, to personal friends and family members. Specific locations are known for some correspondents, so that it is possible to pinpoint the precise address of some noble families, for example, whose houses are part of the cultural heritage; such is the case for Federico Cesi's family residence and palazzo in Acquasparta, a small town in the province of Terni today, and for cultural institutions such as the Accademia dei Lincei that Cesi founded in Rome. Specific locations are available, as well, for the Collegio Romano and Jesuit schools in Rome and throughout Europe. Other certain addresses are also given for people who lived in convents and for Venetian and Medici state representatives. It is not possible, however, to know a specific address for most people writing to Galileo.

An exploratory map via Recogito shows all the identifiable place-names for letters written in Italy, Europe, Asia, and Africa (Fig. 3). The points on the map mark over 100 locations named on the headers of the letters. Map visualizations, like the one presented here, show some patterns. This map allows us to identify the dominance of Rome as a main center of discussion of Galileo's ideas for scientists, politicians, artists, and enthusiasts; it also calls attention to outliers like Aleppo, Vilnius, and the general unspecified area of Morocco. The map's greatest value is in quickly and easily identifying concurrent centers of astronomical discussions such as Venice (384), Florence (271), and Pisa (186) in a panoramic view that complements the tabular dataset.

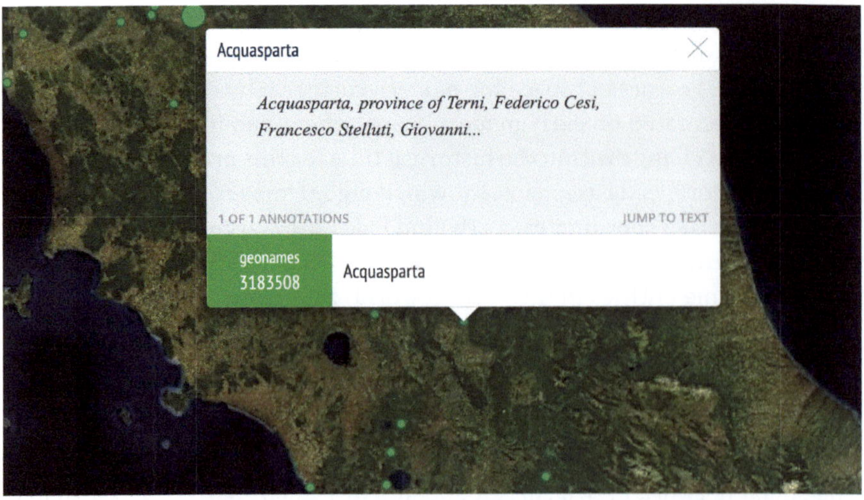

Figure 3. A detail of the Recogito map visualization, zooming in on the location of Acquasparta, where Prince Federico Cesi's villa was located, and where he gathered scholars belonging to the Accademia dei Lincei that he had founded and sponsored.

A place-name, however, usually appears more than once, except for approximately 50 locales from where Galileo received only one letter. The base map is shown in the "basic" layer, which provides terrain features. The very small circles on the Palladio and Recogito map visualizations represent only one or two individuals, and the largest circle represents Rome, with a total of 755 letters. In my dataset, correspondents are listed with basic demographic information (name, city, letter dates, gender, approval or disapproval of Galileo's ideas, and occupation as a scientist, philosopher, writer, politician, religious official, or artist); also listed are individuals' affiliations with cultural institutions, religious orders, political positions, and figurative arts based on the various places where they wrote letters (Fig. 4).

A	B	C	D	E	F	G	H	I	J	K	L	M	N	O	P
Recipient	Sender	City	Date	Volume and pages	approval	POL	REL	ART	SCI	PHIL	WRIT	Topic	Non-Italian L	Volume	Years
Galileo	Christopher Clavius	Rome	16/01/1588	24	Y	N	N	N	Y	N	Y	astronomy	Latin	10	1574-1610

Figure 4. An entry in the dataset of Galileo's correspondence, with an item from a Jesuit scholar, Christopher Clavius, writing from Rome.

As shown in the tabular form of my dataset, I found the number of occurrences of each location and each correspondent, so on map visualizations, locations are shown in the form of smaller or bigger points, reflecting quantities associated with a particular place, for example, quantities of correspondents. For Palladio map visualizations, a column containing geocoordinates of latitude and longitude was also needed ("LatLong"). In all but two of letters examined, specific locales are mentioned; one exception is found in a letter of Gianfrancesco Sagredo, which only names a larger region, the country Morocco, and in another case, the name of a villa, "Dalle Rose," is given, which cannot be connected to a specific geographic location. Having unidentified data confirms the process of collecting the names of correspondents and geospatial information from each letter, including variations in the spelling, followed by an electronic search through the textual data.

Since we know the location of origin for all but two of the letters from the 370 correspondents, we can conclude that letters sent from Rome represent one-third of the known letter locations. This sort of visualization allows us to quickly see which people moved to Rome or out of Rome, such as in the case of Giovanni Ciampoli, who was sent away from Rome to some small towns in the Marche region in central Italy when Pope Urban VIII punished him for his support of Galileo after the *Dialogue Concerning the Two Chief World Systems* was published in 1632. Other areas with more people writing were connected to academies, and in Acquasparta we find an early meeting place for the Accademia dei Lincei, a scientific institution that supported the work of Galileo. This information is facilitated by or only made understandable through the Dear Galileo project, where users encounter the map and can parse the information mapped. The data can be manipulated with other filters, such as time and author, from the dataset or the visualization alike.

In Europe, cities associated with political and cultural institutions appear, such as in the case of Alfonso Antonini, a patron of the arts and military at the service of the Venetian Republic who appears closely associated with the United Provinces of the Low Countries. There are, however, clusters where several correspondents wrote, as did astronomers Johannes Kepler, Thomas Seget, and Martin Hasdale, and diplomats Giuliano de' Medici, Giovanni Pieroni, and Giovanni Marco Marci from Prague. But the cultural dominance of Rome, Venice, and Florence among this majority group is further seen in that only a few correspondents wrote from other areas in Europe, or from Asia and Africa. Gianfrancesco Sagredo is one notable example, writing from Venice and the family properties in Veneto and adjacent regions, but also from his political posts in Palmanova, Aleppo, and Morocco. Thanks to his international connections, Sagredo managed to collect and compare astronomical times at various longitudes (*OG* 11:524–25).[6] When hostilities

[6] Their friendship also became an inspiration to the fictional settings for two of

escalated between Venice and the Vatican, and Pope Paul V issued the Venetian Interdict in 1606, Sagredo was appointed treasurer of the fortress of Palmanova in Friuli. When the Interdict was revoked in April 1607, Sagredo returned to Venice and was appointed consul in Syria later that year, in November. Once Sagredo returned to Venice, however, Galileo had already left his position at the University of Padua and moved to Florence. The two friends only communicated through letters afterwards, and they exchanged portraits in June 1619. While Sagredo's correspondence was connected to his political appointments, Leiden is an example of a city connected to friends and friends of friends. Leiden entered the circuit of Galileo's correspondence through Elias Diodati, a scholar from an Italian Calvinist family residing in Geneva. Diodati wished for Galileo's books to be published abroad in mainland Europe in a city unconnected to Rome and the Vatican, and the Elzevirs became the printing press that would publish his new books after the Inquisition trial.

Based on the dataset I built, network diagrams are applicable visualizations to display connections among correspondents, however, for the scope of the current investigation, the recipient is Galileo, across Pisa, Padua, Florence, and a few other locations where he was transitioning. There are no significant examples of people, in that era or location, who would have had access to other channels and modes of communication, but digital humanities methods might open up new perspectives in that regard. In a network diagram, nodes and edges would represent scholars and correspondence, since Galileo is the main connection of the correspondence on the topic of astronomy, and given that he was both the letters' recipient and the inspirer of new astronomical knowledge and discussions. Expanding the directions of early modern science scholarship would enhance insights to a network of correspondents who were or were not all connected one to the other.

Astronomical Observations, Books, and Letters

One benefit of having digital maps is the ability to showcase geographic information from Galileo's correspondents, thus selecting specific aspects in

---

Galileo's books: the *Dialogue Concerning the Two Chief World Systems* (1632) and the *Two New Sciences* (1638), both of which cast Sagredo as a leading character in the fictional dialogue presenting scientific treatises on astronomy and mechanics, respectively. Sagredo was such a good friend that his portrait, currently in the Ashmolean Museum, used to be in Galileo's rooms while he wrote the *Dialogue* and *Two New Sciences*. The *Dialogue* was set in Sagredo's house, now the Palazzo Morosini Sagredo in Venice (Wilding 2014, 6–19).

the dataset to visualize them geographically. Communication that occurred through correspondence completes the scientific information that Galileo shared in his books, all of which were very successful. Beginning in 1609, Galileo used a new instrument, the telescope, to observe the night sky, and he discussed anomalies about the Moon and the planets Jupiter, Venus, and Saturn in the book *Sidereus Nuncius*, or *Starry Messenger*, first published in 1610.[7] The position of the Sun in the solar system and the Sun's irregular surface were the topic of three letters that Galileo published in *Istoria e dimostrazioni intorno alle macchie solari e loro accidenti*, or *Letters on Sunspots* (1613), in response to Mark Scheiner's three letters sent to him on sunspots in 1611. Later, Galileo discussed comets as temporary, transient phenomena in *Il saggiatore*, or *The Assayer* (1623), and the Earth's motions, tides, and Copernican theories were leading topics in *Dialogo sopra i due massimi sistemi del mondo*, or *Dialogue Concerning the Two Chief World Systems* (1632). But in stating that the Earth is not the center of the universe, Galileo ran into problems of compatibility between scientific beliefs and Catholic doctrines.

Such controversies led to discussions and letters exchanged between the Jesuits conducting leading research and patrons supporting Galileo at the Republic of Venice and, later, the Medici family. Correspondence was a fundamental medium to communicate in the early modern period, and Galileo exchanged ideas regularly with scholars, artists, and scientists, near and far, by letter. The Dear Galileo project is a geospatial investigation that visualizes correspondence on astronomy, a topic which was initially allowed, then limited in 1616, and then forbidden after the Inquisition trial against Galileo in 1633.[8] For Galileo, correspondence became as important as his published

[7] An Italian translation of *Sidereus Nuncius* was commissioned and published later. Illustrations and diagrams accompanied the text of *Sidereus Nuncius* to help readers understand what one could see through a telescope, since media "muddy the map. Like old art, old media remain meaningful" (Gitelman 2014, 4). Observational astronomy through the telescope confirmed Galileo's use of the instrument as a medium and inspired his correspondents' use of the telescope as well. As Gitelman (2014, 2) has maintained, the telescope "is a medium. It doesn't squint around on its own except in a metaphoric sense; it mediates between our eyes and the sites of space that it helps us to experience as sights."

[8] Having access to current astronomical books and instruments such as telescopes confirms Gitelman's (2014, 5) theories that "one helpful way to think of media may be as the scientific instruments of a society at large. Since the late seventeenth century, scientific instruments have emerged as matters of consensus within a community of like-minded and fairly well-to-do people, eventually called scientists. If one scientist

books, because letters complemented his published writings to validate and improve scientific arguments and theories. The locational information about correspondence addressed to Galileo is significant in that it demonstrates who reached out to him and who kept communicating with him—a pressing cultural concern considering the import and consequences of the Inquisition trial, when Galileo was tried and forced to recant his theories in June 1633. The letters that Galileo wrote, on the other hand, invite editorial and stylistic research for scholars, given the high incidence of edits, drafts, and multiple versions of the letters that he intentionally wrote and circulated. Some letters in Galileo's correspondence were intended to address a wider readership, such as the so-called Copernican letters that Galileo wrote to Piero Dini, Father Benedetto Castelli, and the Grand Duchess Christina of Lorraine between 1612 and 1615; the main topic in those letters is the discussion of Copernican concepts. Philological attention to editorial notes in letters has profound implications, especially when letters would be written to their addressees but also transcribed and copied for a wider audience, the equivalent of modern-day journal publications.[9]

In 1613, Galileo wrote a controversial letter to Father Benedetto Castelli, a mathematician and Galileo's former student, that would spark many astronomical controversies on what pertains to the Book of Nature and the Bible (Fig. 5). He made two different copies of that letter, with the proper, "safe" version being transcribed and circulated independently for a wider audience (Abbott 2018). As a result of Galileo's two copies of the letter to Father Castelli, we now have two versions containing different information for different readerships. One version was safely edited for the Inquisition at Rome and circulated in more than a dozen copies, still extant in different collections worldwide today, including a copy now housed at the Vatican Secret Archives. The other version, of which a single copy survives at the Library

or a group of scientists invents a new instrument, they must demonstrate persuasively that the instrument does or means what they say, that it represents the kind and order of phenomena they intend. Other scientists start using the instrument, and ideally, its general acceptance soon helps to make it a transparent fact of scientific practice. . . . They look through the instrument the way one looks through a telescope, without getting caught up in battles already won over whether and how it does the job. The instrument and all of its supporting protocols (norms about how and where one uses it, but also standards like units of measure) have become self-evident as the result of social processes that attend both laboratory practice and scientific publication."

[9] As Boyle (1997, 6) states, "The power to gather, manipulate, retrieve, and commodify information has always been important."

and Archives of the Royal Society, was intended for a readership of experts in astronomy unaffected by theological regulations (see also Camerota, Giudice, and Ricciardo 2019). The stronger, more authentic astronomical message preserved in the letter is one of the cases in which "Galileo did the editing, it seems," to update and control the circulation of his own works as "mixed messages" (Abbott 2018); though the date was incorrectly marked as 21 October 1613, the letter was written on 21 December 1613, to present stronger arguments in support of Copernican ideas. According to Alison Abbott (2018), the letter "provides the strongest evidence yet that, at the start of his battle with the religious authorities, Galileo actively engaged in damage control and tried to spread a toned-down version of his claims." In that letter, Galileo substituted ambiguous words with socially acceptable ones that would pass the scrutiny of print officers, censors, and Inquisitors.

While, according to the original phrasing, certain propositions in the Bible might sound "false if one goes by the literal meaning of the words," in the revised version Galileo replaced the word "false" by crossing it out and instead writing "looking different from the truth." He also did not refer to the Scriptures as "concealing" its most basic dogmas, using the term "veiling" instead, a point that supports my reading of Galileo's scientific writing as a practice of simulation and dissimulation of literal statements, thus following Baroque communicative strategies that Torquato Accetto would describe as the best defense an intellectual could have. In the preface to his *Della dissimulazione onesta* (1641), Accetto wrote on conformity and dissimulation as a form of affectation that is required to protect your own reputation and deepest thoughts, as he himself had to do. According to Accetto (1641, ch. 6), the notions we express are related to the concept one has of our own knowledge. Dissimulation could involve your behavior and thoughts but also your intentions and messages, so that all communicative functions could be veiled and unveiled when needed, at the right time:

> . . . dissimulating consisting in a veil of honest darkness and violent respect, from which one does not find falsehood, but a pause to the truth, in order to show at the right time. As nature wanted both day and night in the order of the universe, thus befits in human vicissitudes to have both light and shadow, I mean, the clear and hidden ways of handling things, appropriate to the use of reason that regulates life and everything occurring in it. (Accetto 1641, ch. 4; my trans.)[10]

---

[10] ". . . non essendo altro il dissimulare, che un velo composto di tenebre oneste e

A clear definition of such strategic thinking and acting is that, by dissimulating, one does not show things as they are in order to feign what is not and, at the same time, to deny what truly is.[11] Familiarity with international areas and their local traditions helps one to dissimulate (see Accetto 1641, ch. 7), and those Baroque conventions confirm the importance and scope of Galileo's local and international correspondence as textual evidence of scientific communication.

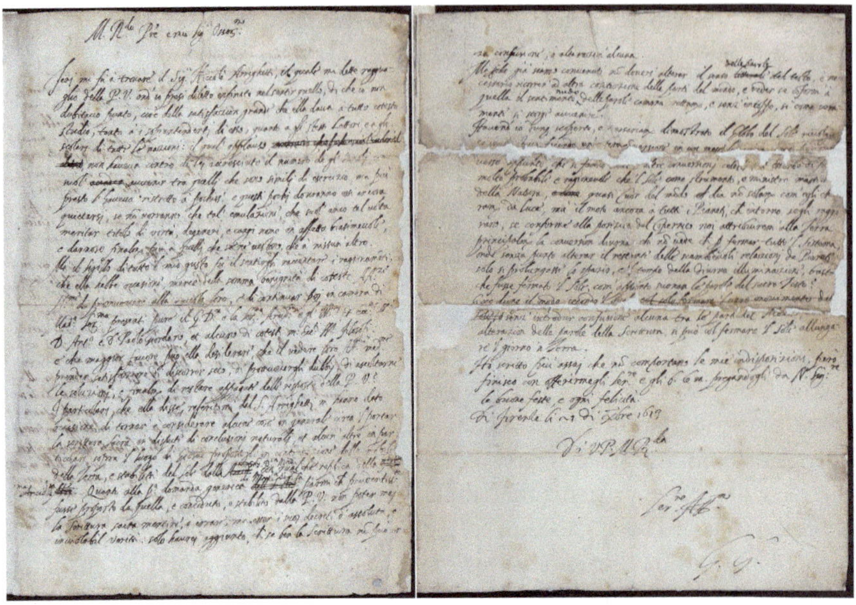

Figure 5. A letter by Galileo Galilei to Father Benedetto Castelli, a former student of Galileo who became a prominent mathematician, defending the role of science in investigating nature (21 December 1613). Wikimedia Commons.

---

di rispetti violenti: da che non si forma il falso, ma si dà qualche riposo al vero, per dimostrarlo a tempo; e come la natura ha voluto che nell'ordine dell'universo sia il giorno e la notte, così convien che nel giro delle opere umane sia la luce e l'ombra, dico il proceder manifesto e nascosto, conforme al corso della ragione, ch'è regola della vita e degli accidenti che in quella occorrono."

11 "La dissimulazione è una industria di non far veder le cose come sono. Si simula quello che non è, si dissimula quello ch'è" (Duplicity is an endeavour not to show things the way they are. One pretends what is not and conceals what is) (Accetto 1641, ch. 8; my trans.).

Given that prudence and secrecy were necessary to discuss Copernican astronomy, textual aspects of prose, poetry, truthfulness, and Baroque deceit or *dissimulazione* also posed a question in terms of style and genre in Galileo's books and the letters he exchanged with his correspondents. Galileo had first been open about his support of Copernicus, whereas Accetto wrote that the unconditional love of truth could have damaged one who is too frank about his own beliefs. In my analysis of the letters that Galileo received, there are several possible levels of interpretation based on a textual and historical study of the contents and historical contexts to assess scientific approval or, conversely, criticism of Galileo's work that shows in the chronological selection of data and by classifying them as letters of approval or disapproval. Thus, I have read the letters in Favaro's edition to determine the type of reception, support, or criticism that the correspondents shared in the letters they sent to Galileo. Examining correspondents as part of support networks before and after the Inquisition trial reveals a social network of individuals who supported Galileo's theories, and another network of individuals who criticized Galileo on several levels—as a scholar, innovator, and writer. Some people wrote angry letters or refutations to Galileo; others debated heliocentrism and other astronomical topics. Given the more informal mode of communication, I consider letters to be the primary means available to modern readers to ascertain discussions that were not recorded in printed books.

In Galileo's correspondence, there were both formal and informal letters, a distinction that can be made based on content, style, and language or multilingual modes. There are advantages in selecting letters based on Galileo being their addressee, particularly when transferring such knowledge into digital formats and visualizations. Correspondents would usually receive a written answer from Galileo, as one easily guesses that communication benefits from a mutual exchange of ideas, explanations, and updates. From renowned Jesuit scholars to science enthusiasts, people wrote letters to Galileo in Italian, Latin, French, and at times even local dialects such as Venetian and Paduan.[12] Informal letters were those exchanged between Galileo and friends or former students to express personal opinions, at times in opposition to the official views of religious and cultural establishments.[13] The editorial and

---

[12] Giuseppe Gagliardi, for example, wrote a letter in the dialect of Padua in March 1608; no location, though, is known for that letter (*OG* 10:196).

[13] Connections with former students lasted for decades, as was the case with Father Benedetto Castelli, who later advocated for Galileo and his theories. As Schaberg (2018, 61) has argued, "These small things [bonding professors and students] add up,

printing process of Galileo's books was also discussed in letters with friends and colleagues, so one can see the support of Galileo's followers—Federico Cesi and Giovanni Ciampoli around Rome, Francesco Rinuccini and Fulgenzio Micanzio in Venice, and Elias Diodati in Paris. Furthermore, the Elzevirs in Leiden edited, prepared for publication, and managed to print Galileo's books in Italy and abroad after theological bans, and they even published his new book, *Discorsi e dimostrazioni matematiche intorno a due nuove scienze*, or *Discourses on Two New Sciences*, in 1638 after it had been sent to them by Diodati (*OG* 17:365; see also Eisenstein 2013, 281–84).

With tools from geospatial humanities, it is possible to visualize correspondents and go-betweens on a map, and to locate letters as texts belonging to a larger scientific and literary corpus.[14] Additionally, having comprehensive structured data of the astronomical correspondence gives us some flexibility to select smaller datasets by filtering by topic, astronomical events, or publications at that time. By integrating official scientific writings with formal and informal correspondence exchanged by Galileo, I have expanded traditional literary perspectives into the contexts of letter writing in the Italian vernacular(s) in Italy and abroad to introduce themes of "Italian diaspora" in the early modern period for scientific topics, with a prevailing Tuscan vernacular (Gabaccia 2013, 16).[15] In terms of methods, Carlo Dionisotti first discussed the geography and history of Italian literature as connected aspects of literary history.[16] He associated both aspects in the title of

in at least two ways: they are the uncompensated, incalculable parts of the job; but they are also the things that can result in lifelong memories for students."

[14] Texts give the opportunity to modulate and edit, express, and share ideas in writing. I second the view expressed by Schaberg (2018, 45) that literature "gives us space to think. It is quite literally *thinking space*. But it can also be a way to think *about* space" (emphasis in original).

[15] At the time, the Tuscan vernacular was shaped to become the leading Italian vernacular. For reference, see the legal terminology used in the trial in which Galileo accused Baldassarre Capra of plagiarism: "di Toscano in Latino" ([a translation] from Tuscan into Latin) (*OG* 2:544). Boyle (1997) discusses plagiarism in chapter 6 of his *Shamans, Software, and Spleens*, arguing that "our notion of 'authorship' is a concept of relatively recent provenance" (53) and discussing how property and originality are opposed, conceptually, to fraud and plagiarism (108–18) and piracy and classroom copies (119–13); some of these themes are still current. See the Bellagio Declaration on cultural agency and authority: case.edu/affil/sce/BellagioDec.html.

[16] For general principles on digital projects and topics in history, see Cohen and Rosenzweig 2006, 189–219; McGann 2014, 90–112.

his book, *Geografia e storia della letteratura italiana* (The geography and history of Italian literature), in which he discusses Italian authors as intellectuals equally connected to their hometowns and to the current historical and political circumstances in which they wrote their books (Dionisotti 1967, 23–45, 47–73). The type of connection that emerges through correspondents and their language(s) reveals friends and friends of friends, which leads me to consider future developments that will allow for the study of the type of relationship between correspondents through social network diagrams and analysis.

Dionisotti (1967, 45) suggested that introducing Italian literature solely from historical viewpoints had likely made Tuscan literature become *the* literature of Italy in a seemingly unifying cultural project of language and geography.[17] Such perspectives have been updated, and studies in early modern literature and digital humanities have called attention to Galileo's readings and his own library; accordingly, his textual quotations and cross-references have been interpreted as evidence of advanced humanistic and scientific skills (Hall 2019). Based on my findings, geospatial information can be traced prior to interpretation in datasets, and their visualizations—maps—become a digital medium of representation. This will prove valuable for the history of science and the gradual introduction of new ideas in astronomy—for example, planetary motions and structures first expressed by Copernicus in the heliocentric model of the universe (see Eisenstein 2013, 231–54). Consequently, interpretations of textual analysis and digital mapping through the lens of correspondence show the growing importance of several Italian vernaculars (Florentine, Venetian, and Paduan, to name a few present in Galileo's correspondence) as a linguistic medium worthy of official academic discussions beyond printed scientific books.

The Inquisition Trial

Conflicts with the Church and the Inquisition trial took place mainly over the course of a year (from the summer of 1632 to the summer of 1633), which means that those debates occurred during the plague outbreak of 1630–33, a set of historical circumstances that made letters a vital substitute for human interaction. Then toward the end of that outbreak, the Inquisition trial

[17] He noted, however, that two foundational authors, Dante and Petrarch, wrote their major works while away from Tuscany (Dionisotti 1967, 34). Since scientific texts are not usually included in the Italian literary canon, Dionisotti mentioned Galileo only briefly in the context of clergymen and laypeople (71–72).

took place in Rome (*OG* vols. 14–15).[18] At that time, Galileo and his friends and colleagues needed to work around quarantines and travel restrictions because travel was restricted for people as well as objects, and letters were carried with more care, at times fumigated or left outside to avoid any risks of contamination. Scholars became isolated, yet they stayed connected thanks to correspondence. Quarantine had not hindered Galileo's scientific work during the plague, but it had delayed the publication of his *Dialogue*. As revealed in a letter of 28 March 1962, Galileo resisted the idea of sending the whole work to Rome, because communications between Florence and Rome were interrupted during the outbreak and fumigation was needed for items traveling from areas stricken by the plague, books included (*OG* 14:339). Still, communication regarding those challenging circumstances occurred through letters. Galileo's former student, mathematician Bonaventura Cavalieri, wrote from Bologna on 3 December 1630, relieved to know that Galileo was fine even though he had been in areas of high plague incidence; he was looking forward to the publication of the *Dialogue* and the progress of Galileo's book on motion, *Two New Sciences* (*OG* 14:170–71). In the intellectual process of coping with illness, personal and collective, scholars benefitted from personal communication and the exchange of letters with Galileo's supporters, including Benedetto Castelli, Piero Dini, and Giovanni Ciampoli in Italy, and Giovanni Pieroni in Prague after the Inquisition trial.[19] Those friends supported Galileo and Copernican ideas unconditionally, to the point that Ciampoli was exiled to central Italy, in the Marche region, as a punishment for his support of Galileo's theories and the publication of his books.

The *Dialogue* was quickly approved by the censors in Florence, where the book was printed by Giovanni Battista Landini in 1632. Pope Urban VIII and the Jesuits saw the book in July 1632, when copies made it to Rome, and the pope expressed his disapproval and anger at seeing the liberties that Galileo had taken in times of plague. Another cause for papal and inquisitorial concern was the publication and distribution of the *Dialogue* across Europe, though a few copies had been lost and quarantined at state borders, as revealed in a

[18] On the plague in Florence, see geospatial work documented in Eckstein 2016; Henderson and Rose 2016.

[19] Eisensten (2013, 109–10) writes about "a distinctive subculture . . . the development of a profitable clandestine book trade and black markets for forbidden books . . . vernacular Bibles . . . [and] Galileo's evasion of the officials who placed him under house arrest." See also Eisenstein 2013, 254–85.

letter of 4 September 1632 (*OG* 14:379–82). The book was banned, and Galileo was summoned to Rome to testify before the Roman Inquisition in September 1632 (Shea and Artigas 2005, 158–200). The Inquisition trial against Galileo took place in a room attached to the church of Santa Maria sopra Minerva on 22 June 1633. During the trial, Galileo was condemned for holding an opinion that had been declared contrary to Scripture, namely that the Earth moves around the Sun. Although his book had been banned, absolution would be available to him if he formally recanted his errors. He had to recant his scientific theories about the motion and position of the Earth (*OG* 19, document 24).

After the Inquisition trial, secretive support of Copernican theories and displays of affection for Galileo show repeatedly, though with discretion, in letters addressed to him. Among Galileo's international correspondents there was concern and anxiety even years after the Inquisition trial and the end of the plague, and it is possible to trace those correspondences on a map. For example, looking at the map visualization reveals correspondents from Paris and Amsterdam after the Inquisition trial, whereas cross-referencing the visualization with the tabular dataset completes the information on letters sent to Galileo. For example, Pierre Gassendi wrote on 13 October 1627 from Marseille that he was so happy to know Galileo was recovering and that he planned to visit him in Arcetri (*OG* 17:197). Ismael Boulliau wrote from Paris on 30 October 1637 that he had decided to contact Galileo in Florence as soon as possible, after hearing from a friend that Galileo had recovered his health in such challenging times of war and dangers (*OG* 17:207). On 28 May 1638, Hugo Grotius, living in Paris, urged Gerardus Vossius in Amsterdam to communicate with Galileo, who was ill (*OG* 17: 335). In a letter of 20 March 1639 to Caspar Hofmann, a physician in Altorf, Matthias Bernegger apologized for not reorganizing Galileo's letters yet (*OG* 18:31–32). Bernegger was a philologist and was commissioned to translate the *Dialogue* into Latin by Elias Diodati, who advertised cultural initiatives to defend and promote Galileo's theories in Europe.

Galileo's astronomical books might have been banned, but as Copernican ideas were defended and proven correct, ways were found to publish these debates. In Galileo's books and letters, recurrent topics included the theoretical foundations of astronomy connected to classical texts, such as those of Ptolemy, with their notions on geography and astronomy in a geocentric system as well as ancient and medieval astronomical tables, recent astronomical observations explained with Galileo's new theories and Copernican hypotheses,[20] and new scientific instruments such as the telescope. By adopting Copernican views on the universe, Galileo was debating both an astronomical and philosophical topic that also had theological implications. Although it was not until the Inquisition trial against Galileo in 1633 that scientific communication was regulated by doctrinal concerns, Cardinal Roberto Bellarmino had already issued an injunction and warning against defending Copernican theories and notified Galileo in 1616.[21] A renewed ban on Copernican ideas, though, made discussion of astronomy impossible, and the revival of Counter-Reformation doctrines promoted a form of "cancel culture" in Italy and in all Catholic countries, so that one could not teach, hold, or defend Copernican theories in speaking or writing. The condemnation of Galileo's theories also extended to any text on banned topics published before the trial; books on those astronomical topics would not be allowed because the supervising authority of the Holy Office would not release their printing permissions (in Latin, *imprimatur*).

Copernican ideas continued to influence many readers for centuries, often regardless of their familiarity with his book, *On the Revolutions of the Heavenly Spheres*, as Owen Gingerich (2004, 29–30) has shown.[22] The fact that Galileo used Copernican statements, and that he wanted to use and prove them as theories, not only opened conflicts with the Church and the Inquisition but also raised debates among professors of philosophy and theologians. Material evidence of those contrasts are found in Galileo's own copy of the *Dialogue* (Fig. 6), which contains handwritten editorial notes documenting his revisions of the text as well as his frustration with opponents and censorship (Favaro 1880). A main interest of the Dear Galileo project is thus to reconstruct the reception of Galileo's theories through the perspectives of those who wrote to him, because scholars could still communicate evolving ideas and unorthodox themes on astronomy through letters.

---

[20] Nicolaus Copernicus had been very influential when he stated that the Earth was not at the center of the universe, and he used that opinion as a working hypothesis for the reform of the calendar in the treatise *De revolutionibus orbium coelestium*, or *On the Revolutions of the Heavenly Spheres* (1543).

[21] On limitations to scientific research starting in 1616, see Eisenstein 2013, 254–85.

[22] For a census of extant books by Copernicus, see Gingerich 2004.

Figure 6. Galileo's personal, annotated copy of the *Dialogo sopra i due massimi sistemi del mondo* (*Dialogue Concerning the Two Chief World Systems*). Photo courtesy of the Biblioteca del Seminario Vescovile, Padua, Italy. The book has many handwritten marginal notes in Galileo's own hand. While the book preserves an internal conversation that Galileo was having with himself when revisiting his own book after it was printed, the letters he exchanged, conversely, show an interconnected community of readers and writers discussing astronomical topics, looking for more information but also supporting or criticizing the new discoveries as well.[23]

Correspondence as Primary Sources and Data

Correspondence, however, is subject to the passing of time, as are all primary sources documenting history and the circumstances of their respective traditions, and many of Galileo's letters have been lost because recipients destroyed them when attempting to avoid any association with the scientist who was tried by the Inquisition. For example, Sister Maria Celeste, Galileo's daughter, helped her father's friends hide or destroy compromising papers to protect his reputation in front of the Inquisition.[24] When surveying

---

[23] Indeed, when Galileo's theories became popular, some cases of plagiarism occurred, a process which Gitelman (2014, 6) identifies, for intellectuals, "at the intersection of authority and amnesia."

[24] Some letters to Galileo document measures taken to protect his reputation and safety; for example, Sister Maria Celeste's letter of 13 July 1633 (*OG* 15:179); Geri Bocchineri's letters of 15 and 16 September 1633 (*OG* 15:263–65); and Niccolò Aggiunti's

letters sent to Galileo, I considered the state of the textual tradition to be a principal factor in the textual analysis of the corpus, being aware that not all letters, both those sent and those received, have survived to this day. While Galileo's letters would have a higher survival rate than most letters, estimates of the overall availability of what was written and exchanged are tentative at best. Thus, I chose to emphasize places and dates, and the people writing from each location, while also considering that several correspondents moved often, as did diplomatic envoys and members of religious orders, for example.

In letters discussing astronomy, correspondents debated theoretical and practical aspects, shared records from personal logbooks with astronomical measurements, and at times sketched planetary features.[25] Spatial information on observational astronomy also differs based on the area where observations are made, so that space as place and space as astronomy are aspects of the same scientific questions that interested Galileo. Astronomy was thus viewed both as a computational and philosophical discipline, relying on the importance of instruments and the measurements they afford, as well as the reasoning of those looking at the night sky. Specifically, the apparent motion of the celestial sphere depends on the observer's latitude, and precise astronomical measurements, in degrees and minutes, were important to confirm observational data. Other variables included stellar aberrations (the so-called parallax), for which information from other areas could be exchanged through letters. Geospatial methodologies illuminate the width of scientific networks as well as support networks around Galileo. Such correspondence was useful to validate observations and integrate data that one could not have in their area of residence.

Important letters by Galileo circulated in multiple drafts, with several intentionally written and distributed versions. When Galileo announced his telescope, he wrote a letter to Doge Leonardo Donato (early 1610), who ruled in Venice from 1606 to 1612 (Fig. 7). This letter became very famous and was forged in the 20th century, with the intent to profit from the false attribution to Galileo (now housed at the University of Michigan Library).

letter of 27 December 1633 (*OG* 15:364). See also Favaro 1887.

25 According to some scholars, Galileo might have had "dubious practices" with his data. Hand (2021, 200) thus sees a presence of "dark data" in science as part of the process of discovery.

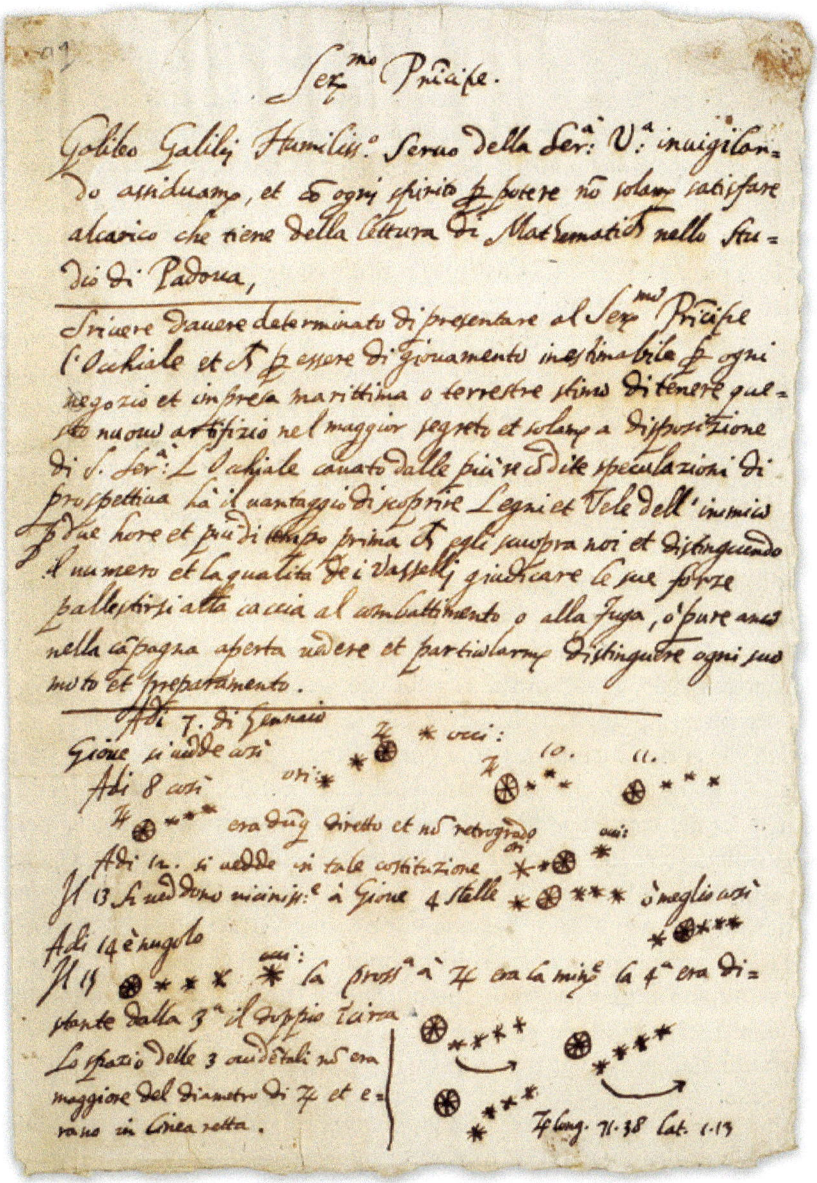

Ser.mo Principe.

Galileo Galilei Humiliss.o Servo della Ser.tà V.a invigilando assiduamente, et con ogni spirito per potere non solamente satisfare al carico che tiene della lettura di Matematico nello Studio di Padova,

Scrive d'avere determinato di presentare al Ser.mo Principe l'Occhiale et di poter essere di giovamento inestimabile per ogni negozio et impresa marittima o terrestre stima di tenere questo nuovo artifizio nel maggior segreto et solamente a disposizione di S. Ser.tà L'Occhiale cavato dalle più recondite speculazioni di prospettiva ha il vantaggio di scoprire Legni et Vele dell'inimico per due hore et più di tempo prima che egli scuopra noi et distinguendo il numero et la qualità dei Vasselli giudicare le sue forze pallestirsi alla caccia al combattimento o alla fuga, o pure ancora nella campagna aperta vedere et particolarmente distinguere ogni suo moto et preparamento.

Adi 7. di Gennaio Giove si vedde così … così: … 10. … 11.

Adi 8 così … era dunque diretto et non retrogrado … così:

Adi 12. si vedde in tale costituzione …

Il 13 si veddono vicinissime à Giove 4 stelle … o meglio così

Adi 14 è nugolo

Il 15 … la pross.a à Giove era la minore la 4.a era distante dalla 3.a il doppio circa.

Lo spatio delle 3 occidentali non era maggiore del diametro di Giove et erano in linea retta.

Giove long. 71.38 lat. 1.13

Figure 7. Letter by Galileo Galilei to Doge Leonardo Donato (early 1610), who ruled in Venice from 1606 to 1612. This manuscript, housed at the University of Michigan Library, is actually a 20th-century forgery. Wikimedia Commons.

Galileo's Correspondents

Who wrote to Galileo? Scholars, friends, and former students who had become mathematicians, astronomers, or physicians, but also diplomats and secretaries writing on behalf of Galileo's patrons at the Republic of Venice and, later, the Medici court in Florence (Fig. 7). For Galileo, it was also important to keep professional connections with renowned scholars, such as the imperial astronomer Johannes Kepler as well as Jesuit scholars in Italy and Europe, all of whom constitute a professional and scientific network. Galileo admired Copernicus, but he mostly ignored another leading astronomer, Tycho Brahe, whose theory reconciled both Ptolemaic and Copernican ideas; only one letter was exchanged with him, from Benátky nad Jizerou in the Central Bohemian Region of the Czech Republic on 4 May 1600 (*OG* 10:79). As William Shea and Mariano Artigas (2005) have shown, the Jesuits were leading mathematicians and theologians in the early modern period, and their cultural and scientific influence spread throughout Europe. In his scientific agenda, Galileo wanted approval for his *Dialogue* from the pope; he went to Rome six times throughout his life to meet high-ranking cardinals, humanists, and scientists. Consequently, Galileo communicated with Jesuit fathers to test, verify, and confirm his own theories and discoveries (Shea and Artigas 2005, 1–18). In the case of the Jesuits, their role in intellectual investigations justified their active participation in scientific discussions, Galileo's theories included. Galileo hoped that the *Dialogue* would be published in Rome with the patronage of Prince Cesi, as *The Assayer* had been in 1623. Some correspondents, however, had never met Galileo in person, while others were introduced to Galileo by correspondence through common friends. That was the case also for a letter of 5 July 1619 from Cardinal Maffeo Barberini, who would later become Pope Urban VIII (*OG* 12:463). Barberini's case is an example of a person shifting opinions from approval to condemnation of Galileo's theories, to the point that he started the Inquisition trial a few months after Galileo had published the *Dialogue*, which the pope found controversial.

Mapping place-names with digital tools supplies another perspective on textual, historical, and scientific topics. Such map visualizations can expand the perspectives on Galileo's connections by looking at interests in astronomy from a variety of geographic areas. For example, the discussion of scientific instruments was influential in showing the role of the scientist, since observation only depended on the view of celestial bodies through a tube and lenses (Bucciantini, Camerota, and Giudice 2015, 118, 146). Alongside his scientific books, Galileo was also marketing his scientific instruments, in particular the telescope. In fact, within Galileo's lifetime we see some scholars writing about scientific discoveries and instruments as early as the 1590s and others as late as the 1930s. The response was both theoretical and practical, with Galileo explaining what the telescope allowed one to see, and public demonstrations of it in use thanks to his friends, as the Grand Duke of Madrid Esau del Borgo did at the Spanish court.[26] Some adventurous exchanges ensued: when Esau del Borgo wished to advertise the telescope on behalf of Galileo at the Spanish court, he wrote on 13 May 1631 that he needed new lenses, while aware that there might be shipping delays because of the current plague (*OG* 14:260). The wife of the ambassador of Florence in Rome, Caterina Riccardi Niccolini, reassured Galileo that they had sent a telescope to replace the one Esau had, but the item was returned to Florence because of safety checkpoints at the borders during the plague; when her mother-in-law received the returned package, she did not accept it, fearing it was not wise to do so (*OG* 14:305). Some passages of the correspondence thus provide information about the mail shipment of the telescope and the historical circumstances of a plague outbreak. Studying Galileo's correspondents seems essential to reveal more about Galileo's scientific and personal connections including those connections he gained through his books and scientific instruments.

Some correspondents wrote from their consular posts, for example David Ricquet from Constantinople, Gianfrancesco Sagredo from Aleppo, and others from Paris, Brussels, Madrid, Munich, and Prague. Most letters are from Rome, Venice, Florence, Pisa, Bologna, Arcetri, Padua, and Siena. From this analysis, it appears that official residences of diplomats and political rulers were in the urban areas in other countries and in the countryside mansions of political rulers and nobility. Diplomatic seats were the biggest European cities of that time from which Medici secretaries of state and diplomats wrote to Galileo. For Galileo, the main political connections were the Republic of Venice, which had hired Galileo as a professor of mathematics at the University of Padua, and the Medici family. Galileo, however, had communicated with more diplomats and even with kings when he tried to circulate his discoveries in the courts of Mantua, Bavaria, Poland, the Netherlands,

---

[26] On media being "always already new," Lisa Gitelman (2014, 1) insists on "the truism that all media was once new." She also discusses "technological methods and devices . . . modern ideas of communication . . . modes and habits of perception . . . [and] political choices and structures (1–22). Conversely, David J. Hand (2021, 110–11) talks about "instrumental limitations" related to historical circumstances in 1609, when "Galileo began exploring the heavens with his telescope, with a magnification of about 30, and this revealed the existence of stars which had not been previously suspected."

and Spain. Non-linear connections appear throughout the study of the corpus of Galileo's letters, as each correspondent wrote more than one letter to Galileo, discussing astronomy and other scientific topics, and more research questions could arise, so that having a dataset is helpful to consult, repurpose, and visualize data.[27]

Collecting geospatial information, categorizing those facts, and applying those units of knowledge to digital tools is a humanistic task that relies on digital resources. What is clear already from the pattern in these birth and death places is, once again, the predominance of Rome, Venice, and Florence as hubs in the correspondents' network. By finding the letters in a specific period and classifying them as letters of approval, or disapproval, of Galileo's astronomical experiments, discoveries, and theories, we can gain a perspective on the geographical proximity of the different networks of people of power in the different social layers of Italy and Europe at a time when competing theories on astronomy were still allowed. While the primary areas of interest and outreach to Galileo were the towns where he lived (Pisa, Padua, Florence, Arcetri, and Bellosguardo), one of the surprising findings of the current project is how few and infrequently letters came from Italian cities outside of Florence, Venice, and Rome after the Inquisition trial.

Among scholarly methods, inductive reasoning guides provisional approaches to computational tools, where several tools would be applicable to map geospatial knowledge related to Galileo's correspondents (see Giordano and Olson 2018). Turning information on correspondence into data works well, namely structured data to apply to geospatial and network-oriented knowledge deriving from and revisiting geospatial datasets. I have explored two main findings related to Galileo's correspondence and map visualizations of those who wrote to him: first, questions leading to a new dataset for letters sent to Galileo on the topic of astronomy, and second, digital maps with points sized according to the number of letters sent from each location and for displaying static geographic information. The geography of Galileo's correspondents could be further developed by studying the effects of time, nationality, and social status, all categories included in my dataset.

Digital data and maps visualizing correspondence on astronomy can trace the width of geographic networks whose key elements are the common addressee, Galileo Galilei, and the historical fundamental divide following the

[27] On data structures, modeling, and visualizations in historical projects documenting the early modern period, specifically in Florence and Tuscany, see Fabbro 2016 and Rose 2016.

trial when Galileo was tried and condemned by the Inquisition. Through letters sent to Galileo, but also digital maps visualizing such locational information, a community of Galileo's correspondents emerges from the locations where they were living or traveled. Approval and criticism of scientific discoveries is a gradual process in intellectual history. Galileo's correspondents were among the people who made scientific expression possible in those years, in Italy and in Europe, and their communication with Galileo survives in letters where they debated astronomical topics.

WORKS CITED

Abbott, Alison. 2018. "Discovery of Galileo's Long-Lost Letter Shows He Edited His Heretical Ideas to Fool the Inquisition." *Nature*, 21 September 2018. doi.org/10.1038/d41586-018-06769-4.

Accetto, Torquato. 1641. *Della dissimulazione onesta*. Napoli: Egidio Longo.

Boyle, James. 1997. *Shamans, Software, and Spleens: Law and the Construction of the Information Society*. Cambridge, MA: Harvard University Press.

Braudel, Fernand. 1980. *On History*. Translated by Sarah Matthews. Chicago: University of Chicago Press.

Bucciantini, Massimo, Michele Camerota, and Franco Giudice. 2015. *Galileo's Telescope: A European Story*. Translated by Catherine Bolton. Cambridge, MA: Harvard University Press.

Camerota, Michele, Franco Giudice, and Salvatore Ricciardo. 2019. "The Reappearance of Galileo's Original Letter to Benedetto Castelli." *Notes and Records: The Royal Society Journal of the History of Science* 73, no. 1 (March): 11–28. doi.org/10.1098/rsnr.2018.0053.

Cohen, Daniel J., and Roy Rosenzweig. 2006. *Digital History: A Guide to Gathering, Preserving, and Presenting the Past on the Web*. Philadelphia: University of Pennsylvania Press.

Conroy, Melanie. 2017. "Visualizing Social Networks: Palladio and the Encyclopédistes, Pt I." *Age of Revolutions*, 25 September 2017. ageofrevolutions.com/2017/09/25/visualizing-social-networks-palladio-and-the-encyclopedistes-pt-i.

Dionisotti, Carlo. 1967. *Geografia e storia della letteratura italiana*. Turin: Einaudi.

Eckstein, Nicholas A. 2016. "Mapping Fear: Plague and Perception in Florence and Tuscany." In *Mapping Space, Sense, and Movement in Florence: Historical GIS and the Early Modern City*, edited by Nicholas Terpstra and Colin Rose, 69–186. New York: Routledge. doi.org/10.4324/9781315639314.

Eide, Øyvind. 2015. *Media Boundaries and Conceptual Modelling: Between Texts and Maps*. Basingstoke, Hampshire: Palgrave Macmillan. doi.org/10.1057/9781137544582.

Eisenstein, Elizabeth L. 2013. *The Printing Revolution in Early Modern Europe*. 2nd ed. Cambridge: Cambridge University Press. doi.org/10.1017/CBO9781139197038.

El Khatib, Randa, and Marcel Schaeben. 2020. "Why Map Literature? Geospatial Prototyping for Literary Studies and Digital Humanities." *Digital Studies/Le champ numérique* 10 (1): 1–22. doi.org/10.16995/dscn.381.

Fabbro, Eduardo. 2016. "From the Decima to DECIMA and Back Again: The Data behind the Data." In *Mapping Space, Sense, and Movement in Florence: Historical GIS and the Early Modern City*, edited by Nicholas Terpstra and Colin Rose, 53–62. New York: Routledge. doi.org/10.4324/9781315639314.

Favaro, Antonio. 1880. *Le aggiunte autografe di Galileo al* Dialogo sopra i due massimi sistemi *nell'esemplare posseduto dalla Biblioteca del Seminario di Padova*. Modena: Società tipografica.

———. 1887. "Serie seconda di scampoli galileiani." *Atti e Memorie della R. Accademia di scienze, lettere ed arti in Padova*, n.s., 3:11–40.

Gabaccia, Donna R. 2013. *Italy's Many Diasporas*. London: Routledge. doi.org/10.4324/9781315072630.

Galilei, Galileo. 1890–1909. *Le opere di Galileo Galilei: Edizione nazionale sotto gli auspicii di sua maesta il re d'Italia*. Edited by Antonio Favaro. 20 vols. Florence: Barbèra.

Gingerich, Owen. 2004. *The Book Nobody Read: Chasing the Revolutions of Nicolaus Copernicus*. London: Arrow.

Giordano, Andrea, and Mark Olson. 2018. "Visualizing Venice: Developing a Methodology for Historical Visualization." In *Visualizing Venice: Mapping and Modeling Time and Change in a City*, edited by Kristin L. Huffman, Andrea Giordano, and Caroline Bruzelius, 20–25. New York: Routledge.

Gitelman, Lisa. 2014. *Always Already New: Media, History, and the Data of Culture*. Cambridge, MA: MIT Press. doi.org/10.7551/mitpress/1208.001.0001.

Hall, Crystal. 2019. "Galileo's Library at the Intersection of Digital Humanities and Italian Studies." *Italian Culture* 37 (2): 159–66. doi.org/10.1080/01614622.2019.1717788.

Hand, David J. 2021. *Dark Data: Why What You Don't Know Matters*. Princeton, NJ: Princeton University Press. doi.org/10.1515/9780691198859.

Henderson, John, and Colin Rose. 2016. "Plague and the City: Methodological Considerations in Mapping Disease in Early Modern Florence." In *Mapping Space, Sense, and Movement in Florence: Historical GIS and the Early Modern City*, edited by Nicholas Terpstra and Colin Rose, 125–46. New York: Routledge. doi.org/10.4324/9781315639314.

Marcus, Hannah, and Paula Findlen. 2019. "Deciphering Galileo: Communication and Secrecy before and after the Trial." *Renaissance Quarterly* 72, no. 3 (Fall): 953–95. doi.org/10.1017/rqx.2019.253.

McGann, Jerome. 2014. *A New Republic of Letters: Memory and Scholarship in the Age of Digital Reproduction*. Cambridge, MA: Harvard University Press.

Midura, Rachel. 2019. "Publishing the Baroque Post: The Postal Itinerary and the Mailbag Novel." In *The Renaissance of Letters: Knowledge and Community in Italy, 1300–1650*, edited by Paula Findlen and Suzanne Sutherland, 255–71. London: Routledge. doi.org/10.4324/9780429429774.

Murrieta-Flores, Patricia, and Bruno Martins. 2019. "The Geospatial Humanities: Past, Present and Future." *International Journal of Geographical Information Science* 33 (12): 424–29. doi.org/10.1080/13658816.2019.1645336.

Ray, Meredith K. 2016. *Margherita Sarrocchi's Letters to Galileo: Astronomy, Astrology, and Poetics in Seventeenth-Century Italy*. New York: Palgrave Macmillan. doi.org/10.1057/978-1-137-59603-1_3.

Rose, Colin. 2016. "Thinking and Using DECIMA: Neighborhoods and Occupations in Renaissance Florence." In *Mapping Space, Sense, and Movement in Florence: Historical GIS and the Early Modern City*, edited by Nicholas Terpstra and Colin Rose, 15–32. New York: Routledge. doi.org/10.4324/9781315639314.

Schaberg, Christopher. 2018. *The Work of Literature in an Age of Post-Truth*. New York: Bloomsbury Academic. doi.org/10.5040/9781501334337.

Shea, William R., and Mariano Artigas. 2005. *Galileo in Rome: The Rise and Fall of a Troublesome Genius*. New York: Oxford University Press.

Southall, Humphrey, Ruth Mostern, and Merrick Lex Berman. 2011. "On Historical Gazetteers." *International Journal of Humanities and Arts Computing* 5 (2): 127–45. doi.org/10.3366/ijhac.2011.0028.

Wilding, Nick. 2014. *Galileo's Idol: Gianfrancesco Sagredo and the Politics of Knowledge*. Chicago: University of Chicago Press.

Wrisley, David Joseph. 2017. "Locating Medieval French, or Why We Collect and Visualize the Geographic Information of Texts." *Speculum* 92, no. S1 (October): 145–69. doi.org/10.1086/694300.

Chapter 9: Penelope Rich: Mapping the Mobility of a Sixteenth-Century Aristocratic Woman

Gerit Quealy
Botanical Shakespeare

Her name alone—Penelope Devereux Rich Blount, Lady Rich, Baroness of Essex[1] and later Countess of Devonshire[2]—is testament to her lineage, her status, and her connections. But it could also function as the major plot points on a map that includes the family seat of the Devereux via hereditary titles: Chartley Manor in Staffordshire, England, and attendant properties at Lamphey in Wales as well as Carmarthen, where her father Walter Devereux had been born. After Penelope's marriage to Robert, Lord Rich, in November of 1581, Robert's primary estate of Leighs (or Leez) Priory in East Anglia also becomes a major plot point on her personal map, as do Lord Rich's other family properties, which include the priory at St. Bartholomew's in West Smithfield, London. Later, Penelope had a designated suite of rooms at her

[1] This is a somewhat unusual attribution since she was married to Robert, Lord Rich, which made her Lady Rich or Baroness Rich (see Kinney 2014), but because her patrilineal family of origin was descended from the Earls of Essex from her father Walter Devereaux as well as the Bouchiers before him, King James I on 17 August 1603 at Farnham Castle granted "licence to Lady Rich, descended from the Bourchiers, Earls of Essex, to take precedence accordingly" (Calendar of State Papers 1857, 32).

[2] The dedication by dramatist John Ford for his *Fames Memoriall*, published in 1606 (Charles Blount died 3 April 1606) is "To the Rightly Right Honorable Lady, The Lady Penelope, Countess of Devonshire," so their marriage on 26 December 1605 was public knowledge. A portrait of Penelope Rich, labeled "A Countess of Devonshire" on its reverse, is in the holdings of Lambeth Palace. In his own way, composer John Coprario also defended her right to the title in "Funeral Teares" (1606), written upon Devonshire's death: "For beauty more adorned no age shall know / Than hers whom he his own for ever named." However, King James I never recognized the marriage, as it was against canon law to remarry while a divorced spouse was still alive. At Blount's lavish funeral in Westminster Abbey, Penelope's family arms were not quartered with her husband's as was the custom, which signals that the legitimacy of her title as Countess would also stand in question. See also Van Evera and Morrongiello 2005; Varlow 2009.

ISBN 978-1-64959-119-7 (paper) ISBN 978-1-64959-120-3 (pdf) ISBN 978-1-64959-121-0 (epub)
New Technologies in Medieval and Renaissance Studies 12 (2025) 227–59

brother Robert Devereux's London seat, Essex House, and subsequently added the homesteads she shared with her lover and second husband, Charles Blount, Earl of Devonshire, particularly Wanstead, previously occupied by her stepfather, Robert Dudley, Earl of Leicester, her mother's husband after Earl Walter's death (see Fig. 1).

In distilling these intimate connections—parents, siblings, husbands, and lovers—to their attendant estates and plotting them on the landscape of Britain, a baseline sphere of influence begins to emerge when studying Penelope's life,[3] offering rich insight into not only the frequency of aristocratic female travel but also Penelope's own personal concerns, private affairs, family loyalties, and even her pregnancies. Plotting all the properties connected to her name(s) on a map was the first point of curiosity: How much literal ground did she covered in name alone? And how often did she move between these spheres? Establishing specifically where she went, and how often, could also perhaps provide a template from which to compare and contrast other women of her time. Highlighting her personal map as a standalone focus in bas-relief became a compelling notion to clarify not only the practical and logistical parameters of her life but also a more intimate understanding of her place in her world and the Elizabethan world at large.

[3] Penelope Rich is how we will refer to her predominantly throughout this chapter, as that is how she was primarily known during her lifetime—although perhaps more often as simply Penelope, as here. A discussion of female identification was initiated in the 3:00 p.m. session at the Berkshire Conference of Women Historians in Toronto on 23 May 2015, where it was considered reductive to call a woman by her prenom as opposed to her surname, as men were/are commonly identified, since it immediately implies an inferior status to the female historical figures under discussion. But as author and feminist leader Gloria Feldt (quoted in Quealy 2013) has pointed out, a woman's surname come from the male line, either her father's or her husband's, so the prenom is the only name that is arguably purely her own (except in rare instances such as pseudonyms; e.g., George Sand, George Elliot). And as Jane Lawson explained (private email exchange, 30 August 2020), a woman did not take her husband's name if her rank was higher than his. So, Lady Mary Cheke married Henry Mackwilliam but was never known as Mrs. Mackwilliam; Frances Brandon Grey, Duchess of Suffolk, married Adrian Stokes but remained Duchess of Suffolk. Many common female names also derive from male names, such as Julia from Julius, Emily from Emilio; Patricia, Judith, and Jane are obvious.

Figure 1. Penelope Devereux Rich Blount, Lady Rich, Baroness of Essex, Countess of Devonshire represented as a map. Each surname and title has attendant estates that become the baseline for Penelope's personal map, anchoring her movement throughout her life. Chartley, for example, the Devereux family seat where she was born, also becomes a favored haven near the end of her life when her brother Robert is in possession of the property. Each destination is associated with one of her surnames.

A second set of plot points derived from all the familial connections her initial list of names pulls in: Ferrers, de Bohuns, and Bourchiers on her father's side, and perhaps more importantly, the Carey and Knollys families through her mother's lineage. Lettice was the daughter of Sir Francis Knollys and his wife Catherine Carey, in turn the daughter of Mary Boleyn during her clandestine affair with Henry VIII.[4] Thus, Penelope and her siblings were direct descendants of not only Queen Elizabeth's aunt but also her father.[5] At the

[4] Sally Varlow (2009, 21–22) claims proof—the discovery of detailed notes inside a Latin dictionary belonging to Sir Francis Knollys—that in fact Henry VIII sired Catherine Carey with Mary Boleyn, under the guise of her husband William Carey.

[5] Michele Margetts (1992, 31) explains a key aspect of all these contacts: "If the Knollyses were unable to display an impressive pedigree centuries long, they had in their

time this was a pervasive rumor (later substantiated), but it could explain the queen's partiality toward the children. Extended relations also pulled in Hunsdons, Howards, Huntingdons, Digbys, Dudleys, and more, all with attendant properties to add to Penelope's personal map (see Appendix A in Margetts 1992).

A distinct advantage to having a big family is the many places it offers to stay. But a static map offers a static experience—distant and diminished somehow—especially for a woman who was always on the move. Penelope was nothing if not fluid.[6] Finding a way to track her movements seemed integral to understanding her mindset and motivations. But capturing that fluidity was a challenge.

To create the maps that would lift Penelope's whereabouts from a linear litany on the page to, if not 3D, at least a more dimensional, textured, and active understanding of her movements required first gathering the data points of her travel. In addition to her names and relations mentioned above, primary sources such as her correspondence were consulted. Her various biographies, both published and unpublished, court records, New Years' gift rolls, and the Elizabethan Court Day by Day on Folgerpedia (folgerpedia.folger.edu) were also compared and contrasted, particularly for her interactions with the queen. With the assistance of Rebecca Webb and Nick Bombicino, these data points were culled into a spreadsheet that became plot points for two different types of maps, since no software seemed to exist to serve the full scope of our needs on a single interface.

The fully animated maps track Penelope's movements chronologically using existing technology from PictraMap, with extra editing and embellishments completed in Final Cut Pro. These maps allow a user to experience her journeys—to the extent that we know them thus far—in order to observe not only where and when she went to a particular destination but also—in an attempt to provide the fullest account possible of her movements—how frequently. However, we were forced to break these maps into sections since they could not accommodate the extent of the data points for her life as a whole; ergo, there is a childhood map, a breakout map for her time as Maid of Honor to Elizabeth (1581), and a map of her adulthood.

---

short family stemma the living cousin [Queen Elizabeth I] who mattered more than illustrious forebears, one who opened all doors."

[6] Varlow's (2009) characterization of Penelope often dashing here or racing there was a major impetus for exploring her travel patterns.

In addition, an interactive map needed to be created to give a "face" to each destination and explanatory information as to its significance; this was accomplished using ArcGIS StoryMaps. Here, plot points were mapped only once; her path was not traced because the software did not allow for it. Here, London required a breakout map due to the many locations Penelope moved between when residing there.

In a perfect future, a platform will become available (or be built by us) that will allow for all of these elements to be present in a single map—and an interactive overlay of a contemporaneous London map especially—to see the full scope of Penelope's movements throughout her life. A pop-up window similar to StoryMaps would explain each visit, although the current structure allows for an understanding of each specific destination as a whole, which is useful. The animated maps, however, currently require a re-rendering with any new data point introduced; this is inefficient, and will become even more so as research continues to unfold and Penelope's movements become increasingly granular.

The first animated map (see Video 1 on the companion website) spans Penelope's childhood, from her birth at Chartley Manor in Staffordshire up to the beginning of 1581 when she becomes, for a brief set of months, Maid of Honor to Queen Elizabeth. While we do not have a record of *every* time she visited aunts, uncles, grandparents, and cousins, the proximity and regularity of the trips allows for the assumption of convenience in transit. The abrupt change toward the end of this timespan is particularly accentuated by the moving map after Penelope's father Walter died in 1576, setting her off on a peripatetic year with her mother and sister for most of 1577.

An important connection, Lady Margaret Douglas Stuart, Countess of Lennox, daughter of Henry VIII's sister Margaret Tudor, could be considered family given that the illegitimate Henry VIII/Mary Boleyn lineage seemed to be an open secret. And perhaps Margaret, as the niece of Henry VIII, was acknowledging it when she invited Lettice and her daughters to stay with her at King's Place in Hackney, a suburb of the City of London, in autumn 1577 during their "homeless" year, since Earl Walter's death left them deprived of the family seat at Chartley.[7]

---

[7] Robert Devereux became the 2nd Earl of Essex upon his father Walter's death, and although he would eventually inherit Chartley Manor when he reached his majority, at 10 years old he became a ward of the court and the family had to vacate the property.

Prior to her father's death in 1576, Penelope's experience of travel had been very much as part of the family unit, with stopovers with grandparents and other relations on summer trips back and forth from their Welsh estates where Walter was born (and subsequently buried). From Chartley in Staffordshire, the homestead where she was presumably born in late January 1563, Penelope would have observed firsthand and probably been involved in the packing of the household for cross-country travel.[8] Large households and "close living made long occupancy of any one residence hygienically unwise," so "summers in Wales near Pembroke and . . . visits to Clifford, Vernon, Knollys and Hastings relatives in Huntingdonshire, Shropshire, Oxfordshire, and Leicestershire" offered familiarity with a pattern of movement that included practicalities of health and maintenance of allies (Margetts 1992, 29).

The Welsh properties, roughly 150–200 miles away from Chartley, required at minimum a week's travel, but with the various stops and stays along the way, that time expanded, with the familial respites providing a degree of comfort and safety. Additionally, travel was not solely by horse and carriage; discussing the Devereux family pilgrimages, Margetts (1992, 40) notes that travel was hard work and uncomfortable, even with the newer coaches "an uncomfortable springless conveyance. Rather than brave the mud of the track-like roads and the increasingly rough terrain they would encounter as they penetrated ever further into Wales, the family probably took to the water at the earliest opportunity, barging down the Severn and taking ship to sail west through the Bristol Channel past Swansea and Carmarthen Bays, round Stacks Rocks and into Milford Haven. Their destination, now only three miles inland."

Mapping Penelope's travel—or anyone's—under these conditions and circumstances is particularly revealing.[9] Rather than understanding it as a direct route from plot point to plot point, the movement forces the reader to consider the paraphernalia included in that journey: horses, carts, coaches, satchels, packs, provisions, and trunks, conveyed over rutted roads, in rough

[8] All dates conform to the New Style/Gregorian calendar, although it was not implemented until 1752 in England. Margetts (1993) is responsible for determining the approximate birth date for Penelope and her christening. She also describes Penelope's childhood as relatively stable, punctuated by "intermittent packing for moves from one great house to another" (Margetts 1992, 28–29).

[9] In another project for RSA 2021, we mapped Elizabeth's progresses throughout her reign and found there is a distinct shift in perception when you see her actual movements across the landscape (see Quealy 2021).

weather, onto boats, back to land—all this allows for a much more distinct and nuanced picture of the human experience unfolding.

In 1577, sans paternal protection and authority, the female Devereux trio's itinerant year brings into focus the travel ban—less a statute and more a stigma at this juncture—for women in the sixteenth century, particularly if travel was deemed outside the domestic sphere. Travel advice books found the prospect of female travel morally repulsive, suggesting that it invited a wanton lasciviousness to women who allowed themselves to be easily seen and accessible outside the home (hence the phrase, she "got around"). It could be argued that Lettice, Penelope, and Penelope's younger sister Dorothy constituted a family unit and hence a sort of mobile domestic sphere. But it is more likely that their aristocratic rank, and the fact that they would have been traveling with a cadre of male domestic servants, might have exempted them from this general stigma. Nevertheless, the wantonness connected with traveling women (and in fact a stigma did later attach itself to all three women, though not solely related to travel) saw them lumped in with "Fooles," "Madmen," "Lunaticke(s)," and "Decrepite persons," as explored in Patricia Akhimie and Bernadette Andrea's *Travel and Travail* (2019).[10] This volume's commitment to "examining familiar sources in new ways" (Akhimie and Andrea 2019, 1) is in part what inspired a fresh look at Penelope Rich's movements as singular and noteworthy.[11] The authors cite evidence of the travel ban in a book published just a year before Earl Walter's death: *The Traveiler of Jerome Turler* (1575), which "warns that 'the wide wandring of Women cannot want suspicion, & bringeth some toke[n] of dishonesty.

[10] The introduction to this collected volume explores the many travel guides, advice manuals, and tracts that elucidate the many constraints, prohibitions, and assumptions surrounding women who might venture forth from the home (Akhimie and Andrea 2019). Akhimie's (2019) own chapter, "Gender and Travel Discourse," discusses issues and perceptions that more directly pertain to Penelope's life and lifestyle, such as the mention of her classical namesake in Homer's *Odyssey*; Odysseus's wife Penelope keeps her son Telemachus too much at home, in effect emasculating him, whereas Penelope Rich more often left her children at home while she was *hic et ubique.*

[11] It turns out we were not the first to notice the abundance of Penelope Rich's travel destinations; Tudor Times, a website dedicated to the period, notes on a map a list of houses she visited or in which she dwelled (see tudortimes.co.uk/people/lady-penelope-devereux). Our original concept to plot her movements differs from this approach, but we have included and significantly expanded upon those points to further illuminate the scope and frequency of Penelope's activity and clarify the particulars involved in the extent of her travel.

Whereupon the Tragicall and Comicall Poets, when they bringe in any car traveling Woman, for the most parte they feine her to be incontinent,' or unchaste" (quoted in Akhimie and Andrea 2019, 1).

After the 1577 New Year festivities at court,[12] Penelope and Dorothy moved with their mother to Grey's Court in Oxfordshire, the home of Lettice's parents, Sir Francis Knollys and Catherine Carey, although the couple were mostly away in service to the queen. Penelope must have known the story of her grandfather once begging the queen to allow his wife a trip home because she was ill and "moderate travayle and qwyatnes of mynde" would do her good, but the queen wanted her close by and claimed the journey "myghte be to hyr danger or discomoditie" (quoted in Doran 2015, 115–17). Perhaps an object lesson for Penelope is the privilege travel could be, even as she was picking up stakes again in late April to stay with her Digby cousins at Coleshill in Warwickshire before landing at King's Place with Lady Lennox that autumn, as mentioned above, and finishing the year "with the Russells at Bedford House in Westminster, four doors down the Strand from Leicester House" (Margetts 1992, 124).[13]

In a certain light, the Devereux women's travel in 1577 could be seen as echoing one of Elizabeth's progresses, albeit a protracted version. The queen's regular rotation was her greater London palaces: Whitehall, Greenwich and Richmond, Hampton Court, and Nonsuch, but court was "in session" further afield when she was on her multi-week summer tours as well. In his study of Henry VIII's progresses, Neil Samman (1995, 59) points out that "the progress left a lasting impression upon contemporaries and was of great political significance," engendering goodwill as well as reinforcing sovereignty.[14] As Elizabeth traveled about the country to see her courtiers, scholars, favorites, local governments, and general populace, she expected some to follow along or visit at one of her destinations, including foreign dignitaries. Elizabeth's progresses set a precedent for an extraordinary amount of travel as a woman within the confines of her realm.

---

[12] Lettice gave a gift of satin clothing, sleeves, and such to the queen and received a gilt bowl in return. For more on New Years gift exchanges, see Lawson 2013.

[13] Given the proximity to Robert Dudley's London home, it is presumed that the affair between him and Lettice had already begun.

[14] As Samman (1995, 59) goes on to say, "The progress is recognised as an important instrument of Tudor government. By visiting the localities a monarch reinforced his authority and was presented to his subjects against a background of ceremony and ritualised splendour: the progress left a lasting impression upon contemporaries."

The progresses of Elizabeth and James are not an entirely fair comparison to Penelope Rich's travel considering they derive from political and dynastic traditions of medieval and Renaissance monarchical public relations, however they do provide a baseline for aristocratic movement and, as such, do prove useful. For Penelope, they set a powerful example, particularly during her roughly seven months in service to the queen as a Maid of Honor, of not only how to pack and move masses of personal paraphernalia but also how to wield influence and form alliances through in-person contact.

Figure 2. A sample progress of James I from 1617, adapted from Cole 2010. James traveled further distances, in part to visit his home country, but he also tended to stay with the same hosts rather than create a diversified itinerary.

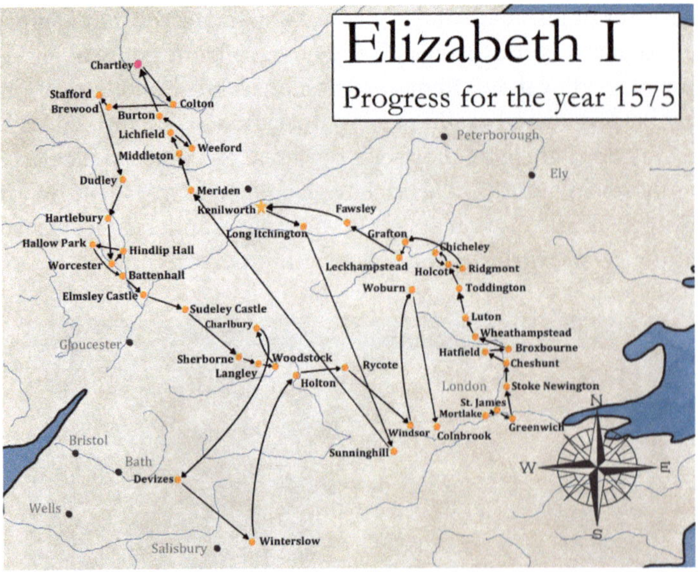

Figure 3.

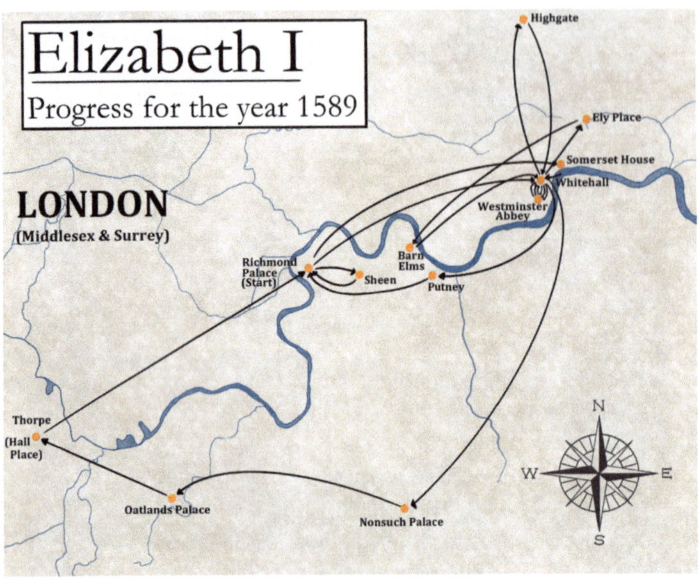

Figure 4.

Figures 3–4. Elizabeth on progress in 1575 (chosen because she visited the Devereux at Chartley that year) and in 1589 (chosen because Penelope began secret missives to James VI in this year). Primarily derived from Colthorpe 2017.

As Penelope probably first met Elizabeth on one of the queen's summer progresses, the girl was schooled in travel by her example, as well as from her own family's excursions. The queen visited the Devereux family seat during her 1575 progress (Fig. 3) after the storied Kenilworth entertainments staged by Robert Dudley, Earl of Leicester, in what was perhaps his last-ditch attempt to win Elizabeth's hand before secretly marrying Penelope's mother. As it happened, his nephew, the fledgling poet and emissary Philip Sidney, was also in attendance during this progress (Falls 1955, 55). When forced to return from Europe, Sidney logged an epistolary complaint that he "was compelled to travel with such haste, by the command of the Queen and [his] family" in order to be present for his uncle's July festivities (quoted in Duncan-Jones 1991, 84). While it is unclear whether Penelope attended the Kenilworth fête with her parents, it certainly seems possible given that it was the event of the decade and only half a day's ride away. Katherine Duncan-Jones (1991, 107) asserts that "Sidney may have had a chance to renew his acquaintance with the Devereux children when the royal progress stopped at Chartley in August 1575."[15] But Sidney's father, Sir Henry, who had joined the Kenilworth party for family solidarity, was then reappointed lord deputy of Ireland at Litchfield, a stop on the queen's progress while at Kenilworth, and it is possible both he and his son departed the entourage after this event (Colthorpe 2017, 3–4 August 1575; Duncan-Jones 1991, 99).[16] With the queen continuing to Chartley almost directly afterward, this confluence of personalities made the summer of 1575 a significant crossroads for Penelope that would impact the rest of her life. By the turn of the decade, Penelope would be traveling *with* the queen as an understudy Maid of Honor, as well as traveling even further afield, figuratively speaking, as the glittering "Stella" of Sidney's widely circulated sonnet cycle, *Astrophil and Stella* (1591).[17]

---

[15] Many scholars still seem to pin the point of initiation for the Philip–Penelope connection as sometime around 1580/81, but in addition to marking 1575 as a significant meeting, Duncan-Jones (1991, 33) cites the late 1560s as *the first* point of contact; at that time, Walter Devereux had seen fit to gift young Sidney with a "red horse" to make his travel easier while attending the Shrewsbury School.

[16] Philip Sidney's mother was Mary, Robert Dudley's sister and the wife of Henry Sidney.

[17] In chapter 11 of *Sir Philip Sidney and the Circulation of Manuscripts*, H. R. Woudhuysen (1996, 365) conducts an extensive exploration of the circumstances of circulation for the *Astrophil and Stella* song and sonnet cycle, citing its "complicated and difficult textual history" and noting Sidney's own references to its circulation: "he boasts that 'my verse best wits doth please' . . . as if he proudly made his poems available to some." Woudhuysen (1996, 219) also stresses the strong possibility that "Sidney gave a copy of *Astrophil and Stella* to Penelope Rich."

An undeniable advantage of providing cartographic representation of Penelope's movements on a digital platform is the possibility of filling out the landscape as new research is uncovered. But beyond that, the spatial humanities approach has offered unexpected insights and allowed for an intimacy with the living Penelope. Animating her personal map creates a more immediate sense of her mobility, its far-reaching scope, and its often distinctly female sphere—aside from traveling with the queen and other maids, she often traveled with or to her mother, her sister, and her cousins and intimates. While male servants obviously did the heavy lifting, both literally and figuratively, Penelope's travels seem to connect a nucleus of powerfully positioned women, a network or web just underneath the frontline players.

An enticing additional layer would be to compare Penelope's map with one of her male counterparts, such as Lord Rich or her brother Robert Devereux, to discover, perhaps, the extent of their companionship and see where they intersect. Robert seemed to employ his sister's natural magnetism with foreign dignitaries to shore up his political aspirations, or was it the other way around? In addition, contrasting the movements of Penelope's female contemporaries, such as Frances Walsingham or Lucy Russell, would provide helpful data to develop a baseline for female aristocratic travel.

The mapping also opened an unanticipated window into the childhood experience of the aristocracy. Common practice for families of rank was to move between properties, which allowed for the thorough cleaning and airing out of unoccupied manses. With the Devereux moving between their estates in Staffordshire and Wales, we see this practice in action. Traveling that distance every summer and stopping at the homes of their many relations along the way not only reinforced familial ties but also acted as a conduit of information—and strengthened allegiances, a lesson Penelope seems to have internalized.

A more granular understanding of how Penelope navigated her life begins to emerge when plotting seemingly incidental points, such as her brief trip to Epsom (was she going to Nonsuch?) gleaned from a 1595 letter that Rowland White sent to Robert Sidney, her almost brother-in-law.[18] Notions of marriage between the fathers of Philip Sidney and Penelope began to foment probably prior to 1575, but the death of Penelope's father in Ireland the following year made the financial aspect of such a union impossible; Walter

[18] We have also included a few other plot points on the maps where she is presumed to have visited, such as Appleton Hall, site of the peculiar song, "Pretty Royal," which has been connected to both Penelope and her brother Robert.

Devereux's promised dowry for Penelope in his will was in doubt given his copious debts. "All these lords that wishe well to the Children and, I suppose, all best Sort of the Englishe lords besides, doe expect what will become of the Treaty between Mr. Phillip and my Lady Penelop," the lawyer Edward Waterhouse wrote to Henry Sidney in Ireland in November 1576, two months after Devereux's death (quoted in Falls 1955, 55).

"Treaty" implies some sort of political alliance, but biographers have dismissed the terminology as casual usage. A footnote in Margetts's (1992, 109n14) thesis on Penelope's early life, however, illuminates why "treaty" was both precise and apt; she explains that the marriage negotiations had clearly not reached contract status, but that Waterhouse's "insistent tone" was meant to provoke Sir Henry's honor to fulfill Earl Walter's dying wish by citing other honorable men and by stressing assurance that Walter's debts would be remitted. "Treaty" also suggests an agreed peace; there had been an undercurrent of friction between the two fathers on various issues, including a disparity of means (Sir Henry had been embarrassed that his own financial constraints had prevented him from attending Sir Walter's elevation to earl in 1572). As Margetts (1992, 63n62) notes, "Sidney's defensive confrontation with the new Earl of Essex over the Welsh sheriffs later that year" drove Secretary of State Francis Walsingham to intercede and pour oil on the waters, a necessity since both men held prominent posts in Ireland; the rift even dated back to a conflict around Edward VI's death. Philip and Penelope's marriage would not mend these fences without a financial boon as incentive. The Christmastide festivities at court in 1577/78 may have brought Philip and Penelope together again, but in a few short years Penelope Devereux would be wed, against her will, to the aptly named Lord Rich.

At that time, the majority of aristocratic women's marriages were by necessity some kind of political or dynastic alliance—to consolidate properties, bolster flagging fortunes, or ensure heirs to vast estates. Most of these women were aware of and perhaps resigned to the practicality of these societal norms. But Penelope's model was the movements and machinations of her monarch, who already operated outside proscriptive social norms for women of the day by refusing to marry and procreate. The autonomy Penelope cultivated, which included her frequent travel, owed a debt to her permissive husband Lord Rich, to the standing of her brother, the Earl of Essex, as favorite of the queen, and perhaps especially to her almost-fiancé Philip Sidney in launching her brilliant career as professional muse—the shining star of *Astrophil and Stella*. Sidney admits, if only via *Astrophil and Stella*, that he was not initially smitten, but his sonnet cycle is rich with lavish praise for

Penelope, including recognizable physical descriptions, and, as if to allow no doubt in the reader's mind, he laces many verses with her conveniently evocative married name, Rich (Duncan-Jones 1991, 201, 242).[19]

But before Penelope came into her own as wealthy wife and exalted goddess of the arts, some rough terrain lay ahead while her future was yet to be determined. Her seemingly endless road trip of 1577 gave way by February 1578 to a period of subdued existence in faraway York under the tutelage of her prudent and pious guardians, Henry Hastings and his wife Katherine, the Earl and Countess of Huntingdon, Walter Devereux's cousin and Robert Dudley's sister, respectively. At King's Manor (and sometimes at Ashby de la Zouch), she and her siblings (excepting Robert, who was then at Cambridge) fine-tuned their education and musicianship, alongside hefty doses of religious doctrine. One cannot help but surmise that this was when Penelope honed her kind and generous nature but also fomented what would become a radically expansive view of religion. The countess was also adamant about preparing the girls to be adept at running a noble household, which would have included how to maintain several residences and the necessities for travel between them (Margetts 1992, 135–36).

When the Countess of Huntingdon decided Penelope was ready to bring to London in 1581 in order to secure her future, a fortuitous slot as Maid of Honor to the queen had unexpectedly opened up.[20] For seven months this allowed Penelope a rarefied view inside court society as one of the half-dozen women closest to the queen. With that came the opportunity to display her commodious talents, impressing visiting dignitaries with her language skills and charming the court with her dancing, lute-playing, and singing. Given that the Maids of Honor always traveled with the queen, she also adapted to a frenetic pace of packing and unpacking, with the court moving from palace to palace and place to place for dinner engagements and entertainments, sometimes every day.

---

[19] As Jean Robertson (1964, 296) also notes, "In Astrophil and Stella Sidney went out of his way to identify himself as Astrophil and Lady Penelope Rich as Stella; and after his death it would seem, from the many illusions in books dedicated to her, that Lady Rich liked to be reminded that she had been Sidney's Stella."

[20] Margetts (1992, 160) explains the sudden opening of a coveted Maid of Honor position as due to Anne Vavasor falling pregnant; she describes how Anne's "prospects for advancement, a good marriage, royal favor, [and] a stable future" all vanished—her life, "thereafter fraught with insecurity and shame," was a cautionary lesson for Penelope.

After 15 years Penelope had become accustomed to frequent travel, both from family visits, including lengthy ones to Wales and a number of nomadic months with her mother and sister in 1577, as well as from her bustling seven months in service to her queen (with a two-year respite of study in between the latter period). She seems to have developed a taste for frequent peregrination, as opposed to a more sedentary existence, which she evidently accomplished with facility and ease. Adding this interdisciplinary element of cartography to represent Penelope's life allows for an alternate accessibility to understanding her place in this world; her interactions with her peers, superiors, and subordinates; her growth as a woman; and, we hope ultimately, a more integrative approach to seeing her as a three-dimensional human as opposed to a distant historical figure.

Sometime in 1581, while Penelope was on the road with the queen, her guardians the Huntingdons determined that Lord Rich would be the ideal husband for Penelope, despite her vocal opposition. As Andrea van Deijck (2009, 29n4) frames it, "Devereux never consented to the match . . . but faced with little alternative, went through with the ceremony. . . . [She] did not develop affection for her husband, always calling him 'Lord Rich' as though he was an acquaintance rather than the usual 'my lord' or 'my lord husband.'" Yet van Deijck grants that "even in the cases of unwanted marriages women often still retained a sense of self and agency in bestowing themselves in marriage" (2).

Penelope certainly exhibited a high degree of agency, and she was a Rich now.[21] Sidney may not have married her, but with the *Astrophil and Stella* sonnet cycle, he wed Penelope to the artistic ideal established by Petrarch and his Laura, a Renaissance exemplar. As chronicled by Sidney, Penelope's reputation for perpetual motion is noted early on in his travel to her in sonnets 84 and 85, and in her own travel here in sonnet 105:

> Unhappy sight, and hath she vanished by,
> So near, in so good time, so free a place?
> Dead glass, dost thou thy object so embrace
> As what my heart still sees, thou canst not spy?
> I swear by her I love and lack, that I

[21] The resolve to Sidney's sonnet 37—"Hath no misfortune, but that Rich she is"—was thought to so clearly identify Penelope Rich as Stella that it was withheld from the 1591 publications of *Astrophil and Stella*, although it was restored to the sequence in Mary Sidney Herbert's folio of her brother's works, published in 1598 after Burghley's death. The original sonnet cycle is assumed to have been composed c. 1582.

Was not in fault, who bent thy dazzling race
Only unto the heaven of Stella's face,
Counting but dust what in the way did lie.
But cease, mine eyes, your tears do witness well
That you, guiltless thereof, your nectar missed.
Cursed be the page from whom the bad torch fell,
Cursed be the night which did your strife resist,
Cursed be the coachman which did drive so fast,
With no worse curse than absence makes me taste.[22]

"Stella has left the speaker at night," writes Jonathan C. Smith, emeritus professor of English at Hanover College, in an online blog examining the sonnets: "This poem laments the speed with which she 'vanished' from sight though still nearby. . . . Adding to the frustration, the second line suggests that she leaves at the very time, and in the very place, where the speaker's fortunes in love might have advanced" (J. C. Smith 2016).[23] Sidney also mentions her travel by water in sonnet 103: "O happy Thames, that didst my Stella bear!"

Sidney also seemed cavalier about revealing her secret lineage. Nicola Tallis (2018, 8) notes that Sidney describes her as "the richest gem of love and life," playing on "Penelope's surname, 'Rich,' throughout," but also that the poem is "littered with references to royalty that seem to openly confirm Penelope's royal heritage." Tallis gives as example these lines from sonnet 37:

Rich in the treasure of deserv'd renown,
Rich in the riches of a royal heart,
Rich in those gifts which give the eternal crown.

Sidney also waxed poetic about her physical attributes: her complexion, "built of alabaster pure," in sonnet 9; her eyes in sonnet 7 ("When Nature made her chief work, Stella's eyes / In color black why wrapt she beams so bright?"); and her cheeks in sonnet 13 ("Rose gules are borne in silver field").[24] Sidney's sonnet cycle is credited with launching the Elizabethan

---

[22] The quotations from Philip Sidney's *Astrophil and Stella* given here are taken from Jonathan C. Smith's *Blogging Sidney's Sonnets*. The original site is now offline, but all blog posts have been archived and can be accessed here: https://sonnets40.rssing.com/chan-9770791/all_p5.html.

[23] Perhaps this is where so many of her biographers absorb the notion of speed in relation to her travels.

[24] Sidney was not the first; Penelope seemed to bring out the poetic impetus in men.

sonnet craze, but it also established Penelope as the paragon of beauty. Woudhuysen (1996, 219, 291, 366) explains that this sonnet cycle circulated widely and was well-known, and both he and Duncan-Jones (1991, 200, 218, 239) agree that Penelope was an early and intended reader.[25]

Other poets followed suit, including Richard Barnfield, John Davies of Hereford, and, later, Alexander Craig. Henry Constable, a devoted fan, lauded her "lightning eyes" and "black sparckling eyes," lilies and roses were enlisted to praise her eyes and face, and the ubiquitous wordplay on her surname—"And *rich* it was as by the gold appears / So happy which in his arms it beares"—all appear in his *Diana* sonnet cycle (Constable 1859).[26] Some poets liberally employed star metaphors drawn from Sidney's *Stella*; the *Diella* (1596) sonnet cycle, for example, is thought to be a conflation of Diana and Stella. Samuel Daniel's *Delia* (1592) is posited to be about Penelope, as is Bartholomew Griffin's *Fidessa, More Chaste Than Kind* (1596)—Homer's constant Penelope with her many suitors is often called upon as stand-in and wordplay for Lady Rich.[27]

Margetts (1992, 120) cites the first known appearance in verse of Penelope Devereux in a Welsh sermon by Huw Llŷn written for her father's death in 1576, noting, "it seems appropriate somehow that [it was] an elegy written in Welsh, the language of her childhood summers." Also, Sidney's use of rose and silver is clever here, referencing the Devereux coat of arms with its argent, or silver, ground with three rose gules at the top.

[25] Margetts (1992, 208n12) also cites agreement with John Buxton (1987, 22).

[26] The "black sparckling eyes" comes from Constable's sonnet "To Mr. Hilliard, upon occasion of a picture he made of my Ladie Rich" (Constable 1859, 44–45), which concludes with another pun on her name: "Doth make the jewell which you paynt seeme Rich."

[27] Even Shakespeare seems to give nod to the zeitgeist with Boyet's line in *Love's Labour's Lost* (act 5, scene 2, line 2048): "Beauties no richer than rich taffeta." Varlow (2009, 169–70) cites Shakespeare's attraction to the Essex circle as fertile fodder soon upon his entry into London in the 1590s as reason for sonnet 84 acknowledging Lady Rich, as well as plot aspects of his plays; she would not be the first to suggest Penelope as the "Dark Lady"—scholars over the last century have posited as much, including those at the British Library (see bl.uk/collection-items/philip-sidneys-astrophil-and-stella-1591). Woudhuysen (1996, 253) acknowledges the preponderance of Penelope poems but exempts Spenser's *Amoretti* 23, however that is probably her, too. J. William Hebel (1924) argued for identifying Anne Goodere as the subject of Michael Drayton's *Sirena*, but if every other poet was seduced by the "cult of Penelope" (Varlow's term), it seems unlikely that Drayton would choose to be exempt; his Sirena lived

Does poet Barnabe Barnes pass the "Rich test"?[28] His *Madrigal* 9 is one of the places Penelope's prime identifier shows up, alongside other oft-used references for and to her:

> For glory, pleasure, and fair flourishing
> Sweet singing, courtly dancing, curious love
> A *rich* remembrance; virtue's nourishing . . .[29]

As previously noted, Penelope was renowned as an adept lutenist and for her high, clear singing voice; with that, an impressive list of sixteenth- and seventeenth-century musical luminaries flocked to write and dedicate music to her, such as William Byrd (possibly via Edward Paston of Appleton Hall), Charles Tessier, Robert Jones, John Dowland, Anthony Holborne, and perhaps John Bartlet. In a relatively recent reassessment of *The Triumphes of Oriana*, published by Thomas Morley, Jeremy L. Smith (2005, 558) asserts that "Morley and his mentor William Byrd were strongly linked to the Sidney/Essex complex of ideals" and convincingly argues for "a different allegorical identity not only for 'Oriana' (James's wife Anna) but also for the character 'Diana' (Essex's sister Penelope Rich), who appears in key works by Byrd and in all the Oriana madrigals as well." Smith clarifies that the work was only reconfigured as a tribute to Queen Elizabeth around 1601, after the fatal events surrounding the Essex Rebellion.

Dedications flowed, too, in works such as John Florio's 1603 translation of Montaigne's *Essays* and a curious poem, *Devoreux, Vertues Teares*, ostensibly by a French woman, Geneviève Petau, on the death of Penelope's brother Wat in 1591 and translated "paraphrastically" by Gervase Markham c. 1597.[30]

"near to the silver Trent," where sat Penelope's ancestral home of Chartley; she was also often linked with silver in her admirers' poetry referencing her complexion, the clarity of her singing voice, and that silver was an element of the Devereux family coat of arms. (It might be useful in a future project to create a table for all the marker words for Penelope.)

28 The "Rich test" is a useful term, I think, for determining whether a poem, sonnet/sonnet cycle, song, or other work is referring to Penelope Rich. Philip Sidney initiated the identifier with rich/Rich in *Astrophil and Stella* (in various songs and sonnets beyond the infamous sonnet 37), which other writers adopted, along with *star* from the titular Stella, among other markers discussed above.

29 Emphasis added. For *Madrigal* 9 specifically, which has been modernized here, see quod.lib.umich.edu/e/eebo/A04567.0001.001/1:4.61?rgn=div2;view=fulltext.

30 Gervase Markham himself describes the narrative poem as "paraphrastically trans-

Penelope's fame traveled far and wide and she herself was not far behind it. Favored by the queen and funded by a husband a bit intimidated by her pedigree and connections, she was free to move about as she pleased.

But that freedom had a lease, and the aforementioned stigma regarding travel for women in the Jacobethan period, with its assumptions of wantonness and immorality, was to prove a discomfiting foreshadow. Certainly Penelope's early travels discussed above, between family properties and relatives' estates, fell squarely within the "domestic sphere" approved of and assigned to women. She would have experienced firsthand what was involved in transporting the necessary household, with its attendant servants and provisions, what was necessary as a visiting guest, and what would need to be brought for a lengthy stay at a family-owned property (see, again, Video 1).

Once Penelope was moved to London from York and installed as a Maid of Honor to Queen Elizabeth, she had a crash course on how to travel on a grand scale, moving with the entire court from the queen's palaces to the estates of the landed gentry during the months of her "apprenticeship." Traveling with the queen, in company with the other five unmarried maids and their servants, would require a great deal of additional provisions and accommodation, most notably in the accoutrements of personal adornment: wigs, makeup, hot curling tongs, tooth cloths and other personal hygiene

---

lated," and in the dedicatory verse he writes, "if such like be my Paraphras vpon this French ground" (see name.umdl.umich.edu/A09513.0001.001). The work is dedicated to Penelope and her sister Dorothy, the full title being *Deveraux: Vertues Teares for the Loss of the Most Christian King Henry, Third of that Name, King of Fraunce; and the Untimely Death, of the Most Noble & Heroicall Gentleman, Walter Devoreux, who was Slaine before Roan in Fraunce*. Anne Lake Prescott (2008) sheds some light on this mysterious poem, the original of which is apparently lost. It is unclear how this work would have come about. Was Petau acquainted with Penelope? Gervase Markham certainly was—she was his patron. Prescott (2008, 228) notes that Petau "also apparently did a translation of James I's *Basilikon Doron* that Jean Hotman, son of the famous Huguenot, had suppressed" as inferior. Hotman, a private secretary to Penelope's stepfather, Robert Dudley, married Penelope's gentlewoman, Jeanne St. Martin, and was later in her service after the earl's death, so perhaps that was the conduit for this work. Prescott (2008, 228) assesses that "the work's agenda seems to be to encourage admiration of Essex, older brother of the fallen Walter, and perhaps to encourage the Devereux family to admire Petau/Markham." Incidentally, the poem also passes the "Rich test" in several places, most notably in stanza 18 (of 257!): "And thou rich *Rich*, richest did ere compile."

items, scents and tinctures, hoods, veils, coifs and cauls, fans, gloves, jewels, and other adornments to organize, pack, and carry.[31] There were as well the many articles of women's clothing including but not limited to starched ruffs, hooped farthingales, foreparts, kirtles, partlets, hanging sleeves, shoe ties, bodies, and bum rolls.

Outfitting the queen was of particular significance in 1581, as Elizabeth contemplated a pivotal marriage alliance with France. Her public face was always carefully cultivated—it was rumored to take hours to assemble her—and the Maids of Honor, while not as elaborately dressed, were symbols of status and purity, often clad all in white, neatly coifed, and pristinely presentable. Maintaining these fashion norms took considerably more effort while on the road (Arnold 2018, 110–2).[32] The queen was anxious to put distance between her court and London when plague broke out, so "for her ladies it meant hurriedly packing up ready for the baggage wagons" (Varlow 2009, 71) to another palace further afield (see Video 2 on the companion website).

Penelope's marriage to Lord Rich in November 1581 does not mean she was immediately whisked off to the country. Particularly in situations such as hers—she expressed opposition to the match at the wedding itself—women were eased into unwanted marriages by initially delaying the onset. Penelope seems to have stayed on in London, perhaps elevated in her now-married status to lady of the privy chamber (Margetts 1992, 237–47). The Earl of Leicester, now her stepfather, having married her mother in 1578, chose to dedicated a suite of rooms for her in his London estate of Leicester House (that suite would remain hers when her brother Robert took over the property the following decade), as well as at his estate at Wanstead (where he and Lettice had wed, and where, ironically, she would spend her final

---

[31] In the compelling double portrait of Dorothy and Penelope Devereux, both sisters have the distinctive Tudor red-gold hair, but later poetry and portraits highlight Penelope's golden tresses, so she must have had to utilize some of the kit listed here, along with saffron or marigold, to alter the hair color. Margetts (1992, 166) also mentions makeup concoctions that women used, making them in essence traveling chemists with substances such as "white fucus made of ground hog bones or mercury sublimate laid on with oil of white poppy and patted over with a lead-based powder." Simon Schama (2000, 372) notes that Queen Elizabeth's cosmetic regime consisted of pulverized borax, alum, and millwater.

[32] Elsewhere, Janet Arnold (1985, 15) quotes seventeenth-century writer Thomas Tomkis: "a ship is sooner rigged by far, than a gentlewoman made ready." Margetts (1992, 165) also notes that Penelope had never been so well dressed in her life.

days with Charles Blount). She never behaved as her husband's property and seemed to move about with "considerable freedom," as Margetts terms it, between court circles, relatives' domains, and her estates by marriage. It may have been during this period that Philip Sidney, Leicester's nephew, took up his pen and began to write the sonnet cycle that would launch Penelope's renown. As noted, poets, musicians, and others fell in line to fawn over her, which gave her a sort of celebrity status and a certain latitude to forge her own route. In a curious way, Sidney did marry her—to fame.

Sometime in 1582, Penelope had finally taken her place as the mistress of Lord Rich's various estates, particularly Leez Priory in Essex. For aristocratic women with aspirations beyond household governance, the umbrella of "domesticity" perhaps provided a convenient cover of superabundant industry in promoting the family's social standing. In Penelope's case, her habitual movements expanded beyond the parameters of domestic public relations. While she was known "as an active participant in the life of the county" (Margetts 1992, 286)—goddaughters and namesakes proliferated, and the country was dotted with Penelopes, a testament to both her reputation and accessibility[33]—she also kept current with court life. Penelope is always described as kind and generous, and, like Katharina in *The Taming of the Shrew*, she seems to have ultimately acquiesced to her married life and perhaps began to realize the advantages of a stable financial position and the armor of a wealthy husband she could wield to her will,[34] coupled with easy proximity to London, powerful friends and relations, assured accommodation, and the ability to move back and forth between these lives with a certain effortlessness.

The frequency of Penelope's travel, however, does call into question the ease of such mobility. Like the copious list of personal accoutrements necessary when traveling with the queen, a broader understanding of what travel required in terms of logistics comes via Lady Anne Clifford (1590–1676), who, while 27 years younger than Penelope, was a near-contemporary in status and social circles, particularly in the early reign of King James. She is also

---

[33] Margetts (1992, 286) notes the frequency of the name Penelope among daughters born in Essex—at least eight at last count. She also comments on the rarity of the prenom, noting that it was not a family name, and that "[b]ooks I and II of Homer's *Odyssey*, with their descriptions of Odysseus' faithful wife, were available at the time of her birth in the French translation of Peletier (1547) and might have provided inspiration to her parents" (37n22).

[34] An example of Robert Rich's tolerance of his wife's behavior is his appearance with her at court in 1600 alongside her lover Charles Blount (Varlow 2009, 201).

perhaps the only woman to record in detail the particulars of aristocratic travel at that time.[35] As early as 1603, Clifford recounts in her diary having ridden so fast with her beloved mother to catch up with the incoming Queen Anne's train—which also saw Penelope racing up to meet the new queen at Berwick-on-Tweed (see Varlow 2009, 227–28)—that they "killed three horses that day" of overexertion (quoted in Ambrose 2019, 164). Laura Williamson Ambrose (2019, 164) describes Clifford's young life as "swirled with movement," a phrase that could equally describe over three decades of Penelope's life beginning in the late 1560s. Clifford's scramble to see Queen Anne may even have included Penelope; she says, "I went the same night and overtook my aunt at Tyttenhanger, my Lady Blount's house, where my mother came the next day noon" (quoted in Ambrose 2019, 164).[36]

Clifford continues the harrowing tale: "[We] came to Wrest, my Lord of Kent's, where we found the doors shut and none in the house but one servant who only had keys of the hall, so that we were enforced to lie in the hall all night, till towards morning at which time came a man and let us in to the higher rooms, where we slept three or four hours" (quoted in Ambrose 2019, 164). We learn from her also that horses needed to be swapped out every 20–30 miles or rested for 24 hours before they could be ridden again. Among other things, her report underscores the importance of planning for overnight stays and sending messengers ahead to ensure access, but it also reveals that impetuosity did occur despite all the provisions required for a safe journey. Ambrose (2019, 165) highlights the insight Clifford provides into the "practice of borrowing horses for each leg of a journey" as well as a "marked nonchalance" and "the ubiquity of aristocratic domestic mobility," which is germane to Penelope's movements as well. A letter Penelope sent to her companion, Jeanne Hotman, bears this out as she expresses impatience in waiting for her

---

[35] Although a generation younger than Penelope, Anne Clifford later married Philip Sidney's sister's son and namesake, Philip Herbert, Earl of Pembroke, thus marring into the Herbert family. Clifford also performed in Queen Anne's masks, although in the years after Penelope, and comments at the outset of King James's reign about Queen Anne's social circle: "Now was my Lady Rich grown great with the queen, in so much as my Lady of Bedford was somewhat out with her [Penelope]" (quoted in Varlow 2009, 231). Clifford also became great friends with Penelope's eldest son Robert and his wife (Varlow 2009, 269).

[36] But a study of the maps suggests that this was more probably Penelope's mother, Lettice, having married Christopher Blount (a distant cousin of Penelope's lover, Charles Blount) after the Earl of Leicester's death; her estate is closest in proximity to these events. See also Ioppolo 2015, 79.

husband's return so horses can be sent for her (Penelope is apparently at Leighs after the delivery of her fifth child), he being so long coming that she deliberates over finding another option (see Margetts 1992, 365).

With the unexpected always a factor in travel, Clifford relates perils such as a horse falling off a bridge into the water and a carriage that needed to be carried down a hill to avoid upending. She describes traveling on horseback, in carriages, and in "my Horslitter, (my women riding in my Coach drawn with six Horses, and my Menservants on horseback)" (quoted in Ambrose 2019, 169). Accompanying servants were a necessity for women traveling "alone" for protection as much as for assistance and manpower; Ambrose (2019, 169) notes that one particular trip had Clifford traveling with "four wagons, more than thirty carts, horses, and twenty-one cartloads of goods." She also notes that Lady Anne Clifford's well-documented movements "echo the royal summer progresses of the Elizabethan and Jacobean monarchs" (169). Had Penelope written of her time with the queen or her own travels, she might have recorded similar experiences.

As the 1580s progressed, Penelope's luster continued to advance; she was often at court between pregnancies, and, as Jean Robertson (1964) pointed out, she liked being identified as Sidney's Stella. More poets and musicians joined the "cult of Penelope" to spread her fame even further—the many verses, madrigals, and other forms of music did some of the traveling for her. She was a copious letter writer as well, which extended her reach even further. She continued, all the while, to bear Lord Rich children, but by the end of the decade, perhaps giddy from all the attention and overly persuaded by her brother Robert's charisma, she began to move into dangerous territory. In 1589, she began a covert correspondence with King James—which was of course intercepted by Lord Burghley's vast spy network (Laoutaris 2013). She had perhaps been seduced by the power of her own beauty, even sending him a portrait miniature of herself in lieu of travel, with the aim of forging a powerful alliance with the man assumed to be the heir to Elizabeth's throne and tempting his alignment with her brother's agenda. Styling herself as "Rialta" (bearing news) in letters to the Scottish king, she had increasing involvement with the Earl of Essex as he expanded his power base with spies and foreign correspondents of his own, which necessitated more travel for Penelope.

Her beauty already abundantly acknowledged, Penelope's epistolary skill should also be mentioned here, since her words, traveling such a distance and to such highly placed people, had an impact on the breadth and ease of her movements. Friends in high places who were allies offered accommodation and assignations. As Margetts (1992, 330) frames it, her letters reveal "an interesting and international cross section of court society." King James, referencing her secret letters, had "com[m]ended muche the fyn[n]es of hir wit the Invencyon and well wrytyng" (Thomas Fowler's letter to Lord Burghley, quoted in Margetts 1992, 358). When assisting her sister Dorothy with her clandestine marriage to Sir Thomas Perrot, their correspondence mentions Penelope's "Excellent Gifte in speakinge" (quoted in Margetts 1992, 251). Margetts (1992, 251) emphasizes that "this is not part of the usual repertoire of compliment for women," noting that in context Perrot is referring to her writing talents, another aspect of her powers of persuasion beyond charm and beauty.

By the 1590s, if Penelope herself was not traveling between court and country (she was known to attend servants' weddings and stood godmother at baptisms) or visiting relatives and influential friends such as Frances Walsingham (Philip Sidney's widow who would marry her brother) or Elizabeth Vernon (a beloved cousin for whom Penelope would advance a match with her ally, Henry Wriothesley, 3rd Earl of Southampton and the dedicatee of Shakespeare's narrative poems in 1593 and 1594), she was represented by either her own letters or the artistic output extolling her virtues. With Sidney as the font of her initial fame—*Astrophil and Stella* achieved print beginning in 1591—her presence became somewhat of a celebrity sighting, with subsequent poets and artists vying to lay praise at her feet.[37]

What could be considered a third strata of plot points to be added to Penelope's map is derived from an ever-expanding set of alliances, employees, and confidantes over the years. These include the famed portrait miniaturist Nicholas Hilliard, for whom Penelope sat on several occasions; the writer Gervais Markham; Philip Sidney's daughter Elizabeth Manners (later Countess of Rutland) and her mother Frances Walsingham, who later married Penelope's brother; and émigré Jean Hotman, the Earl of Leicester's personal secretary who transferred to Penelope's employ and married her lady-in-waiting (see note 30 above). Marking these connections in terms of destinations affords a visual understanding of Penelope's expanded sphere of influence and a more nuanced understanding of where she was situated in this world at various points in time.

---

[37] As previously mentioned, *Astrophil and Stella* is said to have launched the Elizabethan sonnet craze, but Woudhuysen (1996) tracks how the poems were disseminated even before their first publication in 1591.

The pivotal event defining the 1590s for her was falling in love with Charles Blount, Lord Mountjoy, and effectively cohabiting with him (facilitated by her brother) and bearing him children. Verses in George Peele's *Polyhymnia* referencing this turn of events were in circulation at the time, clearly passing the "Rich test":

> Comes Sir Charles Blunt in Or and Azure dight,
> Rich in his colours, richer in his thoughts,
> Rich in his Fortune, Honor, Armes and Arte. (sigs. A4v–B1)

The poetry, proximity to her brother, the Earl of Essex, and wealth gave her a prominence and influence that seemed to fuel a desire for power as well. And this desire fueled her travel; Penelope learned, perhaps from the queen, the power of persuasion and the impact of her beauty and presence. Hiring Jean Hotman after Robert Dudley's death in 1588 was probably as much a political maneuver as a kindness to her beloved lady-in-waiting, whom he married.[38] Via French Hugenot Hotman's connections and correspondence, Penelope pulled several foreign diplomats into her sphere and sent another Hilliard miniature of herself to the French ambassador when she could not see him in person.

While society seemed to turn a blind eye to her affair with Mountjoy—and her seemingly blithe traversing between that world and the one she shared with Lord Rich—her alliance with her brother and her assistance with his political agenda was more problematic. His disastrous Irish campaign got him in serious trouble with the queen,[39] and his mounting desperation eventually led to his ill-advised rebellion on 8 February 1601. But Penelope, for whom inconstancy was anathema, stood by him throughout, taunting Elizabeth's

---

[38] Penelope's biographers differ in their views about her motivations for political power, with Margetts (1992, 1–3) asserting that Penelope craved a sphere of her own but had to achieve it through her brother, and Varlow (2009, 273) believing it was less about being hungry for power and more about dynastic desserts.

[39] Even though Penelope never traveled outside England—although a curious phrase by Woudhuysen (1996, 289) seems to suggest she went to Edinburgh in c. 1589 to curry favor with James VI—her life was inextricably linked to Ireland. It could be said that Penelope lost all three of the deep loves of her life to that country: her father died a painful death there; her brother's fateful Irish campaign led to his execution; and her beloved Charles sacrificed his health in service there and died not long after his final return. Even her poetic champion, Philip Sidney, had his family fortune swallowed up there when his own father was lord deputy of Ireland.

emissaries when they came to arrest Essex for his treasonous act.[40] That very morning she had rustled up carriage and grooms and driven "fast to the earl of Bedford's London home," to shore up support (Varlow 2009, 201). After her brother's beheading, she was repeatedly called in for interrogation regarding her involvement in printing the letter by Lord Treasurer Buckhurst over the ensuing months, but she often retreated to the country to avoid her interrogators.[41]

When considering women's travel in the sixteenth century, our perspective can be skewed because of perceptions derived from plays of the time. Shakespeare's Viola and Rosalind set off on adventures with only a brief pause to dress as boys for safety, Helena simply dons a pilgrim's equipage, and Desdemona insists on traveling with her new husband Othello to a war zone. In 1586 it was rumored that Penelope's mother sought to join her husband and son in the Netherlands "with such a train of ladies and gentlewomen and such rich coaches, litters and side saddles as Her Majesty had none such; and that there should be such a court of ladies as should pass Her Majesty's Court here" (Bruce 1844, 47, quoted in Laoutaris 2013, 209). Like Lettice, these female characters, while traveling for love, were also involved in the political sphere of their respective worlds, but Lettice in fact did not go. Her daughter-in-law, however, a pregnant Frances Walsingham, *did* go to attend her dying husband, Philip Sidney, in Zutphen (Margetts 1992, 285).[42]

In looking at Penelope Rich's travel patterns, we might gain a broader view of other women in this class in the sixteenth century, as she often traveled in the company of or to rendezvous with other female travelers including her mother; her sister; her guardian, the Countess of Huntingdon; her brother's wife, Frances Walsingham; her cousin, Elizabeth Vernon; Philip Sidney's daughter Elizabeth, Countess of Rutland; and perhaps Lucy Russell, Countess

[40] It must be said that soon after the Earl of Essex's arrest, he blamed his sister for urging him on to rebellion.

[41] Julie Crawford (2014) notes the correspondence between Robert Sidney, Philip's brother, and his secretary Rowland Whyte, who relays Robert's wife's advice about Lord Buckhurst's love for Sidney. This may be why Penelope was able to writhe out of the charges against her to the point where Robert Cecil felt he had to advise Buckhurst on sterner tactics with her.

[42] Lady Frances Sidney was detained in Utrecht after Philip's death by Robert, Earl of Leicester, due to his concerns for her travel over the Channel given her grief; she returned to London safely but lost the baby.

of Bedford—to name a handful in her immediate social circle (Tallis 2018, 8).[43]

The map of Penelope's "progresses" is further populated when this social circle is layered in. Although she was an active correspondent, she also understood the value of employing her position as a "mediatrix"—a term for women who functioned as influential go-betweens—in person. As Crawford (2014, 3) states, "Printed texts represent only a fraction of the ways in which women participated in literary culture." Penelope's epistolary "travels" were often augmented by her physical presence. Perhaps she learned from the queen when traveling with the sovereign as a Maid of Honor, coupled with the impact her own physical presence seemed to have on poets and others, that *in-person* persuasion could be her most powerful tool. While all her destinations seem perfectly reasonable within the context of circumstances, what appears unusual is the frequency with which she traveled between her various destinations.

Susan Doran (2015, 193, 207, 211) often takes issue with the highly gendered perspectives of sexual jealousy scenarios in regard to Queen Elizabeth and reframes them from the perspective of statecraft and governance. We might extrapolate that attitude for Penelope as regards her frequent travels. Rather than view Penelope as a social butterfly and fairy godmother, we would do better to consider her travels, at least by the 1590s, under the umbrella of political maneuvering and covert influence from a perspective of legacy, proximity, and preparedness. Was facilitating the secret wedding between her cousin Elizabeth Vernon and Henry Wriothesley, 3rd Earl of Southampton, an act of felicity or a shoring up of the amalgamated Leicester-Sidney-Essex-Herbert faction? The latter looks more likely when viewed in the light of her friend Lucy Russell aligning with William Herbert, 3rd Earl of Pembroke (Sidney's nephew), to lead by each hand George Villiers to and for the delight of King James (Crawford 2014, 8, 14).[44]

---

[43] Lucy, Countess of Bedford, is also said to have "ridden hard" to Edinburgh ahead of a party of gentlewomen (one of whom was Penelope) sent by Robert Cecil to the Scottish border to meet the incoming queen, Anne of Denmark, resulting in her becoming Lady of the Bedchamber and her closest confidant (Barroll 2001; Varlow 2009).

[44] Also, her cousin Vernon was pregnant at the time of the marriage in 1598, although Christopher Hibbert (2001, 73) asserts with surety that Henry Wriothesley was homosexual. While Penelope's marriage brokering is debatable pandering, the latter situation is far less so.

What Penelope did foresee (albeit not for her brother) via James's accession was her exalted status after more than a decade of covert loyalty. She instantly became a favorite of Queen Anne and a "star" in two of the dazzling masques by Ben Jonson presented at the outset of the glittering new reign, all of which must have been a dizzying relief after her brother's downfall and execution just a few years prior. But her preferment might have led her to believe that, as she did during Elizabeth's reign, she could pretty much do as she pleased. This proved untrue. Her long liaison with Charles Blount, with numerous acknowledged children, was "secret" in label only. The couple could not have predicted the severity of the king's wrath when she and Blount wed, disregarding canon law, on 26 December 1605—not long after her divorce from Lord Rich. Within a month, she was ousted from court and in deep disgrace. King James purportedly told Blount that he had won "a fair woman with a black soul"—although this is unconfirmed—and Penelope was subsequently whitewashed from history.[45]

Charles Blount was dead less than four months after their marriage. Here again Penelope moved quickly, while pregnant, to get from London to his bedside at Wanstead, but his lung disease was too far advanced.[46] She miscarried and, it was rumored, sat splayed in a corner on the floor veiled in black, weeping for days after his death on 3 April 1606. She had achieved everything she had striven for—political prominence, acknowledged precedence, and favor and standing at court—but the union with her beloved, to whom

[45] Although Penelope was known for her flashing black eyes and for her fondness for decorating with black, this oft-repeated quote does not appear to be sufficiently sourced. Varlow (2009, 248) claims James's obsession with black and white as justification for this quote and cites both Frederick M. Jones (1958) and Cyril Falls (1955), but neither cite its origin. Penelope was certainly derided viciously in the last year of her life for her marriage to Blount, his subsequent death, her adultery, and her children born out of wedlock, but all this was primarily in connection with lawsuits over Blount's estate. Some poets picked up on the slander and, as noted at the beginning of this chapter, King James did not allow her arms to be a quartered with her husband's at his funeral, but a reliable record of *this* quote has not yet been located.

[46] Doran (2015, 206) writes, "Another 'extraordinary woman'—Lady Anne Heneage (wife of Sir Thomas)—was said to be 'so seldome' at home because of her duties at court. . . . Married women were also expected to continue their service throughout their pregnancies. In the summer of 1565, Cobham bitterly complained to Cecil that his six-month pregnant wife had to travel down to Dover on the queen's behalf to welcome a Swedish princess (who was herself heavily pregnant)."

she had been devoted for over a decade, she only secured for little more than three months.

The remaining 15 months of her life were riven with lawsuits over his estate as she strove to protect her children's inheritance.[47] Libels and slander against her abounded over her liaison with Blount and the illegitimate children it produced, even though their hasty and ill-advised marriage had been to rectify that. She moved back and forth between the law courts and the home she had shared with Mountjoy, and she took refuge with her mother, probably at Drayton Basset, but the stress and strife of the constant court battles and accusations, not to mention her miscarriage, sapped Penelope of her strength. She died on 6 July 1607. She was 44.

Some poets still lauded her as the renowned great lady that she was, but there were perverse rhymes and ballads, too.[48] No one knows where she is buried. For someone who moved around as much as she did, it seems tragic that Penelope's final resting place is unknown, much less that there is no monument to the most celebrated muse of the age, save Elizabeth herself.[49] But maybe that allows us to see her as perpetually in motion, never ceding to a final stopping point. Perhaps she is still in motion.

---

[47] As Varlow (2009, 17) writes, "Mountjoy died a very wealthy man and his relations pursued his estate and Penelope, through every court open to them. She was not, they insisted, his 'lawful wife but an harlot, adulteress, concubine and whore,' and she had obtained his lands 'by devices and deceits.'"

[48] Varlow (2009, 226) cites Thomas Campion's Latin tribute, "Stella Britanna, Penelope," as well as ribald rhymes such as the following: "The devil men say is dead in Devonshire late / Of late did Devonshire live in Rich estate / The which with toys did Devonshire bewitch / That Devonshire died and left the devil Rich."

[49] It would stand to reason that if Penelope died at Essex House, she would be buried at the nearest parish, St. Clement Danes, which was so oft frequented by her during her lifetime. Sylvia Freedman (1983, 195) believed she had identified "A Lady Devereux" in the parish records as confirmation of her burial in All Hallows, Barking-by-the-Tower (several of her brother's children are interred there), but a rereading of the document, available on Ancestry.com, clearly states the burial entry as "Alce Deuorax" on 7 October 1607. Sans confirmation, her final resting place remains unknown, as yet.

WORKS CITED

Akhimie, Patricia. 2019. "Gender and Travel Discourse: Richard Lassels's *The Voyage of the Lady Catherine Whetenall from Brussels into Italy*." In *Travel and Travail: Early Modern Women, English Drama, and the Wider World*, edited by Patricia Akhimie and Bernadette Andrea, 121–38. Lincoln: University of Nebraska Press. doi.org/10.2307/j.ctv8xnh57.11.

Akhimie, Patricia, and Bernadette Andrea. 2019. "Introduction: Early Modern Women, English Drama, and the Wider World." In *Travel and Travail: Early Modern Women, English Drama, and the Wider World*, edited by Patricia Akhimie and Bernadette Andrea, 1–16. Lincoln: University of Nebraska Press. doi.org/10.2307/j.ctv8xnh57.5.

Ambrose, Laura Williamson. 2019. "Lady Anne Clifford's Way and Aristocratic Women's Travel." In *Travel and Travail: Early Modern Women, English Drama, and the Wider World*, edited by Patricia Akhimie and Bernadette Andrea, 158–78. Lincoln: University of Nebraska Press. doi.org/10.2307/j.ctv8xnh57.14.

Arnold, Janet. 1985. *Patterns of Fashion: The Cut and Construction of Clothes for Men and Women, c. 1560–1620*. London: Drama Books.

———. 2018. *Queen Elizabeth's Wardrobe Unlock'd*. London: Routledge.

Barnes, Barnabe. [1593?]. *Parthenophil and Parthenophe Sonnettes, Madrigals, Elegies and Odes*. [London: J. Wolfe]. name.umdl.umich.edu/A04567.0001.001.

Barroll, Leeds. 2001. *Anna of Denmark, Queen of England: A Cultural Biography*. Philadelphia: University of Pennsylvania Press.

Bruce, John, ed. 1844. *Correspondence of Robert Dudley, Earl of Leycester, during His Government of the Low Countries, in the Years 1585 and 1586*. London: J. B. Nichols and Son.

Buxton, John. 1987. *Sir Philip Sidney and the English Renaissance*. 3rd ed. London: Palgrave Macmillan. doi.org/10.1007/978-1-349-19023-2.

Calendar of State Papers. 1857. "James I: Volume 3, August–September, 1603." In *Calendar of State Papers Domestic: James I, 1603–1610*, edited by Mary Anne Everett Green, 26–43. London: Her Majesty's Stationery Office. british-history.ac.uk/cal-state-papers/domestic/jas1/1603-10/pp26-43.

Cole, Emily V. 2010. "The State Apartment in the Jacobean Country House, 1603–1625." PhD diss., University of Sussex. sro.sussex.ac.uk/id/eprint/6337.

Colthorpe, Marion E. 2017. "The Elizabethan Court Day by Day." Folgerpedia. folgerpedia.folger.edu/The_Elizabethan_Court_Day_by_Day.

Constable, Henry. 1859. *Diana: The Sonnets and Other Poems*. London: Pickering. archive.org/details/dianasonnetsothe00consuoft/mode/2up.

Coprario, John. 1606. "Funeral Teares: For the Death of the Right Honorable the Earle of Devonshire [. . .]." London: John Windet. name.umdl.umich.edu/A19264.0001.001.

Crawford, Julie. 2014. *Mediatrix: Women, Politics, and Literary Production in Early Modern England*. Oxford: Oxford University Press.

Doran, Susan. 2015. *Elizabeth I and Her Circle*. Oxford: Oxford University Press.

Duncan-Jones, Katherine. 1991. *Sir Philip Sidney: Courtier Poet*. New Haven, CT: Yale University Press.

Falls, Cyril. 1955. *Mountjoy: Elizabethan General*. London: Odhams Press.

Ford, John. 1606. *Fames Memoriall; or, The Earle of Devonshire deceased with his honourable life, peacefull end, and solemne funerall*. London: [R. Bradock]. name.umdl.umich.edu/A01048.0001.001.

Freedman, Sylvia. 1983. *Poor Penelope: Lady Penelope Rich, an Elizabethan Woman*. Bourne End, UK: Kensal Press.

Griffin, Bartholomew. 1596. *Fidessa, More Chaste Than Kind*. London. shakespeares-sonnets.com/Archive/Fidessa.htm.

Hebel, J. William. 1924. "Drayton's Sirena." *PMLA* 39, no. 4 (December): 814–36. doi.org/10.2307/457250.

Hibbert, Christopher. 2001. *Elizabeth I: A Personal History of the Virgin Queen*. London: Penguin.

Ioppolo, Grace. 2015. "Those Essex Girls: The Lives and Letters of Lettice Knollys, Penelope Rich, Dorothy Perrott Percy, and Frances Walsingham." In *The Ashgate Research Companion to the Sidneys, 1500–1700*, edited by Margaret P. Hannay, Michael G. Brennan, and Mary Ellen Lamb, 77–92. Vol. 1, *Lives*. Farnham: Ashgate.

Jones, Frederick M. 1958. *Mountjoy, 1563–1606: The Last Elizabethan Deputy*. Dublin: Clonmore and Reynolds.

Kinney, Arthur F. 2014. *Titled Elizabethans: A Directory of Elizabethan Court, State, and Church Officers, 1558–1603*. Edited by Jane A. Lawson. 2nd ed. New York: Palgrave Macmillan.

Laoutaris, Chris. 2013. "'Toucht with Bolt of Treason': The Earl of Essex and Lady Penelope Rich." In *Essex: The Cultural Impact of an Elizabethan Courtier*, edited by Annaliese Connolly and Lisa Hopkins, 201–36. Manchester: Manchester University Press. jstor.org/stable/j.ctv18b5n68.16.

Lawson, Jane A., ed. 2013. *The Elizabethan New Years Gift Exchanges, 1559–1603*. Oxford: Oxford University Press.

Margetts, Michele. 1992. "Stella Britanna: The Early Life (1563–1592) of Lady Penelope Devereux, Lady Rich (d. 1607)." PhD diss., Yale University.

———. 1993. "A Christening Date for Lady Penelope Rich." *Notes and Queries* 40, no. 2 (June): 152–54.

Peele, George. 1590. *Polyhymnia*. London: Richard Ihones.

Petau, Geneviève, and Gervase Markham. 1597. *Deuoreux Vertues teares* [. . .]. London: I. Roberts. name.umdl.umich.edu/A09513.0001.001.

Prescott, Anne Lake. 2008. "Mary Sidney's *Antonius* and the Ambiguities of French History." *The Yearbook of English Studies* 38 (1/2): 216–33. jstor.org/stable/20479331.

Quealy, Gerit. 2013. "Can We Still Call Her Kate Middleton?" *HuffPost*, 1 March 2013. huffpost.com/entry/kate-middleton_b_2778993.

———. 2021. "Queen Elizabeth and the Ethnobotany of Early Modern England." Paper presented at the 67th Annual Meeting of the Renaissance Society of America, online, 20 April 2021.

Robertson, Jean. 1964. "Sir Philip Sidney and Lady Penelope Rich." *The Review of English Studies* 15, no. 59 (July): 296–97. doi.org/10.1093/res/XV.59.296.

Samman, Neil. 1995. "The Progresses of Henry VIII, 1509–1529." In *The Reign of Henry VIII: Politics, Policy and Piety*, edited by Diarmaid MacCulloch, 59–73. New York: St. Martin's Press. doi.org/10.1007/978-1-349-24214-6.

Schama, Simon. 2000. *A History of Britain*. Vol. 1, *At the Edge of the World? 3000 B.C.–A.D. 1603*. New York: Hyperion.

Smith, Jeremy L. 2005. "Music and Late Elizabethan Politics: The Identities of Oriana and Diana." *Journal of the American Musicological Society* 58 (3): 507–58. doi.org/10.1525/jams.2005.58.3.507.

Smith, Jonathan C. 2016. *Blogging Sidney's Sonnets* [archived]. Accessed 28 August 2020. https://sonnets40.rssing.com/chan-9770791/all_p5.html.

Tallis, Nicola. 2018. *Elizabeth's Rival: The Tumultuous Life of the Countess of Leicester: The Romance and Conspiracy That Threatened Queen Elizabeth's Court*. New York: Pegasus Books.

van Deijck, Andrea. 2009. "'By Gift of My Chaste Body': Women as Gifts in Early Modern England and Its Drama." PhD diss., University of British Columbia. doi.org/10.14288/1.0067208.

Van Evera, Emily, and Christopher Morrongiello. 2005. *My Lady Rich: Her Teares and Joy*. Avie Records.

Varlow, Sally. 2009. *The Lady Penelope: The Lost Tale of Love and Politics in the Court of Elizabeth I*. London: Andre Deutsch.

Woudhuysen, H. R. 1996. *Sir Philip Sidney and the Circulation of Manuscripts: 1558–1640*. Oxford: Oxford University Press.

Chapter 10: GEA: Invisible Sienese Women Made Visible

Elena Brizio
Georgetown University, Villa Le Balze

Luis Meneses
Vancouver Island University

Introduction

The goal of this brief chapter is to present and explain the GEA project (from the ancient Greek Γῆ, which means "earth," chosen because women are the "earth" and the "heart" of the family) through a short description of the work that was undertaken in order to manage thousands of scattered pieces of information that refer to Sienese women in the time span from about 1450 to roughly 1570. By their nature and because they were produced by hand, archival sources (notarial ledgers, baptismal records, last wills, documents produced by public officials, and so on) are diverse, scattered, incomplete, and often too detailed. A simple, continuous, flexible, and reliable database is therefore needed to manage these sources and to help scholars navigate among many documents and the information they contain. Our analysis of fifteenth- and sixteenth-century Sienese women stems from academic work and personal curiosity to identify and study a category of people who, apart from a few exceptions, have aroused very little interest in the Italian historiographic panorama.

The starting point of the research was to try to understand the political history of Siena during a very difficult period in the sixteenth century, when the Republic of Siena was definitively conquered by Spanish and Florentine troops and lost its freedom (1555–59). One might naturally assume that, during these years, at least half of the population of Siena was composed of women—young and old, married and widowed, servants and nuns—but the city, at least officially, seemed to be populated only by men. Men ruled the city, men struggled for power, men held the most prestigious offices, and men were exiled. The initial research question was thus simply, where are the women? Or better yet, who are the women?

A brief case study may be helpful in explaining how GEA works. Aurelia Petrucci, granddaughter of Pandolfo Petrucci, was attributed by a contemporary historian (no documentation survives) only one husband, her cousin Giovanfrancesco. But through the archival information entered into the GEA

ISBN 978-1-64959-119-7 (paper) ISBN 978-1-64959-120-3 (pdf) ISBN 978-1-64959-121-0 (epub)
New Technologies in Medieval and Renaissance Studies 12 (2025) 261–78

database, it was possible to identify a second husband and three children, one from the first marriage and two from the second, who were otherwise unknown.

As stated, the years between 1450 and 1570 are the chronological limits chosen for this work. This period encompasses two very important political moments in Sienese history: (1) around 1450, we see the wealthy and politically well-connected group (called "Monte" in Siena) of the Nove first attempt to seize power and manage the city in a more elitist way; and (2) by the 1570s, historians begin to detect important changes in demographic and social trends after Siena's annexation to the Florentine duchy. As a consequence of its conquest in 1559, it took some time for Siena to reorganize civic life after years of local warfare, invasions by foreign troops, and voluntary—or compulsory—exile for many hundreds of citizens. But around 1570, we see some new economic and social trends begin to emerge. Future studies will thus need to start from here to analyze the latter part of the sixteenth century, still a relatively unstudied period of Sienese history.

In 1487, Pandolfo Petrucci, a member of the Monte dei Nove, returned to Siena after having previously been exiled for political reasons. Until his untimely death in 1512, with only a brief, voluntary absence in 1503 to spare the city from the reprisals of Cesare Borgia, Pandolfo governed the city, mainly for the political and economic benefit of his supporters. His abilities were praised by Francesco Vettori, Niccolò Machiavelli, and Paolo Giovio. Even Francesco Guicciardini (2010, 206), though accusing him of duplicity and propensity to promise more than he could honor, nonetheless recognized Pandolfo's prudence and ability. A long theoretical discussion on the best option between a government *largo* (inclusive) and a government *stretto* (restricted) was highlighted in the words of an anonymous contemporary chronicler, who reported in his diary that "the city is split in two, one part would like the thing to remain as it is while the other would like to live in common and by councils and not by *balìa*" (quoted in Isaacs 1996, 1014; my trans.).[1] His remark clearly illustrates the political difficulties Siena faced, the internal dissension among its citizens, and the economic issues that had been temporarily overcome under Petrucci's rule, but which returned after 1512 and ultimately led to the end of the Republic, first with war and then with submission to Florence.

[1] "la città è partita in due voluntà, una vorrebbe che la cosa stesse come la sta e l'altra vorrebbe che si vivesse a comuno e per conseglio e non a balìa."

The history of Siena after 1512 is not yet known in full detail. Between 1512 and 1555, when Siena was defeated and after the strenuous resistance of a small number of Sienese citizens recovered in Montalcino, we still lack fundamental economic and social information. In 1559, counting in vain on the help of King Henri II of France, the Republic of Siena officially ended. The population, both the inhabitants who still lived in the city, then under Spanish control, and the pro-French opposition who tried to resist in Montalcino, were once again united and subsumed as *Stato Nuovo* (new state) under the rule of Cosimo I de' Medici, duke of Tuscany.

According to some demographic data, the number of Sienese citizens fluctuated greatly in the first half of the sixteenth century. In the years 1501–10, the figure was about 18,500, and in the following decade it had reached 21,000. During the years 1541–50, the approximate figure was 22,500, but in 1556, at the end of the first part of the war, the number dropped to 10,271 *anime* (souls). In 1560, the official population was 13,679 *bocche* (mouths), and by 1569 it had expanded to 19,640 people including the city proper and the nearby *contado* (not included in the previous account) (Pardi 1923, 111–16).

Siena was a city in which endogamy—that is, marriages between the city's inhabitants—was very common due to a variety of social and economic issues. Even more interesting is the fact that only in some cases—due to political choices—were marriages established between people belonging to different political groups. These particular marriage choices presupposed two things. First, that the city, for economic reasons, was no longer involved in opening itself up to the surrounding world: there was no longer any talk of international trade nor of further exclusive European connections or transfers. The medieval "golden age" of Sienese merchants and bankers was over. Second, that marrying "inside" would have offered fewer opportunities to outsiders (specifically, Florence, Siena's encroaching neighbor) to access Sienese possessions and assets through intermarriage. In the eyes of its inhabitants, Siena would in this way maintain its political and economic independence without outside intermingling, and without risking the loss of its future as a free city—even if this result was not ultimately achieved.

Looking for Names

To find women in public records, it is necessary to search a variety of sources, since many different types of archival collections may contain references to women. Consider, for example, court records, which collect records of trials involving women as both defendants and accusers, or notarial records, which usually contain last wills, marriage contracts, and sale and purchase records of different types of property such as land, farms, and stores in which women participated. Women can also be found listed in public government reports (for example, the list of wives or female relatives of exiles) as well as in tax records, if, as widows, they were the head of their household. Unlike Florence, Siena did not have many private archives containing documents written by or belonging to women, even if they were famous and important, nor did it have many *libri di ricordanze* (memoir books) like Florence, where merchants and businessmen listed all their transactions as well as the birth and death of their children and other important facts of their lives. Looking for women, therefore, requires spending a lot of time in public archives, flipping through hundreds of volumes in search of names. On the other hand, Siena was the first town in Europe, starting in 1381, to keep records of all children, both boys and girls, baptized in the Baptistry of St. John. The baptismal registers of the Sienese church survive in their physical form since 1461, while the names of all the children baptized between 1381 and 1460 were copied into a huge volume that was kept in the Biccherna, the city's main financial office, as a kind of municipal civil registry. The GEA project concentrated on the *Battezzati* (the baptized) as a logical starting point, working at the same time, of course, on other archival collections.

Initially, the methodology was simple: randomly select archival volumes from various collections and transcribe the names of the women found, relying on a very basic Word document (and memory) to keep track of them. Figure 1 shows how the baptismal records were organized. For every year (or more), the pages of the log are filled by the day of the ceremony, in successive order, with information about the infants (both girls and boys) who were baptized. While the information is not structurally consistent, some of the data is always the same: the name of the child, the name of the father (and in many cases the grandfather as well), the family surname, and the date of baptism if different from the date of birth. Sometimes, the baptismal record includes additional interesting details, depending on the importance of the family. In the case shown in Figure 1, Aurelia's godfather was the cardinal of Volterra, Francesco Soderini (1453–1524), scion of an important Florentine family and brother of Piero (1451–1522), *gonfaloniere* of Florence in 1502; for a scholar interested in political relations between Siena and Florence, this might be useful information, perhaps found nowhere else. Other information might include the approximate time of birth—useful for drawing up an astrological chart—the day of the week of birth or baptism, and the names of the godparents—less or more important, as in the case of Aurelia. Because of the characteristics of Siena's particular political organization (as we have seen, a technical democracy increasingly tempted by a strong aristocratic drift), many city families carried a surname from ancient times, while newcomers are easily recognizable because the list names the child's father, grandfather, and even great-grandfather.

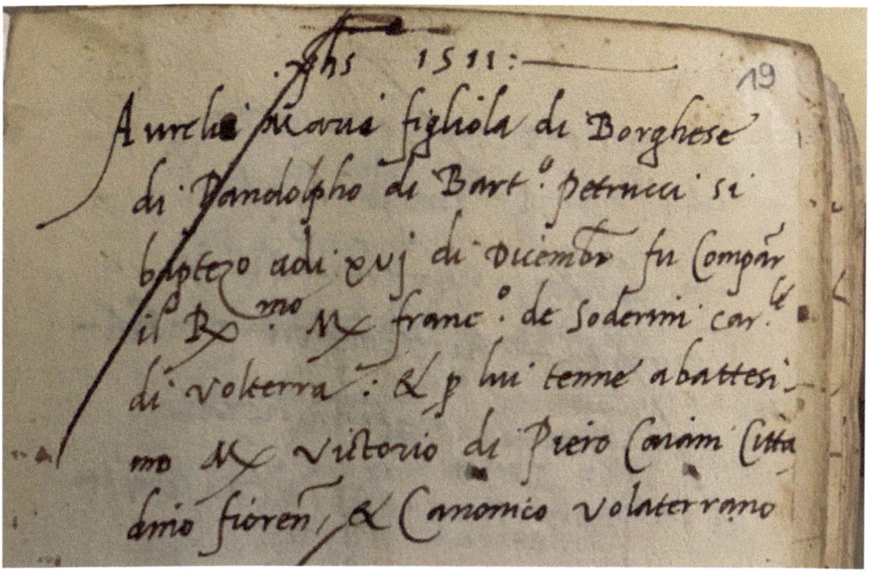

Figure 1. Archivio di Stato di Siena, Pieve di San Giovanni Battista 23, fol. 19r. This is the baptismal record of Aurelia Petrucci, showing the date of her baptism and the names of her father, grandfather, and godparents.

As you can see from the snapshot of the Word document (Fig. 2), details about newborn and baptized girls are listed as they appear in the archival document. There is no option to index personal names or family names. Fathers and grandfathers, though listed, cannot be indexed or searched: no family ties can be built except if done manually. The Word document, initially created as an index, was a static document; it could not be used to build a tool that would have allowed for the desired information to be located at a glance. Because of these limits, the work quickly became overwhelming: there were too many files to check, too many cross-references, too many missing connections, and the result was unmanageable. It therefore became necessary to create a simple relational database, in which all the scattered information—sometimes more or less complete—could be linked to create a more complete biography of the women of Siena. A database organizes data into one or more tables. Tables are made up of columns and rows, where each row is a different record, and each column represents data describing that record. In addition, each row has a unique key that identifies it, decreasing the possibility of duplicates. Relational database management represents the most popular way to create searchable ontologies among computing humanists (see Schreibman, Siemens, and Unsworth 2004).

The Archival Sources

The documents to be covered include women of differing social status—rich and poor, famous and unknown—and residents living both in the city proper and in the countryside. Many women are listed by their first name only, and many first names are extraordinarily common. For example, many women named Margherita or Agnese remain unidentified, which can lead to some uncertainty among the records. Since the issue of correct identification is crucial, we chose to start with women belonging to families with registered surnames, such as the important Piccolomini family and the lesser known (but politically strong) Petrucci family. All of this collected information is reflected in the "Person" table in the database. The "Person" table includes basic details such as each woman's full, modernized name (to make searches more efficient), as well as name variations. In the example shown in Figure 2, you will notice that there is a reference to a girl born into the Griffoli family: her name in the database will be displayed as "Antonia," but "Tonnia" (as it was recorded in the baptismal record) will also be listed in the name variants. Each name can be spelled in different ways, so the database also includes the "original" way the name was spelled.

Pieve San Giovanni 13
1495-1497

01r Panphila Isiphile di Lucia Mora [canc: di] si batteçò adì 6 di giugno [1495] fu commare mana Cristofana

02v Beatrice Francesca figluola d'Antonio di Niccholo Mannucci si battezò adì 17 di giugno [1495] fu compare Alexandro di Bartolomeo di Giacoppo Petrucci

02v Margherita d'Andrea figluola di Iacomo di Giovanni Pini si battezò adì 18 di giugnio [1495]

14v una fanciula naque a Richa... di Lorenzo Grifoli se li pose nome Tonnia [sic] chomare una dona da santo spirito el dì 18 d'otobre [1495]

19v Agnesa figliola di Troilo di Pietropavolo de Boninsegni fu batezata adì 6 di novembre [1495]

29v Battista Antognia figliuola di Fatio di Pietro Pavolo Gallerani fu batteçata addì 17 di ferraio 1495 [1496]

Figure 2. Elena Brizio's transcription of Archivio di Stato di Siena, Pieve di San Giovanni Battista 13. This Word document was a first attempt to make a record of names: simple, but unusable for the goal of connecting information.

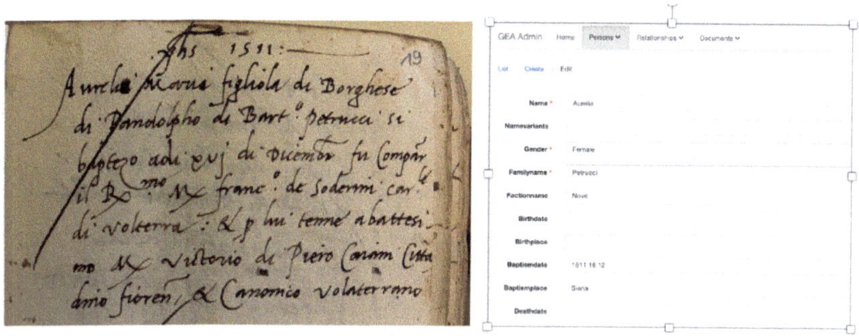

Figure 3. Comparison between the original archival document and the data entered in GEA's "Person" table. As you can see, some information of the original archival document (the godfathers) have not been included in Aurelia's database record.

Other relevant information is the political group identity of the family of origin of both women and men (this information is important to reconstruct family alliances forged mainly through marriages) and the date and place of both birth baptism; if different, the process will involve searching for information in other similar or private archives, but this is work for a future iteration of this project. Finally, the date and place of death are recorded; this information tends to be more difficult to find because we do not have death records to complement the baptismal records. Unfortunately, not all of these women left existing wills or other legal records (inventories, contracts, and so on) in which we could find the exact date of death recorded and the burial place, if known.[2]

The names of the paternal and maternal father and grandfather of the "Person" are extremely important because in Siena, as elsewhere, it was very common to give the same baptismal name (considered a "family" name) to all children born in different branches of the same family. Homonymy has been one of the biggest obstacles in compiling this database, and an example will illustrate this further. The Florentine Medici family is known throughout the world: all of its male children received names chosen from a very short list,

[2] An important caveat: in Siena, as in Florence, the new year began on 25 March, the day of the Annunciation. The days between 1 January and 24 March were therefore considered part of the previous year. In numerical fields containing dates, these have been modernized, with the double entry (e.g., 1531/2) listed in the "Reference note" field (see more below).

which included Cosimo, Piero, Lorenzo, and Giovanni. How might one recognize which Lorenzo or Giovanni is under consideration? It becomes possible through the addition of the father's name and also the grandfather's name. Similarly in Siena, both girls and boys were given the usual "family" names that returned with each generation. Cousins (often many cousins) were identified only by their fathers' and grandfathers' names. There is also another issue, however, that needs to be considered. It was extremely common to give an infant, according to its biological sex, the name of a previous sister or brother who had recently died. The idea was that the "protection" of the dead would be passed on to the infant (Klapisch-Zuber 1988). While this was a meaningful way to honor the dead, it also added countless members of the same family with exactly the same name.

If the record carries information for a woman who was a nun, or for a young girl who later entered a convent, in addition to the required mandatory information we often have the name the woman took when she professed her vows, the name of the convent and the place where the convent was located, and the start and end date of the time she spent in the convent. All these details, as you can imagine, are often incomplete. For many nuns, we only have the religious names they took upon acceptance into the convent. Even the father's name (which would have been helpful in "locating" the girl) was not always listed. A few nuns may have moved from one convent to another, further complicating the picture, and we do not possess complete lists of nuns for every convent of the city or for every year. Our lists, of course, depend on surviving documentation. For the specific time period on which we are focusing, information about nuns is scattered, often lost, and generally confusing. For example, how should the record of a married woman, perhaps with children, who later decided to enter a convent be populated? This was not an uncommon scenario at the time, and it is a case where a relational database does not provide the adequate affordances for documenting it. Figure 4, for example, shows a document of 1531 that provides a list of the nuns of the convent of St. Niccolò. On the one hand, it shows how many votes for the election of the future abbess two of the nuns received (whose names are written in a column on the left of the page), but on the other hand, it does not (with one exception, for "suor Camilla Doccia") provide the family names of the nuns.

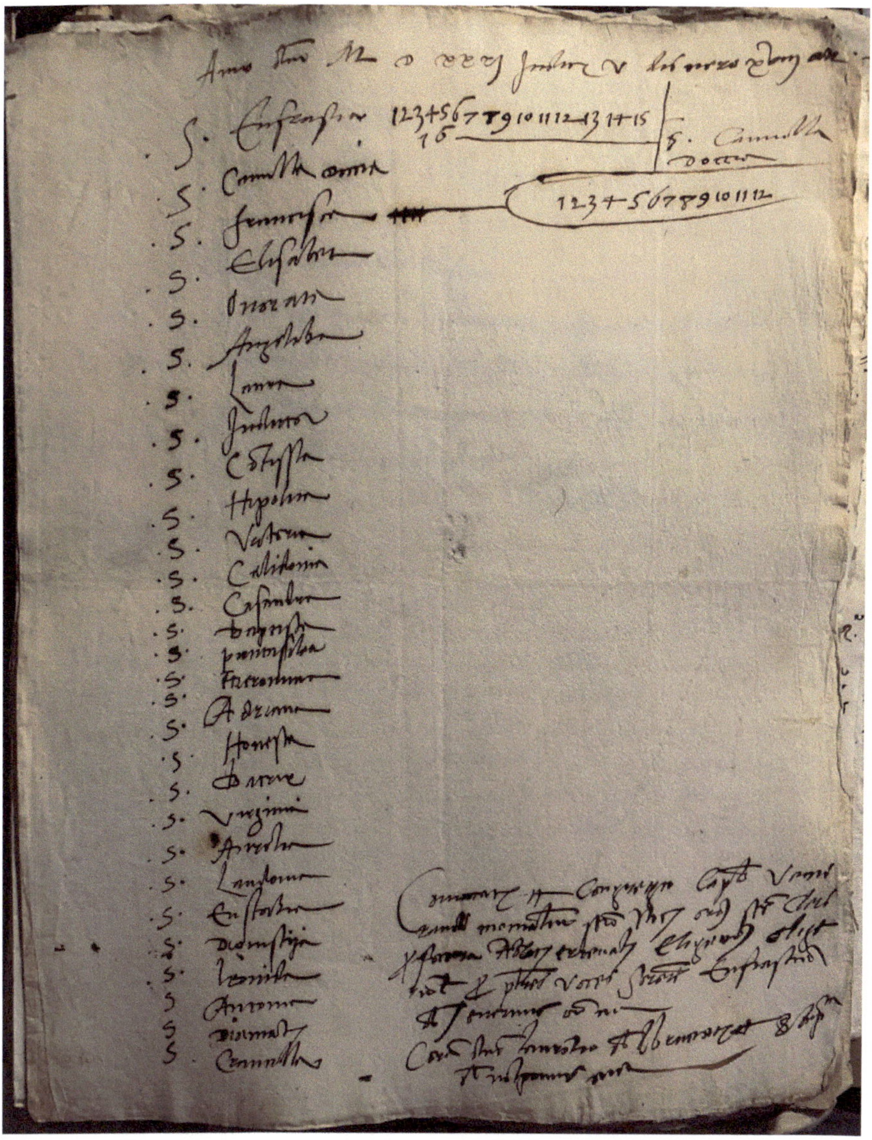

Figure 4. A list of the nuns of the convent of St. Niccolò for the year 1531. Archivio Arcivescovile di Siena, Fondo Storico della Curia Arcivescovile di Siena 3890.

Let us pause the narrative for a moment to analyze this document, located in the Archivio Arcivescovile di Siena, to further illustrate the work. This document is extremely interesting and rare—in fact, it is the only one of its kind yet found—because we can see how many votes for the office of abbess the two candidate nuns each received. It also records who dropped the last ballot that gave the majority to the winner (next to the number "16" there is a line and the name "suor Camilla Doccia"). Unfortunately, however, the document on its own does not help our research into who these nuns were (except for Camilla Docci, here "Doccia"), because we are only given the chosen names of the nuns, not their last names. But through the database—assuming we have collected previous (albeit scattered) information about at least some nuns in this specific convent—we can tentatively attribute a family name to many of them. All the "Record" fields can (and should) also be used to collect information about the men in these families. While we are not primarily interested in these religious men, this is another "open field" for data on the statistical, economic, and power positions of each named entry that will enhance our understanding of Sienese society.

In the future, we also expect to find information about the professions of some of these women. A "Profession" field is thus listed in the "Person" table, as well as related fields for the start and end dates of the occupation. Because we chose to start with known members of upper-class urban families, this field may seem redundant right now, because we know that upper-class women did not work outside the home. But, eventually, this will be the place to list, for example, a famous courtesan or a famous (and clearly identified) prostitute or seamstress or wet nurse.

Finally, at the end of each record there are two extremely important fields. The "Reference note" is a metadata field that references the location of the archival source. Here, the dates, as explained earlier, are in a double year format (e.g., 1531/2). The "Research note" field, on the other hand, resembles a notepad, where details that need to be checked and questions that need to be clarified can be recorded (see Fig. 5). The "Reference note" field should be filled with the appropriate reference when entering any type of record. At the beginning of the project, we enthusiastically started loading names to test the database and then had to spend a large amount of time retrieving the correct references to fill in this critical field.

Relationships between Persons

Once the "Person" table is completed for each individual, it is time to link the information to see the different relationships that a person may be involved in, including marriage, motherhood, and many other types of familial relationships (Fig. 5). On the "Relationship" table we can also report the information that needs to be created to refer to familial and social ties:

"Person 1" and "Person 2" are the people whose relationship needs to be highlighted; the "Relationship name" indicates the type of relationship (e.g., father, mother, cousin, or husband).

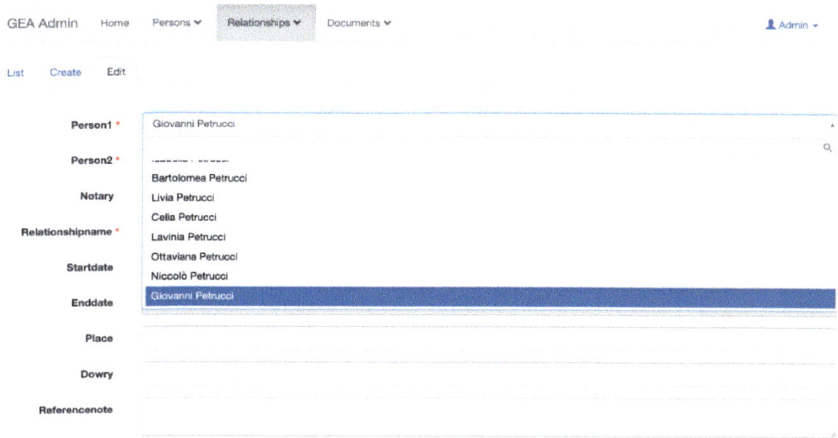

Figure 5. Data entry for GEA's "Relationship" table. Scrolling down the list of names (both female and male) belonging to the Petrucci family, we can locate the individual we are looking for.

If the relationship is a marriage, the name of the notary, if available, is listed, as well as the place where the marriage took place, the start and end date of the relationship, and the amount of the dowry paid by the bride's family. Remarriages occur frequently, and they can be listed by simply adding the new name in the field for "Person 2." If the relationship is a birth, the names of both parents, when available, will each be listed as "Person 2" in the record. It is quite common, however, for the mother's name to be missing (as seen above in Fig. 1). The offspring legally belonged to the paternal family, so mothers are more difficult to find in baptismal records.

Other Documents

As mentioned earlier, women can be found in many different types of archival sources, including notarial or fiscal records. The method for including these additional documents is very simple. Each document can be linked to a "Person" record and includes a "Date" field that refers to the document being analyzed, a "Document name" field (for example, "last will," "sale contract," or "rental contract"), and a "Location" field (Fig. 6). The "Document" table is flexible to allow for the inclusion of different types of documents, which may include various pieces of information such as, for example, a book citation of a woman's name. As usual, the "Reference note" and "Research note" fields are the key working tools for linking and referencing source materials.

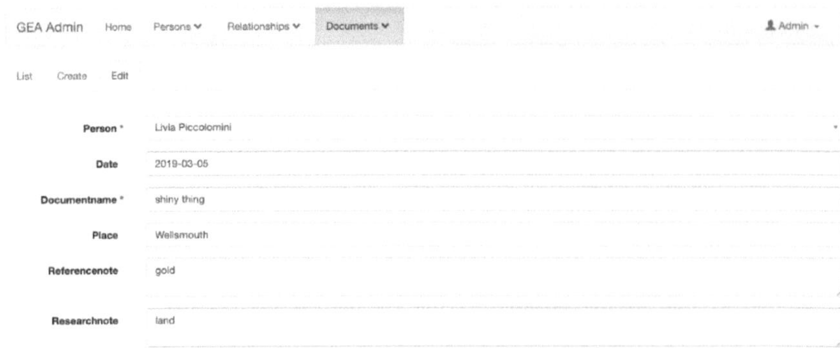

Figure 6. Data entry for GEA's other "Document" table.

One extremely rich source of information, but one that is rather difficult to tap into because of the amount of different information it provides, is the last will. In addition to the date of the will and where it was written, it usually lists the heir(s) and the executor(s) of the will itself. Additionally, several last wills may belong to the same woman, which means we can track her different life choices and see how she adapted her will to changing circumstances. If an heir died unexpectedly, for example, the testatrix would have to change her instructions to make sure there were no problems with the inheritance.

In addition to the still missing "Heirs" field (see more below), which should list heirs in the order in which they appear in the original document and not in order of importance, other fields specifically related to the will should be considered. These include the type of inheritance received and its specification (goods or money), and a description of the inherited property—for example, a house or a convent cell (for a nun). All of this information, which can be quite complex, has no specific place in the current database implementation. This is a case where the "Research note" field may hide some of these important details. A "Substitute heirs" field, which would list the people who were to replace a predeceased heir, as ordered by the testator, could be integrated into future versions of the database.

The Technical Aspects

According to my co-author and webmaster Luis Meneses, GEA is a dynamic site that is deployed on a Linux web server. It is based on Python and relies on open-source libraries.[3] Python was chosen because it supports Unicode, which is an information technology standard for the consistent encoding, representation, and handling of text expressed in most of the world's writing systems. More specifically, GEA's web pages are rendered with Flask (flask.pocoo.org) using the metadata from the records on a MySQL database (mysql.com). Flask is often classified as a microframework because it does not require particular tools or libraries. Moreover, Flask supports extensions that can add application features: for example, Luis used SQLAlchemy (sqlalchemy.org) as a relational mapper for the database models. Flask was chosen because it allows developers to build robust prototypes quickly.

GEA uses a model similar to those employed by other successful projects in the digital humanities that rely on relational databases (where structured records can have predefined relationships between them) as a research tool. For example, the Online Picasso Project (picasso.shsu.edu) consists of a complex system of interrelated databases that include both texts and images pertaining to Pablo Picasso. In this case, the use of relational databases has facilitated the maintenance of a large collection of artworks, along with associated critical narratives, enabling users to create and visualize a dynamic art catalog by combining and linking the different components in the collection and allowing users to analyze artworks in ways not possible with printed versions.

The counterpart to the relational database model is the non-relational model. In the non-relational model, data can be stored in other formats such as XML, which is a markup language and file format for storing, transmitting, and reconstructing data. For example, DEx: A Database of Dramatic Extracts (dex.digitalearlymodern.com) is an online, searchable database of extracts transcribed from seventeenth-century manuscripts. DEx stores its data in XML format and is an example of a successful project that uses a non-relational database. In the case of DEx, XML was chosen because the metadata for each extract was stored in TEI, which uses XML as the basis for its encoding.

On the whole, however, the use of relational databases is common for projects in the digital humanities. As an additional example, the Canadian HSS Commons (hsscommons.ca) aims to connect and support the work of researchers in the humanities and social sciences across Canada and is an instance of a

[3] For a comprehensive tutorial on Python, see Rossum 1995.

large-scale project in the digital humanities that uses a relational database. In the case of GEA, a relational database was chosen because of the speed and convenience that it can provide.

By default, Flask uses the Jinja2 templating system (palletsprojects.com/p/jinja). Jinja2 is one of the most used template engines for Python, and it is distributed under a BSD license, imposing minimal restrictions on the use and distribution of its covered software. Jinja2 is inspired by Django's templating system (djangoproject.com) but extends it with an expressive language that gives template authors a more powerful set of tools with which to work. Taking advantage of this expressiveness, Flask afforded the deployment of a modular master template that allows a chosen layout and structure to be extended onto all the pages of the project. The current version of GEA has views for browsing records for people, factions, families, places, and documents. These records are retrieved and displayed using DataTables (datatables.net) for the browsing view (Fig. 7), while individual details for each record are displayed using a customized view.

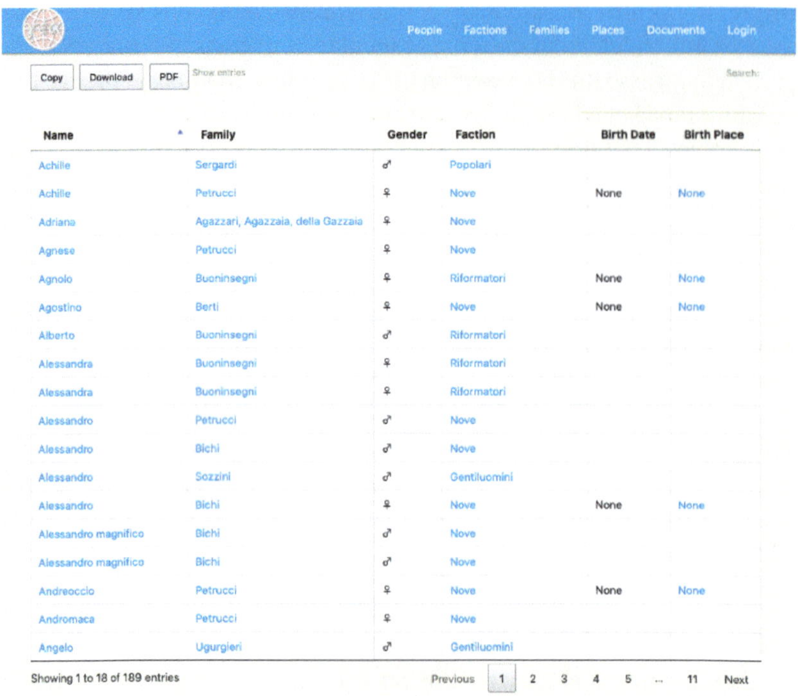

Figure 7. Screenshot of the view to browse records in GEA.

A password-protected administrative section was also incorporated into the current version of GEA (Fig. 8). Since Flask does not natively support user validation, Luis used Flask-Admin (flask-admin.readthedocs.io/en/latest) for this task. Flask-Admin incorporates an administrative interface on top of an existing data model; this was appropriate for our purposes, since GEA does not require a complex framework for user management. The administrative section in GEA provides views and forms for creating, editing, and deleting records. This functionality gives the principal investigators complete control over the content in the project.

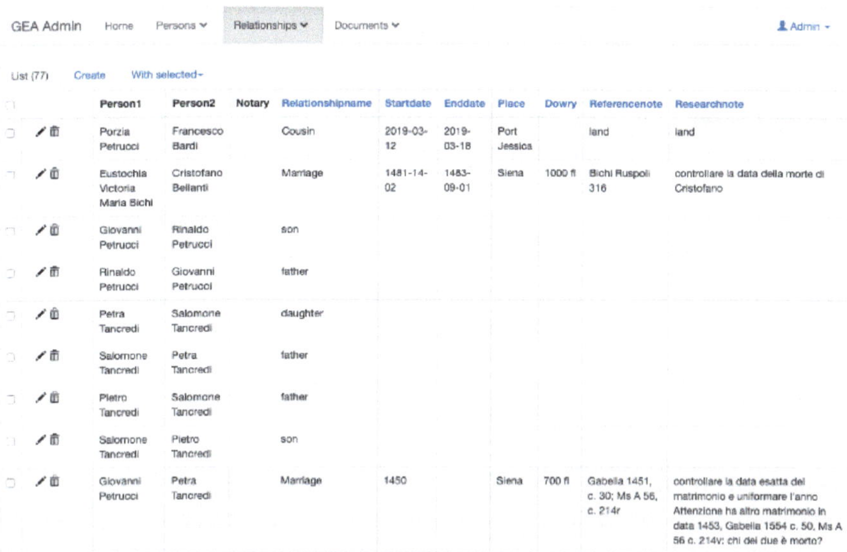
GEA Admin Home Persons Relationships Documents Admin

List (77) Create With selected

Person1	Person2	Notary	Relationshipname	Startdate	Enddate	Place	Dowry	Referencenote	Researchnote
Porzia Petrucci	Francesco Bardi		Cousin	2019-03-12	2019-03-18	Port Jessica		land	land
Eustochia Victoria Maria Bichi	Cristofano Bellanti		Marriage	1481-14-02	1483-09-01	Siena	1000 fl	Bichi Ruspoli 316	controllare la data della morte di Cristofano
Giovanni Petrucci	Rinaldo Petrucci		son						
Rinaldo Petrucci	Giovanni Petrucci		father						
Petra Tancredi	Salomone Tancredi		daughter						
Salomone Tancredi	Petra Tancredi		father						
Pietro Tancredi	Salomone Tancredi		father						
Salomone Tancredi	Pietro Tancredi		son						
Giovanni Petrucci	Petra Tancredi		Marriage	1450		Siena	700 fl	Gabella 1451, c. 30; Ms A 56, c. 214r	controllare la data esatta del matrimonio e uniformare l'anno Attenzione ha altro matrimonio in data 1453, Gabella 1554 c. 50, Ms A 56 c. 214v: chi dei due è morto?

Figure 8. Screenshot of the password-protected administrative section of GEA.

All the software and libraries used in GEA are distributed under an open license, which means that they can be freely used, distributed, and modified. Here, the choices Luis made in terms of the software and technologies used were very intentional. Software and libraries under open licenses are commonly supported by the community over longer periods of time—a crucial aspect for extending the longevity of GEA. However, using software under an open license does have some drawbacks. For example, updates can take some time to be incorporated into the existing codebase, and software libraries are often replaced by new ones that provide similar functionality. Nonetheless, use of an open license is, in Luis's opinion, vital for ensuring the reliability of a digital humanities project over time.

Desiderata *and Future Work*

Among the *desiderata* worthy of future attention is the practical possibility, once the "Person" records are filled in, to quickly highlight different names from that list (e.g., a woman and her second husband) and link them with one click instead of having to scroll through the entire menu to find the right person. Moreover, a populated list would provide two different access options for retrieving names, from women's names but also from men's names. The names would be sorted either by alphabetical order of the family name or by first name, separating and sorting the women's and men's names but listing them alphabetically within the family. To clarify, alphabetical order by family name would look like "Bellanti, Bichi, Chigi" and so on; then, within each family group, female names would be listed one at a time—"Agnese, Alessandra, Andrea" and so on—and then male names—"Bartolomeo, Cristofano, Giovanni." The other option would be first "Agnese, Alessandra, Andrea," then "Bartolomeo, Cristofano, Giovanni," grouped by the alphabetical family name "Bellanti, Bichi, Chigi" and so on. This would streamline the identification of names more quickly and could be used, for example, to show the consistency of certain names within a given family or the shifting trends of name choices.

Other hoped-for additions include a repeatable "Heir" field on the "Document" table to list all the named heirs in a last will; the ability to indicate that a married (or widowed) woman can enter a convent and become a nun; the (very important) inability to continue to upload information if the "Reference note" field is not filled in; and last but not least, that *all* information already uploaded in a given "Person" record will appear immediately when the name is chosen, without the need to re-enter it.

A further question to consider is how best to make use of financial records that include a lot of personal and social information, such as tax forms personally handwritten and filled out by women heads of household. In addition to recording personal details, such as a woman's age and occupation, these records tend to collect familial details, such as whether a woman was married or widowed; the name of her husband or husbands; and the number of children she had (although often they are unnamed and only listed by gender), their approximate ages at the time, and their marital statuses. Financial records also often provide economic details, such as whether a woman had assets and/or property (and if so, what they include and their value), whether she owned her home, and whether any said assets were part of her dowry. Each archival source offers different facts, but GEA allows us to organize and compare each source to better understand Siena in a very nuanced, but also very new, way. No library or archive participated in the creation of this database, but this does not mean that GEA, or its underlying structure, could not be adapted to the diverse needs of other colleagues.

Approaching history from the perspective of women does not mean that men are excluded, but using a gender-oriented approach is quite new and could be fruitful and interesting. Through GEA, many Sienese women (and the men associated with them) will come alive. In the future, we hope that other less prominent family names will be added. Once the basic information is accessible, other scholars studying Siena both before and after the period currently analyzed in GEA will hopefully contribute and collaborate by adding information into the structure of the database. At the moment, the proposed fields for GEA seem sufficient, and we have decided to make them non-editable. We hope, however, that in the near future, other colleagues will use GEA to directly add information about other periods in Siena's history, thus helping us to better understand this beautiful city and the people who populated it. Perhaps there will be an opportunity to create new collaborations (Italian and international) that will allow us to modify GEA, making it even more useful and accessible. GEA was born as a specialized research tool (which means that it is slowly accumulating information), but we hope that its structure can be adapted to similar projects in the digital humanities and be made available as soon as possible.

WORKS CITED

Guicciardini, Francesco. 2010. *Opere*. Vol. 1, *Storie fiorentine, Dialogo del reggimento di Firenze, Ricordi e altri scritti*. Edited by Emanuela Lugnani Scarano. Turin: UTET.

Isaacs, Ann Katherine. 1996. "Cardinali e 'spalagrembi': Sulla vita politica a Siena fra il 1480 e il 1487." In *La Toscana al tempo di Lorenzo il Magnifico*, 1012–50. Vol. 3, *Politica, economia, cultura, arte*. Pisa: Pacini.

Klapisch-Zuber, Christiane. 1988. "Il nome rifatto: La trasmissione dei nomi propri nelle famiglie fiorentine." In *La famiglia e le donne nel Rinascimento a Firenze*, 59–90. Rome: Laterza.

Pardi, Giuseppe. 1923. “La popolazione di Siena e del territorio senese attraverso i secoli.” *Bullettino senese di storia patria* 30:85–132.

Rossum, Guido van. 1995. “Python Tutorial.” Technical Report CS-R9526. Amsterdam: Centrum voor Wikunde en Informatica. ir.cwi.nl/pub/5007/05007D.pdf.

Schreibman, Susan, Ray Siemens, and John Unsworth, eds. 2004. *A Companion to Digital Humanities*. Oxford: Blackwell. doi.org/10.1002/9780470999875.

Chapter 11: Beyond a Digital Catalog: Rethinking Musical and Cartographic Sources through Digital Humanities

Angela Fiore
University of Messina

Sara Belotti
University of Milan

The House of Este was a princely dynasty that played a great part in the history of Renaissance Italy. Ferrara, the first seat of the family, became a significant center of culture thanks to Este patronage (Durante and Martellotti 2005; Lockwood 1984). The family included several patrons of music; in particular, Leonello, Ercole I, and Alfonso II made Ferrara one of the greatest laboratories of musical experimentation of Italy's Renaissance.[1] In 1598, the Papal States, ruled by Clement VIII, came into possession of Ferrara, and following the "Conventions of Faenza," the Este were forced to quickly move to Modena, the duchy's second most important city. The entire cultural heritage of the Este family—consisting of illuminated codices, fine sixteenth-century books, works of art, instruments, and musical manuscripts—was consequently transported in a hurry during the dramatic days of the court's relocation.[2] Following the transfer and the new arrangement of the court, attempts were made to replicate Ferrara's former artistic and musical splendor in the Este's new capital. During the seventeenth century, the three succeeding dukes of Modena—Cesare I, Francesco I, and Francesco II—contributed to the cultural and musical development of the city. The court entertained various relationships with some city institutions, contributing to the cultural growth of the city. However, it was during the reign of Francesco II d'Este,

[1] In particular, the interest of Alfonso II for the music and above all for the madrigal was realized not only in financing the publication of musical works but also in the establishment of musical ensembles, including the famous Concerto delle Dame Principalissime.

[2] This event is known as the "devolution of Ferrara." After the death of Duke Alfonso II, who left no direct heir, the pope did not renew the investiture of the feud of Ferrara to the Este, and it therefore returned to the Papal States. The transfer of the court, led by the new Duke Cesare, took place on the eve of 29 January 1598.

ISBN 978-1-64959-119-7 (paper) ISBN 978-1-64959-120-3 (pdf) ISBN 978-1-64959-121-0 (epub)
New Technologies in Medieval and Renaissance Studies 12 (2025) 279–305

the tenth duke of Modena and Reggio Emilia from 1674 to 1694, that the city's cultural splendor reached its peak.[3]

Francesco II promoted extensive cultural initiatives in the city, including the renewal of the university, the activities of literary academies, the continuation of artistic and architectural works in the Palazzo Ducale, and the reorganization of the ducal library. The ducal court welcomed new musical genres and forms under the cultural stimulus of Francesco II: oratorios, operas, and cantatas by the leading composers of the time, such as Alessandro Stradella, Alessandro Scarlatti, Giovanni Bononcini, Bernardo Pasquini, and Alessandro Melani, were performed in Modena.[4] In particular, from the mid-seventeenth century, several theaters in the city also began to host opera performances, offering a busy, high-quality calendar of events supported by the court. With the investiture of Modena as the capital of the Este duchy, we see not only a cultural and musical development but also a process of urban renewal to give the city an aspect more suited to its new function.

The musical history of this city and its urban evolution are attested today by the music and cartographic collections kept at Modena's Estense Library (Biblioteca Estense Universitaria). While the music collection of the Estense Library testifies how, over the centuries, the Este dukes were generous patrons of music, the cartographic collection shows how the Este court saw the world outside the duchy, thus describing the cultural landscape and interactions with other geographical and cultural contexts. Their differences notwithstanding, the two collections contain common elements concerning the history of Modena, and their comparative study aids our understanding of the urban and cultural evolution of the city.

This chapter describes how our study, initially dedicated to the cataloging and digitization of sources, has given rise to the creation of a digital project dedicated to the reconstruction of the historical soundscape of early modern Modena. As we will explain, the digital tools applied to this historical research could be useful in demonstrating significant relationships between

[3] Francesco I was succeeded by Alfonso IV. Following Alfonso IV's death in 1662, the heir to the throne, Francesco II, was only two years old, and Alfonso IV's widow, Laura Martinozzi, took charge of the duchy's governance. Laura Martinozzi's reign ended in 1674 when her son Francesco II regained power by conspiring against her.

[4] Duke Francesco II had a special admiration for Stradella's musical works and collected his compositions even after the musician's death. Thanks to the Este sovereign, about half of Stradella's musical productions are now preserved in the Estense Library music collection (Gianturco 1983).

data coming from different types of sources and helpful in outlining the process of construction of the sound of a ducal city during the seventeenth century. Therefore, we will show the genesis and the structure of the Este Soundscape project, an online platform dedicated to the reconstruction of the historical soundscape of seventeenth-century Modena. Thanks to the use of state-of-the-art web development tools and geographic information systems (GIS), the platform will feature an interactive search and navigation environment, plus an interactive map with geo-localized objects and events. This will offer new points of view to study a city and its historical and spectacular development.

The Este Heritage

The Biblioteca Estense Universitaria is one of the most important European libraries linked to the history of a princely family. It was, in fact, established by the House of Este in the fifteenth century in Ferrara, Italy, and was subsequently transferred to Modena in the seventeenth century. Throughout the Renaissance and in the following centuries, the Estense Library continued to expand its collection of both local and international materials, including holdings acquired through the suppression of religious orders in Italy and through the bequests of celebrated librarians such as Ludovico Antonio Muratori and Girolamo Tiraboschi. The library moved to its current location at the Palazzo dei Musei in 1882 and became part of the new Gallerie Estensi in 2016. Today, the Estense Library's collections consist of numerous noteworthy manuscripts, illuminated codices, precious printed editions and incunabula, ancient maps, and musical sources.

The Este Digital Heritage project began in 2018 and focused on the creation of the Estense Digital Library (edl.cultura.gov.it), an online digital repository dedicated to the enhancement of the Este manuscript collections. The project is the result of a collaboration between Gallerie Estensi, the Fondazione di Modena, and the University of Modena and Reggio Emilia. Today, the digital library lets us benefit from an important documentary resource by offering the possibility of comparing and annotating over 700,000 pages of manuscripts preserved at the Estense Library. The platform is based on the International Image Interoperability Framework (IIIF), a protocol for standardized image retrieval created by a community of the world's leading research libraries and image repositories (iiif.io). Through this technological tool, high-definition images of the rare manuscripts, maps, and musical sources in the Estense Digital Library can be edited, freely annotated, compared with others, and shared. Furthermore, as we will explain in the following pages, the study and cataloging of this heritage has fostered the creation of a digital platform dedicated to the two most important collections of the Estense Library: the musical sources and the cartographic collection.

The Music Collection and Its Urban Meanings

Toward the mid-seventeenth century, Modena effectively became one of the music capitals of Italy. The city turned into a repository of innovations and artistic trends supported by an enlightened court that was surprisingly sensitive to the musical ferment of the baroque period. Social life in Modena gradually became entwined with art music. The city's physical locations participated in the evolution of musical language, influencing the ways in which music was produced, performed, and listened to. Musical sources produced and collected by the House of Este between the mid-fifteenth and mid-nineteenth centuries form one of the most prestigious Italian music collections today. The study of this collection also helps us reconstruct the city's historical soundscape: in fact, certain sources bear witness to the various sonic experiences in which the court and the city participated.

The collection owes a lot especially to Francesco II: the duke felt compelled to collect and commission music for his own leisure and practice as well as for entertainment at court. The Estense Library today preserves sources related to the musical events commissioned by Duke Francesco II and organized at the court or city's institutions. As an essential part of court life, music accompanied the duke's daily devotional activities as well as extraordinary or dynastic ceremonies, which were often organized in the city's churches. One of the most notable sacred institutions was the Oratorio di San Carlo Rotondo, a place of worship for the Theatine congregation of San Carlo, destined to become a notable center of music production. Built in 1634, the institution hosted the oratorial performances commissioned by Duke Francesco II during Lent.[5] Oratorios took root in Modena thanks to the work of the congregation of San Carlo and Francesco II's personal interest in these compositions. The Estense Library today includes about 80 oratorios relating to the seventeenth century and produced in Modena between 1680 and 1691.[6]

The presence of a ducal theater was an essential requirement for the social life of a duchy's capital. From the mid-seventeenth century, several theaters in the city began to host opera performances, offering a busy and

[5] The oratorio was named *Rotondo* (round) in reference to its octagonal design.

[6] Oratorios were brought to Emilia from Rome by the Philippine Fathers, who originated this genre (see Crowther 1992).

high-quality calendar of events. Scores and libretti of the court's brilliant operatic activity can be found in the collection. Furthermore, sources in the Estense Library also appear to testify to a more intimate and sophisticated musical practice at court: the sounds that accompanied the everyday life of the Este court, in line with the official culture of the Italian courts, consisted of high-quality musical production that coexisted with forms of art inspired by popular culture.[7] The genre of *cantata da camera* is associated with this "reserved" context. The cantata was particularly suitable for performances in the interior spaces of noble palaces, featuring, as it did, poetic and eulogistic texts sometimes written by the nobles themselves. Francesco II was obsessed with this musical genre, as evidenced by the disproportionately large number of cantata anthologies in the Este collection compared to other genres. In fact, around 300 miscellaneous volumes of cantatas have been preserved: some volumes contain just a few dozen pieces; others comprise hundreds. Intended for a select audience of connoisseurs, chamber cantatas became a significant part of Francesco II's cultural agenda, partly thanks to the activities of the literary academies, in particular the Accademia de' Dissonanti. Founded in 1683, the Accademia was a place for cultural exchange between artists, musicians, and poets.[8]

The Estense Library also contains sources related to the outdoor events that characterized the streets and squares of the Duchy of Este's capital. Spectacular feasts included musical accompaniment by mainly wind and percussion instruments such as trumpets, fifes, and drums. Musicians were tasked with filling the streets and squares with sound preceding a procession, emphasizing every ritual and involving the urban fabric.

However, the present collection only partly corresponds to the House of Este's former musical repository. Between the eighteenth and nineteenth centuries, the original corpus was joined by other important assortments of music from foreign collections, bequests, and donations. The largest of these is the collection of the Electoral Prince of Cologne and Archbishop of Bonn

---

[7] The Este music collection also encompasses anthologies of dances, arias, and songs of folk tradition, as well as a large number of madrigals and various forms of poetry for music, which interweave poetry, music, and literature.

[8] The history of the foundation of the Accademia de' Dissonanti is somewhat controversial and debated. It is not clear what role Francesco II played in its creation: the duke probably merely supported its establishment. The repertoire dedicated to this institution mostly consisted of cantatas or *accademie* for vocal soloists and basso continuo with one or more obligato instruments. The texts were part of the academic poetry that aimed to glorify the prestige of the Este family (Jander 1975).

Maximilian Franz of Habsburg. The collection arrived in Modena after the unification of Italy in 1861. Maximilian Franz's collection contains sacred, instrumental, and operatic music from the late eighteenth century, mostly by German, French, Austrian, and Bohemian composers such as Carl Philip Emanuel, Johann Christian Bach, Franz Joseph Haydn, Wolfgang Amadeus Mozart, Josef Myslivecek, Christoph Willibald Gluck, and André Grétry.[9]

Today, the music collection of the Estense Library is therefore the result of the aggregation of multiple groups of musical sources, which arrived in Modena in different periods. Only a part of it is identifiable with the ancient music collection set up by the dukes of Este over the centuries. Over time, the lack of a unique catalog has hindered the understanding of the different aggregation phases of the collection. During the nineteenth century, various inventories and catalogs were made of the collection, their completeness and usefulness depending on the aims of the individual compiler.[10] Hence, our study conducted on musical sources aims at clarifying the formation process of this important collection. At the same time, the digitization and cataloging of sources will organize this heritage collection and make it publicly accessible.

The Cartographic Collection

The cartographic collection of the Estense Library of Modena consists of documents produced between the fifteenth and early twentieth centuries,

[9] Other important groups of music sources present in the Este collection include the music collection of the brothers Luigi, Giovanni, and Bonifazio Asioli; the collection of "fragments," loose parts missing an attribution; the music collection of the marquis Campori; and the music collection of the noble family Forni, recently donated to the Estense Library.

[10] Over time, numerous attempts to reorganize the musical collection by the librarians of the Estense were made. The first inventory, drawn up around 1750, is due to Giovanni Antonio Panelli and Pellegrino Loschi. In 1816, Giovanni Battista dell'Olio compiled a new catalog dedicated to manuscripts and prints, followed by the inventories of Federico Röther and the musicologist Angelo Catelani. However, the above-mentioned catalogs exclude the music collections added to the Estense library later. A more complete examination of the Estense collection and its late aggregations arrived in 1892 with Alessandro Giuseppe Spinelli's handwritten *Catalogo alfabetico descrittivo della Raccolta musicale estense.* Currently, the catalog in use was written by Pio Lodi and published in 1926. It is the most complete among the others at our disposal, even though it excludes several groups of sources. Finally, the more recent reorganization and indexing work carried out by Alessandra Chiarelli should be cited (Chiarelli 1987).

characterized by the presence of some rare handwritten documents of ancient copper engravings and more modern prints. The temporal extension of these documents allows us to appreciate the change in the cartographic technique. At the same time, the collection shows the different visions of the world that have characterized the past centuries.

The current collection had a slow constitution: born from the Este family's interest in geography, it continued to grow, in more recent years, with donations from private libraries of some important Modenese families. As early as the fourteenth century, works of famous travelers such as Marco Polo and Mandeville enriched the Este family's library, as did the great novels of chivalry that narrated imaginary journeys around the world written by Ludovico Ariosto, Matteo Maria Boiardo, and other illustrious authors (Donattini 2000). Subsequently, the geographical horizon progressively widened thanks to the practice of pilgrimage, starting with the one organized by Niccolò III d'Este in the Holy Land in 1413 for both religious and political purposes. In the same period, explorations across the oceans started. This gave rise to an important process of redefining space that aroused interest in European courts, including that of Ferrara, for the opening of new trade routes and the traffic of new raw materials.

The Estense Library preserves numerous cartographical treatises. Among them is a famous copy of the *Geografia di Tolomeo*,[11] dedicated to Borso d'Este in 1466 (Bertoni 1903). Other cartographic works of inestimable value are the *Mappamondo catalano estense* (1450–60) and the *Carta del Cantino* (1502), one of the first representations of the American coast. The Este family's interest in geography represents a particularly important means of facing the challenge of Ferrara's spatial and political marginality,[12] since these maps summarize the information brought to Europe by explorers, navigators, and markets, which was useful in establishing new trade agreements and alliances (Salmson and Moretti 1984).

---

[11] It is a richly decorated, handwritten reproduction of the treatise written in Greek by Claudius Ptolemy in Alexandria around 150 CE. It was translated into Latin in 1406 and was highly influential on the geographical knowledge and cartographic traditions of Renaissance Europe.

[12] After the opening of new trade routes through the oceans (thanks to the impulse of the Portuguese Prince Henry the Navigator), the Mediterranean Sea lost its central role in trade, the Mediterranean courts were thrown into crisis, and the world balance was changed.

In 1859, due to riots unleashed by the arrival in Modena of the army of King Vittorio Emanuele II, some documents were stolen from the library and disappeared. The *Mappamondo catalano estense* and the *Carta del Cantino*, for example, were only found 11 years later by the Modenese collector Giuseppe Boni, who donated them to the Estense Library (Milano 1991; Milano and Battini 1995). Then, the annexation of the Este Duchy to the Kingdom of Sardinia in 1860 marked a new phase for the library; in this period, the collection of geographical maps expanded thanks to numerous donations from several Modenese noble families. Due to these events, the maps of the Estense Library are now included in various catalogs. The main one is the *Inventario dei portolani, carte nautiche e geografiche della R. Biblioteca Estense*, transcribed in 1892 by Clemente Lazzarini, a single list relating to all the maps owned by the library up to the unification of Italy.[13]

Besides this, there are catalogs of the collections donated, acquired, or purchased by the library. Among them, the most notable is the map collection of the Modenese nobleman Giuseppe Campori. Deposited in the library in 1893, the collection contains few, but unique, manuscripts of nautical cartography of the seventeenth century as well as some handwritten atlases. In 1920, the Estense Library map collection increased with the collection donated by Chiaffredo Hugues, a Modenese intellectual. The Hugues collection preserves over 100 topographic maps and city plans, mainly from the nineteenth century produced by the main topographic institutes of the time, such as the Royal Austrian Military Geographical Institute and the Italian Geographic Military Institute. After about 20 years, between 1945 and 1946, the collection of Antonio Bertacchini-Mattioli enriched the Estense Library: it is based on 18 maps produced in the second half of the nineteenth century, some printed in Gotha (Germany) by Justus Perthes, a famous publishing house of geographical maps of the time.

In 2007, the collection of the Forni family was added to the Estense Library. The history of this collection begins with the Modenese cleric Matteo Pagliaroli (1716–77), who in the first half of the eighteenth century formed a rich library; later, it passed to the Forni counts by inheritance and over time expanded with new accessions until it was donated to the Estense Library. The Forni's collection holds several geographical maps, divided into two groups. The first consists of four albums bound in 1834 by Francesco Vignoli:

---

[13] No previous catalogs are present today in the Estense Library; only some sporadic lists of the maps can be found. This situation does not make it easy to reconstruct the original nucleus of the collection.

it contains over 200 maps produced by various cartographers between the eighteenth and nineteenth centuries. The second group consists mainly of topographic maps, plans, and city views made in the nineteenth century.[14]

Over time, these donations were also accompanied by important purchases, including the Pio Falcò di Savoia collection, containing a dozen maps produced between the end of the seventeenth and the beginning of the nineteenth century.[15] Another excellent purchase by the Ministry for Cultural Heritage and Activities in 2000 is the *Planisfero Castiglioni*, created in 1525. According to tradition, the Planisphere was donated as a sign of benevolence by the Emperor Charles V to Baldassarre Castiglioni, a talented military man and man of letters and the apostolic nuncio to Spain. This Planisphere is one of the most important documents currently owned by the Estense Library. It represents an example of the so-called *Padrón Real*, a secret Spanish master map.[16]

Finally, two series of maps are also part of the Estense cartographic heritage: the *Piante di Modena e dello Stato*, in which about 30 maps of the city and province have been grouped, and the *Serie Atlantica*, containing about 60 maps from different parts of the world, both created between the eighteenth and nineteenth centuries by various authors, including Guillaume De L'Isle. Overall, the collection now includes about 1,000 maps in loose sheets and numerous atlases, including those of Gerhard Kremer and the Blaeu family.[17]

Considering the richness and heterogeneity of the material present in the Estense Library, the project started in 2018 to create the Estense Digital Library was focused in particular on cartography in loose sheets. The aim was to prepare a unique inventory of the maps owned by the Estense Library with a descriptive entry for each map. A unique, digital catalog now provides users today with a better knowledge of and accessibility to this important heritage.

---

[14] This part of the collection is currently being cataloged and has only been partially digitized.

[15] The Pio Falcò di Savoia collection was purchased by the Italian Ministry for Cultural Heritage and Activities (Ministero per i Beni e le Attività Culturali, MiBAC) and then gifted to the Estense Library in 2001.

[16] The *Padrón Real* map was constantly updated based on the news that came from exploration trips. It was jealously guarded by the Spanish crown to avoid commercial espionage.

[17] Gherard Kremer (Gerardus Mercator) was a geographer and cartographer who introduced the use of the term *atlas* for a collection of maps. The Blaeu family ran a famous workshop of maps and globes in Flanders.

Investigating the Historical Soundscape

The study and cataloging that we have conducted on these collections has permitted us to read these sources from a wide-ranging perspective. Comparing musical manuscripts, historical maps, and archival sources is particularly useful for grasping the multiform connections between court, city, and territory, offering many details in the complex relationships between sound and space within the urban context. Therefore, our idea has been to fully exploit the potential of digital humanities and to go beyond the simple digitization of sources.

Despite the digitization of a large number of sources, the use that libraries, archives, and museums make of their digital heritage still very often follows the model of the printed catalog, enriched with some interactive functionality. However, digital humanities offer many more opportunities to use cataloging data for research purposes. Unfortunately, digital cataloging projects supported by the libraries themselves often do not include related research projects. To take full advantage of digital resources it is necessary to rethink their ways of use that can allow us to access metadata with a view to *knowledge-sharing*—that is, the means to provide and propose a contextualization of content, documents, and their relationships beyond the simple availability of data and digital objects. In particular, the comparison and cross-referencing of data through new display modes offer the opportunity to highlight the existence of networks and relationships that cannot otherwise be analyzed. Thanks to information technology (IT) tools, we can therefore improve multidisciplinary research and propose different ways of communicating and interacting.[18] In this sense, our project permits users to access the data of musical and cartographic sources and at the same time to discover places, institutions, and events that led Modena to become a center of music production.

Reading and interpreting places and spaces through the sound production that took place in them constitutes a point of confluence between musicology and geography (Giuriati 2015, 115). Sound, indeed, can be interpreted as a form of knowledge of the environment around us. The music itself has

[18] The cataloging promoted by the Estense Library has led to the creation of a digital library, where today the metadata of the cataloged objects are freely accessible. The digitized materials are not downloadable but only viewable. On the other hand, the Este Soundscape project proposes a different reading of these data, allowing the comparison between apparently different sources that belong to the same context.

helped to define the identity of a place, influencing in some cases its architecture (Dell'Agnese and Tabusi 2016; Rocca 2013). Often, sound production has influenced the architectural features of environments (e.g., theaters, churches, and concert halls); conversely, the performance practice of a city has sometimes contributed to the creation of urban spaces (e.g., squares, parks, and public gardens) suitable to host festive occasions. In this sense, sound has been one of the essential components in the development of city spaces.[19] Even in the course of history, musical production has been conditioned by the place for which and in which it was performed (Knighton and Mazuela-Anguita 2018). At the same time, the city represents a privileged environment for musical creation, showing through its history the complex network of institutional relationships that made it possible; the methods of circulation of music, sources, and genres; and the social status and mobility of musicians (Bombi, Carreras, and Marín 2005, 18).

In the Estense context, an analysis of the different types of music production gives us an understanding of how city spaces cannot be considered simple places: they allow us to identify times, ceremonies, and spontaneous practices; perception skills; and a culture of performance and listening. While the Modenese cartographic resources allow us to observe the changes in the territory and in the urban landscape, the Estense musical sources tell us how that same territory produced music. The comparative study of these sources made possible through digital technology help to demonstrate how musical sources can be interpreted as a product of the interaction between court and city, since they are proof of the musical production and practices of some city institutions (e.g., the Oratorio di San Carlo Rotondo, the Accademia de' Dissonanti, and certain theaters in the city). Musical and cartographic sources also

---

[19] Music has always had a political and social significance, influencing and enriching the scenarios in which it was produced. Sometimes the construction of music venues has had a symbolic meaning, as illustrated, for example, in Woolf's (1988) discussion of the pivotal position of the opera house in the reconstruction of nineteenth-century Paris and its role as a locus of diplomatic activity, as analyzed by Everist (2021). Our project aims at analyzing the historical soundscape of Modena from this perspective, considering the music not only as a merely artistic activity but also as a social, political, and cultural activity. Studying the musical activities of the various institutions in Modena has enabled us to understand the extent to which music has been a central part of the city's culture and has contributed to the development of its sonic identity over the centuries. In this sense, external sounds not strictly related to musical production (i.e., not traceable through scores or historical sources) have not been considered in the reconstruction of the historical soundscape.

tell us about spectacular outdoor events that involved both the court and the city. The open spaces of Modena's squares and streets were often the settings for masquerades, tournaments, and jousting matches, featuring floats and theatrical performances. These occasions were not only intended as a means of celebrating an anniversary, entertaining the court and the people, or organizing cultural events but were also excellent opportunities for dukes to demonstrate the magnificence of the court. In the late seventeenth century, the music of the Este family in Modena thus became a social art designed to be displayed and used as a tool for building consensus and publicly affirming the prince's power.

The Digital Project

The Este Soundscape project will create a digital platform through which to reconstruct and explore the sounds, places, events, and people who contributed to the creation of a city's musical identity. The online platform, which is currently under construction, will enable the user to explore and see the urban landscape of early modern Modena, to hear the sounds and music of this city, to access resources dedicated to different sonic events, to read musical sources, and to have data about the context of their production.[20] Thanks to the use of state-of-the-art web development tools and GIS,[21] the platform will feature an interactive search and navigation environment, plus an interactive map with geo-localized objects and events. The chronological period considered by the project is the seventeenth century; it is in fact in this century that Modena becomes a first-rate cultural center and creates its "sound identity."

The "Este Soundscape" Cartographic System

Among digital tools, cartographic supports can contribute to new data visualizations, thanks to the development of numerous mapping tools and GIS. Territorial information systems allow users to acquire, store, organize, catalog, modify, re-elaborate, integrate, and return data concerning phenomena that take place in the territory. The structure of these systems, based on

---

[20] Initially conceived at the Interdepartmental Research Center on Digital Humanities, University of Modena and Reggio Emilia, the project is currently being developed independently by the authors.

[21] A geographic information system (GIS) is a computer system that analyzes and displays geographically referenced information. Among the GIS applications currently available for use in this project is QGIS (qgis.org), a free and open-source cross-platform desktop GIS.

a database, is associated with geographic information (i.e., coordinates) for the georeferencing[22] of the data. A GIS uses a logical model that subdivides the elements (streets, buildings, rivers, land uses, administrative boundaries, etc.) into superimposed layers with numerous technical and data management benefits, allowing simultaneous queries on the various information levels and extraction of information based on their positioning (e.g., count of elements in a specific area, selection of elements based on the distance to another element) (Fea and Loret 2010).

The use of GIS, which began in the 1960s mainly in public administration or in the field of earth sciences, has progressively spread to numerous sectors, including archaeology, cultural heritage, and marketing. Considerable success can also be found in the application of GIS to historical analysis. In fact, GIS tools are useful not only for the creation of maps but also for the extrapolation and reworking of information relating to a particular territory in various historical phases, allowing one to detect its changes in time (Vagnini 2010).

These tools can also be used in various disciplinary fields interested in urban history, such as musicology. Cartographic tools, facilitating the visualization of places, institutions, urban areas, and paths affected by the musical activities of a city, allow us to investigate, through a wide-ranging perspective, the sound landscape of cities and "place identity" more generally. Constituting the cornerstone of numerous social and cultural activities, with their social and cultural resources, cities have been a prerequisite for the growth of music production.

Digital cartography, with the support of the latest digital tools, such as GIS, enables observation of changes in the local area, for example by superimposing historical maps on satellite images. For musicological research purposes, cartography is very useful for locating music production centers within the urban context, improving knowledge of places and music production and dissemination methods. Above all, it is useful for understanding how geographical areas and musical expression have interacted with and influenced each other. Starting from this assumption, the fulcrum of the Este Soundscape project is the presence of an interactive map within the platform. The map, as we will see in the following pages, will allow users to identify the musical centers of early modern Modena, to carry out advanced searches, to

[22] The term *georeferencing* is commonly used in the field of geographic information systems to describe the process of associating elements represented on a map with spatial coordinates, thus locating digital data in the real world.

filter the data, and to view the insights through pop-ups and hypertext. For the creation of the digital map, the Google satellite web mapping service was used as a basis onto which a historical map of the collection of the Estense Library was superimposed.

The map chosen is an eighteenth-century reproduction of the famous 1684 map by Giovan Battista Boccabadati,[23] made by Domenico Vandelli.[24] The representation shows both the above-ground Modena, with plan drawings of buildings and streets, as well as the underground Modena, with its canals and drains already partially buried. This detailed map points out the *forma urbis* of the city after changes that occurred in the sixteenth and seventeenth centuries, including the Herculean addition, the Citadel of Castellamonte and the Palazzo Ducale.[25] Modena maintained this structure until the end of the eighteenth century, when various interventions, promoted by both Francesco III and his son Ercole III, completely modified the urban aspect (Bertuzzi 2001). Therefore, Vandelli's map describes the city in detail, and it is particularly suitable for our project because it permits us to identify

[23] Giovan Battista Boccabadati (1635–96) was a lawyer who was also involved in mathematical and scientific studies. In 1671 he was appointed court librarian by Duke Francesco II, and in 1681 the duke appointed him court engineer. In 1684 he was commissioned by the Municipality of Modena to create a map of the city. The original map of Giovan Battista Boccabadati is today preserved in the Archivio Storico del Comune di Modena.

[24] Domenico Vandelli (1691–1754) studied with the Jesuits (later becoming an abbot) and at the University of Modena, applying himself in philosophy, mathematics, and theology. Thanks to his studies, he became professor of mathematics and engineering at the University of Modena. He was also a geographer of the Este court and an antiquarian, as well as an inspector of rivers and drainage.

[25] With the investiture of Modena as the capital of the Este duchy, a process of urban renewal began to give the city an aspect more suited to its new function. In the second half of the sixteenth century, the Herculean addition had expanded the urban area to the north, although the city still preserved a medieval-type layout. During the seventeenth century, numerous construction sites were opened (for the construction of churches and the embellishment of noble palaces). The most important projects carried out in this period were the construction of the military citadel between 1635 and 1642, and the Ducal Palace to replace the old castle. Afterwards, in the second half of the eighteenth century, the city was partially renovated through the revision of the urban plan implemented by Francesco III. The project, inspired by the ideals of rationality and regularity typical of the Enlightenment, aimed at improving the services and demolishing the unhealthy houses.

buildings, streets, squares, and main infrastructures thanks to its numerous labels. Finally, Vandelli's map constitutes a significant testimony for the city of Modena, created to pay homage to the city itself. The map, commissioned by the Municipality of Modena in 1684, was displayed in the Council Room "in the service of the city," with the order never to remove it from that place (Quaderni dell'Archivio Storico di Modena 2009, 4).

Structure and Function

The platform is based on a relational database system, containing data derived from the analysis and study of musical, cartographic, historical, and archival sources. The interface is currently provided in Italian.

The database created in Django framework is divided into interrelated entities called "Sources" (*Fonti*), "People" (*Persone*), "Genres" (*Generi*), "Events" (*Eventi*), and "Institutions" (*Istituzioni*). The database offers various possibilities for accessing the data including the free text search and browse resources, search indices, and a time slider.

The Sources entity represents the main core of the database and contains records of musical sources examined. The People entity stores data related to musicians and composers. In the Genres entity, musical sources are divided according to their musical form. In Events, one can find all spectacular and musical events realized in the public spaces of the city. Finally, the Institutions entity holds records related to the center of music production in Modena. The Institutions are the connecting element between the relational database system and the virtual map, called EsteWebGIS; each institution is georeferenced through the OpenStreetMap plug-in present in the database, showing the location of each institution on the map. The virtual map provides an interactive city navigation environment through the Google satellite web mapping service. Thanks to the features of the QGIS software, the historical map of Domenico Vandelli has been georeferenced, matching it with the satellite image of modern Modena. By simply ticking or deselecting the layer of the historical map, this overlap allows the user to compare the historic city structure to the present day (Fig. 1). Furthermore, centers of music production in the city can be identified on the map using polygons (Fig. 2). They have been divided in four categories: "Theaters" (*Teatri*), "Squares" (*Piazze*), "Palaces" (*Palazzi*), and "Churches" (*Chiese*).

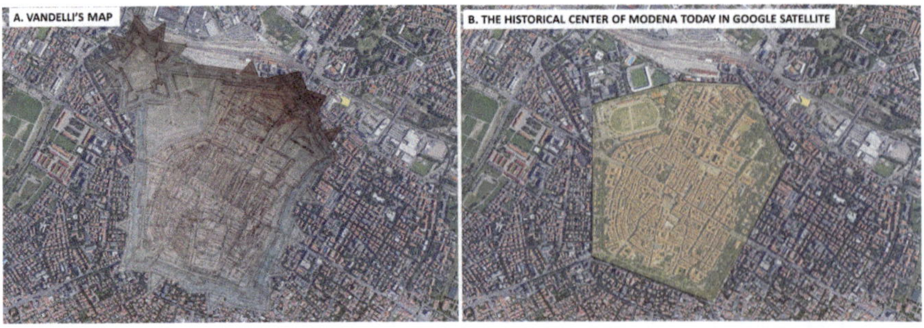

Figure 1. Screenshot of EsteWebGIS showing Vandelli's map. The interactive map will permit users to compare Vandelli's map (A) and the historical center of Modena as it appears today in the Google satellite web mapping service (B).

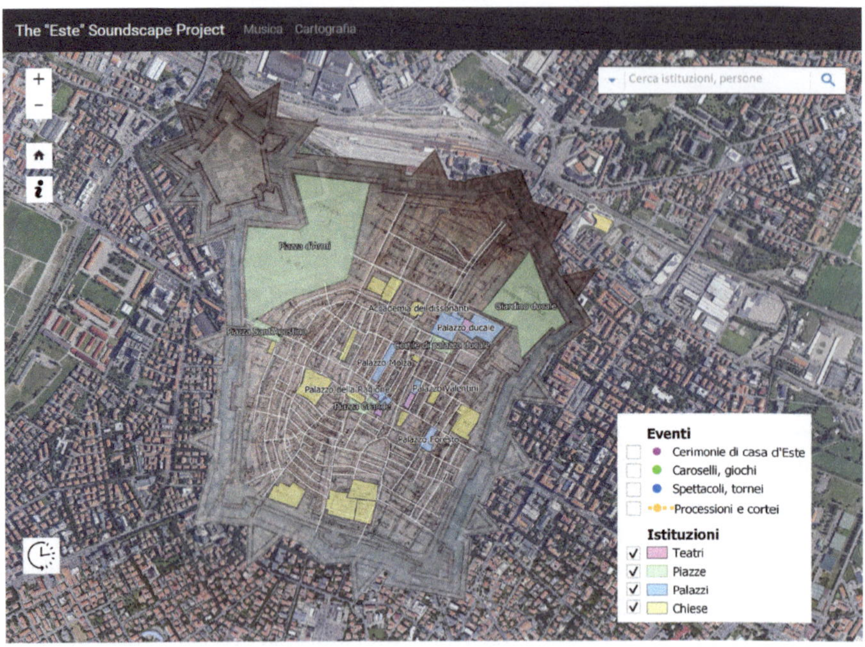

Figure 2. Screenshot of EsteWebGIS showing centers of music production.

Thanks to the map layers, the EsteWebGIS offers different views: it is possible to select a specific category (Theaters, Squares, Palaces, or Churches) or view all categories from the menu. For example, theaters can be highlighted rather than churches or squares (Fig. 3). In addition, informative pop-ups display information regarding institutions and their musical activities and give direct access to the related musical sources. Moreover, using queries, it will be possible to filter and to cross-reference data to obtain re-elaborations of the base map according to specific criteria (e.g., to discover which places in Modena hosted events linked to the anniversary of the House of Este).

Figure 3. Screenshot of EsteWebGIS showing theaters.

During the seventeenth century, several theaters in the city began to host opera performances, offering a busy calendar of high-quality events supported by various dukes. The city's first theatrical activity was carried out at the Teatro della Spelta, built at the behest of duke Francesco I, who was keen to provide the duchy's new capital with a theater that met the needs of the court. Instead, the first court theater, housed in the Palazzo Ducale, dates back to 1669. It was a small theater exclusively intended for the court's private use. The most interesting theater, which managed to combine the needs of the court with those of the city, was the Teatro Valentini. Initially, it was a large "show room" located in the noble Palazzo Valentini, which was built around 1542 by Giovanni Andrea Valentini. In 1683, the theater was bought by another Modenese nobleman, Marquis Decio Fontanelli, who made it the most important theater in the Este duchy, directly linked to the duke's cultural policy. The theater, renamed Teatro Fontanelli, was chosen by Francesco II as the place to host theatrical performances that were sponsored by the court but open to a paying audience.[26] The auditorium contained 136 boxes arranged in five rows with a gallery, with a total capacity of around 1,000 seats (Martinelli Braglia 1985). The Estense Library now preserves nine opera scores and the Fontanelli family's collection of librettos.[27] The presence and correspondence of archival documentation, musical sources, and libretti allows us to reconstruct the whole operatic activity of the Teatro Fontanelli, providing at the same time an accurate portrait of the court opera in Modena.

The Teatro Fontanelli does not exist today. Its location remains visible only in some historical maps of Modena, like the Vandelli one. A pop-up displays brief explanatory notes, the number of sources and people associated with the theater, and a hyperlink to the corresponding institution record (Fig. 4). The record contains data about the history of the institution and bibliographic and archival sources connected to it so that the user can visualize the list of musical sources linked to the institution and access the specific entry for every source (Fig. 5).

Another useful example is the drama *Flavio Cuniberto* by Domenico Gabrielli, staged in 1688 at the Teatro Fontanelli. Like a catalog entry, the record contains several fields related to the bibliographic, physical, and analytical description of the source including its proper title, dimensions, paper type, shelf marks, watermarks, composer, and so on. It also includes archival and

---

[26] In 1705, the son of Decio Fontanelli, the Marquis Giulio, sold "the public theatre of comedies" to Count Teodoro Rangoni. In the nineteenth century, the theater was expanded in various ways; in 1816 it was renamed the Teatro Comunale di Via Emilia, and in 1842 the new, present-day Teatro Comunale was opened (see Martinelli Braglia 2007, 20).

[27] The Fontanelli family collection consists of 1,352 music librettos, all printed and dated from the early seventeenth century to around 1760. Many of them relate to Modenese performances of musical dramas that took place at the Teatro Fontanelli during the reign of Francesco II.

historical information about the context of the production of this drama, and a link to the Estense Digital Library gives access to the digital scores and libretto. In the same way, from the record of the musical source it is possible to access information about the composer and genre (Fig. 6), and, where possible, an audio track can be accessed.

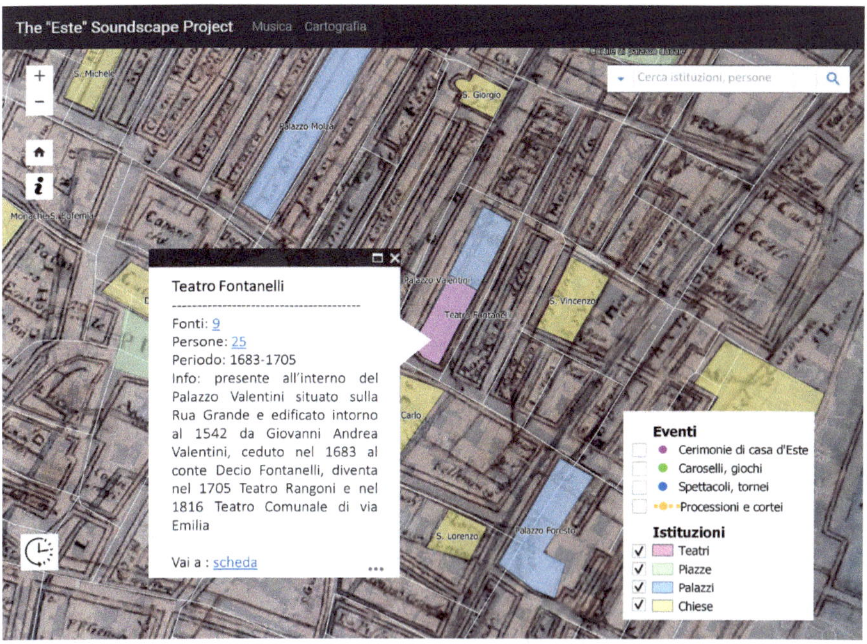

Figure 4. Screenshot of EsteWebGIS showing the Teatro Fontanelli.

Figure 5. Screenshot of the record for the Teatro Fontanelli showing information about the history of the theater and archival, bibliographic, and musical sources related to it.

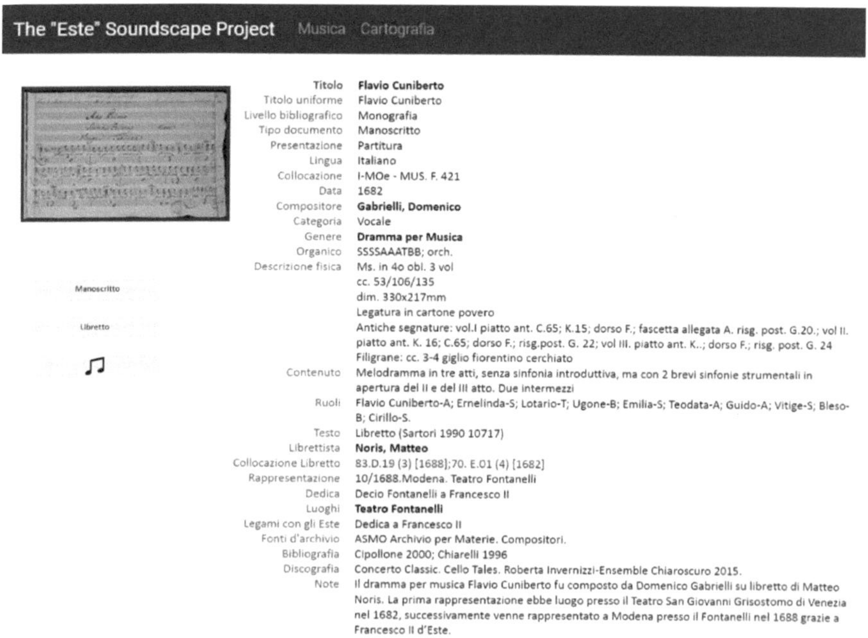

Figure 6. A screenshot showing the record dedicated to the *Flavio Cuniberto* by Domenico Gabrielli, an opera in three acts, on a libretto by Matteo Noris, represented at Teatro San Giovanni Grisostomo in Venice in 1682. Today, the Estense Library preserves the manuscript of the second representation that took place in Modena at the Teatro Fontanelli in 1688.

Our virtual map will also be able to display a series of external events—"Carousels" (*Caroselli e giochi*), "Shows" (*Spettacoli e tornei*), "Ceremonies" (*Cerimonie di casa d'Este*), and "Processions" (*Processioni*)—through which the court interacted with the city (Fig. 7).

For example, throughout the sixteenth century, Piazza Grande was one of the city's key locations. The main buildings of civic and religious power stood on either side of the square: the Cathedral with its bell tower, known as the Ghirlandina, the Palazzo Comunale, and the Palazzo della Ragione. The main religious ceremonies were also held in this square in the seventeenth century, especially liturgies related to the liturgical year, the Cathedral, and the rites of San Geminiano, patron saint of Modena. Piazza Grande was also the setting for masquerades during the Carnival and representations organized for birthday celebrations, illustrious visits, or political events. Historical chronicles provide some information on how these events unfolded, testifying to their splendor and the number of citizens involved.[28]

Figure 7. Screenshot of EsteWebGIS showing "Events."

In 1654, Francesco I married Lucrezia Barberini. The wedding was celebrated by proxy at the Santa Casa in Loreto on 15 April 1654, followed by celebrations in Modena organized with great pomp: lights, music, tournaments, and floats. The chronicler Leone Allacci describes this event: Francesco I's third bride entered Modena on the night of 24 April 1654, greeted by the sound of the city's bells. The festivities enlivened the city for several days. An oval-shaped theater was constructed by Gaspare Vigarani in Piazza Grande with platforms for spectators and spaces for musicians. Several ephemeral machines, created for a play entitled *Gli Amori d'Alessandro con Rossane*, were introduced by the sound of fifes and a chorus of trumpets. The chronicler

[28] For instance, Giovanni Battista Spaccini's chronicle is a valuable account that offers vivid insight into the most important events in the city of Modena. Spaccini produced nine volumes of chronicles: the first two rework the diaries of Iacopino and Tommasino Lancellotti, while the rest report the episodes that Spaccini witnessed between 1588 and 1636 (see Spaccini 1993–2008).

reports that about 40 different instruments were assembled for the occasion in order to produce particular harmonic effects (Allacci 1654, 93–94). Although the musical source of this event has been lost, the virtual map shows the place and space of performance (Fig. 8).

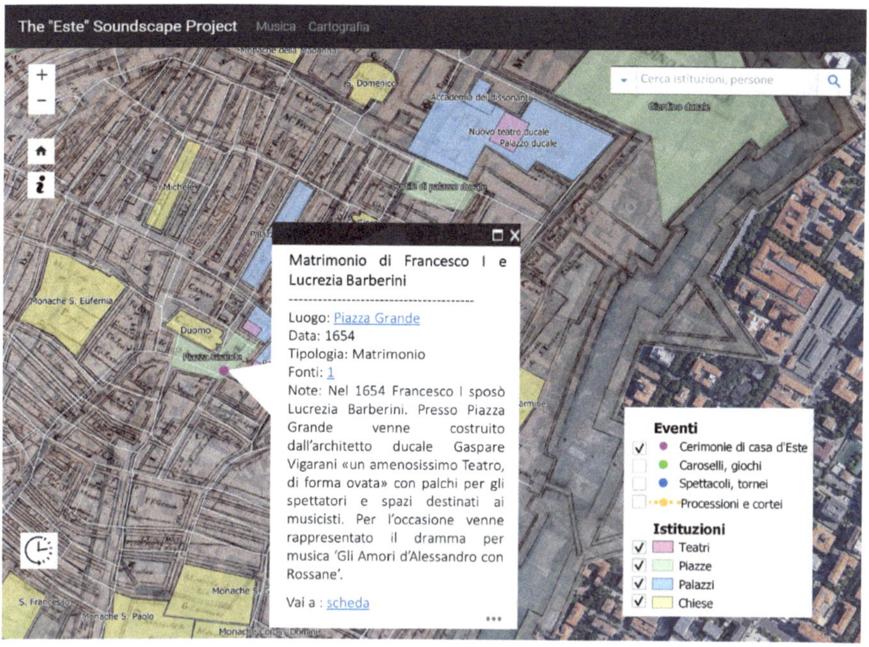

Figure 8. Screenshot of EsteWebGIS showing the Piazza Grande. The pop-up briefly explains the wedding of Francesco I d'Este in 1654. On this occasion, an oval-shaped theater was constructed by Gaspare Vigarani in Piazza Grande with platforms for spectators and spaces for musicians.

A concise pop-up links to a specific record describing the event and offers access to related historical and bibliographic sources and image galleries. Furthermore, if several events have been carried out in the same place, a cluster will indicate the total number (see Fig. 7). Through the search function it will also be possible to filter results. A time slider will allow users to discover the chronological evolution of the spectacular events and will also be useful for obtaining information on the period of activity of an institution present on the map. For example, by superimposing the institutions and time grids, one can learn how many performances were represented in an institution in a certain period. In this way, aggregating data by institution and year, the identification of the important centers of musical production in the city is possible.

Conclusions

In conclusion, this innovative approach demonstrates the utility of using digital tools and many different types of sources to bring to life a historical soundscape, allowing users to discover the musical culture of an early modern city with an online interactive map. The possibility of cross-references between several types of documents gives users an impression of the multifaceted network of musicians and musical activities realized both in and by the Este court. Moreover, the map provides users with new points of view from which to study a city and its historical and spectacular development. In this sense, the EsteWebGIS can be a valid tool for analyzing the artistic and spatial context of a city in a more general sense.

In fact, the project aims to fill several fundamental gaps in the global reconstruction of the musical and cultural view of a city. The development of a digital project dedicated to a city's soundscape can open a discussion in geographical fields on music and landscape in the early modern era, also providing a useful tool for the representation of the city. Because of the key role that the House of Este played in the development of European musical culture, the knowledge obtained will allow a more balanced historiographical view of the overall social history of music in seventeenth-century Italy.

Finally, the project wants to propose a collaborative and multidisciplinary model for historical research and provide new ideas for the enhancement of cultural heritage. In particular, the interactive map can be used to query the database, but it also offers a starting point for the development of teaching tools for scholars dealing with early modern cities in several respects. To foster reuse, reproducibility, and further adoption by other scholars, the source code of the platform will be made publicly available. The Este Soundscape project offers new opportunities to animate academic teaching according to the methodologies related to "action research" (Elliott, Giordan, and Scurati 1993). In particular, EsteWebGIS will be an interdisciplinary digital tool that connects social aspects, landscape perception, and musical sources with urban spaces.[29]

---

[29] Authors' contributions: A. F. paragraphs: The Este Heritage; The Music Collection and Its Urban Meanings; Investigating the Historical Soundscape; Structure and Function. S. B. paragraphs: The Cartographic Collection; The Digital Project; The "Este Soundscape" Cartographic System; Conclusions.

WORKS CITED

Allacci, Leone. 1654. *Del viaggio della Signora D. Lucretia Barberini Duchessa di Modena da Roma a Modena: Lettere di Leone Allacci. All'ill.mo Sig.r il Sig.r Marcantonio Spinola*. Genova.

Bertoni, Giulio. 1903. *La Biblioteca Estense e la coltura ferrarese ai tempi del duca Ercole I (1471–1505)*. Turin: Ermanno Loescher.

Bertuzzi, Giordano. 2001. "Rinnovamento edilizio di una capitale." In *Lo Stato di Modena: Una capitale, una dinastia, una civiltà nella storia d'Europa. Atti del convegno, Modena, 25–28 marzo 1998*, edited by Angelo Spaggiari and Giuseppe Trenti, 93–104. Rome: Ministero per i beni e le attività culturali, Direzione generale per gli archivi.

Bombi, Andrea, Juan José Carreras, and Miguel Ángel Marín. 2005. *Música y cultura urbana en la edad moderna*. Valencia: Universitat de Valencia.

Chiarelli, Alessandra. 1987. *I codici di musica delle raccolte estensi: Ricostruzione dell'inventario settecentesco*. Florence: Olschki.

Crowther, Victor. 1992. *The Oratorio in Modena*. Oxford: Clarendon Press.

Dell'Agnese, Elena, and Massimiliano Tabusi. 2016. "Introduzione." In *La musica come geografia: Suoni, luoghi, territori*, edited by Elena Dell'Agnese and Massimiliano Tabusi, 5–12. Rome: Società Geografica Italiana. societageografica.net/wp/wp-content/uploads/2016/09/La_musica_come_geografia_ebook.pdf.

Donattini, Massimo. 2000. "Cultura geografica ferrarese del Rinascimento." In *Storia di Ferrara*, edited by Adriano Prosperi, 407–58. Vol. 6, *Il Rinascimento: Situazioni e personaggi*. Ferrara: Corbo.

Durante, Elio, and Anna Martellotti. 2005. "Vicende della musica ferrarese dopo la morte di Alfonso II." In *Quaderni degli annali dell'Università di Ferrara*, 357–70. Florence: Le Lettre.

Elliott, John, André Giordan, and Cesare Scurati. 1993. *La ricerca-azione: Metodiche, strumenti, casi*. Turin: Bollati Boringhieri.

Everist, Mark. 2021. "Music, Theatre and Diplomacy: The Paris Opéra during the Second Empire." *Diplomatica* 3 (2): 278–301. doi.org/10.1163/25891774-03020002.

Fea, Maurizio, and Emanuele Loret. 2010. "Che cos'è un GIS: Esempi di applicazioni scientifiche." In *GIS tra natura e tecnologia: Strumento per la didattica e la diffusione della cultura scientifica*, edited by Simone Bozzato, 53–76. Rome: Carocci.

Gianturco, Carolyn, ed. 1983. *Alessandro Stradella e Modena: Atti del convegno internazionale di studi*. Modena: Coptip.

Giuriati, Giovanni. 2015. "Il suono come forma di conoscenza dello spazio che ci circonda: Una prospettiva musicologica." *Semestrale di studi e ricerche di geografia* 27 (2): 115–28. rosa.uniroma1.it/rosa03/semestrale_di_geografia/article/view/15094/14559.

Jander, Owen. 1975. "The Cantata in Accademia: Music for the Accademia de' Dissonanti and Their Duke, Francesco II d'Este." *Rivista Italiana di Musicologia* 10:519–44. rosa.uniroma1.it/rosa03/semestrale_di_geografia/article/view/15094.

Knighton, Tess, and Ascensión Mazuela-Anguita, eds. 2018. *Hearing the City in Early Modern Europe*. Turnhout: Brepols.

Lockwood, Lewis. 1984. *Music in Renaissance Ferrara 1400–1505: The Creation of a Musical Center in the Fifteenth Century*. Oxford: Oxford University Press. doi.org/10.1093/acprof:oso/9780195378276.001.0001.

Lodi, Pio. 1926. *Catalogo delle opere musicali: Città di Modena. Biblioteca Estense*. Parma: Fresching.

Martinelli Braglia, Graziella. 1985. "Il Teatro Fontanelli: Note su impresari ed artisti nella Modena di Francesco II e Rinaldo." In *Alessandro Stradella e Modena: Atti del Convegno internazionale di studi*, edited by Carolyn Gianturco, 138–59. Modena: Coptip.

———. 2007. "Luoghi e artefici dello spettacolo nella Modena di Orazio Vecchi." In *Il Theatro dell'udito: Società, Musica, Storia e Cultura nell'epoca di Orazio Vecchi*, edited by Ferdinando Taddei and Alessandra Chiarelli, 17–50. Modena: Mucchi.

Milano, Ernesto. 1991. *La Carta del Cantino e la rappresentazione della Terra nei codici e nei libri a stampa della Biblioteca Estense e Universitaria*. Modena: Il Bulino.

Milano, Ernesto, and Annalisa Battini, eds. 1995. "Il Mappamondo Catalano Estense." In *Il Mappamondo Catalano Estense*, 7–63. Dietikon-Zürich: Urs Graf Verlag.

Quaderni dell'Archivio Storico di Modena. 2009. *La "Rappresentazione" della Città di Modena: Gian Battista Boccabadati Poeta, Letterato, Cartografo*. Modena: Archivio Storico di Modena.

Rocca, Lorena. 2013. "Le impronte del paesaggio sonoro: Un'opportunità per la didattica della storia e della geografia." *Ri-Vista ricerche per la progettazione del paesaggio* 11 (1): 17–25. oaj.fupress.net/index.php/ri-vista/issue/view/215.

Salmson, June, and Walter Moretti, eds. 1984. *The Renaissance in Ferrara and Its European Horizons*. Ravenna: Edizioni del Girasole.

Spaccini, Giovanni Battista. 1993–2008. *Cronaca di Modena (1588–1636)*. Edited by Albano Biondi, Rolando Bussi, and Carlo Giovannini. 6 vols. Modena: Panini.

Vagnini, Alessandro. 2010. "Il GIS come strumento dell'analisi storica." In *GIS tra natura e tecnologia: Strumento per la didattica e la diffusione della cultura scientifica*, edited by Simone Bozzato, 217–29. Rome: Carocci.

Woolf, Penelope. 1988. "Symbol of the Second Empire: Cultural Politics and the Paris Opera House." In *The Inconography of Landscape: Essays on the Symbolic Representation, Design and Use of Past Environments*, edited by Denis Cosgrove and Stephen Daniels, 214–35. Cambridge: Cambridge University Press.

Chapter 12: Interacting with Big Historical Data of the Dutch Golden Age: Golden Agents and Virtual Interiors

Charles van den Heuvel
Huygens Institute

Golden Agents and Virtual Interiors: Use and Reuse of Big Historical Data

The development of digital infrastructures and the digitization of cultural heritage collections require huge investments. How can these infrastructures and big data—often created with a future, yet unknown, public in mind—be best prepared for use and reuse in historical research? To answer that question, two projects will be discussed: one that creates facilities to involve researchers in data handling, and the other that lets researchers interact with virtual representations of data. The first project, "Golden Agents: Creative Industries and the Making of the Dutch Golden Age" (2017–22), hereafter "Golden Agents," is a digital infrastructure with an emphasis on tools and interfaces that allow users to interact in all phases of the preparation, harmonization, and assessment of the quality of its big data. The second project, "Virtual Interiors as Interfaces for Big Historical Data Research: Spatially Enhanced Publications" (September 2018–22), hereafter "Virtual Interiors," makes use of the data of the Golden Agents project and other collections to confront methodological issues related to interacting with multidimensional representations (2D, 3D, and 4D of data with all its uncertainties herein) and annotations of said data.[1]

---

[1] The Golden Agents project (goldenagents.org) is funded by the Large Investments program of the Netherlands Organization of Scientific Research (NWO) (dossier number 380-98-003). The consortium partners are the Huygens Institute, the University of Amsterdam, VU Amsterdam, Utrecht University, Rijksmuseum, KB National Library of the Netherlands, City Archives of Amsterdam, the RKD Netherlands Institute for Art History, and Lab1100. The principal investigator (PI) is the author Charles van den Heuvel (Huygens Institute). The Virtual Interiors project (virtualinteriorsproject.nl) is funded by NWO Smart Culture – Big Data/Digital Humanities (dossier number 314-99-302). The consortium partners consist of the Huygens Institute, the University of Amsterdam, the City of Amsterdam, Brill, and the Netherlands Institute for Sound and Vision. Applicants are Charles van den Heuvel (PI), Julia Noordegraaf (professor

ISBN 978-1-64959-119-7 (paper) ISBN 978-1-64959-120-3 (pdf) ISBN 978-1-64959-121-0 (epub)
New Technologies in Medieval and Renaissance Studies 12 (2025) 307–39

The Golden Agents project consists of a consortium of computer scientists, information specialists, collection curators, and humanities researchers of all sorts of disciplines (art historians, literary historians, linguists, etc.) from academic and national cultural heritage institutions in the Netherlands. Their aim is to develop a distributed research infrastructure to analyze interactions between the producers and consumers of creative goods, and between the various branches of the creative industries of the Dutch Golden Age. Similar to the Italian Renaissance, the Spanish Golden Age, and Victorian England, nineteenth- and twentieth-century historians created the Dutch Golden Age. Although the aim was likewise to shape a national identity, the term "Golden Age" was already used by the most prominent Dutch poet of the seventeenth century, Joost van den Vondel, to capture this period of prosperity and creativity in which he and his contemporary citizens of the Dutch Republic and its capital Amsterdam lived (Helmers and Janssen 2018).

Like every historical construct of a golden era, the Dutch Golden Age is multifaceted. Some historians refer in nostalgic terms to this era as a period of political freedom and tolerance amidst military and religious conflicts. Others have stressed the development of one of the strongest global economies at that time based on the Netherlands' seafaring and land reclamation. Others still point to painters such as Rembrandt, Vermeer, and Hals, or to the publishers of atlases and maps such as the Blaeu family to underpin the creativity of the Dutch Republic, and of Amsterdam in particular, in this prosperous period. Although most historians accept the multifaceted character of the Dutch Golden Age, their attempts to better understand this period have been largely based on disciplinary approaches and directed by elitist perspectives. These disciplinary and even biased historical approaches also resonate in the digital infrastructures that are created by research and cultural heritage institutions.

Several databases on production within the creative industries do already exist—of artists in the Low Countries, for instance, and of book production in the Netherlands and of theater plays in Amsterdam's public theater in the seventeenth and eighteenth centuries. However, this digital information

---

in digital cultural heritage, University of Amsterdam), and Gabri van Tussenbroek (professor in building history, University of Amsterdam). The research team consists of postdocs Chiara Piccoli (archeology, University of Amsterdam) and Hugo Huurdeman (interface design, University of Amsterdam), PhD student Weixuan Li (art history, Huygens Institute), junior researcher Bart Reuvekamp (urban history, University of Amsterdam), and Saan Rashid (software engineer, University of Amsterdam).

is separated in silos. The Golden Agents project aims to integrate existing and new data collections on the production and consumption (of which far less information is digitally available) of creative goods to enable analyses of crossovers and interactions between the branches of these creative industries.

In the early modern period, for instance, occasional poems written for events such as weddings were presented at the same time as paintings. To give an example, Joost van den Vondel wrote a poem about Rembrandt's portrait of Anna Wijmer, wife of Jan Six who also commissioned a self-portrait from the master. Both works of Rembrandt and the glove that Anna is wearing in the painting are still present in the house of the family Six, together with 2,000 prints, drawings, and paintings; 100,000 archival documents; and cupboards full of glass- and silverware. This information is based on a monograph by Geert Mak (2016), but even if it was already digitally available, multiple databases would need to be consulted separately just to learn more about the people and products present(ed) at this one wedding event. The Short-Title Catalogue Netherlands (data.cerl.org/stcn/) or the Digitale Bibliotheek der Nederlanden (dbnl.org) might provide more information about the occasional poems of Joost van den Vondel. The RKD Netherlands Institute for Art History (rkd.nl/nl/explore/artists) and Remdoc (remdoc.huygens.knaw.nl) also hold documentation about Rembrandt. Additional information about the consumers, Jan Six and Anna Wijmer, would be harder to find, most likely via the indexes to the various dispersed documents in the City Archives of Amsterdam.

This is just one, luckily well-documented cluster of commissioners and artists. However, there are many more well-known families with rich collections that could inform us about the production and consumption of creative goods of the Dutch Golden Age. But this information would still only provide insights into commissions by the elite, hardly informing us about the ways art production was also tailored for "mass consumption." Angela Jager's (2020) analysis of the enormous market of cheap history paintings in seventeenth-century Amsterdam has challenged the existing art-historical canon in which this genre seemed exclusively reserved for the happy few. The promising research of Jager was based on the close reading of just a small number of seventeenth-century probate inventories. The Golden Agents infrastructure that develops tools for analysis and distant reading of the big data of the Dutch Golden Age will provide a better understanding of the consumption of cultural goods in all societal layers of Amsterdam in the Dutch Golden Age and holds the promise for new views of the history of the creative industries and the art-historical canon of the seventeenth century.

To get access to all societal layers of Amsterdam in the Dutch Golden Age, names, locations, and artefacts listed in various types of notarial deeds (probate inventories, pre-nuptial agreements, testaments) are extracted from about 2,500,000 scans of the City Archives of Amsterdam. By bringing together big historical data on the interactions between the producers and consumers of creative goods as well as the interactions between the various branches of the creative industries in a digital research infrastructure for further analysis, annotation, and interpretation, we hope to get more insight into the ways the art market adapted to the needs of consumers and come closer to answering overarching questions regarding the history of taste and of innovation. The infrastructure allows us to test existing hypotheses that are often extrapolations based on small data selections.

This chapter will first describe in more detail the various technologies and methods that were used in the development of the digital infrastructure of the Golden Agents project, which combines Semantic Web solutions, multi-agent technology, handwritten text recognition, and crowdsourcing to get a grip on the big historical data of the creative industries of the Dutch Golden Age. By bringing together big data from multiple, heterogeneous collections that were selected based on various criteria, data is often connected that differs in quality or is just not suitable for the research in question. Developers of distributed collections should not assess data quality on behalf of researchers but only assist them in making such assessments. I will discuss a pipeline of human–computer interfaces, already existing or developed in the context of the Golden Agents project, for ontology alignment, data alignment, entities extraction and identification, queries, and annotations that allow end users to assign values to the quality of the process in all stages of data curation and (re)use of the data for historical research.

This step-by-step description of the interaction possibilities with the big data of the Golden Agents infrastructure will be followed by a discussion of the second project: Virtual Interiors. This project was set up a year after the start of the Golden Agents project for two reasons. First, the conditions of the funding program only allowed for the hiring of developers for the Golden Agents project, not researchers. The involvement of researchers was needed to bring in research questions and test cases to validate the quality of algorithms, ontologies, data, methods, tools, and interfaces produced during the project's construction and to guarantee the future use of the infrastructure. Although the participating universities brought in domain knowledge as matching in kind, we did not want to be fully dependent on the input of their individual scholars given their teaching obligations and understandable different priorities in their scarce time for research. Second, although the Semantic Web technologies used in the Golden Agents project can bring together data of academic and cultural heritage institutions, the representation of linked data is still very abstract, and the notorious user-unfriendly query language SPARQL hardly facilitates interactions by humanities researchers and curators, let alone by the public. Therefore, we felt the need to create within the context of the Semantic Web interfaces for critical, trustworthy readings of big data for humanities research, cultural heritage, and the creative industries.

In the Virtual Interiors project, the research team set up innovative experiments to explore methodological issues in the development of multilayered 2D/3D/4D user interfaces to the linked data of the Semantic Web (Huurdeman, Piccoli, and van Wissen 2021). The project builds upon the linked data of the persons, locations, and cultural goods of the Golden Agents project, and on other sources such as building plans, elevations, topographical views, and diaries to reconstruct the seventeenth-century houses in which the objects are virtually recreated as best as possible in their original setting. The team focuses on the representation of uncertainty in the virtual reconstructions and explains how the reconstructions of Virtual Interiors can provide input for the development and evaluation of more generic, trustworthy interfaces to interact with 2D, 3D, and 4D data in the digital humanities and beyond.

As principal investigator and project lead of both projects, I will conclude the chapter with a personal assessment of how the digital infrastructure and big data of Dutch Golden Age could be reused in other research environments for Renaissance studies. In my view, future reuse would acknowledge the growing awareness in society that the glitter of "golden ages," such as that of the Dutch Republic, often blinds us to very dark histories based on slavery and other forms of institutionalized oppression. Thus, before data is reused in the context of such important societal debates, historians need to be able to provide historical evidence and be transparent in what they know and, even more importantly, what they do not know. Such research requires that users can interact with all processes of big data creation and representation.

Golden Agents: A Pipeline of Human-Computer Interfaces

The process for the creation and representation of linked data for the history of the creative industries of the Dutch Golden Age contains multiple steps. First, multiple, often heterogeneous collections—for the greater part, handwritten archival documents—need to be digitized and converted into a machine-readable standard. Then, entities (e.g., personal names, dates, places, cultural objects) that are needed to get a better understanding of interactions between producers and consumers, and between the various branches of the creative industries, need to be extracted from the data. This entity extraction is particularly difficult due to differences in handwriting and spelling variation and requires disambiguation.

To improve the quality of handwritten text recognition, and to handle this process of disambiguation, artificial intelligence was combined with crowd-sourcing. Further tools applying natural language techniques and network analysis have also been developed for the Golden Agents infrastructure to pre-classify and identify persons, locations, and cultural objects. These entities extracted from archival documents then need to be combined with metadata coming from multiple collections and therefore converted into an interchangeable standard for linked data: Resource Description Frame-work (RDF). To exchange this data between distributed and heterogeneous collections in a meaningful way requires further organization, modeling, and contextualization in so-called ontologies. In every step of this process, data changes and has an impact on the use of the infrastructure and its tools (Koolen, Gorp, and Ossenbruggen 2018, 379). Therefore, the research infrastructure and its tools need to be created in a transparent way so that users know what the state and quality of the data is at every step. The way we model and test each step in the development of the Golden Agents infrastructure as a pipeline with successive interfaces for human–computer interaction is described here below.

Digitization, Automatic Handwritten Text Recognition, and Crowdsourcing

In the quest to bring information together about the consumption of cultural goods in all societal layers of Amsterdam in the Dutch Golden Age, the Golden Agents project has tried to get a grip on the thousands of names, locations, and artefacts (in all sorts of spelling variations) listed in notarial deeds in the City Archives of Amsterdam. The Herculean task of digitizing and disclosing the archive's three kilometers of notarial archives of 731 notaries over the period from 1578 to 1915 was broken into two smaller projects. In the first, All Amsterdam Acts, volunteers indexed the person names and all geographical locations outside of Amsterdam. In a more recent project, Crowd Teaches the Computer How to Read, volunteers corrected automatically transcribed acts generated by the handwritten text recognition (HTR) tool Transkribus (readcoop.eu/transkribus) to train the computer algorithm to learn.

To teach a computer how to read handwritten texts—in our case, in seventeenth- and eighteenth-century Dutch—it needs sufficient examples of high-quality transcriptions created by people to evaluate and validate the results of those generated by the computer. These examples are called "ground truth." Although the number of words that are automatically recognized by the computer are increasing rapidly, creating sufficient ground truth by manually controlled transcriptions to search and to query the data in a trustworthy way is a time-consuming process. Moreover, indexing person names and geographical locations outside of Amsterdam is too limited for the overall scope of the Golden Agents research infrastructure. Therefore, alternative methods were developed within the Golden Agents project to select the data needed, to correct the HTR, and to extract entities relevant for the analysis of interactions between the production and consumption of cultural goods of various branches of the creative industries of Amsterdam in the Dutch Golden Age before the transcriptions were ready for publication.

Pre-classification and Data Alignment of Person Names with Network Analysis

Just the indexing of person names alone in the notary acts of the Amsterdam City Archive results in such huge a number of name variants that they could never be identified without the help of automated techniques. In the Golden Agents project, experiments with artificial intelligence have been set up to pre-classify this unstructured data of name variants mentioned in baptism acts, pre-nuptial agreements, and burial acts and to compare these to the structured data of identified names—for instance, those of married people in the ECARTICO (vondel.humanities.uva.nl/ecartico) database of biographies of more than 50,000 painters, engravers, printers, booksellers, gold- and silversmiths, and others involved in the cultural industries of the Low Countries (Baas 2023; Baas, Dastani, and Feelders 2019).

However, for the majority of person names, in particular of the lesser known citizens of Amsterdam of the Dutch Golden Age, there is hardly structured data available as ground truth to identify the people behind these names. Experiments have therefore been set up with the disambiguation tool Lenticular Lenses (see Idrissou et al. 2018, 2019), which has been further developed in the context of the Golden Agents project.

The functionalities of this disambiguation tool go beyond those of the very popular OpenRefine tool used for semi-automated data clean up and transformation of said data to other formats. Although OpenRefine has been adapted with success in the Getty Vocabularies' OpenRefine Reconciliation service (getty.edu/research/tools/vocabularies/obtain/openrefine.html) to allow users to compare and map their local data—for instance, comparing internal lists of artists and their artefacts to a corresponding set of record identifiers of the Getty's Union List of Artist Names (ULAN) or its Art and Architecture Thesaurus (AAT)—the enormous amount of unstructured person and object names in the City Archives of Amsterdam require further automated processes to assist researchers and collection curators in data curation.

The challenge is to combine these automated processes with human–computer interfaces that allow users to verify step by step the quality of the data selection, disambiguation, and reconciliation. To this end, the visual clustering of person names on the basis of the pre-classification with artificial intelligence is used as input for network analysis for disambiguation. Given the fact that the enormous quantities of person names would clutter the screen with overlapping labels, a hierarchical network visualization is used that allows the user to zoom in on or out from particular clusters of variants of certain names.

Although this first clustering of name variants is useful, further disambiguation is necessary to establish whether these clusters simply contain different spellings of the name of one person, or if they belong to different persons with similar names. This disambiguation is based on the idea that the names of people were registered at least a couple of times during their lifetimes—in birth acts, pre-nuptial agreements, marriage acts, transport acts, property acts, business agreements, burial acts, and so on—and often mentioned in combination with the names of family, spouses, witnesses, and others. The underlying assumption is that if more combinations of names are mentioned in successive shared events and can be interlinked in networks, the probability increases that the named individual can be identified.

To support the researcher or data curator in this process of disambiguation based on networks, Al Idrissou et al. (2018, 2019) introduced the specific concepts of "associated networks" and "identity link networks." Associated networks are networks that combine names of people who participated in the same events and form the basis of the identity link networks, which rely on the context of multiple associated networks so a person can more likely be identified. At the same time, we are aware that many of these names—some names are far more common than others—will never result in the identification of a person. Nevertheless, the disambiguation and undoubling of names is important, not only for the identification of named persons but also for further prosopographical research. For that reason, future users of the Golden Agents infrastructure are supported in the decision of how trustworthy the identification of a person is by guiding them step by step through this disambiguation process in the interactive interface of Lenticular Lenses (Fig. 1).

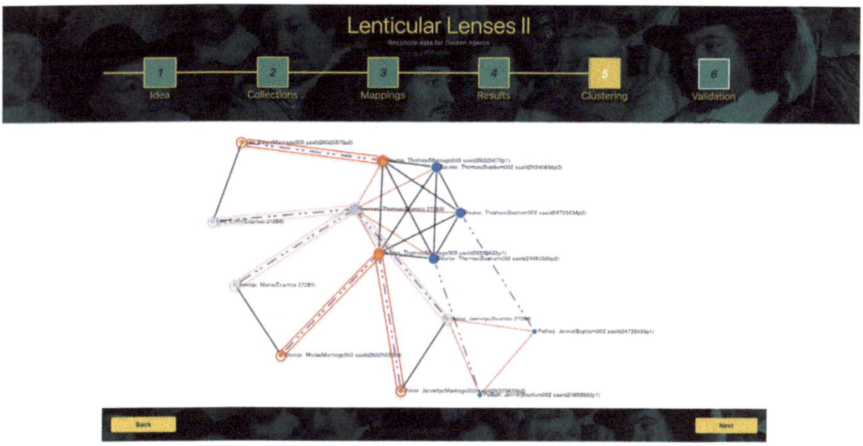

Figure 1. Lenticular Lenses. User interface for disambiguation supported by network analysis. Image credit: Al Idrissou.

Entity Extraction and Visualization of Cultural Objects with Lexicographic Natural Language Processing (NLP) Techniques

As previously noted, we not only need data about people but also about the cultural goods they had in their houses. Also previously mentioned, the projects of the City Archives of Amsterdam do not currently annotate this data for indexing. Finally, the quality of the HTR as delivered by Transkribus, albeit promising, is still too low to completely index and fruitfully search the transcribed texts. But apart from the quality of the transcriptions, keyword search is hampered by the fact that we may not even know the exact words we are looking for, or their many diachronic and regional spelling variants, let alone all the potentially related historical terms. To get a better understanding of the exact requirements for such queries to be satisfactory, a small experiment was set up to automatically locate, identify, and extract information—so-called automated entity extraction of cultural goods in notary acts of the City Archives of Amsterdam, and in the Montias databases of the Getty Research Institute and of the Frick Collection.

For this experiment, we used the Text-Induced Corpus Correction and Lexical Assessment Tool (TICCLAT) developed by Martin Reynaert, which is built on top of a comprehensive lexical database that represents a compendium of over 1.5 million human-attested lexical resources (i.e., Dutch diachronic word forms and names). The compendium is being further extended based on the 18.5 billion word-tokens of the Nederlab corpus (nederlab.nl). This collection of Dutch texts from 800 CE to the present (including, for instance, the crowd-sourced and well-curated seventeenth-century Dutch National Library Newspaper Collection) comes in a unified text format, Folia XML. Word form variation can be visualized in TICCLAT to explore the dispersion of words and their related forms through time and across different sub-corpora (Reynaert, Bos, and van der Zwaan 2019; Reynaert, van der Zwaan, and Bos 2019).

A particularly interesting functionality of TICCLAT is that not only can it be used to find spelling variants, but its linked related word forms in combination with Word2Vec word embeddings also allow for retrieving semantically related words—so-called semantic near neighbors, such as *portret* (portrait) and *tronie* (a Dutch equivalent of "mug" for face) (Reynaert 2020)—which are extracted from external vocabularies. In this experiment, TICCLAT extracted word variants from 794,000 word-tokens, primarily of painting descriptions in the Montias databases from the Getty and Frick collections, and 1 million word-tokens of ground truth transcribed notarial deeds were checked and manually corrected by volunteers. The yet "unknown" word forms and names identified and thereby linked to humanly attested known words and names amount to 17,000 "new" word forms from the Montias collections and 32,000 from the ground truth samples of notarial deeds. To give an example, 17 humanly attested variants of the Dutch word *schilderij* (painting) resulted in 249 previously unattested variants in the Montias databases. Next steps will be to check these words against existing thesauri and catalogs such as AAT, Iconclass, and the Short Title Catalogue of the Netherlands (STCN), and to present newfound words in a temporary thesaurus for later inclusion in such vocabularies at will.

Finally, the code of TICCLAT has been rewritten and its database used as an input lexicon in the development of a new tool, Analiticcl (github.com/proycon/analiticcl), for incorporation in the pipeline of the Golden Agents infrastructure to post-correct all scans and transcriptions by Transkribus. This must allow for recognizing entities of the handwritten notary acts of the Dutch Golden Age supported by a thesaurus with geographical names and object names developed by the Golden Agents project that complements existing standardized vocabularies such as GeoNames (geonames.org) and AAT (getty.edu/research/tools/vocabularies/aat). The terms in these vocabularies and thesauri are mapped to ontologies developed for the Golden Agents project. All these processes of combining artificial intelligence with crowdsourcing and additional methods of network analysis and natural language processing for disambiguation and entity extraction are aimed at translating the original unstructured data of archival resources or of other relevant documents into the common linked data structure of RDF. This Golden Agents data in RDF format is brought together in a so-called triple store, Timbuctoo, where they can be linked with the various other external national and international datasets, as illustrated in Figures 2 and 3.

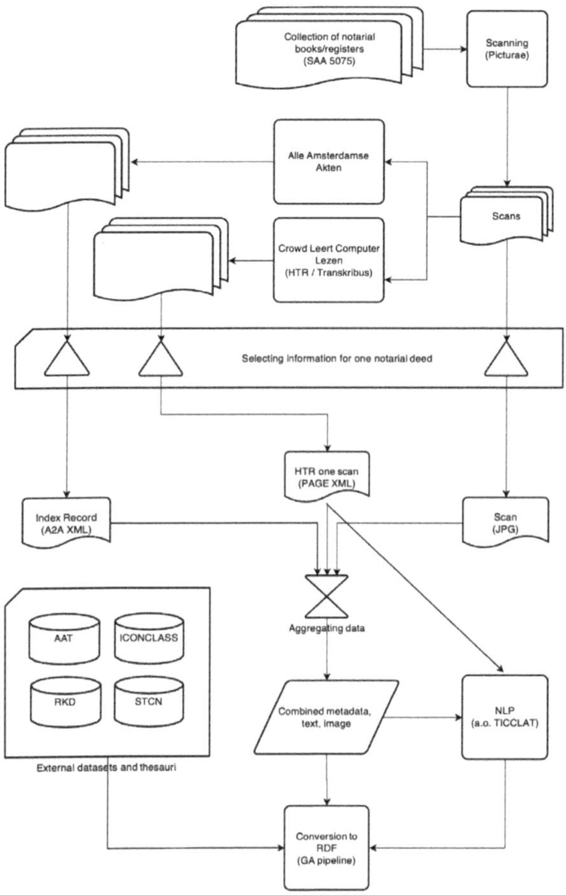

Figure 2. Pipeline for preprocessing archival data and representation in RDF annotations hereof. Image credit: Leon van Wissen.

Textual references to paintings, books, or other cultural goods mentioned in probate inventories are represented in a simplified RDF schema. Moreover, the references to these objects in archival documents can be connected to external thesauri and datasets while keeping the provenance chain by pointing back to their location in the archival document. Figure 3, for instance, shows how a reference to a painting of the Good Samaritan as an object is linked to the term "easel painting" in the Getty vocabulary and to an image in the database of the RKD Netherlands Institute of Art History and its subject to art classification system Iconclass (iconclass.org).

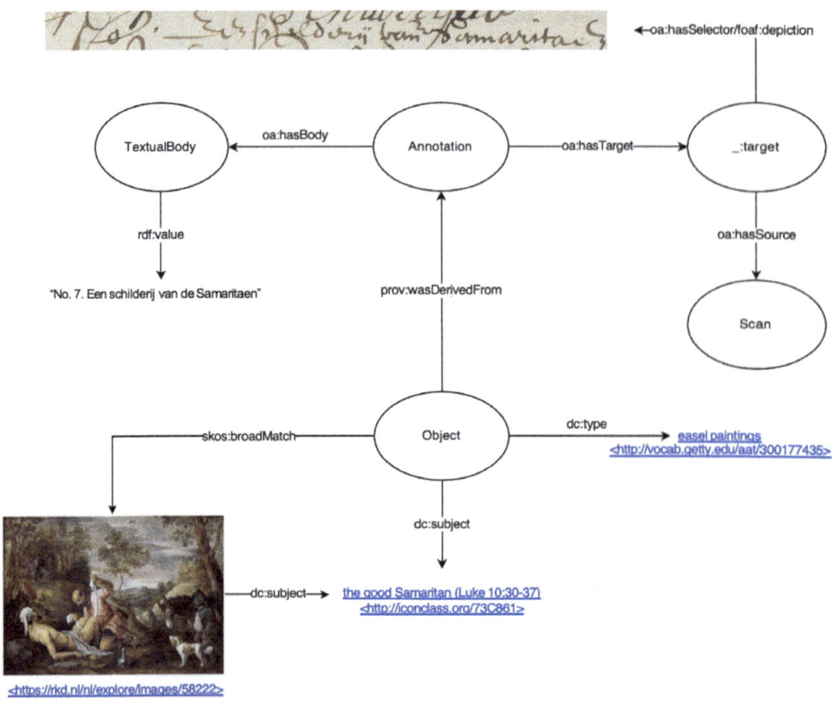

Figure 3. Simplified RDF representation of a painting of the Good Samaritan with reference to Iconclass. Image credit: Leon van Wissen.

Opening Ontological Models

It is not sufficient to convert (meta)data from heterogenous collections into RDF to allow for meaningful use of linked data. When reading the word "Renaissance" in RDF format, for instance, the computer does not distinguish between the understanding of this term by many members of the Renaissance

Society of America (RSA) community and by researchers of manuscripts of the Carolingian Renaissance. To enable that distinction, the computer needs further contextualization by a formal, explicit, and shared conceptualization, in this case of the term Renaissance by both groups of researchers. Such formal groupings of concepts into basic categories are called ontologies. The development of such ontological models for specific (sub)domains or research themes is not straightforward but rather a continuous process of (re)negotiating shared concepts.

It is important to realize that cultural heritage and research institutions have different missions with implications for their ontological models and metadata standards. The commonly used ontological model in exchanges of data between cultural heritage institutions and academic institutions in the humanities is CIDOC Conceptual Reference Model (CRM). However, researchers in the humanities often consider this model developed in the realm of cultural heritage either to be too abstract or to be lacking relevant classes for their specific data. For instance, for historians with a strong focus on processes and archival sources, it is sometimes hard to find the right classes in this cultural heritage model that is predominantly designed to organize concepts that are strongly related to objects and artefacts. Nevertheless, the same historians might want to make use of the full operability of data exchange allowed by existing standards.

To overcome that problem, the Data for History consortium (dataforhistory.org), of which the Golden Agents project is a founding member, took the initiative to develop ontologies for humanities disciplines that are not only fully compliant with standards (such as CIDOC CRM) according to the FAIR Principles (go-fair.org/fair-principles) but also complement them. These ontologies are brought together by the Data for History consortium in an ontological management environment called OntoME (ontome.net) to create, model, align, and export ontologies. The approach is like the development of more specific ontology design patterns described by Cogan Shimizu, Quin Hirt, and Pascal Hitzler (2019). The co-design of such ontology patterns by researchers and curators can certainly contribute to bridging the gap between generic collection ontologies and domain specific ones for research.

The Golden Agents project has contributed to the Data for History consortium by developing two ontological models. The first one, Reconstructions and Observations in Archival Resources (ROAR++), models entities extracted from archivalia. Reconstructions are derived from observations in archival resources. For instance, a person can be mentioned in various sources such as a birth certificate or a notary deed; these we call person observations, which can be combined into a one-person reconstruction. These derivations based on documents or inferred from other observations are recorded in a provenance ontology (PROV) so that the user can always trace back the decisions on which the reconstructions are based. The observations can provide provenance in more or in less detail and are therefore supported by an uncertainty model (Engelse and Wissen 2019; Wissen and Zamborlini 2020).

ROAR++ makes part of the second, more generic and encompassing model, called Storylines of Historical Evidence (Heuvel and Zamborlini 2019, 2021; Zamborlini, Betti, and Heuvel 2017), in which all unstructured data derived from archival sources with information about persons, locations, and cultural goods are organized in "views" to be linked with the structured metadata of the information about the creative industries of the Dutch Golden Age brought together in the Golden Agents infrastructure (see Figs. 4a–b). One of the challenges in the development of this encompassing model is to capture these views on historical processes of the interactions between various branches, and between the production and consumption of these industries. These processes are described as multiple narratives, for which we use the concept of "storifying data."[2]

We already noted that the Golden Agents project tries to break with the canon of art history by analyzing the consumption of cultural goods in all layers of society instead of in elite culture. Nevertheless, for the development of the ontological model, the most famous painter of the Dutch Golden Age, Rembrandt, and his most famous painting, *The Night Watch* (1642), were chosen as a test case. We opted for a painter with many pupils and copyists as well as a work of art with multiple archival sources of commissions and provenance, with a rich material history of production, reuse, and restoration and with contemporary copies and later derivatives in other formats, such as sculptures and even tattoos to make a rich model that included as many past and present stories and perspectives as possible.

[2] The concept of storifying data has been used more generally in the context of data management. We introduce it here specifically in the context of modeling ontologies.

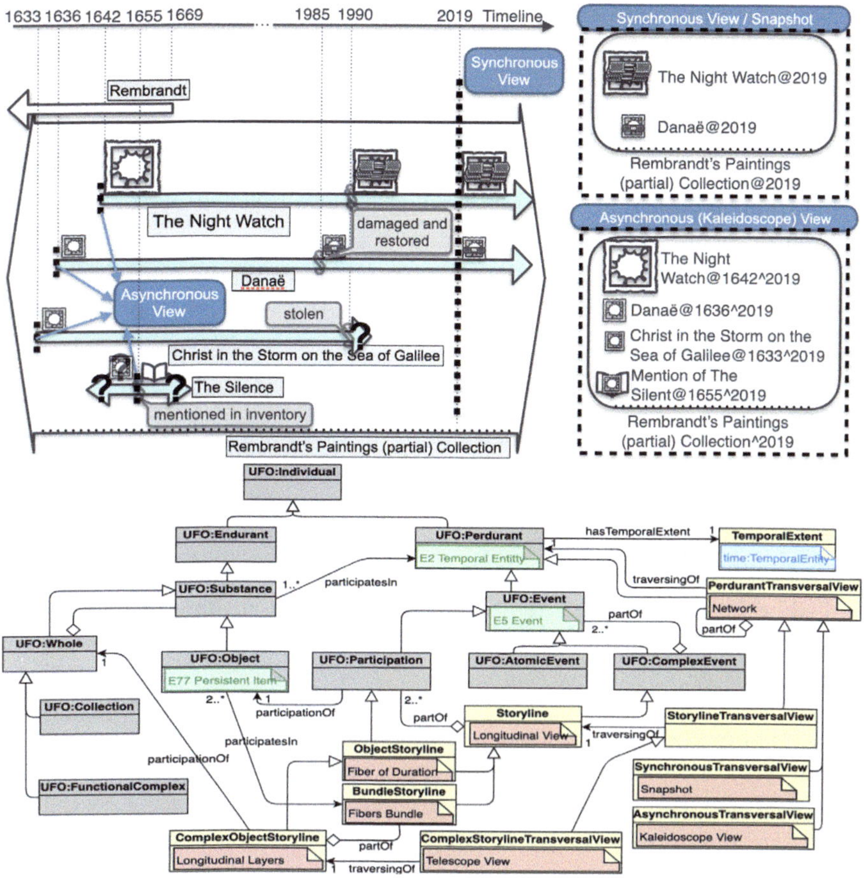

Figures 4a–b. Golden Agents project model: Storylines of Historical Evidence and representation of the ontological model in a Unified Modeling Language (UML) diagram with mapping to CIDOC CRM. Image Credit: Veruska Zamborlini.

The aim of the experiment was to capture the order in the making of an object (from idea to final product), the order of an object in the artistic life or oeuvre of its maker, the order between the original object and copies and transformations hereof, and finally the order of the object within history or in fictional time depicted in paintings or other works of art in parallel storylines that have their own dynamics but sometimes interact. The final aim was to describe these multiple orders in the making of creative products of the Dutch Golden Age and the consumption hereof in events that are underpinned with references to the sources to create the encompassing ontological model: storylines of historical evidence.

Small teams of humanities researchers, computer scientists, and information specialists of the Golden Agents consortium tested (parts of) the model in small experiments. One team, for instance, focused on the use of the storylines model to capture interactions between producers, consumers, and various branches of the creative industries at events such as weddings. Another group investigated its potential use for "processes of creativity" to get a better grip on innovation and its impact on the art market in the Dutch Golden Age.

Sometimes experiments were set up with an external partner. For instance, the ROAR++ model was tested with data of the Getty Research Institute in the context of their Provenance Index Remodel project. Enriched provenance data brought together by the economist and art historian John Michael Montias dispersed over two datasets in the Getty Provenance Index and the Frick Collection's Montias Database of 17th Century Art Inventories were directly linked back to transcribed items of cultural goods mentioned in the notary acts of the City Archives of Amsterdam (Wissen, Latronico, van Ginhoven et al. 2020; Wissen, Latronico, Zamborlini et al. 2020).

We explained the multiple steps of the pipeline with interfaces for human–computer interaction to create meaningful linked data for the history of the creative industries of the Dutch Golden Age. Furthermore, we stressed the importance of making the provenance chain visible by pointing back to the original (re)sources. But how can we inform users about the development of the Golden Agents infrastructure and about the progress in linking it with other distributed collections with metadata and enrichments hereof that vary in completeness and in quality?

Representation and Annotation of Completeness and Quality of Data Based on Provenance

Between and within academic and research institutions there are many differences in completeness and detail in which collections are described and in the ways the quality of the metadata is verified and represented (Helmreich, Lincoln, Heuvel 2021). Differences in detail not only relate to the number of metadata fields but also to the completeness of the data described in each field separately. In quantitative analysis, such differences matter, and for that reason the completeness of the Golden Agents data is indicated in the user interface of the Timbuctoo triple store in a little box with a color that represents the percentage of processed metadata in a particular field. Another step that might be considered for the future is to make the user aware of the quality of the interoperability of the metadata of the Golden Agents project. Here, a similar color scheme in a box represents the percentage of metadata that has been checked and mapped against certain vocabularies. Finally, we are exploring the possibility of allowing users to annotate the quality of the metadata themselves based on the provenance of the data and annotations hereof provided to them (Fig. 5).

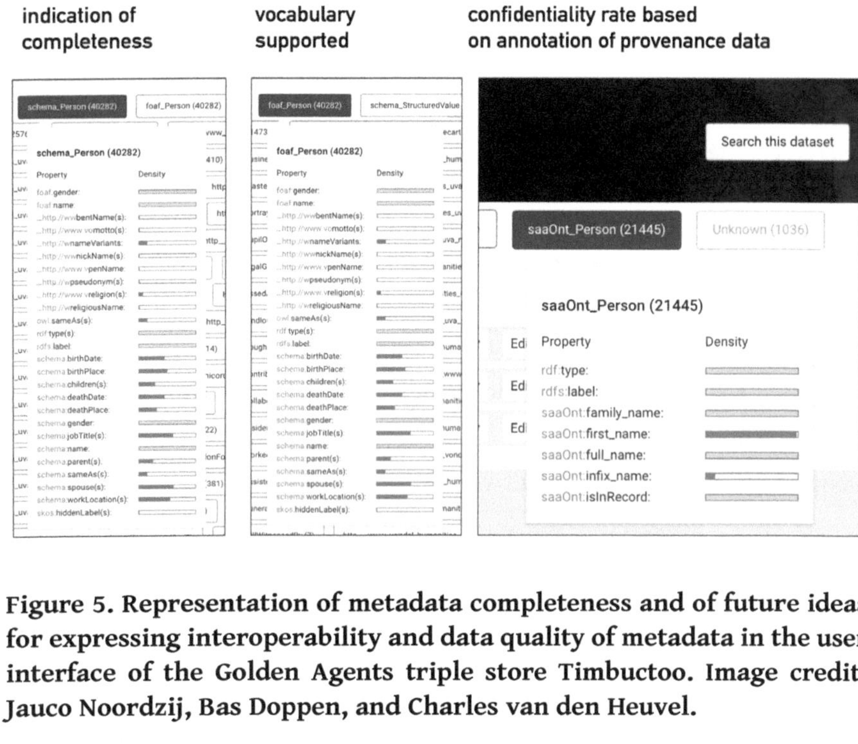

Figure 5. Representation of metadata completeness and of future ideas for expressing interoperability and data quality of metadata in the user interface of the Golden Agents triple store Timbuctoo. Image credit: Jauco Noordzij, Bas Doppen, and Charles van den Heuvel.

Although the creations of such features in the user interface of the triple store can enhance the data control of the user to some extent, extra steps are needed to query the Semantic Web in more user-friendly ways than SPARQL. The same applies to representations of big data in historical networks or in Geographical Information Systems (GIS) that are still too abstract and lacking contextual information to exploit them in depth for historical research in the humanities or for the disclosure of cultural heritage (Bodenhamer 2010; Presner, Shepard, and Kawano 2014). Humanities scholars such as Johanna Drucker (2011, 2013) have challenged the use of digital analytical methods of patterns in big data borrowed from the natural and social sciences. Valuable as the proposals in these critical humanities studies are for close readings of small data, they do not provide solutions yet for handling big data and visualizations hereof. How can we embrace complexity, ambiguity, and uncertainty in the analysis and visualization of big data? This question is central in the Virtual Interiors project.

Virtual Interiors as Interfaces for Big Historical Data Research

Although Virtual Interiors partially builds upon data of the Golden Agents project, the purposes of the development of their respective interfaces are quite different. While the Golden Agents interfaces are merely intended to support users in all phases of data handling that meet the FAIR Principles, the Virtual Interiors project is more concerned with methodological issues related to the interaction of users with multidimensional representations of data (with all its uncertainties herein) and annotations hereof. To this end, experiments were set up to create multilayered 2D, 3D, and 4D user interfaces in the form of digital "deep maps" and virtual rooms of spatial data of Amsterdam in the Dutch Golden Age (Li, Piccoli, and Heuvel 2019). Furthermore, the project explores new ways of archiving these multidimensional digital maps and virtual reconstructions (and their annotations) and of making these available to various audiences in different formats, such as enhanced publications.

Deep Maps and Historical Networks as 2D Interfaces for Spatial Data

During the Dutch Golden Age, between 1585 and 1700, Amsterdam housed more than 1,000 painters. Art historians have tried to understand the impact of this abundance of painters on art production by conducting microlevel studies on specific artists, but they lack a comprehensive view. Economic historians brought in macrolevel mechanisms to explain the art market, but they lost touch with place and people. In her PhD research "Painters' Playbooks: Deep Mapping Socio-spatial Strategies in the Art Market of Seventeenth-Century Amsterdam" (2023), Weixuan Li explores the dynamics between individual artists and their clientele by looking into the connections between where painters lived and worked and their specific painting commissions and business practices (see also Li 2018, 2019a, 2019b). She tries to bridge the gap between art-historical and socioeconomical approaches by looking into the locations of artists' and art dealers' workshops on seventeenth-century maps to capture the interplay between artistic and economic considerations behind artworks and to contextualize the places in which artworks were created and consumed. In short, she tries to find where artists lived—and, in particular, *why* they lived there—by using historical data of the Golden Agents project about paintings applying spatial analytical tools. With these tools she creates "deep maps."

The concept of deep mapping was introduced by David Bodenhamer (2010) to enrich GIS—considered by many humanities scholars to be one-dimensional and "flat"—with contextual information. Instead of minimizing complexities, uncertainties, and ambiguities in a reductionist way, deep maps should include these to account for the imprecise, fluid nature of historical sources. While current discussions of deep mapping are mostly conceptual, Weixuan Li tries to operationalize this concept with concrete examples and advance the methodologies in practice within the domain of the history of art of the Dutch Golden Age. One example concerns the mapping of the original workplaces and the creation of historical networks of artists that lived in Amsterdam in the seventeenth century (Li 2018, 2023).

The place of Rembrandt's original workshop is known and can still be visited today. For most of the 1,000 painters who lived in Amsterdam between 1585 and 1700, however, their exact workplace is not clear, even if their original locations are mentioned in historical documents. The reason is that houses did not have their own house numbers until the French administrative system of cadastral plans, introduced after Napoleon's annexation of Holland, was fully implemented in the Netherlands in 1832.

Although locations can sometimes be inferred from references in archival sources, there is an imbalance in information about the urban fabric and citizens of Amsterdam in the Golden Age that results in ambiguities and uncertainties. For instance, tax registration and property transaction data that provide detailed information about the presence of creative industries, such as of painters' workshops in particular areas of Amsterdam, are only available for some annual intervals during the seventeenth century and do not necessarily coincide with the publication years of the historical maps to which this data is linked.

For a city like Amsterdam, with its concentric canal plan resulting in a half onion-shaped street plan, it is therefore quite difficult to pinpoint the exact location of a house mentioned in the notary acts of the early modern period. In the outer rings of this plan, a street could even run for miles. Of course, there are means to find these houses. People decorated their houses with recognizable gable stones, for instance. When they moved house, however, these beautiful stones—often related to their family name—moved with them. In short, there are many uncertainties in the geo-locations when we project a seventeenth-century map, such as the panoramic view of Balthasar Florisz. van Berckenrode of 1625 (see Fig. 6), onto the cadastral map of 1832. Nevertheless, the location of a house on a particular street can be approximated by looking for references to landmarks, buildings, and so on in additional archival sources.

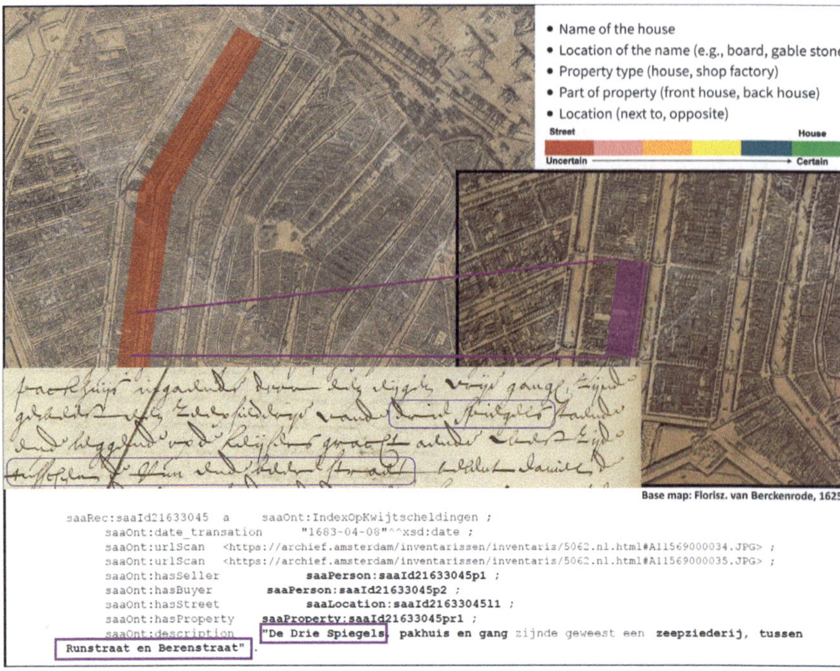

Figure 6. Color code for representing levels of uncertainty of geodata and annotations on the historical map of Balthasar Florisz. van Berckenrode of 1625. Image credit: Weixuan Li and Leon van Wissen.

For instance, in a testimony in the notary acts of the City Archives of Amsterdam (published in Bredius 1915–21, 7:136n2) of the lesser-known painter Jacob Lyon de Fuijter, we can read that his wife indicated that her family lived "op de Keysersgraft in 't Wapen van Oostvriesland t naest de Seepsiedery van de drie Spiegels" (on the Keizersgracht in the Coat of Arms of East Friesland, next to a soap factory called Three Mirrors; my trans.). Without any context, the description "t Wapen van Oostvrieslandt" cannot narrow down the search within hundreds of houses along the Keizersgracht. Nonetheless, the painter's neighboring house, "de Seepsiedery van de drie

Spiegels," is mentioned in the transport acts in more detail: "op de Keyersgraft aen de westzyde tuysschen de run en de berestraet" (on the west side of Keizersgracht between Run and Berenstraat quoted in Li 2018, 2019a). This way we can narrow down its original location and give it a new color code to represent a different level of uncertainty (see Fig. 6). In the future, we hope to extract this kind of approximative geo information automatically using the above mentioned Analiticcl tool, supported by a thesaurus derived from entities in seventeenth-century Dutch archival sources for equivalents in English such as "opposite," "in front of," "next to," "between," "at the corner," and "along."

Representing Uncertainties in Virtual Reconstructions of Interiors

The well-known 2009 London Charter for the Computer-Based Visualisation of Cultural Heritage (londoncharter.org) issued guidelines for best practices to create historically reliable 3D reconstructions in a transparent way, taking ambiguities and uncertainties into account (Denard 2012). However, despite these very useful guidelines, we need experimental case studies to assess whether they can be well implemented. Even though the Virtual Interiors project makes use of the big historical data of the Golden Agents projects, the selection of suitable case studies for its 3D/4D reconstructions is still far from straightforward. The reconstructions of seventeenth-century houses and their interiors rely first on the current state of the houses themselves. If their interiors have changed over time, historical plans and elevations, preferably from the period itself, are necessary to make reconstructions to avoid assumptions based on restorations. Once we have sufficiently reliable information about the original layout of a house, additional archival sources are needed of the goods originally present therein to enable a virtual reconstruction.

As one might imagine, it is almost impossible to find an interior that meets all these criteria. It is more likely that a house owned by a rich merchant, for instance, which later became protected as a historical monument, will have stood the test of time, and we will therefore have more exact information about his cultural goods than those in the lodgings of less wealthy citizens, whose possessions are often only described in very generic terms (e.g., "a painting," with no reference to its maker, title, subject, or genre, or "a book" listed among linen and other domestic goods).

To optimize the use of big data, the Virtual Interiors project has developed a typology of 3D/4D reconstructions based on the minimal required information needed to answer research questions about the original historical situations of houses and their interiors with an acceptable degree of uncertainty. However, even when an optimal selection meets all criteria of necessary information, such as of the well-documented house Herengracht 573, many uncertainties remain that raise all sorts of methodological questions about how to best analyze and visualize the data.

Restoration reports of the Monuments and Archaeology Department of the City of Amsterdam and several building and elevation plans provide much information about material aspects of Herengracht 573, while an extensive probate inventory of the seventeenth-century owners, the regent Pieter de Graeff (1638–1707) and his very politically influential wife Jacoba Bicker (1640–95), listed their goods (almost 1,000 objects) room by room. Moreover, a diary of Pieter de Graeff not only provides additional information about the household properties but also about the craftsmen and painters to whom he commissioned works and about the types of materials for which he paid.[3] From the probate inventory, for instance, it can be deduced that Lundens's copy of Rembrandt's *Night Watch* (before it was resized) hung in the dining room and Frans Hals's portrait of Pieter de Graeff's mother Catherina Hooft hung in the "green room" on the second floor. The diary also provides information about the dimensions of the marble tiles that De Graeff had ordered, necessary to virtually reconstruct the original floor of the hallway; the same applies to a map of an estate of the family that hung in the same entrance. In other cases, however, information does not go beyond indications such as "two chairs." To make users of the Virtual Interiors project aware of such differences in uncertainties in data, we have developed confidence indexes[4] of objects and their original locations (Fig. 7).

---

[3] For this diary as well as the historical documents of Herengracht 573 and of the De Graeff family as its inhabitants, see Piccoli 2024.

[4] The confidence index is based on levels of uncertainties for objects—(1) original; (2) primary source analogy without doubt; (3) primary source analogy with doubt; and (4) uncertain—and for locations—(1) known in original location; (2) inferred with certainty; (3) inferred with doubt; and (4) uncertain. See further, Huurdeman and Piccoli 2020, 2021.

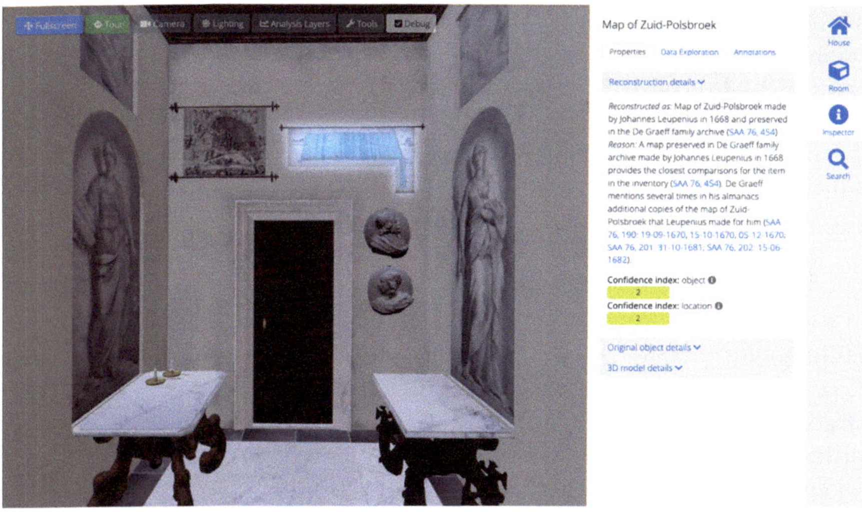

Figure 7. Virtual Interiors project experiment with user interface: visualization of the level of confidence of the map of Zuid Polsbroek (object) and its original location in the hallway of the House of De Graeff. Image credit: Hugo Huurdeman and Chiara Piccoli.

Hyperspaces for Research: Interfaces and Enhanced Publications of Multiple Perspectives

Although Amsterdam in the Dutch Golden Age is used to test how the concept of deep maps and historic reconstructions in 3D/4D can be implemented, the question of how we tell, edit, and represent stories in virtual reconstructions with incomplete/inconsistent data has relevance far beyond this historic case. While it is impossible to make direct extrapolations from the above-described limited case studies of deep maps of Amsterdam and of 3D/4D reconstructions of the interiors of its seventeenth-century houses, the aim is to generalize the results of the development of these human–computer interfaces as best as possible for reuse in digital humanities research, cultural heritage, and publication in this field.

For that reason, postdoc researcher Hugo Huurdeman is embedded in two different organizations: Sound and Vision, a multimedia cultural heritage institute that archives and discloses all radio and television programs of the Dutch national and commercial broadcasting stations, and Brill, a well-known publisher in the field of the humanities with a focus on antiquity, the Middle Ages, and the early modern period. Sound and Vision, together with another Dutch museum that specializes in architecture and multimedia, Het Nieuwe Instituut in Rotterdam, is interested both in new ways of archiving these virtual reconstructions and their annotations and in the manners to make these available to various audiences. Meanwhile, Brill is exploring how the created knowledge of human–computer interfaces can be translated in enhanced publications. In both cases, the provenance of information and the visualization of what we know and do not know is crucial.

Despite some experiments with combinations of analog and web-based publications, the traditional book format is still predominant in the humanities (as in other disciplines) in today's computer age. Affordances of digital publication methods to represent research results or to tell stories in alternative ways are not yet fully exploited let alone implemented. Together with Brill, we are trying to translate the virtual research environment (VRE) into a more interactive, enhanced publication with annotations. Annotations of media, such as tags of fragments in storylines, are highly conditioned by the linear character of many media types (such as books, film, and television). Designing a system for annotating interactive virtual worlds in 3D/4D (but also for games) provides completely new challenges, technically and conceptually, in dealing with the identification of locations and events in changing orders and configurations.

Contextualizing these virtual historic reconstructions with annotations that can be preserved provides input for the creation of what Todd Presner, David Shepard, and Yoh Kawano (2014, 17–18) described as more generic, multidimensional "hyperspaces as contextual realities in which human beings act and create." In short, the aim is to create human–computer interfaces in the form of hyperspaces in which users can navigate and annotate virtual historic reconstructions of the past.

The translation of demonstrators of specific reconstructions of virtual interiors of houses of the Dutch Golden Age into more generic, multidimensional "hyperspaces" for research in the digital humanities, cultural heritage, creative industries, and beyond requires three levels of research. First, it requires additional research into the representation of heterogeneous and ambiguous information in these virtual environments and into the various ways users interact in these areas to come to meaningful interpretations. Second, it needs to establish how this information can be assembled, edited, enriched, and preserved in a sustainable way in enhanced publications. Finally, we need to know not only how meaningful interpretations of the presented knowledge based on the assembled and annotated information can be shared for reuse but also how these enhanced publications can be developed into commercial products of the creative industries using sound business models.

These different uses require different user interfaces to query the multidimensional multimedia. Common ways to explore and experience 3D virtual environments include first person views (i.e., moving around in a multidimensional space) and third-person orbit views in which objects can be freely rotated. In the Virtual Interiors project, however, the number of 3D objects can amount to hundreds in just one environment with potentially multiple audiences. For that reason, Hugo Huurdeman and Chiara Piccoli (2020) set up a test to explore the role of context of search user interfaces (SUIs) and evaluated approaches to contextualize queries of historical 3D objects. It is with this combination of embedding of researchers in practical settings and further user studies that we seek to prepare the human–computer interfaces as best as possible for reuse in digital humanities research, cultural heritage, and publications in this field.

Epilogue: Big Historical Data and Renaissance Studies in Current Societal Debates

Given the huge investments involved, large digital infrastructures are often approached with a discerning eye. It is therefore hardly surprising that the initiative to develop a European Time Machine (timemachine.eu), with the largest funding ever seen in the domains of the humanities and cultural heritage, has met with criticism because its content selection is predominantly centered around Western history and culture and its focus has been deemed too technologically centered. One of the often-expressed fears that deserves full scrutiny is that the development of the numerous tools and technologies and the use of big data in the context of the European Time Machine would challenge and might even ignore the involvement of historians and humanists. This criticism was foremost voiced in discussions around the first of the many satellites of virtual reconstructions that formed the technological basis of the European Time Machine, the Venice Time Machine project (epfl.ch/research/domains/venice-time-machine).

To take away the fear for leaving out the role of the historian, we regard the discussed methodological issues around the use of big historical data and virtual reconstructions as interactive interfaces addressed in the Golden Agents and Virtual Interiors projects as critical test cases of another satellite in this program, the Amsterdam Time Machine (amsterdamtimemachine.nl). However, it is not sufficient to address methodological issues and to test out interfaces with user groups. To legitimize the large investments needed for digital infrastructures of big historical data they need to have societal relevance. Digital infrastructures need to support argumentation based on historical perspectives and evidence in current debates in society. Debates concerning, for instance, the question of whether to remove the statues of "heroes" or "benefactors" who contributed to the wealth of nations but who also have darker histories, including histories of colonialism and the unequal treatment of women. This requires a critical reflection on the future of the above discussed Golden Agents and Virtual Interiors projects.

In recent years, the term "Dutch Golden Age" has become more and more contested. Statues erected in the past to honor Dutch "seafaring heroes" have been graffitied with strong terms of abuse, and in 2019 the Amsterdam Museum decided to remove all references to this so-called Golden Age from its collections. Although we questioned whether the name of the Golden Agents project should be changed for similar reasons, we ultimately decided to stick with it. Not only had many contracts already been signed under this name with external partners but changes to the funded project would also have required authorization. Of course, we could have asked for such permission, which may have been granted, but we also kept the adjective "golden" in part because it provides opportunities to contextualize the contested term. Moreover, societal discussions about the colonial history of the Netherlands and its link to the Dutch Golden Age only took off in earnest when the project was already well underway. Reports about the role of slavery in Dutch cities such as Amsterdam, Rotterdam, and Utrecht saw the light in late 2020 and 2021. These reports were largely based on data of the Dutch West India Company (WIC), and one of their conclusions was that the role of the Dutch East India Company in the history of slavery is still in its infancy (Brandon et al. 2020; Jouwe, Kuipers, and Raben 2021; Stipriaan 2020). Therefore, it seemed better not to include data yet beyond the original scope of the creative industries but just to point to the information about slavery that has recently become available and that might be combined with our datasets to come to a more critical study of the Dutch Golden Age in the future.

Although part of the wealth of the Dutch Republic was due to conditions in place long before its Golden Age and based on different sources of income, such as maritime trade and even the creative industries—for instance the book/printing industries and the art market as described by Claartje Rasterhoff (2017)—the mentioned studies commissioned by the cities already reveal that the slave trade contributed considerably. Historians differ in their opinions on how much the slave trade contributed to the Dutch Golden Age.

Pepijn Brandon and Ulbe Bosma (2019) claimed that by the end of the Dutch Golden Age in the second half of the eighteenth century, 10 percent of the income of the global city of Amsterdam was based on Atlantic slavery. This industry was in the hands of the WIC, in which top administrators of Amsterdam were in charge in the organization of its logistics and/or invested privately. Recent research commissioned by the City of Amsterdam brought to light that 50 percent of its burgomasters in the seventeenth and eighteenth centuries had an administrative function in the Dutch East India Company that invested in the slave trade in Asia (Brandon et al. 2020). By connecting the data of the slave trade to the data of the Golden Agents project, we might get better insight into the extent that the consumption of cultural goods by these wealthy administrators of Amsterdam was related to this "business." We might even literally put faces to the names of these administrators, as we have included Amsterdam Corporate Group Portraits, brought together by Norbert Middelkoop, in the Golden Agents database. Between 1617 and 1650, 80 percent of the 600 regents, guilds, or arquebusiers active in Amsterdam were portrayed in such portraits (Middelkoop 2019, 717). By connecting these persons to the big data of consumption, and by reconstructing the cultural goods in their households to other data relevant for the history of slavery, we might be able to contribute to the Black Lives Matter movement from a historical perspective.

The same applies to criticisms about the exclusive Western perspective of the Dutch Golden Age or the ignored role of women in this rich history. New research projects open new opportunities to come to a more nuanced historical depiction of the Dutch Golden Age. The project Freedom of the Streets (freedomofthestreets.org) focuses on gender and urban space in Eurasia by comparing the ways women navigated the streets of Amsterdam and of Edo in the period between 1600 and 1850. Another recently started project, The Female Impact (thefemaleimpact.org), investigates the impact of women on the art market of the Dutch Republic in the seventeenth century by analyzing their roles as both professionals and clients.[5] Such research can easily be linked with data of the Golden Agents and Virtual Interiors projects. In an internship with the Golden Agents project as part of her master's research thesis, Marleen Puyenbroek (2019) added data about the so-called *schatsers*, (almost always) women who, on behalf of notaries or the City of Amsterdam, evaluated the value of the (cultural) goods in houses for testaments, auctions, and the like.

[5] The PI, Judith Noorman, published a book titled *Gouden Vrouwen* (2020), written together with 34 undergraduate students in her course.

Considering historic inequities from a historical perspective is an important step forward for Renaissance studies. And it is important in that regard to provide historical evidence. Often debates are based on extrapolations of small datasets in which uncertainties are ignored or at best hidden away in footnotes. Bringing data together from multiple projects and creating big data can be beneficial in answering big questions, not only in research of the Dutch Golden Age but in Renaissance studies in general as well. The challenge is to combine big data without losing the richness of the datasets brought together, reflecting the multiple dimensions and perspectives for which they were created. The infrastructure must therefore provide insight into the provenance of the individual datasets and their enrichments, and it requires user interfaces to interact with the data to assess whether said data can be reused with acceptable uncertainties to answer new research questions to contribute to these societal challenges. Interacting with big historical data might be challenging, but it can at the same be promising and give a new creative role to Renaissance studies. To say it in the words of the intellectual historian Randall Collins (1998, 76), "Creativity is the friction of the attention space at the moments when the structural blocks are grinding against one another the hardest."

WORKS CITED

Baas, Jurian. 2023. "Entity Resolution on Historical Knowledge Graphs." PhD diss., Utrecht University.

Baas, Jurian, Mehdi Dastani, and Ad Feelders. 2019. "Graph Embeddings for Enrichment of Historical Data." Paper presented at the European Conference on Machine Learning and Principles and Practice of Knowledge Discovery in Databases, Wurzburg, Germany, 16–20 September 2019.

Bodenhamer, David J. 2010. "The Potential of Spatial Humanities." In *The Spatial Humanities: GIS and the Future of Humanities Scholarship*, edited by David J. Bodenhamer, John Corrigan, and Trevor M. Harris, 14–30. Bloomington: Indiana University Press.

Brandon, Pepijn, and Ulbe Bosma. 2019. "De betekenis van de Atlantische Slavernij voor de Nederlandse economie in de tweede helft van de achttiende eeuw." *Tijdschrift voor Sociaal Economische Geschiedenis* 16 (2): 5–45. doi.org/10.18352/tseg.1082.

Brandon, Pepijn, Guno Jones, Nancy Jouwe, and Matthias van Rossum. 2020. *De Slavernij in Oost en West: Het Amsterdam Onderzoek*. Amsterdam: Spectrum.

Bredius, Abraham. 1915–21. *Künstler-Inventare: Urkunden zur Geschichte der holländischen Kunst des 16ten, 17ten und 18ten Jahrhunderts*. The Hague: M. Nijhoff.

Collins, Randall. 1998. *The Sociology of Philosophies: A Global Theory of Intellectual Change*. Cambridge, MA: Belknap Press of Harvard University Press.

Denard, Hugh. 2012. "A New Introduction to the London Charter." In *Paradata and Transparency in Virtual Heritage*, edited by Anna Bentkowska-Kafel, Hugh Denard, and Drew Baker, 57–71. Farnham: Ashgate. doi.org/10.4324/9781315599366.

Drucker, Johanna. 2011. "Humanities Approaches to Graphical Display." *Digital Humanities Quarterly* 5 (1). digitalhumanities.org/dhq/vol/5/1/000091/000091.html.

———. 2013. *Graphesis: Visual Forms of Knowledge Production*. Cambridge, MA: Harvard University Press.

Engelse, Menno den, and Leon van Wissen. 2019. *Reconstructions and Observations in Archival Resources: Ontology Specification*. Accessed 8 January 2021. w3id.org/roar.

Helmers, Helmer J., and Geert H. Janssen. 2018. "Introduction: Understanding the Dutch Golden Age." In *The Cambridge Companion to the Dutch Golden Age*, edited by Helmer J. Helmers and Geert H. Janssen, 1–12 Cambridge: Cambridge University Press. doi.org/10.1017/9781316771549.004.

Helmreich, Anne, Matthew Lincoln, and Charles van den Heuvel. 2021. "Data Ecosystems and Futures of Art Histories." *Histoire de l'Art. Humanités Numériques: De Nouveaux Récits en Histoire de l'Art?* 87 (1): 45–54.

Heuvel, Charles van den, and Veruska Zamborlini. 2019. "Storifying Data: Modeling Historical Processes in Knowledge Graphs. Kubler's Shape of Time Revisited." Paper presented at ADHO LOD SIG Pre Conference Workshop: Ontologies for Linked Data in the Humanities DH2019 Conference, Utrecht, Netherlands, 8 July 2019. cwrc.ca/islandora/object/islandora%3A82042a5e-35bd-4986-8465-429dea5ae64e.

———. 2021. "Modeling and Visualizing Storylines of Historical Interactions: Kubler's Shape of Time and Rembrandt's *Night Watch*." In *Linking Knowledge: Linked Open Data for Knowledge Organization and Visualization*, edited by Richard P. Smiraglia and Andrea Scharnhorst, 99–141. Würzburg: Ergon Verlag. doi.org/10.5771/9783956506611-99.

Huurdeman, Hugo, and Chiara Piccoli. 2020. "'More than just a Picture': The Importance of Context in Search User Interfaces for Three-Dimensional Content." In *CHIIR '20: Proceedings of the 2020 Conference on Human Information Interaction and Retrieval*, 338–42. New York: Association for Computing Machinery. doi.org/10.1145/3343413.3377994.

———. 2021. "3D Reconstructions as Research Hubs: Geospatial Interfaces for Real-Time Data Exploration of Seventeenth-Century Amsterdam Domestic Interiors." *Open Archaeology* 7 (1): 314–36. doi.org/10.1515/opar-2020-0142.

Huurdeman, Hugo, Chiara Piccoli, and Leon van Wissen. 2021. "Linked Data in a 3D Context: Experiential Interfaces for Exploring the Interconnections of 17th-Century Historical Data." Paper presented at DH Benelux Conference 2021: The Humanities in a Digital World, Leiden, Netherlands, 2–4 June 2021. doi.org/10.5281/zenodo.4889856.

Idrissou, Al, Veruska Zamborlini, Chiara Latronico, Frank van Harmelen, and Charles van den Heuvel. 2018. "Amsterdamers from the Golden Age to the Information Age via Lenticular Lenses." Paper presented at DH Benelux Conference 2018, International Institute for Social History, Amsterdam, 6–8 June 2018.

Idrissou, Al, Veruska Zamborlini, Frank van Harmelen, and Chiara Latronico. 2019. "Contextual Entity Disambiguation in Domains with Weak Identity Criteria: Disambiguating Golden Age Amsterdamers." In *K-CAP '19: Proceedings of the 10th International Conference on Knowledge Capture September 2019*, 259–62. doi.org/10.1145/3360901.3364440.

Jager, Angela. 2020. *The Mass Market for History Paintings in Seventeenth-Century Amsterdam: Production, Distribution, and Consumption.* Amsterdam: Amsterdam University Press. doi.org/10.1515/9789048553983.

Jouwe, Nancy, Matthijs Kuipers, and Remco Raben. 2021. *Slavernij en de stad Utrecht*. Zutphen: Walburg Pers.

Koolen, Marijn, Jasmijn van Gorp, and Jacco van Ossenbruggen. 2018. "Toward a Model for Digital Tool Criticism: Reflection as Integrative Practice." *Digital Scholarship in the Humanities* 34, no. 2 (October): 368–85. doi.org/10.1093/llc/fqy048.

Li, Weixuan. 2023. "Painters' Playbooks: Deep Mapping Socio-spatial Strategies in the Art Market of Seventeenth-century Amsterdam." PhD diss., University of Amsterdam.

———. 2018. "Beyond Location: Deep Mapping Artist's Workshops in Early Modern Amsterdam." Paper presented at Spatial Humanities 2018 Conference, Lancaster University, 20–21 September 2018.

———. 2019a. "Innovative Exuberance: Visualizing the Fluctuations in Painting Production in the 17th-Century Northern Netherlands." *Arts* 8 (2): 72. hdl.handle.net/11245.1/0415bb7d-96f9-475b-b835-8ba392632bcc.

———. 2019b. "Mapping Uncertainty in Golden Age Amsterdam." Paper presented at *28th International Conference on the History of Cartography*, Amsterdam, 14–19 July 2019.

Li, Weixuan, Chiara Piccoli, and Charles van den Heuvel. 2019. "Embracing Complex Interfaces: Linking Deep Maps and Virtual Interiors to Big Data of the Dutch Golden Age." Paper presented at DH Conference 2019, Utrecht, Netherlands, 9–12 July 2019.

Mak, Geert. 2016. *De levens van Jan Six: Een familiegeschiedenis*. Amsterdam: Uitgeverij Atlas Contact.

Middelkoop, Norbert E. 2019. "Schutters, gildebroeders, regenten en regentessen: Het Amsterdamse corporatiestuk 1525–1850." PhD diss., University of Amsterdam.

Noorman, Judith. 2020. *Gouden Vrouwen van de 17de eeuw: Van kunstenaars tot verzamelaars*. Zwolle: wBooks.

Piccoli, Chiara. 2024. *Pieter de Graeff (1638–1707) and his treffelyke bibliotheek: Exploring and Reconstructing an Early Modern Private Library as a Book Collection and as a Physical Space*. (The Library of the Written Word). Leiden: Brill.

Presner, Todd, David Shepard, and Yoh Kawano. 2014. *HyperCities: Thick Mapping in the Digital Humanities*. Cambridge, MA: Harvard University Press.

Puyenbroek, Marleen. 2019. "Gezworen Schatsers: Taxeersters van huisraad en kunst in vroegmodern Amsterdam." MA thesis, University of Amsterdam.

Rasterhoff, Claartje. 2017. *Painting and Publishing as Creative Industries: The Fabric of Creativity in the Dutch Republic, 1580–1800*. Amsterdam: Amsterdam University Press.

Reynaert, Martin. 2020. "Nederlab Word Embeddings and Their Context." Poster presented at CLIN Conference 2020, Utrecht, Netherlands, 30 January 2020. ticclops.uvt.nl/CLIN2020.SemVecNederlab.MRE.pdf.

Reynaert, Martin, Patrick Bos, and Janneke van der Zwaan. 2019. "Granularity versus Dispersion in the Dutch Diachronical Database of Lexical Frequencies (TICCLAT)." In *CLARIN Annual Conference Proceedings*, edited by Kiril Simov and Maria Eskevich, 169–72. Leipzig: CLARIN. office.clarin.eu/v/CE-2019-1512_CLARIN2019_ConferenceProceedings.pdf.

Reynaert, Martin, Janneke van der Zwaan, and Patrick Bos. 2019. "TICCLAT: A Dutch Diachronical Database of Linked Word-Variants." Paper presented at DH Benelux Conference 2019, Liège, Belgium, 11–13 September 2019.

Shimizu, Cogan, Quinn Hirt, and Pascal Hitzler. 2019. "MODL: A Modular Ontology Design Library." In *Proceedings of the 10th Workshop on Ontology Design and Patterns, Auckland, New Zealand, October 27, 2019*. CEUR-WP. doi.org/10.48550/arXiv.1904.05405.

Stipriaan, Alex van. 2020. *Rotterdam in slavernij*. Amsterdam: Boom.

Wissen, Leon van, Chiara Latronico, Sandra van Ginhoven, and Veruska Zamborlini. 2020. "The Montias Case: An Experiment with Data Reconciliation and Provenance between Research and Cultural Institutions." Paper presented at DH2020 Conference, Ottawa, 20–24 July 2020. lvanwissen.github.io/ga-dh2020-demo.

Wissen, Leon van, Chiara Latronico, Veruska Zamborlini, Jirsi Reinders, and Charles van den Heuvel. 2020. "Unlocking the Archives: A Pipeline for Scanning, Indexing, Transcribing, and Modelling Entities of Archival

Documents into Linked Open Data." Paper presented at DH Benelux Conference 2020 #GoesOnline, 3–5 June 2020. doi.org/10.5281/zenodo.3862817.

Wissen, Leon van, and Veruska Zamborlini. 2020. "Reconstructions and Observations in Archival Sources – LODLAM 2020 Challenge Entry." YouTube video, 17:12. 20 January 2020. youtube.com/watch?v=JMO35VmUadk.

Zamborlini, Veruska, Arianna Betti, and Charles van den Heuvel. 2017. "Toward a Core Conceptual Model for (Im)material Cultural Heritage in the Golden Agents Project: Storifying Data." Paper presented at Semantics 2017 Workshop, Amsterdam, 11–14 September 2017. ceur-ws.org/Vol-2063/events-paper1.pdf.

Chapter 13:
Northeye (Re)Constructed: Augmented Reality of an Abandoned Medieval Village[1]

Steven Bednarski
St. Jerome's University

T. C. Nicholas Graham
Queen's University

Robin Harrap
Queen's University

Zack MacDonald
Western Libraries

Andrew Moore
University of Saskatchewan

Sweet Auburn, loveliest village of the plain,
Where health and plenty cheared the labouring swain,
Where smiling spring its earliest visit paid,
And parting summer's lingering blooms delayed
—Oliver Goldsmith, *The Deserted Village* (1770)

Introduction

With these words, an eighteenth-century Irishman mused upon the tragedy of settlements depopulated. For Oliver Goldsmith (1728–74), the veiled critique in his *Deserted Village* was against migration to America, the moral corruption of urbanity, and the flagrant pursuit of wealth. In the closing lines of the poem, Goldsmith remarks pointedly that the culprit is "trade's proud empire," which "hastes to swift decay." But causes of desertion vary over time and space. While, in the late Middle Ages, economics certainly played its part, the impetus was just as much environmental. After all, in the preindustrial world, there was a clear connection between agricultural production and wealth. Changing natural conditions, therefore, including access to food and potable water, the spread of pandemic disease, inundation, or soil deple-

[1] The authors gratefully acknowledge the generous support of the Social Sciences and Humanities Research Council of Canada (SSHRC) for this project. We are equally indebted to several talented research assistants—Kyle Laporte, Connor Ibach, Codie McConkey, and Joseph Gravenor—and to Leah Fusco, our project collaborator and local Northeye expert. Any errors herein are our fault, not theirs.

ISBN 978-1-64959-119-7 (paper) ISBN 978-1-64959-120-3 (pdf) ISBN 978-1-64959-121-0 (epub)
New Technologies in Medieval and Renaissance Studies 12 (2025) 341–80

tion, all account for many of the UK's deserted medieval villages (DMVs), of which over 3,000 have been identified in England alone.

In Sussex, the locus of our team's investigations, the abandoned settlement of Northeye offers a potentially telling case study on the relationship between human wetland and coastal settlements, everyday life, politics, and economics at a time of rapidly changing natural conditions.[2] Northeye has received little scholarly attention and, indeed, has left virtually nothing in the way of evidence. The village, whose occupants worked the nearby land and sea, sat perched on a tidal island in the Pevensey Levels, surrounded by a lagoon that had been partially drained by the late Middle Ages. Northeye had existed since at least the early thirteenth century but was likely abandoned sometime around 1400. Today, blanketed by thick green sod in a farmer's field, lie the remains of the Chapel of St. James, nearby depressions likely left from clustered homes and garden plots, a sunken trackway, and fragments of collapsed flint walls. Still, for modern visitors, it is difficult to visualize the busy little settlement that once stood on the site. This is unfortunate since, without a clear capacity to understand the physical space occupied by Northeye in relation to its surrounding landscape, it is all but impossible for modern observers to understand the complexities of life in a medieval coastal marshland. It is all the more difficult, absent complex modeling, to apprehend the impact of changing climate conditions at the onset of the Little Ice Age, notably increased annual precipitation, more frequent and powerful North Atlantic storms, and shifting sea levels over the period of Northeye's occupancy.[3] Without a plausible reconstruction, therefore, few students (but also tourists and scholars) can fully grasp how land, sea, politics, and economics intersected in and shaped this tiny village.

To reconstruct the village as authentically as possible, we draw upon very limited archival records, haphazard archaeological investigations, artistic

[2] This project is part of a longer eight-year research partnership (2019–27), Environments of Change (medieval-environment.com). Our project connects some 30 researchers from across a dozen disciplines in the sciences, environmental sciences, social sciences, and humanities. Our aim is to develop technologies that instruct on the historical relationship between humans and the natural world in late medieval and early modern Sussex.

[3] Broadly, Northeye appears to have been settled at the end of what climatologists deem the Medieval Climate Optimum, a period of generally warmer and dryer conditions, and the onset of what is somewhat misleadingly labelled the Little Ice Age, a protracted period of generally cooler and wetter conditions in Northern Europe. For the best surveys on the topic, see Brázdil 2002, 2003.

works, and, importantly, detailed cartographic and geospatial evidence, including high-resolution Light Detection and Ranging (LiDAR) imagery, a remote sensing method that uses a pulsed laser to measure distances. Emerging trends in computer graphics, video gaming, and augmented reality (AR) allow us to synthesize and graft evidence onto informed imagination. The net result is a proof-of-concept game that allows users to experience a dynamic augmented reality simulation of *Virtual Northeye*, one that draws upon cutting edge procedural generation processes (outlined below) and mobile AR game development practices.

Through *Virtual Northeye*, we present users (students, teachers, scholars, and tourists) with a more immediate, more instructive appreciation of a lost past, one with significant pedagogical possibilities. The Northeye AR experience allows users to explore a recreated settlement from different perspectives: different scales, close-up or bird's eye, exterior or interior. It even allows for the integration of digitized textual, artistic, and physical artefacts. The net result is that users may conduct self-directed exploration through AR. This experience will provide a richer, more immersive and engaging experience than traditional static and two-dimensional models. Our intention is to generate a plausible facsimile of this forgotten settlement to assist the user's visualization of the settlement's coastal dynamic at a time of storms and plague. In so doing, we provide an immersive—and, we hope, memorable—model to help students and other observers appreciate the fragile symbiotic relationship between human settlement and nature. It is worth noting that this interactive visualization also offers the possibility of linking to additional pedagogical meta-content such as voice-overs, text pop-ups, and videos.

Virtual Northeye is intended for deployment in elementary schools to help teach topics as diverse as medieval history, geography, and civics. Students will benefit from the interactive and cooperative nature of gameplay, which will allow them to experience the village of Northeye as a living and changing place. Students will see crops growing in the fields and villagers going about their everyday business. They will be able to experience the dangers of medieval life, such as loss of crops and homes due to flooding, and participate in problem-solving around how to mitigate such dangers. The use of AR increases the immersion and sense of immediacy of the game, allowing students to move around physically and manipulate the scene.

In this chapter, we document our process of creating a tablet-based AR experience of the reconstructed medieval village of Northeye. We begin by presenting the extant historical evidence, then survey the piecemeal archeology, then turn to cartographic and geospatial evidence, and finally summarize the ways in which procedural generation techniques imported from geologically informed computer science can enhance the experience of Northeye (re)constructed.

Summary of Virtual Northeye *Game*

Virtual Northeye is a tablet-based (i.e., iPad) cooperative pedagogical video game created from actual historical scenarios. These scenarios come from scholarly investigations into late medieval Sussex, England. The game will be free to download via the Apple Store, and accompanying teacher resources will be made available at no cost on an accompanying website.

Virtual Northeye targets pre-adolescent and adolescent learners in a formal classroom setting. We designed the interface, specifically, to be of interest and manageable for learners ranging from about 10 to 15 years of age. While the game itself will remain fairly static regardless of the age of its users, we are producing analogue companion materials to support classroom teachers, and these may be scaled up or down in complexity, depending on the age of the players. So, for example, a Canadian classroom of grade 4 students may play the game while their teacher explores accompanying resources with them that focus on medieval village life or farming. The same game, however, can be contextualized for more sophisticated learners when their classroom teacher engages accompanying resources that lay out historical precipitation and storm patterns, which consider how historians gather proxy data and rely on palaeoclimatological modeling, or how knowledge of engineering supported late medieval large-scale drainage. In this respect, the game itself is "scalable" to the learner.

The interface supports a compelling and historically accurate AR experience. It allows players to navigate a recreated medieval village, but one crafted using extant physical and archival evidence. The player may zoom the perspective in or out, depending on the scenario, to encounter virtual villagers and interact with them up close, or, at times, to adopt more of a "god's eye" view of their world.

The game fosters problem-solving and historical and environmental awareness. At various points in the game, the player will be faced with certain challenges related to the natural world. For example, a virtual villager non-player character (NPC) might alert the player to the problems Northeye has been encountering lately due to flooding. The player must then deploy a group of villagers to attempt various flood mitigation strategies, such as sending them out to the countryside to dig irrigation canals, to unclog open sewers, to build and deploy dams and sluices at different points in a waterway, and so on.

Finally, the game fosters collaboration and movement. Just as no one person or group can solve major environmental challenges, no player can resolve the challenges independently. The game thus embeds various mechanisms that require learners to cooperate to solve complex tasks. The game also encourages players to move about physically while they play, holding their tablets at times as "windows" through which they can "see" Northeye and its environs. A single player will find that their view alters significantly when they hold their tablet up to the tablet of a peer.

Like all satisfying games, Northeye has an element of risk to it, a sense of urgency. Players must race against a clock or risk losing villagers, livestock, farmland, or, worse, their very homes! As a pedagogical tool, though, the game encourages experimentation through trial and error. Players are given the opportunity to see how, for example, the different placement of a sluice will alter a watercourse. In time, players can master the environmental lessons of *Virtual Northeye*, but never perfectly, since the simulated natural elements will always present a certain randomness, so successive gameplay may yield different results. Ultimately, the historical village of Northeye was doomed to become deserted. Its residents abandoned the site because it was no longer viable to their needs. But in *Virtual Northeye*, players can learn how successful mitigation strategies can delay that outcome—at least for a time.

Virtual Northeye builds on an increasing literature of the use of classroom-based educational games. Researchers have found that such games produce positive motivational effects and problem-solving skills (Yang 2012), and improve accessibility of education, for example for children learning outside their native tongue (Kim and Chang 2010). The efficacy of educational games is contingent upon how they are designed and deployed within the classroom; thus, a survey of 12 educational games in mathematics found that seven improved educational outcomes while five did not (Backlund and Hendrix 2013). AR-based games have the particular advantage of affording interactive exploration, face-to-face interaction, and accessibility to persons with little computing background (Billinghurst 2002). They have been found to help with increased content understanding, long-term memory retention, motivation, and collaboration (Radu 2012). AR experiences have been used to teach topics as diverse as exploration of World War I tunnels at Vauquois (Duer et al. 2020), climate change strategies (Fernández Galeote and Hamari 2021), and techniques for identifying fake news (Paraschivoiu et al. 2021).

Through *Virtual Northeye*, we build on the interactivity, collaboration, and support for problem-solving inherent in AR to produce an experience that facilitates exploration, experimentation, and immersion.

Historical Context

Like all European regions inhabited in the Middle Ages (c. 500–1500 CE), the English countryside conceals a number of deserted, ruined, or "lost" medieval settlements. In East Sussex, a southeastern coastal county, this includes the abandoned settlement of Northeye, a small village whose existence is known today through written data and incomplete archaeological excavations. These sources point to a small community that flourished in the thirteenth century, declined in the fourteenth, and was likely abandoned by around the start of the fifteenth (Burleigh 1973, 72).[4] The most enduring evidence of the community comes from a stone chapel with extant subsurface foundations, and from visible earthworks and a sunken roadway most evident through aerial surveillance. The site has long been the subject of scholarly interest in DMVs (Beresford and Hurst 1971, 301; Burleigh 1973; Turner 1867)—mostly by curious locals keen on preserving patrimony, or by national scholars intent on cataloging all such locations—but it has yet to be reconstructed archaeologically. Successive centuries of ploughing by local farmers have disturbed much of the site's surface, making it difficult to conceptualize.[5] For these reasons, there is historical and pedagogical value in recreating a virtual Northeye founded on extant evidence.

The Northeye site (50.839°N 0.388°E) sits at a higher elevation than most of the surrounding land in the Pevensey Levels, a low-lying natural marshland formed by a tidal lagoon.[6] Much of the Levels is situated approximately at sea level. In premodern eras, this meant the region was subject to constant inundation both from coastal flooding and from runoff and rainfall, especially in times of increased precipitation. During the medieval period, human inter-

[4] Northeye is mentioned in sporadic documents from the sixteenth and seventeenth centuries, but these likely refer to the manor rather than the village itself. The chapel may have been used into the sixteenth century, and its ruins were visible until the mid-nineteenth century (Turner 1867).

[5] Since 1973, when G. R. Burleigh completed his survey, roughly 30 per cent of the overall site has been compromised by commercial turf-growing and stripping. The chapel site, roadway, and embankments remain intact beneath pasturage (Historic England Research Records n.d.).

[6] Northeye sits, more specifically, within the Hooe Level, which forms part of the larger Pevensey Levels.

ventions began to transform the marshlands, redirecting and draining accumulated waters out to sea and repelling seawater. Through a complex series of drains, ditches, dikes, sewers, sluices, and sea walls, medieval inhabitants reclaimed the mineral-rich alluvial soils and grazing lands on most of the Levels. In a few cases, though, natural elevations provided protection when the Levels did flood. Toponymic evidence today marks such locations within the Levels. The Anglo-Saxon suffix *-ey* thus points to the higher elevations, or "islands," of Bowley, Whelpley, Horse Eye, Manxey, Rickney, Glyndley, Chilley, Pevensey, Southeye, and Northeye. Each of these locations, hills in an otherwise flat agricultural landscape today, were, in fact, tidal islands at the onset of the Middle Ages. This means that the topographical and ecological contexts of medieval Northeye were visibly different than what is apparent today, a factor that must be considered in any reconstruction.

Politically, thirteenth-century Northeye was noteworthy as a dependent of the important coastal town of Hastings, the leading member of the so-called Cinque Ports. This confederation of prominent coastal towns in Sussex, Kent, and Essex protected England from potential maritime invasion via the Channel and promoted domestic and continental trade.[7] From at least 1229, when it is mentioned as a dependent limb, Northeye fulfilled a supportive role for Hastings. The village's inclusion as a subsidiary of the Cinque Ports signals that shipping in and out of the village was not unimportant. Inland water transport flourished in nearby parts of the Levels, including shipping of resources to outlying communities and a ferry from Pevensey to Bexhill (Gardiner 2014). Northeye's location, as well as the probable existence of medieval docks, suggests that it participated in similar commercial ventures (Historic England n.d.). Northeye thus maintained an active maritime pres-

---

[7] The original Cinque Ports comprised Hastings, New Romney, Hythe, Dover, and Sandwich. By the early thirteenth century, environmental changes led to the inclusion of two previously dependent "ancient towns," Rye and Winchelsea. Over time, the crown added other smaller dependent ports, like Northeye, as "limbs." In general, throughout the Middle Ages, the crown required the Cinque Ports to provide 57 ships, annually and collectively, for 15 days of naval service. In return for providing an early version of a royal navy, the Crown conferred certain tax exemptions; judicial, regulatory, prosecutorial, and penal powers; and maritime salvage rights. King Edward I confirmed the traditional rights of the Cinque Ports into statute through article 9 of his 1297 repetition of the Magna Carta. For a modern translation, see Vincent 2007. For more on the Cinque Ports, see McBain 2013. For more on the founding charters, see Jeake 1728.

ence, at least on some scale, and acted as a support for England's coastal defense efforts via Hastings.

Due to its location near the confluence of natural waterways in the Levels, Northeye found itself at the forefront of medieval drainage efforts in the region. The Sussex coast was at constant risk of saline inundation and, due to increased frequency and severity of Channel storms, freshwater flooding. Local landowners (and the English Crown) worked tirelessly to expel unwanted water from fields.[8] These efforts included collaboration with powerful institutions in the surrounding area. For example, Battle Abbey invested heavily in its satellite settlement at Barnhorne, and in doing so, cultivated a long-term relationship with Northeye (Brandon 1971, 78–79; Dulley 1966, 31; Turner 1867, 14; Whittick 2017, 256).[9] In 1322, moreover, Thomas of Hastings granted to John of Cooden all his lands at Bexhill, along with the waters, walls, ditches, and drains, and 25 acres elsewhere in the saltmarsh, except for the hedges and right-of-way to the marsh, on the condition that John and his heir maintain the infrastructure in the same or better condition (and also pay rent at Thomas's manor of Northeye) (Papers of John Ernest Ray of Hastings 1873–1951). This small settlement of Northeye, which had been so involved in the use of natural waterways, thus grew to become instrumental in the elaboration of thirteenth- and fourteenth-century aquatic infrastructure.

Archaeological Context

There have been several notable investigations of the Northeye site, in 1867, 1939, 1952, and 2009. The report from 1867 was based on field walking during a dry summer with the local farmer, when some ruins had become visible due to the arid conditions. The excavation of 1939 was well documented and has provided photographic evidence as well as physical objects. A subsequent excavation in 1952 supposedly uncovered foundations of a medieval struc-

[8] For a detailed case study, see Moore and Bednarski 2022.

[9] In 1248, the abbot of Battle Abbey granted part of the marsh there to William de Northeye, in exchange for the right to drain the remainder of the land through William's land, which blocked the way to the sea. The abbot agreed to cover two-thirds of the expense if William paid for the remaining third. This partnership lasted until at least 1304, when William of Hastings, then lord of Northeye, allowed the abbot of Battle to drain water from Barnhorne through his lands. In fact, 10 extant Battle Abbey charters between c. 1210 and 1310 describe the drainage of newly reclaimed lands on the Pevensey Levels, either through a 16-feet-wide waterlode near Hooe or a creek called Meneflete leading to Northeye and Cooden.

ture, but no official report was ever published.[10] A recent 2009 study, detailed below, provides mostly a geological analysis.

The first scholarly discussion of Northeye appears in an 1867 journal article by Edward Turner.[11] Turner's primary interest, though, was in determining whether the ruined village was, in fact, the Northeye mentioned in medieval records. He surveyed medieval documents and compared them to observations made while walking the fields in and around Northeye. Far more noteworthy for archeology was the amateur excavation of 1939, which focused on the ruined Chapel of St. James of Northeye. Though in 1939, as today, the foundations of the chapel were subsurface, its location was known locally. Visible remains had stood as recently as the seventeenth century, and the chapel's location was marked on a number of well-known historical maps, including John Speed's 1610 map of Sussex (Fig. 1). So, it was perhaps only natural that the industrious school children from the nearby Normandale School, and their teacher, L. Beasley, were curious about the chapel in 1939, though the brief amateur report their school produced is of limited scientific value.

An extant deed of endowment reveals that the chapel dates to 1262 and notes the following:

> Know all men by these presents that I, William de Northeye, Knight, have given and granted, and by this my present deed confirmed, for the salvation of my own soul, and of the souls of my predecessors and successors, to God and the Chapel of St. James of Northeye, in pure and perpetual alms, for the support of a chaplain continually to reside, and to perform divine service in the said Chapel, 20 acres of marsh land in the parish of Hooe, in the place which is called Tunge, and which is situated between the Hooe ditch to the north and the land of the Abbot of Battle to the south, and heads up to the lands of Richard le Gardener to the east, and my own demesne to the west. (quoted in Turner 1867, 23)

---

[10] Aside from some local extant photographic evidence, there does not appear to be any formal catalog, report, or inventory from this excavation.

[11] The author makes a confused case conflating records and evidence. Nonetheless, this article still preserves important evidence of now lost archaeological evidence, including carved stone ornamentation from the chapel.

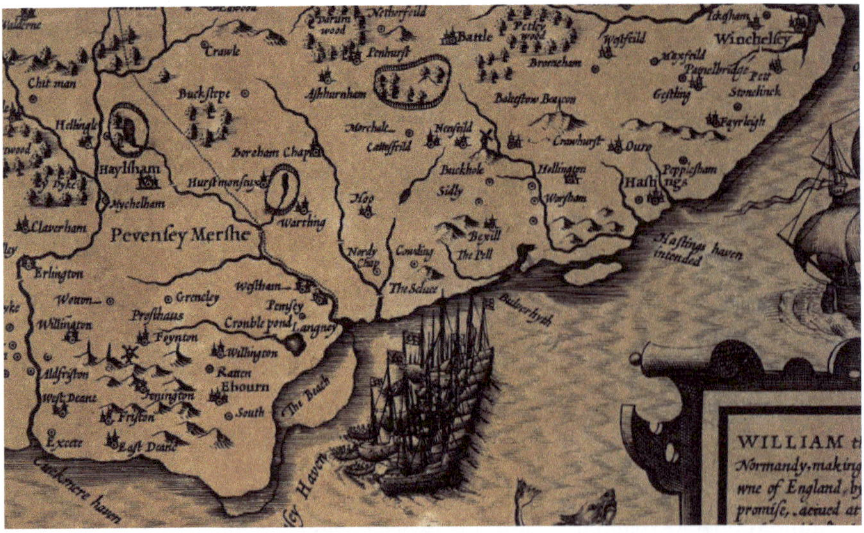

Figure 1. Detail of Speed's map of Sussex (1610) showing "Nordy Chap."

The Normandale excavation unearthed flint walling from the chapel, typical of the region and period, the remains of ashlar dressings (an ancient, finely cut masonry whose precise cuts allow for tightly aligned units), and "carved stones and pillars . . . ecclesiastical in appearance" along with the foundations of walls and "carved mullions of windows, parts of the iron framework, carved pillars of a vertical column, a Roman horseshoe, various kinds of bones, pottery, oyster shells, and two kinds of roofing tiles, slate and red brick" (Normandale Preparatory School 1939, 13). The existence of two different types of tiles led Beasley to conclude that there must have been an earlier Roman building on the same site. In an early experiment with aerial photography to support archeology, the Normandale School hired an airplane with a photographer to document the excavation site.

The archaeological and archival record allows us to posit plausible 3D models of missing Northeye structures. The methodology we deployed to create the 3D model of the Chapel of St. James, and others, draws on techniques developed by virtual archaeologists and historic building information modelers.[12] We constructed a digital rendering of the Chapel of St. James using

[12] For a comprehensive introduction to the methods and implementation of virtual archeology, see Ioannides, Magnenat-Thalmann, and Papagiannakis 2017. For an overview of methods in and applications of historic building information modeling (HBIM), see Bastem and Cekmis 2021.

SketchUp Pro (Fig. 2). To do this, we manually derived a 2D floor plan from the archaeological plan preserved in the 1952 excavation plan sketch. Next, we consulted historical paintings of the ruins of the chapel preserved at the Bexhill Museum and details from contemporaneous ecclesiastical architecture. These sources allowed us to recreate a viable facsimile of the chapel's vertical structure and architectural features. We derived, moreover, the dimensions of the vertical features from pixel calculations, wherein the known physical length and width of the floor plan helped us to calculate the relative pixel length and width of the scanned historical documentation. We then applied that value to the pixel height of the image to estimate the chapel's physical height. Within each 3D model, we tracked the decision-making processes, source materials, uncertainty values, and metadata linked to individual structural components.[13] To illustrate, this uncertainty value tracking is evident in Figure 2 through the color-coded visualization of the secular structure adjacent to the chapel. Recreating the village's lost structures in 3D is an important first step on the path to visualizing Northeye in preparation for our AR experiment.

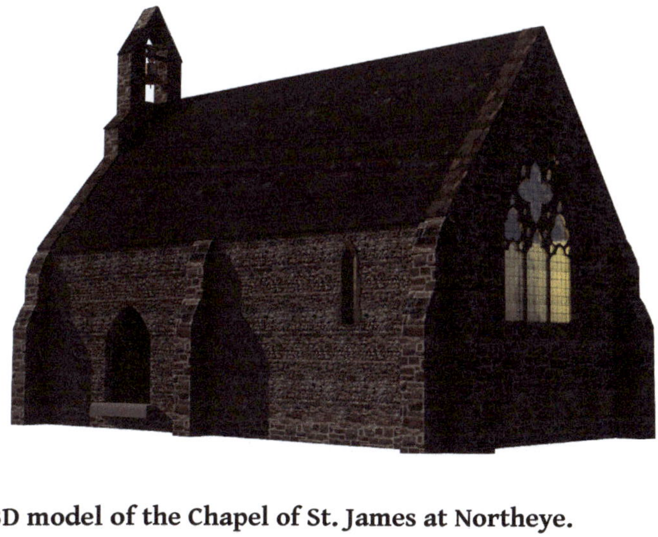

Figure 2. 3D model of the Chapel of St. James at Northeye.

Though the 1952 excavation team published no findings, the survey commissioned in 2009 by Natural England on behalf of the local landowners resulted in a report, produced by Oxford Archaeology (OA), which underscores the site's significance. OA surveyed the 8.3-hectare Northeye site, which is today

[13] This process is modeled after the data capture method outlined in Apollonio 2016.

a scheduled monument (S.M. MES93)—that is, a historical site of particular national importance—and dug a series of boreholes and auger holes to confirm the composition of the site's sediment. In addition to remarking upon soil composition, the report produced by OA notes the following:

> The natural shallow embayments of the island were likely a significant factor in the growth of salt working in this area. The abandonment of the village was most likely partly due to a decline in the salt works. . . . Significant early salt working sites and other medieval features such as jetties may be found around the edges of the Northeye Island. Such discoveries could help inform about the activities associated with the medieval village. Within the area immediately surrounding the bedrock island these deposits are less than 1 metre from the surface and would therefore be vulnerable to direct impacts [from farming, etc.]. (OA 2009, ii–iii)[14]

In fact, this part of Sussex was well-known in the Middle Ages for salt making. Visible evidence of numerous saltworks remains, especially surrounding the elevated bedrock islands of the region (OA 2009, 2). Domesday Book, the extensive survey of England undertaken following the Norman Conquest of 1066, notes sites of salt production throughout Sussex and around the Pevensey Levels.[15] At these saltworks, workers evaporated seawater to form consumable crystals. Over time, earthen mounds formed as the workers discarded the residue left over from the boiling process. These mounds, located near existing waterways, generally predate embankments constructed to block the sea. Today, the remains of the premodern Sussex salt industry are still visible in the Pevensey Levels and can be quite large.[16] Modern British Ordnance Surveys, furthermore, note the locations of medieval saltworks close to Northeye (see, for example, Historic England n.d.).

---

[14] In fact, LiDAR and cartographic analysis confirm that the most likely location of the saltworks was to the north of the village along Waterlot Stream, a few hundred meters away from the settlement. For the cartography, see Yeakell and Gardner 1783; Ordnance Survey 1895, 1899.

[15] See, for example, the entry for another nearby settlement, Hooe, which had a population of 73 households in 1086. Included in its holdings are the lands belonging to Count Robert of Mortain, who operated four salthouses there (as well as others in nearby settlements such as Willingdon) (Open Domesday n.d.).

[16] They are generally around 1–1.5 meters high and around 50 meters in diameter (Rippon 2000, 187).

By the time of the 2009 survey by OA, little physical evidence remained at Northeye, save some structural remnants. Today, the skeleton of the village is still visible to the naked eye through topography and landscape features. For example, the Northeye site remains connected to the nearby deserted medieval village and manor of Barnhorne via a sunken lane. That laneway, running east–west, is marked on the tithe map as a "droveway" (OA 2009, 2). On either side of the road, undulations in the ground indicate the likely presence of several medieval houses. Linear earthworks, clearly visible, also run north–south across the village site (Historic England n.d.).

In addition to the historical records and this limited archaeological evidence, the local Bexhill Museum preserved a few physical objects from premodern Northeye (see Fig. 3). These include fragments of stained glass, a piece of polished Sussex marble, a cairn stone, and various objects of everyday life going back to the Mesolithic. This is the sum total of the historical and archaeological evidence that has survived from the deserted village of Northeye. Though the site is today accessible to the public, it is virtually impossible to interpret in the absence of a reliable reconstruction. The site does have a long history of cartographic representation, however, which can inform any potential reconstruction.

Figure 3. Medieval sheet bronze cauldron from Northeye, Bexhill Museum.

Cartographic and Geospatial Evidence

As noted, Northeye appears on historical maps as far back as the seventeenth century, though such hand-drawn maps do not provide details as to the village's layout, prominent features, or even, frankly, its precise location.[17] By the time of the first series of Ordnance Survey (OS) maps in the late nineteenth century, maps of coastal Sussex increasingly provided annotations of the area's historical landscape.[18] Modern remote sensing data and aerial photographs can augment this nineteenth-century evidence. To map Northeye, therefore, we consulted Yeakell and Gardner's 1783 Survey of Sussex; first, second, and third series OS maps; local thematic maps; and remote sensing data. We deployed extant cartographic and geospatial data in concert with artistic and archival evidence to synthesize Northeye's historic landscape using Esri's ArcGIS Online (arcgis.com), an online geographic information system (GIS) used to create maps by compiling geographic data.

We began with hand-drawn representations prepared by our project collaborator, Leah Fusco, a visual artist and expert on the Northeye site. These representations were based on her interpretation of the site as informed by direct experience and evidence preserved in the Bexhill Museum.[19] We corroborated

---

[17] Several prominent eighteenth-century European cartographers included Northeye on county maps of Sussex. John Speed's map of Sussex from 1610 included "Nordy Chap," indicating that the remnants of the Chapel of St. James was known at the time (see envf.port.ac.uk/geo/research/historical/webmap/sussexmap/speedhastingsl-rg.html). Dutch cartographer Joan Blaeu also included "Nordy Chap" on his map of Sussex (*Svthsexia; vernacule Svssex*) in 1646, and German geographers and engravers Gerard Valk and Peter Schenk did the same on their map of Sussex (*Suthsexia vernacule Sussex*) in 1670 and 1690. In 1695, Robert Morden replicated much of Speed's work, including "Nordy Chap," on his own county map (see envf.port.ac.uk/geo/research/historical/webmap/sussexmap/morden106smallframeset.html). While these references confirm continued knowledge of the lost village of Northeye, or at least of the ruined chapel, they do not provide sufficient detail of the built or natural environments around the village necessary to complete a reconstruction. Data from later maps can help to fill in some of these details.

[18] See, for example, Christopher Macdonald Hewitt's (2018) analysis of the Battle Abbey site.

[19] The hand-drawn maps created by Leah Fusco, and a significant amount of digitized material she shared with us, were invaluable. We are also thankful to Julian Porter, curator of the Bexhill Museum, for his suggestions and feedback, and for making the museum's repositories available remotely to Canadian scholars working during a pandemic.

and expanded upon her initial sketches by identifying historic features, land use, roads, waterways, and drainage noted on eighteenth-century survey maps, first and third series OS maps, and local thematic maps. Next, we identified other features in the village and environs via remote sensing data available from 1-meter resolution LiDAR and early aerial photographs (UK Environment Agency 2019).[20] Finally, we digitized these features and compared them to images and anecdotal descriptions preserved in the archaeological dig reports to create a 2D reconstruction of Northeye. This cartographic compilation provided the basis for our augmented reality work (Figs. 5a–b).

Figure 4. Line-drawn OS six-inch map (1899) overlaid with 50 percent transparency of Esri World Imagery to show green fields. Map includes East Stream, Waterlot, and drainage ditches around the village of

[20] There is more still we can do with LiDAR. As our project progresses, we will explore, for example, the potential of image processing to refine the locations of edges around terrain or archaeological features, effectively enhancing detail and sharpening the image.

Northeye, including the "New Cut" of Waller's Haven at the bottom. Image credit: Reproduced with the permission of the National Library of Scotland.

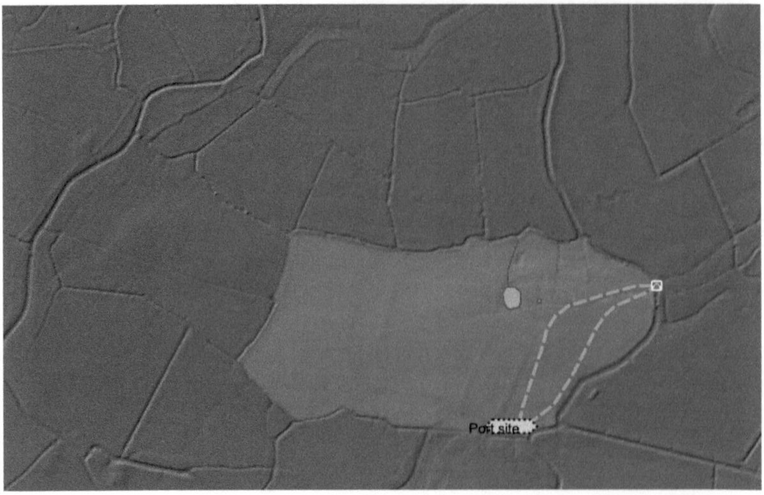

Figure 5a. Showing Northeye in the green area: 1-m LiDAR with sunken trackways in gray dashed lines leading from "stone bridge" to the presumed port site.

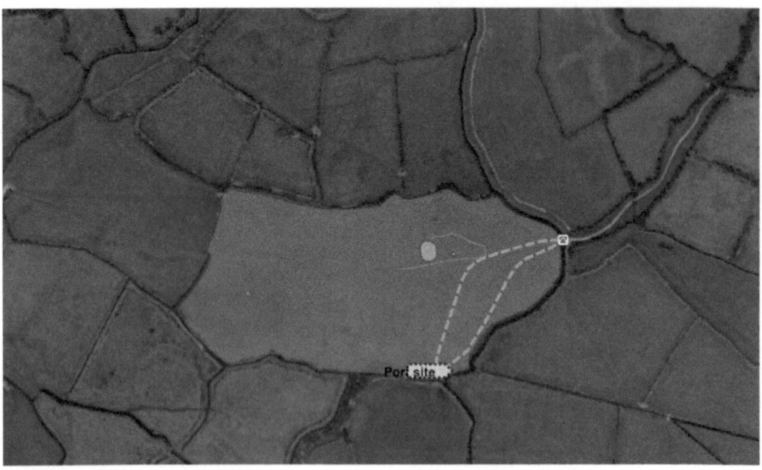

Figure 5b. Showing Northeye in the green area: sunken trackways in gray dashed lines leading from the "stone bridge" to the port, Esri satellite imagery.

Preindustrial maps, which we have georeferenced, and early OS maps allowed us to reconstruct fairly accurately the historical topography of Northeye. Pre-nineteenth-century maps were especially helpful in this regard due to the slow rate of change of the Sussex landscape prior to the nineteenth century (Hoskins 1977, 79). The detailed depiction of the road and waterways, drainage, field boundaries, and woodland on Yeakell and Gardner's 1783 Survey of Sussex thus provides a sound foundation on which to begin reconstructing Northeye's topography. East Stream—an important local drainage route in the Middle Ages—still forms the eastern boundary of Northeye. Furthermore, the drainage cuts described in the agreement between Battle Abbey and William of Hastings remain more or less unchanged (Brandon 1971, 78). The primary drainage ran through Waterlot Stream (*Waterlode*) to the north and west of Northeye, and through East Stream (*Meneflete*) to the east and south (Salzmann 1910). First series Ordnance Survey maps further suggest that these drainage systems have remained relatively unchanged since the initial medieval land reclamation around Northeye (Ordnance Survey 1899).

Cartographic and remote sensing data also suggest the location of Northeye's medieval docks (Fig. 6). East Stream is the most likely of the waterways around Northeye to have had a dock on its banks. It was and remains still the largest waterway, and it offered the most direct route to the coast from the island. With the location of "stone bridge" leading to Barnhorne on the east side of the village, we deduced that the docks would likely have been located somewhere on the southeast embankment of Northeye.[21] Indeed, several trackways lead from the village to the southeast corner of the island, where LiDAR shows a lower, level strip of land 1 meter above the surface of East Stream (which flows at 28 cm below average sea level) along the embankment, evidence that supports this deduction.

[21] This stone bridge is noted on every significant map and appears as "stone bridge" on the early OS maps. It is also noted in the archaeological literature. So, we assume there was a medieval bridge at or near this location. Based on that assumption, medieval inhabitants would have had to construct the docks on the coastal side, as any such bridge would likely have been too low to allow passage beneath.

Figure 6. Detail of a composite map of medieval Northeye with building mounds, salt mounds, and port site in gray.

Remote sensing data also allows us to discern important features of the village.[22] Using 1-meter resolution LiDAR revealed the general location of building foundations along the central east–west trackway. The chapel excavation site forms a distinct depression on the high point of the island, and aerial photographs taken during the 1952 excavation confirm the layout. Finally, a circular depression on the north side of the central trackway, a few meters east of the chapel site, suggests the location of the village well.[23]

As an island village with little access to timber, the builders of Northeye would have relied on resources collected from further afield for building materials and fuel. Yeakell and Gardner's 1783 Survey of Sussex and the Ordnance Surveys identify several possible sources to the east of Barnhorne. The closest significant wooded area was the "High Wood," approximately 2.25 kilometers northeast of Northeye by road through Barnhorne Hill. Taken

[22] Identifying these features was complicated by decades of heavy machine ploughing in the late twentieth and early twenty-first century. This ploughing has reduced to mounds the more defined building platforms that were no doubt once visible even to the naked eye. Prior to the ploughing, the size and orientation of the structures may have been identifiable.

[23] The well and adjacent pond are noted on a sketch of Northeye derived from the aerial photographs, perhaps as part of the 1952 excavation.

together, archival, archaeological, cartographic, and remote sensing image data allows us to compile with a high degree of certainty the general contours and features of Northeye.

For our project, it was important that, having scraped and compiled the available data, and having produced preliminary models of missing structures, we made our reconstructed visualizations interactive, accessible, and instructive, all of which we resolved to accomplish through the creation of a pedagogical video game. The purpose of the game is to immerse learners in an augmented reality simulation to engender a sense of proximity to lost Northeye, and to provide a virtual field of exploration onto which we can graft specific learning outcomes tied to environmental history.

Video Game as Pedagogy

Game-based learning, and especially the use of digital games in the classroom, is becoming increasingly popular (Dicheva et al. 2015). Research into game-based learning has provided frameworks for the design of digital games for educational purposes but rarely investigates the integration of the digital tools into standing curricula or even course design.[24] Several history classes have simulated the economic, social, and political atmosphere of historical cultures through games via popular franchises such as *Civilization* or *Assassin's Creed* (McCall 2016; Shaffer et al. 2005). While no doubt amusing to students, such examples rely on games not designed to be educational. The teacher, in those instances, uses preexisting, commercial games to represent "authentic" past environments to convey historical lessons.[25] Our project seeks to improve this model further by designing, creating, and implementing our own pedagogical video game based on cutting-edge scholarly research. Particularly novel aspects of our Northeye game are its use of AR to provide kinesthetic, small group interactions; its easy configurability through the use of AR station markers; and the development of a "Northeye Engine" that makes it easier for developers to create and experiment with new stations without the considerable technical overhead of developing a networked, real-time AR application.

---

[24] On integrating video games into the class, see, for example, Kotini and Tzelepi 2015; Urh et al. 2015. On the lack of integration within courses or curricula, see Whitton 2014.

[25] For those unfamiliar with authenticity in video games, the technology has advanced to a sophisticated stage. Games such as *Assassin's Creed*, produced by Ubisoft, have recreated fully explorable and highly detailed cityscapes.

The game provides an interactive experience where players can explore different aspects of Northeye. Interaction is supported in small groups to allow shared experience and is based on physical interaction techniques to provide kinesthetic (i.e., an individual's awareness of bodily position and movement by means of the sensory organs)—and therefore more active—engagement with the subject matter. The central presentation of the game world is through a series of interactive stations. A station is similar to an exhibit that one might find in a museum, but fully interactive and explorable, without the glass walls of a physical exhibit.

Participants enter a station by pointing an iPad in its proximity. They are able to see the station "through" the iPad, and moving the iPad around allows the player to see the exhibit from different perspectives and distances. For example, when exploring the Northeye Village station (Fig. 7), the player of the virtual village might sit on a physical table; moving the iPad around the village allows the player to see it from above, from the side, or zoomed right into a village street. This form of interaction is termed a "magic lens," where the iPad serves as a viewport into the virtual environment (Brown and Hua 2006). The object being viewed has a static position and size, so that movement of the iPad allows views from different distances and perspectives.

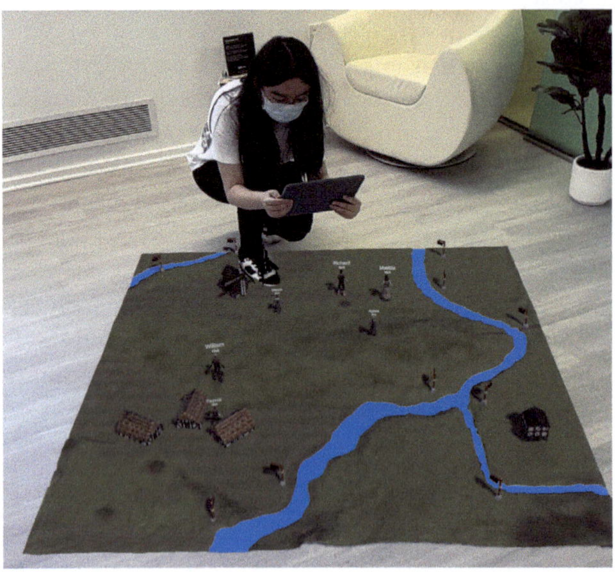

Figure 7. View of Northeye Village station, showing a villager heading to work. A station marker is shown in the background.

Several types of stations have been developed, providing exterior, interior, or video experiences. Exterior stations use a "drone" perspective that allows users to see a large portion of space (Fig. 8). This allows for interaction types that are inspired by real-time strategy (RTS) games and "god games." This aspect of the video game will utilize two examples of an Exterior station: "Northeye Village" and "Northeye Environs." Interior stations fix the player's position within an interior space, such as the inside of a building. Moving the iPad around allows the users to look around within the space. For example, a "barn" station might show the interior of a plausible historical barn structure we reconstructed using historical architectural records and photographic evidence from the nearby Herstmonceux manor and then placed near the Northeye site. Finally, a video station places the player in the center of a 360-degree video. By moving the iPad, the player can see a video representation of a scene from different angles. This could be used, for example, to show a video of the current Northeye site.

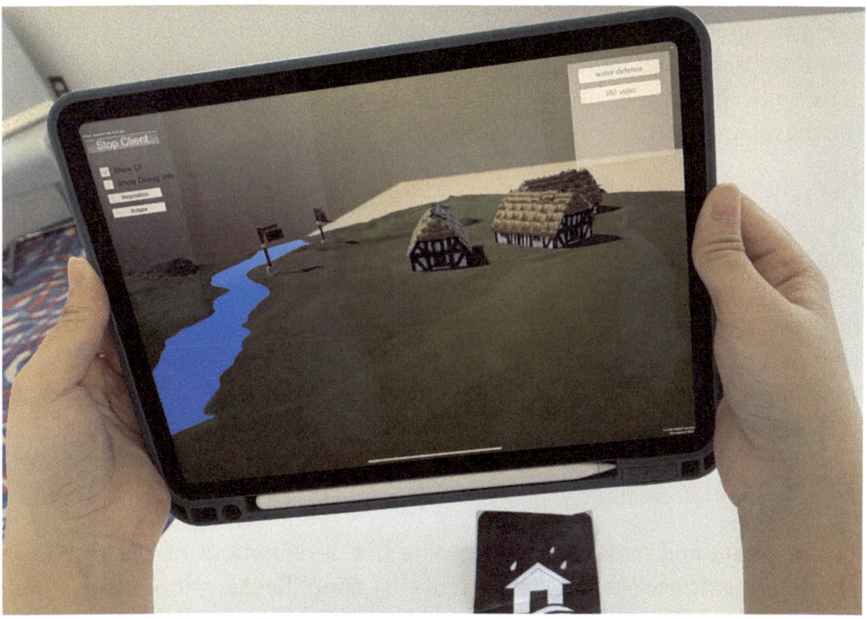

Figure 8. Station showing the environs around Northeye. A player can select farmland within this station and specify that villagers are to cultivate it. Crops will grow in real time.

By using printed markers placed around a room, an instructor (or guide at a visitor center, or a parent who is home-schooling a child, etc.) establishes which stations are active and where they are located. Users move iPads around the room to point at a station's card marker, which the iPad recognizes and uses to initiate the station associated with that card. All users gathered at a station are able to view a common representation of the activities and thereby engage in multiplayer sessions.

By using these physical markers, this model brings a physical element to station-based interaction. Game players must move to a particular physical location within the learning environment in order to access the station they wish to visit. To visit a different station, they must again physically move to the new station's location. While at a station, players both move their iPads to change their views of the station and change their own postures: standing upright, pointing the iPad down, kneeling on the ground pointing the iPad forward or upward, and so on. This form of kinesthetic interaction contrasts with the static interaction typical of most computer use wherein the player is immobile in their chair and focused only on a screen directly in front of them. By requiring game players to move, we hope to engage them more actively in the stations, increasing their involvement in the virtual world of Northeye, and integration collaboration.

The physical placement of markers and the need to move around a room raises legitimate questions of accessibility. Since the classroom teacher is able to position the paper markers anywhere, it should be possible to reduce barriers to play for students who experience mobility challenges. That said, the game does require the use of a tablet, and so there may be some learners who require assistance in manipulating the physical hardware that supports gameplay. We are interested to know how students with different levels of mobility and physical dexterity are able to interact with Northeye, and so part of the data we will gather during the classroom testing phase will address issues of accessibility.

To accelerate and make more accessible the development of the game, we have built a "Northeye Engine," a tool that simplifies development and experimentation with the interactive stations. Creation of a game such as *Virtual Northeye* requires significant technical expertise in areas including augmented reality, artificial intelligence, and game networking. The purpose of the engine is to hide this complex code in reusable components, which administrative users can simply plug into our three types of station. Developers of our Northeye game platform can then be divided into two distinct groups: station developers, who generate game activities and content, and engine developers focused on developing tools for the station developers and the overall game design. This opens the possibility, for example, for station developers to be student programmers who may be with the project for a short duration and may not have the time to develop the technical expertise to become an engine developer.

As we move beyond the prototype stage, some of our team's developers will be tasked with building tools that enable other developers to create new stations and to extend existing ones. We will also task some developers with implementing systems that work between stations, by creating additional required infrastructure for the game (networking, post-processing, asset pipeline improvement, etc.). Still others will build the stations that will be available for the play sessions.

We have designed *Virtual Northeye* around an interdisciplinary and scaffolded collaboration process. Within this process, faculty researchers work alongside postgraduate and undergraduate students. Already, several student research assistants have contributed to the development of the tools described in this chapter. Two fourth-year project students in computer science and a professional programmer developed the first version of the Northeye Engine and created a set of example stations. A fourth-year project student created a prototype version of the village in which villagers can be seen walking around and engaging in their daily tasks. An MSc student in computer science created a prototype station allowing interactive gameplay where placement of water defenses can mitigate the effects of flooding. Finally, a doctoral candidate in history provided valuable historical consultation. As the project grows over time, it promises to engage students from a range of other fields including geology, sedimentology, GIS, and more. Having to pull together disparate areas of expertise, share supervision of diverse students, and work collaboratively requires a conscious effort to move toward a common vocabulary, to become aware of disciplinary differences, and to learn to explain concepts plainly. Ultimately, this reflexive practice inevitably supports the production of a more accessible educational tool.

To align our game with local needs, we turn to the Ontario Curriculum for elementary grades. It provides the framework for the implementation of our educational video game based on medieval environment and culture. One of the core requirements of the grade 4 curriculum is that educators should

> *formulate questions* to guide investigations into ways of life and relationships with the environment in a few early societies,

> including at least one First Nation and one Inuit society, with an emphasis on aspects of the *interrelationship between the environment and life in those societies* (e.g., connections between the local environment and settlement, art, medicine, religion, spirituality, types of work; the impact on the environment of agriculture or the development of towns, cities, settlements, communities, and/or villages). (Government of Ontario 2018, 101; emphasis added)

In terms of *Virtual Northeye*, student-users should thus understand how people in medieval Sussex might have structured their villages and shared common spaces. The village layout in the game, with a particular focus on how the local wetland/coastal environment affected the ways in which people met their physical needs (e.g., food, housing, clothing), addresses educators' responsibility to show students how to "evaluate evidence and draw conclusions about ways of life and relationships with the environment in a few early societies . . . with an emphasis on aspects of the interrelationship between the environment and life in those societies." Some of the ways they can do this is through using digital tools to "analyse a climate map to determine the climatic challenges facing early settlements; construct soil and vegetation maps to determine the connection between soil type and agricultural activity; analyse maps to determine the proximity of early settlements to water" (Government of Ontario 2018, 102). Our Northeye game will therefore include many of these features in its virtual depiction of the surrounding landscape.

Through the simulation of the village, we hope to teach about the social structure of its inhabitants, their dwellings and other structures, and their routines. NPCs will spawn from a list of "job areas" to perform daily activities. Such activities will include, for example, ploughing, sweeping, and fetching water. The NPCs will choose between these activities based on their needs. Certain activities will be exclusive to defined areas. For example, the NPCs will not have the option to plough fields when their assigned job area is a house. Some actions will be shared. For example, the NPCs can talk to those around them in their houses and on the fields. By combining utility AI with existing behavior trees, the game projects verisimilitude, making villagers act in ways that are dynamic and believable.[26] And just as in *The Sims* games, NPC villagers will have basic needs, such as hunger and tiredness. One possibility for the future of *Virtual Northeye* is to turn it into a RTS-style game,

---

[26] According to Bill Merrill (2019, 84), "As it applies to game artificial intelligence behavior, utility theory is simply the process of measuring the relative suitability of a particular action."

where players must order the villagers around, trying to maximize their productivity while minimizing dangers due to overwork or starvation.

To build a farming simulation, we decided which aspects of farming would be simulated and, consequently, what parameters should be used to decide outcomes such as crop yields or degradation of soil quality. We intend for users to learn from the simulation by recognizing patterns (e.g., land in basins is more likely to flood; cycling crops helps to reintroduce nutrients and thus leads to better yields), and by allowing them to experiment with pattern modification. Still, all simulation parameters will accurately capture medieval farming practices. So, in order to accomplish this, the following parameters affect gameplay:

- Nitrogen levels: allows us to enforce crop cycling to reintroduce nitrogen into the soil.
- Fertilizer: players must create, store, and use fertilizer to add to their fields, or have animals in pasture.
- Moisture: aside from enabling flooding and arid condition disasters, the moisture parameter forces players to water/irrigate their crops.
- Isolation: approximates a plot's protection from the elements to incentivize forward thinking when buying/leasing plots.
- Fallow: rating determines the level of weeds in the plot.
- Season: weather and environment are heavily dependent on the season, which has both explicit and implicit impacts.

In addition, virtual villagers will have their own resources that they must manage, which inherently affect the simulation:

- Stamina
- Economic resources
- Animals/seeds
- Social status/communal resources

Any simultion will be limited if the players do not engage with it. Thus, in the example of farming, players will need to interact with the simulated village and its environs. Initially, players might realize that no plants are growing in their fields. Having started out with access to three fields and five cows, players will with practice learn to place all cows on the plot with the highest fallow rating, and to plant one of the other two fields with wheat and the third with beans. The game will then decrease the fallow rating as the cows feed and fertilize the soil with their manure. Meanwhile, the nitrogen and fertilizer ratings on the wheat field will decrease, and on the bean field, the nitrogen level will increase while the fertilizer level decreases. By rotating the crops in the order cereal -> legume -> fallow -> cereal, the player will learn to balance the nutrients of the field so that, barring flooding, they can grow their crops indefinitely. Flooding in the simulation will encourage players to consider additional variables of their farms' geography, such as height above sea level or its protection from inundation.

From Static Image to Procedural Generation Models

The greatest challenge in making the jump from model to augmented reality game was in moving beyond a high-level, birds-eye view of topography, roads, and structures to make the landscape interactive. In a game world, everything—terrain, buildings, trees, even the blades of grass—is a geometric object that requires definition in terms of shape and appearance. Typical video games, pedagogical or otherwise, incorporate any number of objects, beginning with the terrain itself and ending with tiny objects. Often, these include findable objects that many players will never discover. In the case of the Northeye game, these might include game models of archaeological artifacts.

In the game, anything with which a player might interact, or which is dynamic within the game (such as a smoking chimney), requires computer code to define its operation. In building *Virtual Northeye*, we began with the birds-eye view evidence noted above and then added features, constrained by direct historical evidence or placed for historical plausibility. We thus placed the plausible chapel model depicted above (Fig. 2) in its correct archaeological location, upon accurate geometric terrain. The other buildings in the village are grounded in historical or physical data to a lesser degree since less physical evidence of their appearance survives. The same applies for other historically reasonable but unconstrained features, such as fences or the location and geometry of surface features like gardens.

Game worlds, therefore, are replete with objects both constrained and unconstrained, and those visual objects sometimes interact to foster a more authentic user experience. Believability includes not only physical realism but also interactive realism—when a player interacts with an object such as a door, it has to behave in a physically and sonically realistic way. In the case of a historical game, we aim for the game not only to appear realistic but also to honor historical evidence—a complex and, at times, daunting task. As an example, we have researched the extent and form of the chapel on the property to constrain the model. This raises an issue that occupies and informs both budgeting and the mindset of game designers: how to fill a virtual world with realistic objects that behave plausibly and integrate them coherently.

The available historical, physical, and cartographic data presented at the outset of this chapter provides a framework to pin key features, such as the chapel, in place. We may continue to place features manually, using a library of game objects (many of which we will need to create, with others sourced from available game design libraries) to populate the village and its environs. As noted, the objects we create will include not only the large but also the innumerable small items found in any scene, such as tools or personal possessions, some of which are visually necessary but whose exact details do not require the attention of a game designer. Completing a game world without spending a very large number of resources on placing such features poses an ongoing challenge. This challenge multiplies if we seek to create multiple versions of the game world, perhaps representing different interpretations of historical conditions, or supporting gameplay where the players modify the environment as they play.

Techniques that allow designers to place real or abstract objects based on a mixture of rules and randomness are called procedural generation tools. While they do take significant work to prepare, these tools can save developers significant time that they would otherwise devote to the placement of features. To create a plausible and playable Northeye, our team identified four procedural generation processes, distinct ways to integrate generated objects into the simulation: (1) pre-game planning; (2) during game design; (3) during game load; and (4) during game play. First, in the pre-game planning stage, we used existing game design tools to build objects using independent game design software from outside of the game itself. Second, members of the team supported the game design process by providing tools that run independently or within game engines to place individual items or collections, thereby filling in the details for a given setting. As one example of these sorts of experiments, we mentored a summer student to generate realistic forests using the Houdini special effects tool.

These placements can be static or dynamic, allowing for real-time alterations to the planned virtual environment. So, for example, our team was able to move roads or trackways and adjust the forest. Both of these approaches allow significant enhancement to the productivity of the game design without requiring that the object designers actually be part of the final game: the tools they deploy, therefore, are made available autonomously or by the designer purposefully, but they are part of the game design toolkit, not part of the game. Object generation relied on a combination of preexisting object libraries and mathematical randomness to fill in details. For example, *Virtual Northeye* required a plausible natural ecosystem including trees. For this, we deployed a procedural generation tool that used random numbers and an ecosystem description to populate a realistic forest.[27] Procedural techniques like this are now sufficiently powerful that they can be used to simulate realistic ecosystems; the tool has encoded knowledge about where plants grow, how they interact, and how they change with time. As we continue to refine *Virtual Northeye*, we will look to integrate emerging plant and wetland data into our generation tools and models.[28]

Third, we explored how procedural generation processes might be used during the period when the game loads (e.g., spontaneous terrain variation, water elevation, and weather generation). These processes might vary the actual details of the virtual Northeye rendered by the game each time it loads. So, tree lines might subtly move, the height of houses shift, the surrounding water level alter, NPCs might change position or disposition, the weather might change, and so on. This kind of "during play" support can be used to provide a more varied experience each time the game is loaded within constraints from historical data and game objectives.

Fourth and finally, we began to contemplate whether we might want to allow players to control object generation—that is, to design the game to allow players to choose how much plant, weed, wood, and so on is available to help resolve a given challenge. In cases where the object—in this case the plant—is part of the game goals, having scenarios where a player or teacher can alter the available resources can result in significantly different challenges to the player. Provided that the science behind the modeled system is cor-

---

[27] The creators of such tools might collaborate with ecologists to define which collections are realistic and where they can be placed. They might then collaborate with artists to make realistic models of plants. In our case, for this prototype, we relied on a preexisting forest generation tool. Over time, we will incorporate actual local data to refine the model.

[28] We need not separate such a tool from the game itself. Procedural generation tools can be embedded within a game design and delivery. A noteworthy example of why one might do this is the 1980s game *Elite*, which shipped on a single low-density floppy disk but contained an infinite universe, generated procedurally during play.

rect—that is, the game designers had access to realistic models of how plants and flooded fields actually work—then the game becomes an educational simulation that accurately models causality and effect. Repeated play—iterating through different choices—allows learning by trial and, perhaps more often, error.

Many software tools exist to achieve these four sorts of procedural supports, but in our prototype stage, as noted, our team focused on one available tool: Houdini (sidefx.com). Our team selected Houdini because it is widely used in game design and Hollywood special effects shops for all the tasks described above. It is quite capable of handling our needs, is well documented, and integrates easily into our selected game engine. We deployed the various procedural support possibilities outlined above (pre-game, game design, during load, and during play) on three scenarios: rapid transformation of landscape geometry; erosion processes on landscape; and forest growth and regrowth.

First, we attempted to transform landscape geometry—in other words, to alter the geometry of the landscape itself, changing hill shape and height. To do this, we loaded available digital elevation data into Houdini, initially to carry out simple transformations and then to project these transformations forward into the Unity game engine (unity.com), a popular cross-platform engine. One transformation involved the types of landscape flexure associated with post-glacial rebound. When an ice sheet builds up, it depresses the crust slowly, and when it melts, the uplift—the relaxation of this downwarp—is also slow; southern Canada, for example, is still undergoing significant uplift from the Wisconsin glaciation event that ended approximately 10,000 years ago. The effect beyond the ice sheet is more complex, with an area of downwarp followed by an area of mild uplift, as opposed to a simple depression. As the ice loads and moves, the uplifted area moves like a wave, and it does the same in the opposite direction when the ice melts. This overall effect is likely significant (on the scale of several meters) in the Pevensey Levels and might contribute to the overall timing and magnitude of flooding in the area because slight differences in topography have a significant effect on flooding in low-lying areas. Post-glacial rebound operates on the scale of centuries, and so through the history of the site significant changes to flood events may have occurred, compounding other factors such as deliberate landscape change, sea-level change, and changes in storm intensity.

Second, we attempted a transformation by modifying the terrain using the effect of water. Tools like Houdini are capable of simulating erosion of soft materials like soil to form gullies, river valleys, and even simple delta systems, although as with all special effects tools the emphasis is on appearing credible rather than accurate scientific modeling. In most games the distinction is insignificant because scientific modeling is not being done. In our case it may lead to opportunities for examining trade-offs between approaches as our work continues. Steep hillslopes such as those undercut to form cliffs are more difficult to model since the mechanical simulation is more sensitive to parameters. Our team members had prior experience simulating both the nature of processes on steep slopes and the consequences of rockfalls on the immediate environment. For example, they built slope models and investigated different geological scenarios for rockfalls (Fig. 9). In this case, for the prototype and to measure effect, the slope used came from British Columbia and not Sussex. Moving forward, we will substitute for local conditions. This will contribute to areas where there are steep cut banks or coastlines with significant wave cutting taking place.

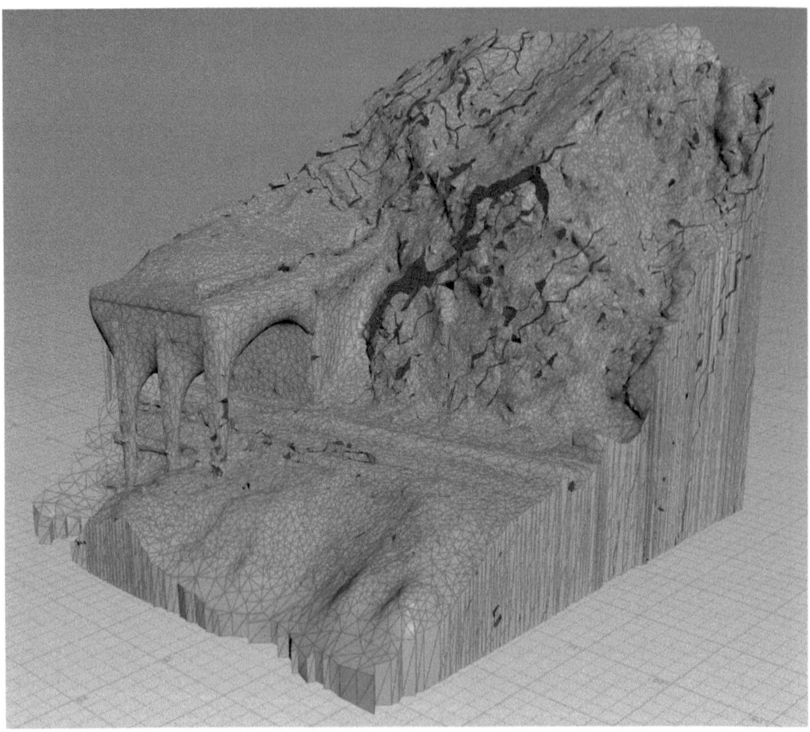

Figure 9. Slope failure model in Houdini. The triangular mesh is the terrain, and the purple areas have cracked (linear zones) or failed and fallen (larger areas) due to slope processes.

Both the soft sediment erosion and the steep rockfall models might be applicable to regional simulations in the area around Northeye, though it appears more likely that the soft sediment erosion models will be most applicable in the short term. Given the strong relationship between type of land cover and erosion rates, we anticipate that erosion and sedimentation models for fields and disturbed ground will be achievable both as a task during game design, and as a live simulation during play.

As noted, another key area for the use of procedural systems is in ecosystem representation and models. To aid in the rapid construction of vegetated landscapes in and around Northeye, we investigated the use of Houdini and Unity to constrain species distribution using parameters of the landscape. For example, we scattered plants only in land areas, not in water, constrained others to be near water, and constrained some by elevation (Fig. 10). Tying the vegetation to the soil type as well as to climate effects could also be done. In these cases, the distribution is done pre-game and the result is loaded into the game engine. There is no temporal component; the distribution is a mix of randomness and preset exclusion rules. This of course raises the question of what could be done with an actual simulation of species growth and spread. In a game where significant time passes during play, the outcome of player decisions such as placing protection from flooding or planting specific plants would alter subsequent gameplay significantly.

Figure 10. Random placement of trees and undergrowth in a landscape with local pools of water, built in Houdini and visualized in Unity using simple example vegetation models as placeholders. The trees prefer slopes and avoid pools of water, while the sedges prefer flat ground and do not avoid water.

In the case of Sussex vegetation, pioneer and successor species (the first plants to grow in clearings and abandoned fields) were well established by the Middle Ages. Although our broader team's work on the specific plants in the area at the time—constrained by palynology and proxy data drawn from written records—is still ongoing, we made a first attempt at a model that simulates the spread of species at varying rates and under different physical constraints such as elevation, soil type, and proximity to water sources (Figs. 11a–c). This first-pass model can not only simulate plants spreading through an area but can also expose some of these controls for during-play use so that learners can experiment with different assumptions about how seeds are distributed and the influence of barriers and the like. The model also allows grown areas to be disturbed—by clearing or fire, for example—and will then model the regrowth into the cleared patch. The plan is to calibrate both the ecosystem guilds, the basic structural units of ecological communities, and the rates of migration against local data in the near future to model change over time.

Procedural techniques, combined with manual placement of key features, allow us to produce more efficiently pedagogical game environments for the Northeye area. They also permit us to begin to explore how interactive simulations of the environment render that environment more compelling in the service of educational goals; more realistic simulations prevent the need, among other things, for having to bring students *in situ*. It is important to add that such techniques are now widespread in desktop gaming and are on the cusp of becoming practical in mobile gaming. As mobile technologies continue to improve, these techniques will become more and more common in mobile gaming. In that respect, we anticipate that *Virtual Northeye* will be at the cutting edge of available mobile game pedagogies.

Figure 11a.

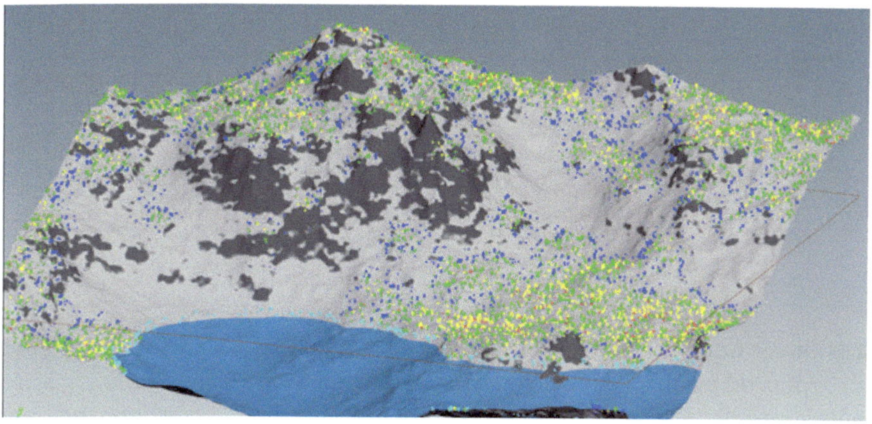

Figure 11b.

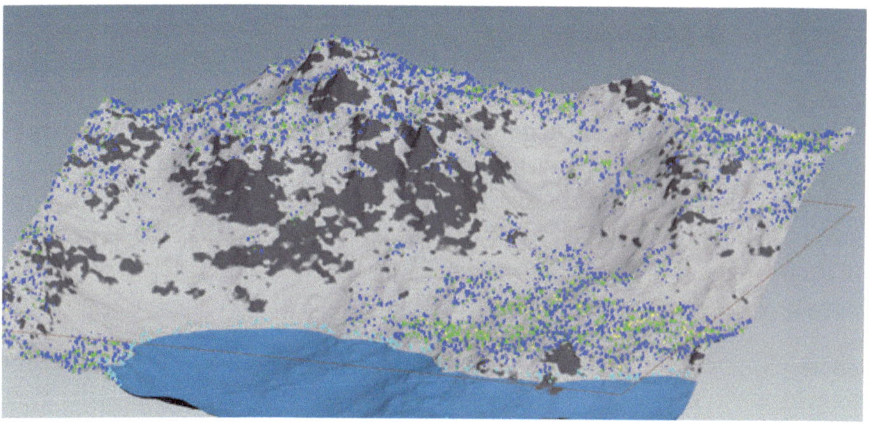

Figure 11c.

Figures 11a–c. Ecosystem evolution on a simulated landscape. The three images show species spreading, with successor species moving in to replace them over time. Note the presence of species that prefer to be along shorelines.

Conclusion

Up yonder hill the village murmur rose
. . .
But now the sounds of population fail
No cheerful murmurs fluctuate in the gale
No busy steps the grass-grown foot-way tread
For all the bloomy flush of life is fled.
—Oliver Goldsmith, *The Deserted Village* (1770)

For Oliver Goldsmith, these words expressed the sadness and ephemerality experienced by all whose meanderings lead them to deserted villages; sites where people once worked, loved, fought, and laughed, but where they did so no longer. There is a familiar sadness in this for those who spend their lives studying the Middle Ages, whose vacations and research time are often passed amidst ruined structures or, in the case of Northeye, within empty fields.

And yet, this ephemerality of time and space, a gap that makes the past all the more unknowable and distant, is now at least partially navigable thanks to emerging digital tools. With the evolution of AR, Canadian students can now experience firsthand a sort of echo of life in rural thirteenth-century Sussex. Through the glass screens of their iPads, they can navigate roadways that no longer exist, explore a demolished chapel, and interact with simulations of villagers to develop a sense of their connection to land and sea.

These experiences, of course, are artificial approximations, but they serve to bridge the gap in a novel, sensory way between what is and what was. In so doing, *Virtual Northeye* offers new ways of thinking about the past and the present. The challenges faced by long-dead English villagers with regard to coastal flooding, food production, preservation, and distribution, as well as commerce and trade, all resonate with twenty-first-century challenges. While it would be a mistake to claim that our historical study of Northeye has direct implications for the modern world, it does serve to inculcate what Sam Wineberg (2001, 5) calls historical thinking, or the "tension between the familiar and the strange, between feelings of proximity and feelings of distance." This, in turn, encourages our young learners to draw lessons from past paradigms, which they can take with them in the world today (van Drie and van Boxtel 2007). This sort of historical awareness is, we argue, invaluable to solving complex problems.

Virtual Northeye is a starting point in our research, a first attempt to lay out how historians, archivists, archaeologists, sedimentologists, geologists, and video game developers can work collaboratively to create plausible facsimiles of past environments that inform important lessons about human culture and the natural world. As we continue to learn to work together, and to develop common vocabularies and tools, it becomes increasingly apparent to us that the applications we have identified here are but a first step. The capacity to expand these sorts of tools to include not just environmental history but also, potentially, politics, economics, cultural studies, and much more is within reach. In this chapter, we have outlined a method that begins a new process to bring to life a deserted village in a fragile historical ecosystem. Through Northeye and the students who play within its virtual streets and fields, we hope to continue to learn and to develop ever better ways to teach the past.

WORKS CITED

Apollonio, Fabrizio I. 2016. "Classification Schemes for Visualization of Uncertainty in Digital Hypothetical Reconstruction." In *3D Research Challenges in Cultural Heritage II: How to Manage Data and Knowledge Related to Interpretative Digital 3D Reconstructions of Cultural Heritage*, edited by Sander Münster, Mieke Pfarr-Harfst, Piotr Kuroczyński, and Marinos Ioannides, 173–97. Cham: Springer. doi.org/10.1007/978-3-319-47647-6_9.

Backlund, Per, and Maurice Hendrix. 2013. "Educational Games: Are They Worth the Effort? A Literature Survey of the Effectiveness of Serious Games." In *2013 5th International Conference on Games and Virtual Worlds for Serious Applications (VS-GAMES)*, 1–8. Piscataway, NJ: IEEE. doi.org/10.1109/VS-GAMES.2013.6624226.

Bastem, Sumeyye Sena, and Asli Cekmis. 2021. "Development of Historic Building Information Modelling: A Systematic Literature Review." *Building Research & Information* 50, no. 5 (June): 527–58. doi.org/10.1080/09613218.2021.1983754.

Beresford, Maurice, and John G. Hurst, eds. 1971. *Deserted Medieval Villages: Studies*. New York: St. Martin's Press.

Billinghurst, Mark. 2002. "Augmented Reality in Education." *New Horizons for Learning* 12 (5): 1–5.

Brandon, P. F. 1971. "Agriculture and the Effects of Floods and Weather at Barnhorne, Sussex, during the Late Middle Ages." *Sussex Archaeological Collections* 109:69–93. doi.org/10.5284/1085874.

Brázdil, Rudolf. 2002. "Patterns of Climate in Central Europe since Viking Times." In *Climate Development and History of the North Atlantic Realm*, edited by Gerold Wefer, Wolfgang H. Berger, Karl-Ernst Behre, and Eystein Jansen, 355–68. Berlin: Springer. doi.org/10.1007/978-3-662-04965-5_22.

———. 2003. "Historical Climatology and Its Progress after 1900." In *People and Nature in Historical Perspectives*, edited by József Laszlovsky and Péter Szabó, 197–228. Budapest: Central European University, Department of Medieval Studies; Archaeolingua.

Brown, Leonard D., and Hong Hua. 2006. "Magic Lenses for Augmented Virtual Environments." *IEEE Computer Graphics and Applications* 26, no. 4 (July–August): 64–73. doi.org/10.1109/MCG.2006.84.

Burleigh, G. R. 1973. "An Introduction to Deserted Medieval Villages in East Sussex." *Sussex Archaeological Collections* 111:45–83.

Dicheva, Darina, Christo Dichev, Gennady Agre, and Galia Angelova. 2015. "Gamification in Education: A Systematic Mapping Study." *Journal of Educational Technology & Society* 18, no. 3 (June): 75–88. jstor.org/stable/jeductechsoci.18.3.75.

Duer, Zach, Todd Ogle, David Hicks, Scott Fralin, Thomas Tucker, and Run Yu. 2020. "Making the Invisible Visible: Illuminating the Hidden Histories of the World War I Tunnels at Vauquois through a Hybridized Virtual Reality Exhibition." *IEEE Computer Graphics and Applications* 40, no. 4 (July–August): 39–50. doi.org/10.1109/mcg.2020.2985166.

Dulley, A. J. F. 1966. "The Level and Port of Pevensey in the Middle Ages." *Sussex Archaeological Collections* 104:26–45.

Fernández Galeote, Daniel, and Juho Hamari. 2021. "Game-Based Climate Change Engagement: Analyzing the Potential of Entertainment and Serious Games." *Proceedings of the ACM on Human-Computer Interaction* 5, no. CHI PLAY (October): 1–21. doi.org/10.1145/3474653.

Gardiner, Mark. 2014. "Hythes, Small Ports, and Other Landing Places in Later Medieval England." In *Waterways and Canal-Building in Medieval England*, edited by John Blair, 85–109. Oxford: Oxford University Press. doi.org/10.1093/acprof:osobl/9780198723134.003.0005.

Government of Ontario. 2018. "The Ontario Curriculum: Social Studies, Grades 1 to 6, History and Geography, Grades 7 and 8." Toronto: Ministry of Education.

Hewitt, Christopher Macdonald. 2018. "How Did East Sussex Really Appear in 1066? The Cartographic Evidence." *Digital Studies* 8 (1): 1–25. doi.org/10.16995/dscn.278.

Historic England. n.d. "Deserted Medieval Village of Northeye, 885m South-West of Old Road Farm." Accessed 10 August 2020. historicengland.org.uk/listing/the-list/list-entry/1002240.

Historic England Research Records. n.d. "Northeye." Heritage Gateway. Accessed 10 August 2020. pastscape.org.uk/hob.aspx?hob_id=411707.

Hoskins, W. G. 1977. *The Making of the English Landscape*. London: Hodder and Stoughton.

Ioannides, Marinos, Nadia Magnenat-Thalmann, and George Papagiannakis, eds. 2017. *Mixed Reality and Gamification for Cultural Heritage*. Cham: Springer. doi.org/10.1007/978-3-319-49607-8.

Jeake, Samuel. 1728. *Charters of the Cinque Ports: Two Ancient Towns and Their Members*. London: Bernard Lintot.

Kim, Sunha, and Mido Chang. 2010. "Computer Games for the Math Achievement of Diverse Students." *Journal of Educational Technology & Society* 13, no. 3 (July): 224–32. jstor.org/stable/jeductechsoci.13.3.224.

Kotini, Isabella, and Sofia Tzelepi. 2015. "A Gamification-Based Framework for Developing Learning Activities of Computational Thinking." In *Gamification in Education and Business*, edited by Torsten Reiners and Lincoln C. Wood, 219–52. Cham: Springer. doi.org/10.1007/978-3-319-10208-5_12.

McBain, Graham S. 2013. "The Charters of the Cinque Ports—Are They Still Needed?" *Review of European Studies* 5 (2): 90–126. doi.org/10.5539/res.v5n2p90.

McCall, Jeremiah. 2016. "Teaching History with Digital Historical Games: An Introduction to the Field and Best Practices." *Simulation & Gaming* 47 (4): 517–42. doi.org/10.1177/1046878116646693.

Merrill, Bill. 2019. "Building Utility Decisions into Your Existing Behavior Tree." In *Game AI Pro 360: Guide to Architecture*, edited by Steve Rabin, 81–90. Boca Raton, FL: CRC Press. doi.org/10.1201/9780429055058.

Moore, Andrew, and Steven Bednarski. 2022. "Draining the Swamp: National and Local Regulation of Drainage in a 1396 Sewer Commission Report." *Speculum* 97, no. 2 (April): 322–48. doi.org/10.1086/718759.

Normandale Preparatory School. 1939. "Archaeological Excavations at Northeye." *The Norman*. Brexhill, East Sussex.

Open Domesday. n.d. "Hooe." Accessed 7 August 2020. opendomesday.org/place/TQ6809/hooe.

Ordnance Survey. 1895. "Sheet 320: Hastings." National Library of Scotland. Accessed 29 January 2021. maps.nls.uk/view/101169047.

———. 1899. "Sussex LXX.5." National Library of Scotland. Accessed 29 January 2021. maps.nls.uk/view/103674691.

Oxford Archaeology (OA). 2009. "Northeye, Pevensey Levels, East Sussex: Geological Assessment Report." Oxford: Oxford Archaeology. eprints.oxfordarchaeology.com/342/1/Northeye_Assessment_Report.pdfA.pdf.

Papers of John Ernest Ray of Hastings (1873–1951). RAY 4/1/3. East Sussex Records Office, The Keep, Brighton.

Paraschivoiu, Irina, Josef Buchner, Robert Praxmarer, and Thomas Layer-Wagner. 2021. "Escape the Fake: Development and Evaluation of an Augmented Reality Escape Room Game for Fighting Fake News." In *Extended Abstracts of the 2021 Annual Symposium on Computer-Human Interaction in Play*, edited by Günter Waller, Alexander Meschtscherjakov, and Max Birk, 320–25. New York: Association for Computing Machinery. doi.org/10.1145/3450337.3483454.

Radu, Iulian. 2012. "Why Should My Students Use AR? A Comparative Review of the Educational Impacts of Augmented-Reality." In *2012 IEEE*

International Symposium on Mixed and Augmented Reality (ISMAR), 313–14. Piscataway, NJ: IEEE. doi.org/10.1109/ISMAR.2012.6402590.

Rippon, Steven. 2000. *The Transformation of Coastal Wetlands: Exploitation and Management of Marshland Landscapes in North West Europe during the Roman and Medieval Periods*. Oxford: Oxford University Press.

Salzmann, L. F. 1910. "The Inning of Pevensey Levels." *Sussex Archaeological Collections* 53:32–62. doi.org/10.5284/1085629.

Shaffer, David Williamson, Kurt R. Squire, Richard Halverson, and James P. Gee. 2005. "Video Games and the Future of Learning." *Phi Delta Kappan* 87, no. 2 (October): 105–11. doi.org/10.1177/003172170508700205.

Turner, Edward. 1867. "The Lost Towns of Northeye and Hydneye." *Sussex Archaeological Collections* 19:1–35.

UK Environment Agency. 2019. "LIDAR Composite DTM 2019 - 1m." Last modified 1 July 2021. data.gov.uk/dataset/3fc40781-7980-42fc-83d9-0498785c600c/lidar-composite-dtm-2019-1m.

Urh, Marko, Goran Vukovic, Eva Jereb, and Rok Pintar. 2015. "The Model for Introduction of Gamification into E-learning in Higher Education." *Procedia: Social and Behavioral Sciences* 197 (July): 388–97. doi.org/10.1016/j.sbspro.2015.07.154.

van Drie, Jannet, and Carla van Boxtel. 2007. "Historical Reasoning: Toward a Framework for Analyzing Students' Reasoning about the Past." *Educational Psychology Review* 2 (20): 87–110.

Vincent, Nicholas, trans. 2007. "Magna Carta Translation." National Archives. archives.gov/exhibits/featured-documents/magna-carta/translation.html.

Whittick, Christopher, ed. 2017. *The Calendar of the Battle Abbey Archive*. San Marino, CA: Huntingdon Library.

Whitton, Nicola. 2014. *Digital Games and Learning: Research and Theory*. New York: Routledge. doi.org/10.4324/9780203095935.

Wineberg, Sam. 2001. *Historical Thinking and Other Unnatural Acts*. Philadelphia: Temple University Press.

Yang, Ya-Ting Carolyn. 2012. "Building Virtual Cities, Inspiring Intelligent Citizens: Digital Games for Developing Students' Problem Solving and Learning Motivation." *Computers & Education* 59, no. 2 (September): 365–77. doi.org/10.1016/j.compedu.2012.01.012.

Yeakell, Thomas, and William Gardner. 1783. *An Actual Topographical Survey of the County of Sussex*. Old Sussex Mapped. University of Portsmouth.

Chapter 14:
The Place of Reading in VR: Pedagogy, Spenser's Kilcolman Castle, and *Amoretti* 65

Thomas Herron
East Carolina University

What is the optimal reading experience using virtual reality (VR)? Not many people feel comfortable for any length of time with a clunky headset on, and this discomfort makes reading and concentration on complex topics difficult. A gamer will be distracted by constant action; as a result, she won't notice the helmet on her head. Pity the virtual museumgoer, however: how many pictures can he stand to look at? How many corridors will he cross and how many placards will he read before he fidgets in his plastic helmet and longs for a real museum, a non-virtual café, or an outdoor sculpture garden?

Imagine, then, trying to appreciate literary works through a headset. If reading museum placards in VR becomes a chore and looking at the paintings themselves feels overly artificial, what about combing through 20 pages' worth of text detached from any real volume? Or 10? What about five? Or even just one dense, difficult page, or a short poem that takes prolonged concentration? What if you need annotations and spot translations to help you along? Do you have the patience to go look for them inside your virtual world? VR and extensive and/or intensive reading seem incompatible.

Yet, whatever our initial frustrations with the technology, reading shorter pieces of prose or poetry, no matter how complex, can be effectively enhanced by the VR experience, as this chapter will argue based on three different ways of reading with VR. All three examples suggest ways to heighten the reading experience through VR by connecting a text to a particular place. These ways of reading are currently being actively developed and explored in an interdisciplinary pedagogical project in the digital humanities, Castle to Classrooms: Developing an Irish Castle in Virtual Reality, described below.

One way that reading enhances the VR experience, and vice-versa, is through VR recreation of cultural monuments associated with famous works of writing. By placing ourselves inside a recreation of the original cultural sphere of the work, we can better appreciate that work and the world that produced it.

ISBN 978-1-64959-119-7 (paper) ISBN 978-1-64959-120-3 (pdf) ISBN 978-1-64959-121-0 (epub)
New Technologies in Medieval and Renaissance Studies 12 (2025) 381–95

This approach is fully in line with an interdisciplinary approach to the study of literature.

Another way to heighten the reading experience of complex texts through VR is to richly annotate the literature using the technology at hand: thanks to memory and the Internet, VR can offer truly multifaceted and entertaining editions with illustrations (and translations) galore. Annotations can also be verbal and provided in real time by professors and students to each other while occupying (as their classroom for the day) an exciting architectural space. Imagine strolling through an Athenian garden with your philosophy professor who asks you questions in the guise of Socrates, the professor's avatar in the VR program. Or, as in the case below, imagine discussing the creative content of an Elizabethan sonnet in the intimate domestic spaces of a medieval castle.

A third way to heighten the VR experience of reading is to probe analogies between the VR experience itself and the practice of reading literature. Literature, as a written art, creatively occupies a confined space (i.e., the page), not unlike a virtual world in a headset. Any building, like a castle, is fast bound by walls. When situated inside a VR device, a complex poem (for example) can encourage a "meta" awareness of the expansive applicability and analogous nature of language, architecture, and VR.

A test case for these three types of VR-enhanced reading is made here using a small selection from the early modern English poet Edmund Spenser's well-known collection of verse, *Amoretti and Epithalamion* (1595). This collection was written while Spenser (1554–99) lived at his adopted home at Kilcolman Castle, County Cork, in the southwest of Ireland, as a colonial administrator and landowner in the late 1580s and 1590s.[1] The main building structure at Kilcolman, known as a tower house, was a common type of small castle throughout late medieval and early modern Ireland (Fig. 1). Spenser's poetry focuses on this fortified home in abstract and concrete ways: for example, the part of the volume known as *Amoretti* consists of a lengthy sonnet sequence that refers, in sonnet 65, to a "brazen tower" that could be Kilcolman, and to a "sacred bowre," either a bedroom or other pleasurable environs (perhaps a garden), relative to it. Subsequently, the concluding poem in the volume,

[1] Spenser's vital dates are taken from Brink 2019. For discussion of Spenser's life in Ireland, including at Kilcolman Castle, see Hadfield 2012. For recent in-depth discussion of Spenser's dwelling at Kilcolman, see the repartee in the online *Spenser Review*: Herron 2019; O'Keeffe 2018, 2019. The tower house at Kilcolman today stands in ruins, and traces of additional side buildings, including a great hall, are found below ground.

Epithalamion, is explicitly set at Kilcolman and a nearby town on Spenser's wedding day, 11 June 1594. *Epithalamion* refers to the topography around the castle as well as to the moon shining into the couple's bedroom chamber, among other details.[2]

Figure 1. Ruins of Kilcolman Castle from the northwest, c. 1996. Image credit: Thomas Herron.

For the sake of concision, only sonnet 65 of the *Amoretti* will be discussed here in the context of ongoing digital work, including website and VR development, that places the sonnet in its cultural/material setting in early modern Ireland: the sonnet offers a short (14-line) but exciting and complex reading experience that calls attention to Spenser's immediate physical environs at Kilcolman, since Kilcolman is the likely (but not certain) place where the sonnet was written. Understanding the dynamic between text and place deepens both the reading experience of the sonnet as well as any visit to the castle ruins; experience of both the sonnet and castle can in turn be enhanced through digital modeling and creative instruction in VR. The

[2] Citations from Spenser's poetry included in this chapter are from *The Yale Edition of the Shorter Works of Edmund Spenser* (see Spenser 1989). Sonnet 65 is on pp. 639–40 of this edition.

Castle to Classrooms project achieves these goals and offers food for thought on how to best enable and highlight the act of reading through location-specific VR.

Setting: Digitizing a Cultural Monument

A preexisting, highly detailed 3D digital model of a hypothetically reconstructed Kilcolman Castle is to be found on the open-access website Centering Spenser: A Digital Resource for Kilcolman Castle (Fig. 2). The Centering Spenser website (core.ecu.edu/umc/Munster), directed by the present author, has been episodically developed since 2010 at East Carolina University by a technical team led by Laurie Godwin. It is intended as a resource for research and teaching as well as for better understanding and appreciating Spenser's controversial experience in Ireland and the literature that came from it (Herron 2016; Lyttleton and Herron 2019). The website is keyed toward educating students, faculty, and the general public alike. Besides the digital model of the castle, the website has many essays on and present-day and historic illustrations of Kilcolman's building fabric in relation to Spenser's life and writings in Ireland, as well as those of famous fellow colonials in Ireland such as Sir Walter Raleigh and the early scientist and explorer Thomas Harriot. The website also has some pedagogical features, including teaching modules focused on sonnets 65 and 75 with analyses of both poems and follow-up questions for students. It also includes a teaching module geared toward Spenser's infamous political tract in prose, *A View of the Present State of Ireland* (c. 1596, published 1633).

Doug Barnum, IT technician and director of the Virtual Reality Lab at East Carolina University, has adapted the existing digital castle model for use in a prototype VR tour on the web-based platform WondaVR (wondavr.com), which can be openly accessed on both a desktop and, for the true VR 360-degree experience, on phones placed into Google Cardboard-type headsets as well as on the Meta Quest VR headset. Barnum has experimented with adapting the castle to the Microsoft HoloLens augmented reality (AR) headset as well, and he has constructed a more fully interactive version of the prototype VR tour using Unreal Engine software for the Oculus Rift and Quest devices.

Figure 2. Overhead view from the south of the reconstructed Kilcolman Castle, from the digital model on the Centering Spenser website. Note both the tower house as well as surrounding buildings and garden within a *bawn*, or fortified yard. Image credit: Thomas Herron, Laurie Godwin, and East Carolina University.

The prototype WondaVR tour allows for room-to-room exploration of the castle compound, while true interactivity is restricted to a few key pop-up features or "interpretive stations" that explore select objects within each room (Fig. 3).[3] This tour is expanded and developed in further, discipline-specific ways as part of the Castle to Classrooms project, funded through a National Endowment for the Humanities (NEH) Stage 2 Digital Humanities Advancement Grant begun in the fall of 2020. The two-year grant allowed four university faculty (Ruth Canning, Thomas Herron, Victoria McAlister, and Susannah Ottaway) and one high school teacher (Sara Painter) to work with Barnum and Godwin to develop innovative teaching modules in VR for undergraduates in history, architecture, archaeology, Irish studies, and English literature, as well as for high school students of English Renaissance poetry. Students who progress through these modules can follow classroom instructions and are asked to read pop-up primary sources and/or other instructional texts keyed toward objects inside the castle. The completed

[3] The "Kilcolman Foundation Tour" can be accessed here: player.wondavr.com/p/ab8ebc52-bd03-445d-ae9c-851423ec1e5d. A link to a more basic VR tour of the castle only (with one pop-up sonnet inserted) is found on the Centering Spenser website home page.

modules with instructional materials were posted on the Web in the fall of 2022 (core.ecu.edu/herront/Castles-Classrooms-Teaching/index.html).

Beyond classroom specifics designed by each collaborator, the project engages with medieval, Renaissance, Irish, colonial, and English-literature topics more generally. The teaching modules also function as exciting tours for the general public, being easily and openly accessible on the Web, attractively designed, and adapted to VR use on computers, headsets, and phones (the tours can be explored on a desktop or laptop using a mouse, albeit without the fully immersive 3D effect of using a headset or phone-in-headset). Like the Centering Spenser website, the modules employ images, music, text, and the spoken word in poetry and prose to create a virtual, lived-in experience of Kilcolman Castle. East Carolina University's usage agreement with WondaVR allows up to 50,000 users at a time to openly access the uploaded castle material at no cost to the individual viewer. Near-ubiquity of cell phones and computers among students today ensure the accessibility and easy use of the VR castle programming (costs increase significantly once programming is adapted and/or developed for Meta Quest-type headsets, however). An open-access companion website introduces each module and provides instruction for teachers on their use as well as further teaching resources related to the Castle to Classrooms project.

Contextualizing a Cultural Monument and Exploring a Cultural Text

Once a historicized context and place for a particular literary work is created in the imagination, or otherwise, that work can be read in the context of that place. When reading *The Tower* (1928) by W. B. Yeats or the *Essaies* (late sixteenth century) of Michel de Montaigne, for example, we can get a better "feel" for the originating environment of these works by imagining the writer at his desk (or chair or bed) scribbling away in his tower. Simultaneously, we can better understand the importance of the architectural monument through the work that describes it, however obliquely.[4] This process of place-reading loops back upon itself when a passage about a tower is read in the actual tower, or in a VR recreation of that tower. In such cases, VR allows a user the unique opportunity to appreciate the value of a "literary" place and the act of authorship through its associated self-referencing literary activity.

[4] For example, Montaigne describes his tower in his third essay, "De trois commerces," in the third part of his *Essaies*.

Sonnet 65 of *Amoretti* is just such a self-reflective literary work aware of important places. It mentions in its concluding lines what could be the "tower" of Kilcolman Castle; if it isn't *literally* the tower—for the tower in the poem is also a complex symbol—a real tower will probably be evoked in the mind of any reader, especially those who are aware that Spenser probably wrote the poem around the time that he occupied Kilcolman Castle and wooed his second wife, Elizabeth Boyle, from there with manuscript versions of what became *Amoretti*. Kilcolman as a real location certainly pops up later in the same volume: the work's concluding *Epithalamion* is largely set at the castle, where the couple's wedding morning and night are celebrated and consummated.

As a result, key details of physical surroundings possibly alluded to in the sonnets and concretely mentioned in *Epithalamion*, like the marshy terrain outside where frogs croak (l. 349), or the glimmer of moonlight through a bedroom window (ll. 37–73, 372–75), can be heightened for the reader through the recreative VR experience. Sonnet 65 of *Amoretti* is not set in any identifiable place, but it has architectural markers (i.e., a "tower" and a "bowre") that represent in symbolic and *potentially* literal terms facets of Kilcolman Castle. In the poem, the poet-speaker's anxious affection for his beloved is clear, as he implores her not to doubt their love and future together:

> THE doubt which ye misdeeme, fayre loue, is vaine,
> That fondly feare to loose your liberty,
> when loosing one, two liberties ye gayne,
> and make him bond that bondage earst dyd fly.
> Sweet be the bands, the which true loue doth tye,
> without constraynt or dread of any ill:
> the gentle birde feeles no captiuity
> within her cage, but singes and feeds her fill.
> There pride dare not approach, nor discord spill
> the league twixt them, that loyal loue hath bound:
> but simple truth and mutuall good will,
> seekes with sweet peace to salue each others wound:
> There fayth doth fearlesse dwell in brasen towre,
> and spotlesse pleasure builds her sacred bowre.

The sonnet is best understood in the context of Elizabethan love poetry, with its sharply contrasted physical and spiritual longings and witty language. It should also be understood within the context of Spenser's entire sonnet sequence, wherein the poet's speaker charts the pleasures, pitfalls, ecstasies, and anxieties of wooing his wife-to-be and (among other things) persuading her to come to Kilcolman to live with him. We see this wooing encouragement in sonnet 65 and many others around it. In sonnet 69, for example, the speaker celebrates the success of his "loves conquest . . . gotten at last with labour and long toyle." His "labour" in wooing Elizabeth Boyle finally concludes in the sequence in his "purchase," or attainment, of her (the word has strong financial overtones, as any marriage at the time did). Edmund and Elizabeth are simultaneously made "eternal" by virtue of being the subjects of the "immortal monument" that is the poem itself: the poet uses the time-honored trope of making his love, who is his muse, and his own genius immortal through his poetry.

As noted, Spenser's wooing was perilous, not only because Elizabeth could be proud and disdainful of the speaker's love (like a classic Petrarchan mistress would be) but also due to the immediate political context of the poem's conception. Spenser inhabited Kilcolman in the late 1580s as an English Protestant colonist who received his estate from dead or disgruntled Irish Catholics, who had recently lost it because of rebellion against the English Crown. Spenser and his wife Elizabeth then lost their castle in turn when they were burned out by another native rebellion, in 1597 or 1598, during the so-called Nine Years' War led by the Catholic earl of Tyrone against English rule in Ireland. Edmund died a few months later as a refugee in London while Elizabeth returned to Ireland after the war and remarried.[5] Understanding Spenser's perilous position as a Protestant colonial settler in a potentially hostile foreign land helps explain the anxieties attendant upon living in a castle—if it is that castle—described as a "brazen tower" in sonnet 65.[6]

Likewise, in sonnet 65, the speaker touchingly and disturbingly uses the language of captivity and protection when referring to the "sacred bowre" he will occupy at Kilcolman with his bride. A "bowre" could connote a place of pleasure and leisure, like a cultivated garden; it could also be a place of hidden shelter and amorous activity, like a bedroom, and here it is imagined as "sacred" rather than illicit or sinful. Captivity and protection seem to be intersecting and inseparable concepts in the speaker's mind throughout the sequence. The speaker tries to convince his bride in sonnet 65 to accept him

[5] For details of Spenser's life, see Hadfield 2012. Against the conventional narrative in Hadfield and elsewhere, Hiram Morgan (2021) provides evidence that the sacking of Kilcolman happened in 1597, not 1598.

[6] "Brazen" means *bold* or *brassy*.

and the "bond" of marriage, which is alluded to in the word "bands."[7] With these bands, bonds, and ring, he tries to capture her and bind her to him. Yet the meaning of line 4 is ambiguous: is it the speaker or his bride who is fleeing the potential "bondage" of marriage? (Perhaps both of them are?) Apparently, Elizabeth still "doubts" whether or not she should marry him. Like most young women who forfeited their property, many of their rights, and their bodies upon marriage, she would have to adjust to the idea of being captured amorously while being virtually owned by her husband. Simultaneously, she is empowered, as she is capturing him as an amorous prize, future spouse, and proud new owner of Kilcolman Castle.

As noted, this eroticized anxiety over who captures whom in the courtship occurs within the larger political anxiety of potentially being captured or killed by the Irish around them, many of whom resented the presence of the new English settlers (Fleming 2000; Hadfield 2012). These dangerous undertones come to the fore at the end of the poem, when the speaker tries to assure his love that their union will be founded on "simple truth and mutuall good will" and filled with a healing "sweet peace"—for the couple and presumably (the speaker hopes) for their neighbors as well. The poem ends with a central vision of the couple in a love nest in the tower infused with their sacred faith for each other: "There fayth doth fearlesse dwell in brasen towre, / and spotlesse pleasure builds her sacred bowre." In this tower, they, as "spotlesse" Protestants, can rest "fearlesse" of each other, presumably insulated from any outside threats—personal or political—that may arise. It is an optimistic vision on Spenser's part.

A real Spenser tower exists today, so these words in the poem have a strongly biographical and architectural resonance that we can appreciate when visiting the site. Seeing the castle in reality or online provides one with a greater sense of the stony fortitude and fertility that surrounded its inhabitants for hundreds of years. The castle stood in rich fields not far south of the Golden Vale of County Limerick. What one also discovers through research into castles is that, while a tower house of Kilcolman's type was "brazenly" fortified, it was also comfortable. A tower house's upper stories usually had larger windows than those below it in order to let in more light and air. While the castle might therefore resemble a "brassy" fortress that could be converted into an oppressive "cage," or prison, especially from down below, it also functioned as a home and airy roost for love birds, with its upper stories high in the sky,

---

[7] The word alludes to a wedding *band*, or ring. Note also the echo of the word *banns*, or an announcement of betrothal.

above all cares, and (most likely) overlooking a pleasant garden down below. At the top, a short step outside onto the castle ramparts would have revealed a marvelous view of the rich north Cork countryside from five or six stories above ground (we are hoping to one day develop this view of the surrounding landscape in the VR model of the castle).

By better comprehending Kilcolman Castle's environs through VR, we not only "see" and "feel" the place that helped to inspire the subject matter of the poem, but we also gain a better appreciation of the thematic tensions built into the poem itself. We appreciate how any politicized anxiety felt by Edmund and/or Elizabeth over their personal security can be compared with anxieties in their relationship, and these anxieties contrast in turn with the speaker's sense of poetic and loving confidence and fertile pleasure that come with gaining the hand of his beloved in a strong castle in a rich land. These interactions and ambiguities are captured in nebulous terms in love sonnets written within or without the walls of both an imagined and very real "brazen tower" with its "sacred bowre."

Technological Annotations and Performative Variations in Pedagogy

The power of VR can enliven, emphasize, and animate a text in many ways. For example, key words can be highlighted visually for quick reference in a glossary, or a pop-up text can be accompanied by audio or video recordings. Depending on the sophistication and memory of the machinery, animation can also be employed to emphasize any aspect of the text at hand. Concepts in the reading material can thereby be reified or personified in some way. For example, beginning with the first poem in the sequence, Spenser repeatedly calls attention to the pages on which the poems are written. These pages, like the wings of a cupid or "little love" figure, find their way to the eyes of the beloved (appropriately, *amoretti* means "little loves" in Italian, and can refer to diminutive love figures, including cupids or *putti*). Each sonnet sent to Elizabeth is, in this sense, a message from the speaker's heart delivered by Cupid. Using the digital model of Kilcolman and enough technical resources, VR could illustrate this connection with animated models for students to easily grasp. Pages could flutter and morph into Renaissance *putti* or present-day Valentine's Day cards or any sort of imaginative connection: perhaps even legal bills. This could in turn encourage students to find and forge their own visual connections with the poems, and students could simultaneously learn about the properties of figurative language, including metaphors, in this way.

Were the VR truly interactive and able to allow fresh content to be uploaded by students into it, then the entire castle model could be appropriated by the student/viewer and filled with additional text (including analyses), images, memes, links, or whatever; a student could work on such a project over the course of a semester and turn in a self-annotated version of the castle to the professor as an assignment. A regular viewer could have fun making a custom-decorated Kilcolman. Engineering or computer design students could in turn tinker with the fabric of the castle itself in ways that are genuinely investigative: how many stories did the castle actually have? (In the present-day ruin, four can barely be detected.) What kinds of rooms would you put into it? Where would you place the bedroom and why? What is the best kind of fortification for defense?[8]

A standard benefit of online learning is, of course, its audio capabilities. In the recreation of Spenser's bedroom on the Centering Spenser website, a copy of *Amoretti and Epithalamion* has been placed on the bed, which logically emphasizes the volume's (and the bed's) erotic function(s). In the prototype WondaVR tour based on the model, the viewer can enter the bedroom and activate a pop-up version of sonnet 65 and see the poem in its original typed setting (in a photograph from the 1595 edition) and/or in a modern transcription. Showing the poem in its original form can make it feel more tangible, exotic, and exciting for students, especially for those who cannot visit a research library's special collections to experience the real thing. The viewer can also hear a machine-generated spoken version of the poem to read along with (Fig. 3).[9] Eventually, the machine-read version in the current prototype may be replaced by a different, more human voice.[10] Similarly, interactive links could one day be made to other open-source recordings found on the web.

---

[8] Professor Edward Triplett currently teaches an art history course at Duke University, Medieval Castles of Europe, which involves just such digital castle-building by students; see his course catalog entry at aahvs.duke.edu/courses/medieval-castles-europe. For more ideas on the potential of VR for interactive student learning, see Craig and Georgieva 2017; and Evenson 2018.

[9] See the bedroom in the "Kilcolman Foundation Tour" at player.wondavr.com/p/ab8ebc52-bd03-445d-ae9c-851423ec1e5d#4th.

[10] See, for example, the audio recording of sonnet 75, read by Julian Lethbridge, on the Centering Spenser website: core.ecu.edu/umc/Munster/teaching-Amoretti-75.html. The sonnet is also inserted into the study in the "Kilcolman Foundation Tour": player.wondavr.com/p/ab8ebc52-bd03-445d-ae9c-851423ec1e5d#4s.

Figure 3. Pop-up version of *Amoretti* sonnet 65 in facsimile, as located in Spenser's bedroom in the prototype WondaVR castle "Kilcolman Foundation Tour." The viewer can hear a mechanized voice-over of the sonnet and can also activate the "Modern Text" function to read it in typed transcription instead. Image credit: Thomas Herron, Doug Barnum, and East Carolina University.

Moreover, any teacher or student can provide a basic yet essential way to appreciate any poem from multiple perspectives by reading the poem aloud in the classroom. Powerful VR programs like those on Oculus Rift or Quest can facilitate this activity by accommodating multiple interacting viewers at once. VR can copy the educational facets of Second Life (secondlife.com) and similar programs by fully replicating a classroom filled with teacher and student avatars. Student Susan could then hear student Xi read out the poem in real time, while both sit virtually in Spenser's hypothetical castle instead of on campus in front of a chalkboard. In another scenario, a teacher could lead a tour through the castle and wind upstairs to the more personal quarters of the tower before arriving at the sonnet by the bed. The teacher could then ask questions of the students about public versus private domestic spaces, love and/or sex, marital relations, and so on before pointing at the small volume on the bed and opening the sonnet in both original facsimile and transcription, so as to explore it *in situ* with the class. When discussion turns to the sonnet's concluding lines about "tower" and "bowre," the teacher could turn the class discussion to the larger colonial context of the sonnet before leading the students through other parts of the castle, like the armory, that provoke the same themes. In this way, poetic text and architecture speak intimately to one another as the class progresses from one castle space to another in a historical tour of their environs.

Infinite Riches in a Little Room

Thinking more broadly, the entire collection of *Amoretti and Epithalamion* is like a little room, or container, showcasing its *putti* or fluttering thoughts. By way of analogy, the virtual tower can be seen as a cabinet that needs to be opened to reveal the textual treasures inside of it. Students can be asked to make bold conceptual leaps between the architecture of a bound text and the rooms of a building, as both are navigated in a flexible narrative order. In this way, the students continue to conceive of the tower house in figurative terms, as (for example) akin to a sequence of texts.

Experiencing the tower house space in VR helps us understand how confined spaces are manipulated and/or enlivened by the creative imagination. Castle walls are usually heavy and closed in, but they provide egress to much wider vistas. So too the burdensome headset of a VR device. You can sit in a real castle bedroom and feel cramped, but once you start reading a sonnet there, larger worlds open up within the imaginative world of the poem and castle. The VR headset by comparison holds fantastic thoughts and visions within it: it is a confining piece of equipment but with a window to outside. A teacher can focus on just these analogies and metaphors of physical restriction and imaginative release. Yes, you may be uncomfortable reading in that space with a VR headset on, but you can move into a different room when you wish and find new spaces and objects there; then, you can climb yet higher onto the castle ramparts to see the landscape all around, which may remind you of Spenser's poetry on Irish rivers (for example). Perhaps, in a night scene, you could find animated above you the astral figures of a sixteenth-century horoscope. The sky is literally the limit in VR, and the possibilities for creative reconstruction of texts, places, and ideas are limitless.[11]

[11] I would like to thank Professors Jonathan Reid and Anne-Hélène Miller for their valuable insights on an earlier draft of this paper.

WORKS CITED

Brink, Jean R. 2019. *The Early Spenser, 1554–80: "Minde on honour fixed."* Manchester: Manchester University Press.

Craig, Emory, and Maya Georgieva. 2017. "VR and AR: Transforming Learning and Scholarship in the Humanities and Social Sciences." *EDUCAUSE Review*, 6 October 2017. er.educause.edu/blogs/2017/10/vr-and-ar-transforming-learning-and-scholarship-in-the-humanities-and-social-sciences.

Evenson, Kai. 2018. "Putting Immersive Technology to Work: Examples from the Digital Humanities." *EDUCAUSE Review*, 26 June 2018. educause.edu/blogs/2018/6/putting-immersive-technology-to-work-examples-from-the-digital-humanities.

Fleming, James. 2000. "A *View* from the Bridge: Ireland and Violence in Spenser's *Amoretti*." *Spenser Studies* 15 (1): 135–64. doi.org/10.1086/SPSv15p135.

Hadfield, Andrew. 2012. *Edmund Spenser: A Life*. Oxford: Oxford University Press.

Herron, Thomas. 2016. "New Technologies, Old Approaches: Material Culture, Digital Modeling, and Spenser's Texts." *Sixteenth Century Journal* 47, no. 4 (Winter): 987–93.

———. 2019. "Spenserian Ambitions at Kilcolman, Mallow, and Rycote: A Response to Tadhg O'Keeffe." *Spenser Review* 49, no. 2 (Spring–Summer). english.cam.ac.uk/spenseronline/review/item/49.2.4.

Lyttleton, James, and Thomas Herron. 2019. "Through the Virtual Keyhole." *Archaeology Ireland* 33, no. 1 (Spring): 30–34. jstor.org/stable/26844444.

Morgan, Hiram. 2021. "Preamble: Portions of a Manuscript History Related to Ireland." *CELT*. Last modified 1 February 2021. research.ucc.ie/celt/document/E590002.

O'Keeffe, Tadhg. 2018. "Home Truths about Raleigh and Spenser: Sir Thomas Norris and the Rebuilding of Mallow Castle." *Spenser Review* 48, no. 3 (Fall). english.cam.ac.uk/spenseronline/review/volume-48/483/home-truths-about-raleigh-and-spenser-sir-thomas-norris-and-the-rebuilding-of-mallow-castle-1/home-truths-about-raleigh-and-spenser-sir-thomas-norris-and-the-rebuilding-of-mallow-castle-1.

———. 2019. "Don't Worry, Be Happy: Reading Herron Reviewing O'Keeffe Making Spenser Envy Norris." *Spenser Review* 49, no. 2 (Spring–Summer 2019). english.cam.ac.uk/spenseronline/review/volume-49/492/dont-worry-be-happy-reading-herron-reviewing-okeeffe-making-spenser-envy-norris.

Spenser, Edmund. 1989. *Amoretti and Epithalamion*. In *The Yale Edition of the Shorter Works of Edmund Spenser*, edited by William Oram, Einar Bjorvand, Ronald Bond, Thomas H. Cain, Alexander Dunlop, and Richard Schell, 583–679. New Haven, CT: Yale University Press.

Chapter 15: Designing an Educational Video Game for Shakespeare's *Hamlet*

John Misak
New York Institute of Technology

Kevin LaGrandeur
Global AI Ethics Institute

Introduction

Our project, *Perchance*, uses the gaming medium to deliver the cultural and historical contexts of Shakespeare's *Hamlet* for introductory literature classes—especially classes for non-English majors. Having taught the play for decades, we sought a modernized modality to replace class-length lectures or passive video watching for this task. Game theory and high-impact practices guided our project, and student feedback helped shape the final product. We found *Hamlet* a perfect play to gamify as it contains elements of mystery, a genre common to video games nearly since their inception. It also helps that the play has dense contexts many students and professors find difficult for introductory literature classes. We discovered in creating a video game for learning purposes that we needed to find a balance between entertainment and learning outcomes. Players need a reason to continue to play, and classroom activities should provide a learning profit. In this chapter, we will outline our goals and the strategies we implemented to reach them. We will also highlight how the moving targets of student attention and evolving technologies changed our creative process several times. Game development on its own takes enormous effort and resources. Adding learning outcomes central to a game based on *Hamlet* complicates this further.

Because we started with no game development experience, we centered our efforts on creating something to impart the dense contexts of *Hamlet*, and then beta tested it with students for feedback.[1] Most of our polling centered on students' opinion of the value of using this technology for contextual background about the play instead of using traditional lectures, video clips, or summary sites before reading. By creating the application from this starting point, we overlooked the basic tenets of both game design and pedagogy. Both have requirements, and by seeking a balance between the two we

[1] Student polling was gathered anonymously and with the permission of the students involved.

ISBN 978-1-64959-119-7 (paper) ISBN 978-1-64959-120-3 (pdf) ISBN 978-1-64959-121-0 (epub)
New Technologies in Medieval and Renaissance Studies 12 (2025) 397–421

found, after testing, that we had given neither gaming nor pedagogy enough initial attention. Instead, the technology guided us. We suspect this happens often to beginner designers; indeed, overemphasis on flashy technology is a common lament about first-generation software on new game consoles.[2] Our initial prototypes interested both students and colleagues, so we understood we had a working concept. We only needed the proper balance of technological intervention.

Ultimately, we created a 3D model of Castle Elsinore (Fig. 1) where players can interact with characters from the play. In this way, our approach intersects with others in this volume, specifically Steven Bednarski et al.'s augmented reality (AR) recreation of Northeye in chapter 13. However, our implementation also incorporates mystery game elements that encourage student-players to investigate a key plot point: Hamlet's state of mind. Did Hamlet really encounter his father's ghost, or did his mental instability cause him to hallucinate the conversation? The game can be played in AR, virtual reality (VR), or a web browser in 3D. The player assumes the role of an actor in the traveling group that performs "The Mousetrap," the play that Hamlet puts on to try to trap Claudius into revealing his guilt. An opening text crawl informs players of the King's death and Claudius's assumption of power. The user, in the third-person role of one of the traveling players, navigates the castle grounds and talks to characters to gain information regarding the circumstances at Elsinore. The user thus witnesses the meeting between Hamlet and the ghost both in-game and through cinematic video clips. Afterward, players answer questions regarding their findings, helping them to work through their observations on Hamlet's state of mind.

The actual gameplay includes interactions with non-player characters (NPCs), who provide clues and direction for the user. These interactions include dialogue options that can affect NPC reactions. Players navigate using a keyboard and mouse or game controller for computers and their mobile device for the mobile version of the game. Players interact with NPCs in the hopes of uncovering the mystery surrounding King Hamlet's death while gauging the actions of these characters, Hamlet included. This sets up a dynamic wherein students play the game and, at the same time, come to conclusions regarding key tenets of the play. Much like Thomas Herron's

---

[2] "Launch titles," games that release at the same time as a new game console, often focus on the graphic capabilities of the console. This leaves fewer resources for sophisticated gameplay. Launch titles serve to showcase the improved graphics technology of the console and little else.

contribution to this volume in chapter 14, we hope that by immersing students in a recreation of Shakespeare's work they can "better appreciate that work and the world that produced it" (381).

Figure 1. An aerial view of the courtyard of *Perchance*'s representation of Castle Elsinore.

Gamifying Shakespeare's Masterpiece

Why *Hamlet*?

Informal research informed us that many college English professors assign *Hamlet*. Though different instructors do so for varying reasons, one key attraction is the ease with which students empathize with the main character. When introduced properly to the play, many students can relate to Hamlet's struggles with his sense of identity and the pain he experiences at his father's death. If given a more direct pathway to Hamlet's plight, students may grasp the play's greater contexts. That pathway may be paved with technology. In *Hamlet on the Holodeck*, Janet Murray (1997) prophesied *Hamlet*'s move into the digital age when she called for the use of more digital technologies for such a play. We sought much of what Murray proposed, specifically a more active and accessible form of literary representation. Though her predictions focus on "future" tech from decades ago, Murray's book did provide us with much of the theoretical and pedagogical framework we needed to build a game based on *Hamlet*.

We took direction from Murray and some later projects that attempted to realize Murray's prediction. Such projects include *Play the Knave* (playtheknave.org); *Hamlet 360: Thy Father's Spirit*, a performance and set design–based mixed reality game (see GBH 2019); and, notably, a recently released adventure game, *Elsinore* by Golden Glitch (goldenglitch.itch.io/elsinore). The latter brings *Hamlet* into the video game medium and provides players with *Hamlet*-based context, specifically focusing on Ophelia, who in the game has the ability to prevent the deaths of the characters in the play. The plot of *Hamlet* exists in *Elsinore*, but it serves as more of a backdrop and thus provides an alternate-reality experience. Our game, *Perchance*, focuses more on teaching the elements of the play, couched in its historical and cultural contexts, with an eye on learning outcomes for an introductory English literature course. In a sense, our approach melds the ambitions of *My Father's Spirit*, the performative aspects of *Play the Knave*, and *Elsinore*'s adventure game elements by attempting to "teach" *Hamlet* through the incorporation of cutting-edge AR technology, faithful representation, and the inclusion of an entertaining video game element. In this sense, our project breaks new ground with this combination of accessibility, technology, and learning.

Many have attempted to heed Murray's call and modernize Shakespeare's play, and with wide-ranging levels of success. Few, however, have involved a microlearning transaction, the imparting of a specific learning outcome, through the medium of video games. The companion to Kenneth Branaugh's *Hamlet* release, *Hamlet: A Murder Mystery*, did incorporate similar elements, albeit with mixed results due to the time of its release in 1997, when video games were not yet considered a serious storytelling medium. That game also changes the narrative of *Hamlet*, something we wanted to avoid in order to achieve our learning outcomes, which had to do specifically with the narrative of the play. Other games have been loosely based on the play, but our goal remains gamification rather than creating a game derived from the plot of *Hamlet*. Gamification refers to the practice of applying game elements or functionalities such as points, rewards, tasks, challenges, goals, or immediate feedback for learning purposes. It aims at fostering playful and gameful attitudes, which are considered beneficial for learning (Lämsä et al. 2018). As Koskimaa and Fenyvesi (2015) note, games "have the potential to enhance [student] engagement with literacy . . . foster skill reinforcement and empower learners' perceptions of their reading progress" (quoted in Lämsä et al. 2018, 596).

Hugh Richmond's (2015) comparison of *Hamlet* to a mystery suggests a successful path to creating games. Mysteries gained early success in video games with *Suspect*, *Deadline*, and some early Sherlock Holmes titles. All-time bestseller lists include classics such as *Myst*, *The 7th Guest*, and the Tex Murphy series. And the genre has continued with more recent successes including *Firewatch*, the *Batman: Arkham* series, *Disco Elysium*, and *The Outer Wilds*. Several other bestselling games incorporate mystery elements (e.g., *Grand Theft Auto*), indicating significant player interest. Since the vast majority of college-aged Americans play video games, we considered the application of gaming to *Hamlet* a perfect vehicle through which to deliver our desired learning outcomes and to engage students with familiar technology. Utilizing the mystery elements of *Hamlet* helps create a pathway to video games and, subsequently, to student interest. With *Perchance*, we hoped to transform the often dull lecture or unengaging video about the play's contexts into a high-impact, interactive classroom experience.

A number of studies illustrate the effectiveness of video games on learning (Chian et al. 2011; Clark, Tanner-Smith, and Killingsworth 2016; Crocco, Offenholley, and Hernandez 2016; Yang, Chen, and Jeng 2010). Also, students have a positive attitude toward using games for educational purposes (Prensky 2006). Such research bolstered our notion that, rather than a passive interaction with a written text, lecture, or learning resources, students would benefit by actively participating within *Hamlet*'s environs to elicit comprehension of the greater contexts at play. The game informs students about history and culture through *doing* rather than *telling*, as a video or lecture might. The game medium also allows for a more personal experience, enabling each student to feel as though they came to an understanding via their own actions and pace. Steinkuehler (2010, 61) notes that "games are narrative spaces that the player inscribes with his or her own intent"; by playing *Perchance*, students have the opportunity to temporarily make their mark on *Hamlet* through their actions within the game. The game creates a personal experience that falls between attending and acting in a play, creating a stronger bond than watching a video or reading for homework.

Choosing a Scene

We wanted to provide students with an entrance to *Hamlet* and its plot through a recognizable medium. We did not seek to replace reading; we wanted to enhance it. The game should not provide students with everything they need to understand the play. It should instead encourage them to investigate further after making individual decisions on small, key elements of the plot. We also didn't want *Perchance* to alter the events in *Hamlet*. Though we desire a personal experience of the play that students will better recall, the plot must remain untouched so that we are still teaching *Hamlet* and not something else; changes for gaming purposes to the structure of *Hamlet*'s plot could prevent a clear understanding of the play. Any instructor who shows the Laurence Olivier or Mel Gibson movie versions to an introductory class understands the confusion that can result from a performance that differs from the original text.

Another concern involved action. A game that was merely a walk-through of the historical and cultural background of the play would serve merely as a kind of digital diorama. Earlier versions of our application enacted this kind of passive discovery, and after tepid student reactions, we decided we wanted more high-impact activity. Games succeed when players find reason to continue to play and when they exit with a sense of accomplishment. Exploration of the culture and history behind Shakespeare's Elsinore might entertain a scholar, but it was too esoteric for our students and thus did not serve our purpose. Students we surveyed indicated an acceptance of playing a game for learning purposes; however, they also stressed *play* in this sentiment. Many students made comments such as, "It's interesting, but the game should include decision-based action." This led us to consideration of scenes that might help to make the game more active. *Hamlet* contains several turning points requiring an understanding of the cultural and historical contexts behind them. A student may easily spot the antiquated treatment of Ophelia yet miss the importance of her compliance in duping Hamlet. Though her "betrayal" of Hamlet in act 3, scene 1 is pivotal, we sought something earlier that students did not need plot background to understand. We sought an introductory moment where players could make decisions while gaining insight into later events in the play. The ghost scene at the ramparts, act 1, scenes 4 and 5, looked promising for that purpose.

To the casual observer, the scene reveals a melancholy son witnessing an apparition along with a friend and guards. The presence of others and their belief that they have seen something supernatural support Hamlet's belief that the ghost is his father. Like all scenes in the play, the reader must peel back several layers of context to ascertain a clearer meaning. The reader's choice of whether Hamlet sees the true ghost of his father or hallucinates their interaction colors their interpretation of the entire play. Therefore, having students decide on this before reading provides them with a firmer understanding of ancillary elements that can guide them throughout the reading. If they feel that they "know" Hamlet's mind,[3] they will feel more confident reading and attempting interpretations of later scenes. As Eithne Kennedy (2018, 716) states, "Students' motivation, engagement and self-confidence also exert a powerful influence on academic achievement."

Hamlet's meeting with his father illuminates his struggle within. He expresses doubts about his mother's remarriage, and questions arise regarding the state of the country. The ghost forces Hamlet to zero in on these issues. He can no longer merely suspect treachery; he must contemplate direct action. Students may see an unequivocal need for Hamlet to act and yet, after they play *Perchance*, come to understand the source of his hesitation because they have actually experienced the early modern cultural context of this situation—that is, they have experienced Hamlet's encounter with the ghost, which claims to be his father and demands that Hamlet avenge his death; yet, the uncertainty about whether the ghost is actually his father or a demon or an hallucination means that, in an early modern Christian context, Hamlet could face damnation for murder. If he does not kill Claudius, on the other hand, he will, according to the mores of the time, be derelict in his filial duty and suffer the torture of knowing that. Students can experience this conundrum vicariously in the action of the game.

Understanding these concepts can inform key aspects of students' interpretative attempts later in the play. Experiencing Hamlet's struggle after the initial encounter at the ramparts helps students comprehend the tension within both Hamlet and Denmark. Hamlet's later commentary about his home as a prison makes more sense when the reader knows Hamlet faces two poor options for his future: one where he follows cultural expectations and kills his uncle, and another where he suffers madness among a tortured populace run by an incestuous royal family. What initially may appear as simple cowardice or overthinking becomes a more complex matrix of feelings and reactions rooted in a concrete early modern context. These contexts can be conveyed through gameplay with students acting in the "fly on the wall" role at the ramparts (Fig. 2).

---

[3] We say this in the sense that students believe they understand Hamlet's thinking. We acknowledge the complexity of such an understanding and do not mean to dismiss the long history of literary criticism arguing this. Giving students confidence by encouraging decisions, even if they are at first an over-simplification, can improve self-confidence and motivate students to read what many consider an extremely difficult text.

Figure 2. The ramparts scene rendered in the Unity game engine, depicting character models for Hamlet, Marcellus, Bernardo, and Horatio.

Another reason we chose to build our game around the ramparts scene in act 1 is because we wanted to economize the time necessary to impart the contexts of *Hamlet*. There is only so much time in a class period, so we allotted 15 minutes for gameplay within the classroom. With little time for setup, we found the ramparts scene fit, since users can jump into the play's environment and start their quest.

Creating a Learning Experience

Our gamification project also afforded an opportunity to consider how we wanted students to experience Elsinore. Unlike most literary texts, plays have a dual existence: they are both written and visual experiences. Normally, students have the option of reading or watching *Hamlet*. *Perchance* enables an experience where students interact with literature-based visual stimuli, thus creating an intersection of visual experience and textual imagination. *Perchance* enables an experience where players see and interact with the characters in *Hamlet*, which provides the users with information to impart better context to our chosen scene. Actors in a play have this interactive experience too, but the virtual interface we use has added dimensions. The virtual user chooses what they see and when, and this interaction stimulates memory differently than only reading or viewing. As Clemenson and Stark (2015, 16116) have found, 3D video games with rich environments "improve hippocampal function and performance on hippocampally mediated memory tasks." Thus, they go on to say, "the exploration of vast and visually stimulating environments within modern-day video games can act as a human correlate of environmental enrichment." Accordingly, we liked the possibilities for memory retention with gaming, and we hoped to use this modality to increase the chance of students retaining material. That is, we hoped to capitalize on the fact that these neurologists found that game players remember major moments in video games differently than a film viewer does, because video games stimulate the hippocampus in a way that situates players within the environment.

Much like other previous attempts at a *Hamlet*-based game, we considered whether we wanted a game couched specifically within the context of the play or inspired by it. We chose the former because we desired a learning experience about the play first and foremost. Our design presents the setting of *Hamlet* to students in a 3D video game environment for learning purposes. Therefore, the setting becomes central for learning. Through several iterations, we created and abandoned different versions of Castle Elsinore and its grounds. Because of technical concerns we will discuss later, we also had to find a balance between graphic fidelity and resource considerations. A photorealistic version of the castle looked impressive, but its realism stood out against the game engine's lower-resolution graphics. Other castles looked dated by comparison, something students were quick to point out in the feedback (Fig. 3).[4] We settled on a fabrication of the castle and grounds using one game engine so that all elements looked coordinated. This version had enough graphic fidelity to appear realistic, thus increasing the chances for the "visually stimulating environments" that Clemenson and Stark mention and thus the hippocampal stimulation and greater memory retention. We imported 3D models of major characters to increase realism and graphic flow between the setting and the people. We did so to minimize distraction; students should feel a seamlessness within the environment, thus creating a sense of suspended disbelief, so that they can achieve learning outcomes.

---

[4] Students' comments included "Great game but graphics look old" and "Graphics too choppy." Nearly half of the negative feedback on the first versions of *Perchance* focused on the quality of the graphics.

Figure 3. An early, low-resolution representation of Castle Elsinore we created in SketchUp.

The Role of the Player/Why Gamify?

Nearly all games studies arguments begin with James Paul Gee's statements on gaming and literacy because they create a framework from which to build. Notably, Gee (2007) states that players often dive into games and learn afterward, without referring to the manual. This is the reverse of the learning environment where educators often ask students to read a text before grounding them in the literary environment. Having literature students play *Perchance* before reading aligns better with players' and students' preferred learning acquisition methods. Since his study, video games have become considered less of a distraction or detraction from learning and more of a contribution to it. They have gained acceptance within learning environments.

In keeping with Gee's definitions of discourse/Discourse, we seek to enable students to decode the contexts and Discourse of Shakespeare's *Hamlet* through the discourse of video games. Gee separates *discourse* and *Discourse* through two definitions: *discourse* is any "stretches of language" (spoken, written, signed) that "hang together" to make sense to some community of people who use that language. As he writes, "Making sense is always a social and variable matter: what makes sense to one community of people may not make sense to another" (Gee 1990, 103). On the other hand, *Discourse* can be "a socially accepted association among ways of using language, of thinking, feeling, believing, valuing, and of acting that can be used to identify oneself as a member of a socially meaningful group or 'social network,' or to signal that one is playing a socially meaningful role" (Gee 1990, 143). A key method to understanding a new Discourse is demystifying it, and we hope the familiarity students have with video game codes can serve as a gateway to *Hamlet* through gameplay. Familiarity with a concept or skill increases the chance of transfer across curricula (Brent 2012). Game-based learning (GBL) helps students achieve learning outcomes coded into a game through a student-centered activity suited for modern classrooms.

To be sure, "transfer" of decoding does not happen automatically. Additionally, merely creating a game for learning purposes will not guarantee student engagement nor success in achieving learning outcomes. For GBL to be effective, the designer of a learning game must seek cues from two sources: the action/entertainment/purpose elements that deem a traditional video game a success or failure, and the pedagogical framework that gauges student acquisition of desired skills and learning outcomes. We must design a game that sustains player interest and provides a clear pathway to the achievement of the game's goals. Since this is a student-centered activity, we want players to follow the purpose of the game and not need much guidance from an instructor. Educational games often fail to engage students as a result of poor design (Lämsä et al. 2018). *Hamlet*-based games often try to either recreate productions of the play or attempt to capture certain elements of it and break the narrative. Ours seeks to provide ancillary information and stimulate cognitive decisions on the part of the student-player. In addition, games must involve a significant amount of discovery activity inspired by design-level instigation of curiosity. Designers need to leave a trail of crumbs for players to follow, but players must understand the importance of moving forward and must want to go in the right direction. Educational games, especially, must adhere more to this design principle because students do not specifically choose to play them out of genuine interest; such interest is created through the game's design.

In contrast, an educational game designed solely to be a good game, without emphasis on course level outcomes (CLOs), offers little for a literature classroom because students would not achieve significant learning applicable to the play. Any game centered on narrative elements may have some merit, but in our case, we also wanted to impart the cultural and historical contexts of Shakespeare's Elsinore. For gaming purposes, though, this all needs to be done subtly so as not to draw too much attention to the educational aspects of the game, because we don't want to kill the very sense of fun that helps motivate students to engage with it in the first place. Doing so would mimic the theatrical production-style games (e.g., *Hamlet: A Murder Mystery*) that merely recreate the play as a passively absorbed artifact with limited interactivity. Our design concept keeps with most gaming and learning research in identifying the entertainment elements as primary, using play to teach rather than hoping that an educational game also has ludic value.

One such way to ensure the success of CLOs involves the incorporation of pauses at significant learning moments. This sort of implementation has existed in games nearly since their inception. Even modern, non-educational games, such as *Red Dead Redemption*, give players moments devoid of plot-progressing action. The series' new release, *Red Dead Redemption 2*, provides campsite scenes where players can sit and interact with NPCs without impact on game progression. These areas allow for character exploration and relationship building and help players better understand the game's world and populace. This affords players a chance to understand why they care about the cause of the game and thereby encourages a sense of purpose. Pauses answer the "why" of plot progression. Our game will similarly slow down or pause completely for student reflection, albeit on a smaller scale, since our game finishes in a fraction of the time. When Hamlet meets the ghost on the ramparts, students must come to important conclusions that can serve as catalysts for play-specific learning. Without prompts pushing them forward in the game, students can process what they experience at their own pace. This kind of reflection allows students to make contextual decisions and increases the probability of learning outcome success.

The Traveling Actor

Student-players will assume the role of an actor in the traveling troupe hired by the king and guided by Hamlet. The game begins with the player entering the castle courtyard and interacting with NPCs in the form of guards and the royal family. Similar to how the film *Rosencrantz and Guildenstern Are Dead* enables further exploration of *Hamlet*'s plot without directly impacting it,[5] having students take on the role of a member of the acting troupe allows them to

---

[5] This film follows two minor characters from *Hamlet* within the same plot timeline of the original play, providing viewers a glimpse at what they *may have* not seen going on in *Hamlet*. It tells a different story about many elements of *Hamlet* without altering the play itself (see Stoppard 1990).

gain a new perspective of the larger play without altering its intrinsic action. In other words, the game does not allow intentional or accidental tampering with *Hamlet*'s plot, and yet at the same time it allows the creation of a near open-world experience. The student-players control how they experience the castle and its grounds and have some freedom in terms of the order in which they encounter characters and areas. This interactive freedom helps facilitate memory retention through the gameplay mechanism's hippocampal stimulation, as discussed earlier.

Having students assume this role helps create a sense of immersion and connection to the play since there are actors in *Hamlet*'s cast. We considered several other options, ranging from the game player taking on the role of a major character to the users acting as themselves "time-traveling" back to the early modern era. Our ultimate choice made design decisions less complicated. The traveling actors in *Hamlet* have a presence in the play but no real identity that might impact it. Student perspectives on the characters and the play remain intact as they transfer from the game to the text. The character of the actor in Hamlet's meta-drama also offers endless choices for student personalization (see Figure 4), as movie versions depict the actors diversely. Students assume the role of a common person, which helps them identify with the player-character more readily than if they controlled Hamlet or another notable major player. It also freed us to allow greater exploration since the player is not limited by the plot within our chosen scene.

Creating a Sense of Purpose

Much of video games' classroom benefits come from their ability to hold players' attention. They achieve this through constant calls to action that encourage the player to move forward in the game. Something similar exists in course- and department-level pedagogy. As teachers, we do not merely want students' eyes to gloss over text; we want their curiosity piqued to get them to investigate and move forward in the work. Similarly, game players do not continue a game that does not provide an impetus. We hoped to inspire the desire to move forward with investigative curiosity instilled by both the literary and gaming elements of *Perchance*. *Hamlet*'s mystery-like plot helps set an investigative tone. We needed to create a sense of urgency within the narrative elements of the game.

We can leverage the entertainment element of games, a distinct advantage over videos or lectures. The purpose of *Perchance* is to increase access to the enjoyment and analysis of early modern literature for students who may feel denied entry. Once inside, we want to foster a sense of literary curiosity that will lead to future engagement with similar literature. We designed *Perchance* to inspire students to question character motivations, plot twists, and setting choices. Games like *Civilization* and *The Elder Scrolls* series piqued our interest in history and early modern settings. Both games succeeded in pushing players to continue, turn after turn, while imparting historical facts and/or providing players with a sense of place in a historical time. We wanted to provide the same for today's students of *Hamlet*. Through interaction with *Perchance*, students may desire a better understanding of the characters or historical elements within *Hamlet*. The hippocampal stimulation video games provide can elicit concrete memories of our 3D modeled Elsinore. By having students take on the role of an actor in a virtual world so that they might experience some feeling of mystery and active involvement (Fig. 4), we hoped to inspire curiosity in the seemingly small but contextually dense significance of the scene on the ramparts.

Figure 4. Four different character models (in different poses) we used in the game. Choosing character models for a realistic depiction of the play helps students feel connected to the game.

The Pedagogy of Playing a Play to Learn

In creating this game, we found ourselves re-engaging with the pedagogy of teaching literature. We realized the need to incorporate learning outcomes in the game. However, when viewed through the game designer lens, it became apparent we needed to drill down to a more granular level and find the basic elements of these outcomes. While our desired learning outcome of "learning historical and/or cultural contexts" makes sense on a broader level, it does not translate well into game design. A game cannot expect a successful delivery of learning outcomes through the mere presentation of graphics and audio of the literary work. Such design would suffer the same failures as the methods we seek to improve upon. Therefore, we realized more specific outcomes would assist in delivery. Inviting students to play a video game to discover the cultural context of Hamlet's obligation as a son, or of the historical context of a dead king walking the country in battle armor represents outcomes better suited for gaming. We also wanted to avoid the "broccoli and chocolate" approach to learning games design where the learning outcomes do not match the game structure (Kellinger 2017). Students should learn through play that mimics the ultimate task. For us that means interaction with literature. Therefore, we wanted to structure a game where students investigate the game similarly to how we want them to investigate the text. *Perchance* aims to develop critical thinking about *Hamlet* that translates to reading.

We sought a technological intervention to increase access to dense texts and also realized we could modernize learning in the process. College students (especially non-English majors) think texts like *Hamlet* are too difficult to learn, and according to a report of the Higher Education Academy, their professors agree (Thew 2006). This clearly indicates a problem. Modern learning focuses on students' desire to learn through problem-solving (Kellinger 2017). However, students may not necessarily view their self-perceived deficiencies in understanding literature as a problem. In *Perchance*, we present key elements of *Hamlet*'s plot and characterization as a problem students must navigate. Ultimately, we see the presentation of story through interactive games meeting students at their interest points better than more traditional methods of imparting contexts.

Design Questions

A Brief History: From Augmented to Virtual Reality and Back Again

We first envisioned an AR application to illustrate the Globe Theatre and Old London to provide visual context of the time. This proved illogical for classroom implementation since it catered more to Shakespeare scholars than students new to the playwright. We then transitioned to VR and a replication of Castle Elsinore for students to explore. AR uses a device to superimpose a 3D model on the real world, enabling a player to "walk through" a model of Castle Elsinore on their living room floor. VR involves a wearable headset so that the player feels immersed in a completely fabricated alternate reality: navigating through the castle as if actually there, for instance. Both AR and VR have high memory retention rates (Cho 2018; Radu 2014), which suited our learning outcomes. Players could interact with objects and characters and witness the appearance of the ghost in act 1, scene 5. The cultural contexts of the ghost and its armor along with the implied call to action for Hamlet suited our goals; however, we found VR tricky to implement in a classroom. The cost of VR headsets proved prohibitive, and the time required to have all students participate negated our initial intent of saving class time.[6] Thus, we found ourselves looking for a better technology and reverted back to AR since it had a strong educational track record (Di Serio, Ibánez, and Delgado Kloos 2013; Radu 2014).

We developed our first working prototype in SketchUp and exported into Kubity AR. It included a detailed model of Castle Elsinore and several characters from the play. Students could interact with our app on mobile devices or computers (without the AR element in the latter case). They superimposed the castle onto the classroom floor and navigated through it or used the computer mouse and keyboard. Initial responses of our student beta testers applauded the interactivity but complained of battery drain. We found AR used tremendous power and processing resources, especially on smartphones, and for this reason many students suggested we implement it sparingly. Students also questioned the purpose of playing with our app. We hadn't thought of interaction with the app as play before this. We created a digital diorama, and we thought exploration within the environment would impart

[6] In other research, we noted it takes roughly 30 minutes for a student to put on a headset, orient themselves, and engage with a learning experience. This means six or more hours for a class of 25 with two headsets. This could be streamlined or mitigated with more headsets, but the cost of over $300 per headset is prohibitive.

the contexts we wanted to convey. We also noted students engaging with the 3D game elements more than with the AR, akin to a child playing with the box a toy came in rather than the toy itself.

This discovery that users expected gameplay encouraged us to gamify our presentation of *Hamlet*. Via the beta testing we had come to understand the importance of purpose—again, a tenet of both game design and teaching pedagogy—and saw how we could keep student interest through the incorporation of game elements to inspire them to move forward. Having recovered from technology intoxication, we scaled back our design to create a mystery game based on the events in the first act of the play. Richmond (2015) says *Hamlet* most closely resembles the plot of a mystery novel. We therefore shaped our design using mystery game elements that we thought would pique player interest. Familiar with the Royal Shakespeare Company's mid-2000's manifesto,[7] we realized having students perform through the act of gameplay suited the RSA's call. Gameplay as performance inspires students to physically interact with drama in ways that the text and videos cannot. Games, although often social, enable shy students to experience this performative interaction with drama without having to perform on stage themselves.

We both previously incorporated games in our classes and found the vast majority of students were not only familiar with them, but that they also enjoyed them. Nearly 90 percent of student-aged Americans play video games. A slightly higher percentage own a smartphone (Anderson and Jingjing 2018). Thus, we reshaped our project into a mobile game accessible on as many devices as possible. We did this with the use of a game design program, Unity (unity.com), which can create games for Windows, Mac, iPhone, and Android devices (Fig. 5). Current educational practices focus on *doing*, on "active learning." Games employ this strategy, and *Perchance* creates active learning of cultural and historical contexts. We iterated from an interactive but passive presentation of Castle Elsinore to a student-oriented game that immerses players in the medieval atmosphere of *Hamlet*. Student polling came from both our classes (seven sections of introductory and advanced literature courses and other writing courses) and two events held on campus to gauge student interest and gather feedback.

---

[7] The Royal Shakespeare Company's "Stand Up for Shakespeare" encourages students to perform elements of Shakespeare's plays in the classroom for more engagement. Game play and AR also gets students out of their seats but does not require them to perform in front of their peers, a certain cause for concern for shy students.

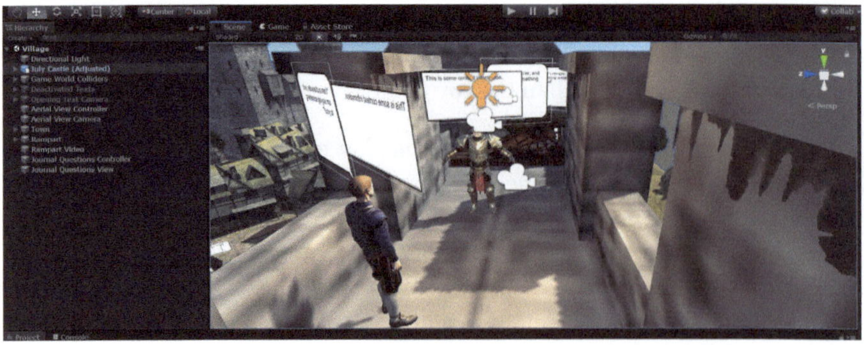

Figure 5. Coding the ramparts scene in the Unity game design software with dialogue bubbles.

Other Technological Considerations

Through our research and beta testing of early game iterations, we discovered a paradox between student engagement and technology, specifically AR. As stated earlier, we experimented with a full AR experience, noting research showed an increased level of retention with this technology (Radu 2014). However, students who tested this version complained of battery drain. Some showed a reluctance to download a school application on their personal device, preferring to use the desktop computers in our lab instead. This initially surprised us, but further polling revealed a distinct tendency for students to be protective of their mobile devices. Students clearly preferred separation between their personal mobile devices and their schoolwork. The battery issue stemmed from the intensive third-party application we used, although students indicated they experienced similar problems with AR-based games like *Pokémon GO* and said they often turned off the AR features to save the battery.

We still saw value in using AR to make an interactive experience and for its memory retention potential. Having weaned ourselves off the "wow" factor of this technology, we sought one short moment within our game to incorporate AR for maximum impact. It didn't take long to pinpoint the depiction of the ghost Hamlet meets on the ramparts for this purpose. This moment provides two key opportunities. First, we can have students to enter into AR (if they want) and explore the armor closely. This allows them to discover specifics about the armor and the very context we seek to impart. The ghost and its armor also serve as a moment of reflection, allowing students to process the information provided. Using AR at this point enables a slowdown of the game because the technology impresses users enough to hold their attention. Students engage with the ghost to explore the technology and realize the message behind the armor. More effective than viewing a film or even seeing the ghost during normal gameplay, the AR element zooms in on the armor and its portent of war for Denmark.

Accessibility

Technology in learning provides students with familiar tools to tackle unfamiliar tasks. At issue is the availability of technologies for learners. We teach at a technical university that provides significant technological resources for students, yet we understand that tech access varies at different institutions. Though over 90 percent of college-aged Americans have a mobile device or computer, we cannot assume all potential users of our game have access to such technology; therefore, we designed our application so that it can be accessed by as many devices as possible at the same time through a simple web browser. Feedback about our initial builds focusing on VR helped lead us away from higher resource requirements, and as we edited further, we simplified more. Much like *Hamlet* confuses new readers with complicated relationships and language, an application or game with high technological requirements could prevent potential users from ever experiencing our design.

Perchance comes with several options to enable the greatest possible compatibility. By using the Unity game engine, we can export into several different formats. Though currently only available for PCs and iOS, we can modify our game for play on Android devices, game consoles, and Macs. The AR elements currently work with PCs and mobile devices. Moreover, a fortunate consequence of cutting back AR elements is the increased accessibility for vision-impaired users. Other parts of the game can utilize screen readers and other accessibility tools. This is more difficult with AR. Thus, our revamped approach resulted in a more accessible design.

Melding the Literary with Gaming

When first-year composition students see *Hamlet*, or even Shakespeare, on a syllabus, they see this monolith towering over the text and often feel overwhelmed. This problem creates another guard standing before the gateway to experiencing such literature. The game environment changes this, creating what psychologist Erik Erickson calls "a learning space in which the learner can take risks where real-world consequences are lowered" (quoted in Gee, 2007, 59). By moving the entry point for appreciating *Hamlet* from a stodgy historical lineage students may not understand to the familiar medium of gaming, we hope the easier access games provide will help students cross the threshold into literary analysis they may otherwise avoid. As Steinkuehler (2010, 63) has noted, "Because [video games] are an area of passionate interest for many young [people], they are one place where you can see what they are truly capable of." This governs our design principle stated earlier; we immerse students in a free-movement game environment and allow them to carry out our coded possibilities in the order of their choosing. Our introductory literature course aims for students to achieve the primary learning outcome of "the analysis of visual media, print and electronic texts." Since the course also expects students to "synthesize coherent responses to diverse narrative perspectives," our game design provides a shift in perspective while preserving the plot and helping student-players achieve the primary learning outcome of literary analysis across different mediums.

Figure 6. The castle courtyard where players will interact with characters and investigate the mystery behind *Hamlet*.

Another design concern involves student sentiment. Students may push back against a game that announces its primary purpose as learning. Gaming narrative and the meta-narrative that arises around gameplay should play a central role in allaying this. Most games have narrative elements, and even those that don't create a sense of narrative in the community of players. Message boards light up with discussions of the history of a game series like *Mortal Kombat*, which had little of its own narrative clearly explained. Though a story existed in the first game, players created their own narratives through arcade community discourse. Our design attempts to encourage student-players to express their reactions to the game with peers, fulfilling another course learning outcome centered on collaboration. The narrative of our game comes from its source material, but we expect students will share perspectives and formulate their own views based on the game through peer interaction.

Presenting *Hamlet* as a game and focusing on the elements that cater to game design, we can attract the attention of students and bring them closer to understanding texts they often mystify. Using their existing game narrative experience and their consequent understanding of the relationship between narrative and play, students can explore *Perchance* and succeed in analyzing the play's narrative across mediums and synthesizing responses to different narrative perspectives. The added element of peer discourse and collaboration, something inherent in games, helps foster an environment where achieving course learning outcomes becomes more likely.

Literature courses encourage students to read from an investigative perspective. This can only be achieved through curiosity, which can often be dampened by the prospect of a play like *Hamlet* because of its perceived difficult language and the density of its contexts. By incorporating the freer atmosphere around gaming, we can sidestep this negative perception of Shakespeare's *Hamlet* and immerse students in its environment before their instinctive barriers engage. Students can witness the characterization of key players through interactive dialogue. They see Hamlet's reaction to his father's ghost and the guards' edginess throughout the opening of the play, and they come to understand the relationship between these two things. Games enable an active narrative workspace for students to intuit literary meaning (Steinkuehler 2010). Our implementation leverages these workspaces for literary analysis of Shakespeare, granting access that some students may not instinctively experience.

Conclusion: Current Design Status/Moving Forward

Of primary importance in this design is student experience. We must focus on meeting students at their entry points. Since our target audience is first-year college students, we have designed our game around what they know and need to discover in order to better experience dense literature like *Hamlet*. This game should encourage students to investigate the text to validate their newly formed perspective on Hamlet's mental state or the existence of the ghost. Our game seeks to invest students in the experience through decisions made in-game and thus create enough curiosity to seek answers in the play. Our first designs came solely from our experience and perceptions of student attitudes toward Shakespeare. Though informative, our early iterations could not hold the interest of students because they created no call to action. We packed the application with information and technology without enough consideration for how the two blended together. The program suffered from the same problems we sought to alleviate in the text, namely, density and confusion.

Through extensive testing and student feedback, we landed on a more concrete model that included gamifying the experience. This created an interactive element that holds student attention long enough to impart the contexts our learning goals outline. We must continue to consider the student experience as we shape our design toward a final product. One such method is the creation of a Twine (twinery.org) experience based on our Unity game design (Fig. 7). This branch of our project enables an automatic storyboard of actions and consequences and clearly indicates where player choice exists. Students can interact with this spinoff of our design and point us toward better decisions as we edit the game. Changing scenes and decisions in Twine takes mere minutes compared to hours of coding for Unity. We can perform the edits ourselves in Twine, removing the need for a coder and the costs of hiring one. Students from all majors can assist in these edits, as Twine uses a simple engine. In essence, we made a game about a game about *Hamlet* so students and peers can provide feedback more readily. It also enables direct interaction with students who contribute to the code.

One gamification element we have explored and intend to implement is a reward system. Many gamified learning studies center on reward systems as a primary game element. A review of 15 studies illustrates how digital badges, leaderboards, and points systems are the most common and successful gamification element for learning. Our goal will be to base the reward system on our learning outcomes, providing students with a mastery path for learning expected in the course.

The feedback from Twine and our Unity game build will inform our final design. Having uncovered unexpected pushback from AR implementation and use of personal devices for learning, we continue to develop a game that takes advantage of AR and mobile technologies but does not require all students to buy into them. Our build works with PCs and Macs, and the Twine game can be accessed from a web browser on any device. We originally set out to create a technologically groundbreaking application to teach *Hamlet*. Now we realize the ground we need to break exists in the delivery of dense contexts with the simplest gaming medium that engages students.

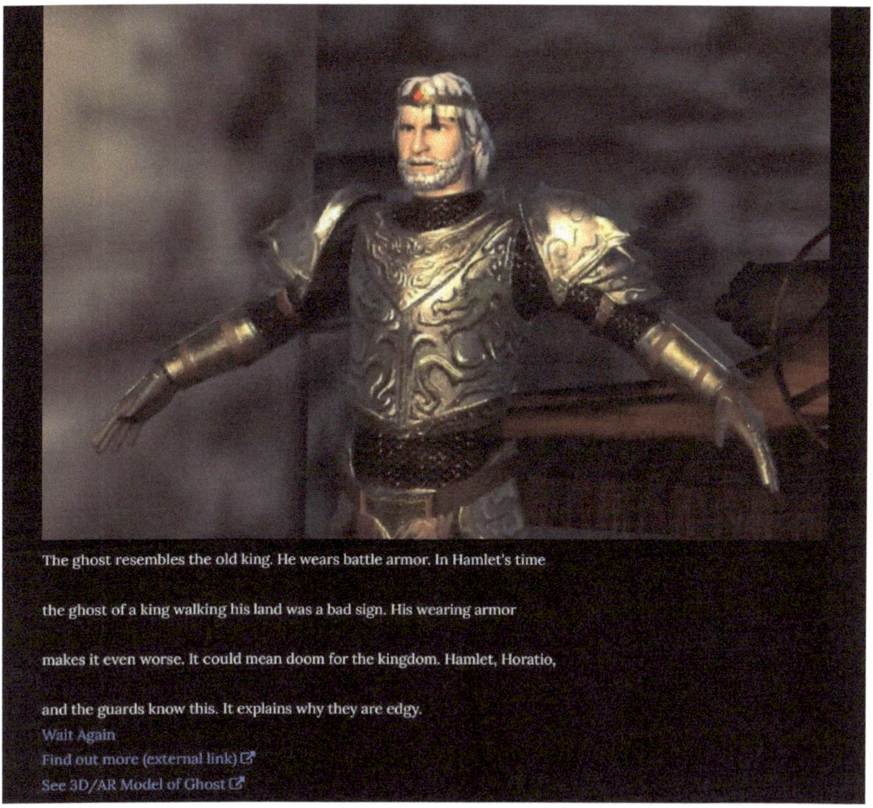

Figure 7. The appearance of the ghost in the Twine game engine.

WORKS CITED

Anderson, Monica, and Jiang Jingjing. 2018. "Teens, Social Media and Technology 2018." Pew Research Center, 31 May 2018. pewresearch.org/internet/2018/05/31/teens-social-media-technology-2018.

Brent, Doug. 2012. "Crossing Boundaries: Co-op Students Relearning to Write." *College Composition and Communication* 63, no. 4 (June): 558–92. doi.org/10.58680/ccc201220299.

Chian, Yu-Tzu, Sunny Lin, Chao-Yang Cheng, and Eric Zhi-Feng Liu. 2011. "Exploring Online Game Players' Flow Experiences and Positive Affect." *Turkish Online Journal of Educational Technology* 10, no. 1 (January): 106–14.

Cho, Yeonhee. 2018. "How Spatial Presence in VR Affects Memory Retention and Motivation on Second Language Learning: A Comparison of Desktop and Immersive VR-Based Learning." MA thesis, Syracuse University. surface.syr.edu/thesis/204.

Clark, Douglas, Emily Tanner-Smith, and Stephen Killingsworth. 2016. "Digital Games, Design, and Learning: A Systematic Review and Meta-Analysis." *Review of Educational Research* 86, no. 1 (March): 79–122. doi.org/10.3102/0034654315582065.

Clemenson, Gregory, and Craig Stark. 2015. "Virtual Environmental Enrichment through Video Games." *The Journal of Neuroscience* 35, no. 49 (December): 16116–25. doi.org/10.1523/JNEUROSCI.2580-15.2015.

Crocco, Francesco, Kathleen Offenholley, and Carlos Hernandez. 2016. "A Proof-of-Concept Study of Game-Based Learning in Higher Education." *Simulation and Gaming* 47, no. 4 (August): 403–22. doi.org/10.1177/1046878116632484.

Di Serio, Ángela, María Ibánez, and Carlos Delgado Kloos. 2013. "Impact of an Augmented Reality System on Students' Motivation for a Visual Art Course." *Computers and Education* 68 (October): 586–96. doi.org/10.1016/j.compedu.2012.03.002.

GBH. 2019. "*Hamlet 360: Thy Father's Sprit*—Shakespeare in VR." Directed by Steven Maler. YouTube video, 1:01:09. 24 January 2019. youtube.com/watch?v=Jc88G7nkV-Q.

Gee, James Paul. 1990. *Social Linguistics and Literacies: Ideology in Discourses.* London: Falmer Press.

———. 2007. *What Video Games Have to Teach Us about Learning and Literacy.* New York: Palgrave Macmillan.

Kellinger, Janna Jackson. 2017. *A Guide to Designing Curricular Games: How to Game the System.* Boston: Springer.

Kennedy, Eithne. 2018. "Engaging Children as Readers and Writers in High-Poverty Contexts." *Journal of Research in Reading* 41, no. 4 (December): 716–31. doi.org/10.1111/1467-9817.12261.

Koskimaa, Raine, and Kristóf Fenyvesi. 2015. "A Mission Impossible? Learning the Logic of Space with Impossible Figures in Experience-Based Mathematics Education." *Opus et Educatio* 2 (1): 70–84. doi.org/10.3311/ope.24.

Lämsä, Joni, Raija Hämäläinen, Mikko Aro, Raine Koskimaa, and Sanna-Mari Äyrämö. 2018. "Games for Enhancing Basic Reading and Maths Skills: A Systematic Review of Educational Game Design in Supporting Learning by People with Learning Disabilities." *British Journal of Educational Technology* 49, no. 4 (July): 596–607. doi.org/10.1111/bjet.12639.

Murray, Janet. 1997. *Hamlet on the Holodeck: The Future of Narrative in Cyberspace.* New York: Simon & Schuster.

Prensky, Martin. 2006. *"Don't Bother Me Mom—I'm Learning!"* St. Paul, MN: Paragon House.

Radu, Iulian. 2014. "Augmented Reality in Education: A Meta-Review and Cross-Media Analysis." *Personal and Ubiquitous Computing* 18, no. 6 (January): 1533–43. doi.org/10.1007/s00779-013-0747-y.

Richmond, Hugh Macrae. 2015. *Shakespeare's Tragedies Reviewed: A Spectator's Role.* New York: Peter Lang. doi.org/10.3726/978-1-4539-1480-9.

Steinkuehler, Constance. 2010. "Video Games and Digital Literacies." *Journal of Adolescent & Adult Literacy* 54, no. 1 (September): 61–63. jstor.org/stable/20749077.

Stoppard, Tom, dir. 1990. *Rosencrantz and Guildenstern Are Dead.* New York: Thirteen / WNET.

Thew, Neill. 2006. *Teaching Shakespeare: A Survey of the Undergraduate Level in Higher Education.* Higher Education Academy. advance-he.ac.uk/knowledge-hub/report-13-teaching-shakespeare-survey-undergraduate-level-higher-education.

Yang, Jie Chi, Chih Hung Chen, and Ming Chang Jeng. 2010. "Integrating Video-Capture Virtual Reality Technology into a Physically Interactive Learning Environment for English Learning." *Computers and Education* 55, no. 3 (November): 1346–56. doi.org/10.1016/j.compedu.2010.06.005.

Chapter 16: Does the *kunstkammer* Need a Digital Future?[1]

Andrea M. Gáldy
Collecting Central Europe

For over 100 years, art historians investigating the history of collections and their display have been interested in the *kunstkammer* as a type of display room, as an architectural phenomenon as well as a specific form of early museum. When research into the history of museums and the history of collecting intensified in the late 1970s (Cole and Pardo 2005; Impey and MacGregor 1985; Liebenwein 1977, 2005), the *kunstkammer* was among the favorite subjects to be explored, since it offered an attractive topic within a limited chronological and geographical frame, considered by most scholars to include above all medieval and early modern Italy.

From the start, at least two issues complicated making the relevant research more comprehensive and international: considered an Italian phenomenon, the *studiolo* or *scrittoio* was often explored as part of a southern and Catholic Renaissance, whereas the *kunst- und wunderkammer* was seen as belonging to a northern, Protestant, even second-rate Renaissance.[2] Such a view also influenced the judgment of traditions, collecting items, access to markets, and role models. Although the terminology of these European collecting cabinets is still under debate, a current change of definition and geopolitical analysis

[1] This chapter is based on my long-term research on the Scrittoio of Calliope and my deliberations on reconstructions using modern technology. A first exploratory essay was published in early 2020. I had planned to give a paper on the more detailed contents of the present chapter at the RSA annual meeting in Philadelphia in 2020 before it was canceled. I owe particular thanks to Robert Gaston for his help and advice. Thanks also to Jens Blechschmidt for discussing with me the creation process of escape rooms in a museum context. I would like to dedicate this chapter to the late Wolfgang Liebenwein for his pioneering work on the *studiolo*.

[2] In Italy alone several terms were used for these display rooms, sometimes even for one and the same room. I am aware of these variations in terminology, traditions, and origins but have decided to keep "kunstkammer" as the principal name for the purpose of this chapter.

ISBN 978-1-64959-119-7 (paper) ISBN 978-1-64959-120-3 (pdf) ISBN 978-1-64959-121-0 (epub)
New Technologies in Medieval and Renaissance Studies 12 (2025) 423–45

of the early modern period will soon—it is to be hoped—have an impact on how they are regarded and researched in future in a wider context.[3]

As the result of these limitations, art, architectural, and collecting historians have investigated the location and contents, intentions and meanings, sources, and afterlives of the *kunstkammer*, but they often remain focused on individual case studies, with an emphasis on Italian exemplars, and attempt to assess what is lost. They have gathered considerable amounts of data from inventories, building plans, and contemporaneous eye-witness reports, and mostly offer reconstructions of original interiors in the form of drawings.

These days, however, new technology provides the means for more detailed and visually stimulating digital reconstructions that allow the viewer to gain a spatial impression and to interact with the objects on display. The scope of research should be extended by offering the opportunity to draw direct comparisons between sufficiently large numbers of reconstructions. Nonetheless, the question remains: what is the point of digital *kunstkammern*? Are they necessary or simply a case of "we do it because we can"? Are there research issues that can best be answered—or even be triggered—by digital reconstructions? And finally, who will ultimately profit, and how, from digital *kunstkammern* in museums and as part of research projects? To address and discuss these questions and to show what we can learn from digital *kunstkammern* is the aim of my chapter. Finally, the case study of the Florentine Scrittoio of Calliope will serve to point out and illustrate the advantages of digital reconstructions and their use to research and museum practice.

The kunstkammer

A *kunst- und wunderkammer* can best be defined as a room or group of rooms, intimate in scale and filled with small but very valuable collecting pieces displayed as part of a programmatic exhibition supported by a decorative scheme (Liebenwein 1977, 2005). This scheme was meant to give a special sense to the selection of objects and to heighten their significance. Therefore, the *kunstkammer* is related to and in some ways identical with cabinets, study rooms, *studioli*, and *scrittoi*, since all of them attempted to show a very valuable selection of their owners' wider collection and to present wonders of art and nature, of science, and objects originating in exotic places (Christian and Clark 2017). By presenting favorite possessions, the collector often gave an

[3] In this context, I would like to draw attention to the publication on Czech collections and collection rooms, including the discussion of the phenomenon of the *studiolo* in Bohemia: Fornasiero, Zlatohlávková, and Kindl 2020.

account of his or her political and cultural aims and aspirations (Gáldy 2022, 273–289; Liebenwein 1991).

Kunstkammern were set up for and by aristocrats, scholars, and artists (Clark 2013; Thornton 1997). Among the most important examples were Isabella d'Este's *studiolo* in Mantua (Ames-Lewis 2012, 9–17; Brown 2005; Campbell 2006), the study created for the Medici in their family *palazzo* in Florence (Fusco and Corti 2006; Syson 2006), and the *wunderkammer* of the counts of Zimmern in today's Baden-Württemberg, Germany (Barack 1881–82, 3:350; Bastress-Dukehart 2002; Zimmern 1558/1565). In many cases we only have access to partial information about the actual rooms, some of the objects, inventory lists, or descriptions. Therefore, it is often difficult to gain the full picture of what was there when a *kunstkammer* was first constructed, decorated, and furnished. We do not always know exactly when a room was created and furbished or the criteria adopted for the selection of objects. Nonetheless, we often have enough information to gain a rough idea of what such a room may have looked like. Since there existed so many *kunstkammern* in Europe during the fourteenth to sixteenth centuries, judicious comparisons between contemporaneous exemplars facilitate a better understanding of the *kunstkammer*'s principal features.

The *kunstkammern* of the past were assembled in accordance with the tastes and ambitions of their owners. Certainly, they were meant to delight owners as well as occasional visitors who had to negotiate access by invitation rather than by paying for a ticket. While a collectors' standard existed at the time that prompted acquisition in relation to a canon of the most covetable items (Gutfleisch and Menzhausen 1989; Liebenwein 2016; Meadow and Robertson 2013), few of the owners were specialists or had access to professional curators. Artists and antiquarians were the most likely assistants in setting up a *kunstkammer*—in the case of the Scrittoio of Calliope (see below), it was Giorgio Vasari—and at least some of them followed their own agenda rather than modern ideas of scholarship. Nonetheless, Vasari proved himself to be surprisingly capable of insisting on order and categorization as well as on display and storage according to size (Gáldy 2014).

Over the centuries, the *kunstkammer* acquired the reputation of a dusty old place crammed full of oddities, the composition of which made no sense and merely reflected the weird predilections of manic collectors (Scott 1816, ch. 3). Although the *kunstkammer* as a genre enjoyed considerable longevity, in particular if one extends their history to private collections of the nineteenth and early twentieth centuries, they eventually acquired the reputation of locations filled with moth-eaten and dust-covered treasures valuable only to their owners. Apart from spectacular *kunstkammern* in the hands of electors, kings, or emperors, amateur antiquarians and other dilettante collectors became figures of ridicule, and their cabinets were often considered with amusement. Although the past 40 years of research have diminished these prejudices, much work is necessary to uncover and analyze convincingly the history, importance, and context of the European *kunstkammer*. If Julius von Schlosser ([1908] 2021) and much later twentieth-century historians of collecting had not chosen the *kunstkammer* as a worthy research object, we would perhaps not be interested now. In the meantime, the *kunstkammer* in its diverse forms and developments has been recognized as an important subject of study that connects the history of collecting, the history of museums, museology, and virtual museums. It is also part of research into early modern architecture, interior decoration, and court culture. It lends itself to a multidisciplinary approach and can be studied as an international phenomenon.

Once scholars and museum curators understood the historical importance of the *kunstkammer* and started to gather information about (now mostly lost) exemplars, they also looked for ways in which to present their findings to specialists and non-specialists in publications and displays. What makes the *kunstkammer* so attractive for research—its apparent seclusion, specific setup, diverse provenance, and the small scale of its exhibits—also increases its appeal to curators and the public. Should a *kunstkammer* be presented as a kind of treasury, as an archeological museum, or as an ethnographical collection? Should it be presented *in situ* whenever possible if the architectural frame still exists? If it were to be displayed in a museum, whether as a reconstruction or via its former exhibits, into which gallery would it most usefully be integrated? Does it fit most easily into an exhibition of early modern art, a selection of ancient artifacts, objects from the Far East, or a collection of Islamic art (Clark 2020; Laue 2012; Wellington and Troelenberg 2019)? Since a *kunstkammer*'s contents are rarely, if ever, limited to objects of one style, genre, or provenance (Turpin 2013), they challenge many of our modern and contemporary notions of attributions, schools, and origins. In their globalized appropriation of cultural objects they are more modern than many of our great museums today, even though some of them—for example, the Uffizi—once presented a wide range of exhibits, including weapons, mathematical instruments, and stuffed animals (Gáldy 2009b; Groom 2014; Reid forthcoming) next to old master paintings and ancient sculptures.

Although today we know much more about the *kunstkammer*, *studiolo*, *scrittoio*, or cabinet than 100 (or even just 40) years ago, there is still much to do in terms of research and display.[4] As scholarship advances, further information will be gathered and—it is hoped—will increase our knowledge and understanding of this type of collecting room. At the same time, it will become more interesting but also more complicated to find ways of display aimed at an ever wider and varied audience. Issues of categorized museum displays will have to be debated and, possibly, reconsidered to some extent. In this context, it is particularly important to adopt all available modes of museum practice deemed useful for research and display. In the case of the *kunstkammer*, the creation of a digital "time machine" with the possibility of accessing the *kunstkammer*'s original location and finding out more about the collecting pieces could work best at this point.

Benefits to Research in the History of Collecting

In the past, the wealth of archival information and objects preserved prompted reconstruction attempts in the form of descriptions and drawings (e.g., Gáldy 2020, figs. 5 and 7). A digital reconstruction would, however, not only look far more attractive but would also give an impression of the space and furnishings and chart the transfer of successive groups of objects taken to the room. A digital *scrittoio* could also provide the architectural context more clearly than any plan or vertical section and thus show the setting and processional route in which the room was embedded from the start. Finally, and perhaps most importantly, all the above could be done convincingly and to scale without moving the collecting pieces from museums, reapplying wall cladding and cupboards or shelves, or breaking down walled-up doors.

Digital reconstructions therefore make sense for a number of reasons. As a result, academic research more easily lends itself to direct and detailed comparison over wider geographical and chronological areas. Location, decoration, contents, and visitor impressions of northern and southern European *kunstkammern* can more easily be compared to underpin discussion of the terms to be used and functions fulfilled by the rooms and artifacts (Conticelli 2020). The use of standardized enhanced metadata can help with archiving

[4] Therefore, I am currently working on a grant application to finance an international research project, The (Digital) Kunstkammer, as part of the activities organized by the newly established platform Collecting Central Europe, founded in September 2020. The project will focus on Central and Eastern European *kunstkammern* as part of a pan-European network of *kunstkammer* collectors and collections, as well as investigate the possibilities offered by the digital humanities in up-to-date research in the field.

data and facilitating searches across the entire range of investigated examples. It can also answer queries in relation to the categorization of works of art and other collecting items once displayed in a *kunstkammer*, similar to issues discussed in modern museum practice. In addition, "biographies" of rooms and collecting items displayed within individual buildings or courts as well as the transport of pieces from one *studiolo* to the next can be investigated and clearly visualized.

As a result, detailed digital reconstructions that include the possibility of transformative changes can lead to a better understanding of the long histories of study rooms across time and space and help follow the biographies of objects from the moment they were discovered, acquired, or commissioned down to their current exhibition in a museum or private collection. In any case, each stage of such a transformative collecting display would visualize new contexts and open a new dialogue between the objects themselves as well as between objects and their location. Once a particularly well-preserved *kunstkammer* and its history is explored and presented in this way, it could also provide a model for more fragmentarily preserved examples throughout Europe and fill our gaps of knowledge about room, setup, and content by discovering the existence of a historical pattern or being able to prove the lack of one. It could also offer necessary information for the theoretical debate in relation to setup and contents.

Since digital tools allow for more convincing reconstructions based on the data generated so far, they enable specialists in collecting history and museology to bring *kunstkammern*, their decorative schemes, and their contents back to life in a virtual reality through the adoption of twenty-first-century technology. Among the most obvious advantages of digital *kunstkammern* are reconstructions achieved without long-term loans of exhibits, or health and safety hazards caused by the original architectural settings of small rooms in centuries-old buildings with limited access to wide stairs, lifts, and barrier-free fire escapes, as well as a visual attractiveness beyond the capabilities of more traditional means.

Such digital reconstructions are well within the reach of modern technology. Given enough data, it is possible to model city quarters, entire cities, and (parts of) buildings in the virtual world. Projects such as Venice Time Machine (ec.europa.eu/futurium/en/content/venice-time-machine-flagship.html) directly link archival documents to historical city maps and thereby make it possible to gain in-depth knowledge about a past realty. Florence 4D (florence4d.org) by the University of Exeter not only aimed at the reconstruction of the long-demolished church of San Pier Maggiore in Florence but connected this virtual reconstruction to works of art once at the church but now at major museums worldwide. What Jane Saw (whatjanesaw.org) investigated John Boydell's Shakespeare Gallery, reconstructed the display, and connected it to a catalog of works of art displayed in the gallery in 1796.[5] Finally, the IDEA (isabelladestearchive.org/virtual-studiolo) reconstruction of Isabella d'Este's *studiolo* in Mantua, particularly appropriate in this context, creates a detailed digital reconstruction of a Renaissance *kunstkammer*, which attests to the existing level of technical sophistication and suggests further possibilities of application (Shemek et al. 2018).

Although one might argue that digital reconstructions merely function as an improved form of reconstruction and visualization compared to what scholarship achieved by other means in the past, it is clear that they also offer ways in which to present collections and their display in less static fashion and thus to lay the foundations for wider comparison. Digital reconstruction is therefore useful for research in the history of collecting and might be used to attract the interest of scholars and non-specialists. Presented in a suitable format, digital reconstructions can also draw the attention of museum audiences and entice them to engage with the history of this early modern display room.

The kunstkammer *Time Machine*

When museum exhibits started to come out of their glass cases to be displayed in a feasible research-based context, the issue of what constituted "reality" became important. Museum pieces were meant to be shown in such a way that the visitor could enjoy them and learn about their previous "lives." The aim was to take visitors back in time (in something akin to a time machine) and to teach them via a verisimilar display how the objects were perceived and used in the past. This kind of museum concept particularly lent itself to the exhibition of historical and ethnographic collections but can, in theory, also be used for painting galleries, for example, by adding QR codes with retrievable visual information to the labels when works of art are shown without a trace of their original settings.[6] When Robert Lumley published the edited volume *The Museum Time Machine* in 1988, authentic displays, their

[5] I would like to thank one of the peer reviewers for bringing this project to my attention.

[6] QR (quick response) codes constitute (two-dimensional) matrix barcodes. These optical labels can be read by tablets and smartphones and offer a wider range of information, including context, to what can be found on cards and labels.

impact on museum audiences, and the viewers' response were still relatively new ideas. Nonetheless, even then it became clear that a reconstructed setting, no matter how authentic, could only pretend to be the "real thing." Although preferable to a context-free display in vitrines, the reconstruction was to an extent the result of the curator's imagination and interpretation. The main issue, therefore, was that a "film set" was presented as the authentic image of a real past to which the visitor would be transported by means of the museum time machine, as discussed in Lumley's book.

To some extent these issues still exist. Although increasing amounts of data and preserved architecture allow us to reconstruct a *kunstkammer* in a museum or in its original location, curators and visitors face problems of reality and authenticity. A display will take us back to a previously existing state that is verisimilar but cannot be proven to have existed in the same constellation of room and contents. In addition, such a presentation often pretends to display the original by showing how a *kunstkammer* was set up or developed out of a specific collecting room. In this case, the data may be correct and authentic, but the room is a fake.

Museums have dealt with the *kunstkammer* in several ways, from building a substitute architecture mainly filled with pieces we know to have been there (or in another *kunstkammer*) originally (e.g., the Medici *studiolo* at the V&A, London) to modern showcases in the original building in which the collecting items are exhibited in accordance with descriptions and inventory lists and which present early modern attempts at categorization (see Castle Ambras, Innsbruck; Gulyás 2018; Haag 2012; Sandbichler 2012). There are *kunstkammern* that obviously attest to a modern interpretation of an early modern exemplar (see Hofburg, Vienna; Bukovinská 2017; Holzschuh-Hofer 2015), and others that changed so much during the course of their existence that the display takes the visitor back to a period much later than the beginnings of this particular collection (see Grünes Gewölbe, Dresden; Marx and Plassmeyer 2014; Syndram and Minning 2012; Watanabe-O'Kelly 2002). Although all these examples lack a strictly sixteenth-century authenticity, they nonetheless offer important information and give an impression of location, space, collecting objects, and their presentation at some point in the respective *kunstkammer*'s biographies. All of them, however, leave gaps in the historical narrative, the decorative scheme, and the provenance of their exhibits.

A particularly interesting case in the history of recreating Renaissance cabinets is the reconstructed Medici *studiolo* at the V&A, London. The original room in the Palazzo Medici was much admired in the fifteenth century but has long been lost (Bulst 1970; Hatfield 1970). We know its position next to the Medici chapel and have contemporary sources that tell us about its architectural setup and contents. Since the V&A not only owns the *tondi* of the months once presented on the barrel vault of the original cabinet but also several other collecting items typically preserved in a *kunstkammer*, some of them perhaps from Isabella's *studiolo*, it was possible to create a physical reconstruction that is in itself a museum piece at the Mediaeval and Renaissance Galleries (Clark 2020; Syson 2006). It is obviously not the real *studiolo*; still, it manages to take the viewer back in time by presenting a rather convincing reconstruction without pretending to be completely authentic. Therefore, as a reconstruction it goes in the right direction, while in its function as a time machine there are limits to what it can do in terms of authenticity, reality, and historical narrative.

Museum Displays

On a practical, museological level, the concept as well as individual case studies of digital *kunstkammern* ought to result in a more engaging presentation of objects and research to museum audiences, the growing number and diversity of which needs to be taken into account. The expectations of visitors have developed along with museum practice. Unless they belong to a category that enters a museum merely because of its must-see status and to shoot a photo in front of a particular highlight of the collection, the audience usually wishes to be entertained as much as informed and appreciates the possibility to interact with the collection. In my experience, visitors tend to be bored easily; therefore, it is important to stimulate their curiosity, in particular the attention of digital natives. While they do not wish to revisit lessons taught at school, they may have encountered ancient and Renaissance history and its monuments (e.g., the library of Alexandria) through computer games such as *Assassin's Creed* (Leiva Aldea 2017). Even the dwindling public able to appreciate a museum visit when not brightened by excursions to the shops and by tea and cake at the restaurant might be susceptible to (digital) reconstructions that allow for the extension of knowledge by active participation in presentations that provide a feeling of live-and-learn by finding out about an object's historical context.

If digital reconstructions were to be downloadable onto smartphones and tablets, the audience could also use them in preparation for a museum visit. It would be made clear that what they see is an ideal state constructed like a puzzle out of a multitude of elements available at a number of museums that—in combination—can tell them about a reality that no longer exists but is worth finding out about. Elements of up-to-date museum practice and outreach methods could serve as an inducement to use these digital reconstruction in the best possible way. There are several ways to induce the visitor to arrive at a more participatory experience by using the possibilities of modern museum practice in connection with their familiarity with computers and games. The aim would be to use the museum time machine to travel several centuries back for the inspection and study of one or several displays, for example of a *kunstkammer*. Whether on the original premises or, if impossible, in a reconstructed/virtual architecture, the public could enter and move within a study room that looks as much as its analogue model as possible. With the help of a virtual reality (VR) headset, visitors would immerse themselves into a long-lost reality and gain a very similar impression to the one enjoyed by guests invited to the *kunstkammer* during previous centuries. Less didactic than the study of digital reconstructions provided by museums on tablets to facilitate the search for additional information, this type of VR experience would be more immediate and therefore stronger by appealing to both the informed and the new visitor. It would not necessarily require previous knowledge but could pique the curiosity by the visual impact made on the viewer/participant.

Another way to involve the audience and instruct them through participation could be offered in the guise of escape rooms, which have gained great popularity over recent decades. In escape rooms, one plays with objects that are either hidden, changed, or locked up to solve riddles, as in the interactive game *Chaos in den Vatikanischen Museen* (view.genial.ly/618fccd5da47890e05b52dc4/interactive-content-chaos-in-den-vatikanischen-museen). The objects concerned would obviously not be the originals once displayed in a *kunstkammer* or larger museum but, perhaps, abstract, symbolic pieces distributed within an equally symbolic architecture. By moving an object to a particular place, the participant would be able to discover additional information as well as trigger a transmutation from one *studiolo* escape room into another and finally manage to discover the exit.[7] Provided there is enough space, a real-life escape room or even a series of rooms could be set up in a museum to give visitors a more intense and interactive experience of the museum collections' history and its display over the centuries.

---

[7] Jens Blechschmidt kindly shared his experience on how to set up such an escape room in the analogue world and on the possibilities of visualizing the available information for a participating audience.

The same could be done digitally, either before the visit or on screens set up in the galleries. As mentioned above, the same digital reconstruction could be presented in several museums to combine information about the reconstruction of the room with the knowledge about collecting objects now distributed over several museums in the same city or all over the world. This sort of reconstruction would invite the viewer to investigate the provenance, biography, and display of exhibits in their modern settings. While this kind of presentation is bound to attract the attention of a wider section of the museum-going public than traditional displays, it could also be done more entertainingly. If set up in the mode of a digital escape room that opens virtual cupboards, drawers, and doors, the virtual escape room would give access to information more likely to stay in mind since it was gained rather than consumed during a more or less enjoyable tour through the analogue galleries. Indeed, ideally it would serve as an introduction to the proper museum for those who wish to deepen their experience by visiting the collection items in their traditional museum setting.

These are but two examples by which research results, including but not limited to increased knowledge about the *kunstkammer*, can be presented to today's museum visitors. Similar measures have already been adopted at, for example, the Alpines Museum, Munich, where members of the public can participate in a virtual rescue operation strapped into a stretcher and wearing a VR headset that makes them live through a flight from the Alps to safety (Zinnecker 2020). As described above, computer games as well as other modes of participatory activities—whether online or not—may be taken as models for introducing a wider audience to the latest research results by taking advantage of their previous experiences in virtual reality. As a result of a changing degree and mode of preparation, museum practice therefore needs to adapt itself to current consumer requirements so that the visitors may gain the full benefits from entering a museum.

Case Study: The Scrittoio of Calliope

In antiquity, a museum was a place of the Muses in which to worship the godmothers of the arts (Wood 2017). It is no coincidence that early modern collecting rooms, for example the Scrittoio of Calliope in Palazzo Vecchio, were sometimes dedicated to the Muses and bear their names. Calliope was the muse of epic poetry and mother of Orpheus, who was able to tame wild beasts by the sound of his music. These early "museums" cannot be compared closely to our modern public institutions that attract millions of visitors each year, but both are part of the same history and, of course, connected by the display of works of art and other collecting pieces.

We are particularly fortunate in the case of the study of Calliope preserved in Palazzo Vecchio, Florence, set up for Duke Cosimo I de' Medici in the 1550s (Gáldy 2005, 2009a, 61–84, 2012). The Apartment of the Elementi (Fig. 1) includes state rooms dedicated to a number of ancient Roman gods and heroes, which were decorated by Giorgio Vasari and his workshop. The main room is the Hall of the Elements. The Scrittoio of Calliope is accessed through the Hall of Ceres; in the past, one could also enter it secretly via a spiral staircase. Although this study room still exists *in situ*, it has lost its wall cladding, furnishings, and exhibits (Figs. 1–2). Both the ceiling painting of the Muse Calliope (Giorgio Vasari, 1555–58) and the stained-glass window depicting Venus and the three Graces (Gualtiero da Anversa, 1555–58) are still in place, and a dedicated inventory lists the 70-odd pieces transferred to the room in the summer of 1559. A considerable number of these objects can be (tentatively) identified and are today preserved in the National Archaeological Museum of Florence, the Bargello, and other Florentine museums (Gáldy 2009a, 361–458, 524–60, 2012).

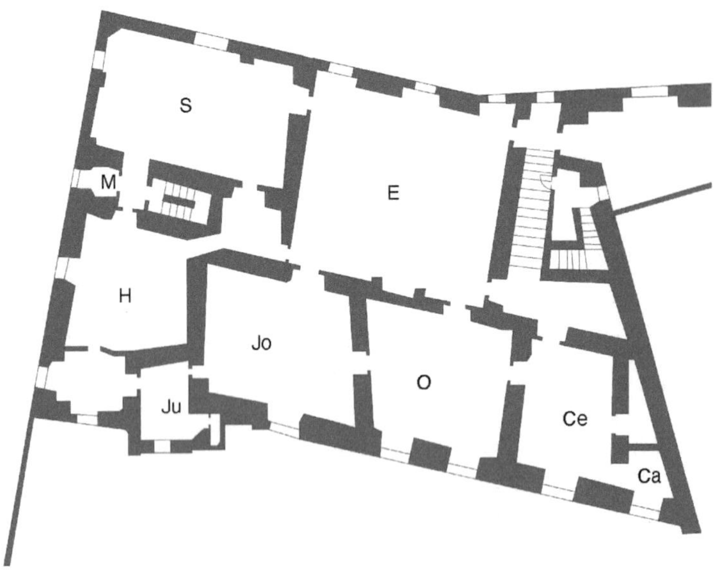

Figure 1. Plan of the Apartment of the Elementi, Palazzo Vecchio, Florence, second floor, including the Scrittoio of Calliope. E = Elements, S = Saturn, M = Minerva, H = Hercules, Jo = Jove, Ju = Juno, O = Ops, Ce = Ceres,

Ca = Calliope. Image credit: Jessica Wright, based on a detail from Prague plan 77, NA Prague, RAT, Mapy, n. 716, B.A. 49, VII 2/1.

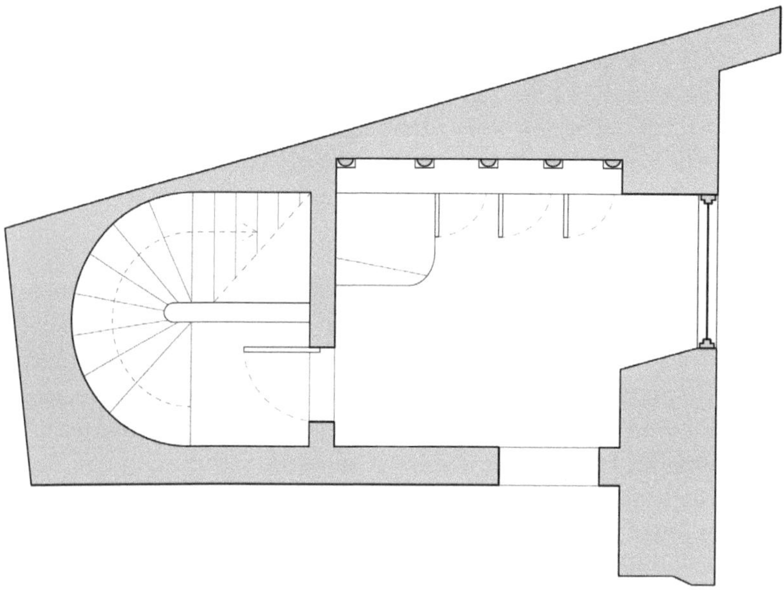

Figure 2. Plan of the Scrittoio of Calliope, Apartment of the Elementi. Image credit: Jessica Wright, based on Liebenwein 1977.

The date of its creation, the location in the state rooms of the Ducal Palace (Palazzo Vecchio), and the type of collecting objects selected for display make it likely that in this *scrittoio* we are dealing with a room set up in conscious imitation of the *kunstkammer* created for Emperor Ferdinand I at the Hofburg, Vienna (Gáldy 2020, 2022). Tracing the objects through the Medici inventories and documents even tells us when many of them were discovered, for example a group of small bronzes in the company of the Etruscan *Chimaera* (Archaeological Museum, Florence) in November 1553 in Arezzo, Italy (Gáldy 2012; Zucchi 2017). Several other pieces had been owned by the duke's family back in the fifteenth century and therefore had familial significance to the Medici (Romualdi and de Marinis 1992).

In the case of the Scrittoio of Calliope, digital visualization could be used to create links to reconstructions of previously existing studies in Florence owned by the Medici (Palazzo Medici), and to later *kunstkammern* set up in other locations in the Ducal Palace as well as in other relevant buildings that belonged to the ducal court (Uffizi). The Ducal Palace included several study rooms, most famously Francesco I's Studiolo (1570–72) next to the Hall of the 500 (Alberts 2018; Conticelli 2006, 2007). Grand Duke Francesco would eventually dissolve his Studiolo and transfer at least some of its contents to the new Tribuna at the Uffizi (Reid forthcoming), where they would be exhibited in a new context and attract a wider audience over the coming centuries. The Tribuna's most famous depiction is Johann Zoffany's painting of 1772–78 (Royal Collection Trust) that shows an ideal Tribuna filled with additional collecting pieces and several admiring (English) visitors and thus presents a kind of imaginary reconstruction of the collection, its display, and audience reactions.

As regards the Scrittoio of Calliope, to my knowledge no physical reconstruction has been attempted so far. Since its architecture and part of the decoration still exist, it would be possible to recreate much of its former setup as documented by letters, descriptions, and inventories. Alternatively, it would also be possible to follow the example from the V&A and construct a copy of the architectural frame and display it filled with the erstwhile exhibits now preserved in the Florentine museums—ideally at the Archaeological Museum but possibly also at the Bargello or the Museo degli Argenti. In such a way, the museum collections would be returned to their former context, or at least to a context that, while not authentic, would contribute to a better understanding of their past collecting and display histories. In this case, many of the objects would be authentic, while both place and setup are not.

A reconstruction *in situ*, however, would avoid these issues of authenticity as far as the place itself is concerned. Nonetheless, the question remains whether the museums of Florence would be ready to lend the collecting pieces once stored and displayed in the Scrittoio to Palazzo Vecchio. If not, it would become necessary to create copies for an "as real as possible" visitor experience. The furnishings and wall cover in "velluto chermisi" (crimson velvet; Vasari 1923) would also need to be reconstructed in a place, the state of which is certainly not what it was in the 1550s, but which might be protected by heritage regulations and thus prevent invasive changes to the architecture. Even if it were possible to do all that—and one must not forget that the furnishings would be based on scant descriptions and therefore not correspond entirely to a past reality (Pegazzano 2014)—the public would see a snapshot reconstruction in a very small location that could admit only a limited number of visitors at a time (Fig. 2). In addition, these visitors would need to be able-bodied people, capable of moving down a steep spiral staircase that forms part of the processional route of the visit (Allegri and Cecchi 1980, xxiv–xxv, 80–82; Cinelli 2006; Jonietz 2017, 73, 98, 138, 188, 235, 255,

273–76). Altogether, it would be easy to mistake the reconstruction for the real thing and assume that what one sees is what was there originally (i.e., accept a fake as real).

All these reservations disappear in the case of a digital reconstruction (Figs. 3a–b), which is obviously not real but contains every bit of information available at the time. There is no pretension of authenticity in terms of place, space or contents, whereas the information provided is as complete and authentic as possible. If updates become necessary, corrections are a matter of programming rather than building work, refurbishing or reordering of the contents. No invasive changes are necessary to the building and images of the collecting pieces are being used. Depending on the type of reconstruction and display, access is easy and can be granted to all visitors; there may be versions for people with vision or hearing impairments. The digital exhibition created for the Scrittoio of Calliope could even become part of the permanent display as a complementary museum piece, even though particular themes might be foregrounded in connection with changing themes.

As discussed above, a digital reconstruction can also present several stages of the biography of one and the same *kunstkammer*, while the development from one *kunstkammer* to the next can be documented as well. The reconstruction could be presented in or near the original location on a screen, or in other locations, for example in the case of the Scrittoio of Calliope at the Palazzo Vecchio, at the Bargello, at the Archaeological Museum, at the Uffizi, and at the Museo degli Argenti to provide the fullest possible picture of the room and collecting items and to connect them to the museums' holdings. By hovering over the objects in the reconstruction, the visitor would be able to access further information about the objects and find out where other pieces once in the room are preserved today. Links could be created to library and museum catalogs as well as online encyclopedias to provide further reading material for the interested. The objects' biographies, including their provenance, use, make, and style, could be addressed and reference could be made to pieces listed in the ducal inventories that can no longer be traced to museum collections in Florence or elsewhere. Such a display would not only be more attractive and engaging than what is offered at present, but it would also enhance the status of several Florentine and international museum collections and encourage visitors to explore them in more detail.

It has been the aim of this chapter to point out the opportunities and potential benefits of digital museum displays, in particular of *kunstkammer* reconstructions, to art historical research, the history of collecting, and museum practice. In this context, we must define the aims and goals of museums in the past as well as now; it is also important to understand how digitization can help to achieve these goals today (Kohle 2018). While many modern museums already use up-to-date technology to present their collections in the best possible way for the instruction and delectation of their audiences, in the case of the *kunstkammer* the way forward is perhaps not so clear. The creation of a digital *kunstkammer* requires funding and effort. How many of them would have to be set up to arrive at the critical mass necessary for an international research project? Should they be used mainly as a (temporary) exhibition, as a tool for research, or as a means of entertainment?

Does the *kunstkammer* really need a digital future? In the light of contemporary research in the history of collecting, modern museum practice, and of the expectations of present museum audiences, it seems a very promising way forward. With the help of digitization and VR technologies, convincing reconstructions of *kunstkammern* are within reach. Why not bring the *kunstkammer* into the twenty-first century? It certainly seems worth a try.

Figure 3a.

Figure 3b.

Figures 3a–b. Reconstruction of the Scrittoio of Calliope at Palazzo Vecchio. Image credit: Jessica Wright.

WORKS CITED

Alberts, Lindsay. 2018. "Francesco I's Museum: Cultural Politics at the Galleria degli Uffizi." *Journal of the History of Collections* 30, no. 2 (July): 203–16. doi.org/10.1093/jhc/fhx017.

Allegri, Ettore, and Alessandro Cecchi. 1980. *Il Palazzo Vecchio e i Medici: Guida storica*. Florence: SPES.

Ames-Lewis, Francis. 2012. *Isabella and Leonardo: The Artistic Relationship between Isabella d'Este and Leonardo da Vinci, 1500–1506*. New Haven, CT: Yale University Press.

Barack, Karl August, ed. 1881–82. *Zimmerische Chronik*. 4 vols. Freiburg: Mohr.

Bastress-Dukehart, Erica. 2002. *The Zimmern Chronicle: Nobility, Memory and Self-Representation in Sixteenth-Century Germany*. Aldershot: Ashgate. doi.org/10.4324/9781315236483.

Brown, Clifford M. 2005. *Isabella d'Este in the Ducal Palace in Mantua: An Overview of Her Rooms in the Castello di San Giorgio and the Corte Vecchia*. Rome: Bulzoni.

Bukovinská, Beket. 2017. "Kunstkammer Ferdinands I: Viele Fragen, wenige Antworten." In *Dresden-Prague um 1600*, edited by Beket Bukovinská and Lubomír Konečný, 69–86. Prague: Artefactum.

Bulst, Wolfger A. 1970. "Die ursprüngliche innere Aufteilung des Palazzo Medici in Florenz." *Mitteilungen des Kunsthistorischen Institutes in Florenz* 14 (4): 369–92. doi.org/10.11588/mkhi.1970.4.41607.

Campbell, Stephen. 2006. *The Cabinet of Eros: Renaissance Mythological Painting and the Studiolo of Isabella d'Este*. New Haven, CT: Yale University Press.

Christian, Kathleen, and Leah Clark, eds. 2017. *European Art and the Wider World, 1350–1550*. Manchester: Manchester University Press.

Cinelli, Carlo. 2006. "Il Quartiere degli elementi." In *Palazzo Vecchio: Officina di opere e di ingegni*, edited by Carlo Francini, 234–45. Cinisello Balsamo: Silvana.

Clark, Leah R. 2013. "Collecting, Exchange, and Sociability in the Renaissance *studiolo*." *Journal of the History of Collections* 25, no. 2 (July): 171–84. doi.org/10.1093/jhc/fhs022.

———. 2020. "Representing the World: Collecting and Display in the Renaissance and Today." In *Collecting and Museology*, edited by Andrea M. Gáldy and Florian Dobmeier, 1–21. Newcastle-upon-Tyne: Cambridge Scholars Publishing.

Cole, Michael, and Mary Pardo, eds. 2005. *Inventions of the Studio: Renaissance to Romanticism*. Chapel Hill: University of North Carolina Press.

Conticelli, Valentina. 2006. "Lo Studiolo di Francesco I." In *Palazzo Vecchio: Officina di opere e di ingegni*, edited by Carlo Francini, 250–57. Cinisello Balsamo: Silvana.

———. 2007. "Guardaroba di cose rare et preziose." In *Lo studiolo di Francesco I de' Medici: Arte, Storia e Significati*. Lugano: Agora.

———. 2020. "Studiolo, Grotta, Cupola e Museum." In *Beyond "Art Collections": Owning and Accumulating Objects from Greek Antiquity to the Early Modern Period*, edited by Gianfranco Adornato, Gabriella Cirucci, and Walter Cupperi, 199–226. Berlin: De Gruyter.

Fornasiero, Alice, Eliška Zlatohlávková, Miroslav Kindl. 2020. *From Studiolo to Gallery: Secular Spaces for Collections in the Lands of the Bohemian Crown on the Threshold of the Early Modern Era*. Prague: Charles University.

Fusco, Laurie S., and Gino Corti. 2006. *Lorenzo de' Medici: Collector and Antiquarian*. Cambridge: Cambridge University Press.

Gáldy, Andrea M. 2005. "The Scrittoio della Calliope, a Tuscan Museum." *Renaissance Studies* 19 (5): 699–709.

———. 2009a. *Cosimo de' Medici as Collector: Antiquities and Archaeology in Sixteenth-Century Florence*. Newcastle-upon-Tyne: Cambridge Scholars Publishing.

———. 2009b. "Medici Collections of Dynastic Ambitions: Arms, Armour and Antiquities." In *Collecting and Dynastic Ambition*, edited by Susan Bracken, Andrea M. Gáldy, and Adriana Turpin, 37–57. Newcastle-upon-Tyne: Cambridge Scholars Publishing.

———. 2012. "A Show of Independence: Collecting and Display of Etruscan Art at the Court of Cosimo I de' Medici (1537–1574)." In *Myth, Allegory, Emblem: The Many Lives of the Chimaera of Arezzo*, edited by G. Carlotta Cianferoni, Mario Iozzo, and Elisabetta Settari, 153–65. Rome: Aracne.

———. 2014. "Vasari, Exhibitor of Art: Medici Collections of Antiquities." In *Giorgio Vasari and the Birth of the Museum*, edited by Maia Wellington Gahtan, 119–30. Farnham: Ashgate.

———. 2020. "The Kunst- und Wunderkammer: Past, Present and Digital Future." In *Collecting and Museology*, edited by Andrea M. Gáldy and Florian Dobmeier, 23–46. Newcastle-upon-Tyne: Cambridge Scholars Publishing.

———. 2022. "A Role Model Twice Removed? Cosimo I de' Medici as New Augustus." In *Augustus through the Ages: Receptions, Readings and*

Appropriations of the Historical Figure of the First Roman Emperor, edited by Marco Cavalieri, Mattia Cavagna, David Engels, and Pierre Assenmaker, 259–71. Brussels: Latomus.

Groom, Angelica. 2014. "Collecting Zoological Rarities and the Medici Court: Real, Stuffed and Depicted Beasts as Cultural Signs." In *Collecting Nature*, edited by Andrea M. Gáldy and Sylvia Heudecker, 19–35. Newcastle-upon-Tyne: Cambridge Scholars Publishing.

Gulyás, Borbála. 2018. "'Achtet Casten, darin allerleÿ Büecher': Prints and Manuscripts in the Kunstkammer of Ferdinand of Tyrol." In *Collecting Prints and Drawings*, edited by Andrea M. Gáldy and Sylvia Heudecker, 105–20. Newcastle-upon-Tyne: Cambridge Scholars Publishing.

Gutfleisch, Barbara, and Joachim Menzhausen. 1989. "'How a Kunstkammer should be formed': Gabriel Kaltemarckt's Advice to Christian I of Saxony on the Formation of an Art Collection, 1587." *Journal of the History of Collections* 1, no. 1 (June): 3–32. doi.org/10.1093/jhc/1.1.3.

Haag, Sabine, ed. 2012. *Dresden and Ambras: Kunstkammerschätze der Renaissance*. Vienna: Kunsthistorisches Museum.

Hatfield, Rab. 1970. "Some Unknown Descriptions of the Medici Palace in 1459." *The Art Bulletin* 52, no. 3 (September): 232–49. doi.org/10.2307/3048729.

Holzschuh-Hofer [Leggatt-Hofer], Renate. 2015. "Wien unter Ferdinand I, 1521–1564: Über die Verflechtungen von Fürst, Stadt und Residenz aus kunsthistorischer Perspektive." *Historie – Otázky – Problémy* 7 (2): 60–70.

Impey, Oliver, and Arthur MacGregor, eds. 1985. *The Origins of Museums: The Cabinet of Curiosities in Sixteenth- and Seventeenth-Century Europe*. Oxford: Clarendon Press.

Jonietz, Fabian. 2017. *Das Buch zum Bild: Die "Stanze nuove" im Palazzo Vecchio, Giorgio Vasaris "Ragionamenti" und die Lesbarkeit der Kunst im Cinquecento*. Berlin: Deutscher Kunstverlag.

Kohle, Hubertus. 2018. *Museen digital: Eine Gedächtnisinstitution sucht den Anschluss an die Zukunft*. Heidelberg: Heidelberg University Publishing.

Laue, Georg. 2012. *Exotica*. Munich: Kunstkammer Georg Laue.

Leiva Aldea, José Manuel. 2017. *Recreación y revisión del Renacimiento en Florencia a través de la franquicia* Assassin's Creed. Málaga: Universidad de Málaga.

Liebenwein, Wolfgang. 1977. *Studiolo: Die Entstehung eines Raumtypes und seine Entwicklung bis um 1600.* Berlin: Gebrüder Mann.

———. 1991. "Lo Studiolo come Luogo del Principe." In *Le Muse e il Principe: Arte di Corte nel Rinascimento Padano*, edited by Alessandro Mottola Malfino and Mauro Natale, 135–44. Modena: Panini.

———. 2005. *Studiolo: Storia e tipologia di uno spazio culturale.* Edited by Claudia Cieri Via. Modena: Panini.

———. 2016. "Gabriel Kaltemarckt und die Vites des Giorgio Vasari." In *Vasari als Paradigma*, edited by Fabian Jonietz and Alessandro Nova, 139–52. Venice: Marsilio.

Lumley, Robert, ed. 1988. *The Museum Time Machine: Putting Cultures on Display.* London: Routledge. doi.org/10.4324/9780203358825.

Marx, Barbara, and Peter Plassmeyer, eds. 2014. *Sehen und Staunen: Die Dresdner Kunstkammer von 1640.* Berlin: Deutscher Kunstverlag.

Meadow, Mark A., and Bruce Robertson, trans. and eds. 2013. *The First Treatise on Museums: Samuel Quiccheberg's Inscriptiones, 1565.* Los Angeles: Getty Research Institute.

Pegazzano, Donatella. 2014. "Giorgio Vasari, Rome and Early Forms of Display of the Medici Collections in Florence: Models and Afterlife." In *Giorgio Vasari and the Birth of the Museum*, edited by Maia Wellington Gahtan, 131–49. Farnham: Ashgate.

Reid, Callum. Forthcoming. *Art's Completest Treasury: The Galleria degli Uffizi in the Grand Ducal Era.* London: Routledge.

Romualdi, Antonella, and Giuliano de Marinis. 1992. *Itinerario Laurenziano nel Museo Archeologico di Firenze.* Florence: Giuntina.

Sandbichler, Veronika. 2012. "Ambras [. . .] worinnen eine wunderwürdig, ohnschäzbare Rüst-Kunst und Raritaeten Kammer anzutreffen." In *Dresden and Ambras: Kunstkammerschätze der Renaissance*, edited by Sabine Haag, 31–41. Vienna: Kunsthistorisches Museum.

Schlosser, Julius von. (1908) 2021. *Art and Curiosity Cabinets of the Late Renaissance: A Contribution to the History of Collecting*. Edited by Thomas DaCosta Kauffmann. Translated by Jonathan Blower. Los Angeles: Getty Reserarch Institute. First published in German.

Scott, Walter. 1816. *The Antiquary*. Edinburgh: Archibald Constable.

Shemek, Deanna, Antonella Guidazzoli, Maria Chiara Liguori, Giovanni Bellavia, Daniele De Luca, Luigi Verri, and Silvano Imboden. 2018. "Renaissance Remix. Isabella d'Este: Virtual Studiolo." *Digital Humanities Quarterly*, 12 (4). digitalhumanities.org/dhq/vol/12/4/000400/000400.html.

Syndram, Dirk, and Martina Minning, eds. 2012. *Die kurfürstlich-sächsische Kunstkammer in Dresden*. Dresden: Sandstein.

Syson, Luke. 2006. "The Medici Study." In *At Home in Renaissance Italy*, edited by Marta Ajmar-Wollheim and Flora Dennis, 288–93. London: V & A.

Thornton, Dora. 1997. *The Scholar in His Study: Ownership and Experience in Renaissance Italy*. New Haven, CT: Yale University Press.

Turpin, Adriana. 2013. "The Display of Exotica in the Uffizi Tribuna." In *Collecting East and West*, edited by Susan Bracken, Andrea M. Gáldy, and Adriana Turpin, 83–117. Newcastle-upon-Tyne: Cambridge Scholars Press.

Vasari, Giorgio. 1923. "Letter CCXLIII (13.11.1556)." In *Der literarische Nachlass Giorgio Vasaris*, edited by Karl Frey, 457. Vol. 1. Munich: Georg Müller.

Watanabe-O'Kelly, Helen. 2002. *Court Culture in Dresden from Renaissance to Baroque*. Basingstone: Palgrave Macmillan. doi.org/10.1057/9780230514492.

Wellington, Maia, and Eva-Maria Troelenberg, eds. 2019. *Collecting and Empires: An Historical and Global Perspective*. London: Harvey Miller Publishers.

Wood, Chris. 2017. "Temple of the Muses: Beyond the Secular Museum." *The Ickeny Collection*. norwichsphere.org.uk/essays/templeofthemuses.pdf.

Zimmern, Froben Christoph von. 1558/1565. *Zimmernsche Chronik*, Württembergische Landesbibliothek, Stuttgart, Cod.Don.580, a–b.

Zinnecker, Andrea. 2020. "Magischer Realismus für Ausstellungsbesucher: VR-Generalprobe im Alpinen Museum München." News release, 8 June 2020, br.de/presse/inhalt/pressemitteilungen/br-digitalprojekt-die-bergrettung-100.html.

Zucchi, Valentina. 2017. "L'Etruscomania di Cosimo I de' Medici." In *Chimera Relocated: Vincere il Mostro*, edited by Sergio Risaliti and Valentina Zucchi, 49–57. Milan: Officina Libraria.

Contributors

Caterina Agostini is a historian of science and Postdoctoral Fellow at Indiana University Bloomington. She is an editor and investigator of the Chymistry of Isaac Newton project (National Science Foundation) and the Harriot Papers (National Endowment for the Humanities, and the Arts and Humanities Research Council). She co-chairs the International Image Interoperability Framework (IIIF), making digital images and texts more accessible to wider audiences. Caterina has published on Galileo Galilei, early modern science, digital editions, maps, and navigation in the Renaissance.

Sarah Banschbach Valles is a literature scholar residing in Lubbock, TX. Her research focuses on early modern Britain and includes women's writing, religious studies, and cultures of the book. She is the Co-Director of the Dalhousie Manuscripts Project, a digital edition of two seventeenth-century verse miscellanies. Her recent work consists of a chapter contribution to *Recognizing Our Religious Allegiances in Early Modern Literary Scholarship* (Baylor 2025), and a co-authored article in the *Journal of Early Modern Studies* (2024).

Steven Bednarski is an award-winning social historian of crime, gender, and natural environment. He is Professor of History at St. Jerome's University at the University of Waterloo, where he also serves as Co-Director of Medieval Studies. In 2017 he won the international D2L Innovation Award in Teaching and Learning, and in 2011 he received the University of Waterloo's Distinguished Teacher Award. Since 2013 he has directed Environments of Change, an international transdisciplinary research collaboration that unites dozens of scholars from across the sciences, social sciences, and humanities into a single research team. Their research, coordinated through the state-of-the-art Digital Research in Arts and Graphical Environmental Networks Laboratory (DRAGEN Lab), centres on finding ways to deploy emerging digital technologies to better understand the relationship between natural environment, climate, and culture. His first book, *Curia: A Social History of a Provençal Criminal Court in the Fourteenth Century* (Presses universitaires de la Méditerranée, 2013), looks at the evolution of late medieval criminal courts in Western Europe. His second book, *A Poisoned Past: The Life and Times of Margarida de Portu, a Fourteenth-Century Accused Poisoner* (University of Toronto Press, 2014), is a pedagogical microhistory that queries how academics write history and proposes a new learner-centred model for the study of the past and present.

ISBN 978-1-64959-119-7 (paper) ISBN 978-1-64959-120-3 (pdf) ISBN 978-1-64959-121-0 (epub)
New Technologies in Medieval and Renaissance Studies 12 (2025) 447–56

Sara Belotti holds a PhD in Geography of Development from the University of Naples "L'Orientale" and the University of Bergamo. She is currently a tenure-track Assistant Professor in the Department of Languages, Literatures, Cultures and Mediations at the University of Milan. Between 2021 and 2023 she was Adjunct Professor of Biodiversity and Geography of Cooperation and Sustainable Development at the University of Bergamo, where she collaborated on several research projects. From 2018 to 2021, as a research fellow at the University of Modena and Reggio Emilia, she collaborated on a digitization project of the cartographic collection of the Estense Library. Her research interests are in the fields of soundscape and cultural heritage enhancement, protected area governance, development cooperation, and the promotion of responsible tourism with participatory methodologies. She pays particular attention to cartographic representation of phenomena using GIS and to disseminating research using digital humanities.

Francesca Bortoletti is Associate Professor at the University of Parma, having previously worked at the University of Minnesota. She was trained at the University of Bologna and the Centre d'etudes supérieures de la Renaissance in Tours. In 2014, she was research fellow at the Italian Academy for Advanced Studies at Columbia University, and subsequently for a European Research Council (ERC) project at the University of Leeds. As visiting fellow, Francesca conducted research at the Getty Research Institute in Los Angeles, the European University Institute in Florence, and the Scuola Superiore Normale in Pisa. She has published three books as well as several book chapters and articles in peer-reviewed international journals. Her research interests include theater history, literature, and visual arts in early modern society, as well as the application of information technologies to digital humanities in order to define new methodologies for analyzing, interpreting, and writing historical phenomena and performing arts. Francesca is currently directing an interdisciplinary digital project on Italian Renaissance festivals, supported by the Italian Academy, the Gladys Krieble Delmas Foundation, the Centro Branca–Fondazione Giorgio Cini Onlus, and a Mellon Foundation–Consortium for the Study of the Premodern World (CSPW) grant.

Elena Brizio teaches medieval and early modern history at Georgetown University Villa Le Balze in Fiesole. She was a visiting fellow at the Newberry Library in Chicago, and at the Pontifical Institute for Mediaeval Studies and the Centre for Reformation and Renaissance Studies (both at the University of Toronto), and she is a Fulbright scholar. She has published on the political and institutional history of Siena of the Trecento, as well as on the *consilia* of medieval jurists Bartolo da Sassoferrato and Otto di Lapo Niccolini. She has been a peer reviewer for major academic journals, and she is currently editor of the Italian Bookshelf at *Annali di Italianistica*. Her current research focuses on the cultural, legal, and social power of Sienese women in the Renaissance, on which she has published extensively. Her most recent publication is *Idealizing Women in the Italian Renaissance* (Centre for Renaissance and Reformation Studies, 2022), co-edited with Marco Piana.

Nadia Cannata is Professor in Italian Philology and History of the Italian Language at Sapienza Università di Roma. Previously, she was a postdoctoral fellow at the British Academy and at Villa I Tatti, Harvard Center for Italian Renaissance Studies, the recipient of a Leverhulme Trust grant, and she taught at Oxford University and in the Department of Italian Studies at the University of Reading (1992–2002). Her main lines of research have concerned the history of the printed book in Italy in the early Renaissance and its relevance for the history of Italian language and literature; the critical edition of vernacular and Neo-Latin poetry in the Renaissance; textual bibliography; the relationship between the figurative arts and literature in the early Italian Renaissance; and treatises on the language and history of linguistics in the Middle Ages and the Renaissance. She directs the Epigraphic Database of Inscriptions in Italian Vernaculars (EDV) project and Eurotales (Museum of the Voices of Europe), based at Sapienza, the first language museum in a European university. She co-edited the first study dedicated to language museums in the world, *Museums of Language and the Display of Intangible Cultural Heritage* (Routledge, 2020).

Giuditta Cirnigliaro received her PhD in Italian Studies with a focus on Art History from Rutgers University in 2018, with a thesis on Leonardo da Vinci's fables and emblems. She holds a laurea in lettere degree from the University of Milan, and a BA and MA in Fine Arts from the Brera Academy and the Glasgow School of Arts, respectively. She is currently a postdoctoral fellow at Roma Tre University, collaborating with academic institutions and museums on projects focusing on recurrent patterns in Leonardo's work, word and image narratives, and material and digital cultures. She has published books and articles on Leonardo's manuscripts, the relationship between word and image in the Renaissance, and the digital humanities, including the monograph *Leonardo's Fables: Sources, Iconography and Science* (Brill, 2022), and the edition *Leonardo da Vinci: Favole e profezie* (Garzanti, 2019) with Carlo Vecce.

Paolo Ciuccarelli, an architect and communication designer, joined Northeastern University in 2019 as founding Director of the Center for Design and Professor of Design. Before that, he spent twenty years at Politecnico di

Milano, where he founded the DensityDesign Research Lab, an award-winning laboratory studying data visualization and information design. Paolo's research aims at improving decision-making processes, especially for non-expert stakeholders in controversial, complex social issues, by integrating data and design processes. He also works in developing tools and methods to understand the evolution of design as a discipline and a practice, with a focus on emerging technologies, including artificial intelligence. Paolo is author of best paper–awarded publications and has lectured at several universities, including the Royal College of Arts, King's College, and Stanford Humanities Center, and has presented at conferences such as Eyeo Festival, TEDx, Visualized, and NetSci. He's Senior Affiliate at Harvard metaLAB and co-editor of the peer-reviewed journal *Big Data & Society*.

Randa El Khatib completed a Postdoctoral Fellowship at the University of Toronto Scarborough and holds a PhD in English from the University of Victoria. She also served as Co-Director of the Digital Humanities Summer Institute and Editor of *Early Modern Digital Review*. Currently, she is an Associate Machine Learning Engineer at Carfax, specializing in model engineering and natural language processing. In 2015, she co-founded the Digital Humanities Institute-Beirut—the first digital humanities training institute in the Middle East. Randa guest edited a special issue on Spatial Humanities published in *EMDR* and *Renaissance and Reformation/Renaissance et Réforme* (2021); her work has also appeared in *Digital Humanities Quarterly*, *Digital Scholarship in the Humanities*, and *Digital Studies/Le champ numérique*, among other venues.

Tommaso Elli is a researcher at Politecnico di Milano, Department of Design. His interests include information visualization, digital humanities, and creative coding. He obtained a PhD in Design in 2022 with a thesis about visualization, literary studies, and design. Since 2016, he has been a member of the DensityDesign Research Lab and has participated in several projects and didactic activities. In 2023, he joined the Fashion in Process group. He is currently working on the PNRR MUSA project (funded by NextGenerationEU), focusing on fashion retail, sustainability, and circularity. He also participates in the development of RAWGraphs, a free, open-source tool to extend access to data visualization. In addition to this work, he is one of the founders of Associazione Abilítiamo Autismo ODV, a non-profit organization.

Angela Fiore earned her PhD at the University of Fribourg, Switzerland, in 2015. She is now a tenure-track Assistant Professor in Musicology at the University of Messina. From 2018 to 2021, as a postdoctoral fellow at the University of Modena and Reggio Emilia, she collaborated on the project sponsored by the Gallerie Estensi dedicated to the digitization of the music collection of the House of Este preserved at the Biblioteca Estense Universitaria, Modena. From 2019 to 2021 she was also Adjunct Professor of Medieval and Renaissance Music at Ca' Foscari University of Venice. Her research fields include digital musicology, musical collections and archives, urban musicology, and soundscape studies. For her research she received grants from the Fondazione Pergolesi Spontini in 2007, the Swiss National Science Foundation in 2011, the Pôle de recherche at the University of Fribourg in 2014, the Jacques-Handschin Prize in 2016, and the American Musicological Society in 2017. Besides this, she holds a diploma in violin and specializes in the baroque violin repertoire.

Andrea M. Gáldy was trained as a classical archaeologist with a special interest in Roman and Etruscan material cultures. In 2002, she gained her PhD at the School of Art History and Archaeology at the University of Manchester with a thesis on the collections of antiquities of Cosimo de' Medici. As a specialist in the history of collecting, she has published widely on collections of antiquities and *kunstkammern* in early modern Europe. She is a former fellow of the Henry Moore Institute (2003) and of the Villa I Tatti (2005), and she currently teaches at Ludwig Maximilian University of Munich. Andrea is one of three founders of the international forum Collecting & Display (London), as well as the founder of Collecting Central Europe (Munich), which she established in 2020.

Giuseppe Gerbino is Professor of Historical Musicology at Columbia University. His research interests include Renaissance theories of cognition and sense perception, the Italian madrigal, the relationship between music and language in the early modern period, and nineteenth-century opera. He is the author of *Canoni ad Enigmi: Pier Francesco Valentini e l'artificio canonico nella prima metà del Seicento* (Edizioni Torre d'Orfeo, 1995) as well as *Music and the Myth of Arcadia in Renaissance Italy* (Cambridge University Press, 2009), which won the 2010 Lewis Lockwood Award of the American Musicological Society. Among his most recent publications is the co-edited volume *Italian Opera in the United States, 1800–1850: At the Origins of a Cultural Migrations* (Libreria Musicale Italiana, 2023), and he is currently at work on a book on music, mind, and soul in the Italian Renaissance.

Beatrice Gobbo a postdoctoral researcher at the Design Department of Politecnico di Milano. She received her PhD in Design from the Design Department of Politecnico di Milano, where she was a member of the DensityDesign Research Lab. Her work and academic interests are positioned at the intersection of information design and computer science. Indeed, in her PhD thesis, "Embalming and Dissecting AI: Visual Explanations for the General Public," she describes a mixed methodology for approaching the Explainable Artificial Intelligence issue from a communication design perspective.

T. C. Nicholas Graham is Professor at the School of Computing at Queen's University and specializes in the human factors of digital games. His notable projects include the Liberi Exergame, a pedal-to-play game designed for children with neurodevelopmental disorders, and the Northeye augmented reality game for teaching elementary school children about daily life in a medieval village. He is a member and former chair of IFIP Working Group 2.7/13.4 on User Interface Engineering, and he is Director of the EQUIS Lab at Queen's for next-generation digital games.

Crystal Hall is Associate Professor of Digital Humanities at Bowdoin College in Brunswick, ME. She is an affiliated faculty member in Italian Studies and a founding member of Digital and Computational Studies at Bowdoin. Her research and teaching focus on the relationship between technology, textual expression, and the creation of knowledge. In addition to collaborating with colleagues across the liberal arts in their use of text analysis, her primary projects and publications relate to the reconstruction and study of Galileo Galilei's personal library. She is author of *Galileo's Reading* (Cambridge University Press, 2013) and co-editor of *German and European Cultural Histories, 1760–1830: Between Network and Narrative* (Liverpool University Press, 2024).

Robin Harrap is Adjunct Professor in the Department of Geological Sciences and Geological Engineering at Queen's University. He did his undergraduate degree in Geological Engineering at Queen's, followed by an MSc in Cordilleran Tectonics and Structural Geology at Carleton University. Since 1990, he has been at Queen's in a variety of roles including as PhD student, research associate, and part-time adjunct. During that time his emphasis has been on the use of technology for all kinds of mapping, with an increasing emphasis on opportunities arising from advances in visualization and game design methods. Rob has worked extensively with GIS, LiDAR scanning, databases, procedural generation methods, and artificial intelligence, with application areas ranging from natural resources and natural hazards to educational game design.

Thomas Herron is Professor of English at East Carolina University in Greenville, NC. He works extensively on Edmund Spenser and Irish history, archaeology, and culture, and he has published widely on Shakespeare and other authors. Thomas's digital work includes the website Centering Spenser: A Digital Resource for Kilcolman Castle. He recently directed a National Endowment for the Humanities (NEH) Digital Humanities Advancement grant, Castle to Classrooms, which developed an architectural model of Spenser's Kilcolman Castle in virtual reality (WondaVR) for teaching purposes in different disciplines.

Charles van den Heuvel is Emeritus Professor of Digital Methods and Historical Disciplines at the University of Amsterdam and former head of the Department of Knowledge and Art Practices of the Huygens Institute of the Royal Netherlands Academy of Arts and Sciences. He has a background in the history of art; has specialized in the history of town planning, fortification, and architecture of the early modern period; and has worked for several cultural heritage institutions. His recent interests are in digital humanities, the history of knowledge, and the history of library and information sciences. He was the PI of the projects Golden Agents: Creative Industries and the Making of the Dutch Golden Age (2017–2022), Virtual Interiors as Interfaces for Big Historical Data Research: Spatially Enhanced Publications (2018–2022), and Through the Lens of Antoni: How Do You Represent What You Cannot See? (2022), all funded by the Dutch Research Council.

Kevin LaGrandeur is Director of Research for the Global AI Ethics Institute, former Professor of Humanities at the New York Institute of Technology, fellow of the Institute for Ethics and Emerging Technologies, co-founder of the NY Posthuman Research Group, and advisory board member of the Lifeboat Foundation, which seeks ways to promote the safe development of new technologies. He specializes in technology and culture, ethics, and education. Kevin is a member of the founding editorial boards of two journals: *AI and Ethics* and the *Journal of Posthumanism*. He has published more than 50 articles and media productions in both professional venues and the popular press as well as two books: *Androids and Intelligent Networks in Early Modern Literature and Culture: Artificial Slaves* (Routledge, 2013), which won a 2014 Science Fiction and Technoculture Studies Book Prize, and *Surviving the Machine Age: Intelligent Technology and the Transformation of Human Work* (Palgrave Macmillan, 2017) with sociologist James J. Hughes.

Zack MacDonald is the Map Librarian for Archives and Special Collections for Western University in London, ON, where he manages geospatial data and cartographic collections ranging from manuscript maps and historic atlases to LiDAR records and aerial photographs. His current work focuses on preservation and enhancing user access through digitization and digitalization. His research interests focus on the use of GIS and remote sensing, 3D modelling, game engines, and immersive technologies to generate navigable and interactive historical reconstructions. His current work explores the application and impact of discovery layers and building information modelling to enhance research data discoverability and access in virtual and augmented reality training and education applications.

Catherine Medici is Coordinator of the Gender and Sexuality Resource Center at the University of Nebraska Medical Center. Her work on women and family networks, especially women of the Dudley-Sidney family, has appeared in the *Oxford Dictionary of National Biography* as well as various book chapters. Her study of gender and family networks has led to digital humanities work on network analysis of the Sidney family letters. She also works in the field of medical humanities on gender and chronic illness and has published in *Early Modern Women: An Interdisciplinary Journal* on chronic illness and disability. She has presented her work widely, including at meetings of the Renaissance Society of America, the Sixteenth Century Society, and the American Historical Association. Catherine completed both her PhD in History and Women's and Gender Studies and an MA in History and Medieval and Renaissance Studies at the University of Nebraska.

Luis Meneses is Professor in the Department of Computer Science at Vancouver Island University. He is a Fulbright scholar and a Mitacs Elevate fellow. He has served on the board of the Text Encoding Initiative (TEI) Consortium and on the IEEE Technical Committee on Digital Libraries. His research interests include digital humanities, digital libraries, information retrieval, and human–computer interaction.

John Misak is Associate Professor of English and Director of the Technical Communication program at New York Institute of Technology in Old Westbury. His research interests center on technologies and learning, specifically video games, augmented and virtual realities, and artificial intelligence. His recent co-authored study, "Metaphors, Mental Model and Multiplicity: Understanding Student Perception of Digital Literacy," published in *Computers and Composition*, won the 2023 Ellen Nold Award for Outstanding Article. His latest book chapter on reverse engineering stories in the literature classroom is part of *Teaching Games and Games Studies in the Literature Classroom* (Bloomsbury, 2022), which was a runner up for the 2023 Best Teaching Literature Book at Iowa State University. His in-progress article will report on the effectiveness of teaching prompt engineering in literature classes.

Andrew Moore is a historian of the preindustrial environment and uses an interdisciplinary methodology to understand how fourteenth-century English rural communities located in environmentally vulnerable areas experienced and reacted to a changing climate. He puts more traditional archival sources, especially manorial court rolls, in conversation with proxy data using dendroclimatology, palynology, and sedimentology to inform conclusions about the interactions between nature and culture in a medieval context. His current postdoctoral research, at the University of Saskatchewan, uses GIS to map the movement of resources and consumption in commercially isolated medieval communities in England. He is also Research Coordinator for the Social Sciences and Humanities Research Council (SSHRC) Partnership Grant, Environments of Change, centred at the University of Waterloo. His PhD dissertation was a finalist for the Governor General's Gold Medal, and he is lead author of an article in the April 2022 issue of *Speculum: A Journal of Medieval Studies.*

Jessica Marie Otis is Assistant Professor of History and Director of Public Projects at the Roy Rosenzweig Center for History and New Media at George Mason University. She received both her PhD in History and her MS in Mathematics from the University of Virginia. Her research explores the ways people adopt and adapt to new information technologies, as well as how those technologies can transform previous understandings of both the natural world and human history. Her most recent book, *By the Numbers: Numeracy, Religion, and the Quantitative Transformation of Early Modern England*, was published by Oxford University Press in 2024.

Gerit Quealy is an independent scholar in New York City. As a journalist, her work has appeared in the *New York Times, Huffington Post, Biography*, and in articles for NBC, among other outlets. She is an avid paleographer and studied at the Folger Institute. Her article accompanying a recently discovered holograph letter from Philip Herbert to Fulke Greville was published in the *Sidney Journal* in 2017, and a 2019 Shakespeare Association of America paper on Greville family tombs is forthcoming in *Church Monuments*. Her presentation titled "Queen Elizabeth and the Ethnobotany of Early Modern England," originally developed for the Annual Meeting of Renaissance Society of America in 2021, expanded into a mapping project for all of Elizabeth's progresses as well as multiple programs and talks. She has been a visiting lecturer and workshop leader at various institutions including Columbia University, Williams College, the City College of New York, and the State University of New York at Albany, among others. A recent paper, "Astrophil's Star: Locating Penelope Rich in the Sidney Constellation," appears in the 2023 special issue of the *Sidney Journal* titled "Penshurst and Beyond." She is the author of *Botanical Shakespeare* (HarperCollins, 2017).

Sarah J. Sprouse is Assistant Professor of English at West Texas A&M University. Her scholarship focuses on the transmission of ideas and literature in the medieval and early modern British Isles. She has published on Middle English romance, Gerald of Wales, and codicology, and recent publications have appeared in journals such as *Arthuriana* and *Manuscript Studies*. Her research has been supported by the Medieval Academy of America, the Huntington Library, and Trinity College Dublin.

Caroline Winter is a former postdoctoral fellow in open social scholarship at the University of Victoria (UVic)'s Electronic Textual Cultures Lab (ETCL). She holds a PhD in English literature (UVic), focusing on British Romantic fiction and the rise of commercial society, with a particular interest in the Gothic novel. Now working at the UVic Libraries, Caroline holds an MLIS (University of Alberta) and is interested in the intersections between library and information science and digital humanities. Caroline's work has appeared in *Pop!*, *Digital Humanities Quarterly*, *Digital Scholarship in the Humanities*, and *Lumen*, among other publications. Together with Randa El Khatib, she co-organized the 2020 New Technologies and Renaissance Studies–Digital Humanities at RSA (NTRS–DH@RSA) online conference upon which this volume is based.

NEW TECHNOLOGIES IN MEDIEVAL AND RENAISSANCE STUDIES

SERIES TITLES

New Technologies and Renaissance Studies
Edited by William R. Bowen and Raymond G. Siemens
Volume 1, 2008

Electronic Publishing: Politics and Pragmatics
Edited by Gabriel Egan
Volume 2, 2010

Digitizing Medieval and Early Modern Material Culture
Edited by Brent Nelson and Melissa Terras
Volume 3, 2012

New Technologies and Renaissance Studies II
Edited by Tassie Gniady, Kris McAbee, and Jessica Murphy
Volume 4, 2014

A Social Edition of the Devonshire Manuscript (BL MS Add 17,492)
Edited by Raymond Siemens, Karin Armstrong, Constance Crompton, and The Devonshire MS Editorial Group
Volume 5, 2015

Early Modern Studies after the Digital Turn
Edited by Laura Estill, Diane K. Jakacki, and Michael Ullyot
Volume 6, 2016

Social Knowledge Creation in the Humanities: Volume 1
Edited by Alyssa Arbuckle, Aaron Mauro, and Daniel Powell
Volume 7, 2017

Social Knowledge Creation in the Humanities: Volume 2
Edited by Aaron Mauro
Volume 8, 2022

New Technologies and Renaissance Studies III
Edited by Matthew Evan Davis and Colin Wilder
Volume 9, 2022

Digital Pedagogy in Early Modern Studies: Method and Praxis
Edited by Andie Silva and Scott Schofield
Volume 10, 2024

The Past, Present, and Future of Early Modern Digital Studies: Iter at 25
Edited by Laura Estill and Ray Siemens
Volume 11, 2025